www.wadsworth.com

wadsworth.com is the World Wide Web site for Wadsworth and is your direct source to dozens of online resources.

At *wadsworth.com* you can find out about supplements, demonstration software, and student resources. You can also send email to many of our authors and preview new publications and exciting new technologies.

wadsworth.com
Changing the way the world learns®

Readings in African-American History

Third Edition

Edited by

THOMAS R. FRAZIER

PROFESSOR EMERITUS

BERNARD M. BARUCH COLLEGE

THE CITY UNIVERSITY OF NEW YORK

WADSWORTH

™

THOMSON LEARNING

Australia • Canada • Mexico • Singapore • Spain
United Kingdom • United States

WADSWORTH
THOMSON LEARNING

History Publisher: *Clark G. Baxter*
Senior Development Editor: *Sharon Adams Poore*
Assistant Editor: *Jennifer Ellis*
Marketing Manager: *Diane McOscar*
Print Buyer: *Robert King*
Permissions Editor: *Stephanie Keough-Hedges*
Production Services and Composition: *Aksen Associates*
Cover Designer: *Ross Carron*
Printer: *Maple-Vail, Binghamton*

ISBN: 0-534-52373-0

Wadsworth/Thomson Learning
10 Davis Drive
Belmont, CA 94002-3098
USA

For more information about our products, contact us:
Thomson Learning Academic Resource Center
1-800-423-0563
http://www.wadsworth.com

International Headquarters
Thomson Learning
International Division
290 Harbor Drive, 2nd Floor
Stamford, CT 06902-7477
USA

UK/Europe/Middle East/South Africa
Thomson Learning
Berkshire House
168-173 High Holborn
London WC1V 7AA
United Kingdom

Asia
Thomson Learning
60 Albert Street, #15-01
Albert Complex
Singapore 189969

Canada
Nelson Thomson Learning
1120 Birchmount Road
Toronto, Ontario M1K 5G4
Canada

Contents

GENERAL READING SUGGESTIONS   449

Preface

Since the first edition of this text was published in 1970, the importance of African-American history has been clearly established among those who study America's past. Before 1970, black history was almost exclusively studied and taught in black colleges in, and outside of, the South. The changes in public consciousness as a result of the struggles for racial equality since the late 1950s, however, have led to the inclusion of African-American history courses in the curricula of predominantly white colleges and universities. The previous systematic, though not always deliberate, denial of a significant past to the African-American community tended to distort the self-image of Americans, black and white. Both public events and academic scholarship in recent years have begun to alter the past misconceptions. Informed citizens now recognize that our history is that of many Americas, not just one.

This book is intended to serve as an introduction to the history of African-Americans through the use of historical documents that originated in the black community. Although the number of documents that could be used was of course limited, a careful attempt has been made to represent the wide range of black life and thought that has contributed to the development of black America.

The material is arranged chronologically into thirteen sections, covering the entire range of American history, from the colonial period to the present. Each section has a brief historical introduction and contains from three to five documents. Each document, in turn, is introduced by a short note giving its specific historical context. The documents were selected on the basis of vividness and pertinence. They are presented in their entirety, or, if abridged, they are complete enough to enable the reader to grasp the range of thought and the frame of reference of their authors. Included are descriptions of black life, statements of black leaders, and position papers of black organizations.

Each section of the book concludes with an annotated bibliography (entitled "Suggestions for Further Reading") to guide readers in further study, and a general bibliography (entitled "General Reading Suggestions") appears at the end of the book. In all the bibliographies, titles available in paperback are marked with an asterisk.

This third edition includes new material on popular culture, and the lives of black youth. I would like to acknowledge the assistance of my agent, David Follmer of Lyceum Books, and Clark Baxter of Wadsworth Publishing in the development and publication of this new edition. I remain grateful for the assistance of John Hope Franklin (Duke University) and James M. McPherson (Princeton University) in the preparation of the earlier editions. The following libraries provided valuable assistance in the gathering of this material: the Harvard College Library, the Massachusetts Historical Society Library, the Boston Public Library, the Boston Athenaeum Library, the New-York Historical Society Library, the New York Public Library (including the Schomburg Collection), the Columbia University Library, the Union Theological Seminary Library, and the University of Michigan Library.

Finally, I want to express my appreciation to several academic reviewers of the manuscript: Alfrieda Watson (West Valley College) Edwin D. Hoffman (California State University, Hayward) and Dr. Fola Soremekun (Citrus College).

Thomas R. Frazier

1

✻

AFRICA AND
THE SLAVE TRADE

INTRODUCTION

Although Moslem traders from north of the Sahara had carried on an extensive trade with the states of West Africa during the Middle Ages, Africa remained the "dark continent" to the light-skinned Christians of the North until the time of the discovery and exploitation of the Americas by the Europeans. Then, as the demand from the New World for cheap labor grew, the Europeans turned to Africa, and the West African coast from the Senegal River south to the mouth of the Congo began to swarm with ships intent on capitalizing on the trade in human beings.

Estimates of the number of Africans taken into slavery in the Americas range from nine million to fifty million, with the true figure probably close to the former. However, this figure does not include all the blacks uprooted from their homes. Millions died fighting in the wars to capture slaves, making the arduous trek to the coast where the slave ships waited, or undergoing the devastating passage across the Atlantic.

As the control of the Atlantic slave trade passed successively through the hands of the Portuguese, the Dutch, the French, and the English (including the American colonists), the typical European cared little and knew less about the land from which the blacks were being taken. Until recent years, with the exception of a few studies of the trade itself, Europeans gave no serious thought to the history of West Africa prior to and during the trade.

Most of coastal Africa—the area with which the slavers dealt—was organized into states rather than into tribes or simple societies. Between the tenth and sixteenth centuries, in the interior, centered around the bend of the Niger

River, the empires of Ghana, Mali, and Songhai flourished. These interior kingdoms had no direct contact with the Atlantic slave trade. The states of the West African coast were so strong and well fortified that the European traders were not able to penetrate the interior in order to capture slaves; instead, they had to depend on the coastal kings for their booty. These African political leaders competed for the monopoly on slaves with the various European traders. The blacks who were sold into slavery usually came from the area just behind the coast, and most were either captured in wars waged for the trade or collected by the coastal rulers as tribute from weaker states.

There is much controversy today about the effect of the slave trade on the coastal states. It is unclear whether the states benefited from the trade in terms of the improved standard of living that resulted from the increased commerce or whether the buying and selling of millions of people only brought about moral degeneration, which eventually led to the decline and virtual disappearance of the coastal kingdoms. The same questions might be asked, of course, of the individual traders and the countries involved in the trade. What is clear is that competition between the African states, fostered by the use of guns as trade goods by the European slavers, led to ruinous wars that weakened the states to the point that they could be taken over during the period of European colonization in the late nineteenth century.

Two of the main reasons Africans were so successfully used as slaves had to do with their physical resistance to European diseases and the high level of commercial organization they had achieved in West Africa. The American Indian population that had been enslaved by the Spanish in the New World was dying out at a startling rate because of the diseases introduced by the Europeans. The same diseases seem to have existed widely enough in Africa to allow the Africans to develop a certain immunity to them. Thus, they were able to endure the conditions of slavery in the New World.

The African states' previous experience in commerce enabled them to adapt easily to dealing in human beings—the commodity then in demand—instead of in gold or salt. And the old trade routes into the interior began to yield the new trade item. Indeed, a high degree of commercial organization was needed to supply up to 100,000 people a year for the trade.

By the seventeenth century, most of the slave trade was carried on in standard commercial patterns. A ship would arrive off the coast of a trading station; depending on the particular arrangement, African businessmen would come aboard the ship to bargain, or the ship's captain would go ashore. Customarily, there would be some haggling over the terms of the trade. European money had no value in Africa, so the blacks were usually bought with rolls of tobacco, rum, guns, or bars of useful metal, such as iron, copper, and brass. From time to time, cowrie shells, widely used in Africa as a medium of exchange, were introduced. After the deal was made, it was necessary to examine the goods. Only the best physical specimens were acceptable. Those who proved fit were branded with the mark of the trader, lest a substitution be made between the examination and the sailing.

When the time came to sail, the slaves were chained together and loaded into the ships. At this point, there were many violent struggles. Sometimes the blacks would capture the ship; sometimes they would break away and dive overboard, preferring to face drowning rather than go as slaves to an unknown fate. The traders considered loading the ship the most dangerous part of the transaction.

Once under way, the traders would relax somewhat and begin the infamous "middle passage," so called because it was the second leg of the triangular pattern characteristic of the Atlantic trade during this period—from Europe or New England to Africa, from Africa to the West Indies, from the West Indies to Europe or New England. Once the ship was at sea, speed was of the essence. The shorter the voyage, the fewer the number of slaves there would be on board who would die. It has been estimated that one of every eight slaves died during this part of the trade. The quickest time between Africa and the New World was three weeks, but when winds were contrary or there was no wind at all, the voyage sometimes lasted over three months.

If weather permitted, the captives were kept on deck during the day and forced to exercise and eat. But when the weather was bad, they were kept chained for most of the voyage in incredibly cramped and poorly ventilated quarters below.

Upon arriving at its destination, the ship would disgorge its contents at a local slave mart, where the entire lot would be bid for on the basis of an average price. The purchaser was usually a slave dealer, who would either resell the slaves on the spot to individuals who had been unable to participate in the initial bidding or transport the slaves elsewhere for resale.

The slave trade was so extensive that, by 1850, one-third of the people in the world with African ancestry lived outside Africa, most of them in the Americas. This forced migration, one of the largest movements of people in the history of the world, had an incalculable effect on both Africa and the New World.

Taken from the
Guinea Coast as a Child

A Narrative of the Life
and Adventures of Venture

VENTURE SMITH

When this narrative was composed, Venture Smith was an old man, living in East Haddam, Connecticut. He had taken his surname from Colonel Oliver Smith, his last owner, who had permitted him to work evenings in order to buy his freedom. After freeing himself, he had bought his wife and children from their master and settled in Connecticut.

The events Smith describes here took place in Africa, the home that he left at the age of six. Though he surely did not have total recall of his life in Africa, his general description is probably quite accurate. Perhaps the most important aspect of this narrative is its depiction of the warfare between the states of the coast and those of the interior, where Smith was born. This commercial warfare, waged for the slave trade, brought about great changes in the political life of Africa.

I was born at Dukandarra, in Guinea, about the year 1729. My father's name was Saungm Furro, Prince of the tribe of Dukandarra. My father had three wives. Polygamy was not uncommon in that country, especially among the rich, as every man was allowed to keep as many wives as he could maintain. By his first wife he had three children. The eldest of them was myself, named by my father, Broteer. The other two were named Cundazo and Soozaduka. My father had two children by his second wife, and one by his third. I descended from a very large, tall and stout race of beings, much larger than the generality of people in other parts of the globe, being commonly considerable above six feet in height, and every way well proportioned.

The first thing worthy of notice which I remember was, a contention between my father and mother, on account of my father marrying his third wife without the consent of his first and eldest, which was contrary to the custom generally observed among my countrymen. In consequence of this rupture, my mother left her husband and country, and travelled away with her three children to the eastward. I was then five years old. She took not the least sustenance along with her, to support either herself or children.

FROM Venture Smith, *A Narrative of the Life and Adventures of Venture, A Native of Africa but Resident about Sixty Years in the United States of America* (New London, 1798), pp. 3–9. Reprinted A.D. 1835 and published by a descendant of Venture.

I was able to travel along by her side; the other two of her offspring she carried one on her back, and the other being a sucking child, in her arms. When we became hungry, our mother used to set us down on the ground, and gather some of the fruits which grew spontaneously in that climate. These served us for food on the way. At night we all lay down together in the most secure place we could find, and reposed ourselves until morning. Though there were many noxious animals there; yet so kind was our Almighty protector, that none of them were ever permitted to hurt or molest us. Thus we went on our journey until the second day after our departure from Dukandarra, when we came to the entrance of a great desert. During our travel in that we were often affrighted with the doleful howlings and yellings of wolves, lions, and other animals. After five days travel we came to the end of this desert, and immediately entered into a beautiful and extensive interval country. Here my mother was pleased to stop and seek a refuge for me. She left me at the house of a very rich farmer. I was then, as I should judge, not less than one hundred and forty miles from my native place, separated from all my relations and acquaintance. At this place my mother took her farewell of me, and set out for my own country. My new guardian, as I shall call the man with whom I was left, put me into the business of tending sheep, immediately after I was left with him. The flock which I kept with the assistance of a boy, consisted of about forty. We drove them every morning between two and three miles to pasture, into the wide and delightful plains. When night drew on, we drove them home and secured them in the cote. In this round I continued during my stay here. One incident which befel me when I was driving my flock from pasture, was so dreadful to me in that age, and is to this time so fresh in my memory, that I cannot help noticing it in this place. Two large dogs sallied out of a certain house and set upon me. One of them took me by the arm, and the other by the thigh, and before their master could come and relieve me, they lacerated my flesh to such a degree, that the scars are very visible to the present day. My master was immediately sent for. He came and carried me home, as I was unable to go myself on account of my wounds. Nothing remarkable happened afterwards until my father sent for me to return home.

Before I dismiss this country, I must just inform my reader what I remember concerning this place. A large river runs through this country in a westerly course. The land for a great way on each side is flat and level, hedged in by a considerable rise in the country at a great distance from it. It scarce ever rains there, yet the land is fertile; great dews fall in the night which refresh the soil. About the latter end of June or first of July, the river begins to rise, and gradually increases until it has inundated the country for a great distance, to the height of seven or eight feet. This brings on a slime which enriches the land surprisingly. When the river has subsided, the natives begin to sow and plant, and the vegetation is exceeding rapid. Near this rich river my guardian's land lay. He possessed, I cannot exactly tell how much, yet this I am certain of respecting it, that he owned an immense tract. He possessed likewise a great many cattle and goats. During my stay with him I was kindly used, and with as much tenderness, for what I saw, as his only son, although I was an entire stranger to him, remote from friends and relations. The principal occupations of the inhabitants there, were the cultivation of the soil and the care of their flocks. They were a people pretty similar in every respect to that of mine, except in their persons, which were not so tall and stout. They appeared to be very kind and friendly. I will now return to my departure from that place.

My father sent a man and horse after me. After settling with my guardian for keeping me, he took me away and went for home. It was then about one year since my mother brought me here. Nothing remarkable occurred to us on our journey until we arrived safe home.

I found then that the difference between my parents had been made up previous to their sending for me. On my return, I was received both by my father and mother with great joy and affection, and was once more restored to my paternal dwelling in peace and happiness. I was then about six years old.

Not more than six weeks had passed after my return, before a message was brought by an inhabitant of the place where I lived the preceding year to my father, that the place had been invaded by a numerous army, from a nation not far distant, furnished with musical instruments, and all kinds of arms then in use; that they were instigated by some white nation who equipped and. sent them to subdue and possess the country; that his nation had made no preparation for war, having been for a long time in profound peace; that they could not defend themselves against such a formidable train of invaders, and must therefore necessarily evacuate their lands to the fierce enemy, and fly to the protection of some chief; and that if he would permit them they would come under his rule and protection when they had to retreat from their own possessions. He was a kind and merciful prince, and therefore consented to these proposals.

He had scarcely returned to his nation with the message, before the whole of his people were obliged to retreat from their country, and come to my father's dominions.

He gave them every privilege and all the protection his government could afford. But they had not been there longer than four days before news came to them that the invaders had laid waste their country, and were coming speedily to destroy them in my father's territories. This affrighted them, and therefore they immediately pushed off to the southward, into the unknown countries there, and were never more heard of.

Two days after their retreat, the report turned out to be but too true. A detachment from the enemy came to my father and informed him, that the whole army was encamped not far out of his dominions, and would invade the territory and deprive his people of their liberties and rights, if he did not comply with the following terms. These were to pay them a large sum of money, three hundred fat cattle, and a great number of goats, sheep, asses, &c.

My father told the messenger he would comply rather than that his subjects should be deprived of their rights and privileges, which he was not then in circumstances to defend from so sudden an invasion. Upon turning out those articles, the enemy pledged their faith and honor that they would not attack him. On these he relied and therefore thought it unnecessary to be on his guard against the enemy. But their pledges of faith and honor proved no better than those of other unprincipled hostile nations; for a few days after a certain relation of the king came and informed him, that the enemy who sent terms of accommodation to him and received tribute to their satisfaction, yet meditated an attack upon his subjects by surprise, and that probably they would commence their attack in less than one day, and concluded with advising him, as he was not prepared for war, to order a speedy retreat of his family and subjects. He complied with this advice.

The same night which was fixed upon to retreat, my father and his family set off about the break of day. The king and his two younger wives went in one company, and my mother and her children in another. We left our dwellings in succession, and my father's company went on first. We directed our course for a large shrub plain, some distance off, where we intended to conceal ourselves from the approaching enemy, until we could refresh ourselves a little. But we presently found that our retreat was not secure. For having struck up a little fire for the purpose of cooking victuals, the enemy who happened to be encamped a little distance off, had sent out a scouting party who discovered us by the smoke of the fire, just as we were extinguishing it, and about to eat. As soon as we had finished eating, my father discovered the party, and immediately began to discharge arrows at them. This was what I first saw, and it alarmed both me and the women, who being unable to make any resistance, immediately betook ourselves to the tall thick reeds not far off, and left the old king to fight alone. For some time I beheld him from the reeds defending himself with great courage and firmness, till at last he was obliged to surrender himself into their hands.

They then came to us in the reeds, and the very first salute I had from them was a violent blow on the back part of the head with the fore part of a gun, and at the same time a grasp round the neck. I then had a rope put about my neck, as had all the women in the thicket with me, and was immediately led to my father, who was likewise pinioned and haltered for leading. In this condition we were all led to the camp. The women and myself being pretty submissive, had tolerable treatment from the enemy, while my father was closely interrogated respecting his money which they knew he must have. But as he gave them no account of it, he was instantly cut and pounded on his body with great inhumanity, that he might be induced by the torture he suffered to make the discovery. All this availed not in the least to make him give up his money, but he despised all the tortures which they inflicted, until the continued exercise and increase of torment, obliged him to sink and expire. He thus died without informing his enemies where his money lay. I saw him while he was thus tortured to death. The shocking scene is to this day fresh in my mind, and I have often been overcome while thinking on it. He was a man of remarkable stature. I should judge as much as six feet and six or seven inches high, two feet across his shoulders, and every way well proportioned. He was a man of remarkable strength and resolution, affable, kind and gentle, ruling with equity and moderation.

The army of the enemy was large, I should suppose consisting of about six thousand men. Their leader was called Baukurre. After destroying the old prince, they decamped and immediately marched towards the sea, lying to the west, taking with them myself and the women prisoners. In the march a scouting party was detached from the main army. To the leader of this party I was made waiter, having to carry his gun, &c. As we were a-scouting we came across a herd of fat cattle, consisting of about thirty in number. These we set upon, and immediately wrested from their keepers, and afterwards converted them into food for the army. The enemy had remarkable success in destroying the country wherever they went. For as far as they had penetrated, they laid the habitations waste and captured the people. The distance they had now brought me was about four hundred miles. All the march I had very hard tasks imposed on me, which I must perform on pain of punishment. I was obliged to carry on my head a large flat stone used for grinding our corn, weighing as I should suppose, as much as twenty-five pounds; besides victuals, mat and cooking utensils. Though I was pretty large and stout of my age, yet these burdens were very grievous to me, being only six years and a half old.

We were then come to a place called Malagasco. When we entered the place we could not see the least appearance of either houses or inhabitants, but upon stricter search found, that instead of houses above ground they had dens in the sides of hillocks, contiguous to ponds and streams of water. In these we perceived they had all hid themselves, as I suppose they usually did on such occasions. In order to compel them to surrender, the enemy contrived to smoke them out with faggots. These they put to the entrance of the caves and set them on fire. While they were engaged in this business, to their great surprise some of them were desperately wounded with arrows which fell from above on them. This mystery they soon found out. They perceived that the enemy discharged these arrows through holes on the top of the dens directly into the air. Their weight brought them back, point downwards on their enemies heads, whilst they were smoking the inhabitants out. The points of their arrows were poisoned, but their enemy had an antidote for it, which they instantly applied to the wounded part. The smoke at last obliged the people to give themselves up. They came out of their caves, first spatting the palms of their hands together, and immediately after extended their arms, crossed at their wrists, ready to be bound and pinioned. I should judge that the dens above mentioned were extended about eight feet horizontally into the earth, six feet in height and as many wide. They were arched over head and lined with earth, which was of the clay kind, and made the surface of their walls firm and smooth.

The invaders then pinioned the prisoners of all ages and sexes indiscriminately, took their flocks and all their effects, and moved on their way towards the sea. On the march the prisoners were treated with clemency, on account of their being submissive and humble. Having come to the next tribe, the enemy laid siege and immediately took men, women, children, flocks, and all their valuable effects. They then went on to the next district which was contiguous to the sea, called in Africa, Anamaboo. The enemies' provisions were then almost spent, as well as their strength. The inhabitants knowing what conduct they had pursued, and what were their present intentions, improved the favorable opportunity, attacked them, and took enemy, prisoners, flocks and all their effects. I was then taken a second time. All of us were then put into the castle, and kept for market. On a certain time I and other prisoners were put on board a canoe, under our master, and rowed away to a vessel belonging to Rhode Island, commanded by Captain Collingwood, and the mate Thomas Mumford. While we were going to the vessel, our master told us all to appear to the best possible advantage for sale. I was bought on board by one Robertson Mumford, steward of said vessel, for four gallons of rum, and a piece of calico, and called VENTURE, on account of his having purchased me with his own private venture. Thus I came by my name. All the slaves that were bought for that vessel's cargo, were two hundred and sixty.

The Horrors of
the Middle Passage

The Interesting Narrative of the
Life of Olaudah Equiano

OLAUDAH EQUIANO

Olaudah Equiano, the author of this selection, was from the Ibo country around Benin in what is now Nigeria. He was sold into slavery in 1756 to the British, who brought him to the New World. In 1766, he bought his freedom and went to England, where he worked as a barber and as a personal servant. He became actively involved in the antislavery movement in England and was interested in colonizing freed blacks in Sierra Leone. His autobiography, written in 1789, is one of the most informative of all such narratives by former slaves.

The portion of Equiano's narrative included here describes his experience of the "middle passage" from Africa to the West Indies. He recalled it as a horrifying example of man's inhumanity to his brothers. Included is a reference to the widespread fear among the captured Africans that they were to be eaten by the white men.

The first object which saluted my eyes when I arrived on the coast was the sea, and a slave ship, which was then riding at anchor, and waiting for its cargo. These filled me with astonishment, which was soon converted into terror, when I was carried on board I was immediately handled, and tossed up, to see if I were sound, by some of the crew; and I was now persuaded that I had got into a world of bad spirits, and that they were going to kill me. Their complexions too differing so much from ours, their long hair, and the language they spoke (which was very different from any I had ever heard) united to confirm me in this belief. Indeed such were the horrors of my views and fears at the moment, that, if ten thousand worlds had been my own, I would have freely parted with them all to have exchanged my condition with that of the meanest slave in my own country. When I looked round the ship too and saw a large furnace or copper boiling, and a multitude of black people of every description chained together, every one of their countenances expressing dejection and sorrow, I no longer doubted of my fate; and, quite overpowered with horror and anguish, I fell motionless on the deck and fainted. When I recovered a little I found some black people about me, who I believed were some of those who had brought me on board, and had been receiving their pay; they talked to me in order to cheer me, but all in vain. I asked them if we

FROM Olaudah Equiano, *The Interesting Narrative of the Life of Olaudah Equiano or Gustavus Vasa, The African*, Vol. 1 (New York, 1791), pp. 49–62.

were not to be eaten by those white men with horrible looks, red faces, and long hair. They told me I was not; and one of the crew brought me a small portion of spirituous liquor in a wine-glass; but being afraid of him, I would not take it out of his hand. One of the blacks therefore took it from him and gave it to me, and I took a little down my palate, which, instead of reviving me, as they thought it would, threw me into the greatest consternation at the strange feeling it produced, having never tasted any such liquor before. Soon after this the blacks who brought me on board went off, and left me abandoned to despair. I now saw myself deprived of all chance of returning to my native country, or even the least glimpse of hope of gaining the shore, which I now considered as friendly; and I even wished for my former slavery in preference to my present situation, which was filled with horrors of every kind, still heightened by my ignorance of what I was to undergo. I was not long suffered to indulge my grief; I was soon put down under the decks, and there I received such a salutation in my nostrils as I had never experienced in my life: so that with the loathsomeness of the stench, and crying together, I became so sick and low that I was not able to eat, nor had I the least desire to taste any thing. I now wished for the last friend, death, to relieve me; but soon, to my grief, two of the white men offered me eatables; and, on my refusing to eat, one of them held me fast by the hands, and laid me across, I think the windlass, and tied my feet, while the other flogged me severely. I had never experienced any thing of this kind before: and, although not being used to the water, I naturally feared that element the first time I saw it, yet, nevertheless, could I have got over the nettings, I would have jumped over the side, but I could not; and, besides, the crew used to watch us very closely who were not chained down to the decks, lest we should leap into the water. and I have seen some of these poor African prisoners most severely cut for attempting to do so, and hourly whipped for not eating. This indeed was often the case with myself. In a little time after, amongst the poor chained men, I found some of my own nation, which in a small degree gave ease to my mind. I inquired of these what was to be done with us? They gave me to understand we were to be carried to these white people's country to work for them. I then was a little revived, and thought, if it were no worse than working, my situation was not so desperate: but still I feared I should be put to death, the white people looked and acted, as I thought, in so savage a manner; for I had never seen among any people such instances of brutal cruelty; and this not only shown towards us blacks, but also to some of the whites themselves. One white man in particular I saw, when we were permitted to be on deck, flogged so unmercifully with a large rope near the foremast, that he died in consequence of it; and they tossed him over the side as they would have done a brute. This made me fear these people the more; and I expected nothing less than to be treated in the same manner. I could not help expressing my fears and apprehensions to some of my countrymen: I asked them if these people had no country, but lived in this hollow place (the ship)? they told me they did not, but came from a distant one, "Then," said I, "how comes it in all our country we never heard of them!" They told me, because they lived so very far off. I then asked where were their women? had they any like themselves? I was told they had: "And why," said I, "do we not see them?" they answered, because they were left behind. I asked how the vessel could go? they told me they could not tell; but that there were cloth put upon the masts by the help of the ropes I saw, and then the vessel went on; and the white men had some spell or magic they put in the water when they liked in order to stop the vessel, I was exceedingly amazed at this account, and really thought they were spirits. I therefore wished much to be from amongst them, for I expected they would sacrifice me: but my wishes were vain; for we were so quartered that it was impossible for any of us to make our escape. While we stayed on the coast I was mostly on deck; and one day, to my great astonishment, I saw one of these vessels coming in with the sails up. As soon as the whites saw it, they gave a great shout, at which we were amazed: and the more so as the vessel appeared larger by approaching nearer. At last she came to an anchor in my sight, and when the anchor was let go I and my countrymen who saw it were lost in astonishment to observe the vessel stop; and were now convinced it was done by magic. Soon after this the other ship got her boats out, and they came on board of us, and the people of both ships seemed very glad to see each other. Several of the strangers also shook hands with us black people, and made motions with their hands, signifying I suppose, we were to go to their country; but we did not understand them. At last, when the ship we were in, had got in all her cargo, they made ready with many fearful noises, and we were all put under deck, so that we could not see how they managed the vessel. But this disappointment was the least of my sorrow. The stench of the hold while we were on the coast was so intolerably loathsome, that it was dangerous to remain there for any time, and some of us had been permitted to stay on the deck for the fresh air; but now that the whole ship's cargo were confined together, it became absolutely pestilential. The closeness of the place, and the heat of the climate, added to the number in the ship, which was so crowded that each had scarcely room to turn himself, almost suffocated us. This produced copious perspirations, so that the air soon became unfit for respiration, from a variety of loathsome smells, and brought on a sickness amongst the slaves, of which many died, thus falling victims to the improvident avarice, as I may call it, of their purchasers. This wretched situation was again aggravated by the galling of the chains, now become insupportable; and the filth of the necessary tubs, into which the children often fell, and were almost suffocated. The shrieks of the women, and the groans of the dying, rendered the whole a scene of horror almost inconceivable. Happily perhaps for myself I was soon reduced so low here that it was thought necessary to keep me almost always on deck; and from my extreme youth I was not put in fetters. In this situation I expected every hour to share the fate of my companions, some of whom were almost daily brought upon deck at the point of death, which I began to hope would soon put an end to my miseries. Often did I think many of the inhabitants of the deep much more happy than myself, I envied them the freedom they enjoyed, and as often wished I could change my condition for theirs. Every circumstance I met with served only to render my state more painful, and heightened my apprehensions

and my opinion of the cruelty of the whites. One day they had taken a number of fishes; and when they had killed and satisfied themselves with as many
as they thought fit, to our astonishment who were on the deck, rather than
give any of them to us to eat, as we expected, they tossed the remaining fish
into the sea again, although we begged and prayed for some as well as we
could, but in vain; and some of my countrymen, being pressed by hunger, took
an opportunity, when they thought no one saw them, of trying to get a little
privately; but they were discovered, and the attempt procured them some very
severe floggings. One day, when we had a smooth sea and moderate wind, two
of my wearied countrymen who were chained together (I was near them at
the time), preferring death to such a life of misery, somehow made through
the nettings and jumped into the sea: immediately another quite dejected fellow, who on account of his illness, was suffered to be out of irons, also followed
their example; and I believe many more would very soon have done the same
if they had not been prevented by the ship's crew who were instantly alarmed.
Those of us that were the most active were in a moment put down under the
deck, and there was such a noise and confusion amongst the people of the ship
as I never heard before, to stop her, and get the boat out to go after the slaves.
However two of the wretches were drowned, but they got the other, and afterwards flogged him unmercifully for thus attempting to prefer death to slavery.
In this manner we continued to undergo more hardships than I can now
relate, hardships which are inseparable from this accursed trade. Many a time
we were near suffocation from the want of fresh air, which we were often
without for whole days together. This, and the stench of the necessary tubs,
carried off many. During our passage I first saw flying fishes, which surprised
me very much: they used frequently to fly across the ship, and many of them
fell on the deck. I also now first saw the use of the quadrant; I had often with
astonishment seen the mariners make observations with it, and I could not
think what it meant. They at last took notice of my surprise: and one of them,
willing to increase it, as well as to gratify my curiosity, made me one day look
through it. The clouds appeared to me to be land, which disappeared as they
passed along. This heightened my wonder; and I was now more persuaded
than ever that I was in another world, and that every thing about me was
magic. At last we came in sight of the island of Barbadoes, at which the whites
on board gave a great shout, and made many signs of joy to us. We did not
know what to think of this; but as the vessel drew nearer, we plainly saw the
harbour, and other ships of different kinds and sizes; and we soon anchored
amongst them off Bridge-Town. Many merchants and planters now came on
board, though it was in the evening. They put us in separate parcels, and examined us attentively. They also made us jump, and pointed to the land, signifying we were to go there. We thought by this we should be eaten by these ugly
men, as they appeared to us; and, when soon after we were all put down under
the deck again, there was much dread and trembling among us, and nothing
but bitter cries to be heard all the night from these apprehensions, insomuch
that at last the white people got some old slaves from the land to pacify us.
They told us we were not to be eaten, but to work, and were soon to go on

land, where we should see many of our country people. This report eased us much; and sure enough, soon after we landed, there came to us Africans of all languages. We were conducted immediately to the merchant's yard, where we were all pent up together like so many sheep in a fold, without regard to sex or age. As every object was new to me, every thing I saw filled me with surprise. What struck me first was that the houses were built with bricks and stories, and in every other respect different from those I had seen in Africa: but I was still more astonished on seeing people on horseback. I did not know, what this could mean; and indeed I thought these people were full of nothing but magical arts. While I was in this astonishment one of my fellow prisoners spoke to a countryman of his about the horses, who said they were the same kind they had in their country. I understood them, though they were from a distant part of Africa, and I thought it odd I had not seen any horses there; but afterwards when I came to converse with different Africans, I found they had many horses amongst them, and much larger than those I then saw. We were not many days in the merchant's custody before we were sold after their usual manner, which is this:—On a signal given, (as the beat of a drum) the buyers rush at once into the yard where the slaves are confined, and make choice of that parcel they like best. The noise and clamour with which this is attended, and the eagerness visible in the countenances of the buyers, serve not a little to increase the apprehension of terrified Africans, who may well be supposed to consider them as the ministers of that destruction to which they think themselves devoted. In this manner, without scruple, are relations and friends separated, most of them never to see each other again. I remember in the vessel in which I was brought over, in the men's apartment, there were several brothers, who, in the sale were sold in different lots; and it was very moving on this occasion to see and hear their cries at parting. O, ye nominal Christians! might not an African ask you, learned you this from your God, who says unto you, Do unto all men as you would men should do unto you? Is it not enough that we are torn from our country and friends, to toil for your luxury and lust of gain? Must every tender feeling be likewise sacrificed to your avarice? Are the dearest friends and relations, now rendered more dear by their separation from their kindred, still to be parted from each other, and thus prevented from cheering the gloom of slavery with the small comfort of being together, and mingling their sufferings and sorrows? Why are parents to lose their children, brothers their sisters, or husbands their wives? Surely this is a new refinement in cruelty, which, while it has no advantage to atone for it, thus aggravates distress, and adds fresh horrors even to the wretchedness of slavery.

A Devout Moslem
Sold to the Infidels

Autobiography

OMAR IBN SEID

By the year 1100, the states of West Africa had come under the influence of Islam, and the rulers of Mali and Songhai were devout Moslems. It comes as no surprise, then, that many slaves brought to America were Moslem and spoke Arabic.

Omar ibn Seid, the author of the following sketch, was a member of the Fula tribe from what is now called Senegal. He was born about 1770. After being trained in Arabic and mathematics by his uncle, he became a merchant dealing primarily in cotton cloth. Subsequently, he was captured and sold into slavery in Charleston, South Carolina, by the infidels—in this case, the Christians.

He ran away from his master in South Carolina and was arrested in Fayetteville, North Carolina. While in jail, he began writing on the walls of his cell in Arabic, a feat that brought him to the attention of General James Owen, who purchased him. Although Omar was still a devout Moslem when bought by General Owen, he later converted to Christianity.

This brief autobiography is translated from the Arabic and begins with scattered selections from the Koran that Omar considered relevant to the story he had to tell.

In the name of God, the merciful the gracious.—God grant his blessing upon our Prophet Mohammed. Blessed be He in whose hands is the kingdom and who is Almighty; who created death and life that he might test you; for he is exalted; he is the forgiver (of sins), who created seven heavens one above the other. Do you discern anything trifling in creation? Bring back your thoughts. Do you see anything worthless? Recall your vision in earnest. Turn your eye inward for it is diseased. God has adorned the heavens and the world with lamps, and has made us missiles for the devils, and given us for them a grievous punishment, and to those who have disbelieved their Lord, the punishment of hell and pains of body. Whoever associates with them shall hear a boiling caldron, and what is cast therein may fitly represent those who suffer under the anger of God.—Ask them if a prophet has not been sent unto them. They say, "Yes, a prophet has come to us, but we have lied to him." We said, "God has not sent us down anything, and you are in grievous error." They say, "If we had listened and been wise we should not now have been suffering the punishment of the Omniscient." So they have sinned in destroying the

FROM "Autobiography of Omar ibn Seid, Slave in North Carolina, 1831," *American Historical Review*, Vol. 30 (July 1925), pp. 791–95.

followers of the Omniscient. Those who fear their Lord and profess his name, they receive pardon and great honor. Guard your words, (ye wicked), make it known that God is all-wise in all his manifestations. Do you not know from the creation that God is full of skill? that He has made for you the way of error, and you have walked therein, and have chosen to live upon what your god Nasûr has furnished you? Believe on Him who dwells in heaven, who has fitted the earth to be your support and it shall give you food. Believe on Him who dwells in Heaven, who has sent you a prophet, and you shall understand what a teacher (He has sent you). Those that were before them deceived them (in regard to their prophet). And how came they to reject him? Did they not see in the heavens above them, how the fowls of the air receive with pleasure that which is sent them? God looks after all. Believe ye: it is He who supplies your wants, that you may take his gifts and enjoy them, and take great pleasure in them. And now will you go on in error, or walk in the path of righteousness. Say to them, "He who regards you with care, and who has made for you the heavens and the earth and gives you prosperity, Him you think little of. This is He that planted you in the earth, and to whom you are soon to be gathered." But they say, "If you are men of truth, tell us when shall this promise be fulfilled?" Say to them, "Does not God know? and am not I an evident Prophet?" When those who disbelieve shall see the things draw near before their faces, it shall then be told them, "These are the things about which you made inquiry." Have you seen that God has destroyed me or those with me? or rather that He has shewn us mercy? And who will defend the unbeliever from a miserable punishment? Say, "Knowledge is from God." Say, "Have you not seen that your water has become impure? Who will bring you fresh water from the fountain?"

O Sheikh Hunter, I cannot write my life because I have forgotten much of my own language, as well as of the Arabic. Do not be hard upon me, my brother.—To God let many thanks be paid for his great mercy and goodness.

In the name of God, the Gracious, the Merciful.—Thanks be to God, supreme in goodness and kindness and grace, and who is worthy of all honor, who created all things for his service, even man's power of action and of speech.

FROM OMAR TO SHEIKH HUNTER

You asked me to write my life. I am not able to do this because I have much forgotten my own, as well as the Arabic language. Neither can I write very grammatically or according to the true idiom. And so, my brother, I beg you, in God's name, not to blame me, for I am a man of weak eyes, and of a weak body.

My name is Omar ibn Seid. My birthplace was Fut Tur, between the two rivers. I sought knowledge under the instruction of a Sheikh called Mohammed Seid, my own brother, and Sheikh Soleiman Kembeh, and Sheikh Gabriel Abdal. I continued my studies twenty-five years, and then returned to my home where I remained six years. Then there came to our place a large army, who killed many men, and took me, and brought me to the great sea, and sold me into the hands of the Christians, who bound me and sent me on board a great ship and we sailed upon the great sea a month and a half, when we came to a place called Charleston in the Christian language. There they sold me to a small, weak, and wicked man, called Johnson, a complete infidel, who had no fear of God at all. Now I am a small man, and unable to do hard work so I fled from the hand of Johnson and after a month came to a place called Fayd-il [Fayetteville]. There I saw some great houses (churches). On the new moon I went into a church to pray. A lad saw me and rode off to the place of his father and informed him that he had seen a black man in the church. A man named Handah (Hunter?) and another man with him on horseback, came attended by a troop of dogs. They took me and made me go with them twelve miles to a place called Fayd-il, where they put me into a great house from which I could not go out. I continued in the great house (which, in the Christian language, they called *jail*) sixteen days and nights. One Friday the jailor came and opened the door of the house and I saw a great many men, all Christians, some of. whom called out to me, "What is your name? Is it Omar or Seid?" I did not understand their Christian language. A man called Bob Mumford took me and led me out of the jail, and I was very well pleased to go with them to their place. I stayed at Mumford's four days and nights, and then a man named Jim Owen, son-in-law of Mumford, having married his daughter Betsey, asked me if I was willing to go to a place called Bladen. I said, Yes, I was willing. I went with them and have remained in the place of Jim Owen until now.

Before [after?] I came into the hand of Gen. Owen a man by the name of Mitchell came to buy me. He asked me if I were willing to go to Charleston City. I said "*No, no, no, no, no, no, no,* I not willing to go to Charleston. I stay in the hand of Jim Owen."

O ye people of North Carolina, O ye people of S. Carolina, O ye people of America all of you; have you among you any two such men as Jim Owen and John Owen? These men are good men. What food they eat they give to me to eat. As they clothe themselves they clothe me. They permit me to read the gospel of God, our Lord, and Saviour, and King; who regulates all our circumstances, our health and wealth, and who bestows his mercies willingly, not by constraint. According to power I open my heart, as to a great light, to receive the true way, the way of the Lord Jesus the Messiah.

Before I came to the Christian country, my religion was the religion of "Mohammed, the Apostle of God—may God have mercy upon him and give him peace." I walked to the mosque before day-break, washed my face and head and hands and feet. I prayed at noon, prayed in the afternoon, prayed at sunset, prayed in the evening. I gave alms every year, gold, silver, seeds, cattle, sheep, goats, rice, wheat, and barley. I gave tithes of all the above-named things. I went every year to the holy war against the infidels. I went on pilgrimage to Mecca, as all did who were able.— My father had six sons and five daughters, and my mother had three sons and one daughter. When I left my country I was thirty-seven years old; I have been in the country of the Christians twenty-four years. —Written A. D. 1831.

O ye people of North Carolina, O ye people of South Carolina, O all ye people of America—

The first son of Jim Owen is called Thomas, and his sister is called Masajein (Martha Jane?). This is an excellent family.

Tom Owen and Nell Owen have two sons and a daughter. The first son is called Jim and the second John. The daugher is named Melissa.

Seid Jim Owen and his wife Betsey have two sons and five daughters. Their names are Tom, and John, and Mercy, Miriam, Sophia, Margaret and Eliza. This family is a very nice family. The wife of John Owen is called Lucy and an excellent wife she is. She had five children. Three of them died and two are still living.

O ye Americans, ye people of North Carolina—have you, have you, have you, have you, have you among you a family like this family, having so much love to God as they?

Formerly I, Omar, loved to read the book of the Koran the famous. General Jim Owen and his wife used to read the gospel, and they read it to me very much, —the gospel of God, our Lord, our Creator, our King, He that orders all our circumstances, health and wealth, willingly, not constrainedly, according to his power. —Open thou my heart to the gospel, to the way of uprightness. —Thanks to the Lord of all worlds, thanks in abundance. He is plenteous in mercy and abundant in goodness.

For the law was given by Moses but grace and truth were by Jesus the Messiah.

When I was a Mohammedan I prayed thus: "Thanks be to God, Lord of all worlds, the merciful the gracious, Lord of the day of Judgment, thee we serve, on thee we call for help. Direct us in the right way, the way of those on whom thou hast had mercy, with whom thou hast not been angry and who walk not in error. Amen." —But now I pray "Our Father", etc., in the words of our Lord Jesus the Messiah.

I reside in this our country by reason of great necessity. Wicked men took me by violence and sold me to the Christians. We sailed a month and a half on the great sea to the place called Charleston in the Christian land. I fell into the hands of a small, weak, and wicked man, who feared not God at all, nor did he read (the gospel) at all nor pray. I was afraid to remain with a man so depraved and who committed so many crimes and I ran away. After a month our Lord God brought me forward to the hand of a good man, who fears God, and loves to do good, and whose name is Jim Owen and whose brother is called Col. John Owen. These are two excellent men. —I am residing in Bladen County.

I continue in the hand of Jim Owen who never beats me, nor scolds me. I neither go hungry nor naked, and I have no hard work to do. I am not able to do hard work for I am a small man and feeble. During the last twenty years I have known no want in the hand of Jim Owen.

SUGGESTIONS FOR FURTHER READING

A good place to begin a study of African history is with Robert O. Collins (ed.) *Problems in African History* (1967) or Basil Davidson, *Africa in History*★ (1969). Two works treating the background of the area from which most New World blacks came are J. D. Fage, *History of West Africa* (1962) and Basil Davidson, *A History of West Africa, 1000 to 1900*★ (1965). Documents illustrative of African history are collected in Philip Curtin (ed.), *Africa Remembered: Narratives by West Africans from the Era of the Slave Trade*★ (1968) and Basil Davidson (ed.) *The African Past: Chronicles from Antiquity to Modern Times* (1964).

The prime source for information about the Atlantic slave trade is Elizabeth Donnan (ed.), *Documents Illustrative of the History of the Slave Trade to America*, 4 vols. (1930–1935). The definitive history of the trade is Hugh Thomas, *The Slave Trade*★ (1997). Two briefer works are Basil Davidson, *The African Slave Trade*★ (1961) and Daniel P. Mannix and Malcolm Cowley, *Black Cargoes* (1962). The extent of the trade is explored in Philip D. Curtin, *The Atlantic Slave Trade: A Census* ★(1969).

Special studies include Jay Coughtry, *The Notorious Triangle: Rhode Island and the African Slave Trade, 1700–1807* (1981), John Thornton, *Africa and Africans in the Making of the Atlantic World, 1400–1800*★, 2 ed., (1998), and Joseph E. Inikori and Stanley Engerman (eds.), *The Atlantic Slave Trade: Effects on Economics, Societies, and Peoples in Africa, the Americas, and Europe* ★(1992).

A pioneering study of attempts to end the trade can be found in W. E. B. Du Bois' Harvard dissertation, *The Suppression of the African Slave Trade to the United States, 1638–1870*★ (1896). The impact of the abolition of the slave trade is found in David Eltis and James Walvin (eds.), *The Abolition of the Atlantic Slave Trade: Origins and Effects in Europe, Africa, and the Americas* (1981). An important analysis of the economic impact of the establishment of slavery in the New World is Eric Williams, *Capitalism and Slavery*★ (1944).

★ Books marked by an asterisk are available in paperback.

2

✵

The African-American Before 1800

INTRODUCTION

In 1619, the year before the *Mayflower* crossing, twenty blacks were brought to Jamestown, Virgina, by a Dutch man-of-war. It appears that the Africans had been pirated from a Spanish slave vessel bound for the Caribbean. The blacks were sold by the master of the ship into indentured servitude, thus becoming the first black inhabitants of the English colonies.

In the beginning, it seems that no clear-cut distinction was made between black and white indentured servants, but by 1640 a clear difference in treatment had emerged. In 1641, Massachusetts became the first colony to legally recognize slavery. After the middle of the century, all blacks—and only blacks—entering the colonies came under the slave laws.

Not all Africans in the English colonies were slaves: The original twenty, their descendants, and others who gained their freedom in various ways lived in all parts of the colonies. By the middle of the century, several of these free blacks had become prosperous enough to import white indentured servants to work on their lands.

Black slavery grew slowly in the South until the end of the century, when the rapid growth of plantation agriculture and the opening up of the slave trade on a nonmonopoly basis led to a large increase in the number of Africans imported to the English colonies. This increase in the number of slaves led to the adoption of legal codes designed to limit the activity of the slaves and, hopefully, prevent insurrection and rebellion. These codes generally prohibited the slaves from owning property, carrying weapons, and traveling without a pass. After several abortive insurrections in New York City and in the Southern colonies, the laws became even more repressive.

The slaves were never an important part of the economy of the Northern colonies. Blacks, both slave and free, worked in a variety of capacities in the cities, primarily as domestic servants, artisans, and unskilled laborers. It was customary for slaves to hire themselves out and then pay the masters the wages received. Sometimes the owner allowed the slaves to work out their freedom in this way.

In several Northern cities, white artisans found themselves competing regularly with blacks for the available work. On more than one occasion, the blacks provided such a threat that attempts were made to have them legally barred from doing certain kinds of skilled labor.

As the agitation for self-government grew in the colonies, so the agitation for liberty grew on the part of the slaves, particularly in Massachusetts. In that colony, several slaves sued for their freedom in the courts and won, but each case was separate, and no general ruling was made. Many slaves gained their freedom by fighting in the War for American Independence. Although blacks for the most part had been prohibited from serving in the military, a shortage of troops in 1777 led to a relaxation of the laws, and blacks entered the service of the Continental Army.

As slavery began to be abolished in the North about the time of the war, the racist ideology of the English colonists was threatened by the emergence of the "natural rights" ideas expressed in the Declaration of Independence. But the Constitutional Convention of 1787 got back down to practical matters, and the Great Compromise, which stated that five slaves were to be considered the equivalent of three free persons in determining representation in the lower house of Congress, gave slavery a clear legal basis. As an institution, it was now backed up by the federal Constitution and the strength of federal authority. The retrogressive Constitution, coupled with new technological developments in Southern agriculture, led to a rapid increase in the slave trade, both external and internal. The number of slaves in the United States increased from 697,624 in 1790 to 3,953,760 in 1860—an average increase per decade of 28.2 percent.

Because of widespread racial prejudice, even the free blacks in the North suffered from the indifference and the outright hostility of white society. The extent of this prejudice can be seen, for example, in the development of black religion. When the Africans were first brought to this country, Protestant Christians were reluctant to allow them to be exposed to the teachings of Christianity for fear that they would be converted and thereby gain a claim to freedom. This particular problem was solved when the Virginia legislature ruled in 1677 that becoming a Christian did not alter the status of the convert in this world. No great rush to convert the slaves was made, however, and very few blacks, slave or free, became even nominal Christians during the colonial period.

Only with the growth of Methodist and Baptist churches after the War for American Independence did large numbers of blacks become Christian. Even within these churches, however, they met with so much discrimination, that before the end of the century, several separate black religious societies had been founded.

The free blacks began to realize that individually they were powerless. Only when they began to organize themselves would they have any force in society. Beginning in the 1770s, groups of free blacks began appealing for redress of their grievances to such groups as the Boston Town Selectmen and the Massachusetts legislature. Though their petitions were not always granted, their efforts had a positive effect: The records of those official bodies reflect an attitude of greater respect than before toward the black population. Such groups as the African Society and the African Lodge in Boston and the Free African Society in Philadelphia gave blacks a voice in the public arena that was not easily ignored. Societies like these also provided blacks with financial protection in the form of insurance, a training ground for leadership, and a place where group solidarity could be affirmed.

Though many blacks, both slave and free, had learned to read and write in informal ways before the war, progress in black education was slow in coming. By the end of the eighteenth century, several private schools for blacks had been founded—through white benevolence, as well as black initiative. But no public schools for black children were established in the eighteenth century, and the few black children who attended white schools did not remain long, because of the discrimination they met there.

Organization of free blacks for self-help and self-protection grew apace after the War for American Independence and continued until the Civil War, when the victory of the North led the black population to assume it would be able to move more freely than before within the structure of white institutions, both political and religious.

Blacks Serve the City
in a Time of Crisis

A Narrative of the Proceedings
of the Black People during the Late
Awful Calamity in Philadelphia

ABSALOM JONES AND RICHARD ALLEN

In 1793, an epidemic of yellow fever broke out in Philadelphia. Since an eminent physician of that city, Benjamin Rush, believed that blacks were immune to its ravages, the Free African Society was asked by the mayor to supply nurses and men for burial duty. Hundreds of blacks responded, and—contrary to current medical supposition—hundreds of blacks contracted the disease and died.

At the conclusion of the epidemic, a pamphlet entitled A Short Account of the Malignant Fever, lately prevalent in Philadelphia ... appeared. The author, Matthew Carey, accused some blacks of having looted the possessions of the dead and charged exorbitantly for their services. Although they themselves were specifically exempted from the accusation, Absalom Jones and Richard Allen, who had founded the Free African Society in 1787, replied to the charges in detail.

Their pamphlet of reply, reprinted in the pages that follow, gives a vivid idea of the terror that struck the city along with the disease. As the black leaders point out, profiteering certainly took place during the epidemic, but there was no color line in the matter.

In consequence of a partial representation of the conduct of the people who were employed to nurse the sick, in the late calamitous state of the city of Philadelphia, we are solicited, by a number of those who feel themselves injured thereby, and by the advice of several respectable citizens, to step forward and declare facts as they really were; seeing that from our situation, on account of the charge we took upon us, we had it more fully and generally in our power, to know and observe the conduct and behavior of those that were so employed.

Early in September, a solicitation appeared in the public papers, to the people of colour to come forward and assist the distressed, perishing, and neglected sick; with a kind of assurance, that people of our colour were not liable to take the infection. Upon which we and a few others met and consulted how to act on so truly alarming and melancholy an occasion. After some conversation, we found a freedom to go forth, confiding in him who can preserve in

FROM A. J. and R. A. (Absalom Jones and Richard Allen), *A Narrative of the Proceedings of the Black People during the Late Awful Calamity in Philadelphia in the Year 1793 ...* (Philadelphia, 1794).

the midst of a burning fiery furnace, sensible that it was our duty to do all the good we could to our suffering fellow mortals. We set out to see where we could be useful. The first we visited was a man in Emsley's alley, who was dying, and his wife lay dead at the time in the house, there were none to assist but two poor helpless children. We administered what relief we could, and applied to the overseers of the poor to have the woman buried. We visited upwards of twenty families that day—they were scenes of woe indeed! The Lord was pleased to strengthen us, and remove all fear from us, and disposed our hearts to be as useful as possible.

In order the better to regulate our conduct, we called on the mayor next day, to consult with him how to proceed, so as to be most useful. The first object he recommended was a strict attention to the sick, and the procuring of nurses. This was attended to by Absalom Jones and William Gray; and, in order that the distressed might know where to apply, the mayor advertised the public that upon application to them they would be supplied. Soon after, the mortality increasing, the difficulty of getting a corpse taken away, was such, that few were willing to do it, when offered great rewards. The black people were looked to. We then offered our services in the public papers, by advertising that we would remove the dead and procure nurses. Our services were the production of real sensibility;—we sought not fee nor reward, until the increase of the disorder rendered our labour so arduous that we were not adequate to the service we had assumed. The mortality increasing rapidly, obliged us to call in the assistance of five[1] hired men, in the awful discharge of interring the dead. They, with great reluctance, were prevailed upon to join us. It was very uncommon, at this time, to find any one that would go near, much more, handle, a sick or dead person.

Mr. Carey, in page 106 of his third edition, has observed that, "for the honor of human nature, it ought to be recorded, that some of the convicts in the gaol, a part of the term of whose confinement had been remitted as a reward for their peaceable, orderly behavior, voluntarily offered themselves as nurses to attend the sick at Bush-hill; and have, in that capacity, conducted themselves with great fidelity, &c." Here it ought to be remarked, (although Mr. Carey hath not done it) that two-thirds of the persons, who rendered these essential services, were people of colour, who, on the application of the elders of the African church, (who met to consider what they could do for the help of the sick) were liberated, on condition of their doing the duty of nurses at the hospital at Bush-hill; which they as voluntarily accepted to do, as they did faithfully discharge, this severe and disagreeable duty. —May the Lord reward them, both temporally and spiritually.

When the sickness became general, and several of the physicians died, and most of the survivors were exhausted by sickness or fatigue; that good man, Doctor Rush, called us more immediately to attend upon the sick, knowing we could both bleed; he told us we could increase our utility, by attending to

---

[1] Two of whom were Richard Allen's brothers.

his instructions, and accordingly directed us where to procure medicine duly prepared, with proper directions how to administer them, and at what stages of the disorder to bleed; and when we found ourselves incapable of judging what was proper to be done, to apply to him, and he would, if able, attend them himself, or send Edward Fisher, his pupil, which he often did; and Mr. Fisher manifested his humanity, by an affectionate attention for their relief. — This has been no small satisfaction to us; for, we think, that when a physician was not attainable, we have been the instruments in the hand of God, for saving the lives of some hundreds of our suffering fellow mortals.

We feel ourselves sensibly aggrieved by the censorious epithets of many, who did not render the least assistance in the time of necessity, yet are liberal of their censure of us, for the prices paid for our services, when no one knew how to make a proposal to any one they wanted to assist them. At first we made no charge, but left it to those we served in removing their dead, to give what they thought fit—we set no price, until the reward was fixed by those we had served. After paying the people we had to assist us, our compensation is much less than many will believe.

We do assure the public, that all the money we have received, for burying, and for coffins which we ourselves purchased and procured, has not defrayed the expense of wages which we had to pay to those whom we employed to assist us. The following statement is accurately made:

CASH RECEIVED

The whole amount of Cash we received for burying the dead, and for burying beds, is,	£233 10 4

CASH PAID

For coffins, for which we have received nothing,	£33 0 0	
For the hire of five men, 3 of them 70 days each, and the other two, 63 days each, at 22/6 per day,	378 0 0	
		411 0 0
Debts due us, for which we expect but little,	£110 0 0	
From this statement, for the truth of which we solemnly vouch, it is evident, and we sensibly feel the operation of the fact, that we are out of pocket,		£177 9 8

Besides the costs of hearses, the maintenance of our families for 70 days, (being the period of our labours) and the support of the five hired men, during the respective times of their being employed; which expenses, together with sundry gifts we occasionally made to poor families, might reasonably and properly be introduced, to show our actual situation with regard to profit—but it is enough to exhibit to the public, from the above specified items, of *Cash paid and Cash received*, without taking into view the other expenses, that, by the employment we were engaged in, we lost £ 177 9 8. But, if the other expenses, which we have actually paid, are added to that sum, how much then may we not say we have suffered! We leave the public to judge.

It may possibly appear strange to some who know how constantly we were employed, that we should have received no more Cash than £ 233 10 4. But we repeat our assurance, that this is the fact, and we add another, which will serve the better to explain it: We have buried *several hundreds* of poor persons and strangers, for which service we have never received, nor never asked any compensation.

We feel ourselves hurt most by a partial, censorious paragraph, in Mr. Carey's second edition, of his account of the sickness, &c. in Philadelphia; pages 76 and 77, where he asperses the blacks alone, for having taken the advantage of the distressed situation of the people. That some extravagant prices were paid, we admit; but how came they to be demanded? the reason is plain. It was with difficulty persons could be had to supply the wants of the sick, as nurses; —applications became more and more numerous, the consequence was, when we procured them at six dollars per week, and called upon them to go where they were wanted, we found they were gone elsewhere; here was a disappointment; upon enquiring the cause, we found, they had been allured away by others who offered greater wages, until they got from two to four dollars per day. We had no restraint upon the people. It was natural for people in low circumstances to accept a voluntary, bounteous reward; especially under the loathsomeness of many of the sick, when nature shuddered at the thoughts of the infection, and the task assigned was aggravated by lunacy, and being left much alone with them. Had Mr. Carey been solicited to such an undertaking, for hire, *Query*, "what would *he* have demanded?" but Mr. Carey, although chosen a member of that band of worthies who have so eminently distinguished themselves by their labours, for the relief of the sick and helpless—yet, quickly after his election, left them to struggle with their arduous and hazardous task, by leaving the city. 'Tis true Mr. Carey was no hireling, and had a right to flee, and upon his return, to plead the cause of those who fled; yet, we think, he was wrong in giving so partial and injurious an account of the black nurses; if they have taken advantage of the public distress, is it any more than he hath done of its desire for information? We believe he has made more money by the sale of his "scraps" than a dozen of the greatest extortioners among the black nurses. The great prices paid did not escape the observation of that worthy and vigilant magistrate, Mathew Clarkson, mayor of the city, and president of the committee—he sent for us, and requested we would use our influence, to lessen the wages of the nurses, but on informing him the cause, i.e. that of the people overbidding one another, it was concluded unnecessary to attempt any thing on that head; therefore it was left to the people concerned. That there were some few black people guilty of plundering the distressed, we acknowledge; but in that they only are pointed out, and made mention of, we esteem partial and injurious; we know as many whites who were guilty of it; but this is looked over, while the blacks are held up to censure. —Is it a greater crime for a black to pilfer, than for a white to privateer?

We wish not to offend, but when an unprovoked attempt is made, to make us blacker than we are, it becomes less necessary to be over cautious on that account; therefore we shall take the liberty to tell of the conduct of some of the whites.

We know six pounds was demanded by, and paid, to a white woman, for putting a corpse into a coffin; and forty dollars was demanded, and paid, to four white men, for bringing it down the stairs.

Mr. and Mrs. Taylor both died in one night; a white woman had the care of them; after they were dead she called on Jacob Servoss, esq. for her pay, demanding six pounds for laying them out; upon seeing a bundle with her, he suspected she had pilfered; on searching her, Mr. Taylor's buckles were found in her pocket, with other things.

An elderly lady, Mrs. Malony, was given into the care of a white woman, she died, we were called to remove the corpse, when we came the woman was laying so drunk that she did not know what we were doing, but we know she had one of Mrs. Malony's rings on her finger, and another in her pocket.

Mr. Carey tells us, Bush-hill exhibited as wretched a picture of human misery, as ever existed. A profligate abandoned set of nurses and attendants (hardly any of good character could at that time be procured,) rioted on the provisions and comforts, prepared for the sick, who (unless at the hours when the doctor attended) were left almost entirely destitute of every assistance. The dying and dead were indiscriminately mingled together. The ordure and other evacuations of the sick, were allowed to remain in the most offensive state imaginable. Not the smallest appearance of order or regularity existed. It was in fact a great human slaughter house, where numerous victims were immolated at the altar of intemperance.

It is unpleasant to point out the bad and unfeeling conduct of any colour, yet the defence we have undertaken obliges us to remark, that although "hardly any of good character at that time could be procured" yet only two black women were at this time in the hospital, and they were retained and the others discharged, when it was reduced to order and good government.

The bad consequences many of our colour apprehend from a partial relation of our conduct are, that it will prejudice the minds of the people in general against us—because it is impossible that one individual, can have knowledge of all, therefore at some future day, when some of the most virtuous, that were upon most praise-worthy motives, induced to serve the sick, may fall into the service of a family that are strangers to him, or her, and it is discovered that it is one of those stigmatised wretches, what may we suppose will be the consequence? Is it not reasonable to think the person will be abhored, despised, and perhaps dismissed from employment, to their great disadvantage, would not this be hard? and have we not therefore sufficient reason to seek for redress? We can with certainty assure the public that we have seen more humanity, more real sensibility from the poor blacks, than from the poor whites. When many of the former, of their own accord rendered services where extreme necessity called for it, the general part of the poor white people were so dismayed, that instead of attempting to be useful, they in a manner hid themselves—a remarkable instance of this—A poor afflicted dying man, stood at his chamber window, praying and beseeching every one that passed by, to help him to a drink of water; a number of white people passed, and instead of being moved by the poor man's distress, they hurried as fast as they could out of the sound of his cries—until at length a gentleman, who seemed to be a foreigner came up, he could not pass by, but had not resolution enough to go into the house, he held eight dollars in his hand, and offered it to several as a reward for giving the poor man a drink of water, but was refused by every one, until a poor black man came up, the gentleman offered the eight dollars to him, if he would relieve the poor man with a little water, "Master" replied the good natured fellow, "I will supply the gentleman with water, but surely I will not take your money for it" nor could he be prevailed upon to accept his bounty: he went in, supplied the poor object with water, and rendered him every service he could.

A poor black man, named Sampson, went constantly from house to house where distress was, and no assistance without fee or reward; he was smote with the disorder, and died, after his death his family were neglected by those he had served.

Sarah Bass, a poor black widow, gave all the assistance she could, in several families, for which she did not receive any thing; and when any thing was offered her, she left it to the option of those she served.

A woman of our colour, nursed Richard Mason and son, when they died, Richard's widow considering the risk the poor woman had run, and from observing the fears that sometimes rested on her mind, expected she would have demanded something considerable, but upon asking what she demanded, her reply was half a dollar per day. Mrs. Mason, intimated it was not sufficient for her attendance, she replied it was enough for what she had done, and would take no more. Mrs. Mason's feelings were such, that she settled an annuity of six pounds a year, on her, for life. Her name is Mary Scott.

An elderly black woman nursed—with great diligence and attention; when recovered he asked what he must give for her services—she replied "a dinner master on a cold winter's day," and thus she went from place to place rendering every service in her power without an eye to reward.

A young black woman, was requested to attend one night upon a white man and his wife, who were very ill, no other person could be had; —great wages were offered her—she replied, I will not go for money, if I go for money God will see it, and may be make me take the disorder and die, but if I go, and take no money, he may spare my life. She went about nine o'clock, and found them both on the floor; she could procure no candle or other light, but staid with them about two hours, and then left them. They both died that night. She was afterward very ill with the fever—her life was spared.

Caesar Cranchal, a black man, offered his services to attend the sick, and said, I will not take your money, I will not sell my life for money. It is said he died with the flux.

A black lad, at the Widow Gilpin's, was intrusted with his young Master's keys, on his leaving the city, and transacted his business, with the greatest honesty, and dispatch, having unloaded a vessel for him in the time, and loaded it again.

A woman, that nursed David Bacon, charged with exemplary moderation, and said she would not have any more.

It may be said, in vindication of the conduct of those, who discovered ignorance or incapacity in nursing, that it is, in itself, a considerable art, derived from experience, as well as the exercise of the finer feelings of humanity—this experience, nine-tenths of those employed, it is probable were wholly strangers to.

We do not recollect such acts of humanity from the poor white people, in all the round we have been engaged in. We could mention many other instances of the like nature, but think it needless.

It is unpleasant for us to make these remarks, but justice to our colour, demands it. Mr. Carey pays William Gray and us a compliment; he says, our services and others of their colour, have been very great &c. By naming us, he leaves these others, in the hazardous state of being classed with those who are called the "vilest." The few that were discovered to merit public censure, were brought to justice, which ought to have sufficed, without being canvassed over in his "Trifle" of a pamphlet—which causes us to be more particular, and endeavour to recall the esteem of the public for our friends, and the people of colour, as far as they may be found worthy; for we conceive, and experience proves it, that an ill name is easier given than taken away. We have many unprovoked enemies, who begrudge us the liberty we enjoy, and are glad to hear of any complaint against our colour, be it just or unjust; in consequence of which we are more earnestly endeavouring all in our power, to warn, rebuke, and exhort our African friends, to keep a conscience void of offence towards God and man; and, at the same time, would not be backward to interfere, when stigmas or oppression appear pointed at, or attempted against them, unjustly; and, we are confident, we shall stand justified in the sight of the candid and judicious, for such conduct.

Mr. Carey's first, second, and third editions, are gone forth into the world, and in all probability, have been read by thousands that will never read his fourth—consequently, any alteration he may hereafter make, in the paragraph alluded to, cannot have the desired effect, or atone for the past; therefore we apprehend it necessary to publish our thoughts on the occasion. Had Mr. Carey said, a number of white and black Wretches eagerly seized on the opportunity to extort from the distressed, and some few of both were detected in plundering the sick, it might extenuate, in a great degree, the having made mention of the blacks.

We can assure the public, there were as many white as black people, detected in pilfering, although the number of the latter, employed as nurses, was twenty times as great as the former, and that there is, in our opinion, as great a proportion of white, as of black, inclined to such practices. It is rather to be admired, that so few instances of pilfering and robbery happened, considering the great opportunities there were for such things: we do not know of more than five black people, suspected of any thing clandestine, out of the great number employed; the people were glad to get any person to assist them—a black was preferred, because it was supposed, they were not so likely to take the disorder, the most worthless were acceptable, so that it would have been no cause of wonder, if twenty causes of complaint occurred, for one that hath. It has been alledged, that many of the sick, were neglected by the nurses; we do not wonder at it, considering their situation, in many instances, up night and day, without any one to relieve them, worn down with fatigue, and want of sleep, they could not in many cases, render that assistance, which was needful: where we visited, the causes of complaint on this score, were not numerous. The case of the nurses, in many instances, were deserving of commiseration, the patient raging and frightful to behold; it has frequently required two persons, to hold them from running away, others have made attempts to jump out of a window, in many chambers they were nailed down, and the door was kept locked, to prevent them from running away, or breaking their necks, others lay vomiting blood, and screaming enough to chill them with horror. Thus were many of the nurses circumstanced, alone, until the patient died, then called away to another scene of distress, and thus have been for a week or ten days left to do the best they could without any sufficient rest, many of them having some of their dearest connections sick at the time, and suffering for want, while their husband, wife, father, mother, &c. have been engaged in the service of the white people. We mention this to shew the difference between this and nursing in common cases, we have suffered equally with the whites, our distress hath been very great, but much unknown to the white people. Few have been the whites that paid attention to us while the blacks were engaged in the other's service. We can assure the public we have taken four and five black people in a day to be buried. In several instances when they have been seized with the sickness while nursing, they have been turned out of the house, and wandering and destitute until taking shelter wherever they could (as many of them would not be admitted to their former homes) they have languished alone and we know of one who even died in a stable. Others acted with more tenderness, when their nurses were taken sick they had proper care taken of them at their houses. We know of two instances of this.

It is even to this day a generally received opinion in this city, that our colour was not so liable to the sickness as the whites. We hope our friends will pardon us for setting this matter in its true state.

The public were informed that in the West-Indies and other places where this terrible malady had been, it was observed the blacks were not affected with it. Happy would it have been for you, and much more so for us, if this observation had been verified by our experience.

When the people of colour had the sickness and died, we were imposed upon and told it was not with the prevailing sickness, until it became too notorious to be denied, then we were told some few died but not many. Thus were our services extorted *at the peril of our lives*, yet you accuse us of extorting *a little money from you*.

The bill of mortality for the year 1793, published by Matthew Whitehead, and John Ormrod, clerks, and Joseph Dolby, sexton, will convince any reasonable man that will examine it, that as many coloured people died in proportion as others. In 1792, there were 67 of our colour buried, and in 1793 it amounted to 305; thus the burials among us have increased more than fourfold, was not this in a great degree the effects of the services of the unjustly vilified black people?

Perhaps it may be acceptable to the reader to know how we found the sick affected by the sickness; our opportunities of hearing and seeing them have been very great. They were taken with a chill, a headach, a sick stomach, with pains in their limbs and back, this was the way the sickness in general began, but all were not affected alike, some appeared but slightly affected with some of these symptoms, what confirmed us in the opinion of a person being smitten was the colour of their eyes. In some it raged more furiously than in others—some have languished for seven and ten days, and appeared to get better the day, or some hours before they died, while others were cut off in one, two, or three days, but their complaints were similar. Some lost their reason and raged with all the fury madness could produce, and died in strong convulsions. Others retained their reason to the last, and seemed rather to fall asleep than die. We could not help remarking that the former were of strong passions, and the latter of a mild temper. Numbers died in a kind of dejection, they concluded they must go, (so the phrase for dying was) and therefore in a kind of fixed determined state of mind went off.

It struck our minds with awe, to have application made by those in health, to take charge of them in their sickness, and of their funeral. Such applications have been made to us; many appeared as though they thought they must die, and not live; some have lain on the floor, to be measured for their coffin and grave. A gentleman called one evening, to request a good nurse might be got for him, when he was sick, and to superintend his funeral, and gave particular directions how he would have it conducted, it seemed a surprising circumstance, for the man appeared at the time, to be in perfect health, but calling two or three days after to see him, found a woman dead in the house, and the man so far gone, that to administer any thing for his recovery, was needless— he died that evening. We mention this, as an instance of the dejection and despondence, that took hold on the minds of thousands, and are of opinion, it aggravated the case of many, while others who bore up chearfully, got up again, that probably would otherwise have died.

When the mortality came to its greatest stage, it was impossible to procure sufficient assistance, therefore many whose friends, and relations had left them, died unseen, and unassisted. We have found them in various situations, some laying on the floor, as bloody as if they had been dipt in it, without any appearance of their having had, even a drink of water for their relief; others laying on a bed with their clothes on, as if they had came in fatigued, and lain down to rest; some appeared, as if they had fallen dead on the floor, from the position we found them in.

Truly our task was hard, yet through mercy, we were enabled to go on.

One thing we observed in several instances—when we were called, on the first appearance of the disorder to bleed, the person frequently, on the opening a vein before the operation was near over, felt a change for the better, and expressed a relief in their chief complaints; and we made it a practice to take more blood from them, than is usual in other cases; these in a general way recovered; those who did omit bleeding any considerable time, after being taken by the sickness, rarely expressed any change they felt in the operation.

We feel a great satisfaction in believing, that we have been useful to the sick, and thus publicly thank Doctor Rush, for enabling us to be so. We have bled upwards of eight hundred people, and do declare, we have not received to the value of a dollar and a half, therefor: we were willing to imitate the Doctor's benevolence, who sick or well, kept his house open day and night, to give what assistance he could in this time of trouble.

Several affecting instances occurred, when we were engaged in burying the dead. We have been called to bury some, who when we came, we found alive; at other places we found a parent dead, and none but little innocent babes to be seen, whose ignorance led them to think their parent was asleep; on account of their situation, and their little prattle, we have been so wounded and our feelings so hurt, that we almost concluded to withdraw from our undertaking, but seeing others so backward, we still went on.

An affecting instance. —A woman died, we were sent for to bury her, on our going into the house and taking the coffin in, a dear little innocent accosted us, with, mamma is asleep, don't wake her; but when she saw us put her in the coffin, the distress of the child was so great, that it almost overcame us; when she demanded why we put her mamma in the box? We did not know how to answer her, but committed her to the care of a neighbour, and left her with heavy hearts. In other places where we have been to take the corpse of a parent, and have found a group of little ones alone, some of them in a measure capable of knowing their situation, their cries and the innocent confusion of the little ones, seemed almost too much for human nature to bear. We have picked up little children that were wandering they knew not where, (whose parents were cut off) and taken them to the orphan house, for at this time the dread that prevailed over people's minds was so general, that it was a rare instance to see one neighbour visit another, and even friends when they met in the streets were afraid of each other, much less would they admit into their houses the distressed orphan that had been where the sickness was; this extreme seemed in some instances to have the appearance of barbarity; with reluctance we call to mind the many opportunities there were in the power of individuals to be useful to their fellow-men, yet through the terror of the times was omitted. A black man riding through the street, saw a man push a woman out of the house, the woman staggered and fell on her face in the gutter, and was not able to turn herself, the black man thought she was drunk, but observing she was in danger of suffocation alighted, and taking the woman up found her perfectly sober, but so far gone with the disorder that she was not able to help herself; the hard hearted man that threw her down, shut the door and left her—in such a situation, she might have perished in a few minutes; we heard of it, and took her to Bush-hill. Many of the white people, that ought to be patterns for us to follow after, have acted in a manner that would make humanity shudder. We remember an instance of cruelty, which we trust, no black man would be guilty of: two sisters orderly, decent, white women were sick with the fever, one of them recovered so as to come to the door; a neighbouring white man saw her, and in an angry tone asked her if her sister was dead or not? She answered no, upon which he replied, damn her, if she don't die before morning, I will make her die. The poor woman shocked at such an expression, from this monster of a man, made a modest reply, upon which he snatched up a tub of water, and would have dashed it over her, if he had not been prevented by a black man; he then went and took a couple of fowls out of a coop, (which had been given them for nourishment) and threw them into an open alley; he had his wish, the poor woman that he would make die, died that night. A white man threatened to shoot us, if we passed by his house with a corpse: we buried him three days after.

We have been pained to see the widows come to us, crying and wringing their hands, and in very great distress, on account of their husbands' death; having nobody to help them, they were obliged to come to get their husbands buried, their neighbours were afraid to go to their help or to condole with them; we ascribe such unfriendly conduct to the frailty of human nature, and not to wilful unkindness, or hardness of heart.

Notwithstanding the compliment Mr. Carey hath paid us, we have found reports spread, of our taking between one, and two hundred beds, from houses where people died; such slanderers as these, who propagate such wilful lies are dangerous, although unworthy notice. We wish if any person hath the least suspicion of us, they would endeavour to bring us to the punishment which such atrocious conduct must deserve; and by this means, the innocent will be cleared from reproach, and the guilty known.

We shall now conclude with the following old proverb, which we think applicable to those of our colour who exposed their lives in the late afflicting dispensation: —

God and a soldier, all men do adore,
In time of war, and not before;
When the war is over, and all things righted
God is forgotten, and the soldier slighted.

Black People Organize
for Self-Protection
The Rules of the African Society

In 1693, the Puritan leader Cotton Mather printed what he called "Rules for a Society of Negroes." These rules were designed to guide the blacks in becoming docile, obedient, loyal, sober Christians. They showed little understanding of the black man's need for freedom and self-expression. Although Mather was a zealous advocate of education for blacks, his recommendations seemed to be primarily in the interests of white society.

When blacks began to organize themselves, it became clear that their interests were a good deal less abstract than Mather's. True, they were interested in moral uplift; but their major concern was economic protection—protection of themselves and of their families. Hence, most of the early African societies stressed the need for life (actually death) insurance and for legal protection of heirs, lest they be sold into slavery on one pretext or another.

The document that follows is a simple and straightforward list of the rules of the African Society of Boston, formed in 1796. In 1802, when this list was published in pamphlet form, the society had forty-four members.

1st. We, the African Members, form ourselves into a Society, under the above name, for the mutual benefit of each other, which may from time to time offer; behaving ourselves at the same time as true and faithful Citizens of the Commonwealth in which we live; and that we take no one into the Society, who shall commit any injustice or outrage against the laws of their country.

2d. That before any person can become a Member of the Society, he must be presented by three of the Members of the same; and the person, or persons, wishing to become Members, must make application one month at least beforehand, and that at one of the monthly, or three monthly meetings. Person, or persons if approved of shall be received into the Society. And, that before the admittance of any person into the Society, he shall be obliged to read the rules, or cause the same to be read to him; and not be admitted as a member unless he approves them.

3d. That each Member on admittance, shall pay one quarter of a Dollar to the Treasurer; and be credited for the same, in the books of the Society; and his name added to the list of the Members.

FROM *Laws of the African Society, Instituted at Boston Anno Domini, 1796* (Boston, 1802). Reprinted by permission from a pamphlet in the Library of the Boston Athenxum.

4th. That each Member shall pay one quarter of a Dollar per month to the Treasurer, and be credited for the same on the book; but no benefit can be tendered to any Member, until he has belonged to the Society one year.

5th. That any Member, or Members, not able to attend the regular meetings of the Society, may pay their part by appointing one of their brothers to pay the same for him: So any traveling, at a distance by sea, or land, may, by appointing any person to pay their subscription, will be, though absent for any length of time, or on their return, will pay up the same, shall still be considered as brothers, and belonging to the Society.

6th. That no money shall be returned to any one, that shall leave the Society; but if the Society should see fit to dismiss any one from their community, it shall then be put to a vote, whether the one, thus dismissed shall have his money again, if he should have any left, when the expences he may have been to the Society are deducted.

7th. That any Member, absenting himself from the Society, for the space of one year, shall be considered as separating himself from the same; but, if he should return at the end of that time, and pay up his subscription, he shall in six months be re-established in all the benefits of a Societain: But after that time he shall be considered as a new Member.

8th. That a committee, consisting of three, or five persons, shall be chosen by the members every three months; and that their chief care shall be, to attend to the sick, and see that they want nothing that the Society can give, and inform the Society, at their next meeting of those who stand in need of assistance of the Society, and of what was done during the time of their committeement. The committee shall likewise be empowered to call the Society together as often as may be necessary.

9th. That all monies, paid into the Society, shall be credited to the payers; and all going out, shall be debted to whom, or what for; and a regular account kept by one, chosen by the Society for that purpose.

10th. When any Member, or Members of the Society is sick, and not able to supply themselves with necessaries, suitable to their situations, the committee shall then tender to them and their family whatever the Society have, or may think fit for them. And should any Member die, and not leave wherewith to pay the expences of his funeral, the Society shall then see that any, so situated, be decently buried. But it must be remembered, that any Member, bringing on himself any sickness, or disorder, by intemperance, shall not be considered, as entitled to any benefits, or assistance from the Society.

11th. Should any Member die, and leave a lawful widow and children, the Society shall consider themselves bound to relieve her necessities, so long as she behaves herself decently, and remains a widow; and that the Society do the best in their power to place the children so that they may in time be capable of getting an honest living.

12th. Should the Society, with the blessing of Heaven, acquire a sum, suitable to bear interest, they will then take into consideration the best method they can, of making it useful.

13th. The Members will watch over each other in their Spiritual concerns; and by advice, exhortation, and prayer excite each other to grow in Grace, and in the knowledge of our Lord and Saviour Jesus Christ, and to live soberly, righteously and Godly, in this present world, that we may all be accepted of the Redeemer, and live together with him in Glory hereafter.

14th. That each Member traveling for any length of time, by Sea or Land, shall leave a Will with the Society, or being married, with his wife, all other Members to leave a Will with the Society, for to enable them to recover their effects, if they should not return, but on their return, this Will is to be returned to the one that gave it, but if he should not return, and leave a lawful heir, the property is to be delivered to him; otherwise deemed to the Society.

☞ The African Society have a Charity Lecture quarterly, on the second Tuesday in every third month.

A Plea for Federal Protection
for Manumitted Slaves
in the South

Petition of Four Free Blacks to the United States House of Representatives, 1797

Toward the close of the eighteenth century, the Southern states were beginning to fear the large number of free blacks living in their midst. As a result, they passed laws severely restricting the freeing, or manumission, of slaves. In 1775, North Carolina passed a law forbidding manumission not previously approved by a county court. Certain whites, however, continued to free their slaves; so, in 1778, North Carolina passed another law, providing a reward for the capture and resale of illegally freed blacks.

Needless to say, all free blacks were soon threatened by roving bands of whites intent on collecting the rewards. Many blacks left the state and settled in the North. In 1797, four of these "fugitive" free men filed a petition in the House of Representatives seeking federal protection for themselves and freedom for their relatives who had been freed and then sold again into slavery. The petition is reprinted here in its entirety.

After some debate, the House voted not to accept the petition, and the fate of black men was left to the discretion of the individual states.

To the President, Senate, and House of Representatives

The Petition and Representation of the under-named Freemen, respectfully showeth: —

That, being of African descent, late inhabitants and natives of North Carolina, to you only, under God, can we apply with any hope of effect, for redress of our grievances, having been compelled to leave the State wherein we had a right of residence, as freemen liberated under the hand and seal of humane and conscientious masters, the validity of which act of justice, in restoring us to our native right of freedom, was confirmed by judgment of the Superior Court of North Carolina, wherein it was brought to trial; yet, not long after this decision, a law of that State was enacted, under which men of cruel disposition, and void of just principle, received countenance and authority in violently seizing, imprisoning, and selling into slavery, such as had been so emancipated; whereby we were reduced to the necessity of separating from some of our nearest and most tender connexions, and of seeking refuge in such

FROM *Annals of the Congress of the United States*, 4th Congress, 2nd Session (1796–97), pp. 2015–18.

parts of the Union where more regard is paid to the public declaration in favor of liberty and the common right of man, several hundreds, under our circumstances, having in consequence of the said law, been hunted day and night, like beasts of the forest, by armed men with dogs, and made a prey of as free and lawful plunder. Among others thus exposed, I, Jupiter Nicholson, of Perquimans county, North Carolina, after being set free by my master, Thomas Nicholson, and having been about two years employed as a seaman in the service of Zachary Nickson, on coming on shore, was pursued by men with dogs and arms; but was favored to escape by night to Virginia, with my wife, who was manumitted by Gabriel Cosand, where I resided about four years in the town of Portsmouth, chiefly employed in sawing boards and scantling; from thence I removed with my wife to Philadelphia, where I have been employed, at times, by water, working along shore, or sawing wood. I left behind me a father and mother, who were manumitted by Thomas Nicholson and Zachary Nickson; they have since been taken up, with a beloved brother, and sold into cruel bondage.

I, Jacob Nicholson, also of North Carolina, being set free by my master, Joseph Nicholson, but continuing to live with him till, being pursued night and day, I was obliged to leave my abode, sleep in the woods, and stacks in the fields, &c, to escape the hands of violent men who, induced by the profit afforded them by law, followed this course as a business; at length, by night, I made my escape, leaving a mother, one child, and two brothers, to see whom I dare not return.

I, Job Albert, manumitted by Benjamin Albertson, who was my careful guardian to protect me from being afterwards taken and sold, providing me with a house to accommodate me and my wife, who was liberated by William Robertson; but we were night and day hunted by men armed with guns, swords, and pistols, accompanied with mastiff dogs; from whose violence, being one night apprehensive of immediate danger, I left my dwelling, locked and barred, and fastened with a chain, being at some distance from it, while my wife was by my kind master locked up under his roof. I heard them break into my house, where, not finding their prey, they got but a small booty, a handkerchief of about a dollar value, and some provisions; but, not long after, I was discovered and seized by Alexander Stafford, William Stafford, and Thomas Creesy, who were armed with guns and clubs. After binding me with my hands behind me, and a rope around my arms and body, they took me about four miles to Hartford prison, where I lay four weeks, suffering much from want of provision; from thence, with the assistance of a fellow-prisoner, (a white man,) I made my escape and for three dollars was conveyed, with my wife, by a humane person, in a covered wagon by night, to Virginia, where, in the neighborhood of Portsmouth, I continued unmolested about four years, being chiefly engaged in sawing boards and plank. On being advised to move Northward, I came with my wife to Philadelphia, where I have labored for a livelihood upwards of two years, in Summer mostly, along shore in vessels and stores, and sawing wood in the Winter. My mother was set free by Phineas Nickson, my sister by John Trueblood, and both taken up and sold into slavery, myself deprived of the consolation of seeing them, without being exposed to the like grievous oppression.

I, Thomas Pritchet, was set free by my master Thomas Pritchet, who furnished me with land to raise provisions for my use, where I built myself a house, cleared a sufficient spot of woodland to produce ten bushels of corn; the second year about fifteen, and the third, had as much planted as I suppose would have produced thirty bushels; this I was obliged to leave about one month before it was fit for gathering, being threatened by Holland Lockwood, who married my said master's widow, that if I would not come and serve him, he would apprehend me, and send me to the West Indies; Enoch Ralph also threatening to send me to jail, and sell me for the good of the country; being thus in jeopardy, I left my little farm, with my small stock and utensils, and my corn standing, and escaped by night into Virginia, where shipping myself for Boston, I was, through stress of weather landed in New York, where I served as a waiter for seventeen months; but my mind being distressed on account of the situation of my wife and children, I returned to Norfolk in Virginia, with a hope of at least seeing them, if I could not obtain their freedom; but finding I was advertised in the newspaper, twenty dollars the reward for apprehending me, my dangerous situation obliged me to leave Virginia, disappointed of seeing my wife and children, coming to Philadelphia, where I resided in the employment of a waiter upward of two years.

In addition to the hardship of our own case, as above set forth, we believe ourselves warranted, on the present occasion, in offering to your consideration the singular case of a fellow-black now confined in the jail of this city, under sanction of the act of General Government, called the Fugitive Law, as it appears to us a flagrant proof how far human beings, merely on account of color and complexion, are, through prevailing prejudice, outlawed and excluded from common justice and common humanity, by the operation of such partial laws in support of habits and customs cruelly oppressive. This man, having been many years past manumitted by his master in North Carolina, was under the authority of the aforementioned law of that State, sold again into slavery, and, after serving his purchaser upwards of six years, made his escape to Philadelphia, where he has resided eleven years, having a wife and [f]our children; and, by an agent of the Carolina claimer, has been lately apprehended and committed to prison, his said claimer, soon after the man's escaping from him, having advertised him, offering a reward of ten silver dollars to any person that would bring him back, or five times that sum to any person that would make due proof of his being killed, and no questions asked by whom.

We beseech your impartial attention to our hard condition, not only with respect to our personal sufferings, as freemen, but as a class of that people who, distinguished by color, are therefore with a degrading partiality, considered by many, even of those in eminent stations, as unentitled to that public justice and protection which is the great object of Government. We indulge not a hope, or presume to ask for the interposition of your honorable body, beyond the extent of your constitutional power or influence, yet are willing to believe your serious, disinterested, and candid consideration of the premises, under the benign impressions of equity and mercy, producing upright exertion of what is in your power, may not be without some salutary effect, both for our relief as a people, and toward the removal of obstructions to public order and well-being.

If, notwithstanding all that has been publicly avowed as essential principles respecting the extent of human right to freedom; notwithstanding we have had the right restored to us, so far as was in the power of those by whom we were held as slaves, we cannot claim the privilege of representation in your councils, yet we trust we may address you as fellow-men, who, under God, the sovereign Ruler of the Universe, are intrusted with the distribution of justice, for the terror of evil-doers, the encouragement and protection of the inno-cent, not doubting that you are men of liberal minds, susceptible of benevo-lent feelings and clear conception of rectitude to a catholic extent, who can admit that black people (servile as their condition generally is throughout this Continent) have natural affections, social and domestic attachments and sensi-bilities; and that, therefore, we may hope for a share in your sympathetic attention while we represent that the unconstitutional bondage in which mul-titudes of our fellows in complexion are held, is to us a subject sorrowfully affecting; for we cannot conceive this condition (more especially those who have been emancipated and tasted the sweets of liberty, and again reduced to slavery by kidnappers and man-stealers) to be less afflicting or deplorable than the situation of citizens of the United States, captured and enslaved through the unrighteous policy prevalent in Algiers. We are far from considering all those who retain slaves as wilful oppressors, being well assured that numbers in the State from whence we are exiles, hold their slaves in bondage, not of choice, but possessing them by inheritance, feel their minds burdened under the slavish restraint of legal impediments to doing justice which they are convinced is due to fellow-nationals. May we not be allowed to consider this stretch of power, morally and politically, a Governmental defect, if not a direct violation of the declared fundamental principles of the Constitution; and finally, is not some remedy for an evil of such magnitude highly worthy of the deep inquiry and unfeigned zeal of the supreme Legislative body of a free and enlightened people? Submitting our cause to God, and humbly craving your best aid and influence, as you may be favored and directed by that wisdom which is from above, wherewith that you may be eminently dignified and rendered conspicuously, in the view of nations, a blessing to the people you represent, is the sincere prayer of your petitioners.

–JACOB NICHOLSON,
–JUPITER NICHOLSON, his mark,
–JOB ALBERT, his mark,
–THOMAS PRITCHET, his mark.

Philadelphia, January 23, 1797.

SUGGESTIONS FOR FURTHER READING

In recent years, many excellent studies of African–American life in the colonial period have appeared. Some of the best of these are Ira Berlin, *Many Thousand Gone: The First Two Centuries of Slavery in North America*★ (1998), Mechal Sobel, *The World They Made Together: Black and White Values in Eighteenth Century Virginia*★ (1987), Marvin L. Michael Kay and Lorin Lee Cary, *Slavery in North Carolina, 1748–1775*★ (1995), Robert Olwell, *Masters, Slaves, and Subjects: The Culture of Power in the South Carolina Low Country, 1740–1790*★ (1998), Philip D. Morgan, *Slave Counterpoint: Black Culture in the 18th Century Chesapeake and Lowcountry*★ (1998), and Gwendolyn Midlo Hall, *Africans in Colonial Louisiana: The Development of Afro-Creole Culture in the Eighteenth Century*★ (1995). Older works include Peter Wood, *Black Majority: Negroes in Colonial South Carolina from 1670 through the Stono Rebellion*★ (1974), Edmund S. Morgan, *American Slavery—American Freedom: The Ordeal of Colonial Virginia*★ (1975), and Allan Kulikoff, *Tobacco and Slaves: The Development of Southern Cultures in the Chesapeake, 1680–1800*★ (1986).

Works that describe the formation of racial attitudes that led to the adoption and maintenance in British America are Winthrop Jordan, *White over Black: American Attitudes toward the Negro, 1550–1812*★ (1968), and two books by David D. Davis, *The Problem of Slavery in Western Culture*★ (1966) and *The Problem of Slavery in the Age of Revolution, 1770–1823*★ (1975).

Two books on slave rebellion are Gerald Mullin, *Flight and Rebellion: Slave Resistance in Eighteenth Century Virginia*★ (1972) and T. J. Davis, *A Rumor of Revolt: The "Great Negro Plot" in Colonial New York* (1985). A successful slave revolt in the Caribbean that had a great effect on nineteenth century slavery is treated by C. L. R. James in *Black Jacobins: Toussaint L 'Ouverture and the San Domingo Revolution*★ (1938).

★ Books marked with an asterisk are available in paperback.

3

✪

Slavery in the Nineteenth Century

INTRODUCTION

Slavery was virtually eliminated in the North, except in New York and New Jersey, before the end of the eighteenth century. It had proved to be economically unviable, and under pressure from free labor, abolitionists, and the blacks themselves, the new state constitutions and the various legislatures had ruled the enslavement of human beings illegal. It is sometimes suggested that slavery was on its way out in the South at the same time. Although this view has been discredited, there is no doubt that slavery in the South changed character and dimension radically in the nineteenth century.

The invention of the cotton gin in 1793, which made it possible to separate the seeds from the fiber of cotton quickly and on a large scale, and the purchase of the Louisiana Territory in 1803, which freed the Gulf Coast and the Mississippi River for the transportation of cotton bales, made short-staple cotton king in the Deep South. By the early nineteenth century, cotton had become the basic crop of Georgia and the Carolina foothills. In 1811, two-thirds of all the cotton grown in the United States came from this region. The cultivation of cotton rapidly spread farther south, however, and as it became clear that the rich soil of the Deep South provided ideal conditions for the growing of cotton, the center of production shifted. By 1860, the states of the Deep South and the Southwest as far as Texas were producing three-fourths of the cotton grown in the United States.

Many yeoman farmers found that cotton could be a money crop, even on a small farm, but the plantation system came to be the most profitable one for cotton production. The backbone of the plantation system was, of course, the field slave. As cotton production moved south into the coastal and delta lands, plantations that were often quite large were set up there, and large numbers of slaves were called for. There were two obvious ways to procure the needed slaves—through the external and the internal slave trades. Although the external trade was declared illegal by the federal government in 1808, only token attempts were made to enforce this legislation, and it is estimated that from 250,000 to 300,000 African slaves were brought into the South between 1808 and 1860. More important, however, was the internal trade.

As the slave system became less viable in the Southeast because of the havoc wrought with the soil through intensive tobacco farming, the surplus of slaves could be sold to the new cotton-producing areas at great profit. Soon, then, the Southeast found itself literally breeding slaves for the market. The selling of slaves became a major item in Virginia's economy, and the sight of a hundred or more slaves chained together, walking from the upper to the lower South, was not uncommon.

Even though cotton was king, just under half the slaves in the South were engaged in cotton production. The rest were engaged in other kinds of agricultural work or—in the case of the 400,000 who lived in towns or cities—were involved in various trades, both skilled and unskilled.

When considering the creative role played in American history by blacks, one must note first of all that most slaves were merely victims. There were, however, many who found ways of seeking deliverance from the system that denied them even the most fundamental of human rights. It was in this search for freedom and self-expression that the slaves made their most important contributions to our heritage.

The first and most obvious way of seeking deliverance was through organized rebellion or insurrection. There is much controversy over the number of slave rebellions that actually occurred in the South. Many of the so-called uprisings undoubtedly took place only in the minds of an increasingly fearful white slave-owning population. But the threat of insurrection was real, and the slave-owners' fear was historically justified, for groups of slaves had been rebelling ever since the Africans arrived in the New World. In the Caribbean and in Brazil, for instance, large numbers of slaves had fought for freedom from their masters and had succeeded in setting up independent states. And Southern whites were well informed about the role played by the slaves in establishing Haiti as a free black state and thus destroying Napoleon's dream of a Western empire.

The three most widely publicized slave conspiracies in the United States were those led by Gabriel Prosser in Richmond, Virginia, in 1800; by Denmark Vesey in Charleston, South Carolina, in 1822; and by Nat Turner near Southampton, Virginia, in 1831. As a result of these conspiracies, the laws restricting the freedom of slaves and free blacks in the South were made even more oppressive. The very heavy-handedness of the measures taken to suppress the slaves indicates that the slave masters lived in great fear of black rebellion—

a fact that belies the pious utterings of those who have sought to defend slavery on the grounds that the slaves themselves were content.

A second form of revolt for the slave was simply running away. From the beginning of slavery in the colonies, large numbers of slaves won their freedom in this way. Some of them joined Indian tribes; others formed bands that terrorized white settlers in Virginia, the Carolinas, and Alabama. Many of the runaways must have died in the forest, forgotten, but free. It is estimated that by 1855 as many as 60,000 slaves had fled toward the North, sometimes leaving behind dead or wounded masters. By that time, the Underground Railroad, conducted primarily by blacks, was in operation, aiding fugitives as they sought to escape not only the South, but also the enforcement of the federal Fugitive Slave Laws in the free states.

A third way of seeking deliverance was through noncooperation with the system. Slaves soon earned a reputation for being lazy, refusing to work hard; clumsy, breaking tools and other equipment; and dishonest, stealing food and valuables of all kinds. These characteristics were often cited as evidence of the inferiority of the slave. Indeed, much of the writing that has been done about the uncivilized nature of the blacks is based on such testimony from former slave owners. Needless to say, this behavior can be interpreted another way. By such deliberate gestures, the slaves were able to indicate their hostility to the system.

The Christian religion provided the slaves with their ultimate means of deliverance. As the spiritual says of the promise of heaven, "Free at last, free at last,/I thank God I'm free at last."

Rebellion

The Confessions of Nat Turner

Whites who were reluctant to allow slaves to hear about Christianity had a good sense of the danger inherent in the gospel of liberation: Several of the leaders of slave insurrections considered themselves called by God to free their people. The most famous of these was Nat Turner, who led a rebellion of slaves in Virginia in 1831. Approximately seventy slaves were involved in the uprising, and some fifty-five whites were killed. The rebellion was finally put down with the use of local militia, and many prisoners were taken. About twenty were tried and executed for their part in the disturbance, and at least a hundred innocent blacks were murdered in the weeks that followed by vigilante bands of whites that roamed the Virginia countryside. Nat Turner himself was tried, found guilty, and hanged. Subsequently, the work of black ministers in the South was severely circumscribed, and whites tried to extend their control over the religious life of the slaves.

The text that follows is the entire confession of Nat Turner as taken down by a white lawyer immediately before the trial.

Agreeable to his own appointment, on the evening he was committed to prison, with permission of the jailor, I visited Nat on Tuesday the 1st November, when, without being questioned at all, he commenced his narrative in the following words: —

Sir, –You have asked me to give a history of the motives which induced me to undertake the late insurrection, as you call it—To do so I must go back to the days of my infancy, and even before I was born. I was thirty-one years of age the 2d of October last, and born the property of Benj. Turner, of this county. In my childhood, a circumstance occurred which made an indelible impression on my mind, and laid the ground work of that enthusiasm, which has terminated so fatally to many, both white and black, and for which I am about to atone at the gallows. It is here necessary to relate this circumstance— trifling as it may seem, it was the commencement of that belief which has grown with time, and even now, sir, in this dungeon, helpless and forsaken as I am, I cannot divest myself of. Being at play with other children, when three or four years old, I was telling them something, which my mother overhearing, said it had happened before I was born—I stuck to my story, however, and related some things which went, in her opinion, to confirm it—others being called on were greatly astonished, knowing that these things had happened, and caused them to say in my hearing, I surely would be a prophet, as the Lord had shewn me things that had happened before my birth. And my father and

FROM *The Confessions of Nat Turner, the leader of the late insurrection in Southampton, Va. As fully and voluntarily made to Thomas R. Gray* ... (Baltimore, 1831).

mother strengthened me in this my first impression, saying in my presence, I was intended for some great purpose, which they had always thought from certain marks on my head and breast—[a parcel of excrescences which I believe are not at all uncommon, particularly among negroes, as I have seen several with the same. In this case he has either cut them off or they have nearly disappeared]—My grand mother, who was very religious, and to whom I was much attached—my master, who belonged to the church, and other religious persons who visited the house, and whom I often saw at prayers, noticing the singularity of my manners, I suppose, and my uncommon intelligence for a child, remarked I had too much sense to be raised, and if I was, I would never be of any service to any one as a slave—To a mind like mine, restless, inquisitive and observant of every thing that was passing, it is easy to suppose that religion was the subject to which it would be directed, and although this subject principally occupied my thoughts—there was nothing that I saw or heard of to which my attention was not directed—The manner in which I learned to read and write, not only had great influence on my own mind, as I acquired it with the most perfect ease, so much so, that I have no recollection whatever of learning the alphabet—but to the astonishment of the family, one day, when a book was shewn me to keep me from crying, I began spelling the names of different objects—this was a source of wonder to all in the neighborhood, particularly the blacks—and this learning was constantly improved at all opportunities—when I got large enough to go to work, while employed, I was reflecting on many things that would present themselves to my imagination, and whenever an opportunity occurred of looking at a book, when the school children were getting their lessons, I would find many things that the fertility of my own imagination had depicted to me before; all my time, not devoted to my master's service, was spent either in prayer, or in making experiments in casting different things in moulds made of earth, in attempting to make paper, gun-powder, and many other experiments, that although I could not perfect, yet convinced me of its practicability if I had the means.[1] I was not addicted to stealing in my youth, nor have ever been—Yet such was the confidence of the negroes in the neighborhood, even at this early period of my life, in my superior judgment, that they would often carry me with them when they were going on any roguery, to plan for them. Growing up among them, with this confidence in my superior judgment, and when this, in their opinions, was perfected by Divine inspiration, from the circumstances already alluded to in my infancy, and which belief was ever afterwards zealously inculcated by the austerity of my life and manners, which became the subject of remark by white and black. —Having soon discovered to be great, I must appear so, and therefore studiously avoided mixing in society, and wrapped myself in mystery, devoting my time to fasting and prayer—By this time, having arrived to man's estate, and hearing the scriptures

---

[1] When questioned as to the manner of manufacturing those different articles, he was found well informed on the subject.

commented on at meetings, I was struck with that particular passage which says: "Seek ye the kingdom of Heaven and all things shall be added unto you." I reflected much on this passage, and prayed daily for light on this subject—As I was praying one day at my plough, the spirit spoke to me, saying "Seek ye the kingdom of Heaven and all things shall be added unto you." *Question*— what do you mean by the Spirit. *Ans.* The Spirit that spoke to the prophets in former days—and I was greatly astonished, and for two years prayed continually, whenever my duty would permit—and then again I had the same revelation, which fully confirmed me in the impression that I was ordained for some great purpose in the hands of the Almighty. Several years rolled round, in which many events occurred to strengthen me in this my belief. At this time I reverted in my mind to the remarks made of me in my childhood, and the things that had been shewn me—and as it had been said of me in my childhood by those by whom I had been taught to pray, both white and black, and in whom I had the greatest confidence, that I had too much sense to be raised, and if I was, I would never be of any use to any one as a slave. Now finding I had arrived to man's estate, and was a slave, and these revelations being made known to me, I began to direct my attention to this great object, to fulfil the purpose for which, by this time, I felt assured I was intended. Knowing the influence I had obtained over the minds of my fellow servants, (not by the means of conjuring and such like tricks—for to them I always spoke of such things with contempt) but by the communion of the Spirit whose revelations I often communicated to them, and they believed and said my wisdom came from God. I now began to prepare them for my purpose, by telling them something was about to happen that would terminate in fulfilling the great promise that had been made to me—About this time I was placed under an overseer, from whom I ran away—and after remaining in the woods thirty days, I returned, to the astonishment of the negroes on the plantation, who thought I had made my escape to some other part of the country, as my father had done before. But the reason of my return was, that the Spirit appeared to me and said I had my wishes directed to the things of this world, and not to the kingdom of Heaven, and that I should return to the service of my earthly master—"For he who knoweth his Master's will, and doeth it not, shall be beaten with many stripes, and thus have I chastened you." And the negroes found fault, and murmured against me saying that if they had my sense they would not serve any master in the world. And about this time I had a vision— and I saw white spirits and black spirits engaged in battle, and the sun was darkened—the thunder rolled in the Heavens, and blood flowed in streams— and I heard a voice saying, "Such is your luck, such you are called to see, and let it come rough or smooth, you must surely bear it." I now withdrew myself as much as my situation would permit, from the intercourse of my fellow servants, for the avowed purpose of serving the Spirit more fully—and it appeared to me, and reminded me of the things it had already shown me, and that it would then reveal to me the knowledge of the elements, the revolution of the planets, the operation of tides, and changes of the seasons. After this revelation in the year 1825, and the knowledge of the elements being made known to me, I sought more than ever to obtain true holiness before the great day of judgment should appear, and then I began to receive the true knowledge of faith. And from the first steps of righteousness until the last, was I made perfect; and the Holy Ghost was with me, and said, "Behold me as I stand in the Heavens"—and I looked and saw the forms of men in different attitudes— and there were lights in the sky to which the children of darkness gave other names than what they really were—for they were the lights of the Saviour's hands, stretched forth from east to west, even as they were extended on the cross on Calvary for the redemption of sinners. And I wondered greatly at these miracles, and prayed to be informed of a certainty of the meaning thereof—and shortly afterwards, while laboring in the field, I discovered drops of blood on the corn as though it were dew from heaven—and I communicated it to many, both white and black, in the neighborhood—and I then found on the leaves in the woods hieroglyphic characters, and numbers, with the forms of men in different attitudes, portrayed in blood, and representing the figures I had seen before in the heavens. And now the Holy Ghost had revealed itself to me, and made plain the miracles it had shown me—For as the blood of Christ had been shed on this earth, and had ascended to heaven for the salvation of sinners, and was now returning to earth again in the form of dew— and as the leaves on the trees bore the impression of the figures I had seen in the heavens, it was plain to me that the Saviour was about to lay down the yoke he had borne for the sins of men, and the great day of judgment was at hand. About this time I told these things to a white man, (Etheldred T. Brantley) on whom it had a wonderful effect—and he ceased from his wickedness, and was attacked immediately with a cutaneous eruption, and blood oozed from the pores of his skin, and after praying and fasting nine days, he was healed, and the Spirit appeared to me again, and said, as the Saviour had been baptised so should we be also—and when the white people would not let us be baptised by the church, we went down into the water together, in the sight of many who reviled us, and were baptised by the Spirit—After this I rejoiced greatly, and gave thanks to God. And on the 12th of May, 1828, 1 heard a loud noise in the heavens, and the Spirit instantly appeared to me and said the Serpent was loosened, and Christ had laid down the yoke he had borne for the sins of men, and that I should take it on and fight against the Serpent, for the time was fast approaching when the first should be last and the last should be first. *Ques.* Do you not find yourself mistaken now? *Ans.* Was not Christ crucified. And by signs in the heavens that it would make known to me when I should commence the great work—and until the first sign appeared, I should conceal it from the knowledge of men—And on the appearance of the sign, (the eclipse of the sun last February) I should arise and prepare myself, and slay my enemies with their own weapons. And immediately on the sign appearing in the heavens, the seal was removed from my lips, and I communicated the great work laid out for me to do, to four in whom I had the greatest confidence, (Henry, Hark, Nelson, and Sam)—It was intended by us to have begun the work of death on the 4th July last—Many were the plans formed and rejected by us, and it affected my mind to such a degree, that

I fell sick, and the time passed without our coming to any determination how to commence—Still forming new schemes and rejecting them, when the sign appeared again, which determined me not to wait longer.

Since the commencement of 1830, I had been living with Mr. Joseph Travis, who was to me a kind master, and placed the greatest confidence in me; in fact, I had no cause to complain of his treatment to me. On Saturday evening, the 20th of August, it was agreed between Henry, Hark and myself, to prepare a dinner the next day for the men we expected, and then to concert a plan, as we had not yet determined on any. Hark, on the following morning, brought a pig, and Henry brandy, and being joined by Sam, Nelson, Will and Jack, they prepared in the woods a dinner, where, about three o'clock, I joined them.

Q. Why were you so backward in joining them.

A. The same reason that had caused me not to mix with them for years before.

I saluted them on coming up, and asked Will how came he there, he answered, his life was worth no more than others, and his liberty as dear to him. I asked him if he thought to obtain it? He said he would, or loose his life. This was enough to put him in full confidence. Jack, I knew, was only a tool in the hands of Hark, it was quickly agreed we should commence at home (Mr. J. Travis') on that night, and until we had armed and equipped ourselves, and gathered sufficient force, neither age nor sex was to be spared, (which was invariably adhered to.) We remained at the feast, until about two hours in the night, when we went to the house and found Austin; they all went to the cider press and drank, except myself. On returning to the house, Hark went to the door with an axe, for the purpose of breaking it open, as we knew we were strong enough to murder the family, if they were awakened by the noise; but reflecting that it might create an alarm in the neighborhood, we determined to enter the house secretly, and murder them whilst sleeping. Hark got a ladder and set it against the chimney, on which I ascended, and hoisting a window, entered and came down stairs, unbarred the door, and removed the guns from their places. It was then observed that I must spill the first blood. On which, armed with a hatchet, and accompanied by Will, I entered my master's chamber, it being dark, I could not give a death blow, the hatchet glanced from his head, he sprang from the bed and called his wife, it was his last word, Will laid him dead, with a blow of his axe, and Mrs. Travis shared the same fate, as she lay in bed. The murder of this family, five in number, was the work of a moment, not one of them awoke; there was a little infant sleeping in a cradle, that was forgotten, until we had left the house and gone some distance, when Henry and Will returned and killed it; we got here, four guns that would shoot, and several old muskets, with a pound or two of powder. We remained some time at the barn, where we paraded; I formed them in a line as soldiers, and after carrying them through all the manoeuvres I was master of, marched them off to Mr. Salathul Francis', about six hundred yards distant. Sam and Will went to the door and knocked. Mr. Francis asked who was there, Sam replied it was him, and he had a letter for him, on which he got up and came to the door; they immediately seized him, and dragging him out a little from the door, he was dispatched by repeated blows on the head; there was no other white person in the family. We started from there for Mrs. Reese's, maintaining the most perfect silence on our march, where finding the door unlocked, we entered, and murdered Mrs. Reese in her bed, while sleeping; her son awoke, but it was only to sleep the sleep of death, he had only time to say who is that, and he was no more. From Mrs. Reese's we went to Mrs. Turner's, a mile distant, which we reached about sunrise, on Monday morning. Henry, Austin, and Sam, went to the still, where, finding Mr. Peebles, Austin shot him, and the rest of us went to the house; as we approached, the family discovered us, and shut the door. Vain hope! Will, with one stroke of his axe, opened it, and we entered and found Mrs. Turner and Mrs. Newsome in the middle of a room, almost frightened to death. Will immediately killed Mrs. Turner, with one blow of his axe. I took Mrs. Newsome by the hand, and with the sword I had when I was apprehended, I struck her several blows over the head, but not being able to kill her, as the sword was dull. Will turning around and discovering it, despatched her also. A general destruction of property and search for money and ammunition, always succeeded the murders. By this time my company amounted to fifteen, and nine men mounted, who started for Mrs. Whitehead's, (the other six were to go through a byway to Mr. Bryant's, and rejoin us at Mrs. Whitehead's), as we approached the house we discovered Mr. Richard Whitehead standing in the cotton patch, near the lane fence; we called him over into the lane, and Will, the executioner, was near at hand, with his fatal axe, to send him to an untimely grave. As we pushed on to the house, I discovered some one run round the garden, and thinking it was some of the white family, I pursued them, but finding it was a servant girl belonging to the house, I returned to commence the work of death, but they whom I left, had not been idle; all the family were already murdered, but Mrs. Whitehead and her daughter Margaret. As I came round to the door I saw Will pulling Mrs. Whitehead out of the house, and at the step he nearly severed her head from her body, with his broad axe. Miss Margaret, when I discovered her, had concealed herself in the corner, formed by the projection of the cellar cap from the house; on my approach she fled, but was soon overtaken, and after repeated blows with a sword, I killed her by a blow on the head, with a fence rail. By this time, the six who had gone by Mr. Bryant's, rejoined us, and informed me they had done the work of death assigned them. We again divided, part going to Mr. Richard Porter's, and from thence to Nathaniel Francis', the others to Mr. Howell Harris', and Mr. T. Doyles'. On my reaching Mr. Porter's, he had escaped with his family. I understood there, that the alarm had already spread, and I immediately returned to bring up those sent to Mr. Doyles', and Mr. Howell Harris'; the party I left going on to Mr. Francis', having told them I would join them in that neighborhood. I met these sent to Mr. Doyles' and Mr. Harris' returning, having met Mr. Doyle on the road and killed him; and learning from some who joined them, that Mr. Harris was from home, I immediately pursued the course taken by the party gone on before; but knowing they would complete the work of death and pillage, at Mr. Francis' before

I could get there, I went to Mr. Peter Edwards', expecting to find them there, but they had been here also. I then went to Mr. John T. Barrow's, they had been here and murdered him. I pursued on their track to Capt. Newit Harris', where I found the greater part mounted, and ready to start; the men now amounting to about forty, shouted and hurraed as I rode up, some were in the yard, loading their guns, others drinking. They said Captain Harris and his family had escaped, the property in the house they destroyed, robbing him of money and other valuables. I ordered them to mount and march instantly, this was about nine or ten o'clock, Monday morning. I proceeded to Mr. Levi Waller's, two or three miles distant. I took my station in the rear, and as it 'twas my object to carry terror and devastation wherever we went, I placed fifteen or twenty of the best armed and most to be relied on, in front, who generally approached the house as fast as their horses could run; this was for two purposes, to prevent their escape and strike terror to the inhabitants—on this account I never got to the houses, after leaving Mrs. Whitehead's, until the murders were committed. except in one case. I sometimes got in sight in time to see the work of death completed, viewed the mangled bodies as they lay, in silent satisfaction, and immediately started in quest of other victims—Having murdered Mrs. Waller and ten children, we started for Mr. William Williams'— having killed him and two little boys that were there; while engaged in this, Mrs. Williams fled and got some distance from the house, but she was pursued, overtaken, and compelled to get up behind one of the company, who brought her back, and after showing her the mangled body of her lifeless husband, she was told to get down and lay by his side, where she was shot dead. I then started for Mr. Jacob Williams, where the family were murdered—Here we found a young man named Drury, who had come on business with Mr. Williams—he was pursued, overtaken and shot. Mrs. Vaughan was the next place we visited—and after murdering the family here, I determined on starting for Jerusalem—Our number amounted now to fifty or sixty, all mounted and armed with guns, axes, swords and clubs—On reaching Mr. James W. Parkers' gate, immediately on the road leading to Jerusalem, and about three miles distant, it was proposed to me to call there, but I objected, as I knew he was gone to Jerusalem, and my object was to reach there as soon as possible; but some of the men having relations at Mr. Parker's it was agreed that they might call and get his people. I remained at the gate on the road, with seven or eight; the others going across the field to the house, about half a mile off. After waiting some time for them, I became impatient, and started to the house for them, and on our return we were met by a party of white men, who had pursued our blood-stained track, and who had fired on those at the gate, and dispersed them, which I knew nothing of, not having been at that time rejoined by any of them—immediately on discovering the whites, I ordered my men to halt and form, as they appeared to be alarmed—The white men, eighteen in number, approached us in about one hundred yards, when one of them fired, (this was against the positive orders of Captain Alexander P. Peete, who commanded, and who had directed the men to reserve their fire until within thirty paces). And I discovered about half of them retreating, I then

ordered my men to fire and rush on them; the few remaining stood their
ground until we approached within fifty yards, when they fired and retreated.
We pursued and overtook some of them who we thought we left dead; (they
were not killed) after pursuing them about two hundred yards, and rising a little hill, I discovered they were met by another party, and had halted, and were
re-loading their guns, (this was a small party from Jerusalem who knew the
negroes were in the field, and had just tied their horses to await their return
to the road, knowing that Mr. Parker and family were in Jerusalem, but knew
nothing of the party that had gone in with Captain Peete; on hearing the firing they immediately rushed to the spot and arrived just in time to arrest the
progress of these barbarous villains, and save the lives of their friends and fellow citizens.) Thinking that those who retreated first, and the party who fired
on us at fifty or sixty yards distant, had all only fallen back to meet others with
ammunition. As I saw them re-loading their guns, and more coming up than
I saw at first, and several of my bravest men being wounded, the others became
panick struck and squandered over the field; the white men pursued and fired
on us several times. Hark had his horse shot under him, and I caught another
for him as it was running by me; five or six of my men were wounded, but
none left on the field; finding myself defeated here I instantly determined to
go through a private way, and cross the Nottoway river at the Cypress Bridge,
three miles below Jerusalem, and attack that place in the rear, as I expected
they would look for me on the other road, and I had a great desire to get there
to procure arms and ammunition. After going a short distance in this private
way, accompanied by about twenty men, I overtook two or three who told me
the others were dispersed in every direction. After trying in vain to collect a
sufficient force to proceed to Jerusalem, I determined to return, as I was sure
they would make back to their old neighborhood, where they would rejoin
me, make new recruits, and come down again. On my way back, I called at
Mrs. Thomas's, Mrs. Spencer's, and several other places, the white families having fled, we found no more victims to gratify our thirst for blood, we stopped
at Maj. Ridley's quarter for the night, and being joined by four of his men,
with the recruits made since my defeat, we mustered now about forty strong.
After placing out sentinels, I laid down to sleep, but was quickly roused by a
great racket; starting up, I found some mounted, and others in great confusion;
one of the sentinels having given the alarm that we were about to be attacked,
I ordered some to ride round and reconnoitre, and on their return the others
being more alarmed, not knowing who they were, fled in different ways, so
that I was reduced to about twenty again; with this I determined to attempt
to recruit, and proceed on to rally in the neighborhood, I had left. Dr. Blunt's
was the nearest house, which we reached just before day; on riding up the
yard, Hark fired a gun. We expected Dr. Blunt and his family were at Maj.
Ridley's, as I knew there was a company of men there; the gun was fired to
ascertain if any of the family were at home; we were immediately fired upon
and retreated, leaving several of my men. I do not know what became of them,
as I never saw them afterwards. Pursuing our course back and coming in sight
of Captain Harris', where we had been the day before, we discovered a party

of white men at the house, on which all deserted me but two, (Jacob and Nat,) we concealed ourselves in the woods until near night, when I sent them in search of Henry, Sam, Nelson, and Hark, and directed them to rally all they could, at the place we had had our dinner the Sunday before, where they would find me, and I accordingly returned there as soon as it was dark and remained until Wednesday evening, when discovering white men riding around the place as though they were looking for some one, and none of my men joining me, I concluded Jacob and Nat had been taken, and compelled to betray me. On this I gave up all hope for the present; and on Thursday night after having supplied myself with provisions from Mr. Travis's, I scratched a hole under a pile of fence rails in a field, where I concealed myself for six weeks, never leaving my hiding place but for a few minutes in the dead of night to get water which was very near; thinking by this time I could venture out, I began to go about in the night and eaves drop the houses in the neighborhood; pursuing this course for about a fortnight and gathering little or no intelligence, afraid of speaking to any human being, and returning every morning to my cave before the dawn of day. I know not how long I might have led this life, if accident had not betrayed me, a dog in the neighborhood passing by my hiding place one night while I was out, was attracted by some meat I had in my cave, and crawled in and stole it, and was coming out just as I returned. A few nights after, two negroes having started to go hunting with the same dog, and passed that way, the dog came again to the place, and having just gone out to walk about, discovered me and barked, on which thinking myself discovered, I spoke to them to beg concealment. On making myself known they fled from me. Knowing then they would betray me, I immediately left my hiding place, and was pursued almost incessantly until I was taken a fortnight afterwards by Mr. Benjamin Phipps, in a little hole I had dug out with my sword, for the purpose of concealment, under the top of a fallen tree. On Mr. Phipps' discovering the place of my concealment, he cocked his gun and aimed at me. I requested him not to shoot and I would give up, upon which he demanded my sword. I delivered it to him, and he brought me to prison. During the time I was pursued, I had many hair breadth escapes, which your time will not permit you to relate. I am here loaded with chains, and willing to suffer the fate that awaits me.

I here proceeded to make some inquiries of him, after assuring him of the certain death that awaited him, and that concealment would only bring destruction on the innocent as well as guilty, of his own color, if he knew of any extensive or concerted plan. His answer was, I do not. When I questioned him as to the insurrection in North Carolina happening about the same time, he denied any knowledge of it; and when I looked him in the face as though I would search his inmost thoughts, he replied, "I see sir, you doubt my word; but can you not think the same ideas, and strange appearances about this time in the heavens might prompt others, as well as myself, to this undertaking." I now had much conversation with and asked him many questions, having forborne to do so previously, except in the cases noted in parenthesis; but during his statement, I had, unnoticed by him, taken notes as to some particular circumstances, and having the advantage of his statement before me in writing, on the evening of the third day that I had been with him, I began a cross examination, and found his statement corroborated by every circumstance coming within my own knowledge or the confessions of others who had been either killed or executed, and whom he had not seen nor had any knowledge since 22d of August last, he expressed himself fully satisfied as to the impracticability of his attempt. It has been said he was ignorant and cowardly, and that his object was to murder and rob for the purpose of obtaining money to make his escape. It is notorious, that he was never known to have a dollar in his life; to swear an oath, or drink a drop of spirits. As to his ignorance, he certainly never had the advantages of education, but he can read and write, (it was taught him by his parents,) and for natural intelligence and quickness of apprehension, is surpassed by few men I have ever seen. As to his being a coward, his reason as given for not resisting Mr. Phipps, shews the decision of his character. When he saw Mr. Phipps present his gun, he said he knew it was impossible for him to escape as the woods were full of men; he therefore thought it was better to surrender, and trust to fortune for his escape. He is a complete fanatic, or plays his part most admirably. On other subjects he possesses an uncommon share of intelligence, with a mind capable of attaining any thing; but warped and perverted by the influence of early impressions. He is below the ordinary stature, though strong and active, having the true negro face, every feature of which is strongly marked. I shall not attempt to describe the effect of his narrative, as told and commented on by himself, in the condemned hole of the prison. The calm, deliberate composure with which he spoke of his late deeds and intentions, the expression of his fiend-like face when excited by enthusiasm, still bearing the stains of the blood of helpless innocence about him; clothed with rags and covered with chains; yet daring to raise his manacled hands to heaven, with a spirit soaring above the attributes of man; I looked on him and my blood curdled in my veins.

I will not shock the feelings of humanity, nor wound afresh the bosoms of the disconsolate sufferers in this unparalleled and inhuman massacre, by detailing the deeds of their fiend-like barbarity. There were two or three who were in the power of these wretches, had they known it, and who escaped in the most providential manner. There were two whom they thought they left dead on the field at Mr. Parker's, but who were only stunned by the blows of their guns, as they did not take time to re-load when they charged on them. The escape of a little girl who went to school at Mr. Waller's, and where the children were collecting for that purpose, excited general sympathy. As their teacher had not arrived, they were at play in the yard, and seeing the negroes approach, she ran up on a dirt chimney, (such as are common to log houses,) and remained there unnoticed during the massacre of the eleven that were killed at this place. She remained on her hiding place till just before the arrival of a party, who were in pursuit of the murderers, when she came down and fled to a swamp, where, a mere child as she was, with the horrors of the late scene before her, she lay concealed until the next day, when seeing a party go up to the house, she came up, and on being asked how she escaped, replied with the utmost simplicity, "The Lord helped her." She was taken up behind a gentleman of the party, and returned to the arms of her weeping mother. Miss Whitehead concealed herself between the bed and the mat that supported it, while they murdered her sister in the same room, without discovering her. She was afterwards carried off, and concealed for protection by a slave of the family, who gave evidence against several of them on their trial. Mrs. Nathaniel Francis, while concealed in a closet heard their blows, and the shrieks of the victims of these ruthless savages; they then entered the closet where she was concealed, and went out without discovering her. While in this hiding place, she heard two of her women in a quarrel about the division of her clothes. Mr. John T. Baron, discovering them approaching his house, told his wife to make her escape, and scorning to fly, fell fighting on his own threshold. After firing his rifle, he discharged his gun at them, and then broke it over the villain who first approached him, but he was overpowered, and slain. His bravery, however, saved from the hands of these monsters, his lovely and amiable wife, who will long lament a husband so deserving of her love. As directed by him, she attempted to escape through the garden, when she was caught and held by one of her servant girls, but another coming to her rescue, she fled to the woods, and concealed herself. Few indeed, were those who escaped their work of death. But fortunate for society, the hand of retributive justice has overtaken them; and not one that was known to be concerned has escaped.

Life as a Slave

A Narrative

MARY REYNOLDS

During the Great Depression of the 1930s, the Federal Writers' Project, one of the New Deal programs, recorded the reminiscences of a large number of former slaves who were still living. Over ten thousand manuscript pages were collected in this fashion. A selection from them was published in 1945 in a book entitled Lay My Burden Down: A Folk History of Slavery. *An exceedingly rich source of folk recollection about slavery, the book includes folk-tales, stories about plantation life, and memories of the freedom that the Civil War brought.*

Reprinted here is the reminiscence of Mary Reynolds, of Dallas, Texas, who was almost a hundred years old at the time of her interview. She had been a slave on a big cotton plantation in Louisiana, and the wit and vigor with which she describes her life there make this narrative one of the liveliest documents of its kind.

My paw's name was Tom Vaughn, and he was from the North, born free man and lived and died free to the end of his days. He wasn't no educated man, but he was what he calls himself a piano man. He told me once he lived in New York and Chicago and he built the insides of pianos and knew how to make them play in tune. He said some white folks from the South told he if he'd come with them to the South he'd find a lot of work to do with pianos in them parts, and he come off with them.

He saw my maw on the place and her man was dead. He told my massa he'd buy my maw and her three children with all the money he had, iffen he'd sell her. But Massa was never one to sell any but the old niggers who was past working in the fields and past their breeding times. So my paw married my maw and works the fields, same as any other nigger. They had six gals: Martha and Panela and Josephine and Ellen and Katherine and me.

I was born same time as Miss Dora. Massa's first wife and my maw come to their time right together. Miss Dora's maw died, and they brung Miss Dora to suck with me. It's a thing we ain't never forgot. My maw's name was Sallie and Miss Dora always looked with kindness on my maw. We sucked till we was a fair size and played together, which wasn't no common thing. None the other little niggers played with the white children. But Miss Dora loved me so good.

I was just 'bout big 'nough to start playing with a broom to go 'bout sweeping up and not even half doing it when Massa sold me. They was a old white man in Trinity, and his wife died and he didn't have chick or child or slave or nothing. Massa sold me cheap, 'cause he didn't want Miss Dora to play with no nigger young-un. That old man bought me a big doll and went off and left me all day, with the door open. I just sot on the floor and played with that doll. I used to cry. He'd come home and give me something to eat and then go to bed, and I slept on the foot of the bed with him. I was scared all the time in the dark. He never did close the door.

Miss Dora pined and sickened. Massa done what he could, but they wasn't no pertness in her. She got sicker and sicker, and Massa brung 'nother doctor. He say, "You little gal is grieving the life out her body, and she sure gwine die iffen you don't do something 'bout it." Miss Dora says over and over, "I wants Mary." Massa say to the doctor, "That a little nigger young-un I done sold." The doctor tells him he better git me back iffen he wants to save the life of his child. Massa has to give a big plenty more to git me back than what he sold me for, but Miss Dora plumps up right off and grows into fine health.

Then Massa marries a rich lady from Mississippi, and they has children for company to Miss Dora and seem like for a time she forgits me.

Massa wasn't no piddling man. He was a man of plenty. He had a big house with no more style to it than a crib, but it could room plenty people. He was a medicine doctor, and they was rooms in the second story for sick folks what come to lay in. It would take two days to go all over the land he owned. He had cattle and stock and sheep and more'n a hundred slaves and more besides. He bought the best of niggers near every time the speculators come that way. He'd make a swap of the old ones and give money for young ones what could work.

He raised corn and cotton and cane and 'taters and goobers, 'sides the peas and other feeding for the niggers. I 'member I held a hoe handle mighty unsteady when they put a old woman to larn me and some other children to scrape the fields. That old woman would be in a frantic. She'd show me and then turn 'bout to show some other little nigger, and I'd have the young corn cut clean as the grass. She say, "For the love of God, you better larn it right, or Solomon will beat the breath out you body." Old Man Solomon was the nigger driver.

Slavery was the worst days was ever seed in the world. They was things past telling, but I got the scars on my old body to show to this day. I seed worse than what happened to me. I seed them put the men and women in the stock with they hands screwed down through holes in the board and they feets tied together and they naked behinds to the world. Solomon the overseer beat them with a big whip and Massa look on. The niggers better not stop in the fields when they hear them yelling. They cut the flesh 'most to the bones, and some they was when they taken them out of stock and put them on the beds, they never got up again.

When a nigger died, they let his folks come out the fields to see him afore he died. They buried him the same day, take a big plank and bust it with a ax in the middle 'nough to bend it back, and put the dead nigger in betwixt it. They'd cart them down to the graveyard on the place and not bury them deep 'nough that buzzards wouldn't come circling round. Niggers mourns now, but in them days they wasn't no time for mourning.

The conch shell blowed afore daylight, and all hands better git out for roll call, or Solomon bust the door down and git them out. It was work hard, git beatings, and half-fed. They brung the victuals and water to the fields on a slide pulled by a old mule. Plenty times they was only a half barrel water and it stale and hot, for all us niggers on the hottest days. Mostly we ate pickled pork and corn bread and peas and beans and 'taters. They never was as much as we needed.

The times I hated most was picking cotton when the frost was on the bolls. My hands git sore and crack open and bleed. We'd have a little fire in the fields, and iffen the ones with tender hands couldn't stand it no longer, we'd run and warm our hands a little bit. When I could steal a 'tater, I used to slip it in the ashes, and when I'd run to the fire I'd take it out and eat it on the sly.

In the cabins it was nice and warm. They was built of pine boarding, and they was one long row of them up the hill back of the big house. Near one side of the cabins was a fireplace. They'd bring in two-three big logs and put on the fire, and they'd last near a week. The beds was made out of puncheons fitted in holes bored in the wall, and planks laid 'cross them poles. We had ticking mattresses filled with corn shucks. Sometimes the men build chairs at night. We didn't know much 'bout having nothing, though.

Sometimes Massa let niggers have a little patch. They'd raise 'taters or goobers. They liked to have them to help fill out on the victuals. 'Taters roasted in the ashes was the best-tasting eating I ever had. I could die better satisfied to have just one more 'tater roasted in hot ashes. The niggers had to work the patches at night and dig the 'taters and goobers at night. Then if they wanted to sell any in town, they'd have to git a pass to go. They had to go at night, 'cause they couldn't ever spare a hand from the fields.

Once in a while they'd give us a little piece of Saturday evening to wash out clothes in the branch. We hanged them on the ground in the woods to dry. They was a place to wash clothes from the well, but they was so many niggers all couldn't git round to it on Sundays. When they'd git through with the clothes on Saturday evenings, the niggers which sold they goobers and 'taters brung fiddles and guitars and come out and play. The others clap they hands and stomp they feet and we young-uns cut a step round. I was plenty biggity and liked to cut a step.

We was scared of Solomon and his whip, though, and he didn't like frolicking. He didn't like for us niggers to pray, either. We never heared of no church, but us having praying in the cabins. We'd set on the floor and pray with our heads down low and sing low, but if Solomon heared he'd come and beat on the wall with the stock of his whip. He'd say, "I'll come in there and tear the hide off you backs." But some the old niggers tell us we got to pray to God that He don't think different of the blacks and the whites. I know that Solomon is burning in hell today, and it pleasures me to know it.

Once my maw and paw taken me and Katherine after night to slip to 'nother place to a praying and singing. A nigger man with white beard told us a day am coming when niggers only be slaves of God. We prays for the end of tribulation and the end of beatings and for shoes that fit our feet. We prayed that us niggers could have all we wanted to eat and special for fresh meat. Some the old ones say we have to bear all, 'cause that all we can do. Some say they was glad to the time they's dead, 'cause they'd rather rot in the ground than have the beatings. What I hated most was when they'd beat me and I didn't know what they beat me for, and I hated them stripping me naked as the day I was born.

When we's coming back from that praying, I thunk I heared the nigger dogs and somebody on horseback. I say, "Maw, it's them nigger hounds and they'll eat us up." You could hear them old hounds and sluts a-baying. Maw listens and say, "Sure 'nough, them dogs am running and God help us!" Then she and Paw talk and they take us to a fence corner and stands us up 'gainst the rails and say don't move and if anyone comes near, don't breathe loud. They went to the woods, so the hounds chase them and not git us. Me and Katherine stand there, holding hands, shaking so we can hardly stand. We hears the hounds come nearer, but we don't move. They goes after Paw and Maw, but they circles round to the cabins and gits in. Maw say it the power of God.

In them days I weared shirts, like all the young-uns. They had collars and come below the knees and was split up the sides. That's all we weared in hot weather. The men weared jeans and the women gingham. Shoes was the worstest trouble. We weared rough russets when it got cold, and it seem powerful strange they'd never git them to fit. Once when I was a young gal, they got me a new pair and all brass studs in the toes. They was too little for me, but I had to wear them. The brass trimmings cut into my ankles and them places got miserable bad. I rubs tallow in them sore places and wrops rags round them and my sores got worser and worser. The scars are there to this day.

I wasn't sick much, though. Some the niggers had chills and fever a lot, but they hadn't discovered so many diseases then as now. Massa give sick niggers ipecac and asafetida and oil and turpentine and black fever pills.

They was a cabin called the spinning-house and two looms and two spinning wheels going all the time, and two nigger women sewing all the time. It took plenty sewing to make all the things for a place so big. Once Massa goes to Baton Rouge and brung back a yaller gal dressed in fine style. She was a seamster nigger. He builds her a house 'way from the quarters, and she done fine sewing for the whites. Us niggers knowed the doctor took a black woman quick as he did a white and took any on his place he wanted, and he took them often. But mostly the children born on the place looked like niggers. Aunt Cheyney always say four of hers was Massa's, but he didn't give them no mind. But this yaller girl breeds so fast and gits a mess of white young-uns. She larnt them fine manners and combs out they hair.

Oncet two of them goes down the hill to the dollhouse, where the Missy's children am playing. They wants to go in the dollhouse and one the Missy's boys say, "That's for white children." They say, "We ain't no niggers, 'cause we got the same daddy you has, and he comes to see us near every day and fotches us clothes and things from town." They is fussing, and Missy is listening out her chamber window. She heard them white niggers say, "He is our daddy and we call him daddy when he comes to our house to see our mama."

When Massa come home that evening, his wife hardly say nothing to him, and he ask her what the matter, and she tells him, "Since you asks me, I'm studying in my mind 'bout them white young-uns of that yaller nigger wench from Baton Rouge." He say, "Now, honey, I fotches that gal just for you, 'cause she a fine seamster." She say, "It look kind of funny they got the same kind of hair and eyes as my children, and they got a nose look like yours." He say, "Honey, you just paying 'tention to talk of little children that ain't got no mind to what they say." She say, "Over in Mississippi I got a home and plenty with my daddyo, and I got that in my mind."

Well, she didn't never leave, and Massa bought her a fine, new span of surrey hosses. But she don't never have no more children, and she ain't so cordial with the Massa. That yaller gal has more white young-uns, but they don't never go down the hill no more to the big house.

Aunt Cheyney was just out of bed with a suckling baby one time, and she run away. Some say that was 'nother baby of Massa's breeding. She don't come to the house to nurse her baby, so they misses her and Old Solomon gits the nigger hounds and takes her trail. They gits near her and she grabs a limb and tries to hist herself in a tree, but them dogs grab her and pull her down. The men hollers them onto her, and the dogs tore her naked and et the breasts plumb off her body. She got well and lived to be a old woman, but 'nother woman has to suck her baby, and she ain't got no sign of breasts no more.

They give all the niggers fresh meat on Christmas and a plug tobacco all round. The highest cotton-picker gits a suit of clothes, and all the women what had twins that year gits a outfitting of clothes for the twins and a double, warm blanket.

Seems like after I got bigger, I 'member more and more niggers run away. They's 'most always cotched. Massa used to hire out his niggers for wage hands. One time he hired me and a nigger boy, Turner, to work for some ornery white trash, name of Kidd. One day Turner goes off and don't come back. Old Man Kidd say I knowed 'bout it, and he tied my wrists together and stripped me. He hanged me by the wrists from a limb on a tree and spraddled my legs round the trunk and tied my feet together. Then he beat me. He beat me worser than I ever been beat before, and I faints dead away. When I come to I'm in bed. I didn't care so much iffen I died.

I didn't know 'bout the passing of time, but Miss Dora come to me. Some white folks done git word to her. Mr. Kidd tries to talk hisself out of it, but Miss Dora fotches me home when I'm well 'nough to move. She took me in a cart and my maw takes care of me. Massa looks me over good and says I'll git well, but I'm ruint for breeding children.

After while I taken a notion to marry and Massa and Missy marries us same as all the niggers. They stands inside the house with a broom held crosswise of the door and we stands outside. Missy puts a little wreath on my head they kept there, and we steps over the broom into the house. Now, that's all they was to the marrying. After freedom I gits married and has it put in the book by a preacher.

One day we was working in the fields and hears the conch shell blow, so we all goes to the back gate of the big house. Massa am there. He say, "Call the roll for every nigger big 'nough to walk, and I wants them to go to the river and wait there. They's gwine be a show and I wants you to see it." They was a big boat down there, done built up on the sides with boards and holes in the boards and a big gun barrel sticking through every hole. We ain't never seed nothing like that. Massa goes up the plank onto the boat and comes out on the boat porch. He say, "This am a Yankee boat." He goes inside and the water wheels starts moving and that boat goes moving up the river, and they says it goes to Natchez.

The boat wasn't more'n out of sight when a big drove of soldiers comes into town. They say they's Federals. More'n half the niggers goes off with them soldiers, but I goes on back home 'cause of my old mammy.

Next day them Yankees is swarming the place. Some the niggers wants to show them something. I follows to the woods. The niggers shows them soldiers a big pit in the ground, bigger'n a big house. It is got wooden doors that lifts up, but the top am sodded and grass growing on it, so you couldn't tell it. In that pit is stock, hosses and cows and mules and money and chinaware and silver and a mess of stuff them soldiers takes.

We just sot on the place doing nothing till the white folks comes home. Miss Dora come out to the cabin and say she wants to read a letter to my mammy. It come from Louis, which is brother to my mammy, and he done follow the Federals to Galveston. A white man down there write the letter for him. It am tored in half and Massa done that. The letter say Louis am working in Galveston and wants Mammy to come with us, and he'll pay our way. Miss Dora say Massa swear, "Damn Louis. I ain't gwine tell Sallie nothing," and he starts to tear the letter up. But she won't let him, and she reads it to Mammy.

After a time Massa takes all his niggers what wants to Texas with him and Mammy gits to Galveston and dies there. I goes with Massa to the Tennessee Colony and then to Navasota. Miss Dora marries and goes to El Paso. She wrote and told me to come to her, and I always meant to go.

My husband and me farmed round for times, and then I done housework and cooking for many years. I come to Dallas and cooked for seven year for one white family. My husband died years ago. I guess Miss Dora been dead these long years. I always kept my years by Miss Dora's years, 'count we is born so close.

I been blind and 'most helpless for five year. I'm gitting mighty enfeebling, and I ain't walked outside the door for a long time back. I sets and 'members the times in the world. I 'members now clear as yesterday things I forgot for a long time. I 'members 'bout the days of slavery, and I don't 'lieve they ever gwine have slaves no more on this earth. I think God done took that burden offen his black children, and I'm aiming to praise Him for it to His face in the days of glory what ain't so far off.

An Ingenious
Escape from Slavery

WILLIAM AND ELLEN CRAFT

So many individual slaves ran away from their masters during the first half of the nineteenth century that a certain Dr. Samuel Cartwright of the University of Louisiana declared that the blacks suffered from a peculiar disease he called: "Drapetomania, or the Disease Causing Negroes to Run Away." The story of the runaways and those who aided them in both North and South is one of the most exciting chapters of American history.

William and Ellen Craft were a slave couple in Macon, Georgia. Their escape plan was made possible by the fact that Ellen was fair-skinned enough to pass for white. They decided to flee to the North by having William pose as the slave of Ellen, who would have to act as though she were his master. The dramatic story of their adventures on their way out of the South and bondage provides many insights into the oppression of the slave system.

After the passage of the new Fugitive Slave Act in 1850, the Crafts realized that the North no longer provided a significant margin of safety for fugitives, and they eventually made their way to England, where their freedom would be secure.

My wife was torn from her mother's embrace in childhood, and taken to a distant part of the country. She had seen so many other children separated from their parents in this cruel manner, that the mere thought of her ever becoming the mother of a child, to linger out a miserable existence under the wretched system of American slavery, appeared to fill her very soul with horror; and as she had taken what I felt to be an important view of her condition, I did not, at first, press the marriage, but agreed to assist her in trying to devise some plan by which we might escape from our unhappy condition, and then be married.

We thought of plan after plan, but they all seemed crowded with insurmountable difficulties. We knew it was unlawful for any public conveyance to take us as passengers, without our master's consent. We were also perfectly aware of the startling fact, that had we left without this consent the professional slave-hunters would have soon had their ferocious bloodhounds baying on our track, and in a short time we should have been dragged back to slavery, not to fill the more favourable situations which we had just left, but to be

FROM *Running a Thousand Miles for Freedom or The Escape of William and Ellen Craft From Slavery.* London: William Tweedie, 337, Strand 1860.

separated for life, and put to the very meanest and most laborious drudgery; or else have been tortured to death as examples, in order to strike terror into the hearts of others, and thereby prevent them from even attempting to escape from their cruel taskmasters. It is a fact worthy of remark, that nothing seems to give the slaveholders so much pleasure as the catching and torturing of fugitives. They had much rather take the keen and poisonous lash, and with it cut their poor trembling victims to atoms, than allow one of them to escape to a free country, and expose the infamous system from which he fled.

The greatest excitement prevails at a slave-hunt. The slaveholders and their hired ruffians appear to take more pleasure in this inhuman pursuit than English sportsmen do in chasing a fox or a stag. Therefore, knowing what we should have been compelled to suffer, if caught and taken back, we were more than anxious to hit upon a plan that would lead us safely to a land of liberty.

But. after puzzling our brains for years, we were reluctantly driven to the sad conclusion, that it was almost impossible to escape from slavery in Georgia, and travel 1,000 miles across the slave States. We therefore resolved to get the consent of our owners, be married, settle down in slavery, and endeavour to make ourselves as comfortable as possible under that system; but at the same time ever to keep our dim eyes steadily fixed upon the glimmering hope of liberty, and earnestly pray God mercifully to assist us to escape from our unjust thraldom.

We were married, and prayed and toiled on till December, 1848, at which time (as I have stated) a plan suggested itself that proved quite successful, and in eight days after it was first thought of we were free from the horrible trammels of slavery, and glorifying God who had brought us safely out of a land of bondage.

Knowing that slaveholders have the privilege of taking their slaves to any part of the country they think proper, it occurred to me that, as my wife was nearly white, I might get her to disguise herself as an invalid gentleman, and assume to be my master, while I could attend as his slave, and that in this manner we might effect our escape. After I thought of the plan, I suggested it to my wife, but at first she shrank from the idea. She thought it was almost impossible for her to assume that disguise, and travel a distance of 1,000 miles across the slave States. However, on the other hand, she also thought of her condition. She saw that the laws under which we lived did not recognize her to be a woman, but a mere chattel, to be bought and sold, or otherwise dealt with as her owner might see fit. Therefore the more she contemplated her helpless condition, the more anxious she was to escape from it. So she said, "I think it is almost too much for us to undertake; however, I feel that God is on our side, and with his assistance, notwithstanding all the difficulties, we shall be able to succeed. Therefore, if you will purchase the disguise, I will try to carry out the plan."

But after I concluded to purchase the disguise, I was afraid to go to any one to ask him to sell me the articles. It is unlawful in Georgia for a white man to trade with slaves without the master's consent. But, notwithstanding this, many persons will sell a slave any article that he can get the money to buy. Not that they sympathize with the slave, but merely because his testimony is not admitted in court against a free white person.

Therefore, with little difficulty I went to different parts of the town, at odd times, and purchased things piece by piece. (except the trowsers which she found necessary to make,) and took them home to the house where my wife resided. She being a ladies' maid, and a favourite slave in the family, was allowed a little room to herself; and amongst other pieces of furniture which I had made in my overtime, was a chest of drawers; so when I took the articles home, she locked them up carefully in these drawers. No one about the premises knew that she had anything of the kind. So when we fancied we had everything ready the time was fixed for the flight. But we knew it would not do to start off without first getting our master's consent to be away for a few days. Had we left without this, they would soon have had us back into slavery, and probably we should never have got another fair opportunity of even attempting to escape.

Some of the best slaveholders will sometimes give their favourite slaves a few days' holiday at Christmas time; so, after no little amount of perseverance on my wife's part, she obtained a pass from her mistress, allowing her to be away for a few days. The cabinet-maker with whom I worked gave me a similar paper, but said that he needed my services very much, and wished me to return as soon as the time granted was up. I thanked him kindly; but somehow I have not been able to make it convenient to return yet; and, as the free air of good old England agrees so well with my wife and our dear little ones, as well as with myself, it is not at all likely we shall return at present to the "peculiar institution" of chains and stripes.

On reaching my wife's cottage she handed me her pass, and I showed mine, but at that time neither of us were able to read them. It is not only unlawful for slaves to be taught to read, but in some of the States there are heavy penalties attached, such as fines and imprisonment, which will be vigorously enforced upon any one who is humane enough to violate the so-called law.

The following case will serve to show how persons are treated in the most enlightened slaveholding community.

"INDICTMENT.

COMMONWEALTH OF VIRGINIA, Norfolk County, *ss.* } *In the Circuit Court.* The Grand Jurors empannelled and sworn to inquire of offences committed in the body of the said County on their oath present, that Margaret Douglass, being an evil disposed person, not having the fear of God before her eyes, but moved and instigated by the devil, wickedly, maliciously, and feloniously, on the fourth day of July, in the year of our Lord one thousand eight hundred and fifty-four, at Norfolk, in said County, did teach a certain black girl named Kate to read in the Bible, to the great displeasure of Almighty God, to the pernicious example of others in like case offending, contrary to the form of the statute in such case made and provided, and against the peace and dignity of the Commonwealth of Virginia.

"Victor Vagabond, *Prosecuting Attorney.*"

"On this indictment Mrs. Douglass was arraigned as a necessary matter of form, tried, found guilty of course; and Judge Scalaway, before whom she was tried, having consulted with Dr. Adams, ordered the sheriff to place Mrs. Douglass in the prisoner's box, when he addressed her as follows: 'Margaret Douglass, stand up. You are guilty of one of the vilest crimes that ever disgraced society; and the jury have found you so. You have taught a slave girl to read in the Bible. No enlightened society can exist where such offences go unpunished. The Court, in your case, do not feel for you one solitary ray of sympathy, and they will inflict on you the utmost penalty of the law. In any other civilized country you would have paid the forfeit of your crime with your life, and the Court have only to regret that such is not the law in this country. The sentence for your offence is, that you be imprisoned one month in the county jail, and that you pay the costs of this prosecution. Sheriff, remove the prisoner to jail.' On the publication of these proceedings, the Doctors of Divinity preached each a sermon on the necessity of obeying the laws; the *New York Observer* noticed with much pious gladness a revival of religion on Dr. Smith's plantation in Georgia, among his slaves; while the *Journal of Commerce* commended this political preaching of the Doctors of Divinity because it favoured slavery. Let us do nothing to offend our Southern brethren."

However, at first, we were highly delighted at the idea of having gained permission to be absent for a few days; but when the thought flashed across my wife's mind, that it was customary for travellers to register their names in the visitors' book at hotels, as well as in the clearance or Custom-house book at Charleston, South Carolina—it made our spirits droop within us.

So, while sitting in our little room upon the verge of despair, all at once my wife raised her head, and with a smile upon her face, which was a moment before bathed in tears, said, "I think I have it!" I asked what it was. She said, "I think I can make a poultice and bind up my right hand in a sling, and with propriety ask the officers to register my name for me." I thought that would do.

It then occurred to her that the smoothness of her face might betray her; so she decided to make another poultice, and put it in a white handkerchief to be worn under the chin, up the cheeks, and to tie over the head. This nearly hid the expression of the countenance, as well as the beardless chin.

The poultice is left off in the engraving, because the likeness could not have been taken well with it on.

My wife, knowing that she would be thrown a good deal into the company of gentlemen, fancied that she could get on better if she had something to go over the eyes; so I went to a shop and bought a pair of green spectacles. This was in the evening.

We sat up all night discussing the plan, and making preparations. Just before the time arrived, in the morning, for us to leave, I cut off my wife's hair square at the back of the head, and got her to dress in the disguise and stand out on the floor. I found that she made a most respectable looking gentleman.

My wife had no ambition whatever to assume this disguise, and would not have done so had it been possible to have obtained our liberty by more simple means; but we knew it was not customary in the South for ladies to travel with male servants; and therefore, notwithstanding my wife's fair complexion, it would have been a very difficult task for her to have come off as a free white lady, with me as her slave; in fact, her not being able to write would have made this quite impossible. We knew that no public conveyance would take us, or any other slave, as a passenger, without our master's consent. This consent could never be obtained to pass into a free State. My wife's being muffled in the poultices, &c., furnished a plausible excuse for avoiding general conversation, of which most Yankee travellers are passionately fond.

There are a large number of free negroes residing in the southern States; but in Georgia (and I believe in all the slave States,) every coloured person's complexion is *primâ facie* evidence of his being a slave; and the lowest villain in the country, should he be a white man, has the legal power to arrest, and question, in the most inquisitorial and insulting manner, any coloured person, male or female, that he may find at large, particularly at night and on Sundays, without a written pass, signed by the master or some one in authority; or stamped free papers, certifying that the person is the rightful owner of himself.

If the coloured person refuses to answer questions put to him, he may be beaten, and his defending himself against this attack makes him an outlaw, and if he be killed on the spot, the murderer will be exempted from all blame; but after the coloured person has answered the questions put to him, in a most humble and pointed manner, he may then be taken to prison; and should it turn out, after further examination, that he was caught where he had no permission or legal right to be, and that he has not given what they term a satisfactory account of himself, the master will have to pay a fine. On his refusing to do this, the poor slave may be legally and severely flogged by public officers. Should the prisoner prove to be a free man, he is most likely to be both whipped and fined.

The great majority of slaveholders hate this class of persons with a hatred that can only be equalled by the condemned spirits of the infernal regions. They have no mercy upon, nor sympathy for, any negro whom they cannot enslave. They say that God made the black man to be a slave for the white, and act as though they really believed that all free persons of colour are in open rebellion to a direct command from heaven, and that they (the whites) are God's chosen agents to pour out upon them unlimited vengeance. For instance, a Bill has been introduced in the Tennessee Legislature to prevent free negroes from travelling on the railroads in that State. It has passed the first reading. The bill provides that the President who shall permit a free negro to travel on any road within the jurisdiction of the State under his supervision shall pay a fine of 500 dollars; any conductor permitting a violation of the Act shall pay 250 dollars; provided such free negro is not under the control of a free white citizen of Tennessee, who will vouch for the character of said free negro in a penal bond of one thousand dollars. The State of Arkansas has passed a law to banish all free negroes from its bounds, and it came into effect on the 1st day of January, 1860. Every free negro found there after that date will be liable to be sold into slavery, the crime of freedom being unpardonable. The Missouri Senate has before it a bill providing that all free negroes above the age of eighteen years who shall be found in the State after September, 1860, shall be sold into slavery; and that all such negroes as shall enter the State after September, 1861, and remain there twenty-four hours, shall also be sold into slavery for ever. Mississippi, Kentucky, and Georgia, and in fact, I believe, all the slave States, are legislating in the same manner. Thus the slaveholders make it almost impossible for free persons of colour to get out of the slave States, in order that they may sell them into slavery if they don't go. If no white persons travelled upon railroads except those who could get some one to vouch for their character in a penal bond of one thousand dollars, the railroad companies would soon go to the "wall." Such mean legislation is too low for comment; therefore I leave the villainous acts to speak for themselves.

But the Dred Scott decision is the crowning act of infamous Yankee legislation. The Supreme Court, the highest tribunal of the Republic, composed of nine judge Jeffries's, chosen both from the free and slave States, has decided that no coloured person, or persons of African extraction, can ever become a citizen of the United States, or have any rights which white men are bound to respect. That is to say, in the opinion of this Court, robbery, rape, and murder are not crimes when committed by a white upon a coloured person.

Judges who will sneak from their high and honourable position down into the lowest depths of human depravity, and scrape up a decision like this, are wholly unworthy the confidence of any people. I believe such men would, if they had the power, and were it to their temporal interest, sell their country's independence, and barter away every man's birthright for a mess of pottage. Well may Thomas Campbell say—

> United States, your banner wears,
>   Two emblems, —one of fame,
> Alas, the other that it bears
>   Reminds us of your shame!
> The white man's liberty in types
>   Stands blazoned by your stars;
> But what's the meaning of your stripes?
>   They mean your Negro-scars.

When the time had arrived for us to start, we blew out the lights, knelt down, and prayed to our Heavenly Father mercifully to assist us, as he did his people of old, to escape from cruel bondage; and we shall ever feel that God heard and answered our prayer. Had we not been sustained by a kind, and I sometimes think special, providence, we could never have overcome the mountainous difficulties which I am now about to describe.

After this we rose and stood for a few moments in breathless silence, —we were afraid that some one might have been about the cottage listening and watching our movements. So I took my wife by the hand, stepped softly to the door, raised the latch, drew it open, and peeped out. Though there were trees all around the house, yet the foliage scarcely moved; in fact, everything appeared to be as still as death. I then whispered to my wife, "Come my dear, let us make a desperate leap for liberty!" But poor thing, she shrank back, in a state of trepidation. I turned and asked what was the matter; she made no reply, but burst into violent sobs, and threw her head upon my breast. This appeared to touch my very heart, it caused me to enter into her feelings more fully than ever. We both saw the many mountainous difficulties that rose one after the other before our view, and knew far too well what our sad fate would have been, were we caught and forced back into our slavish den. Therefore on my wife's fully realizing the solemn fact that we had to take our lives, as it were, in our hands, and. contest every inch of the thousand miles of slave territory over which we had to pass, it made her heart almost sink within her, and, had I known them at that time, I would have repeated the following encouraging lines, which may not be out of place here—

> "The hill, though high, I covet to ascend,
> The *difficulty will not me offend*;
> For I perceive the way to life lies here:
> Come, pluck up heart, let's neither faint nor fear;
> Better, though difficult, the right way to go, —
> Than wrong, though easy, where the end is woe."

However, the sobbing was soon over, and after a few moments of silent prayer she recovered her self-possession, and said, "Come, William, it is getting late, so now let us venture upon our perilous journey."

We then opened the door, and stepped as softly out as "moonlight upon the water." I locked the door with my own key, which I now have before me, and tiptoed across the yard into the street. I say tiptoed, because we were like persons near a tottering avalanche, afraid to move, or even breathe freely, for fear the sleeping tyrants should be aroused, and come down upon us with double vengeance, for daring to attempt to escape in the manner which we contemplated.

We shook hands, said farewell, and started in different directions for the railway station. I took the nearest possible way to the train, for fear I should be recognized by some one, and got into the negro car in which I knew I should have to ride; but my *master* (as I will now call my wife) took a longer way round, and only arrived there with the bulk of the passengers. He obtained a ticket for himself and one for his slave to Savannah, the first port, which was about two hundred miles off. My master then had the luggage stowed away, and stepped into one of the best carriages.

But just before the train moved off I peeped through the window, and, to my great astonishment, I saw the cabinet-maker with whom I had worked so long, on the platform. He stepped up to the ticket-seller, and asked some question, and then commenced looking rapidly through the passengers, and into the carriages. Fully believing that we were caught, I shrank into a corner, turned my face from the door, and expected in a moment to be dragged out. The cabinetmaker looked into my master's carriage, but did not know him in his new attire, and, as God would have it, before he reached mine the bell rang, and the train moved off.

I have heard since that the cabinet-maker had a presentiment that we were about to "make tracks for parts unknown;" but, not seeing me, his suspicions vanished, until he received the startling intelligence that we had arrived safely in a free State.

As soon as the train had left the platform, my master looked round in the carriage, and was terror-stricken to find a Mr. Cray—an old friend of my wife's master, who dined with the family the day before, and knew my wife from childhood—sitting on the same seat.

The doors of the American railway carriages are at the ends. The passengers walk up the aisle, and take seats on either side; and as my master was engaged in looking out of the window, he did not see who came in.

My master's first impression, after seeing Mr. Cray, was, that he was there for the purpose of securing him. However, my master thought it was not wise to give any information respecting himself, and for fear that Mr. Cray might draw him into conversation and recognise his voice, my master resolved to feign deafness as the only means of self-defence.

After a little while, Mr. Cray said to my master, "It is a very fine morning, sir." The latter took no notice, but kept looking out of the window. Mr. Cray soon repeated this remark, in a little louder tone, but my master remained as before. This indifference attracted the attention of the passengers near, one of whom laughed out. This, I suppose, annoyed the old gentleman; so he said, "I will make him hear;" and in a loud tone of voice repeated, "It is a very fine morning, sir."

My master turned his head, and with a polite bow said, "Yes," and commenced looking out of the window again.

One of the gentlemen remarked that it was a very great deprivation to be deaf. "Yes," replied Mr. Cray, "and I shall not trouble that fellow any more." This enabled my master to breathe a little easier, and to feel that Mr. Cray was not his pursuer after all.

The gentlemen then turned the conversation upon the three great topics of discussion in first-class circles in Georgia, namely, Niggers, Cotton, and the Abolitionists.

My master had often heard of abolitionists, but in such a connection as to cause him to think that they were a fearful kind of wild animal. But he was highly delighted to learn, from the gentlemen's conversation, that the abolitionists were persons who were opposed to oppression; and therefore, in his opinion, not the lowest, but the very highest, of God's creatures.

Without the slightest objection on my master's part, the gentlemen left the carriage at Gordon, for Milledgeville (the capital of the State).

We arrived at Savannah early in the evening, and got into an omnibus, which stopped at the hotel for the passengers to take tea. I stepped into the house and brought my master something on a tray to the omnibus, which took us in due time to the steamer, which was bound for Charleston, South Carolina.

Soon after going on board, my master turned in; and as the captain and some of the passengers seemed to think this strange, and also questioned me respecting him, my master thought I had better get out the flannels and opodeldoc which we had prepared for the rheumatism, warm them quickly by the stove in the gentleman's saloon, and bring them to his berth. We did this as an excuse for my master's retiring to bed so early.

While at the stove one of the passengers said to me, "Buck, what have you got there?" "Opodeldoc, sir," I replied. "I should think it's opo*devil*," said a lanky swell, who was leaning back in a chair with his heels upon the back of another, and chewing tobacco as if for a wager; "it stinks enough to kill or cure twenty men. Away with it, or I reckon I will throw it overboard!"

It was by this time warm enough, so I took it to my master's berth, remained there a little while, and then went on deck and asked the steward where I was to sleep. He said there was no place provided for coloured passengers, whether slave or free. So I paced the deck till a late hour, then mounted some cotton bags, in a warm place near the funnel, sat there till morning, and then went and assisted my master to get ready for breakfast.

He was seated at the right hand of the captain, who, together with all the passengers, inquired very kindly after his health. As my master had one hand in a sling, it was my duty to carve his food. But when I went out the captain said, "You have a very attentive boy, sir; but you had better watch him like a hawk when you get on to the North. He seems all very well here, but he may act quite differently there. I know several gentlemen who have lost their valuable niggers among them d—d cut-throat abolitionists."

Before my master could speak, a rough slavedealer, who was sitting opposite, with both elbows on the table, and with a large piece of broiled fowl in his fingers, shook his head with emphasis, and in a deep Yankee tone, forced through his crowded mouth the words, "Sound doctrine, captain, very sound." He then dropped the chicken into the plate, leant back, placed his thumbs in the armholes of his fancy waistcoat, and continued, "I would not take a nigger to the North under no consideration. I have had a deal to do with niggers in my time, but I never saw one who ever had his heel upon free soil that was worth a d—n." "Now stranger," addressing my master, "if you have made up your mind to sell that ere nigger, I am your man; just mention your price, and if it isn't out of the way, I will pay for him on this board with hard silver dollars." This hardfeatured, bristly-bearded, wire-headed, red-eyed monster, staring at my master as the serpent did at Eve, said, "What do you say, stranger?" He replied, "I don't wish to sell, sir; I cannot get on well without him."

"You will have to get on without him if you take him to the North," continued this man; "for I can tell ye, stranger, as a friend, I am an older cove than you, I have seen lots of this ere world, and I reckon I have had more dealings with niggers than any man living or dead. I was once employed by General Wade Hampton, for ten years, in doing nothing but breaking 'em in; and everybody knows that the General would not have a man that didn't understand his business. So I tell ye, stranger, again, you had better sell, and let me take him down to Orleans. He will do you no good if you take him across Mason's and Dixon's line; he is a keen nigger, and I can see from the cut of his eye that he is certain to run away." My master said, "I think not, sir; I have great confidence in his fidelity." "Fi*devil*," indignantly said the dealer, as his fist came down upon the edge of the saucer and upset a cup of hot coffee in a gentleman's lap. (As the scalded man jumped up the trader quietly said, "Don't disturb yourself, neighbour; accidents will happen in the best of families.") "It always makes me mad to hear a man talking about fidelity in niggers. There isn't a d—d one on 'em who wouldn't cut sticks," if he had half a chance."

By this time we were near Charleston; my master thanked the captain for his advice, and they all withdrew and went on deck, where the trader fancied he became quite eloquent. He drew a crowd around him, and with emphasis said, "Cap'en, if I was the President of this mighty United States of America, the greatest and freest country under the whole univarse, I would never let no man, I don't care who he is, take a nigger into the North and bring him back here, filled to the brim, as he is sure to be, with d—d abolition vices, to taint all quiet niggers with the hellish spirit of running away. These air, cap'en, my flat-footed, every day, right up and down sentiments, and as this is a free country, cap'en, I don't care who hears 'em; for I am a Southern man, every inch on me to the backbone." "Good!" said an insignificant-looking individual of the slave-dealer stamp. "Three cheers for John C. Calhoun and the whole fair sunny South!" added the trader. So off went their hats, and out burst a terrific roar of irregular but continued cheering. My master took no more notice of the dealer. He merely said to the captain that the air on deck was too keen for him, and he would therefore return to the cabin.

While the trader was in the zenith of his eloquence, he might as well have said, as one of his kith did, at a great Filibustering meeting, that "When the great American Eagle gets one of his mighty claws upon Canada and the other into South America, and his glorious and starry wings of liberty extending from the Atlantic to the Pacific, oh! then, where will England be, ye gentlemen? I tell ye, she will only serve as a pocket-handkerchief for Jonathan to wipe his nose with."

On my master entering the cabin he found at the breakfast-table a young southern military officer, with whom he had travelled some distance the previous day.

After passing the usual compliments the conversation turned upon the old subject, —niggers.

The officer, who was also travelling with a manservant, said to my master, "You will excuse me, Sir, for saying I think you are very likely to spoil your boy by saying `thank you' to him. I assure you, sir, nothing spoils a slave so soon as saying, `thank you' and `if you please' to him. The only way to make a nigger toe the mark, and to keep him in his place, is to storm at him like thunder, and keep him trembling like a leaf. Don't you see, when I speak to my Ned, he darts like lightning; and if he didn't I'd skin him."

Just then the poor dejected slave came in, and the officer swore at him fearfully, merely to teach my master what he called the proper way to treat me.

After he had gone out to get his master's luggage ready, the officer said, "That is the way to speak to them. If every nigger was drilled in this manner, they would be as humble as dogs, and never dare to run away."

The gentleman urged my master not to go to the North for the restoration of his health, but to visit the Warm Springs in Arkansas.

My master said, he thought the air of Philadelphia would suit his complaint best; and, not only so, he thought he could get better advice there.

The boat had now reached the wharf. The officer wished my master a safe and pleasant journey, and left the saloon.

There were a large number of persons on the quay waiting the arrival of the steamer: but we were afraid to venture out for fear that some one might recognize me; or that they had heard that we were gone, and had telegraphed to have us stopped. However, after remaining in the cabin till all the other passengers were gone, we had our luggage placed on a fly, and I took my master by the arm, and with a little difficulty he hobbled on shore, got in and drove off to the best hotel, which John C. Calhoun, and all the other great southern fire-eating statesmen, made their head-quarters while in Charleston.

On arriving at the house the landlord ran out and opened the door: but judging, from the poultices and green glasses, that my master was an invalid, he took him very tenderly by one arm and ordered his man to take the other.

My master then eased himself out, and with their assistance found no trouble in getting up the steps into the hotel. The proprietor made me stand on one side, while he paid my master the attention and homage he thought a gentleman of his high position merited.

My master asked for a bed-room. The servant was ordered to show a good one, into which we helped him. The servant returned. My master then handed me the bandages, I took them downstairs in great haste, and told the landlord my master wanted two hot poultices as quickly as possible. He rang the bell, the servant came in, to whom he said, "Run to the kitchen and tell the cook to make two hot poultices right off, for there is a gentleman upstairs very badly off indeed!"

In a few minutes the smoking poultices were brought in. I placed them in white handkerchiefs, and hurried upstairs, went into my master's apartment, shut the door, and laid them on the mantel-piece. As he was alone for a little while, he thought he could rest a great deal better with the poultices off. However, it was necessary to have them to complete the remainder of the journey. I then ordered dinner, and took my master's boots out to polish them. While doing so I entered into conversation with one of the slaves. I may state here, that on the sea-coast of South Carolina and Georgia the slaves speak worse English than in any other part of the country. This is owing to the frequent importation, or smuggling in, of Africans, who mingle with the natives. Consequently the language cannot properly be called English or African, but a corruption of the two.

The shrewd son of African parents to whom I referred said to me, "Say, brudder, way you come from, and which side you goin day wid dat ar little don up buckra" (white man)?

I replied, "To Philadelphia."

"What!" he exclaimed, with astonishment, "to Philumadelphy?"

"Yes," I said.

"By squash! I wish I was going wid you! I hears um say dat dare's no slaves way over in dem parts; is um so?"

I quietly said, "I have heard the same thing."

"Well," continued he, as he threw down the boot and brush, and, placing his hands in his pockets, strutted across the floor with an air of independence—"Gorra Mighty, dem is de parts for Pompey; and I hope when you get dare you will stay, and nebber follow dat buckra back to dis hot quarter no more, let him be eber so good."

I thanked him; and just as I took the boots up and started off, he caught my hand between his two, and gave it a hearty shake, and, with tears streaming down his cheeks, said:—

"God bless you, broder, and may de Lord be wid you. When you gets de freedom, and sitin under your own wine and fig-tree, don't forget to pray for poor Pompey."

I was afraid to say much to him, but I shall never forget his earnest request, nor fail to do what little I can to release the millions of unhappy bondmen, of whom he was one.

At the proper time my master had the poultices placed on, came down, and seated himself at a table in a very brilliant dining-room, to have his dinner. I had to have something at the same time, in order to be ready for the boat; so they gave me my dinner in an old broken plate, with a rusty knife and fork, and said, "Here, boy, you go in the kitchen." I took it and went out, but did not stay more than a few minutes, because I was in a great hurry to get back to see how the invalid was getting on. On arriving I found two or three servants waiting on him; but as he did not feel able to make a very hearty dinner, he soon finished, paid the bill, and gave the servants each a trifle, which caused one of them to say to me, "Your massa is a big bug"—meaning a gentleman of distinction—"he is the greatest gentleman dat has been dis way for dis six months." I said, "Yes, he is some pumpkins," meaning the same as "big bug."

When we left Maçon, it was our intention to take a steamer at Charleston through to Philadelphia; but on arriving there we found that the vessels did not run during the winter, and I have no doubt it was well for us they did not; for on the very last voyage the steamer made that we intended to go by, a fugitive was discovered secreted on board, and sent back to slavery. However, as we had also heard of the Overland Mail Route, we were all right. So I ordered a fly to the door, had the luggage placed on; we got in, and drove down to the Customhouse Office, which was near the wharf where we had to obtain tickets, to take a steamer for Wilmington, North Carolina. When we reached the building, I helped my master into the office, which was crowded with passengers. He asked for a ticket for himself and one for his slave to Philadelphia. This caused the principal officer—a very mean-looking, cheese-coloured fellow, who was sitting there—to look up at us very suspiciously, and in a fierce tone of voice he said to me, "Boy, do you belong to that gentleman?" I quickly replied, "Yes, sir" (which was quite correct). The tickets were handed out, and as my master was paying for them the chief man said to him, "I wish you to register your name here, sir, and also the name of your nigger, and pay a dollar duty on him."

My master paid the dollar, and pointing to the hand that was in the poultice, requested the officer to register his name for him. This seemed to offend the "high-bred" South Carolinian. He jumped up, shaking his head; and, cramming his hands almost through the bottom of his trousers pockets, with a slave-bullying air, said, "I shan't do it."

This attracted the attention of all the passengers. Just then the young military officer with whom my master travelled and conversed on the steamer from Savannah stepped in, somewhat the worse for brandy; he shook hands with my master, and pretended to know all about him. He said, "I know his kin (friends) like a book;" and as the officer was known in Charleston, and was going to stop there with friends, the recognition was very much in my master's favour.

The captain of the steamer, a good-looking jovial fellow, seeing that the gentleman appeared to know my master, and perhaps not wishing to lose us as passengers, said in an off-hand sailor-like manner, "I will register the gentleman's name, and take the responsibility upon myself." He asked my master's name. He said, "William Johnson." The names were put down, I think, "Mr. Johnson and slave." The captain said, "It's all right now, Mr. Johnson." He thanked him kindly, and the young officer begged my master to go with him, and have something to drink and a cigar; but as he had not acquired these accomplishments, he excused himself, and we went on board and came off to Wilmington, North Carolina. When the gentleman finds out his mistake, he will, I have no doubt, be careful in future not to pretend to have an intimate acquaintance with an entire stranger. During the voyage the captain said, "It was rather sharp shooting this morning, Mr. Johnson. It was not out of any disrespect to you, sir; but they make it a rule to be very strict at Charleston. I have known families to be detained there with their slaves till reliable information could be received respecting them. If they were not very careful, any d—d abolitionist might take off a lot of valuable niggers."

My master said, "I suppose so," and thanked him again for helping him over the difficulty.

We reached Wilmington the next morning, and took the train for Richmond, Virginia. I have stated that the American railway carriages (or cars, as they are called), are constructed differently to those in England. At one end of some of them, in the South, there is a little apartment with a couch on both sides for the convenience of families and invalids; and as they thought my master was very poorly, he was allowed to enter one of these apartments at Petersburg, Virginia, where an old gentleman and two handsome young ladies, his daughters, also got in, and took seats in the same carriage. But before the train started, the gentleman stepped into my car, and questioned me respecting my master. He wished to know what was the matter with him, where he was from, and where he was going. I told him where he came from, and said that he was suffering from a complication of complaints, and was going to Philadelphia, where he thought he could get more suitable advice than in Georgia.

The gentleman said my master could obtain the very best advice in Philadelphia. Which turned out to be quite correct, though he did not receive it from physicians, but from kind abolitionists who understood his case much better. The gentleman also said, "I reckon your master's father hasn't any more such faithful and smart boys as you." "O, yes, sir, he has," I replied, "lots on 'em." Which was literally true. This seemed all he wished to know. He thanked me, gave me a ten-cent piece, and requested me to be attentive to my good master. I promised that I would do so, and have ever since endeavoured to keep my pledge. During the gentleman's absence, the ladies and my master had a little cosy chat. But on his return, he said, "You seem to be very much afflicted, sir." "Yes, sir," replied the gentleman in the poultices. "What seems to be the matter with you, sir; may I be allowed to ask?" "Inflammatory rheumatism, sir." "Oh! that is very bad, sir," said the kind gentleman: "I can sympathise with you; for I know from bitter experience what the rheumatism is." If he did, he knew a good deal more than Mr. Johnson.

The gentleman thought my master would feel better if he would lie down and rest himself; and as he was anxious to avoid conversation, he at once acted upon this suggestion. The ladies politely rose, took their extra shawls, and made a nice pillow for the invalid's head. My master wore a fashionable cloth cloak, which they took and covered him comfortably on the couch. After he had been lying a little while the ladies, I suppose, thought he was asleep; so one of them gave a long sigh, and said, in a quiet fascinating tone, "Papa, he seems to be a very nice young gentleman." But before papa could speak, the other lady quickly said, "Oh! dear me, I never felt so much for a gentleman in my life!" To use an American expression, "they fell in love with the wrong chap."

After my master had been lying a little while he got up, the gentleman assisted him in getting on his cloak, the ladies took their shawls, and soon they were all seated. They then insisted upon Mr. Johnson taking some of their refreshments, which of course he did, out of courtesy to the ladies. All went on enjoying themselves until they reached Richmond, where the ladies and their father left the train. But, before doing so, the good old Virginian gentleman, who appeared to be much pleased with my master, presented him with a recipe, which he said was a perfect cure for the inflammatory rheumatism. But the invalid not being able to read it, and fearing he should hold it upside down in pretending to do so, thanked the donor kindly, and placed it in his waistcoat pocket. My master's new friend also gave him his card, and requested him the next time he travelled that way to do him the kindness to call; adding, "I shall be pleased to see you, and so will my daughters." Mr. Johnson expressed his gratitude for the proffered hospitality, and said he should feel glad to call on his return. I have not the slightest doubt that he will fulfil the promise whenever that return takes place. After changing trains we went on a little beyond Fredericksburg, and took a steamer to Washington.

At Richmond, a stout elderly lady, whose whole demeanour indicated that she belonged (as Mrs. Stowe's Aunt Chloe expresses it) to one of the "firstest families;" stepped into the carriage, and took a seat near my master. Seeing me passing quickly along the platform, she sprang up as if taken by a fit, and exclaimed, "Bless my soul! there goes my nigger, Ned!"

My master said, "No; that is my boy."

The lady paid no attention to this; she poked her head out of the window, and bawled to me, "You Ned, come to me, sir, you runaway rascal!"

On my looking round she drew her head in, and said to my master, "I beg your pardon, sir, I was sure it was my nigger; I never in my life saw two black pigs more alike than your boy and my Ned." .

After the disappointed lady had resumed her seat, and the train had moved off, she closed her eyes, slightly raising her hands, and in a sanctified tone said to my master, "Oh! I hope, sir, your boy will not turn out to be so worthless as my Ned has. Oh! I was as kind to him as if he had been my own son. Oh! sir, it grieves me very much to think that after all I did for him he should go off without having any cause whatever."

"When did he leave you?" asked Mr. Johnson.

"About eighteen months ago, and I have never seen hair or hide of him since."

"Did he have a wife?" enquired a very respectable-looking young gentleman, who was sitting near my master and opposite to the lady.

"No, sir; not when he left, though he did have one a little before that: She was very unlike him; she was as good and as faithful a nigger as any one need wish to have. But, poor thing! she became so ill, that she was unable to do much work; so I thought it would be best to sell her, to go to New Orleans, where the climate is nice and warm."

"I suppose she was very glad to go South for the restoration of her health?" said the gentleman.

"No; she was not," replied the lady, "for niggers never know what is best for them. She took on a great deal about leaving Ned and the little nigger; but, as she was so weakly, I let her go."

"Was she good-looking?" asked the young passenger, who was evidently not of the same opinion as the talkative lady, and therefore wished her to tell all she knew.

"Yes; she was very handsome, and much whiter than I am; and therefore will have no trouble in getting another husband. I am sure I wish her well. I asked the speculator who bought her to sell her to a good master. Poor thing! she has my prayers, and I know she prays for me. She was a good Christian,

and always used to pray for my soul. It was through her earliest prayers," continued the lady, "that I was first led to seek forgiveness of my sins, before I was
converted at the great camp-meeting."

This caused the lady to snuffle and to draw from her pocket a richly
embroidered handkerchief, and apply it to the corner of her eyes. But my
master could not see that it was at all soiled.

The silence which prevailed for a few moments was broken by the gentleman's saying, "As your 'July' was such a very good girl, and had served you so
faithfully before she lost her health, don't you think it would have been better
to have emancipated her?"

"No, indeed I do not!" scornfully exclaimed the lady, as she impatiently
crammed the fine handkerchief into a little work-bag. "I have no patience
with people who set niggers at liberty. It is the very worst thing you can do
for them. My dear husband just before he died willed all his niggers free. But
I and all our friends knew very well that he was too good a man to have ever
thought of doing such an unkind and foolish thing, had he been in his right
mind, and, therefore we had the will altered as it should have been in the first
place."

"Did you mean, madam," asked my master, "that willing the slaves free was
unjust to yourself, or unkind to them?"

"I mean that it was decidedly unkind to the servants themselves. It always
seems to me such a cruel thing to turn niggers loose to shift for themselves,
when there are so many good masters to take care of them. As for myself,"
continued the considerate lady, "I thank the Lord my dear husband left me and
my son well provided for. Therefore I care nothing for the niggers, on my own
account, for they are a great deal more trouble than they are worth, I sometimes wish that there was not one of them in the world: for the ungrateful
wretches are always running away. I have lost no less than ten since my poor
husband died. It's ruinous, sir!"

"But as you are well provided for, I suppose you do not feel the loss very
much," said the passenger.

"I don't feel it at all," haughtily continued the good soul; "but that is no reason why property should be squandered. If my son and myself had the money
for those valuable niggers, just see what a great deal of good we could do for
the poor, and in sending missionaries abroad to the poor heathen, who have
never heard the name of our blessed Redeemer. My dear son who is a good
Christian minister has advised me not to worry and send my soul to hell for
the sake of niggers; but to sell every blessed one of them for what they will
fetch, and go and live in peace with him in New York. This I have concluded
to do. I have just been to Richmond and made arrangements with my agent
to make clean work of the forty that are left."

"Your son being a good Christian minister," said the gentleman, "It's strange
he did not advise you to let the poor negroes have their liberty and go North."

"It's not at all strange, sir; it's not at all strange. My son knows what's best
for the niggers; he has always told me that they were much better off than the

free niggers in the North. In fact, I don't believe there are any white labouring people in the world who are as well off as the slaves."

"You are quite mistaken, madam," said the young man. "For instance, my own widowed mother, before she died, emancipated all her slaves, and sent them to Ohio, where they are getting along well. I saw several of them last summer myself."

"Well," replied the lady, "freedom may do for your ma's niggers, but it will never do for mine; and, plague them, they shall never have it; that is the word, with the bark on it."

"If freedom will not do for your slaves," replied the passenger, "I have no doubt your Ned and the other nine negroes will find out their mistake, and return to their old home.

"Blast them!" exclaimed the old lady, with great emphasis, "if I ever get them, I will cook their infernal hash, and tan their accursed black hides well for them! God forgive me," added the old soul, "the niggers will make me lose all my religion!"

By this time the lady had reached her destination. The gentleman got out at the next station beyond. As soon as she was gone, the young Southerner said to my master, "What a d—d shame it is for that old whining hypocritical humbug to cheat the poor negroes out of their liberty! If she has religion, may the devil prevent me from ever being converted!"

For the purpose of somewhat disguising myself, I bought and wore a very good second-hand white beaver, an article which I had never indulged in before. So just before we arrived at Washington, an uncouth planter, who had been watching me very closely. said to my master, "I reckon, stranger, you are *'spiling'* that ere nigger of yourn. by letting him wear such a devilish fine hat. Just look at the quality on it; the President couldn't wear a better. I should just like to go and kick it overboard." His friend touched him, and said, "Don't speak so to a gentleman." "Why not" exclaimed the fellow. He grated his short teeth, which appeared to be nearly worn away by the incessant chewing of tobacco, and said, "It always makes me itch all over, from head to toe, to get hold of every d—d nigger I see dressed like a white man. Washington is run away with *spiled* and free niggers. If I had my way I would sell every d—d rascal of 'em way down South, where the devil would be whipped out on 'em."

This man's fierce manner made my master feel rather nervous, and therefore he thought the less he said the better; so he walked off without making any reply. In a few minutes we were landed at Washington, where we took a conveyance and hurried off to the train for Baltimore.

We left our cottage on Wednesday morning, the 21st of December, 1848, and arrived at Baltimore, Saturday evening, the 24th (Christmas Eve). Baltimore was the last slave port of any note at which we stopped.

On arriving there we felt more anxious than ever, because we knew not what that last dark night would bring forth. It is true we were near the goal, but our poor hearts were still as if tossed at sea; and, as there was another great and dangerous bar to pass, we were afraid our liberties would be wrecked, and, like the ill-fated *Royal Charter*, go down for ever just off the place we longed to reach.

They are particularly watchful at Baltimore to prevent slaves from escaping into Pennsylvania, which is a free State. After I had seen my master into one of the best carriages, and was just about to step into mine, an officer, a full-blooded Yankee of the lower order, saw me. He came quickly up, and, tapping me on the shoulder, said in his unmistakable native twang, together with no little display of his authority, "Where are you going, boy?" "To Philadelphia, sir," I humbly replied. "Well, what are you going there for?" "I am travelling with my master, who is in the next carriage, sir." "Well, I calculate you had better get him out; and be mighty quick about it, because the train will soon be starting. It is against my rules to let any man take a slave past here, unless he can satisfy them in the office that he has a right to take him along."

The officer then passed on and left me standing upon the platform, with my anxious heart apparently palpitating in the throat. At first I scarcely knew which way to turn. But it soon occurred to me that the good God, who had been with us thus far, would not forsake us at the eleventh hour. So with renewed hope I stepped into my master's carriage, to inform him of the difficulty. I found him sitting at the farther end, quite alone. As soon as he looked up and saw me, he smiled. I also tried to wear a cheerful countenance, in order to break the shock of the sad news. I knew what made him smile. He was aware that if we were fortunate we should reach our destination at five o'clock the next morning, and this made it the more painful to communicate what the officer had said; but, as there was no time to lose, I went up to him and asked him how he felt. He said "Much better," and that he thanked God we were getting on so nicely. I then said we were not getting on quite so well as we had anticipated. He anxiously and quickly asked what was the matter. I told him. He started as if struck by lightning, and exclaimed, "Good Heavens! William, is it possible that we are, after all, doomed to hopeless bondage?" I could say nothing, my heart was too full to speak, for at first I did not know what to do. However we knew it would never do to turn back to the "City of Destruction," like Bunyan's *Mistrust* and *Timorous*, because they saw lions in the narrow way after ascending the hill Difficulty; but press on, like noble *Christian* and *Hopeful*, to the great city in which dwelt a few "shining ones." So, after a few moments, I did all I could to encourage my companion, and we stepped out and made for the office: but how or where my master obtained sufficient courage to face the tyrants who had power to blast all we held dear, heaven only knows! Queen Elizabeth could not have been more terror-stricken, on being forced to land at the traitors' gate leading to the Tower, than we were on entering that office. We felt that our very existence was at stake, and that we must either sink or swim. But, as God was our present and mighty helper in this as well as in all former trials, we were able to keep our heads up and press forwards.

On entering the room we found the principal man, to whom my master said, "Do you wish to see me, sir?" "Yes," said this eagle-eyed officer; and he added, "It is against our rules, sir, to allow any person to take a slave out of Baltimore into Philadelphia, unless he can satisfy us that he has a right to take him along." "Why is that?" asked my master, with more firmness than could be expected. "Because, sir," continued he, in a voice and manner that almost chilled our blood, "if we should suffer any gentleman to take a slave past here into Philadelphia; and should the gentleman with whom the slave might be travelling turn out not to be his rightful owner; and should the proper master come and prove that his slave escaped on our road, we shall have him to pay for; and, therefore, we cannot let any slave pass here without receiving security to show, and to satisfy us, that it is all right."

This conversation attracted the attention of the large number of bustling passengers. After the officer had finished, a few of them said, "Chit, chit, chit;" not because they thought we were slaves endeavouring to escape, but merely because they thought my master was a slaveholder and invalid gentleman, and therefore it was wrong to detain him. The officer, observing that the passengers sympathised with my master, asked him if he was not acquainted with some gentleman in Baltimore that he could get to endorse for him, to show that I was his property, and that he had a right to take me off. He said, "No;" and added, "I bought tickets in Charleston to pass us through to Philadelphia, and therefore you have no right to detain us here." "Well, sir," said the man, indignantly, "right or no right, we shan't let you go." These sharp words fell upon our anxious hearts like the crack of doom, and made us feel that hope only smiles to deceive.

For a few moments perfect silence prevailed. My master looked at me, and I at him, but neither of us dared to speak a word, for fear of making some blunder that would tend to our detection. We knew that the officers had power to throw us into prison, and if they had done so we must have been detected and driven back, like the vilest felons, to a life of slavery, which we dreaded far more than sudden death.

We felt as though we had come into deep waters and were about being overwhelmed, and that the slightest mistake would clip asunder the last brittle thread of hope by which we were suspended, and let us down for ever into the dark and horrible pit of misery and degradation from which we were straining every nerve to escape. While our hearts were crying lustily unto Him who is ever ready and able to save, the conductor of the train that we had just left stepped in. The officer asked if we came by the train with him from Washington; he said we did, and left the room. Just then the bell rang for the train to leave; and had it been the sudden shock of an earthquake it could not have given us a greater thrill. The sound of the bell caused every eye to flash with apparent interest, and to be more steadily fixed upon us than before. But, as God would have it, the officer all at once thrust his fingers through his hair, and in a state of great agitation said, "I really don't know what to do; I calculate it is all right." He then told the clerk to run and tell the conductor to "let this gentleman and slave pass;" adding, "As he is not well, it is a pity to stop him here. We will let him go." My master thanked him, and stepped out and hobbled across the platform as quickly as possible. I tumbled him unceremoniously into one of the best carriages, and leaped into mine just as the train was gliding off towards our happy destination.

We thought of this plan about four days before we left Maçon; and as we had our daily employment to attend to, we only saw each other at night. So we sat up the four long nights talking over the plan and making preparations.

We had also been four days on the journey; and as we travelled night and day, we got but very limited opportunities for sleeping. I believe nothing in the world could have kept us awake so long but the intense excitement, produced by the fear of being retaken on the one hand, and the bright anticipation of liberty on the other.

We left Baltimore about eight o'clock in the evening; and not being aware of a stopping-place of any consequence between there and Philadelphia, and also knowing that if we were fortunate we should be in the latter place early the next morning, I thought I might indulge in a few minutes' sleep in the car; but I, like Bunyan's Christian in the arbour, went to sleep at the wrong time, and took too long a nap. So, when the train reached Havre de Grace, all the first-class passengers had to get out of the carriages and into a ferry-boat, to be ferried across the Susquehanna river, and take the train on the opposite side.

The road was constructed so as to be raised or lowered to suit the tide. So they rolled the luggage-vans on to the boat, and off on the other side; and as I was in one of the apartments adjoining a baggage-car, they considered it unnecessary to awaken me, and tumbled me over with the luggage. But when my master was asked to leave his seat, he found it very dark, and cold, and raining. He missed me for the first time on the journey. On all previous occasions, as soon as the train stopped, I was at hand to assist him. This caused many slaveholders to praise me very much: they said they had never before seen a slave so attentive to his master: and therefore my absence filled him with terror and confusion; the children of Israel could not have felt more troubled on arriving at the Red Sea. So he asked the conductor if he had seen anything of his slave. The man being somewhat of an abolitionist, and believing that my master was really a slaveholder, thought he would tease him a little respecting me. So he said, "No, sir; I haven't seen anything of him for some time: I have no doubt he has run away, and is in Philadelphia, free, long before now." My master knew that there was nothing in this; so he asked the conductor if he would please to see if he could find me. The man indignantly replied, "I am no slave-hunter; and as far as I am concerned everybody must look after their own niggers." He went off and left the confused invalid to fancy whatever he felt inclined. My master at first thought I must have been kidnapped into slavery by some one, or left, or perhaps killed on the train. He also thought of stopping to see if he could hear anything of me, but he soon remembered that he had no money. That night all the money we had was consigned to my own pocket, because we thought, in case there were any pickpockets about, a slave's pocket would be the last one they would look for. However, hoping to meet me some day in a land of liberty, and as he had the tickets, he thought it best upon the whole to enter the boat and come off to Philadelphia, and endeavour to make his way alone in this cold and hollow world as best he could. The time was now up, so he went on board and came across with feelings that can be better imagined than described.

After the train had got fairly on the way to Philadelphia, the guard came into my car and gave me a violent shake, and bawled out at the same time, "Boy, wake up!" I started, almost frightened out of my wits. He said, "Your master is scared half to death about you." That frightened me still more—I thought they had found him out; so I anxiously inquired what was the matter. The guard said, "He thinks you have run away from him." This made me feel quite at ease. I said, "No, sir; I am satisfied my good master doesn't think that." So off I started to see him. He had been fearfully nervous, but on seeing me he at once felt much better. He merely wished to know what had become of me.

On returning to my seat, I found the conductor and two or three other persons amusing themselves very much respecting my running away. So the guard said, "Boy, what did your master want?"[1] I replied, "He merely wished to know what had become of me." "No," said the man, "that was not it; he thought you had taken French leave, for parts unknown. I never saw a fellow so badly scared about losing his slave in my life. Now," continued the guard, "let me give you a little friendly advice. When you get to Philadelphia, run away and leave that cripple, and have your liberty." "No, sir," I indifferently replied, "I can't promise to do that." "Why not?" said the conductor, evidently much surprised; "don't you want your liberty?" "Yes, sir," I replied; "but I shall never run away from such a good master as I have at present."

One of the men said to the guard, "Let him alone; I guess he will open his eyes when he gets to Philadelphia, and see things in another light." After giving me a good deal of information, which I afterwards found to be very useful, they left me alone.

I also met with a coloured gentleman on this train, who recommended me to a boarding-house that was kept by an abolitionist, where he thought I would be quite safe, if I wished to run away from my master. I thanked him kindly, but of course did not let him know who we were. Late at night, or rather early in the morning, I heard a fearful whistling of the steam-engine; so I opened the window and looked out, and saw a large number of flickering lights in the distance, and heard a passenger in the next carriage—who also had his head out of the window—say to his companion, "Wake up, old horse, we are at Philadelphia!"

The sight of those lights and that announcement made me feel almost as happy as Bunyan's Christian must have felt when he first caught sight of the cross. I, like him, felt that the straps that bound the heavy burden to my back began to pop, and the load to roll off. I also looked, and looked again, for it

---

[1] I may state here that every man slave is called boy till he is very old, then the more respectable slave-holders call him uncle. The women are all girls till they are aged, then they are called aunts. This is the reason why Mrs. Stowe calls her characters Uncle Tom, Aunt Chloe, Uncle Tiff, &c.

appeared very wonderful to me how the mere sight of our first city of refuge should have all at once made my hitherto sad and heavy heart become so light and happy. As the train speeded on, I rejoiced and thanked God with all my heart and soul for his great kindness and tender mercy, in watching over us, and bringing us safely through.

As soon as the train had reached the platform, before it had fairly stopped, I hurried out of my carriage to my master, whom I got at once into a cab, placed the luggage on, jumped in myself, and we drove off to the boarding-house which was so kindly recommended to me. On leaving the station, my master—or rather my wife, as I may now say—who had from the commencement of the journey borne up in a manner that much surprised us both, grasped me by the hand, and said, "Thank God, William, we are safe!" and then burst into tears, leant upon me, and wept like a child. The reaction was fearful. So when we reached the house, she was in reality so weak and faint that she could scarcely stand alone. However, I got her into the apartments that were pointed out, and there we knelt down, on this Sabbath, and Christmas-day, —a day that will ever be memorable to us, —and poured out our heartfelt gratitude to God, for his goodness in enabling us to overcome so many perilous difficulties, in escaping out of the jaws of the wicked.

Let My People Go: *Spirituals*

Little attempt was made to convert the Southern slaves to Christianity until the period of the Second Great Awakening early in the nineteenth century. when Baptist and Methodist churches made great headway among blacks. Although it is impossible to know how many slaves adopted the religion of the slave masters, it is clear that in becoming Christian, the blacks made the religion their own. They saw in the Old Testament story of a captive chosen people many elements that were analogous to their own condition and they drew hope from the gospel of freedom and deliverance preached in the New Testament, finding in it the promise that a righteous God would intervene in this world and establish justice.

Much of our knowledge of slave religion comes from the surviving Spirituals, religious folk songs that originated among the slaves of the South. These songs richly reflect the attitudes of the slaves toward this world and their condition in it. Running through the whole literature of the slave songs are three major themes: dissatisfaction with the conditions of slavery, faith in ultimate deliverance by a righteous God, and anticipation of a better world "over there." "Over there" often refers at the same time to freedom: in this world and freedom in the next. As they sang "Ev'rybody talkin 'bout heab'n ain't goin' dere," the slaves who had adopted Christianity, made it clear that they had little doubt about who the true Christians were—the slaves themselves or the slave masters.

GO DOWN, MOSES

Go down, Moses,
'Way down in Egypt land,
Tell ole Pharaoh,
To let my people go.

Go down, Moses,
'Way down in Egypt land,
Tell ole Pharaoh,
To let my people go.

When Israel was in Egypt land,
Let my people go,
Oppressed so hard they could not stand,
Let my people go,

Thus spoke the Lord, bold Moses said,
Let my people go,
If not I'll smite your first-born dead,
Let my people go.

Go down, Moses,
'Way down in Egypt land,
Tell ole Pharaoh,
To let my people go.

ALL GOD'S CHILLUN GOT WINGS

I got a robe, you got a robe,
All o' God's chillun got a robe.
When I get to heab'n, goin' to put on my robe,
I'm goin' to shout all ovah God's heab'n,
Heab'n, heab'n,
Ev'rybody talkin' 'bout heab'n ain't goin' dere;
Heab'n, heab'n,
I'm goin' to shout all ovah God's heab'n.

I got-a wings, you got-a wings,
All o' God's chillun got-a wings.
When I get to heab'n, goin' to put on my wings,
I'm goin' to fly all ovah God's heab'n,
Heab'n, heab'n,
Ev'rybody talkin' 'bout heab'n ain't goin' dere;
Heab'n, heab'n,
I'm goin' to fly all ovah God's heab'n.

I got a harp, you got a harp,
All o' God's chillun got a harp.
When I get to heab'n, goin' to play on my harp,
I'm goin' to play all ovah God's heab'n,
Heab'n, heab'n,
Ev'rybody talkin' 'bout heab'n ain't goin' dere;
Heab'n, heab'n,
I'm goin' to play all ovah God's heab'n.

I got-a shoes, you got-a shoes,
All o' God's chillun got-a shoes.
When I get to heab'n, goin' to put on my shoes,
I'm goin to walk all ovah God's heab'n,
Heab'n, heab'n,
Ev'rybody talkin' 'bout heab'n ain't goin' dere;
Heab'n, heab'n,
I'm goin' to walk all ovah God's heab'n.

STEAL AWAY TO JESUS

Steal away, steal away, steal away to Jesus!
Steal away, steal away home,

I ain't got long to stay here.
My Lord, He calls me, He calls me by the thunder,
The trumpet sounds within-a my soul,
I ain't got long to stay here.

Steal away, steal away, steal away to Jesus!
Steal away, steal away home,
I ain't got long to stay here.

Green trees a-bending, po' sinner stand a-trembling,
The trumpet sounds within-a my soul,
I ain't got long to stay here.

Steal away, steal away, steal away to Jesus!
Steal away, steal away home,
I ain't got long to stay here.

DIDN'T MY LORD DELIVER DANIEL

Didn't my Lord deliver Daniel,
    deliver Daniel, deliver Daniel,
Didn't my Lord deliver Daniel,
An' why not every man.

He delivered Daniel from the lion's den,
Jonah from the belly of the whale,
An' the Hebrew chillun from the fiery furnace,
An' why not every man.

Didn't my Lord deliver Daniel,
    deliver Daniel, deliver Daniel,
Didn't my Lord deliver Daniel,
An' why not every man.

The moon run down in a purple stream,
The sun forbear to shine,
An' every star disappear,
King Jesus shall-a be mine.

The win' blows eas' an' the win' blows wes',
It blows like the judg-a-ment day,
An' ev'ry po' soul that never did pray'll
Be glad to pray that day.

Didn't my Lord deliver Daniel,
    deliver Daniel, deliver Daniel,
Didn't my Lord deliver Daniel,
An' why not every man.

I THANK GOD I'M FREE AT LAST

Free at last, free at last,
I thank God I'm free at last.
Free at last, free at last,
I thank God I'm free at last.

Way down yonder in the graveyard walk,
I thank God I'm free at last,
Me and my Jesus gonna meet an' talk,
I thank God I'm free at last.

On-a my knees when the light pass by,
I thank God I'm free at last,
Thought my soul would rise an' fly,
I thank God I'm free at last.

One o' these mornin's bright an' fair,
I thank God I'm free at last,
Gonna meet my Jesus in the middle o' the air,
I thank God I'm free at last.

Free at last, free at last,
I thank God I'm free at last,
Free at last, free at last,
I thank God I'm free at last.

SUGGESTIONS FOR FURTHER READING

Standard works on nineteenth century slavery include Kenneth Stampp, *The Peculiar Institution: Slavery in the Ante-Bellum South*★ (1956), Eugene Genovese, *Roll, Jordan, Roll*★ (1974), John Blassingame, *The Slave Community*★, rev. ed. (1979), and Peter Kolchin, *American Slavery, 1619–1877*★ (1993). Other general studies of importance are George Rawick, *From Sundown to Sunup: The Making of the Black Community*★ (1972), Sterling Stuckey, *Slave Culture*★ (1987), and Thomas D. Morris, *Southern Slavery and the Law, 1619–1860*★ (1996).

Studies of special interest on aspects of slavery are Albert Raboteau, *Slave Religion: The "Invisible Institution" in the Antebellum South*★ (1978), Thomas Webber, *Deep Like the Rivers: Education in the Slave Quarter Community. 1835–1865*★ (1978), Barbara J. Fields, *Slavery and Freedom on the Middle Ground: Maryland in the Nineteenth Century*★ (1985), Walter Johnson, *Soul by Soul: Life Inside the Antebellum Slave Market* (2000). See also Michael A. Morrison, *Slavery and the American West*★ (1997) and Albert J. Von Frank, *The Trials of Anthony Burns: Freedom and Slavery in Emerson's Boston*★ (1998). A work of critical importance is Herbert G. Gutman, *The Black Family in Slavery and Freedom, 1750–1925*★ (1977).

The slaves themselves left three kinds of literature that are valuable in a study of African-American life in the nineteenth century: songs (both sacred and secular), folk tales, and the slave narratives (autobiographical descriptions of life under slavery written by fugitives or ex-slaves in the period before the Civil War). The most complete collection of spirituals is that edited by James Weldon Johnson and J. Rosamond Johnson, *The Books of American Negro Spirituals* (1925, 1926). For studies of black folk songs, see Harold Courlander, *Negro Folk Music, U.S.A.,* (1963) and Dena J. Epstein, *Sinful Tunes and Spirituals: Black Folk Music to the Civil War*★ (1977). Folk tales have been gathered together in Richard Dorson (ed.), *American Negro Folktales* (1967) and J. Mason Brewer (ed.), *American Negro Folklore* (1968). The importance of folklore in the black community has been brilliantly analyzed in Lawrence Levine, *Black Culture and Black Consciousness: Afro-American Folk Thought from Slavery to Freedom*★ (1977). Slave narratives have been collected many times and are available in different editions. The most recent and complete of these is the excellent two volume collection edited by Yuval Taylor, *I Was Born a Slave: An Anthology of Classic Slave Narratives*★ (1999).

Slave rebelliousness is dealt with in two works by Herbert Aptheker, *American Negro Slave Revolts*★ (1943) and *Nat Turner's Slave Rebellion* (1966). A failed slave rebellion is described in John Lofton, *Insurrection in South Carolina: The Turbulent World of Denmark Vesey* (1964), published in paperback as *Denmark Vesey's Revolt.*★

★ Books marked by an asterisk are available in paperback

4

✦

The Free Black
Community 1800 –1860

INTRODUCTION

When the first federal census was taken in 1799, there were 59,557 free persons of African descent in the United States. By 1860, the number had risen to 488,070. At this time, the free black population was concentrated in the upper South and the Middle Atlantic States, and about half the total number of free blacks lived in the South. The increase in the number of free blacks was due primarily to the process of manumission, the freeing of slaves through private or public action. In the early decades of the new nation, manumission had proceeded apace in both North and South. But as sectional antagonism increased and the threat of slave insurrection grew, most Southern states prohibited or severely restricted private manumission.

In the South in 1850, mulattoes—persons of mixed white and black parentage—constituted 37 percent of the free black population, but only 8 percent of the slave population. Many of the free mulattoes were children slave women bore to their white masters. The masters regularly freed the children born of these illicit unions. In several Southern cities, there were organizations of free mulattoes that denied membership to blacks of unmixed ancestry.

In both North and South, the free blacks who lived in the cities were usually in a better position economically than those who lived in rural areas. It has been suggested that Southern cities held better economic opportunities for free blacks than did Northern ones, for in the South certain occupations were open to blacks almost exclusively, whereas in the North they had to compete with a growing white immigrant population. Though it may be true that the blacks in Southern cities had certain economic advantages, they were suppressed in many other ways and were not allowed even the small amount of personal freedom that the Northern states offered free blacks. With the exception of New Orleans, Southern cities allowed the blacks virtually no public voice until 1865.

In the Northern cities, on the other hand, the free blacks were able to speak out about their condition with some degree of freedom. Beginning with *Freedom's Journal*, first published in New York City in 1827, several newspapers edited by blacks appeared. The primary purpose of these papers was to give voice to the feelings and the needs of the black people. Despite these printed cries, however, the black people found themselves less and less able to influence public affairs, for throughout the first half of the nineteenth century the political activity of blacks was increasingly restricted by legislation. By the 1840s, all Northern states except Maine, Massachusetts, New Hampshire, Rhode Island, and Vermont had either severely limited or completely abolished the right of the black people to vote.

The Northern blacks were also seriously restricted in the job market. Craft and trade unions would not accept them, so they were generally limited to jobs in unskilled or domestic labor. Toward the end of the antebellum period, even those positions became elusive, because of the massive influx of unskilled white immigrants, particularly the Irish. Several severe clashes between blacks and whites resulted from this development, culminating in the bloody Draft Riots of 1863, when mobs of Irish hoodlums roamed the streets of New York City, beating and burning black people and destroying their homes.

Deprived of the ballot, deprived of economic mobility, and deprived for the most part of public schooling, the blacks developed a variety of responses to their condition—responses that in many cases have continued to this day. Although these responses are sometimes placed on a continuum from accommodation to protest, they must all be considered as protests of some kind. What varies from one to the other is merely the public expression of the rage within.

As has been the case during the entire history of the African-American, most of the black people who lived in the nineteenth century led lives of quiet desperation. To them, the avenues of public protest seemed either closed (as in the South) or futile (as in the North). They had only to struggle through their lives in silent anonymity.

Others were not so quiet in their desperation. Rejecting the notion that protest was useless, they together and singly called out for God's justice. Here and there appeared lonely prophets like David Walker, whose impassioned demand that the slaves rise up and throw off their oppression brought him the enmity of both North and South—and probably hastened his death. More commonly, those who wished to make themselves heard joined together. In the nineteenth century, more and more societies for the self-help and self-protection of black people were organized.

The message of the Christian gospel had given the black man an ideology of freedom and justice. Many of the leaders of black protest in the nineteenth century were clergymen, and many others used the imagery of the Bible as they called for a world in which men were truly equal—equal before one another, as well as before God. Although some of these leaders—Frederick Douglass, for example—rejected the idea of separate religious organizations for blacks, the establishment of all-black churches continued throughout the period.

The black church spawned one of the most important movements of organized protest among black people—the convention movement. The first convention was held in 1830 to protest the suggestion of the white colonizers that free blacks move to Africa in order to eliminate the race problem in the North. Conventions were held from time to time during the rest of the century.

Most of the conventions of the antebellum years emphasized the necessity of alleviating the oppression of free blacks and dealt with problems related to education, suffrage, and job training. Often, however, resolutions of support for the enslaved blacks of the South were passed at the convention meetings. Needless to say, resolutions were not enough, and blacks in the North, many of whom were active in the Underground Railroad, began to form vigilance committees to help protect fugitive slaves from recapture and to find them jobs and housing. Northern blacks were also involved in the work of the many abolitionist organizations.

Although most blacks had rejected emigration as a way to put an end to their difficulties, there was a revival of emigrationist sentiment within the black community toward the middle of the century. Such men as Martin Delany proposed that blacks look elsewhere for the future denied them in the United States. Originally, Delany suggested that Central America become the home of American blacks; later, he advocated a return to Africa and even went so far as to take a lease on some land on the Niger River for resettlement purposes. In the 1850s, several black emigrationist societies were organized. With the outbreak of the Civil War, however, new hope for domestic freedom was aroused in the hearts of the black people.

The White Church's
Oppression of the Black Man

Our Wretchedness in Consequence of the Preachers of the Religion of Jesus Christ

DAVID WALKER

David Walker's Appeal burst like a bomb on the scene of American race relations in 1829. The author's bitter call for slave rebellion frightened the South into taking extraordinary pains to suppress the circulation of the document.

Walker was born in the South in 1785, the son of a free black woman. Since a child assumed the status of his mother under Southern law, he was born free. During his youth he traveled widely, finally setting up an old-clothes shop in Boston in the 1820s. In 1827, he began writing and lecturing on the abolition of slavery. After the publication of his Appeal, there were rumors that a reward was being offered for his head. He died mysteriously on a Boston street in 1830, probably from poison.

The section of the Appeal that follows is an attack on the white Christians who sent missionaries to convert the heathen abroad, but denied the American black man the right to worship in the Christian church. Walker firmly believed that because God was just, America was doomed for its treatment of the African.

Religion, my brethren, is a substance of deep consideration among all nations of earth. The Pagans have a kind, as well as the Mahometans, the Jews and the Christians. But pure and undefiled religion, such as was preached by Jesus Christ and his apostles, is hard to be found in all the earth. God, through his instrument, Moses, handed a dispensation of his Divine will, to the children of Israel after they had left Egypt for the land of Canaan or of Promise, who through hypocrisy, oppression and unbelief, departed from the faith. —He then, by his apostles, handed a dispensation of his, together with the will of Jesus Christ, to the Europeans in Europe, who, in open violation of which, have made *merchandise* of us, and it does appear as though they take this very dispensation to aid them in their *infernal* depredations upon us. Indeed, the way in which religion was and is conducted by the Europeans and their descendants, one might believe it was a plan fabricated by themselves and the devils to oppress us. But hark! My master has taught me better than to believe it—he has taught me that his gospel as it was preached by himself and his

FROM David Walker, "Article III" of *David Walker's Appeal, in Four Articles ...* (Boston, 1829).

apostles remains the same, notwithstanding Europe has tried to mingle blood and oppression with it.

It is well known to the Christian world, that Bartholomew Las Casas, that very very notoriously avaricious Catholic priest or preacher, and adventurer with Columbus in his second voyage, proposed to his countrymen, the Spaniards in Hispaniola to import the Africans from the Portuguese settlement in Africa, to dig up gold and silver, and work their plantations for them, to effect which, he made a voyage thence to Spain, and opened the subject to his master, Ferdinand then in declining health, who listened to the plan: but who died soon after, and left it in the hand of his successor, Charles V.[1] This wretch, ("Las Casas, the Preacher,") succeeded so well in his plans of oppression, that in 1503, the first blacks had been imported into the new world. Elated with this success, and stimulated by sordid avarice only, he importuned Charles V in 1511, to grant permission to a French merchant, to import 4000 blacks at one time.[2] Thus we see, through the instrumentality of a pretended preacher of the gospel of Jesus Christ our common master, our wretchedness first commenced in America—where it has been continued from 1503, to this day, 1829. A period of three hundred and twenty-six years. But two hundred and nine, from 1620—when twenty of our fathers were brought into Jamestown, Virginia, by a Dutch man of war, and sold off like brutes to the highest bidders; and there is not a doubt in my mind, but that tyrants are in hope to perpetuate our miseries under them and their children until the final consummation of all things. —But if they do not get dreadfully deceived, it will be because God has forgotten them.

The Pagans, Jews and Mahometans try to make proselytes to their religions, and whatever human beings adopt their religions they extend to them their protection. But Christian Americans, not only hinder their fellow creatures, the Africans, but thousands of them *will absolutely beat a coloured person nearly to death, if they catch him on his knees, supplicating the throne of grace.* This barbarous cruelty was by all the heathen nations of antiquity, and is by the Pagans, Jews and Mahometans of the present day, left entirely to Christian Americans to inflict on the Africans and their descendants, that their cup which is nearly full may be completed. I have known tyrants or usurpers of human liberty in

---

[1] See Butler's *History of the United States*, vol. 1, page 24. —See also, page 25.

[2] It is not unworthy of remark, that the Portuguese and Spaniards, were among, if not the very first Nations upon Earth, about three hundred and fifty or sixty years ago—But see what those *Christians* have come to now in consequence of afflicting our fathers and us, who have never molested, or disturbed them or any other of the white *Christians*, but have they received one quarter of what the Lord will yet bring upon them, for the murders they have inflicted upon us? —They have had, and in some degree have now, sweet times on our blood and groans, the time however, of bitterness have sometime since commenced with them. —There is a God the Maker and preserver of all things, who will as sure as the world exists, give all his creatures their just recompense of reward in this and in the world to come, —we may fool or deceive, and keep each other in the most profound ignorance, beat, murder and keep each other out of what is our lawful rights, or the rights of man, yet it is impossible for us to deceive or escape the Lord Almighty.

different parts of this country to take their fellow creatures, the coloured people, and beat them until they would scarcely leave life in them; what for? Why they say "The black devils had the audacity to be found *making prayers and supplications to the God who made them!!!!*" Yes, I have known small collections of coloured people to have convened together, for no other purpose than to worship God Almighty, in spirit and in truth, to the best of their knowledge; when tyrants, calling themselves *patrols*, would also convene and wait almost in breathless silence for the poor coloured people to commence singing and praying to the Lord our God, as soon as they had commenced, the wretches would burst in upon them and drag them out and commence beating them as they would rattle-snakes—many of whom, they would beat so unmercifully, that they would hardly be able to crawl for weeks and sometimes for months. Yet the American ministers send out missionaries to convert the heathen, while they keep us and our children sunk at their feet in the most abject ignorance and wretchedness that ever a people was afflicted with since the world began. Will the Lord suffer this people to proceed much longer? Will he not stop them in their career? Does he regard the heathens abroad, more than the heathens among the Americans? Surely the Americans must believe that God is partial, notwithstanding his Apostle Peter, declared before Cornelius and others that he has no respect to persons, but in every nation he that feareth God and worketh righteousness is accepted with him. —"The word," said he, "which God sent unto the children of Israel, preaching peace, by Jesus Christ, (he is Lord of all." [3]) Have not the Americans the Bible in their hands? Do they believe it? Surely they do not. See how they treat us in open violation of the Bible!! They no doubt will be greatly offended with me, but if God does not awaken them, it will be, because they are superior to other men, as they have represented themselves to be. Our divine Lord and Master said, "all things whatsoever ye would that men should do unto you, do ye even so unto them." But an American minister, with the Bible in his hand, holds us and our children in the most abject slavery and wretchedness. Now I ask them, would they like for us to hold them and their children in abject slavery and wretchedness? No, says one, that never can be done—you are too abject and ignorant to do it—you are not men—you were made to be slaves to us, to dig up gold and silver for us and our children. Know this, my dear sirs, that although you treat us and our children now, as you do your domestic beast—yet the final result of all future events are known but to God Almighty alone, who rules in the armies of heaven and among the inhabitants of the earth, and who dethrones one earthly king and sets up another, as it seemeth good in his holy sight. We may attribute these vicissitudes to what we please, but the God of armies and of justice rules in heaven and in earth, and the whole American people shall see and know it yet, to their satisfaction. I have known pretended preachers of the gospel of my Master, who not only held us as their natural inheritance, but treated us with as much rigor as any Infidel or Deist in the world—just as though they were intent only on taking our blood and groans to glorify the

---

[3] See Acts of the Apostles, chap. x. v.—25–27.

Lord Jesus Christ. The wicked and ungodly, seeing their preachers treat us with so much cruelty, they say: our preachers, who must be right, if any body are, treat them like brutes, and why cannot we? —They think it is no harm to keep them in slavery and put the whip to them, and why cannot we do the same! —They being preachers of the gospel of Jesus Christ, if it were any harm, they would surely preach against their oppression and do their utmost to erase it from the country; not only in one or two cities, but one continual cry would be raised in all parts of this confederacy, and would cease only with the complete overthrow of the system of slavery, in every part of the country. But how far the American preachers are from preaching against slavery and oppression, which have carried their country to the brink of a precipice; to save them from plunging down the side of which, will hardly be affected, will appear in the sequel of this paragraph, which I shall narrate just as it transpired. I remember a Camp Meeting in South Carolina, for which I embarked in a Steam Boat at Charleston, and having been five or six hours on the water, we at last arrived at the place of hearing, where was a very great concourse of people, who were no doubt, collected together to hear the word of God, (that some had collected barely as spectators to the scene, I will not here pretend to doubt, however, that is left to themselves and their God.) Myself and boat companions, having been there a little while, we were all called up to hear; I among the rest went up and took my seat—being seated, I fixed myself in a complete position to hear the word of my Saviour and to receive such as I thought was authenticated by the Holy Scriptures; but to my no ordinary astonishment, our Reverend gentleman got up and told us (coloured people) that slaves must be obedient to their masters—must do their duty to their masters or be whipped—the whip was made for the backs of fools, &c. Here I pause for a moment, to give the world time to consider what was my surprise, to hear such preaching from a minister of my Master, whose very gospel is that of peace and not of blood and whips, as this pretended preacher tried to make us believe. What the American preachers can think of us, I aver this day before my God, I have never been able to define. They have newspapers and monthly periodicals, which they receive in continual succession, but on the pages of which, you will scarcely ever find a paragraph respecting slavery, which is ten thousand times more injurious to this country than all the other evils put together; and which will be the final overthrow of its government, unless something is very speedily done; for their cup is nearly full. —Perhaps they will laugh at or make light of this; but I tell you Americans! that unless you speedily alter your course, *you* and your *Country are gone!!!!!!* For God Almighty will tear up the very face of the earth!!! Will not that very remarkable passage of Scripture be fulfilled on Christian Americans? Hear it Americans!! "He that is unjust, let him be unjust still: —and he which is filthy, let him be filthy still: and he that is righteous, let him be righteous still: and he that is holy, let him be holy still." [4] I hope that the Americans may hear, but I am afraid that they have done us so much injury, and are so firm in the belief

---

[4] See Revelation, chap. xxii, 11.

that our Creator made us to be an inheritance to them for ever, that their hearts will be hardened, so that their destruction may be sure. This language, perhaps is too harsh for the American's delicate ears. But Oh Americans! Americans!! I warn you in the name of the Lord, (whether you will hear, or forbear,) to repent and reform, or you are ruined!!! Do you think that our blood is hidden from the Lord, because you can hide it from the rest of the world, by sending out missionaries, and by your charitable deeds to the Greeks, Irish, &c.? Will he not publish your secret crimes on the house top? Even here in Boston, pride and prejudice have got to such a pitch, that in the very houses erected to the Lord, they have built little places for the reception of coloured people, where they must sit during meeting, or keep away from the house of God, and the preachers say nothing about it—much less go into the hedges and highways seeking the lost sheep of the house of Israel, and try to bring them in to their Lord and Master. There are not a more wretched, ignorant, miserable, and abject set of beings in all the world, than the blacks in the Southern and Western sections of this country, under tyrants and devils. The preachers of America cannot see them, but they can send out missionaries to convert the heathens, notwithstanding. Americans! unless you speedily alter your course of proceeding, if God Almighty does not stop, I say it in his name, that you may go on and do as you please for ever, both in time and eternity—never fear any evil at all!!!!!!!!!

☞ ADDITION. —The preachers and people of the United States form societies against Free Masonry and Intemperance, and write against Sabbath breaking, Sabbath mails, Infidelity, &c. &c. But the fountain head,[5] compared with which, all those other evils are comparatively nothing, and from the bloody and murderous head of which, they receive no trifling support, is hardly noticed by the Americans. This is a fair illustration of the state of society in this country—it shows what a bearing *avarice* has upon a people, when they are nearly given up by the Lord to a hard heart and a reprobate mind, in consequence of afflicting their fellow creatures. God suffers some to go on until they are ruined for ever!!!!! Will it be the case with the whites of the United States of America? —We hope not—we would not wish to see them destroyed notwithstanding, they have and do now treat us more cruel than any people have treated another, on this earth since it came from the hands of its Creator (with the exceptions of the French and the Dutch, they treat us nearly as bad as the Americans of the United States.) The will of God must however, in spite of us, *be done.*

The English are the best friends the coloured people have upon earth. Though they have oppressed us a little and have colonies now in the West Indies, which oppress us *sorely.* —Yet notwithstanding they (the English) have done one hundred times more for the melioration of our condition, than all the other nations of the earth put together. The blacks cannot but respect the English as a nation, notwithstanding they have treated us a little cruel.

---

5 Slavery and oppression.

There is no intelligent *black man* who knows any thing, but esteems a real Englishman, let him see him in what part of the world he will—for they are the greatest benefactors we have upon earth. We have here and there, in other nations, good friends. But as a nation, the English are our friends. ☜

How can the preachers and people of America believe the Bible? Does it teach them any distinction on account of a man's colour? Hearken, Americans! to the injunctions of our Lord and Master, to his humble followers.

"And Jesus came and spake unto them, saying, all power is given unto me in Heaven and in earth.[6]

"Go ye, therefore, and teach all nations, baptizing them in the name of the Father, and of the Son, and of the Holy Ghost.

"Teaching them to observe all things whatsoever I have commanded you; and lo, I am with you *always*, even unto the end of the world. Amen."

I declare, that the very face of these injunctions appear to be of God and not of man. They do not show the slightest degree of distinction. "Go ye therefore," (says my divine Master) "and teach all nations," (or in other words, all people) "baptizing them in the name of the Father, and of the Son, and of the Holy Ghost." Do you understand the above, Americans? We are a people, notwithstanding many of you doubt it. You have the Bible in your hands with this very injunction. —Have you been to Africa, teaching the inhabitants thereof the words of the Lord Jesus? "Baptizing them in the name of the Father, and of the Son and of the Holy Ghost." Have you not, on the contrary, entered among us, and learnt us the art of throatcutting, by setting us to fight, one against another, to take each other as prisoners of war, and sell to you for small bits of calicoes, old swords, knives, &c. to make slaves for you and your children? This being done, have you not brought us among you, in chains and hand-cuffs, like brutes, and treated us with all the cruelties and rigour your ingenuity could invent, consistent with the laws of your country, which (for the blacks) are tyrannical enough? Can the American preachers appeal unto God, the Maker and Searcher of hearts, and tell him, with the Bible in their hands, that they make no distinction on account of men's colour? Can they say, O God! thou knowest all things—thou knowest that we make no distinction between thy creatures, to whom we have to preach thy Word? Let them answer the Lord; and if they cannot do it in the affirmative, have they not departed from the Lord Jesus Christ, their master? But some may say, that they never had, or were in possession of religion, which made no distinction, and of course they could not have departed from it. I ask you then, in the name of the Lord, of what kind can your religion be? Can it be that which was preached by our Lord Jesus Christ from Heaven? I believe you cannot be so wicked as to tell him that his Gospel was that of *distinction*. What can the American preachers and people take God to be? Do they believe his words? If they do, do they believe that he will be mocked? Or do they believe, because they are whites and we blacks, that God will have respect to them? Did not

---

[6] See St. Matthew's Gospel, chap. xxviii. 18, 19, 20. After Jesus was risen from the dead.

God make us all as it seemed best to himself? What right, then, has one of us, to despise another, and to treat him cruel, on account of his colour, which none, but the God who made it can alter? Can there be a greater absurdity in nature, and particularly in a free republican country? But the Americans, having introduced slavery among them, their hearts have become almost seared, as with an hot iron, and God has nearly given them up to believe a lie in preference to the truth!!! And I am awfully afraid that pride, prejudice, avarice and blood, will, before long prove the final ruin of this happy republic, or land of *liberty!!!!* Can any thing be a greater mockery of religion than the way in which it is conducted by the Americans? It appears as though they are bent only on daring God Almighty to do his best—they chain and handcuff us and our children and drive us around the country like brutes, and go into the house of the God of justice to return him thanks for having aided them in their infernal cruelties inflicted upon us. Will the Lord suffer this people to go on much longer, taking his holy name in vain? Will he not stop them, PREACHERS and all? O Americans! Americans! I call God—I call angels—I call men, to witness, that your DESTRUCTION *is at hand*, and will be speedily consummated unless you REPENT.

Discrimination
in the Free States

Address to a Legislative Committee in the
Massachusetts House of Representatives,
1842

CHARLES L. REMOND

*Many thoughtful blacks were active in the various abolitionist societies, giving speeches
and writing articles about the evils of slavery. But they were also concerned about the
discrimination free blacks met in the North. Among the most effective of the black
spokesmen was Charles Lenox Remond of Massachusetts, who was employed by the
American Anti-Slavery Society and became one of the most prominent black abolitionists. He attended the London World Anti-Slavery Conference in 1840, then lec-
tured on abolition in the British Isles for two years before returning home. Upon his
return, he met with segregation on the railroads and determined to have it abolished.*

*The address that follows was made by Remond in 1842 to a legislative commit-
tee in the Massachusetts House of Representatives that was studying the problem of
segregation. In the address, he emphasized the contrast between the nondiscriminatory
treatment he received while abroad and the segregation he was forced into at home. A
year later, the Massachusetts legislature abolished segregation.*

Mr. Chairman, and Gentlemen of the Committee

On rising at this time, and on this occasion, being the first person of color who
has ever addressed either of the bodies assembling in this building, I should,
perhaps, in the first place, observe that, in consequence of the many miscon-
structions of the principles and measures of which I am the humble advocate,
I may in like manner be subject to similar misconceptions from the moment
I open my lips in behalf of the prayer of the petitioners for whom I appear,
and therefore feel I have the right at least to ask, at the hands of this intelligent Committee, an impartial hearing; and that whatever prejudices they may
have imbibed, be eradicated from their minds, if such exist. I have, however,
too much confidence in their intelligence, and too much faith in their determination to do their duty as the representatives of this Commonwealth, to
presume they can be actuated by partial motives. Trusting, as I do, that the day
is not distant, when, on all questions touching the rights of the citizens of this

FROM Charles L. Remond, "Before the Legislative Committee in the House of Representatives [Mass.]
respecting the rights of colored citizens in travelling, etc." *Liberator* (February 25, 1842).

State, men shall be considered *great* only as they are *good*—and not that it shall be told, and painfully experienced, that, in this country, this State, ay, this city, the Athens of America, the rights, privileges and immunities of its citizens are measured by complexion, or any other physical peculiarity or conformation, especially such as over which no man has any control. Complexion can in no sense be construed into crime, much less be rightfully made the criterion of rights. Should the people of color, through a revolution of Providence, become a majority, to the last I would oppose it upon the same principle; for, in either case, it would be equally reprehensible and unjustifiable—alike to be condemned and repudiated. It is JUSTICE I stand here to claim, and not FAVOR for either complexion.

And now, sir, I shall endeavor to confine my remarks to the same subject which has occupied the attention of the Committee thus far, and to stand upon the same principle which has been so ably and so eloquently maintained and established by my esteemed friend, Mr. Phillips.

Our right to citizenship in this State has been acknowledged and secured by the allowance of the elective franchise and consequent taxation; and I know of no good reason, if admitted in this instance, why it should be denied in any other.

With reference to the wrongs inflicted and injuries received on railroads, by persons of color, I need not say they do not end with the termination of the route, but, in effect, tend to discourage, disparage and depress this class of citizens. All hope of reward for upright conduct is cut off. Vice in them becomes a virtue. No distinction is made by the community in which we live. The most vicious is treated as well as the most respectable, both in public and private.

But it is said we all look alike. If this is true, it is not true that we all behave alike. There is a marked difference; and we claim a recognition of this difference.

In the present state of things, they find God's provisions interfered with in such a way, by these and kindred regulations, that virtue may not claim her divinely appointed rewards. Color is made to obscure the brightest endowments, to degrade the fairest character, and to check the highest and most praiseworthy aspirations. If the colored man is vicious, it makes but little difference; if besotted, it matters not; if vulgar, it is quite as well; and he finds himself as well treated, and received as readily into society, as those of an opposite character. Nay, the higher our aspirations, the loftier our purposes and pursuits, does this iniquitous principle of prejudice fasten upon us, and especial pains are taken to irritate, obstruct and injure. No reward of merit, no remuneration for services, no equivalent is rendered the deserving. And I submit, whether this unkind and unchristian policy is not well calculated to make every man disregardful of his conduct, and every woman unmindful of her reputation.

The grievances of which we complain, be assured, sir, are not imaginary, but real—not local, but universal—not occasional, but continual—every day matter of fact things—and have become, to the disgrace of our common country, matter of history.

Mr. Chairman, the treatment to which colored Americans are exposed in their own country, finds a counterpart in no other; and I am free to declare, that, in the course of nineteen months' traveling in England, Ireland, and Scotland, I was received, treated and recognised, in public and private society, without any regard to my complexion. From the moment I left the American packet ship in Liverpool, up to the moment I came in contact with it again, I was never reminded of my complexion; and all that know anything of my usage in the American ship, will testify that it was unfit for a brute, and none but one could inflict it. But how unlike that afforded in the British steamer Columbia! Owing to my limited resources, I took a steerage passage. On the first day out, the second officer came to inquire after my health; and finding me the only passenger in that part of the ship, ordered the steward to give me berth in the second cabin; and from that hour until my stepping on shore at Boston, every politeness was shown me by the officers, and every kindness and attention by the stewards; and I feel under deep and lasting obligations to them, individually and collectively.

In no instance was I insulted or treated in any way distinct or dissimilar from other passengers or travelers, either in coaches, rail-roads, steampackets, or hotels; and if the feeling was entertained, in no case did I discover its existence.

I may with propriety here relate an accident, illustrative of the subject now under consideration. I took a passage ticket at the steam packet office in Glasgow, for Dublin; and on going into the cabin to retire, I found the berth I had engaged occupied by an Irish gentleman and merchant. I enquired if he had not mistaken the number of his berth. He thought not. On comparing tickets, we saw that the clerk had given two tickets of the same number; and it appeared I had received mine first. The gentleman at once offered to vacate the berth, against which I remonstrated, and took my berth in an opposite state room. Here, sir, we discover treatment just, impartial, reasonable; and we ask nothing beside.

There is a marked difference between social and civil rights. It has been well and justly remarked, by my friend Mr. Phillips, that we all claim the privilege of selecting our society and associations; but, in civil rights, one man has not the prerogative to define rights for another. For instance, sir, in public conveyances, for the rich man to usurp the privileges to himself, to the injury of the poor man, would be submitted to in no well regulated society. And such is the position suffered by persons of color. On my arrival home from England, I went to the rail way station, to go to Salem, being anxious to see my parents and sisters as soon as possible—asked for a ticket—paid 50 cents for it, and was pointed to the American designation car. Having previously received information of the regulations, I took my seat peaceably, believing it better to suffer wrong than do wrong. I felt then, as I felt on many occasions prior to leaving home, unwilling to descend so low as to bandy words with the superintendents, or contest my rights with conductors, or any others in the capacity of servants of any stage or steamboat company, or rail-road corporation; although I never, by any means, gave evidence that, by my submission, I intended to sanction usages which would derogate from uncivilized, much less long and loud professing and high pretending America.

Bear with me while I relate an additional occurrence. On the morning after my return home, I was obliged to go to Boston again, and on going to the Salem station I met two friends, who enquired if I had any objection to their taking seats with me. I answered, I should be most happy. They took their seats accordingly, and soon afterwards one of them remarked to me—'Charles, I don't know if they will allow us to ride with you.' It was some time before I could understand what they meant, and; on doing so, I laughed—feeling it to be a climax to every absurdity I had heard attributed to Americans. To say nothing of the wrong done those friends, and the insult and indignity offered me by the appearance of the conductor, who ordered the friends from the car in a somewhat harsh manner—they immediately left the carriage.

On returning to Salem some few evenings afterwards, Mr. Chase, the superintendent on this road, made himself known to me, by recalling bygone days and scenes, and then enquired if I was not glad to get home after so long an absence in Europe. I told him I was glad to see my parents and family again, and this was the only object I could have, unless he thought I should be glad to take a hermit's life in the great pasture; inasmuch as I never felt to loathe my American name so much as since my arrival. He wished to know my reasons for the remark. I immediately gave them, and wished to know of him, if, in the event of his having a brother with red hair, he should find himself separated while travelling because of this difference, he should deem it just. He could make no reply. I then wished to know if the principle was not the same; and if so, there was an insult implied by his question. In conclusion, I challenged him as the instrument inflicting the manifold injuries upon all not colored like himself, to the presentation of an instance in any other Christian or unchristian country, tolerating usages at once so disgraceful, unjust and inhuman. What if some few of the West or East India planters and merchants should visit our liberty-loving country, with their colored wives—how would he manage? Or, if R. M. Johnson, the gentleman who has been elevated to the second office in the gift of the people, should be travelling from Boston to Salem, if he was prepared to separate him from his wife or daughters (involuntary burst of applause, instantly restrained.)

Sir, it happens to be my lot to have a sister a few shades lighter than myself; and who knows, if this state of things is encouraged, whether I may not on some future occasion be mobbed in Washington-street, on the supposition of walking with a white young lady! (Suppressed indications of sympathy and applause.)

Gentlemen of the Committee, these distinctions react in all their wickedness—to say nothing of their concocted and systematized odiousness and absurdity—upon those who instituted them; and particularly so upon those who are illiberal and mean enough to practise them.

Mr. Chairman, if colored people have abused any rights granted them, or failed to exhibit due appreciation of favors bestowed, or shrunk from dangers or responsibility, let it be made to appear. Or if our country contains a population to compare with them in loyalty and patriotism, circumstances duly considered, I have it yet to learn. The history of our country must ever testify in their behalf. In view of these and many additional considerations, I unhesitatingly assert their claim, on the naked principle of merit, to every advantage set forth in the Constitution of this Commonwealth.

Finally, Mr. Chairman, there is in this and other States a large and growing colored population, whose residence in your midst has not been from choice, (let this be understood and reflected upon,) but by the force of circumstances over which they never had control. Upon the heads of their oppressors and calumniators be the censure and responsibility. If to ask at your hands redress for injuries, and protection in our rights and immunities, as citizens, is reasonable, and dictated alike by justice, humanity and religion, you will not reject, I trust, the prayer of your petitioners.

Before sitting down, I owe it to myself to remark, that I was not appraised of the wish of my friends to appear here until passing through Boston, a day or two since; and having been occupied with other matters, I have had no opportunity for preparation on this occasion. I feel much obliged to the Committee for their kind, patient, and attentive hearing. (Applause.)

What to the Slave is the Fourth of July?

FREDERICK DOUGLASS

Frederick Douglass was unquestionably the most impressive African-American in nineteenth-century America. Born a slave, he escaped the South in 1838. Almost from the day he arrived in the North, he began working to improve the lot of American black people. His initial appearance as a speaker was so electrifying that he soon became the most sought-after black speaker in the abolitionist movement. While lecturing in England in 1845, he was persuaded by his English supporters to allow them to buy his freedom. In 1847, he started the first of several newspapers he was to edit, in Rochester, New York.

Although Douglass made many speeches calling for the abolition of slavery, it is generally thought that none were more powerful or uncompromising than the one delivered, ironically, on the day in 1852 on which white Americans celebrated their successful struggle for liberty. He condemned whites for their hypocrisy in denying liberty to millions of African-Americans dwelling in the United States while having rallies and parades honoring those patriots who helped bring freedom to themselves in the War for American Independence.

Mr. President, Friends and Fellow Citizens:

He who could address this audience without a quailing sensation, has stronger nerves than I have. I do not remember ever to have appeared as a speaker before any assembly more shrinkingly, nor with greater distrust of my ability, than I do this day. A feeling has crept over me quite unfavorable to the exercise of my limited powers of speech. The task before me is one which requires much previous thought and study for its proper performance. I know that apologies of this sort are generally considered flat and unmeaning. I trust, however, that mine will not be so considered. Should I seem at ease, my appearance would much misrepresent me. The little experience I have had in addressing public meetings, in country school houses, avails me nothing on the present occasion.

The papers and placards say that I am to deliver a Fourth of July Oration. This certainly sounds large, and out of the common way, for me. It is true that I have often had the privilege to speak in this beautiful Hall, and to address many who now honor me with their presence. But neither their familiar faces, nor the perfect gage I think I have of Corinthian Hall seems to free me from embarrassment.

Oration delivered in Corinthian Hall, Rochester, New York, July 5, 1852.

The fact is, ladies and gentlemen, the distance between this platform and the slave plantation, from which I escaped, is considerable—and the difficulties to be overcome in getting from the latter to the former are by no means slight. That I am here to-day is, to me, a matter of astonishment as well as of gratitude. You will not, therefore, be surprised, if in what I have to say I evince no elaborate preparation, nor grace my speech with any high sounding exordium. With little experience and with less learning, I have been able to throw my thoughts hastily and imperfectly together; and trusting to your patient and generous indulgence, I will proceed to lay them before you.

This, for the purpose of this celebration, is the Fourth of July. It is the birthday of your National Independence, and of your political freedom. This, to you, is what the Passover was to the emancipated people of God. It carries your minds back to the day, and to the act of your great deliverance; and to the signs, and to the wonders, associated with that act, and that day. This celebration also marks the beginning of another year of your national life; and reminds you that the Republic of America is now 76 years old. I am glad, fellow-citizens, that your nation is so young. Seventy-six years, though a good old age for a man, is but a mere speck in the life of a nation. Three score years and ten is the allotted time for individual men; but nations number their years by thousands. According to this fact, you are, even now, only in the beginning of your national career, still lingering in the period of childhood. I repeat, I am glad this is so. There is hope in the thought, and hope is much needed, under the dark clouds which lower above the horizon. The eye of the reformer is met with angry flashes, portending disastrous times; but his heart may well beat lighter at the thought that America is young, and that she is still in the impressible stage of her existence. May he not hope that high lessons of wisdom, of justice and of truth, will yet give direction to her destiny? Were the nation older, the patriot's heart might be sadder, and the reformer's brow heavier. Its future might be shrouded in gloom, and the hope of its prophets go out in sorrow. There is consolation in the thought that America is young.—Great streams are not easily turned from channels, worn deep in the course of ages. They may sometimes rise in quiet and stately majesty, and inundate the land, refreshing and fertilizing the earth with their mysterious properties. They may also rise in wrath and fury, and bear away, on their angry waves, the accumulated wealth of years of toil and hardship. They, however, gradually flow back to the same old channel, and flow on as serenely as ever. But, while the river may not be turned aside, it may dry up, and leave nothing behind but the withered branch, and the unsightly rock, to howl in the abyss-sweeping wind, the sad tale of departed glory. As with rivers so with nations.

Fellow-citizens, I shall not presume to dwell at length on the associations that cluster about this day. The simple story of it is, that, 76 years ago, the people of this country were British subjects. The style and title of your "sovereign people" (in which you now glory) was not then born. You were under the British Crown. Your fathers esteemed the English Government as the home government; and England as the fatherland. This home government, you know, although a considerable distance from your home, did, in the exercise of

its parental prerogatives, impose upon its colonial children, such restraints, burdens and limitations, as, in its mature judgment, it deemed wise, right and
proper.

But your fathers, who had not adopted the fashionable idea of this day, of
the infallibility of government, and the absolute character of its acts, presumed
to differ from the home government in respect to the wisdom and the justice
of some of those burdens and restraints. They went so far in their excitement
as to pronounce the measures of government unjust, unreasonable, and oppressive, and altogether such as ought not to be quietly submitted to. I scarcely
need say, fellow-citizens, that my opinion of those measures fully accords with
that of your fathers. Such a declaration of agreement on my part would not be
worth much to anybody. It would certainly prove nothing as to what part I
might have taken had I lived during the great controversy of 1776. To say now
that America was right, and England wrong, is exceedingly easy. Everybody
can say it; the dastard, not less than the noble brave, can flippantly discant on
the tyranny of England towards the American Colonies. It is fashionable to do
so; but there was a time when, to pronounce against England, and in favor of
the cause of the colonies, tried men's souls. They who did so were accounted
in their day plotters of mischief, agitators and rebels, dangerous men. To side
with the right against the wrong, with the weak against the strong, and with
the oppressed against the oppressor! here lies the merit, and the one which, of
all others, seems unfashionable in our day. The cause of liberty may be stabbed
by the men who glory in the deeds of your fathers. But, to proceed.

Feeling themselves harshly and unjustly treated, by the home government,
your fathers, like men of honesty, and men of spirit, earnestly sought redress.
They petitioned and remonstrated; they did so in a decorous, respectful, and
loyal manner. Their conduct was wholly unexceptionable. This, however, did
not answer the purpose. They saw themselves treated with sovereign indifference, coldness and scorn. Yet they persevered. They were not the men to look
back.

As the sheet anchor takes a firmer hold, when the ship is tossed by the
storm, so did the cause of your fathers grow stronger as it breasted the chill-
ing blasts of kingly displeasure. The greatest and best of British statesmen
admitted its justice, and the loftiest eloquence of the British Senate came to its
support. But, with that blindness which seems to be the unvarying characteristic of tyrants, since Pharaoh and his hosts were drowned in the Red Sea, the
British Government persisted in the exactions complained of.

The madness of this course, we believe, is admitted now, even by England;
but we fear the lesson is wholly lost on our present rulers.

Oppression makes a wise man mad. Your fathers were wise men, and if they
did not go mad, they became restive under this treatment. They felt themselves
the victims of grievous wrongs, wholly incurable in their colonial capacity.
With brave men there is always a remedy for oppression. Just here, the idea of
a total separation of the colonies from the crown was born! It was a startling
idea, much more so than we, at this distance of time, regard it. The timid and
the prudent (as has been intimated) of that day were, of course, shocked and
alarmed by it.

Such people lived then, had lived before, and will, probably, ever have a place on this planet; and their course, in respect to any great change (no matter how great the good to be attained, or the wrong to be redressed by it), may be calculated with as much precision as can be the course of the stars. They hate all changes, but silver, gold and copper change! Of this sort of change they are always strongly in favor.

These people were called Tories in the days of your fathers; and the appellation, probably, conveyed the same idea that is meant by a more modern, though a somewhat less euphonious term, which we often find in our papers, applied to some of our old politicians.

Their opposition to the then dangerous thought was earnest and powerful; but, amid all their terror and affrighted vociferations against it, the alarming and revolutionary idea moved on, and the country with it.

On the 2d of July, 1776, the old Continental Congress, to the dismay of the lovers of ease, and the worshipers of property, clothed that dreadful idea with all the authority of national sanction. They did so in the form of a resolution; and as we seldom hit upon resolutions, drawn up in our day, whose transparency is at all equal to this, it may refresh your minds and help my story if I read it.

> "Resolved, That these united colonies are, and of right, ought to be free and Independent States; that they are absolved from all allegiance to the British Crown; and that all political connection between them and the State of Great Britain is, and ought to be, dissolved."

Citizens, your fathers made good that resolution. They succeeded; and to-day you reap the fruits of their success. The freedom gained is yours; and you, therefore, may properly celebrate this anniversary. The 4th of July is the first great fact in your nation's history—the very ringbolt in the chain of your yet undeveloped destiny.

Pride and patriotism, not less than gratitude, prompt you to celebrate and to hold it in perpetual remembrance. I have said that the Declaration of Independence is the ringbolt to the chain of your nation's destiny; so, indeed, I regard it. The principles contained in that instrument are saving principles. Stand by those principles, be true to them on all occasions, in all places, against all foes, and at whatever cost.

From the round top of your ship of state, dark and threatening clouds may be seen. Heavy billows, like mountains in the distance, disclose to the leeward huge forms of flinty rocks! That bolt drawn, that chain broken, and all is lost. Cling to this day—cling to it, and to its principles, with the grasp of a storm-tossed mariner to a spar at midnight.

The coming into being of a nation, in any circumstances, is an interesting event. But, besides general considerations, there were peculiar circumstances which make the advent of this republic an event of special attractiveness.

The whole scene, as I look back to it, was simple, dignified and sublime. The population of the country, at the time, stood at the insignificant number of three millions. The country was poor in the munitions of war. The population was weak and scattered, and the country a wilderness unsubdued. There were then no means of concert and combination, such as exist now. Neither steam nor lightning had then been reduced to order and discipline. From the Potomac to the Delaware was a journey of many days. Under these, and innumerable other disadvantages, your fathers declared for liberty and independence and triumphed.

Fellow Citizens, I am not wanting in respect for the fathers of this republic. The signers of the Declaration of Independence were brave men. They were great men, too—great enough to give frame to a great age. It does not often happen to a nation to raise, at one time, such a number of truly great men. The point from which I am compelled to view them is not, certainly, the most favorable; and yet I cannot contemplate their great deeds with less than admiration. They were statesmen, patriots and heroes, and for the good they did, and the principles they contended for, I will unite with you to honor their memory.

They loved their country better than their own private interests; and, though this is not the highest form of human excellence, all will concede that it is a rare virtue, and that when it is exhibited it ought to command respect. He who will, intelligently, lay down his life for his country is a man whom it is not in human nature to despise. Your fathers staked their lives, their fortunes, and their sacred honor, on the cause of their country. In their admiration of liberty, they lost sight of all other interests.

They were peace men; but they preferred revolution to peaceful submission to bondage. They were quiet men; but they did not shrink from agitating against oppression. They showed forbearance; but that they knew its limits. They believed in order; but not in the order of tyranny. With them, nothing was "settled" that was not right. With them, justice, liberty and humanity were "final"; not slavery and oppression. You may well cherish the memory of such men. They were great in their day and generation. Their solid manhood stands out the more as we contrast it with these degenerate times.

How circumspect, exact and proportionate were all their movements! How unlike the politicians of an hour! Their statesmanship looked beyond the passing moment, and stretched away in strength into the distant future. They seized upon eternal principles, and set a glorious example in their defence. Mark them!

Fully appreciating the hardships to be encountered, firmly believing in the right of their cause, honorably inviting the scrutiny of an on-looking world, reverently appealing to heaven to attest their sincerity, soundly comprehending the solemn responsibility they were about to assume, wisely measuring the terrible odds against them, your fathers, the fathers of this republic, did, most deliberately, under the inspiration of a glorious patriotism, and with a sublime faith in the great principles of justice and freedom, lay deep, the corner-stone of the national super-structure, which has risen and still rises in grandeur around you.

Of this fundamental work, this day is the anniversary. Our eyes are met with demonstrations of joyous enthusiasm. Banners and pennants wave exultingly on the breeze. The din of business, too, is hushed. Even mammon seems to have quitted his grasp on this day. The ear-piercing fife and the stirring drum unite their accents with the ascending peal of a thousand church bells. Prayers are made, hymns are sung, and sermons are preached in honor of this day; while the quick martial tramp of a great and multitudinous nation, echoed back by all the hills, valleys and mountains of a vast continent, bespeak the occasion one of thrilling and universal interest—a nation's jubilee.

Friends and citizens, I need not enter further into the causes which led to this anniversary. Many of you understand them better than I do. You could instruct me in regard to them. That is a branch of knowledge in which you feel, perhaps, a much deeper interest than your speaker. The causes which led to the separation of the colonies from the British crown have never lacked for a tongue. They have all been taught in your common schools, narrated at your firesides, unfolded from your pulpits, and thundered from your legislative halls, and are as familiar to you as household words. They form the staple of your national poetry and eloquence.

I remember, also, that, as a people, Americans are remarkably familiar with all facts which make in their own favor. This is esteemed by some as a national trait—perhaps a national weakness. It is a fact, that whatever makes for the wealth or for the reputation of Americans and can be had cheap! will be found by Americans. I shall not be charged with slandering Americans if I say I think the American side of any question may be safely left in American hands.

I leave, therefore, the great deeds of your fathers to other gentlemen whose claim to have been regularly descended will be less likely to be disputed than mine!

My business, if I have any here to-day, is with the present. The accepted time with God and His cause is the ever-living now.

> Trust no future, however pleasant,
>   Let the dead past bury its dead;
> Act, act in the living present,
>   Heart within, and God overhead.

We have to do with the past only as we can make it useful to the present and to the future. To all inspiring motives, to noble deeds which can be gained from the past, we are welcome. But now is the time, the important time. Your fathers have lived, died, and have done their work, and have done much of it well. You live and must die, and you must do your work. You have no right to enjoy a child's share in the labor of your fathers, unless your children are to be blest by your labors. You have no right to wear out and waste the hard-earned fame of your fathers to cover your indolence. Sydney Smith tells us that men seldom eulogize the wisdom and virtues of their fathers, but to excuse some folly or wickedness of their own. This truth is not a doubtful one. There are illustrations of it near and remote, ancient and modern. It was fashionable, hundreds of years ago, for the children of Jacob to boast, we have "Abraham to our father," when they had long lost Abraham's faith and spirit. That people contented themselves under the shadow of Abraham's great name, while they repudiated the deeds which made his name great. Need I remind you that a similar thing is being done all over this country to-day? Need I tell you that the Jews are not the only people who built the tombs of the prophets, and garnished the sepulchers of the righteous? Washington could not die till he had broken the chains of his slaves. Yet his monument is built up by the price of human blood, and the traders in the bodies and souls of men shout —"We have Washington to *our* father." —Alas! that it should be so; yet so it is.

> The evil that men do, lives after them,
> The good is oft interred with their bones.

Fellow-citizens, pardon me, allow me to ask, why am I called upon to speak here to-day? What have I, or those I represent, to do with your national independence? Are the great principles of political freedom and of natural justice, embodied in that Declaration of Independence, extended to us? and am I, therefore, called upon to bring our humble offering to the national altar, and to confess the benefits and express devout gratitude for the blessings resulting from your independence to us?

Would to God, both for your sakes and ours, that an affirmative answer could be truthfully returned to these questions! Then would my task be light, and my burden easy and delightful. For *who* is there so cold, that a nation's sympathy could not warm him? Who so obdurate and dead to the claims of gratitude, that would not thankfully acknowledge such priceless benefits? Who so stolid and selfish, that would not give his voice to swell the hallelujahs of a nation's jubilee, when the chains of servitude had been torn from his limbs? I am not that man. In a case like that, the dumb might eloquently speak, and the "lame man leap as an hart."

But such is not the state of the case. I say it with a sad sense of the disparity between us. I am not included within the pale of this glorious anniversary! Your high independence only reveals the immeasurable distance between us. The blessings in which you, this day, rejoice, are not enjoyed in common. — The rich inheritance of justice, liberty, prosperity and independence, bequeathed by your fathers, is shared by you, not by me. The sunlight that brought light and healing to you, has brought stripes and death to me. This Fourth July is *yours*, not *mine*. *You* may rejoice, *I* must mourn. To drag a man in fetters into the grand illuminated temple of liberty, and call upon him to join you in joyous anthems, were inhuman mockery and sacrilegious irony. Do you mean, citizens, to mock me, by asking me to speak to-day? If so, there is a parallel to your conduct. And let me warn you that it is dangerous to copy the example of a nation whose crimes, towering up to heaven, were thrown down by the breath of the Almighty, burying that nation in irrevocable ruin! I can to-day take up the plaintive lament of a peeled and woe-smitten people!

"By the rivers of Babylon, there we sat down. Yea! we wept when we remembered Zion. We hanged our harps upon the willows in the midst thereof. For there, they that carried us away captive, required of us a song; and they who wasted us required of us mirth, saying, Sing us one of the songs of Zion.

How can we sing the Lord's song in a strange land? If I forget thee, O Jerusalem, let my right hand forget her cunning. If I do not remember thee, let my tongue cleave to the roof of my mouth."

Fellow-citizens, above your national, tumultuous joy, I hear the mournful wail of millions! whose chains, heavy and grievous yesterday, are, to-day, rendered more intolerable by the jubilee shouts that reach them. If I do forget, if I do not faithfully remember those bleeding children of sorrow this day, "may my right hand forget her cunning, and may my tongue cleave to the roof of my mouth!" To forget them, to pass lightly over their wrongs, and to chime in with the popular theme, would be treason most scandalous and shocking, and would make me a reproach before God and the world. My subject, then, fellow-citizens, is American slavery. I shall see this day and its popular characteristics from the slave's point of view. Standing there identified with the American bondman, making his wrongs mine, I do not hesitate to declare, with all my soul, that the character and conduct of this nation never looked blacker to me than on this 4th of July! Whether we turn to the declarations of the past, or to the professions of the present, the conduct of the nation seems equally hideous and revolting. America is false to the past, false to the present, and solemnly binds herself to be false to the future. Standing with God and the crushed and bleeding slave on this occasion, I will, in the name of humanity which is outraged, in the name of liberty which is fettered, in the name of the constitution and the Bible which are disregarded and trampled upon, dare to call in question and to denounce, with all the emphasis I can command, everything that serves to perpetuate slavery—the great sin and shame of America! "I will not equivocate; I will not excuse"; I will use the severest language I can command; and yet not one word shall escape me that any man, whose judgment is not blinded by prejudice, or who is not at heart a slaveholder, shall not confess to be right and just.

But I fancy I hear some one of my audience say, "It is just in this circumstance that you and your brother abolitionists fail to make a favorable impression on the public mind. Would you argue more, and denounce less; would you persuade more, and rebuke less; your cause would be much more likely to succeed." But, I submit, where all is plain there is nothing to be argued. What point in the antislavery creed would you have me argue? On what branch of the subject do the people of this country need light? Must I undertake to prove that the slave is a man? That point is conceded already. Nobody doubts it. The slaveholders themselves acknowledge it in the enactment of laws for their government. They acknowledge it when they punish disobedience on the part of the slave. There are seventy-two crimes in the State of Virginia which, if committed by a black man (no matter how ignorant he be), subject him to the punishment of death; while only two of the same crimes will subject a white man to the like punishment. What is this but the acknowledgment that the slave is a moral, intellectual, and responsible being? The manhood of the slave is conceded. It is admitted in the fact that Southern statute books are covered with enactments forbidding, under severe fines and penalties, the teaching of the slave to read or to write. When you can point to any such laws in reference to the beasts of the field, then I may consent to argue the manhood of the slave. When the dogs in your streets, when the fowls of the air, when the cattle on your hills, when the fish of the sea, and the reptiles that crawl, shall be unable to distinguish the slave from a brute, *then* will I argue with you that the slave is a man!

For the present, it is enough to affirm the equal manhood of the Negro race. Is it not astonishing that, while we are ploughing, planting, and reaping, using all kinds of mechanical tools, erecting houses, constructing bridges, building ships, working in metals of brass, iron, copper, silver and gold; that, while we are reading, writing and ciphering, acting as clerks, merchants and secretaries, having among us lawyers, doctors, ministers, poets, authors, editors, orators and teachers; that, while we are engaged in all manner of enterprises common to other men, digging gold in California, capturing the whale in the Pacific, feeding sheep and cattle on the hill-side, living, moving, acting, thinking, planning, living in families as husbands, wives and children, and, above all, confessing and worshipping the Christian's God, and looking hopefully for life and immortality beyond the grave, we are called upon to prove that we are men!

Would you have me argue that man is entitled to liberty? that he is the rightful owner of his own body? You have already declared it. Must I argue the wrongfulness of slavery? Is that a question for Republicans? Is it to be settled by the rules of logic and argumentation, as a matter beset with great difficulty, involving a doubtful application of the principle of justice, hard to be understood? How should I look to-day, in the presence of Americans, dividing, and subdividing a discourse, to show that men have a natural right to freedom? Speaking of it relatively and positively, negatively and affirmatively. To do so, would be to make myself ridiculous, and to offer an insult to your understanding. —There is not a man beneath the canopy of heaven that does not know that slavery is wrong *for him.*

What, am I to argue that it is wrong to make men brutes, to rob them of their liberty, to work them without wages. to keep them ignorant of their relations to their fellow men, to beat then with sticks, to flay their flesh with the lash, to load their limbs with irons, to hunt them with dogs, to sell them at auction, to sunder their families, to knock out their teeth, to burn their flesh, to starve them into obedience and submission to their masters? Must I argue that a system thus marked with blood, and stained with pollution, is *wrong*? No! I will not. I have better employment for my time and strength than such arguments would imply.

What, then, remains to be argued? Is it that slavery is not divine; that God did not establish it; that our doctors of divinity are mistaken? There is blasphemy in the thought. That which is inhuman, cannot be divine! *Who* can reason on such a proposition? They that can, may; I cannot. The time for such argument is passed.

At a time like this, scorching irony, not convincing argument, is needed. O! had I the ability, and could reach the nation's ear, I would, to-day, pour out a fiery stream of biting ridicule, blasting reproach, withering sarcasm, and stern rebuke. For it is not light that is needed, but fire; it is not the gentle shower, but thunder. We need the storm, the whirlwind, and the earthquake. The feeling of the nation must be quickened; the conscience of the nation must be roused; the propriety of the nation must be startled; the hypocrisy of the nation must be exposed; and its crimes against God and man must be proclaimed and denounced.

What, to the American slave, is your 4th of July? I answer; a day that reveals to him, more than all other days in the year, the gross injustice and cruelty to which he is the constant victim. To him, your celebration is a sham; your boasted liberty, an unholy license; your national greatness, swelling vanity; your sounds of rejoicing are empty and heartless; your denunciation of tyrants, brass fronted impudence; your shouts of liberty and equality, hollow mockery; your prayers and hymns, your sermons and thanksgivings, with all your religious parade and solemnity, are, to Him, mere bombast, fraud, deception, impiety, and hypocrisy—a thin veil to cover up crimes which would disgrace a nation of savages. There is not a nation on the earth guilty of practices more shocking and bloody than are the people of the United States, at this very hour.

Go where you may, search where you will, roam through all the monarchies and despotisms of the Old World, travel through South America, search out every abuse, and when you have found the last, lay your facts by the side of the everyday practices of this nation, and you will say with me, that, for revolting barbarity and shameless hypocrisy, America reigns without a rival.

Take the American slave-trade, which we are told by the papers, is especially prosperous just now. Ex-Senator Benton tells us that the price of men was never higher than now. He mentions the fact to show that slavery is in no danger. This trade is one of the peculiarities of American institutions. It is carried on in all the large towns and cities in one-half of this confederacy; and millions are pocketed every year by dealers in this horrid traffic. In several states this trade is a chief source of wealth. It is called (in contradistinction to the foreign slave-trade) "*the internal slave-trade.*" It is, probably, called so, too, in order to divert from it the horror with which the foreign slave-trade is contemplated. That trade has long since been denounced by this government as piracy. It has been denounced with burning words from the high places of the nation as an execrable traffic. To arrest it, to put an end to it, this nation keeps a squadron, at immense cost, on the coast of Africa. Everywhere, in this country, it is safe to speak of this foreign slave-trade as a most inhuman traffic, opposed alike to the laws of God and of man. The duty to extirpate and destroy it, is admitted even by our doctors of divinity. In order to put an end to it, some of these last have consented that their colored brethren (nominally free) should leave this country, and establish themselves on the western coast of Africa! It is, however, a notable fact that, while so much execration is poured out by Americans upon all those engaged in the foreign slave-trade, the men engaged in the slave-trade between the states pass without condemnation, and their business is deemed honorable.

Behold the practical operation of this internal slave-trade, the American slave-trade, sustained by American politics and American religion. Here you will see men and women reared like swine for the market. You know what is a swine-drover? I will show you a man-drover. They inhabit all our Southern States. They perambulate the country, and crowd the highways of the nation, with droves of human stock. You will see one of these human flesh jobbers, armed with pistol, whip, and bowie-knife, driving a company of a hundred men, women, and children, from the Potomac to the slave market at New Orleans. These wretched people are to be sold singly, or in lots, to suit purchasers. They are food for the cotton-field and the deadly sugar-mill. Mark the sad procession, as it moves wearily along, and the inhuman wretch who drives them. Hear his savage yells and his blood-curdling oaths, as he hurries on his affrighted captives! There, see the old man with locks thinned and gray. Cast one glance, if you please, upon that young mother, whose shoulders are bare to the scorching sun, her briny tears falling on the brow of the babe in her arms. See, too, that girl of thirteen, weeping, yes! weeping, as she thinks of the mother from whom she has been torn! The drove moves tardily. Heat and sorrow have nearly consumed their strength; suddenly you hear a quick snap, like the discharge of a rifle; the fetters clank, and the chain rattles simultaneously; your ears are saluted with a scream, that seems to have torn its way to the centre of your soul! The crack you heard was the sound of the slave-whip; the scream you heard was from the woman you saw with the babe. Her speed had faltered under the weight of her child and her chains! that gash on her shoulder tells her to move on. Follow this drove to New Orleans. Attend the auction; see men examined like horses; see the forms of women rudely and brutally exposed to the shocking gaze of American slave-buyers. See this drove sold and separated forever; and never forget the deep, sad sobs that arose from that scattered multitude. Tell me, citizens, where, under the sun, you can witness a spectacle more fiendish and shocking. Yet this is but a glance at the American slave-trade, as it exists, at this moment, in the ruling part of the United States.

I was born amid such sights and scenes. To me the American slave-trade is a terrible reality. When a child, my soul was often pierced with a sense of its horrors. I lived on Philpot Street, Fell's Point, Baltimore, and have watched from the wharves the slave ships in the Basin, anchored from the shore, with their cargoes of human flesh, waiting for favorable winds to waft them down the Chesapeake. There was, at that time, a grand slave mart kept at the head of Pratt Street, by Austin Woldfolk. His agents were sent into every town and county in Maryland, announcing their arrival, through the papers, and on flaming "*hand-bills,*" headed cash for Negroes. These men were generally well dressed men, and very captivating in their manners; ever ready to drink, to treat, and to gamble. The fate of many a slave has depended upon the turn of a single card; and many a child has been snatched from the arms of its mother by bargains arranged in a state of brutal drunkenness.

The flesh-mongers gather up their victims by dozens, and drive them, chained, to the general depot at Baltimore. When a sufficient number has been collected here, a ship is chartered for the purpose of conveying the forlorn crew to Mobile, or to New Orleans. From the slave prison to the ship, they are usually driven in the darkness of night; for since the antislavery agitation, a certain caution is observed.

In the deep, still darkness of midnight, I have been often aroused by the dead, heavy footsteps, and the piteous cries of the chained gangs that passed our door. The anguish of my boyish heart was intense; and I was often consoled, when speaking to my mistress in the morning, to hear her say that the custom was very wicked; that she hated to hear the rattle of the chains and the heart-rending cries. I was glad to find one who sympathized with me in my horror.

Fellow-citizens, this murderous traffic is, to-day, in active operation in this boasted republic. In the solitude of my spirit I see clouds of dust raised on the highways of the South; I see the bleeding footsteps; I hear the doleful avail of fettered humanity on the way to the slave-markets, where the victims are to be sold like *horses*, *sheep*, and *swine*, knocked off to the highest bidder. There I see the tenderest ties ruthlessly broken, to gratify the lust, caprice and rapacity of the buyers and sellers of men. My soul sickens at the sight.

> Is this the land your Fathers loved,
>   The freedom which they toiled to win?
> Is this the earth whereon they moved?
>   Are these the graves they slumber in?

But a still more inhuman, disgraceful, and scandalous state of things remains to be presented. By an act of the American Congress, not yet two years old, slavery has been nationalized in its most horrible and revolting form. By that act, Mason and Dixon's line has been obliterated; New York has become as Virginia; and the power to hold, hunt, and sell men, women and children, as slaves, remains no longer a mere state institution, but is now an institution of the whole United States. The power is co-extensive with the star-spangled banner, and American Christianity. Where these go, may also go the merciless slave-hunter. Where these are, man is not sacred. He is a bird for the sportsman's gun. By that most foul and fiendish of all human decrees, the liberty and person of every man are put in peril. Your broad republican domain is hunting ground for men:. Not for thieves and robbers, enemies of society, merely, but for men guilty of no crime. Your law-makers have commanded all good citizens to engage in this hellish sport. Your President, your Secretary of State, your lords, nobles, and ecclesiastics enforce, as a duty you owe to your free and glorious country, and to your God, that you do this accursed thing. Not fewer than forty Americans have, within the past two years, been hunted down and, without a moment's warning, hurried away in chains, and consigned to slavery and excruciating torture. Some of these have had wives and children, dependent on them for bread; but of this, no account was made. The right of the hunter to his prey stands superior to the right of marriage, and to *all* rights in this republic, the rights of God included! For black men there is neither law nor justice, humanity nor religion. The Fugitive Slave *Law* makes mercy to them a crime; and bribes the judge who tries them. An American judge gets ten dollars for every victim he consigns to slavery, and five, when he fails to do so. The oath of any two villains is sufficient, under this hell-black enactment, to send the most pious and exemplary black man into the remorseless jaws of slavery! His own testimony is nothing. He can bring no witnesses for himself. The minister of American justice is bound by the law to hear but *one* side; and *that* side is the side of the oppressor. Let this damning fact be perpetually told. Let it be thundered around the world that in tyrant-killing, king-hating, people-loving, democratic, Christian America the seats of justice are filled with judges who hold their offices under an open and palpable *bribe*, and are bound, in deciding the case of a man's liberty, *to hear only his accusers!*

In glaring violation of justice, in shameless disregard of the forms of administering law, in cunning arrangement to entrap the defenceless, and in diabolical intent this Fugitive Slave Law stands alone in the annals of tyrannical legislation. I doubt if there be another nation on the globe having the brass and the baseness to put such a law on the statute-book. If any man in this assembly thinks differently from me in this matter, and feels able to disprove my statements, I will gladly confront him at any suitable time and place he may select.

I take this law to be one of the grossest infringements of Christian Liberty, and, if the churches and ministers of our country were not stupidly blind, or most wickedly indifferent, they, too, would so regard it.

At the very moment that they are thanking God for the enjoyment of civil and religious liberty, and for the right to worship God according to the dictates of their own consciences, they are utterly silent in respect to a law which robs religion of its chief significance and makes it utterly worthless to a world lying in wickedness. Did this law concern the *"mint, anise, and cummin"*—abridge the right to sing psalms, to partake of the sacrament, or to engage in any of the ceremonies of religion, it would be smitten by the thunder of a thousand pulpits. A general shout would go up from the church demanding *repeal, repeal, instant repeal!*—And it would go hard with that politician who presumed to solicit the votes of the people without inscribing this motto on his banner. Further, if this demand were not complied with, another Scotland would be added to the history of religious liberty, and the stern old covenanters would be thrown into the shade. A John Knox would be seen at every church door and heard from every pulpit, and Fillmore would have no more quarter than was shown by Knox to the beautiful, but treacherous, Queen Mary of Scotland. The fact that the church of our country (with fractional exceptions) does not esteem "the Fugitive Slave Law" as a declaration of war against religious liberty, implies that that church regards religion simply as a form of worship, an empty ceremony, and not a vital principle, requiring active benevolence, justice, love, and good will towards man. It esteems sacrifice above mercy; psalm-singing above right doing; solemn meetings above practical righteousness. A worship that can be conducted by persons who refuse to give shelter to the houseless, to give bread to the hungry, clothing to the naked, and who enjoin obedience to a law forbidding these acts of mercy is a curse, not a blessing to mankind. The Bible addresses all such persons as "scribes, pharisees, hypocrites, who pay tithe of *mint, anise,* and *cummin,* and have omitted the weightier matters of the law, judgment, mercy, and faith."

But the church of this country is not only indifferent to the wrongs of the slave, it actually takes sides with the oppressors. It has made itself the bulwark of American slavery, and the shield of American slave-hunters. Many of its most eloquent Divines, who stand as the very lights of the church, have shamelessly given the sanction of religion and the Bible to the whole slave system. They have taught that man may, properly, be a slave; that the relation of master and slave is ordained of God; that to send back an escaped bondman to his master is clearly the duty of all the followers of the Lord Jesus Christ; and this horrible blasphemy is palmed off upon the world for Christianity.

For my part, I would say, welcome infidelity! welcome atheism! welcome anything! in preference to the gospel, *as preached by those Divines!* They convert the very name of religion into an engine of tyranny and barbarous cruelty, and serve to confirm more infidels, in this age, than all the infidel writings of Thomas Paine, Voltaire, and Bolingbroke put together have done! These ministers make religion a cold and flinty-hearted thing, having neither principles of right action nor bowels of compassion. They strip the love of God of its beauty and leave the throne of religion a huge, horrible, repulsive form. It is a religion for oppressors, tyrants, man-stealers, and *thugs.* It is not that "*pure and undefiled religion*" which is from above, and which is "*first pure, then peaceable, easy to be entreated,* full of mercy and good fruits, *without partiality, and without hypocrisy.*" But a religion which favors the rich against the poor; which exalts the proud above the humble; which divides mankind into two classes, tyrants and slaves; which says to the man in chains, *stay there*; and to the oppressor, *oppress on*; it is a religion which may be professed and enjoyed by all the robbers and enslavers of mankind; it makes God a respecter of persons, denies his fatherhood of the race, and tramples in the dust the great truth of the brotherhood of man. All this we affirm to be true of the popular church, and the popular worship of our land and nation—a religion, a church, and a worship which, on the authority of inspired wisdom, we pronounce to be an abomination in the sight of God. In the language of Isaiah, the American church might be well addressed, "Bring no more vain oblations; incense is an abomination unto me: the new moons and Sabbaths, the calling of assemblies, I cannot away with; it is iniquity, even the solemn meeting. Your new moons, and your appointed feasts my soul hateth. They are a trouble to me; I am weary to bear them; and when ye spread forth your hands I will hide mine eyes from you. Yea! when ye make many prayers, I will not hear. Your hands are full of blood; cease to do evil, learn to do well; seek judgment; relieve the oppressed; judge for the fatherless; plead for the widow."

The American church is guilty, when viewed in connection with what it is doing to uphold slavery; but it is superlatively guilty when viewed in its connection with its ability to abolish slavery.

The sin of which it is guilty is one of omission as well as of commission. Albert Barnes but uttered what the common sense of every man at all observant of the actual state of the case will receive as truth, when he declared that "There is no power out of the church that could sustain slavery an hour, if it were not sustained in it."

Let the religious press, the pulpit, the Sunday School, the conference meeting, the great ecclesiastical, missionary, Bible and tract associations of the land array their immense powers against slavery, and slave-holding; and the whole system of crime and blood would be scattered to the winds; and that they do not do this involves them in the most awful responsibility of which the mind can conceive.

In prosecuting the anti-slavery enterprise, we have been asked to spare the church, to spare the ministry; but *how*, we ask, could such a thing be done? We are met on the threshold of our efforts for the redemption of the slave, by the church and ministry of the country, in battle arrayed against us; and we are compelled to fight or flee. From *what* quarter, I beg to know, has proceeded a fire so deadly upon our ranks, during the last two years, as from the Northern pulpit? As the champions of oppressors, the chosen men of American theology have appeared—men honored for their so-called piety, and their real learning. The Lords of Buffalo, the Springs of New York, the Lathrops of Auburn, the Coxes and Spencers of Brooklyn, the Gannets and Sharps of Boston, the Deweys of Washington, and other great religious lights of the land have, in utter denial of the authority of *Him* by whom they professed to be called to the ministry, deliberately taught us, against the example of the Hebrews, and against the remonstrance of the Apostles, *that we ought to obey man's law before the law of God*.

My spirit wearies of such blasphemy; and how such men can be supported, as the "standing types and representatives of Jesus Christ," is a mystery which I leave others to penetrate. In speaking of the American church, however, let it be distinctly understood that I mean the *great mass* of the religious organizations of our land. There are exceptions, and I thank God that there are. Noble men may be found, scattered all over these Northern States, of whom Henry Ward Beecher, of Brooklyn; Samuel J. May, of Syracuse; and my esteemed friend (Rev. R. R. Raymond) on the platform, are shining examples; and let me say further, that, upon these men lies the duty to inspire our ranks with high religious faith and zeal, and to cheer us on in the great mission of the slave's redemption from his chains.

One is struck with the difference between the attitude of the American church towards the anti-slavery movement, and that occupied by the churches in England towards a similar movement in that country. There, the church, true to its mission of ameliorating, elevating and improving the condition of mankind, came forward promptly, bound up the wounds of the West Indian slave, and restored him to his liberty. There, the question of emancipation was a high religious question. It was demanded in the name of humanity, and according to the law of the living God. The Sharps, the Clarksons, the Wilberforces, the Buxtons, the Burchells, and the Knibbs were alike famous for their piety and for their philanthropy. The anti-slavery movement *there* was not an anti-church movement, for the reason that the church took its full share in prosecuting that movement: and the anti-slavery movement in this country will cease to be an anti-church movement, when the church of this country shall assume a favorable instead of a hostile position towards that movement.

Americans! your republican politics, not less than your republican religion, are flagrantly inconsistent. You boast of your love of liberty, your superior civilization, and your pure Christianity, while the whole political power of the nation (as embodied in the two great political parties) is solemnly pledged to support and perpetuate the enslavement of three millions of your countrymen. You hurl your anathemas at the crowned headed tyrants of Russia and Austria and pride yourselves on your Democratic institutions, while you yourselves consent to be the mere *tools* and *body-guards* of the tyrants of Virginia and Carolina. You invite to your shores fugitives of oppression from abroad, honor them with banquets, greet them with ovations, cheer them, toast them, salute them, protect them, and pour out your money to them like water; but the fugitives from your own land you advertise, hunt, arrest, shoot, and kill. You glory in your refinement and your universal education; yet you maintain a system as barbarous and dreadful as ever stained the character of a nation—a system begun in avarice, supported in pride, and perpetuated in cruelty. You shed tears over fallen Hungary, and make the sad story of her wrongs the theme of your poets, statesmen, and orators, till your gallant sons are ready to fly to arms to vindicate her cause against the oppressor; but, in regard to the ten thousand wrongs of the American slave, you would enforce the strictest silence, and would hail him as an enemy of the nation who dares to make those wrongs the subject of public discourse! You are all on fire at the mention of liberty for France or for Ireland; but are as cold as an iceberg at the thought of liberty for the enslaved of America. You discourse eloquently on the dignity of labor; yet, you sustain a system which, in its very essence, casts a stigma upon labor. You can bare your bosom to the storm of British artillery to throw off a three-penny tax on tea; and yet wring the last hard earned farthing from the grasp of the black laborers of your country. You profess to believe "that, of one blood, God made all nations of men to dwell on the face of all the earth," and hath commanded all men, everywhere, to love one another; yet you notoriously hate (and glory in your hatred) all men whose skins are not colored like your own. You declare before the world, and are understood by the world to declare that you "*hold these truths to be self-evident, that all men are created equal; and are endowed by their Creator with certain inalienable rights; and that among these are, life, liberty, and the pursuit of happiness*; and yet, you hold securely, in a bondage which, according to your own Thomas Jefferson, "*is worse than ages of that which your fathers rose in rebellion to oppose*," a seventh part of the inhabitants of your country.

Fellow-citizens, I will not enlarge further on your national inconsistencies. The existence of slavery in this country brands your republicanism as a sham, your humanity as a base pretense, and your Christianity as a lie. It destroys your moral power abroad: it corrupts your politicians at home. It saps the foundation of religion; it makes your name a hissing and a bye-word to a mocking earth. It is the antagonistic force in your government, the only thing that seriously disturbs and endangers your *Union*. It fetters your progress; it is the enemy of improvement; the deadly foe of education; it fosters pride; it breeds insolence; it promotes vice; it shelters crime; it is a curse to the earth that supports it; and yet you cling to it as if it were the sheet anchor of all your hopes. Oh! be warned! be warned! a horrible reptile is coiled up in your nation's bosom; the venomous creature is nursing at the tender breast of your youthful republic; *for the love of God, tear away*, and fling from you the hideous monster, and *let the weight of twenty millions crush and destroy it forever!*

But it is answered in reply to all this, that precisely what I have now denounced is, in fact, guaranteed and sanctioned by the Constitution of the United States; that, the right to hold, and to hunt slaves is a part of that Constitution framed by the illustrious Fathers of this Republic.

Then, I dare to affirm, notwithstanding all I have said before, your fathers stooped, basely stooped

> To palter with us in a double sense:
> And keep the word of promise to the ear,
> But break it to the heart.

And instead of being the honest men I have before declared them to be, they were the veriest impostors that ever practised on mankind. This is the inevitable conclusion, and from it there is no escape; but I differ from those who charge this baseness on the framers of the Constitution of the United States. It is a slander upon their memory, at least, so I believe. There is not time now to argue the constitutional question at length; nor have I the ability to discuss it as it ought to be discussed. The subject has been handled with masterly power by Lysander Spooner, Esq., by William Goodell, by Samuel E. Sewall, Esq., and last, though not least, by Gerrit Smith, Esq. These gentlemen have, as I think, fully and clearly vindicated the Constitution from any design to support slavery for an hour.

Fellow-citizens! there is no matter in respect to which the people of the North have allowed themselves to be so ruinously imposed upon as that of the pro-slavery character of the Constitution. In that instrument I hold there is neither warrant, license, nor sanction of the hateful thing; but interpreted, as it ought to be interpreted, the Constitution is a glorious liberty document. Read its preamble, consider its purposes. Is slavery among them? Is it at the gateway? or is it in the temple? it is neither. While I do not intend to argue this question on the present occasion, let me ask, if it be not somewhat singular that, if the Constitution were intended to be, by its framers and adopters, a slaveholding instrument, why neither slavery, slaveholding, nor slave can anywhere be found in it. What would be thought of an instrument, drawn up, legally drawn up, for the purpose of entitling the city of Rochester to a tract of land, in which no mention of land was made? Now, there are certain rules of interpretation for the proper understanding of all legal instruments. These rules are well established. They are plain, commonsense rules, such as you and I, and all of us, can understand and apply, without having passed years in the study of law. I scout the idea that the question of the constitutionality, or unconstitutionality of slavery, is not a question for the people. I hold that every American citizen has a right to form an opinion of the constitution, and to propagate that opinion, and to use all honorable means to make his opinion the prevailing one. Without this right, the liberty of an American citizen would be as insecure as that of a Frenchman. Ex-Vice-President Dallas tells us that the constitution is an object to which no American mind can be too attentive, and no American heart too devoted. He further says, the Constitution, in its words, is plain and intelligible, and is meant for the home-bred, unsophisticated understandings of our fellow-citizens. Senator Berrien tells us that the Constitution is the fundamental law, that which controls all others. The charter of our liberties, which every citizen has a personal interest in understanding thoroughly. The testimony of Senator Breese, Lewis Cass, and many others that might be named, who are everywhere esteemed as sound lawyers, so regard the constitution. I take it, therefore, that it is not presumption in a private citizen to form an opinion of that instrument.

Now, take the Constitution according to its plain reading, and I defy the presentation of a single pro-slavery clause in it. On the other hand, it will be found to contain principles and purposes, entirely hostile to the existence of slavery.

I have detained my audience entirely too long already. At some future period I will gladly avail myself of an opportunity to give this subject a full and fair discussion.

Allow me to say, in conclusion, notwithstanding the dark picture I have this day presented. of the state of the nation, I do not despair of this country. There are forces in operation which must inevitably work the downfall of slavery. "The arm of the Lord is not shortened," and the doom of slavery is certain. I, therefore, leave off where I began, with hope. While drawing encouragement from "the Declaration of Independence," the great principles it contains, and the genius of American Institutions, my spirit is also cheered by the obvious tendencies of the age. Nations do not now stand in the same relation to each other that they did ages ago. No nation can now shut itself up from the surrounding world and trot round in the same old path of its fathers without interference. The time was when such could be done. Long established customs of hurtful character could formerly fence themselves in, and do their evil work with social impunity. Knowledge was then confined and enjoyed by the privileged few, and the multitude walked on in mental darkness. But a change has now come over the affairs of mankind. Walled cities and empires have become unfashionable. The arm of commerce has borne away the gates of the strong city. Intelligence is penetrating the darkest corners of the globe. It makes its pathway over and under the sea, as well as on the earth. Wind, steam, and lightning are its chartered agents. Oceans no longer divide, but link nations together. From Boston to London is now a holiday excursion. Space is comparatively annihilated. —Thoughts expressed on one side of the Atlantic are distinctly heard on the other.

The far off and almost fabulous Pacific rolls in grandeur at our feet. The Celestial Empire, the mystery of ages, is being solved. The fiat of the Almighty, "Let there be Light," has not yet spent its force. No abuse, no outrage whether in taste, sport or avarice, can now hide itself from the all-pervading light. The iron shoe, and crippled foot of China must be seen in contrast with nature. Africa must rise and put on her yet unwoven garment. "Ethiopia shall stretch out her hand unto God." In the fervent aspirations of William Lloyd Garrison, I say, and let every heart join in saying it:

> God speed the year of jubilee
>   The wide world o'er!
> When from their galling chains set free,
> Th' oppress'd shall vilely bend the knee,
>
> And wear the yoke of tyranny
>   Like brutes no more.
> That year will come, and freedom's reign,
> To man his plundered rights again
>   Restore.
>
> God speed the day when human blood
>   Shall cease to flow!
> In every clime be understood,
> The claims of human brotherhood,
> And each return for evil, good,
>   Not blow for blow;
>
> That day will come all feuds to end,
> And change into a faithful friend
>   Each foe.
>
> God speed the hour, the glorious hour,
>   When none on earth
> Shall exercise a lordly power.
> Nor in a tyrant's presence cower;
> But to all manhood's stature tower,
>   By equal birth!
> That hour will come, to each. to all,
> And from his prison-house, to thrall
>   Go forth.
>
> Until that year, day, hour, arrive,
> With head, and heart, and hand I'll strive,
> To break the rod, and rend the gyve,
> The spoiler of his prey deprive—
>   So witness Heaven!
> And never from my chosen post.
> Whate'er the peril or the cost.
>   Be driven.

SUGGESTIONS FOR FURTHER READING

The standard work on free blacks in the South during this period is Ira Berlin, *Slaves Without Masters: The Free Negro in the Antebellum South*★ (1981). For the North, see Leon Litwack, *North of Slavery: The Negro in the Free States, 1790–1860*★ (1961). See also Leonard P. Curry, *The Free Black in Urban America, 1800–1850*★ (1981) and Elizabeth Rauh Bethel, *The Roots of African American Identity: Memory and History in Antebellum Free Communities*★ (1997).

Blacks in the antislavery movement are dealt with in Benjamin Quarles, *Black Abolitionists*★ (1969), R. J. M. Blackett, *Building an Antislavery Wall: Black Americans in the Atlantic Abolitionist Movement, 1830–1860* (1983), and C. Peter Ripley and Jeffrey S. Rossbach (eds.), *The Black Abolitionist Papers* (1981–). The career of Frederick Douglass can be followed in Nathan I. Huggins, *Slave and Citizen: The Life of Frederick Douglass*★ (1980), William McFeely, *Frederick Douglass*★ (1991), and the series of volumes in John Blassingame (ed.), *The Frederick Douglass Papers* (1979–). See also Robert S. Levine, *Martin Delany, Frederick Douglass, and the Politics of Representative Identity*★ (1997). Philip Foner's five volume collection of Douglass' works is presented in an abridged one volume edition with the title *Frederick Douglass: Selected Speeches and Writings*★ (1999).

Important works on this period include Peter P. Hinks, *To Awaken My Afflicted Brethren: David Walker and the Problem of Antebellum Slave Resistance*★ (1996), Nell Irvin Painter, *Sojourner Truth: A Life, A Symbol*★ (1996), W. Jeffrey Bolster, *Black Jacks: African American Sailors in the Age of Sail*★ (1997), Carol V. R. George, *Segregated Sabbaths: Richard Allen and the Emergence of Independent Black Churches, 1760–1840* (1973), and Suzanne Lebsock, *The Free Women of Petersburg: Status and Culture in a Southern Town, 1784–1860*★ (1984). Larry Gara explores the escape route of runaway slaves in *The Liberty Line: The Legend of the Underground Radroad*★ (1961).

Philip J. Staudenraus, in *The African Colonization Movement, 1816–1865* (1961), surveys both the attempts of whites to remove black people from the United States and the attempts of blacks to remove themselves. Black emigrationist ideas are presented in two works by Martin R. Delany, *The Condition, Elevation, Emigration and Destiny of the Colored People in the United States* (1852) and *Official Report of the Niger Valley Exploring Party* (1861), and in Robert Campbell, *A Pilgrimage to My Motherland* (1861).

★ Books marked by an asterisk are available in paperback.

5

✪

The Civil War and Reconstruction

INTRODUCTION

When the Civil War began, black people had two major goals: to get into the fight and to see to it that all blacks were free. Blacks had fought in all previous wars of the United States, and they felt that in this war above all, they had a place. The day after Lincoln's call for troops went out, groups of black men all over the North offered themselves for military service. Everywhere they were turned down. The War Department had no intention of using black troops. This attitude might be accounted for in several ways. There was a general feeling among whites that blacks lacked courage; thus, the military leaders may have thought their presence in the ranks would do more harm than good. But there was also an idea among whites that blacks had fiery, impulsive natures. This may have led to the reasoning that if the black men got guns, they would use them to insist on their own equality.

As the war drew on, however, and there was a need for more and more soldiers, certain field commanders began using runaway slaves, or "contraband," as they were called, in the battle lines. In July 1862, Congress passed a bill authorizing the use of black troops, and open recruiting began shortly thereafter. Before the end of the war, about 180,000 black soldiers served in the Union army, making up about 10 percent of the total federal troops, and nearly 29,000 served in the navy, making up about 25 percent of the Union sailors. Some historians feel that the decision to allow blacks to fight was a crucial factor in ultimate Union victory.

Although Lincoln and his cabinet insisted that slavery was not the issue at the heart of the war, the slave question overshadowed all others. Lincoln himself was opposed to slavery in principle, but he was opposed to notions of social or political equality as well. If he had had his way, he would have eliminated the race problem through a program of gradual, compensated emancipation and colonization. When his colonization schemes were made public in 1862, black people throughout the Union held meetings of protest.

One reason Lincoln was urging migration was that he had decided to issue a proclamation of emancipation for the slaves in the rebel territories, and he felt that it would be easier for whites to accept the situation if the freed blacks were to leave the country. When Lincoln issued the Emancipation Proclamation, to take effect on January 1, 1863, it had little but symbolic effect. It took the Thirteenth Amendment, ratified in December 1865, to free the remaining slaves. But the Proclamation did stimulate the enlistment of black troops in the Union army and encourage the runaway slaves.

Black women participated in the war effort also. Many worked in hospitals or in military camps. A group of black women in Washington helped the "contraband" find jobs and homes. School teachers moved into liberated areas of the South in order to set up schools and help the freedmen develop the tools of citizenship.

Even though Union victory was to ensure the legal freedom of the former slaves, many questions about the future of all blacks in America remained unanswered. Blacks were disfranchised in both North and South. Competition for jobs was becoming more and more a source of violent confrontation in Northern cities. What would happen to the freedman who had agricultural skills but no land on which to exercise them?

There was a clear division between the educated blacks of the North and the rural freedmen of the South. The former were interested primarily in obtaining political and civil rights. Most of them had some degree of economic security because of their training and experience; now they sought freedom to participate more actively in the general life of the society. The freedmen, on the other hand, knew little but the farm, and their future was tied up with getting the land necessary to allow them a measure of economic independence. All other rights depended on that one.

Several proposals were made for providing each freedman with "forty acres and a mule" so that he might make a start toward real freedom. As different parts of the South became liberated, however, various plans put into operation by federal authority effectively prevented the freedmen from procuring the needed land. Before the assassination of Lincoln, there was a possibility that land would be confiscated from plantation owners who had supported the Southern war effort and distributed among the former slaves. But, for the most part, the land policy of the Union—even before the end of the war—seemed but another form of slavery. Instead of being given land of their own, the freedmen were required to sign labor contracts with Northern adventurers to whom the former plantations had been leased in order to provide support for federal troops. Many of these lessees were more interested in making money than in aiding the freedmen, and the former slaves often worked as hard as they had in the past at ridiculously low wages.

With the accession of Andrew Johnson to the presidency, the rural freed-men lost all hope. Johnson's policy was to restore as many plantations as possible to their former owners. He felt that this was the way to provide for the South's return to the Union with a minimum of residual hostility. Unfortunately, it was the black people who paid the price of this policy. Most rural freedmen ended up as sharecroppers in a system that drove them deeper and deeper into debt. By the end of the century, they had fallen into a condition that approached serfdom.

During Reconstruction, many blacks in the South participated in elective politics for the first time in American history. There were sixteen black men in Congress during this period, including two in the Senate; of the sixteen, thirteen were former slaves. Even more important, perhaps, were the black members of the various state constitutional conventions and legislatures. Under their influence, the new state constitutions called for an extension of the franchise, free public education, and significant reforms in such areas as state penal and judicial systems. Ironically, although blacks formed a majority in only one Southern state legislature (the lower house in South Carolina), the reforms enacted under their leadership contributed in a major way to the renaissance of the white South.

Free the Slaves and Then Leave Them Alone

Address to the Emancipation League in Boston, 1862

FREDERICK DOUGLASS

When war broke out between the rebellious Confederacy and the United States gov-
ernment, it was not clear to all participants that it was a war over slavery. But it was
clear to Frederick Douglass. He saw slavery on its way to eradication, and he insisted
that African-Americans be allowed to serve in the army that would gain their freedom.
After initial reluctance on the part of the government, blacks began to be enlisted in
the Union army in 1862, and they served with distinction, as they have in all of
America's wars.

Although Douglass got his wish as far as military service for African-Americans
was concerned, his belief that the freedpeople could survive after the war if they were
just given their freedom and left alone to make their way in society without help or
hindrance was less prescient. He was not able to foresee that, without some kind of eco-
nomic support, the freedpeople would find themselves subject to raw economic forces
that would likely doom them to poverty, even if white society had left them alone. The
radical Republicans who proposed that "40 acres and a mule" be given to each for-
merly slave family were better aware of the social and economic forces operative in
American society. Without an underpinning of property, many of the newly freed
African-Americans found themselves slipping into economic dependency. With the
return to political power of the racist Democratic party in the South, the freedpeople
found themselves both politically and economically powerless, and the long, hard strug-
gle to achieve racial equality entered a new phase.

Frederick Douglass remained a militant crusader on behalf of African-Americans.
He held a number of Republican political offices in the postwar years, with the cap-
stone of his career being his appointment in 1889 as United States Minister to Haiti.

Douglass made the following address before the Emancipation League in Boston
in 1862. This organization, which had been founded the year before by prominent
white abolitionists, sought the immediate emancipation of the slaves as the only way
to bring peace to the nation.

Ladies and Gentlemen:

The progress of the present tremendous war has developed great qualities of
mind and heart among the loyal people, and none more conspicuously than

---

FROM Frederick Douglass, "The Future of the Negro People of the Slave States," *Douglass' Monthly* (March 1862).

patience. We have seen our sons, brothers, and fathers led to the battle field by untried and unskillful generals, and have held our breath; we have seen them repeatedly marched in thousands upon concealed batteries of the enemy, to be swept down by storms of iron and fire, and have scarcely murmured: we have seen the wealth of the land poured out at the frightful rate of a million a day without complaint; we have seen our Capital surrounded, hemmed in, blockaded in the presence of a fettered but chafing loyal army of a quarter of a million on the Potomac during seven long months, and still we have cried patience and forbearance. We have seen able and earnest men displaced from high and important positions to make room for men who have yet to win our confidence, and still have believed in the Government. This is all right, all proper. Our Government however defective is still our Government. It is all we have to shield us from the fury and vengeance of treason, rebellion, and anarchy.

If I were asked to describe the most painful and mortifying feature presented in the prosecution and management of the present war on the part of the United States Government, against the slaveholding rebels now marshalled against it, I should not point to Ball's Bluff, Big Bethel, Bull Run, or any of the many blunders and disaster on flood or field; but I should point to the vacillation, doubt, uncertainty and hesitation, which have thus far distinguished our government in regard to the true method of dealing with the vital cause of the rebellion. We are without any declared and settled policy—and our policy seems to be, to have no policy.

The winds and currents are ever changing, and after beating about for almost a whole year on the perilous coast of a wildering ocean unable to find our bearings, we at last discover that we are in the same latitude as when we set sail, as far from the desired port as ever and with much less heart, health and provisions for pursuing the voyage than on the morning we weighed anchor.

If it be true that he that doubteth is condemned already, there is certainly but little chance for this Republic.

At the opening session of the present Congress there was a marked, decided, and emphatic expression against slavery as the great motive power of the present slaveholding war. Many petitions, numerously and influentially signed, were duly sent in and presented to that body, praying, first, for the entire abolition of slavery in all the slaveholding States; secondly, that a just award be made by Congress to loyal slaveholders; and thirdly, that the slaves of rebels be wholly confiscated. The vigor, earnestness, and power with which these objects were advocated, as war measures, by Messrs. Stevens, Bingham, Elliott, Gurley, Lovejoy and others, inspired the loyal friends of Freedom all over the North with renewed confidence and hope, both for the country and for the slave. The conviction was general that at last the country was to have a policy, and that that policy would bring freedom and safety to the Republic.

Thus far, however, this hope, this confidence, this conviction has not been justified. The country is without a known policy. The enemies of the Abolition cause, taking alarm from these early efforts, have earnestly set themselves to the work of producing a reaction in favor of slavery, and have succeeded beyond what they themselves must have expected at the first.

Among other old, and threadbare, and worn out objections which they have raised against the Emancipation policy, is the question as to what shall be done with the four million slaves of the South, if they are emancipated? or in other words, what shall be the future of the four million slaves?

I am sensible, deeply sensible, of the importance of this subject, and of the many difficulties which are supposed to surround it.

If there is any one great, pressing, and all-commanding problem for this nation to solve, and to solve without delay, that problem is slavery. Its claims are urgent, palpable, and powerful. The issue involves the whole question of life and death to the nation.

Some who speak on this subject are already sure as to how this question will finally be decided. I am not, but one thing I know:—If we are a wise, liberty-loving, a just and courageous nation—knowing what is right and daring to do it—we shall solve this problem, and solve it speedily, in accordance with national safety, national unity, national prosperity, national glory, and shall win for ourselves the admiration of an onlooking world and the grateful applause of after-coming generations. If on the other hand, we are a cunning, cowardly, and selfish nation given over—as other nations have been before us—to hardness of heart and blindness of mind, it needs no prophet to foretell our doom.

Before proceeding to discuss the future of the colored people of the slave States, you will allow me to make a few remarks, personal and general, respecting the tremendous crisis through which we are passing. In the first place I have not the vanity to suppose—and I say it without affectation—that I can add any thing to the powerful arguments of the able men who have preceded me in this course of lectures. I take the stand tonight more as an humble witness than as an advocate. I have studied slavery and studied freedom on both sides of Mason and Dixon's line. Nearly twenty-two years of my life were spent in Slavery, and more than twenty-three have been spent in freedom. I am of age in both conditions, and there seems an eminent fitness in allowing me to speak for myself and my race. If I take my stand tonight as I shall do, with the down-trodden and enslaved, and view the facts of the hour more as a bondman than as a freeman, it is not because I feel no interest in the general welfare of the country. Far from it.

I am an American citizen. In birth, in sentiment, in ideas, in hopes, in aspirations, and responsibilities, I am an American citizen. According to Judge Kent there are but two classes of people in America: they are citizens and aliens, natives and foreigners. —Natives are citizens—foreigners are aliens until naturalized.

But I am not only a citizen by birth and lineage, I am such by choice.

I once had a very tempting offer of citizenship in another country; but declined it because I preferred the hardships and duties of my mission here. I have never regretted that decision, although my pathway has been anything than a smooth one; and to-night, I allow no man to exceed me in the desire for the safety and welfare of this country. And just here do allow me to boast a little. There is nothing in the circumstances of the present hour, nothing in the behavior of the colored people, either North or South, which requires apology at my hands. Though everywhere spoken against, the most malignant and unscrupulous of all our slanderers have not, in this dark and terrible hour of the nation's trial dared to accuse us of a want of patriotism or loyalty. Though ignored by our friends and repelled by our enemies, the colored people, both north and south, have evinced the most ardent desire to serve the cause of the country, as against the rebels and traitors who are endeavoring to break it down and destroy it. That they are not largely represented in the loyal army, is the fault of the Government, and a very grievous fault it is. Mark here our nation's degeneracy. Colored men were good enough to fight under Washington. They are not good enough to fight under McClellan. —They were good enough to fight under Andrew Jackson. They are not good enough to fight under Gen. Halleck. They were good enough to help win American independence but they are not good enough to help preserve that independence against treason and rebellion. They were good enough to defend New Orleans but not good enough to defend our poor beleaguered Capital. I am not arguing against, not condemning those in power, but simply stating facts in vindication of my people; and as these facts stand, I do say that I am proud to be recognized here as an humble representative of that rejected race. Whether in peace or in war, whether in safety or in peril, whether in evil report or good report, at home or abroad, my mission is to stand up for the down-trodden, to open my mouth for the dumb, to remember those in bonds as bound with them.

Happily, however, in standing up in their cause I do, and you do, but stand in defense of the cause of the whole country. The circumstances of this eventful hour make the cause of the slaves and the cause of the country identical. They must fall or flourish together. A blow struck for the freedom of the slave, is equally a blow struck for the safety and welfare of the country. As Liberty and Union have become identical, so slavery and treason have become one and inseparable. I shall not argue this point. It has already been most ably argued. All eyes see it, all hearts begin to feel it; and all that is needed is the wisdom and the manhood to perform the solemn duty pointed out by the stern logic of our situation. It is now or never with us.

The field is ripe for the harvest. God forbid that when the smoke and thunder of this slaveholding war shall have rolled from the troubled face of our country it shall be said that the harvest is past, the summer is ended and we are not saved.

There are two classes of men who are endeavoring to put down this strange and most unnatural rebellion. About patriotism and loyalty, they talk alike; but the difference between them is heaven wide—and if we fail to suppress the rebels and restore the country to a condition of permanent safety it will be chargeable less to the skill and power of the rebels themselves, than to this division and conflict among ourselves. Never could it be said more truly and sadly than now, that our enemies are those of our own household. —The traitors of

the South are open, bold, decided. We know just where to find them. —They
are on the battle field, with arms in their hands and bullets in their pockets. It
is easy to deal with them, but it is not so easy to deal with the so-called Union
men in Maryland, Western Virginia, and Kentucky, and those who sympathize
with them in the Northern States.

One class is for putting down the rebellion if that can be done by force and
force alone, and without abolishing slavery, and the other is for putting down
the rebellion by putting down slavery upon every rod of earth which shall be
made sacred by the footprints of a single loyal soldier. One class would strike
down the effect, the other would strike at the cause. Can any man doubt for
a moment that the latter is the wisest and best course? Is it not as plain as the
sun in the heavens, that slavery is the life, the soul, the inspiration, and power
of the rebellion? Is it not equally plain that any peace which may be secured
which shall leave slavery still existing at the South, will prove a hollow and
worthless peace, a mere suspension of hostilities, to be renewed again at the
first favorable opportunity? —Does any man think that the slaveholders would
relinquish all hope of Southern independence in the future because defeated
in the present contest? Would they not come out of the war with a deadlier
hate and a firmer purpose to renew the struggle hereafter, with larger knowledge and better means of success? He who thinks or flatters himself that they
would not, has read history and studied human nature to little purpose.

But why, O why should we not abolish slavery now? All admit that it must
be abolished at some time. What better time than now can be assigned for that
great work? —Why should it longer live? What good thing has it done that it
should be given further lease of life? What evil thing has it left undone?
Behold its dreadful history! Saying nothing of the rivers of tears and streams
of blood poured out by its 4,000,000 victims—saying nothing of the leprous
poison it has diffused through the life blood of our morals and our religion—
saying nothing of the many humiliating concessions already made to it—
saying nothing of the deep and scandalous reproach it has brought upon our
national good name—saying nothing of all this, and more the simple fact that
this monster Slavery has eaten up and devoured the patriotism of the whole
South, kindled the lurid flames of a bloody rebellion in our midst, invited the
armies of hostile nations to desolate our soil, and break down our
Government, is good and all-sufficient cause of smiting it as with a bolt from
heaven. If it is possible for any system of barbarism to sing its own death warrant, Slavery, by its own natural working, is that svstem. All the arguments of
conscience, sound expediency, national honor and safety unite in the fiat—let
it die the death of its own election.

One feature of the passing hour is notable in showing how narrow and limited may be the channel through which a great reformatory movement can
run for long and weary years, without once overflowing its banks and enrich-
ing the surrounding country through which it passes.

Notwithstanding all our books, pamphlets, newspapers, our great conventions, addresses, and resolutions, tens of thousands of the American people are
now taking their *first* lessons as to the character and influence of slavery and

slaveholders. Tongues that used to bless Slavery now curse it, and men who formerly found paragons of the race only among slave mongers and their abettors, are but now having the scales torn from their eyes by slaveholding treason and rebellion. They are just coming to believe what we have all along been trying to tell them, that is: that he who breaks faith with God may not be expected to keep faith with man. I gladly welcome this great change in the public sentiment of the country. And yet I do not rely very confidently upon it. I am not deceived either in regard to its origin or its quality. —I know that national self-preservation, national safety, rather than any regard to the bondman as a man and a brother, is at the bottom of much that now meets us in the shape of opposition to slavery. The little finger of him who denounced slavery from a high moral conviction of its enormity is more than the loins of him that merely denounces it for the peril into which it has brought the country. Nevertheless, I rejoice in this change, the result will be nearly the same to the slave, if from motives of necessity or any other motives the nation shall be led to the extinction of slavery. Every consideration of expediency and justice may be consistently brought to bear against that sum of all villanies.

But to return. What shall be done with the four million slaves, if emancipated. I answer, deal justly with them; pay them honest wages for honest work; dispense with the biting lash, and pay them the ready cash; awaken a new class of motives in them; remove those old motives of shriveling fear of punishment which benumb and degrade the soul, and supplant them by the higher and better motives of hope, of self-respect, of honor, and of personal responsibility. Reverse the whole current of feeling in regard to them. They have been compelled hitherto to regard the white man as a cruel, selfish, and remorseless tyrant, thirsting for wealth, greedy of gain, and caring nothing as to the means by which he obtains it. Now, let him see that the white man has a nobler and better side to his character, and he will love, honor, esteem the white man.

But it is said that the black man is naturally indolent, and that he will not work without a master. I know that this is a part of his bad reputation; but I also know that he is indebted for this bad reputation to the most indolent and lazy of all the American people, the slaveholders—men who live in absolute idleness, and eat their daily bread in the briny sweat of other men's faces. That the black man in Slavery shirks labor—aims to do as little as he can, and to do that little in the most slovenly manner—only proves that he is a man. Thackery says that all men are about as lazy as they can afford to be—and I do not claim that the Negro is an exception to this rule. He loves ease and abundance just as other peole love ease and abundance. If this is a crime, then all men are criminals, and the Negro no more than the rest.

Again, it is affirmed that the Negro, if emancipated, could not take care of himself. My answer to this is, let him have a fair chance to try it. For 200 years he has taken care of himself and his master in the bargain. I see no reason to believe that he could not take care, and very excellent care, of himself when having only himself to support. The case of the freed slaves in the British West Indies has already been dwelt upon in the course of these lectures, and facts, arguments, and statistics have been presented demonstrating beyond all controversy that the black man not only has the ability and the disposition to work, but knows well how to take care of his earnings. The country over which he has toiled as a slave is rapidly becoming his property—that freedom has made him both a better producer and a better consumer.

LIBERTY AN EXPERIMENT

It is one of the strangest and most humiliating triumphs of human selfishness and prejudice over human reason, that it leads men to look upon emancipation as an experiment, instead of being, as it is, the natural order of human relations. Slavery, and not Freedom, is the experiment; and to witness its horrible failure we have to open our eyes, not merely upon the blasted soil of Virginia and other Slave States, but upon a whole land brought to the verge of ruin.

We are asked if we would turn the slaves all loose. I answer, Yes. Why not? They are not wolves nor tigers, but men. They are endowed with reason—can decide upon questions of right and wrong, good and evil, benefits and injuries—and are therefore subjects of government precisely as other men are.

But would you have them stay here? Why should they not? What better is here than there? What class of people can show a better title to the land on which they live than the colored people of the South? They have watered the soil with their tears and enriched it with their blood, and tilled it with their hard hands during two centuries; they have leveled its forests, raked out the obstructions to the plow and hoe, reclaimed the swamps, and produced whatever has made it a goodly land to dwell in, and it would be a shame and a crime little inferior in enormity to Slavery itself if these natural owners of the Southern and Gulf States should be driven away from their country to make room for others—even if others could be obtained to fill their places.

But unjust and revolting to every right-minded and humane man as is this talk of the expatriation of the slaves, the offense is not more shocking than it is unwise. For a nation to drive away its laboring population is to commit political suicide. It is like cutting off one's right hand in order to work the better and to produce the more. To say that Negroes shall not live in the Southern States is like saying that the lands of the South shall be no longer cultivated. The cry has all along been, We must have Negroes to work in the South, for white men cannot stand the hot sun and the fell diseases of the rice swamp and the sugar plantation. Even the leaders of the rebellion made it one of their grievances that they could not get more Negroes, though from motives of policy they have now dropped this plank from their platform. No one doubts that the Gulf States mean to have more slaves from Africa just so soon as they shall get well settled in their independence. Again, why not allow the colored people of the South remain where they are? Will they occupy more room in freedom than slavery? If you could bear them as objects of your injustice, can they be more offensive as objects of your justice and your humanity? Why send them away? Who wants to take their places in the cotton field, in the rice swamp, and sugar fields, which they have tilled for ages? The whole scheme of colonization would be too absurd for discussion, but that the madness of the moment has drowned the voice of common sense as well as common justice.

There is a measure now before Congress duly reported from one of its Committees proposing, first, to make the Negroes leave the land of their birth, and secondly to pay the expense of their enforced removal. If such a measure can become a law, the nation is more deeply wicked than any Abolitionist has hitherto ventured to believe. It is a most mischievous and scandalous proposition, unworthy of any man not dead to the claims of every sentiment of honor and humanity. I predict that if it passes it will become like the Fugitive Slave law—it will die dead upon the statue book—having no other effect than to alarm the freed men of the South and disgrace the Congress by which it is passed.

Once free the slaves, and at once the motives which now require their expatriation will become too weak to breathe. In the single little State of Maryland, with climate and soil which invite the white laborer to its borders, there are at this moment nearly one hundred thousand free colored people. Now, notwithstanding that Maryland is a Slave State, and thus possesses a strong motive for getting rid of their free colored people, the better to hold her slaves—and notwithstanding the circumstances of climate and soil—that Slave State only a year or two ago voted down by a large majority of their people the inhuman and barbarous proposition concerning her free colored population.

The number of colored people now on this continent and in the adjacent islands cannot fall far below twenty millions. An attempt to remove them would be as vain as to bail out the ocean. The whole naval power of the United States could not remove the natural increase of our part of this population. Every fact in our circumstances here marks us as a permanent element of the American people. Mark the readiness with which we adapt ourselves to your civilization. You can take no step in any direction where the black man is not at your back or side. —Go to California and dig gold: the black man is there. Go to war with Mexico, and let your armies penetrate the very heart of the country, and the black man is there. Go down into the coast of North and South Carolina, and the black man is there, and there as your friend, to give you more important and more trustworthy information than you can find among all the loyal poor white trash you can scare up in that region. The Negro is sometimes compared with the Indian, and it is predicted that, like the Indian, he will die out before the onward progress of the Anglo-Saxon race. I have not the least apprehension at this point. In features and complexion, the Negro is more unlike the European than is his Mongolian brother. But the interior resemblance is greater than the exterior difference. The Indian wraps himself in gloom, and proudly glories in isolation—he retreats before the onward march of civilization. The humming of the honey bee warns him away from his hunting grounds. He sees the plowshare of civilization tossing up the bones of his venerated fathers, and he dies of a broken heart. Not so with the Negro. There is a vitality about him that seems alike invincible to hardship and cruelty. Work him, whip him, sell him, torment him, and he still lives, and clings to American civilization—an Uncle Tom in the Church, and an Uncle Ben on the Southern coast, to guide our Burnside expeditions.

My friends, the destiny of the colored American, however this mighty war shall terminate, is the destiny of America. We shall never leave you. The allotments of Providence seem to make the black man of America the open book out of which the American people are to learn lessons of wisdom, power, and goodness—more sublime and glorious than any yet attained by the nations of the old or the new world. Over the bleeding back of the American bondman we shall learn mercy. In the very extreme difference of color and features of the Negro and the Anglo-Saxon, shall be learned the highest ideas of the sacredness of man and the fullness and perfection of human brotherhood.

Throughout the delivery of his address, Mr. Douglass was interrupted with most hearty and enthusiastic applause.—Ed.

Educating the Freedmen of the Sea Islands

Life on the Sea Islands

CHARLOTTE FORTEN

When Northern troops, anxious to blockade the harbor at Charleston, South Carolina, captured Port Royal in the Sea Islands late in 1861, the first major attempt of the war to aid the freedmen got under way. There were about ten thousand "contraband" in the area, and their previous isolation made them perhaps the most un-Americanized of all the slaves in the South. For several years, a serious effort was made to "civilize" the former slaves. New agricultural methods were introduced, schools were established, and troops were recruited. The famous First South Carolina Volunteers, who fought under the leadership of Thomas Wentworth Higginson, a white Boston abolitionist, were from Port Royal.

Charlotte Forten was the granddaughter and daughter of wealthy free blacks from Philadelphia. She lived for a time with the family of the fiery Charles L. Remond in Salem, Massachusetts. When the call for teachers at Port Royal went out, Miss Forten volunteered. She reached the island late in 1862, determined to prove that the blacks were as capable of self-improvement as were whites. The selection that follows is taken from two articles compiled from letters written by Miss Forten to the poet John Greenleaf Whittier, her good friend, who sent them to the Atlantic Monthly *for publication.*

The next morning L. and I were awakened by the cheerful voices of men and women, children and chickens, in the yard below. We ran to the window, and looked out. Women in bright-colored handkerchiefs, some carrying pails on their heads, were crossing the yard, busy with their morning work; children were playing and tumbling around them. On every face there was a look of serenity and cheerfulness. My heart gave a great throb of happiness as I looked at them, and thought, "They are free! so long downtrodden, so long crushed to the earth, but now in their old homes, forever free!" And I thanked God that I had lived to see this day.

After breakfast Miss T. drove us to Oaklands, our future home. The road leading to the house was nearly choked with weeds. The house itself was in a dilapidated condition, and the yard and garden had a sadly neglected look. But

---

FROM Charlotte Forten, "Life on the Sea Islands," *Atlantic Monthly*, vol. 13 (May and June 1864), pp. 588–89, 591–94, 666–67.

there were roses in bloom; we plucked handfuls of feathery, fragrant acacia-
blossoms; ivy crept along the ground and under the house. The freed people
on the place seemed glad to see us. After talking with them, and giving some
directions for cleaning the house, we drove to the school, in which I was to
teach. It is kept in the Baptist Church, —a brick building, beautifully situated
in a grove of live-oaks. These trees are the first objects that attract one's attention here: not that they are finer than our Northern oaks, but because of the
singular gray moss with which every branch is heavily draped. This hanging
moss grows on nearly all the trees, but on none so luxuriantly as on the live-
oak. The pendants are often four or five feet long, very graceful and beautiful,
but giving the trees a solemn, almost funereal look. The school was opened in
September. Many of the children had, however, received instruction during
the summer. It was evident that they had made very rapid improvement, and
we noticed with pleasure how bright and eager to learn many of them
seemed. They sang in rich, sweet tones, and with a peculiar swaying motion of
the body, which made their singing the more effective. They sang "Marching
Along," with great spirit, and then one of their own hymns, the air of which
is beautiful and touching: —

> "My sister, you want to git religion,
>   Go down in de Lonesome Valley;
> My brudder, you want to git religion,
>   Go down in de Lonesome Valley.

> CHORUS
> "Go down in de Lonesome Valley,
> Go down in de Lonesome Valley, my Lord,
> Go down in de Lonesome Valley,
>   To meet my Jesus dere!

> "Oh, feed on milk and honey, my Lord,
> Oh, feed on milk and honey,
> Oh, feed on milk and honey,
>   To meet my Jesus dere!

> "Oh, John he brought a letter,
> Oh, John he brought a letter, my Lord,
> Oh, Mary and Marta read 'em,
>   Meet my Jesus dere!"

> CHORUS
> "Go down in de Lonesome Valley," etc.

They repeat their hymns several times, and while singing keep perfect time
with their hands and feet.

The Sunday after our arrival we attended service at the Baptist Church. The people came in slowly; for they have no way of knowing the hour, except by the sun. By eleven they had all assembled, and the church was well filled. They were neatly dressed in their Sunday attire, the women mostly wearing clean, dark frocks, with white aprons and bright-colored head-handkerchiefs. Some had attained to the dignity of straw hats with gay feathers, but these were not nearly as becoming nor as picturesque as the handkerchiefs. The day was warm, and the windows were thrown open as if it were summer, although it was the second day of November. It was very pleasant to listen to the beautiful hymns, and look from the crowd of dark, earnest faces within, upon the grove of noble oaks without. The people sang, "Roll, Jordan, roll," the grandest of all their hymns. There is a great, rolling wave of sound through it all.

> "Mr. Fuller settin' on de Tree ob Life,
> Fur to hear de ven Jordan roll.
> Oh, roll, Jordan! roll, Jordan! roll, Jordan, roll!
>
> CHORUS
> "Oh, roll, Jordan, roll! oh, roll, Jordan, roll!
> My soul arise in heab'n, Lord,
> Fur to hear de ven Jordan roll!
>
> "Little chil'en, learn to fear de Lord,
> And let your days be long.
> Oh, roll, Jordan! roll, Jordan! roll, Jordan, roll!
>
> CHORUS
> "Oh, march, de angel, march! oh, march, de angel, march!
> My soul arise in heab'n, Lord,
> Fur to hear de ven Jordan roll!"

The "Mr. Fuller" referred to was their former minister, to whom they seem to have been much attached. He is a Southerner, but loyal, and is now, I believe, living in Baltimore. After the sermon the minister called upon one of the elders, a gray-headed old man, to pray. His manner was very fervent and impressive, but his language was so broken that to our unaccustomed ears it was quite unintelligible. After the services the people gathered in groups outside, talking among themselves, and exchanging kindly greetings with the superintendents and teachers. In their bright handkerchiefs and white aprons they made a striking picture under the gray-mossed trees. We drove afterward a mile farther, to the Episcopal Church, in which the aristocracy of the island used to worship. It is a small white building, situated in a fine grove of live-oaks, at the junction of several roads. On one of the tombstones in the yard is the touching inscription in memory of two children, —"Blessed little lambs, and *art thou* gathered into the fold of the only true shepherd? Sweet *lillies* of the valley, and *art thou* removed to a more congenial soil?" The floor of the church is of stone, the pews of polished oak. It has an organ, which is not so entirely out of tune as are the pianos on the island. One of the ladies played, while the gentlemen sang, —old-fashioned New-England church-music, which it was pleasant to hear, but it did not thrill us as the singing of the people had done.

The first day at school was rather trying. Most of my children were very small, and consequently restless. Some were too young to learn the alphabet. These little ones were brought to school because the older children—in whose care their parents leave them while at work—could not come without them. We were therefore willing to have them come, although they seemed to have discovered the secret of perpetual motion, and tried one's patience sadly. But after some days of positive, though not severe treatment, order was brought out of chaos, and I found but little difficulty in managing and quieting the tiniest and most restless spirits. I never before saw children so eager to learn, although I had had several years' experience in New-England schools. Coming to school is a constant delight and recreation to them. They come here as other children go to play. The older ones, during the summer, work in the fields from early morning until eleven or twelve o'clock, and then come into school, after their hard toil in the hot sun, as bright and as anxious to learn as ever.

Of course there are some stupid ones, but these are the minority. The majority learn with wonderful rapidity. Many of the grown people are desirous of learning to read. It is wonderful how a people who have been so long crushed to the earth, so imbruted as these have been,—and they are said to be among the most degraded negroes of the South,—can have so great a desire for knowledge, and such a capability for attaining it. One cannot believe that the haughty Anglo-Saxon race, after centuries of such an experience as these people have had, would be very much superior to them. And one's indignation increases against those who, North as well as South, taunt the colored race with inferiority while they themselves use every means in their power to crush and degrade them, denying them every right and privilege, closing against them every avenue of elevation and improvement. Were they, under such circumstances, intellectual and refined, they would certainly be vastly superior to any other race that ever existed.

After the lessons, we used to talk freely to the children, often giving them slight sketches of some of the great and good men. Before teaching them the "John Brown" song, which they learned to sing with great spirit, Miss T. told them the story of the brave old man who had died for them. I told them about Toussaint, thinking it well they should know what one of their own color had done for his race. They listened attentively, and seemed to understand. We found it rather hard to keep their attention in school. It is not strange, as they have been so entirely unused to intellectual concentration. It is necessary to interest them every moment, in order to keep their thoughts from wandering. Teaching here is consequently far more fatiguing than at the North. In the church, we had of course but one room in which to hear all the children; and to make one's self heard, When there were often as many as a hundred and forty reciting at once, it was necessary to tax the lungs very severely.

My walk to school, of about a mile, was part of the way through a road lined with trees,—on one side stately pines, on the other noble live-oaks, hung with moss and canopied with vines. The ground was carpeted with brown, fragrant pine-leaves; and as I passed through in the morning, the woods were enlivened by the delicious songs of mocking-birds, which abound here, making one realize the truthful felicity of the description in "Evangeline," —

"The mocking-bird, wildest of singers,
Shook from his little throat such floods of delirious music
That the whole air and the woods and the waves seemed silent to listen."

The hedges were all aglow with the brilliant scarlet berries of the cassena, and on some of the oaks we observed the mistletoe, laden with its pure white, pearl-like berries. Out of the woods the roads are generally bad, and we found it hard work plodding through the deep sand.

Harry, the foreman on the plantation, a man of a good deal of natural intelligence, was most desirous of learning to read. He came in at night to be taught, and learned very rapidly. I never saw any one more determined to learn. We enjoyed hearing him talk about the "gun-shoot,"—so the people call the capture of Bay Point and Hilton Head. They never weary of telling you "how Massa run when he hear de fust gun."

"Why did n't you go with him, Harry?" I asked.

"Oh, Miss, 't was n't 'cause Massa did n't try to 'suade me. He tell we dat de Yankees would shoot we, or would sell we to Cuba, an' do all de wust tings to we, when dey come, 'Berry well, Sar,' says I. 'If I go wid you, I be good as dead. If I stay here, I can't be no wust; so if I got to dead, I might's well dead here as anywhere. So I'll stay here an' wait for de "dam Yankees."' Lor', Miss, I knowed he was n't tellin' de truth all de time."

"But why did n't you believe him, Harry?"

"Dunno, Miss; somehow we hear de Yankees was our friends, an' dat we'd be free when dey come, an' 'pears like we believe *dat.*"

I found this to be true of nearly all the people I talked with, and I thought it strange they should have had so much faith in the Northerners. Truly, for years past, they had had but little cause to think them very friendly. Cupid told us that his master was so daring as to come back, after he had fled from the island, at the risk of being taken prisoner by our soldiers; and that he ordered the people to get all the furniture together and take it to a plantation on the opposite side of the creek, and to stay on that side themselves. "So," said Cupid, "dey could jus' sweep us all up in a heap, an' put us in de boat. An' he telled me to take Patience—dat's my wife—an' de chil'en down to a certain pint, an' den I could come back, if I choose. Jus' as if I was gwine to be sich a goat!" added he, with a look and gesture of ineffable contempt. He and the rest of the people, instead of obeying their master, left the place and hid themselves in the woods; and when he came to look for them, not one of all his "faithful servants" was to be found. A few, principally house-servants, had previously been carried away.

In the evenings, the children frequently came in to sing and shout for us. These "shouts" are very strange, —in truth, almost indescribable. It is necessary to hear and see in order to have any clear idea of them. The children form a ring, and move around in a kind of shuffling dance, singing all the time. Four or five stand apart, and sing very energetically, clapping their hands, stamping their feet, and rocking their bodies to and fro. These are the musicians, to whose performance the shouters keep perfect time. The grown people on this plantation did not shout, but they do on some of the other plantations. It is very comical to see little children, not more than three or four years old, entering into the performance with all their might. But the shouting of the grown people is rather solemn and impressive otherwise. We cannot determine whether it has a religious character or not. Some of the people tell us that it has, others that it has not. But as the shouts of the grown people are always in connection with their religious meetings, it is probable that they are the barbarous expression of religion, handed down to them from their African ancestors, and destined to pass away under the influence of Christian teachings. The people on this island have no songs. They sing only hymns, and most of these are sad. Prince, a large black boy from a neighboring plantation, was the principal shouter among the children. It seemed impossible for him to keep still for a moment. His performances were most amusing specimens of Ethiopian gymnastics. Amaretta the younger, a cunning, kittenish little creature of only six years old, had a remarkably sweet voice. Her favorite hymn, which we used to hear her singing to herself as she walked through the yard, is one of the oddest we have heard: —

"What makes ole Satan follow me so?
Satan got nuttin' 't all fur to do wid me.

CHORUS
"Tiddy Rosa, hold your light!
Brudder Tony, hold your light!
All de member, hold bright light
On Canaan's shore!"

This is one of the most spirited shouting-tunes. "Tiddy" is their word for sister.

A very queer-looking old man came into the store one day. He was dressed in a complete suit of brilliant Brussels carpeting. Probably it had been taken from his master's house after the "gun-shoot"; but he looked so very dignified that we did not like to question him about it. The people called him Doctor Crofts,—which was, I believe, his master's name, his own being Scipio. He was very jubilant over the new state of things, and said to Mr. H., —"Don't hab me feelins hurt now. Used to hab me feelins hurt all de time. But don't hab 'em hurt now no more." Poor old soul! We rejoiced with him that he and his brethren no longer have their "feelins" hurt, as in the old time.

A few days before Christmas, we were delighted at receiving a beautiful Christmas Hymn from Whittier, written by request, especially for our children. They learned it very easily, and enjoyed singing it. We showed them the writer's picture, and told them he was a very good friend of theirs, who felt the deepest interest in them, and had written this hymn expressly for them to sing,—which made them very proud and happy. Early Christmas morning, we were wakened by the people knocking at the doors and windows, and shouting, "Merry Christmas!" After distributing some little presents among them, we went to the church, which had been decorated with holly, pine, cassena, mistletoe, and the hanging moss, and had a very Christmas-like look. The children of our school assembled there, and we gave them the nice, comfortable clothing, and the picture-books, which had been kindly sent by some Philadelphia ladies. There were at least a hundred and fifty children present. It was very pleasant to see their happy, expectant little faces. To them, it was a wonderful Christmas-Day, —such as they had never dreamed of before. There was cheerful sunshine without, lighting up the beautiful moss-drapery of the oaks, and looking in joyously through the open windows; and there were bright faces and glad hearts within. The long, dark night of the Past, with all its sorrows and its fears, was forgotten; and for the Future, —the eyes of these freed children see no clouds in it. It is full of sunlight, they think, and they trust in it, perfectly.

After the distribution of the gifts, the children were addressed by some of the gentlemen present. They then sang Whittier's Hymn, the "John Brown" song, and several of their own hymns, among them a very singular one, commencing, —

> "I wonder where my mudder gone;
> Sing, O graveyard!
> Graveyard ought to know me;
> Ring, Jerusalem!
> Grass grow in de graveyard;
> Sing, O graveyard!
> Graveyard ought to know me;
> Ring, Jerusalem!"

They improvise many more words as they sing. It is one of the strangest, most mournful things I ever heard. It is impossible to give any idea of the deep pathos of the refrain, —

> "Sing, O graveyard!"

In this, and many other hymns, the words seem to have but little meaning; but the tones,—a whole lifetime of despairing sadness is concentrated in them. They sing, also, "Jehovyah, Hallelujah," which we like particularly: —

"De foxes hab holes,
An' de birdies hab nes',
But de Son ob Man he hab not where
To lay de weary head.

CHORUS
"Jehovyah, Hallelujah! De Lord He will purvide!
Jehovyah, Hallelujah! De Lord He will purvide!"

They repeat the words many times. "De foxes hab holes," and the succeeding lines, are sung in the most touching, mournful tones; and then the chorus
—"Jehovyah, Hallelujah"—swells forth triumphantly, in glad contrast.

Christmas night, the children came in and had several grand shouts. They
were too happy to keep still.

"Oh, Miss, all I want to do is to sing and shout!" said our little pet,
Amaretta. And sing and shout she did, to her heart's content.

She read nicely, and was very fond of books. The tiniest children are
delighted to get a book in their hands. Many of them already know their letters. The parents are eager to have them learn. They sometimes said to me, —

"Do, Miss, let de chil'en learn everyting dey can. We nebber hab no chance
to learn nuttin', but we wants de chil'en to learn."

They are willing to make many sacrifices that. their children may attend
school. One old woman, who had a large family of children and grandchil-
dren, came regularly to school in the winter, and took her seat among the little ones. She was at least sixty years old. Another woman—who had one of the
best faces I ever saw—came daily, and brought her baby in her arms. It happened to be one of the best babies in the world, a perfect little "model of
deportment," and allowed its mother to pursue her studies without interrup-
tion.

Debate on Compulsory Free Public Education for All

A Record of Proceedings at the Constitutional Convention of South Carolina, 1868

Historians have often misconstrued Reconstruction as an era in which illiterate blacks, aided by white carpetbaggers, rode roughshod over the rights of the native white population of the South. Recently, however, it has become clear that blacks played the same kinds of roles in Reconstruction politics as did whites—some good and some, unfortunately, bad.

Seventy-four black men, a majority of the total delegates, participated in the South Carolina Constitutional Convention of 1868. Fourteen of these were from the North; sixty were from the South, and of these, thirty-eight were former slaves. The constitution they wrote was the most progressive to date in the South.

The except that follows is a transcription of a debate that took place during the convention over whether school attendance should be compulsory. It aptly illustrates many of the concerns of Southern blacks of the time—formerly free or formerly slave. Of the participants in the portion of the debate reprinted here, Leslie, Duncan, and Holmes were white; all others were black. The chairman of the education committee that drew up the proposal under discussion was F. L. Cardozo, a free black educated at Glasgow and London who had returned to the South to teach school.

As can be seen from the passage, the split on the issue was not along racial lines. Both blacks and whites opposed the idea, but for different reasons. Ultimately, the South Carolina Constitution did include a provision for compulsory, nonsegregated schools. Neither aspect of this provision, however, was put into effect by the political authorities of the state.

Mr. R. C. De Large: Although laboring under great inconvenience, I shall attempt to defend the amendment proposing to strike out the word "compulsory." In the first place, we have a report which is to become a portion of the Constitution, and that Constitution emphatically declares, in terms that cannot be misunderstood, that "no distinction shall be made on account of race, color, or previous condition." It has been remarked this morning that in the Constitution of Massachusetts, and other Northern States, the same proviso exists. But any one who reflects for a moment upon the condition of the people of Massachusetts, and those of South Carolina, will fully appreciate the great difference between them. As already stated, I object to the word "compulsory," because it is contrary to the spirit and principles of

FROM *Proceedings of the Constitutional Convention of South Carolina* (Charleston, 1868), pp 686–94.

republicanism. Where is the necessity for placing in the Constitution a proviso that can never be enforced. It is just as impossible to put such a section in practical operation, as it would be for a man to fly to the moon. No one will deny that an attempt to enforce it would entail the greatest trouble and expense. Who, I ask, do we propose to set up as a censor of learning? Perhaps the opponents of the measure will say the School Commissioner. I deny that he can do it. He may be the father of half a dozen children. I, too, am the father of children; but will any body tell me that, as a free citizen of South Carolina, I have not the right to choose whether I shall send those children to school or not. Will any one say I shall not teach my child myself? It may be said, such a right is not denied me. Whether it be so or not, I plant myself upon the broad principle of the equality of all men as the basis of true republicanism; and to compel any man to do what this section provides is contrary to this principle.

Again, this clause will lead to difficulties of a serious character, to which neither you nor myself can blind our eyes. In Massachusetts there is a population cradled in the arms of freedom and liberty, free of all prejudice and devoid of passion, to a great extent. In South Carolina we have an entirely different set of people. We are about to inaugurate great changes, which it is our desire shall be successful.

Mr. C. P. Leslie: Do I understand you to say that the people of Massachusetts have no prejudices of race?

Mr. F. L. Cardozo: I would also like to ask the gentleman where he gets his authority for saying that the people of Massachusetts are cradled in the principles of freedom and liberty. Is it so provided in the Constitution of Massachusetts?

Mr. R. C. De Large: I am not well acquainted with all the clauses in the Constitution of Massachusetts, and speak only from my historic knowledge of that people. This section proposes to open these schools to all persons, irrespective of color, to open every seminary of learning to all. Heartily do I endorse the object, but the manner in which it is to be enforced meets my most earnest disapproval. I do not propose to enact in this report a section that may be used by our enemies to appeal to the worst passions of a class of people in this State. The schools may be opened to all, under proper provisions in the Constitution, but to declare that parents "shall" send their children to them whether they are willing or not is, in my judgment, going a step beyond the bounds of prudence. Is there any logic or reason in inserting in the Constitution a provision which cannot be enforced? What do we intend to give the Legislature power to do? In one breath you propose to protect minor children, and in the next to punish their parents by fine and imprisonment if they do not send their children to school. For these reasons I am opposed to the section, and urge that the word "compulsory" shall be stricken out.

Mr. A. J. Ransier: I am sorry to differ with my colleague from Charleston on this question. I contend that in proportion to the education of the people so is their progress in civilization. Believing this, I believe that the Committee have properly provided for the compulsory education of all the children in this State between the ages named in the section.

I recognize the importance of this measure. There is a seeming objection to the word "compulsory," but I do not think it of grave importance. My friend does not like it, because he says it is contrary to the spirit of republicanism. To be free, however, is not to enjoy unlimited license, or my friend himself might desire to enslave again his fellow men.

Now I propose to support this section fully, and believe that the more it is considered in all its bearings upon the welfare of our people, the greater will be the desire that every parent shall, by some means, be compelled to educate his children and fit them for the responsibilities of life. As to the particular mode of enforcing attendance at school, we leave that an open question. At present we are only asserting the general principle, and the Legislature will provide for its application.

Upon the success of republicanism depends the progress which our people are destined to make. If parents are disposed to clog this progress by neglecting the education of their children, for one, I will not aid and abet them. Hence, this, in my opinion, is an exceedingly wise provision, and I am content to trust to the Legislature to carry out the measures to which it necessarily leads.

Vice and degradation go hand in hand with ignorance. Civilization and enlightenment follow fast upon the footsteps of the schoolmaster; and if education must be enforced to secure these grand results, I say let the compulsory process go on.

Mr. R. C. De Large: Can the gentleman demonstrate how the Legislature is to enforce the education of children without punishment of their parents by fine or imprisonment.

Mr. A. J. Ransier: When that question arises in the Legislature, I hope we shall have the benefit of my friend's counsel, and he himself may possibly answer that question. If there is any one thing to which we may attribute the sufferings endured by this people, it is the gross ignorance of the masses. While we propose to avoid all difficulties which may be fraught with evil to the community, we shall, nevertheless, insist upon our right to provide for the exercise of the great moral agencies which education always brings to bear upon public opinion. Had there been such a provision as this in the Constitution of South Carolina heretofore, there is no doubt that many of the evils which at present exist would have been avoided, and the people would have been advanced to a higher stage of civilization and morals, and we would not have been called upon to mourn the loss of the flower of the youth of our country. In conclusion, I favor this section as it stands. I do not think it will militate against the cause of republicanism, but, on the contrary, be of benefit both to it and to the people whom we represent. Feeling that everything depends on the education of the rising generation, I shall give this measure my vote, and use all my exertions to secure its adoption into this Constitution.

Mr. B. F. Randolph: In favoring, as I do, compulsory attendance at school, I cannot for the life of me see in what manner republicanism is at stake. It seems to have been the fashion on this floor to question a man's republicanism because he chooses to differ with others on general principles. Now this is a question which does not concern republicanism at all. It is simply a matter of justice which is due to a people, and it might be just as consistently urged that it is contrary to republican principles to organize the militia, to force every man to enroll his name, and to arm and equip them, as to urge that this provision is anti-republican because it compels parents to see to the education of their children.

Mr. B. O. Duncan: Does the gentleman propose to educate children at the point of the bayonet, through the militia?

Mr. B. F. Randolph: If necessary we may call out the militia to enforce the law. Now, the gentlemen on the other side have given no reasons why the word "compulsory" should be stricken out.

Mr. R. C. De Large: Can you name any State where the provision exists in its Constitution?

Mr. B. F. Randolph: It exists in Massachusetts.

Mr. R. C. De Large: That is not so.

Mr. F. L. Cardozo: This system has been tested in Germany, and I defy the gentleman from Charleston to deny the fact. It has also been tested in several States of the Union, and I defy the gentleman to show that it has not been a success. It becomes the duty of the opposition if they want this section stricken from the report, to show that where it has been applied it has failed to produce the result desired.

Mr. J. J. Wright: Will you inform us what State in the Union compels parents to send their children to school?

Mr. B. F. Randolph: The State of New Hampshire is one. It may be asked what is the object of law? It is not only for the purpose of restraining men from doing wrong, but for the protection of all the citizens of a State, and the promotion of the general welfare. Blackstone lays it down as one of the objects, the furthering, as far as it can consistently be done, of the general welfare of the people. It is one of the objects of law, as far as practicable, not to restrain wrong by punishing man for violating the right, but also one of its grand objects to build up civilization, and this is the grand object of this provision in the report of the Committee on Education. It proposes to further civilization, and I look upon it as one of the most important results which will follow the defeat of the rebel armies, the establishment among the people who have long been deprived of the privilege of education, a law which will compel parents to send their children to school.

Mr. R. B. Elliott: Is it not regulated by general statutes in the State of Massachusetts, that parents shall be compelled to send their children to school?

Mr. B. F. Randolph: We propose to do that here. I consider this one of the most important measures which has yet come before this body. I think I can read it in the eyes of the members of this Convention to favor this measure. I feel that every one here believes it to be his duty to the people he represents. I believe every one here is zealous in doing all he can to further civilization, in building up educational institutions in the State, and doing all that is calculated to diffuse intelligence among the people generally. I had the honor of being principal of a free school two years; and, in the midst of one of the most intelligent systems of schools, the most trying thing which teachers had to contend with was the want of regular attendance on the part of the children. The most intelligent parents would sometimes neglect to send their children to school. The teachers had to adopt rules closing their doors to those who were irregular in their attendance. This law will assist the teachers and assist our school system. It will prove beneficial to the State not only for the reasons I have given, but for various other reasons. I hope you will all vote for it. I shall vote for it with all my heart, because I believe it to be something beneficial to the welfare of the people of the State.

Mr. A. C. Richmond: I desire to say but a few words on this subject. I shall speak principally in reference to our common schools and public funds. We expect to have a public school fund, although it may not be very large. We expect our parishes to be divided into school districts of convenient size. We can erect only a limited number of school houses each year, and it may be five or ten years before school houses are erected in all the districts, and the fund becomes large enough to assist in the education of all the people. If the word "compulsory" remains, it will be impossible to enforce the law for sometime to come. We say the public schools shall be opened to all. Every school district will have its school houses and its teachers. There is to be a particular school fund, school districts, and school houses. It is supposed by legislators and others that it is an excellent thing to have the children to go to school. It opens up a vast field for discussion, and affords a beautiful opportunity for making buncombe speeches. It is admitted by all legislators in every State of the Union, that cheap education is the best defense of the State. There must be schools to which colored children can go; but we wish to look into the propriety of compelling parents to send their children to school. I believe the efforts of the teachers, preachers, and all those interested in the welfare of the State, and the efforts of all those interested in the welfare of the colored people, will bring out nearly all the colored children. I believe nearly all the colored children of the State will go to school. We have societies that will help to furnish the books; we have preachers who are much interested; we have missionaries, all of whom are interested in this class of our people, and who will see to it that the colored children are educated, so that settles that point. The next point is, how are the white children going to school? By means of moral suasion nearly all the colored children will be brought to school; and by means of white schools, nearly all white children will go to school and be educated. It will regulate itself. The word "compulsory" is used to compel the attendance of children in one or the other class of schools.

Mr. R. C. De Large: What does the tenth section of that report say?

Mr. A. C. Richmond: I believe it is the meaning, that if families of white people are not able to send their children to private schools, they shall be obliged to send their children to the public schools, in which all white and colored shall be educated.

Mr. F. L. Cardozo: We only compel parents to send their children to some school, not that they shall send them with the colored children; we simply give those colored children who desire to go to white schools, the privilege to do so.

Mr. A. C. Richmond: By means of moral suasion, I believe nearly all the colored people, as well as a large number of the children of white parents will go to school; such schools as their parents may select. If parents are too proud to take advantage of the means of education afforded, why then I say let their children grow up in ignorance.

Mr. J. A. Chestnut: So far as I have been able to see and judge, this report of the Committee is a sensible one, and ought to be adopted as it stands. How it can affect the rights of the people, or interfere with the spirit of republicanism, I am at a loss to discover. On the contrary, from all the experience I have had among the people, I unhesitatingly declare that no measure adopted by this Convention will be more in consonance with their wishes than this, or more productive of material blessings to all classes. Sir, you cannot by any persuasive and reasonable means establish civilization among an ignorant and degraded community, such as we have in our country. Force is necessary, and, for one, I say let force be used. Republicanism has given us freedom, equal rights, and equal laws. Republicanism must also give us education and wisdom.

It seems that the great difficulty in this section is in the fact that difficulty may arise between the two races in the same school, or that the whites will not send their children to the same schools with the colored children. What of that? Has not this Convention a right to establish a free school system for the benefit of the poorer classes? Undoubtedly. Then if there be a hostile disposition among the whites, an unwillingness to send their children to school, the fault is their own, not ours. Look at the idle youths around us. Is the sight not enough to invigorate every man with a desire to do something to remove this vast weight of ignorance that presses the masses down? I have no desire to curtail the privileges of freemen, but when we look at the opportunities neglected, even by the whites of South Carolina, I must confess that I am more than ever disposed to compel parents, especially of my own race, to send their children to school. If the whites object to it, let it be so. The consequences will rest with themselves.

I hope, therefore, that the motion to strike out the word "compulsory" will be laid upon the table.

Mr. R. H. Cain: It seems to me that we are spending a great deal of unnecessary time in the discussion of this subject. It is true, the question is one of great interest, and there are few who are not anxious that provisions shall be made by this Convention for the education of all classes in the State. But I am confident that it will not be necessary to use compulsion to effect this object. Hence, I am opposed to the insertion of the obnoxious word. I see no necessity for it. You cannot compel parents to send their children to school; and if you could, it would be unwise, impolitic, and injudicious. Massachusetts is fifty years ahead of South Carolina, and, under the circumstances which exist in that State, I might, if a resident, insist upon a compulsory education; but in South Carolina the case is different. There is a class of persons here whose situation, interests and necessities are varied, and controlled by surroundings which do not exist at the North. And justice is demanded for them. To do justice in this matter of education, compulsion is not required. I am willing to trust the people. They have good sense, and experience itself will be better than all the force you can employ to instill the idea of duty to their children.

Now, as a compromise with the other side, I propose the following amendment, namely that "the General Assembly may require the attendance at either public or private schools," &c.

This is a question that should be left to the Legislature. If the circumstances demand it, compulsion may be used to secure the attendance of pupils; but I do not believe such a contingency ever will occur.

As to the idea that both classes of children will be compelled to go to school together, I do not think it is comprehended in the subject at all. I remember that in my younger days I stumped the State of Iowa for the purpose of having stricken from the Constitution a clause which created distinction of color in the public schools. This was prior to the assembling of the Constitutional Convention. All we claimed was that they should make provision for the education of all the youth. We succeeded, and such a clause was engrafted in the Constitution, and that instrument was ratified by a majority of ten thousand. We said nothing about color. We simply said "youth."

I say to you, therefore, leave this question open. Leave it to the Legislature. I have great faith in humanity. We are in a stage of progress, such as our country never has seen, and while the wheels are rolling on, depend upon it, there are few persons in this country who will not seek to enjoy it by sending their children to school. White or black, all will desire to have their children educated. Let us then make this platform broad enough for all to stand upon without prejudice or objection. The matter will regulate itself, and to the Legislature may safely be confided the task of providing for any emergency which may arise.

Mr. R. G. Holmes: If there is anything we want in this State, it is some measure to compel the attendance of children between the ages of six and sixteen at some school. If it is left to parents, I believe the great majority will lock up their children at home. I hope, therefore, we shall have a law compelling the attendance of all children at school. It is the statute law in Massachusetts, and I hope we will have the provision inserted in our Constitution. The idea that it is not republican to educate children is supremely ridiculous. Republicanism, as has been well said, is not license. No man has the right, as a republican, to put his hand in my pocket, or steal money from it, because he wishes to do it. I can conceive of a way in which my child may be robbed by that system of republicanism which some members have undertaken to defend. My child may be left an orphan, poor and dependent on the kindness of neighbors or friends. They may think it to the best interest of that child to bind it out as an apprentice to some person. My child may be robbed of an education, because the person to whom it was bound does not think it advisable to send that child to school, as there may happen to be some objectionable children in the school. I have seen white children sitting by the side of colored children in school, and observed that there could not have been better friends. I do not want this privilege of attending schools confined to any exclusive class. We want no laws made here to prevent children from attending school. If any one chooses to educate their children in a private school, this law does not debar them that privilege.

But there are some who oppose all education. I remember the case of an individual who refused to have his children educated because, as he said, he himself had got along well enough without it, and he guessed his children could do the same. There is too much of that spirit in our State, and we want to contrive something to counteract it. In the case to which I have alluded, that individual some fifteen years afterwards, when his children had grown up, regretted his action, and was very much mortified because his children had no education. I hope we will engraft something into the Constitution, making it obligatory upon parents to send their children to school, and with that view, I hope the section will pass as it is.

Discrimination in
Mississippi Elections

Address to the United States Senate, 1876

BLANCHE K. BRUCE

Two black men served in the Senate during the Reconstruction period—both, oddly enough, from Mississippi. The first, Hiram Revels, was a free black born in North Carolina. He left the South to study at Knox College in Illinois and then worked in Missouri as an educator and a minister of the African Methodist Episcopal Church. Finally, he settled in Natchez, Mississippi, where he was persuaded to enter politics. In 1870 he was chosen to fill the seat vacated by Jefferson Davis in 1861, when Mississippi seceded from the Union.

The second, Blanche K. Bruce, was an exceedingly skillful politician and the only Mississippi black ever elected to a full term in the Senate. Born a slave in Virginia, he was chosen by his master—who may have been also his father—to be educated by a private tutor. When freed at the end of the Civil War, Bruce organized the first school for blacks in Missouri. Later, he moved to Mississippi and, after making a fortune as a planter, entered politics. In 1874, he was elected to the U. S. Senate, where he served with distinction. After completing his term in the Senate, he filled various appointive positions in Washington until his death.

Bruce made the following speech to the Senate in 1876. In it, he gives some of the details of the discrimination suffered by Mississippi freedmen in the elections of 1875 and offers some suggestions for the solution of the race problem in Mississippi.

Mr. Bruce. Mr. President, I had hoped that no occasion would arise to make it necessary for me again to claim the attention of the Senate until at least I had acquired a larger acquaintance with its methods of business and a fuller experience in public affairs; but silence at this time would be infidelity to my senatorial trust and unjust to both the people and the State I have the honor in part to represent.

The conduct of the late election in Mississippi affected not merely the fortunes of partisans—as the same were necessarily involved in the defeat or success of the respective parties to the contest—but put in question and jeopardy the sacred rights of the citizens; and the investigation contemplated in the pending resolution has for its object not the determination of the question

FROM Blanche K. Bruce, *Congressional Record*, 44th Congress, 1st Session (March 31, 1876), pp. 2101–04.

whether the offices shall be held and the public affairs of that State be administered by democrats or republicans, but the higher and more important end, the protection in all their purity and significance of the political right of the people and the free institutions of the country. I believe the action sought is within the legitimate province of the Senate; but I shall waive a discussion of that phase of the question, and address myself to the consideration of the importance of the proposed investigation.

The demand of the substitute of the Senator from Michigan proceeds upon the allegation that fraud and intimidation were practiced by the opposition in the late State election, so as not only to deprive many citizens of their political rights, but so far as practically to have defeated a fair expression of the will of a majority of the legal voters of the State of Mississippi, resulting in placing in power many men who do not represent the popular will.

The truth of the allegations relative to fraud and violence is strongly suggested by the very success claimed by the democracy. In 1872 the republicans carried the State by 20,000 majority; in November last the opposition claimed to have carried it by 30,000; thus a democratic gain of more than 50,000. Now, by what miraculous or extraordinary interposition was this brought about? I can conceive that a large State like New York, where free speech and free press operate upon intelligent masses—a State full of railroads, telegraphs, and newspapers—on the occasion of a great national contest, might furnish an illustration of such a thorough and general change in the political views of the people; but such a change of front is unnatural and highly improbable in a State like my own, with few railroads, and a widely scattered and sparse population. Under the most active and friendly canvass the voting masses could not have been so rapidly and thoroughly reached as to have rendered this result probable.

There was nothing in the character of the issues nor in the method of the canvass that would produce such an overwhelming revolution in the sentiments of the colored voters of the State as implied in this pretended democratic success. The republicans—nineteen-twentieths of whom are colored—were not brought, through the press or public discussions, in contact with democratic influences to such an extent as would operate a change in their political convictions, and there was nothing in democratic sentiments nor in the proscriptive and violent temper of their leaders to justify such a change of political relations.

The evil practices so naturally suggested by this view of the question as probable will be found in many instances by the proposed investigation to have been actual. Not desiring to anticipate the work of the committee nor to weary Senators with details, I instance the single county of Yazoo as illustrative of the effects of the outrages of which we complain. This country gave in 1873 a republican majority of nearly two thousand. It was cursed with riot and bloodshed prior to the late election, and gave but seven votes for the republican ticket, and some of these, I am credibly informed, were cast in derision by the democrats, who declared that republicans must have some votes in the county.

To illustrate the spirit that prevailed in that section, I read from the Yazoo Democrat, an influential paper published at its county seat:

> Let unanimity of sentiment pervade the minds of men. Let invincible determination be depicted on every countenance. Send forth from our deliberative assembly of the eighteenth the soul-stirring announcement that Mississippians shall rule Mississippi though the heavens fall. Then will woe, irretrievable woe, betide the radical tatterdemalions. Hit them hip and thigh, everywhere and at all times.
>
> Carry the election peaceably if we can, forcibly if we must.

Again:

> There is no radical ticket in the field, and it is more than likely there will be none; for the leaders are not in this city, and dare not press their claims in this county.

Speaking of the troubles in Madison County, the Yazoo City Democrat for the 26th of October says:

> Try the rope on such characters. It acts finely on such characters here.

The evidence in hand and accessible will show beyond peradventure that in many parts of the State corrupt and violent influences were brought to bear upon the registrars of voters, thus materially affecting the character of the voting or poll lists; upon the inspectors of election, prejudicially and unfairly thereby changing the number of votes cast; and, finally, threats and violence were practiced directly upon the masses of voters in such measure and strength as to produce grave apprehensions for their personal safety, and as to deter them from the exercise of their political franchises.

Lawless outbreaks have not been confined to any particular section of the country, but have prevailed in nearly every State at some period in its history. But the violence complained of and exhibited in Mississippi and other Southern States, pending a political canvass, is exceptional and peculiar. It is not the blow that the beggared miner strikes that he may give bread to his children, nor the stroke of the bondsman that he may win liberty for himself, nor the mad turbulence of the ignorant masses when their passions have been stirred by the appeals of the demagogue; but it is an attack by an aggressive, intelligent, white political organization upon inoffensive, law-abiding fellow-citizens; a violent method for political supremacy, that seeks not the protection of the rights of the aggressors, but the destruction of the rights of the party assailed. Violence so unprovoked, inspired by such motives, and looking to such ends, is a spectacle not only discreditable to the country, but dangerous to the integrity of our free institutions.

I beg Senators to believe that I refer to this painful and reproachful condition of affairs in my own State not in resentment, but with sentiments of profound regret and humiliation.

If honorable Senators ask why such flagrant wrongs were allowed to go unpunished by a republican State government, and unresented by a race claiming 20,000 majority of the voters, the answer is at hand. The civil officers of the State were unequal to meet and suppress the murderous violence that frequently broke out in different parts of the State, and the State executive found himself thrown for support upon a militia partially organized and poorly armed. When he attempted to perfect and call out this force and to use the very small appropriation that had been made for their equipment, he was met by the courts with an injunction against the use of the money, and by the proscriptive element of the opposition with such fierce outcry and show of counter-force, that he became convinced a civil strife, a war of races, would be precipitated unless he staid his hand. As a last resort, the protection provided in the national Constitution for a State threatened with domestic violence was sought; but the national Executive—from perhaps a scrupulous desire to avoid the appearance of interference by the Federal authority with the internal affairs of that State—declined to accede to the request made for Federal troops.

It will not accord with the laws of nature or history to brand the colored people as a race of cowards. On more than one historic field, beginning in 1776 and coming down to this centennial year of the Republic, they have attested in blood their courage as well as love of liberty. I ask Senators to believe that no consideration of fear or personal danger has kept us quiet and forbearing under the provocations and wrongs that have so sorely tried our souls. But feeling kindly toward our white fellow-citizens, appreciating the good purposes and offices of the better classes, and, above all, abhorring a war of races, we determined to wait until such time as an appeal to the good sense and justice of the American people could be made.

A notable feature of the outrages alleged is that they have referred almost exclusively to the colored citizens of the State. Why is the colored voter to be proscribed? Why direct the attack upon him? While the methods of violence, resorted to for political purposes in the South, are foreign to the genius of our institutions as applied to citizens generally—and so much is conceded by even the opposition—yet they seem to think we are an exceptional class and citizens, rather by sufferance than right; and when pressed to account for their bitterness and proscription toward us they, with more or less boldness, allege incompetent and bad government as their justification before the public opinion of the country. Now, I declare that neither political incapacity nor venality are qualities of the masses of colored citizens. The emancipation of the colored race during the late civil strife was an expression alike of the magnanimity and needs of the nation; and the subsequent and early subtraction of millions of industrial values from the resources of the insurrectionary States and the presence of many thousand additional brave hearts and strong hands around the flag of the country vindicated the justice and wisdom of the measure.

The close of the war found four millions of freedmen, without homes or property, charged with the duty of self-support and with the oversight of their personal freedom, yet without civil and political rights! The problem presented by this condition of things was one of the gravest that has ever been submitted to the American people. Shall these liberated millions of a separate race, while retaining personal liberty, be deprived of political rights? The practical sense of the American people definitely settled this delicate and difficult question, and the demand for a more pronounced loyal element in the work of reconstruction in the lately rebellious States furnished an opportunity for the recognition of the political rights of the race, both in the interest of justice and good government.

The history of my race since enfranchisement, considered in connection with the difficulties that have environed us, will exhibit hopeful progress and attest that we have been neither ungrateful for the civil and political privileges received nor wanting in appreciation of the correspondingly weighty obligations imposed upon us.

Again, we began our political career under the disadvantages of the inexperience in public affairs that generations of enforced bondage had entailed upon our race. We suffered also from the vicious leadership of some of the men whom our necessities forced us temporarily to accept. Consider further that the States of the South, where we were supposed to control by our majorities, were in an impoverished and semi-revolutionary condition—society demoralized, the industries of the country prostrated, the people sore, morbid, and sometimes turbulent, and no healthy controlling public opinion either existent or possible—consider all these conditions, and it will be seen that we began our political novitiate and formed the organic and statutory laws under great embarrassments.

Despite the difficulties and drawbacks suggested, the constitutions formed under colored majorities, whatever their defects may be, were improvements on the instruments they were designed to supersede; and the statutes framed, though necessarily defective because of the crude and varying social and industrial conditions upon which they were based, were more in harmony with the spirit of the age and the genius of our free institutions than the obsolete laws that they supplanted. Nor is there just or any sufficient grounds upon which to charge an oppressive administration of the laws.

The State debt proper is less than a half million dollars and the State taxes are light. Nor can complaint be reasonably made of the judiciary. The records of the supreme judicial tribunal of the State will show, in 1859–60, 266 decisions in cases of appeal from the lower courts, of which 169 were affirmed and 97 reversed. In 1872–73 the records show 328 decisions rendered in cases of appeal from below, of which 221 were affirmed and 107 reversed; in 1876, of appeals from chancellors, appointed by Governor Ames, up to date, 41 decisions have been rendered, of which 33 were affirmed and 8 reversed. This exhibit, whether of legislation or administration, shows there has been no adequate provocation to revolution and no justification for violence in Mississippi. That we should have made mistakes, under the circumstances, in measures of both legislation and administration, was natural, and that we have had any success is both creditable and hopeful.

But if it can be shown that we have used the ballot either to abridge the rights of our fellow-citizens or to oppress them; if it shall appear that we have ever used our newly acquired power as a sword of attack and not as a shield of defense, then we may with some show of propriety be charged with incapacity, dishonesty, or tyranny. But, even then, I submit that the corrective is in the hands of the people, and not of a favored class, and the remedy is in the honest exercise of the ballot, and not in fraud and violence.

Mr. President, do not misunderstand me; I do not hold that all the white people of the State of Mississippi aided and abetted the white-league organizations. There is in Mississippi a large and respectable element among the opposition who are not only honest in their recognition of the political rights of the colored citizen and deprecate the fraud and violence through which those rights have been assailed, but who would be glad to see the color line in politics abandoned and good-will obtain and govern among all classes of her people. But the fact is to be regretted that this better class of citizens in many parts of the State is dominated by a turbulent and violent element of the opposition, known as the White League—a ferocious minority—and has thus far proved powerless to prevent the recurrence of the outrages it deprecates and deplores.

The uses of this investigation are various. It will be important in suggesting such action as may be found necessary not only to correct and repair the wrongs perpetrated, but to prevent their recurrence. But I will venture to assert that the investigation will be most beneficial in this, that it will largely contribute to the formation of a public sentiment that, while it restrains the vicious in their attacks upon the rights of the loyal, lawabiding voters of the South, will so energize the laws as to secure condign punishment to wrong-doers, and give a security to all classes, which will effectively and abundantly produce the mutual good-will and confidence that constitute the foundations of the public prosperity.

We want peace and good order at the South; but it can only come by the fullest recognition of the rights of all classes. The opposition must concede the necessity of change, not only in the temper but in the philosophy of their party organization and management. The sober American judgment must obtain in the South as elsewhere in the Republic, that the only distinctions upon which parties can be safely organized and in harmony with our institutions are differences of opinions relative to principles and policy of government, and that differences of religion, nationality, or race can neither with safety nor propriety be permitted for a moment to enter into the party contests of the day. The unanimity with which the colored voters act with a party is not referable to any race prejudice on their part. On the contrary, they invite the political co-operation of their white brethren, and vote as a unit because proscribed as such. They deprecate the establishment of the color line by the opposition, not only because the act is unwise and wrong in principle, but because it isolates them from the white men of the South, and forces them, in sheer self-protection and against their inclination, to act seemingly upon the basis of a race prejudice that they neither respect nor entertain. As a class they are free from prejudices, and have no uncharitable suspicions against their white fellow-citizens, whether native born or settlers from the Northern States. They not only recognize the equality of citizenship and the right of every man to hold, without proscription, any position of honor and trust to which the confidence of the people may elevate him; but owing nothing to race, birth, or surroundings, they, above all other classes in the community, are interested to see prejudices drop out of both politics and the business of the country, and success in life proceed only upon the integrity and merit of the man who seeks it. They are also appreciative—feeling and exhibiting the liveliest gratitude for counsel and help in their new career, whether they come from the men of the North or of the South. But withal, as they progress in intelligence and appreciation of the dignity of their prerogatives as citizens, they, as an evidence of growth, begin to realize the significance of the proverb, "When thou doest well for thyself, men shall praise thee"; and are disposed to exact the same protection and concession of rights that are conferred upon other citizens by the Constitution, and that, too, without the humiliation involved in the enforced abandonment of their political convictions.

We simply demand the practical recognition of the rights given us in the Constitution and laws, and ask from our white fellow-citizens only the consideration and fairness that we so willingly extend to them. Let them generally realize and concede that citizenship imports to us what it does to them, no more and no less, and impress the colored people that a party defeat does not imperil their political franchise. Let them cease their attempts to coerce our political co-operation, and invite and secure it by a policy so fair and just as to commend itself to our judgment, and resort to no motive or measure to control us that self-respect would preclude their applying to themselves. When we can entertain opinions and select party affiliations without proscription, and cast our ballots as other citizens and without jeopardy to person or privilege, we can safely afford to be governed by the considerations that ordinarily determine the political action of American citizens. But we must be guaranteed in the unproscribed exercise of our honest convictions and be absolutely, from within or without, protected in the use of our ballot before we can either wisely or safely divide our vote. In union, not division, is strength, so long as White League proscription renders division of our vote impracticable by making a difference of opinion opprobrious and an antagonism in politics a crime. On the other hand, if we should, from considerations of fear, yield to the shot-gun policy of our opponents, the White League might win a temporary success, but the ultimate result would be disastrous to both races, for they would first become aggressively turbulent, and we, as a class, would become servile, unreliable, and worthless.

It has been suggested, as the popular sentiment of the country, that the colored citizens must no longer expect special legislation for their benefit, nor exceptional interference by the National Government for their protection. If this is true, if such is the judgment relative to our demands and needs, I venture to offset the suggestion, so far as it may be used as a reason for a denial of the protection we seek, by the statement of another and more prevalent popular conviction. Back of this, and underlying the foundations of the Republic itself, there lies deep in the breasts of the patriotic millions of the country the conviction that the laws must be enforced, and life, liberty, and property must, alike to all and for all, be protected. But I allege that we do not seek special action in our behalf, except to meet special danger, and only then such as all classes of citizens are entitled to receive under the Constitution. We do not ask the enactment of new laws, but only the enforcement of those that already exist.

The vicious and exceptional political action had by the White League in Mississippi has been repeated in other contests and in other States of the South, and the colored voters have been subjected therein to outrages upon their rights similar to those perpetrated in my own State at the recent election. Because violence has become so general a quality in the political canvasses of the South and my people the common sufferers in each instance, I have considered this subject more in detail than would, under other circumstances, have been either appropriate or necessary. As the proscription and violence toward the colored voters are special and almost exclusive, and seem to proceed upon the assumption that there is something exceptionally offensive and unworthy in them, I have felt, as the only representative of my race in the Senate of the United States, that I was placed, in some sort, upon the defensive, and I have consequently endeavored to show how aggravated and inexcusable were the wrongs worked upon us, and have sought to vindicate our title to both the respect and good-will of the just people of the nation. The gravity of the issues involved has demanded great plainness of speech from me. But I have endeavored to present my views to the Senate with the moderation and deference inspired by the recollection that both my race and myself were once bondsmen, and are to-day debtors largely to the love and justice of a great people for the enjoyment of our personal and political liberty. While my antecedents and surroundings suggest modesty, there are some considerations that justify frankness, and even boldness of speech.

Mr. President, I represent, in an important sense, the interest of nearly a million of voters, constituting a new, hopeful, permanent, and influential political element, and large enough to affect in critical periods the fortunes of this great Republic; and the public safety and common weal alike demand that the integrity of this element should be preserved and its character improved. They number more than a million of producers, who, since their emancipation and outside of their contributions to the production of sugar, rice, tobacco, cereals, and the mechanical industries of the country, have furnished nearly forty million bales of cotton, which, at the ruling prices of the world's market, have yielded $2,000,000,000, a sum nearly equal to the national debt; producers who, at the accepted ratio that an able-bodied laborer earns, on an average $800 per year, annually bring to the aggregate of the nation's great bulk of values more than $800,000,000.

I have confidence, not only in my country and her institutions, but in the endurance, capacity, and destiny of my people. We will, as opportunity offers and ability serves, seek our places, sometimes in the field of letters, arts, sciences, and the professions. More frequently mechanical pursuits will attract and elicit our efforts; more still of my people will find employment and livelihood as the cultivators of the soil. The bulk of this people—by surroundings, habits, adaptation, and choice—will continue to find their homes in the South, and constitute the masses of its yeomanry. We will there probably, of our own volition and more abundantly than in the past, produce the great staples that will contribute to the basis of foreign exchange, aid in giving the nation a balance of trade, and minister to the wants and comfort and build up the prosperity of the whole land. Whatever our ultimate position in the composite civilization of the Republic and whatever varying fortunes attend our career, we will not forget our instincts for freedom nor our love of country. Guided and guarded by a beneficent Providence, and living under the genial influence of liberal institutions, we have no apprehensions that we shall fail from the land from attrition with other races, or ignobly disappear from either the politics or industries of the country.

Mr. President, allow me here to say that, although many of us are uneducated in the schools, we are informed and advised as to our duties to the Government, our State, and ourselves. Without class prejudice or animosities, with obedience to authority as the lesson and love of peace and order as the passion of our lives, with scrupulous respect for the rights of others, and with the hopefulness of political youth, we are determined that the great Government that gave us liberty, and rendered its gift valuable by giving us the ballot, shall not find us wanting in a sufficient response to any demand that humanity or patriotism may make upon us; and we ask such action as will not only protect us in the enjoyment of our constitutional rights, but will preserve the integrity of our republican institutions.

SUGGESTIONS FOR FURTHER READING

The story of blacks during the Civil War is most interestingly told in the collection of primary source material imaginatively edited by James McPherson in *The Negro's Civil War*★ (1956). Secondary works on black troops are Dudley T. Cornish, *The Sable Arm: Negro Troops in the Union Army* (1956) and Benjamin Quarles, *The Negro in the Civil War* (1953). See also *Army Life in a Black Regiment*★ (1870), the story of black troops as told by their white commander, and Bernard C. Nalty, *Strength for the Fight: A History of Black Americans in the Military*★ (1989). See also David W. Blight, *Frederick Douglass' Civil War*★ (1989).

The standard history of Reconstruction is Eric Foner, *Reconstruction, 1863–1877*★ (1988). *Black Reconstruction in America*★ (1935), by W. E. B. Du Bois, was the work that began the revision of Reconstruction historiography that led to Foner's study. Other books in that tradition include Kenneth Stampp, *The Era of Reconstruction, 1865–1877*★ (1965), James McPherson, *The Struggle for Equality: Abolitionists and the Negro in the Civil War and Reconstruction*★ (1964).

The early days of Reconstruction are covered in Willie Lee Rose, *Rehearsal for Reconstruction: The Port Royal Experiment*★ (1964) and Leon F. Litwack, *Been in the Storm so*

Long: The Aftermath of Slavery★ (1979). See also the volumes in Ira Berlin, *et al.*, (eds.), *Freedom: A Documentary History of Emancipation, 1861–1867* (1982–).

Special studies of women during the period are Leslie A. Schwalm, *A Hard Fight for We: Women's Transition from Slavery to Freedom in South Carolina*★ (1997) and Tara W. Hunter, *To 'Joy My Freedom: Southern Black Women's Lives and Labors after the Civil War*★ (1 997). See also Jacqueline Jones, *Labor of Love, Labor of Sorrow: Black Women, Work, and the Family from Slavery to the Present*★ (1985).

The education of the freedmen is treated in Robert Morris, *Reading, 'Riting and Reconstruction: The Education of the Freedmen in the South, 1861–1870* (1981), Jacqueline Jones, *Soldiers of Light and Love: Northern Teachers and Georgia Blacks, 1865–1873* (1980), and the autobiographical *The Journal of Charlotte Forten*★ (1953), edited by Ray A. Billington. Other studies of special interest are Claude F. Oubre, *Forty Acres and a Mule: The Freedman's Bureau and Black Land Ownership* (1978), Gerald David Jaynes, *Branches without Roots: Genesis of the Black Working Class in the American South, 1862–1882* (1986), and Julie Saville, *The Work of Reconstruction: From Slave to Wage Laborer in South Carolina, 1860–1870*★ (1994).

The violence of Reconstruction is the subject of Allen W. Trelease, *White Terror: The Ku Klux Klan Conspiracy and Southern Reconstruction*★ (1972) and George C. Rable, *But There Was No Peace: The Role of Violence in the Politics of Reconstruction*★ (1984).

Individual states are dealt with in Joel Williamson, *After Slavery: The Negro in South Carolina during Reconstruction, 1861–1877*★ (1965), Vernon Lane Wharton, *The Negro in Mississippi, 1865–1890*★ (1947), Peter Kolchin, *First Freedom* [Alabama] (1972), C. Peter Ripley, *Slaves and Freedmen in Civil War Louisiana* (1976), and Thomas Holt, *Black over White: Negro Political Leadership in South Carolina during Reconstruction*★ (1977).

★ Books marked by an asterisk are available in paperback.

6

✦

The Legal Segregation
of Free People

INTRODUCTION

The years from 1877 to 1900 were a period of renewed victimization for the black population of the United States, both North and South. The Republican Party, which had served as a guarantor of black political freedom, withdrew its support in 1877 under President Rutherford B. Hayes and gave the white South the freedom to deal with the black population as it saw fit. Abandoned by the federal government and bereft of Northern support, the blacks of the South were driven rapidly into political impotence, or—what was often worse—they were forced to support political policies that were clearly contrary to their own interests.

Extralegal disfranchisement of the blacks, effected through intimidation and outright violence, was gradually supplanted in the South by legal exclusion from the political process. Mississippi, in 1890, was the first state to apply the new suffrage restrictions in constitutional fashion. The key provision was that each applicant for the vote be able to interpret a portion of the state constitution to the satisfaction of a state-appointed registrar. Although on the face of it the new provision did not call for racial discrimination, it was clearly intended and used to eliminate black people from the voting lists.

In the process of disfranchisement, other states added a "good conduct" clause to their constitutions, requiring each registrant to have a recommendation from a responsible (i. e., white) citizen; a "grandfather" clause, stating that if one's grandfather had voted in 1860, it was not necessary to meet the usual voting requirements; and a ruling that only whites could participate in primary elections, which effectively eliminated the black vote in the one-party South. Some of these restrictions were removed only with the federal Voting Act of 1965.

Along with legal disfranchisement came legal segregation. Many Southerners, black as well as white, were willing to live with the separation of the races that characterized much of Reconstruction life. But fear of a possible breakdown in racial customs led whites to impose legal restrictions on the activities of blacks. The first segregation laws applied in the field of public education. By 1878, most Southern states operated a dual educational system, with blacks receiving a much smaller per capita expenditure than whites. Transportation segregation came next, and though the laws developed at different rates in different places, by the turn of the century most Southern states enforced segregation on streetcars and railroads. When the First World War broke out, segregation was legally maintained in almost every area of social contact.

While their political and social rights were being restricted, black people in Southern cities were losing the economic position they had enjoyed earlier. An influx of white labor, skilled and unskilled, began to edge the blacks out of even the jobs that had traditionally been theirs. When the Civil War ended, five of every six artisans in the South were black; by 1900, only one of every twenty was black.

The condition of the black family in the rural South has already been mentioned. Since land was not made available to them, most black farmers were dependent on the white plantation owners for work. The work consisted of sharecropping, a system in which the cropper existed on credit extended by the landowner. Inevitably, at the end of the year the cropper remained in debt and was required to sign labor contracts that virtually tied them to the soil. Equally discriminatory in effect was the convict-lease system, whereby blacks arrested on minor charges were rented to plantation owners by law-enforcement authorities.

As might have been expected, these conditions led many rural blacks to seek ways to migrate to more promising lands. Some suggested that the Indian Territory (now a part of Oklahoma) be made into an all-black state, and in anticipation of such an event, several all-black towns were founded in the area beginning in 1891. Some of the towns exist to this day and are still all black. The most notable migration of the period, however, occurred in 1879, when over 7,000 poor blacks, under the leadership of an ex-slave, "Pop" Singleton, arrived in Kansas to begin a new life. Unfortunately, there was nothing there for them except a severe winter and white hostility. Many died, and many of those who survived the winter returned home or went elsewhere.

When Reconstruction ended, the hostility of local white authorities caused black people to look to the federal government for legal aid. At that time, the Civil Rights Act of 1875, which provided for protection against segregation in transportation and public accommodations, was in effect, and the blacks had every reason to expect federal support. The Supreme Court, however, struck the struggle for equal rights several near-fatal blows. The first came in 1883, when the Court declared the Civil Rights Act of 1875 unconstitutional on the grounds that the Fourteenth Amendment did not prohibit discrimination by individuals. Later, in 1896, in the *Plessy v. Ferguson* decision, the Court ruled that "separate but equal" facilities were permissible and that states could use police power to enforce segregation law. Shortly thereafter, it ruled that states could limit the franchise in any way that was not explicitly based on race, color, or previous condition of servitude. The federal government's betrayal of the African-American was complete.

There were two short-lived signs of hope during the last quarter of the nineteenth century—one in the area of jobs and the other in politics. The first was the emergence of the Knights of Labor, a group that sought to organize skilled and unskilled industrial workers on an interracial basis. During the 1870s and the 1880s, the Knights worked hard to enlist black members in both the North and the South, and it has been estimated that in 1886, blacks formed from 9 to 11 percent of the total membership of 700,000. A reputation for radicalism and violence cost the Knights their power after the 1880s, however, and they were supplanted by the American Federation of Labor (AFL). Although originally opposed to racial discrimination, by the close of the century the AFL adopted a policy of permitting—even sometimes encouraging—the exclusion of blacks from union locals.

The Populist Movement was the second sign of hope. For a time it looked as though poor white and poor black farmers would be able to cooperate in order to bring about an improvement in the condition of both groups. In many states, black men ran for office on a Populist or fusion ticket. Opportunistic white politicians, however, revived the residual fear of and hostility to the blacks, and in an attempt to maintain political power, the Populist leaders shifted emphasis from interracial cooperation to virulent race hatred. By early in the twentieth century, the racial attitudes of white Populist leaders could hardly be distinguished from those of Southern Democrats; if anything, the former were the more intensely discriminatory.

The Areas of
Racial Discrimination

Report of the Committee on
Grievances at the State Convention of
Colored Men of Texas, 1883

The convention movement among blacks did not cease with emancipation. On the contrary, since its primary concern before the Civil War was the status and the treatment of free blacks, it had even more reason for being after the remaining slaves were freed. When federal support was removed from Southern blacks at the end of Reconstruction and power reverted to the former ruling class, conventions were called to deal with the problem of growing segregation and the raising of new caste barriers.

In 1883, a national convention was scheduled to be held in Louisville, Kentucky; preliminary to that meeting, various state conventions met to elect delegates and draw up recommendations. The document reprinted here is the report made at the Texas convention by its grievance committee. From the document, one can get a clear idea of some of the ways in which legal segregation was beginning to take shape. It is interesting to note that the committee of black Texans was prepared to accept separate facilities if they were truly equal.

Mr. Chairman and Gentlemen

We, your Committee on Grievances, beg leave to make the following report: We find that the denial to the colored people of the free exercise of many of the rights of citizenship, is due to the fact of there being such great prejudice against them as a race. This prejudice was engendered from the belief which underlay the institution of slavery, and which kept that institution alive, and built it to the enormous proportions which it has attained; that is, the belief that the Negro was intended by the Divine Creator as servants and menials for the more favored races; hence, was not to be accorded the rights and privileges exercised by other races. Very naturally, then, was it thought fitting and proper, and in keeping with Divine intention, to keep the Negro bowed down in slavery. The sudden change from a status wherein we were slaves to one in which we were made freemen; and then, further, to that in which we became citizens equal before the law, was so unexpected and contrary, both to the training and teaching of our former owners, that they have

FROM *Proceedings of the State Convention of Colored Men of Texas, Held at the City of Austin, July 10–12, 1883* (Houston, 1883), pp. 12–17. Reprinted by permission from a pamphlet in the Library of the University of Michigan, Ann Arbor.

never fully accepted said changes, though they have affected to accept them, because their acceptance was made the only condition upon which they could regain their former position in the Union. We submit, that it is contrary to the natural order of things for them to have surrendered their belief in the matter simply because they were physically overpowered. And, not only is the belief in the Negro's inferiority and creation for servants, deeply rooted in the minds of its advocates, but it has culminated in what seems to be a bitter hatred and fixed prejudice. This culmination was brought about by the Negro being taken from the position of a slave and forcibly placed equal to his former master; also, by his being subsequently utilized in carrying on the war against the unfortunates of the lost cause after the battle had been transferred from the field to the ballot box; and in doing this he adhered to a political party which he kept up by his support, and which was nearly identical with the triumphant party which had caused their former owners' defeat on the bloody field of battle. This is the outcome of a train of circumstances naturally liable to produce just such a result. The reason given by our debasers, when attempting to justify themselves in regarding us socially so grossly inferior is, that it always has been their policy to do so, and hence it will always be. This remark refers to the fact that they regarded us thus during slavery as a ground upon which they justified slavery, and as they have experienced no change of mind they will continue thus to regard us. Your committee arrived at this conclusion: that if our former owners deny our social equality, they cannot be expected to be swift in respecting our legal equality or equality before the law; for it is the social regard one has for another as a member of society, which impels him to protect and accord unto such a one his legal rights. Hence, if there be a class who socially regard us less favorably than they do other races, to an extent that they are prejudiced, such a class certainly are indifferent as to whether we obtain our legal rights or not. Accordingly, social disregard may well imply absolute indifference as to another's legal rights, but never that mutual regard which is supposed to possess citizens of a common country. It is a true rule that the degree to which any right is enjoyed as a citizen, is measured by the willingness of the whole body of citizens to protect such a right; if there is lack of regard there is, therefore, lack of the will to protect. We find, therefore, that this social disregard is the sole cause of all the infringements upon our rights as a race, as we shall specify:

MISCEGENATION LAW

Prominent among the enactments in furtherance of this social disregard, is a law of this State punishing as felons all persons who intermarry when one is a descendant of the Negro race and the other is not. The same series of laws impose an insignificant fine only for the same persons to live together in unlawful wedlock, or have carnal intercourse with each other without being married. In most cases, say ninety-nine cases in one hundred, parties of the two races thus unlawfully cohabiting are not even reported, or if reported not punished. And, sad to remark, in many cases officers of the law are disqualified to try such cases; in many others, those who would in good faith testify against offenders of this class, would do so at the risk of their lives. The result of this series of crimes, tolerated and encouraged by our Criminal Code, which makes pretensions to preserving public morals, common decency and chastity, is to increase immorality in the lower classes of both races to an alarming extent. The law should never imply that a thing otherwise lawful is a felony, and that a thing of the same nature unlawful in itself is less than a felony. Colored females, victims of this well-laid plan, called a law to protect public morals, and common decency and chastity, are severely censured, and our whole race indiscriminately described as a race without morals. A careful consideration of the operation of the law convinces all fair-minded persons, that the law was intended to gratify the basest passions of certain classes of men who do not seek such gratification by means of lawful wedlock. We are pained to announce that the law bears its evil fruits. The committee dismiss the consideration of this dark subject with the recommendation that the Convention urge upon our next Legislature the necessity of an amendment to this law that will punish as rigidly for all carnal intercourse between the two races, unlawfully carried on, as it punishes them for intermarrying. If the Legislature do this, they will show a willingness to stop the tide of immorality that now makes such inroads upon the morals of some of our most promising females.

FREE SCHOOLS

The Constitution, and laws made in pursuance thereof, make provision for the education of the youth of the State, without regard to race or previous condition. Further, they make provision that cities may assume the control of school affairs within their limits, on condition that they make a special taxation upon their property in order to lengthen the school term to ten months. What we complain of is, that notwithstanding the Constitution, laws, courts, and the Board of Education have decided that provision for each race must be equal and impartial, many cities make shameful discrimination because the colored people do not own as much property on which to pay taxes as the white people do, in proportion to the number of children in each race. They utterly refuse to give colored schools the same provision as to character of buildings, furniture, number and grade of teachers as required by law. The result of this discrimination is, that the white schools of such cities show good fruit, while the colored show poor fruit or none at all. We here say that this charge of discrimination is not made against all cities, but against only such as really discriminate. And again, there are many colored teachers appointed mainly on account of their personal relation with the individuals composing the Boards, and not with reference to the peculiar needs of the pupils to be benefitted, neither the fitness of the teacher nor the wishes of patrons.

We are glad to say, however, that many school boards, exclusively white, do their full duty towards colored schools. Still we deem it proper and just, in recognition of our rights, to assist in supervising and controlling, to have some colored man or men appointed on school boards in cities where there is a large number of colored pupils and patrons—especially where suitable men can be found. We make no complaint against the provision made by the Legislature of our State for the education of our children, but against the partial manner in which those provisions are executed by some of the local authorities.

TREATMENT OF CONVICTS

Another sore grievance that calls for the consideration of this Convention is the treatment of convicts, a large proportion of whom are colored. It is inhuman and cruel in the extreme. We do not refer to those that are kept within the walls. They are under the immediate care and supervision of the management, and we believe considerably treated. But most of the convicts are scattered over the State on farms, having no one to administer to their physical, moral or spiritual needs but a host of inhuman, brutal convict guards. When a fresh convict is carried to the farms, he is taken down by the other convicts and beaten, at the command of the guard, and that, too, with a large piece of cowhide. The guard takes this method of taming the newcomer. Of course this lays him up, but in a few days he is hauled out of his sick quarters and put to work, whether he is physically able to do it or not. The law provides that a convict physically unable to work shall not be required to do so, such inability to be ascertained by the examination of the penitentiary physician. But, convicts on farms, who are mostly colored, have no physician to determine such inability, and even when sick and dying have none, unless the hiring planter, who has no particular interest in saving his life, sees fit to employ one. In many cases sick convicts are made to toil until they drop dead in their tracks. Many again, driven to desperation by inhuman treatment, seek to relieve themselves by attempting to escape when the chances are against them, thus inducing the guards to shoot them, which they are ready to do on the slightest pretext. Others are maltreated by being placed in the pillory or stocks until they are dead or nearly so. When convicts are brutally murdered, nothing is done with their slayers unless the indignant citizens are prompt in insisting upon their punishment. In nine cases out of ten, parties sent to investigate these occurrences report the killing justifiable, because guards and their friends find it convenient to make it appear so. When legislative committees visit one of these convict camps, they always find the convicts ready to report that they are well treated, because all of them, both white and black, are previously warned by their guards to report thus or accept the consequences which will surely follow. Again we will state, although the law justifies the killing of a convict escaping from the penitentiary, when his escape can be prevented in no other way, still we fail to see wherein it can be justified when the convict is carried on a farm, away from the penitentiary, and given a chance to escape only to be deliberately shot down in attempting to do so. We believe such to be deliberate murder, and should be punished as such. Believing that most of the evils can be remedied by the appointment of a colored inspector who is a humane man, having power to investigate the affairs of convict camps and the management of convict labor on private farms, therefore, we recommend to the Governor and Board such an appointment at the earliest possible moment. We recommend also, that as most of the State convicts are colored, that there be appointed at least one colored commissioner of penitentiaries. Though our men and youths are sent to the penitentiary to be reformed, in most cases they are made worse by the inhumanities and immoral habits of their guards, who, in many cases, are worse morally than the convicts themselves. We think that this Convention should pass a resolution condemning, in strongest terms, the practice of yoking or chaining male and female convicts together. This is an act of officials, done only for the purpose of further demoralizing those persons, especially so where they are only county convicts.

RAILWAYS, INNS AND TAVERNS

The criticism and censures of many, that colored persons in demanding admission to first class cars are forcing social intercourse, are unjust and unwarranted. For those who censure know that if the companies were to furnish accommodations for colored passengers holding first class tickets, equal to the accommodations furnished white passengers holding the same, though such accommodations be in separate cars, no complaint will be made. But selling two classes of passengers the same kind of tickets, at the same time and price, certainly sell to them the same accommodations and privileges. The colored people, like any other class of citizens, will contend for the right in this matter as long as our Constitution reads, "all men when they form a social compact have equal rights," and even longer.

We would also state that we do not contend for the privilege of riding in the car with whites, but for the right of riding in cars equally as good, and for the mutual right of riding in their car if they have a separate one, whenever they are permitted to ride in ours if we have a separate one. We believe the State laws to be adequate to protect us in every right, and that there is no necessity of appealing to a law of Congress unless the laws and government of our own State refuse to recognize and protect these rights.

As for accommodations at public inns, taverns and hotels, we have the same right as other races to be accommodated on equal terms and conditions, though we cannot compel them to accommodate us in the same room, at the same table or even in the same building, but the proprietor can be compelled to make provision as good. We recognize the fact that our State law is as adequate to protect a colored man in the exercise of his rights as it is to protect a white man. While not encouraging the contention for our rights at hotels when we can make other provision, we recommend our people to invoke the aid of the courts when their rights with reference to railroads are violated, and ask that they assert our rights thereon by such damages as are sufficient to assert them.

JURIES

The prevailing practice among sheriffs and jury commissioners of summoning jurors exclusively white or nearly so, is in direct violation of the laws of this State, for no person is disqualified as a juror on account of his color. If the sheriff and commissioners exclude any one by practice on account of color, it is such an exclusion as is not contemplated by law, for the parties summoning cannot excuse themselves by saying they knew of none who could read and write, for that is a qualification they are to assume and let the court test jurors' qualifications after they are summoned. A juror who sits in judgment on a case involving the rights of a man whom he regards with less consideration than he does members of his own class, is in law an incompetent juror, and should by law be excluded on evidence of such lack of regard. We deem it to be the duty of all judges to, at all times, specially instruct sheriffs and commissioners with reference to correcting these abuses, so as to secure to every individual, white or black, a fair and impartial trial by a jury composed of men acknowledging themselves to be his peers.

In furtherance of a desire to effectually and legitimately prescribe a remedy for the evils and wrongs complained of, we recommend the formation of an organization to be known and called "The Colored People's Progressive Union." It shall have for its object the protection of the rights of the colored people of Texas, by giving aid and direction in the prosecution of suits in the support of every right guaranteed to colored people as citizens. We recommend that our delegates to the National Convention be instructed to urge upon said Convention the necessity of organizing a national convention of the same name and for the same object, under which, if organized, this State Association shall act as a branch.

All of which is respectfully submitted.

— MACK HENSON, Chairman
— A. R. NORRIS,
— J. N. JOHNSON,
— J. Q. A. POTTS.

Attack on the Supreme Court

The Outrage of the Supreme Court: A Letter from Henry M. Turner

HENRY M. TURNER

The Supreme Court's failure to support the fight for equal rights during the last quarter of the nineteenth century came as a severe blow to the black man. No one expressed the rage and the dismay of the nation's blacks better than Henry M. Turner. Educated in the North to be a clergyman in the African Methodist Episcopal Church, Turner was appointed chaplain to black troops by Lincoln in 1863. After the war, he moved to Georgia, where he became active in Radical Republican politics. In 1868, he was elected to the Georgia state legislature, but because of a Democratic majority, he and twenty-six other black legislators were barred from their seats at the opening session. A massive protest to Washington succeeded in gaining them admittance to the second session of the legislature.

Throughout his political career, Turner served as a minister in Atlanta. When violent attacks on the Supreme Court decisions of 1883 and 1896 came to no avail, he gave up in disgust and joined the emigrationists in advocating a return to Africa for American blacks.

The next document was written in response to a question about Turner's attack on the 1883 decision of the Court declaring the Civil Rights Act of 1875 unconstitutional. Turner's reply makes clear his anger at the Court's decision to leave Southern blacks at the mercy of Southern society.

Editor of the New York Voice

Amidst multitudinous duties I find, calling my attention, your note of recent date, asking me to briefly refer to the "Civil Rights Decisions," which, since their delivery has drawn from me expressions which many are pleased to call severe adverse strictures upon the highest court in this country, and upon all of its judges save one, Mr. Justice Harlan. It is to me a matter of that kind of surprise called wonder suddenly excited to find a single, solitary individual who belongs in the United States, or who has been here for any considerable time, unacquainted with those famous FIVE DEATH DEALING DECISIONS. Indeed, Sir, those decisions have had, since the 15th day of October, A.D. 1883, the day of their pronouncement, more of my study than any other civil subject. I incline to the opinion that I have an argument which, taken as

FROM Henry M. Turner, "Civil Rights: The Outrage of the Supreme Court of the United States upon the Black Man" (Atlanta, 1889).

a concomitant of the learned dissenting sentiments of that eminent jurist, Mr. Justice Harlan, would to a rational mind make the judgment of Justice Bradley and his associates a deliquescence—a bubble on the wave of equity—a legal nothing. You bid me in my reply to observe brevity. Shortness and conciseness seem to be the ever present rule when the Negro and his case is under treatment. However, I am satisfied that in saying this, I do not convey your reason for commanding me to condense, "boil down." The more I ponder the non-agreeing words of that member of our chief assize, who had the moral courage to bid defiance to race prejudice, the more certain am I that no words of mine, condemnatory of that decision, have been sufficiently harsh.

March 1st, 1875, Congress passed an act entitled "An act for the prevention of discrimination on the ground of race, color or previous condition of servitude," said act being generally known as the Civil Rights Bill, introduced during the lifetime of the Negro's champion, the immortal Charles Sumner. The act provided:

"SECTION 1. That all persons within the jurisdiction of the United States shall be entitled to the full and equal enjoyment of the accommodations, advantages, facilities, and privileges of inns, public conveyances on land or water, theaters, and other places of public amusements—subject only to the conditions and limitations established by law and applicable alike to citizens of every color and race, regardless of any previous condition of servitude.

"SEC. 2. That any person who shall violate the foregoing section by denying to any citizen, except for reasons by law applicable to citizens of every race and color, and regardless of any previous condition of servitude, the full enjoyment of any of the accommodations, advantages, facilities or privileges in said section enumerated, or by aiding or inciting such denial, shall for every such offence forfeit and pay the sum of five hundred dollars to the person aggrieved thereby, to be recovered in an action of debt, with full costs; and shall also, for every such offence, be deemed guilty of a misdemeanor, and, upon conviction thereof, shall be fined not less than five hundred, nor more than one thousand, dollars, or shall be imprisoned not less than thirty days nor more than one year. Provided, that all persons may elect to sue for the penalty aforesaid, or to proceed under their rights at common law and by State statutes; and having so elected to proceed in the one mode on the other, their right to proceed in the other jurisdiction shall be barred. But this provision shall not apply to criminal proceedings, either under this act or the criminal law of any State. And provided further, that a judgment for the penalty in favor of the party aggrieved, or a judgment upon an indictment, shall be a bar to either prosecution respectively."

Here we have the exact language of the law:

First, what is forbidden; second, the penalty; third, the mode for gaining redress; and fourth, the defendant's security against excessive punishment. The questions that come forward and will not down are: Was this law just? Did this law violate the principle which should be foremost in every hall of legislation—hurt no one, give unto every man his just due? Should the color of one's skin deny him privileges any more than the color of one's hair, seeing that the individual had nothing to do with the cause for the one or for the other? Before attempting to answer the above questions, which must and will suggest themselves to every *compos mentis*, we state the constitutional amendments upon which the act under consideration was founded and upheld. We cannot see how one so learned in the law as Mr. Justice Bradley is presumed to be, by reason of his exalted position, can see only the Fourteenth Amendment, as the part of the Constitution, relied on. It is undeniably patent to all that the Thirteenth Amendment more nearly expresses the foundation for the "act." The language of the Thirteenth Amendment says:

"SECTION 1. Neither slavery nor involuntary servitude, except as a punishment for a crime, whereof the party shall have duly been convicted, shall exist within the United States, or any place subject to their jurisdiction." This amendment in its second section, declares that "Congress shall have the power to enforce this article by appropriate legislation." Under this article, alone, I am satisfied that our National Legislature had full warrant and authority to enact the law now abrogated. The Fourteenth Amendment to the Constitution provides that "All persons born or naturalized in the United States, and subject to the jurisdiction thereof, are citizens of the United States, and of the State wherein they reside. No State shall make or enforce any law which shall abridge the privileges or immunities of the citizens of the United States; nor shall any State deprive any person of life, liberty or property without due process of law, nor deny to any person in its jurisdiction the equal protection of the laws." Upon these two amendments, say these wise judges, depends the constitutionality of the act or law under discussion.

In October, 1882, five cases were filed or submitted: United States vs. Stanley, from Kansas; United States vs. Ryan, from California; United States vs. Nichols, from Missouri; United States vs. Singleton, from New York; and Robinson and wife vs. Memphis and Charleston Railroad Company, from Tennessee. Our learned (?) judges occupied a year in considering what their dicta should be. October 15, 1883, found Justice Bradley in his place, on the bench, prepared to voice the opinion of the court as to the rights of more than seven millions of human beings. Mr. Solicitor-General Phillips, had delivered his argument for the life of the law to be maintained. The argument of the Solicitor-General had been supplemented by the eloquent efforts of Mr. William M. Randolph, on behalf of Robinson and wife. Numerous authorities were cited to show that where the Constitution guarantees a right, Congress is empowered to pass the legislation appropriate to give effect to that right. It was also maintained and established by judicial precedents, that the constitutionality of the act was not harmed by the nice distinction of "guaranteed rights," instead of "created rights." Justice Bradley consumes seventeen pages, to do what in his conscientious (?) opinion he believes to be right. Justice Harlan, in opposing the position taken by Mr. Bradley, occupies thirty-seven pages. After reciting the law countenancing the actions instituted by the sorely aggrieved persons, the first question which propounded itself to the member reading the opinion was, "Are these sections constitutional?" After taking space and time to tell what it is not the essence of the law to do, the

Honorable Judge in *obiter dictum* language says: "But the responsibility of an independent judgment is now thrown upon this court; and we are bound to exercise it according to the best lights we have."

Why this apologetic language? Are we not acquainted with the functions and duties of our court of last resort? Do we not know that the judges thereof are appointed for life, subject only to their good behavior? This deciding judge says: "The power is sought, first in the Fourteenth Amendment: and the views and arguments of distinguished senators, advanced whilst the law was under consideration, claiming authority to pass it by virtue of that amendment, are the principal arguments adduced in favor of the power. We have carefully considered those arguments, as was due to the eminent ability of those who put them forward, and have felt, in all its force, the weight of authority which always invests a law that Congress deems itself competent to pass." It is not said that arguments opposed to the passage of the act were noticed. It is not said that this Honorable Judge, long before this question of law was brought before him, had predetermined its nonconstitutionality.

It is not hinted that this Republican Supreme Court had caused it to be noised abroad what their "finding" would be if the "law" was inquired into. The court, it is said, could see, and only see, negroes in Kansas and Missouri intermingling with white persons in hotels and inns; negroes in California and New York associating on equal terms with Caucasians in theaters; and negroes in the presence of those free from the taint of African blood in the parlor-cars of Tennessee. These sights completely blinded the eyes of the, at other times, learned judges, and one of their number, not too full of indignation for utterance, proclaimed aloud, these things may not be; these pictures shall not in future be produced; the law is unconstitutional; and all of the other members, save one, said, amen. Negroes may come as servants into all of the hotels, inns, theaters and parlor-cars, but they shall never be received as equals—as are other persons. A negro woman with a white baby in her arms may go to the table in the finest and most aristocratic hotel, and there, as a servant, be permitted to associate with all present, of whatever nationality. The same woman, unaccompanied by said baby, or coming without the distinguished rank of servant, is given to understand that she can not enter. And what is more, by the Bradley infamous decision, may be by force of arms prevented from entering. A negro, whose father is a white man, and whose mother's father was white, if marked sufficiently to tell that he is somewhat negro is denied admission into certain places; the same resorts or places of entertainment being readily granted to the inky dark negro who is accompanying an invalid white man. The gambler, cut-throat, thief, despoiler of happy homes and the cowardly assassin need only to have white faces in order to be accommodated with more celerity and respect than are our lawyers, doctors, teachers and humble preachers. Talk about the "Dred Scott" decision; why it was only a mole-hill in comparison with this obstructing Rocky Mountain to the freedom of citizenship. I am charged by your Pennsylvania correspondent with saying that, "By the decision of the Republican Supreme Court colored people may be turned out of hotels, cheated, abused and insulted on steamboats and railroads without legal redress." I am of the opinion that the reporter on your paper who published the above quotation as coming from me, made no mistake unless it was that of making it more mild than I intended. When I use the term, "cheated," I mean that colored persons are required to pay first-class fare and in payment there for are given no-class treatment, or at least the kind which no other human being, paying first-class fare, is served. Some conveyances excepted, I must say to their credit. Bohemians, Scandinavians, Greasers, Italians and Mongolians all precede negroes. When Mr. Justice Harlan shall have retired from the bench by reason of age and infirmity, I pray him to accept, take and carry with him into his retirement the boiled-down essence of the love of more than eight million negroes, who delight to honor an individual whose vertebra is strong enough to stem the tide of race prejudice. His decision dissenting in favor of equal and exact justice to all men will last always, will never be forgotten as long as there is a descendant of the American negro on the earth: I have no doubt that the feeling of Justice Harlan when seeking rest upon his soft couch on the night of that fateful day in October, was different to the emotions present with Judge Bradley. The latter had doomed seven million human beings and their posterity to "stalls" and "nooks," denoting inferiority: the other had attempted to protect them from American barbarism and vandalism. Seven million persons, many of whom are not only related to Justice Bradley's race by affinity, but by consanguinity, cannot move the bowels of his compassion to the extent of framing or constructing even one sentence in all of that notorious decision which fairly can be interpreted as a friendly regard for the rights of those struggling souls who cried to God, while carrying the burden of bondage for more than two hundred and forty years. God will some day raise up another Lincoln, another Thad. Stevens and another Charles Sumner. In my opinion, if Jesus was on earth, he would say, when speaking of eight members of the Supreme Court and the decision which worked such acerb and cruel wrong upon my people, "Father, forgive them; they know not what they do."

Mr. Justice Harlan, in his protesting language, says many things which stand non-controvertible and may some day be remembered only to be thought about when it is too late. He says: "The opinion in these cases proceeds, it seems to me, upon grounds entirely too narrow and artificial. I cannot resist the conclusion that the substance and spirit of the recent amendments of the Constitution, have been sacrificed by a subtle and ingenious verbal criticism." He then quotes an authority which is so old and well established that the memory of man goeth not to the contrary, which says:

"It is not the words of the law, but the internal sense of it that makes the law; the letter of the law is the body; the sense and reason of the law is the soul." Continuing, he says: "Constitutional provisions, adopted in the interest of liberty, and for the purpose of securing, through national legislation, if need be, rights inhering in a state of freedom, and belonging to American citizenship, have been so construed as to defeat the ends the people desired to accomplish, which they attempted to accomplish, and which they thought they had accomplished by changes in their fundamental law. By this, I do not mean that the determination of these cases should have been materially controlled by considerations of mere expediency or policy. I mean only, in this form, to express an earnest conviction that the court has departed from the familiar rule requiring, in the interpretation of constitutional provisions, that full effect be given to the intent with which they were adopted. The court adjudges, I think, erroneously, that Congress is without power, under either the Thirteenth or Fourteenth Amendment, to establish such regulations, and that the first and second sections of the statute are, in all their parts, unconstitutional and void."

Then follows a great number of authorities maintaining his position. No sane man can read the record, law and authorities relating to these cases, without forming a conclusion that cannot be brushed away, that the bench of judges were narrow even to wicked ingeniousness, superinduced by color-phobeism. Sane men know that the gentlemen in Congress who voted for this act of 1875 understood full well the condition of our country, as did the powers amending the Constitution abolishing slavery. The intention was to entirely free, not to partly liberate. The desire was to remove the once slave so far from his place of bondage, that he would not even remember it, if such a thing were possible. Congress stepped in and said, he shall vote, he shall serve on juries, he shall testify in court, he shall enter the professions, he shall hold offices, he shall be treated like other men, in all places the conduct of which is regulated by law, he shall in no way be reminded by partial treatment, by discrimination, that he was once a "chattel," a "thing." Certainly Congress had a right to do this. The power that made the slave a man instead of a "thing" had the right to fix his status. The height of absurdity, the chief point in idiocy, the brand of total imbecility, is to say that the Negro shall vote a privilege into existence which one citizen may enjoy for pay, to the exclusion of another, coming in the same way, but clothed in the vesture covering the earth when God first looked upon it. Are colored men to vote grants to railroads upon which they cannot receive equal accommodation? When we ask redress, we are told that the State must first pass a law prohibiting us from enjoying certain privileges and rights, and that after such laws have been passed by the State, we can apply to the United States courts to have such laws declared null and void by *quo warranto* proceedings. The Supreme Court, when applied to, will say to the State, you must not place such laws on your statute book. You can continue your discrimination on account of color. You can continue to place the badge of slavery on persons having more than one-eighth part of Negro blood in their veins, and so long as your State legislatures do not license you so to do, you are safe. For if they (the Negroes) come to us for redress, we will talk about the autonomy of the State must be held inviolate, referring them back to you for satisfaction.

Do you know of anything more degrading to our country, more damnable? The year after this decision the Republican party met with defeat, because it acquiesced by its silence in that abominable decision, nor did it lift a hand to strike down that diabolical sham of judicial monstrosity, neither in Congress nor the great national convention which nominated Blaine and Logan. God, however, has placed them in power again, using the voters and our manner of

electing electors as instruments in his hands. God would have men do right,
harm no one, and to render to every man his just due. Mr. Justice Harlan
rightly says that the Thirteenth Amendment intended that the white race
should have no privilege whatsoever pertaining to citizenship and freedom,
that was not alike extended and to be enjoyed by those persons who, though
the greater part of them were slaves, were invited by an act of Congress to aid
in saving from overthrow a government which, theretofore, by all of its departments, had treated them as an inferior race, with no legal rights or privileges
except such as the white race might choose to grant. It is an indisputable fact
that the amendment last mentioned may be exerted by legislation of a direct
and primary character for the eradication, not simply of the institution of slavery, but of its badges and incidents indicating that the individual was once a
slave. The Supreme Court must decide the interstate commerce law to be
unconstitutional on account of interference with the State's autonomy, for it
must be remembered that Mrs. Robinson, a citizen of Mississippi, bought a
ticket from Grand Junction, Tennessee, to Lynchburg, Virginia, and when praying for satisfaction for rough and contumacious treatment, received at the
hands of the company's agent, she was informed by the court, that the court
was without power to act. Congress had constitutional power to pursue a runaway slave into all the States by legislation, to punish the man that would dare
to conceal the slave. Congress could find the poor fellow seeking God's best
blessing to man, liberty, and return him to his master, but Congress cannot, so
say our honorable court, give aid sufficient to the poor black man, to prove
beyond all doubt to him that he is as free as any other citizen. Mr. Justice
Harlan says: "The difficulty has been to compel a recognition of the legal right
of the black race to take the rank of citizens, and to secure the enjoyment of
privileges belonging under the law to them as a component part of the people for whose welfare government is ordained. At every step in this direction,
the Nation has been confronted with class tyranny, which is of all tyrannies the
most intolerable, for it is ubiquitous in its operation, and weighs perhaps most
heavily on those whose obscurity or distance would draw them from the
notice of a single despot. To-day it is the colored race which is denied by corporations and individuals wielding public authority, rights fundamental in
their freedom and citizenship. AT SOME FUTURE TIME IT MAY BE THAT SOME
OTHER RACE WILL FALL UNDER THE BAN OF RACE DISCRIMINATION." This last
preceding sentence sounds like prophecy from on high. Will the day come
when Justice Bradley will want to hide from his decree of the 15th day of
October, 1883, and say *non est factum*? I conclude with great reluctance these
brief lines, assuring you that the subject is just opened and if desired by you, I
will be glad to give it elaborate attention. I ask no rights and privileges for my
race in this country, which I would not contend for on behalf of the white
people were the conditions changed, or were I to find proscribed white men
in Africa where black rules.

A word more and I am done, as you wish brevity. God may forgive this
corps of unjust judges, but I never can, their very memories will also be
detested by my children's children, nor am I alone in this detestation. The eight

millions of my race and their posterity will stand horror-frozen at the very mention of their names. The scenes that have passed under my eyes upon the public highways, the brutal treatment of helpless women which I have witnessed, since that decision was proclaimed, is enough to move heaven to tears and raise a loud acclaim in hell over the conquest of wrong. But we will wait and pray, and look for a better day, for God still lives and the LORD OF HOSTS REIGNS.

I am, sir, yours, for the Fatherhood of God, and the Brotherhood of man.

— H. M. TURNER.
Atlanta, Georgia, January 4, 1889

Peonage in the South

The Life Story of a Negro Peon

Peonage is the system in which a debtor must work out what he owes in compulsory service to his creditor. In the South, this was the condition of the sharecropper, who went deeper and deeper into debt to the planter on whose farm he worked. Since the planter furnished the goods the cropper needed and kept the account books himself, it was virtually impossible for the black cropper to free himself from debt and thus escape the system.

The selection that follows was obtained from an interview with a black peon. It is of particular interest because it describes not only peonage, but also the convict-lease system, whereby black people were arrested for minor offenses then leased to white farmers by the state for a fee. It is needless to say that the number of arrests made rose with the need for labor on farms.

I am a Negro and was born sometime during the war in Elbert County, Ga., and I reckon by this time I must be a little over forty years old. My mother was not married when I was born, and I never knew who my father was or anything about him. Shortly after the war my mother died, and I was left to the care of my uncle. All this happened before I was eight years old, and so I can't remember very much about it. When I was about ten years old my uncle hired me out to Captain—. I had already learned how to plow, and was also a good hand at picking cotton. I was told that the Captain wanted me for his houseboy, and that later on he was going to train me to be his coachman. To be a coachman in those days was considered a post of honor, and young as I was, I was glad of the chance.

But I had not been at the Captain's a month before I was put to work on the farm, with some twenty or thirty other Negroes—men, women and children. From the beginning the boys had the same tasks as the men and women. There was no difference. We all worked hard during the week, and would frolic on Saturday nights and often on Sundays. And everybody was happy. The men got $3 a week and the women $2. I don't know what the children got. Every week my uncle collected my money for me, but it was very little of it that I ever saw. My uncle fed and clothed me, gave me a place to sleep, and allowed me ten or fifteen cents a week for "spending change," as he called it.

I must have been seventeen or eighteen years old before I got tired of that arrangement, and felt that I was man enough to be working for myself and handling my own wages. The other boys about my age and size were

FROM "The Life Story of a Negro Peon," in *The Life Stories of Undistinguished Americans as Told by Themselves*, ed. by Hamilton Holt (New York, 1906), pp. 183–99.

"drawing" their own pay, and they used to laugh at me and call me "Baby," because my old uncle was always on hand to "draw" my pay. Worked up by these things, I made a break for liberty. Unknown to my uncle or the Captain I went off to a neighboring plantation and hired myself out to another man. The new landlord agreed to give me forty cents a day and furnish me one meal. I thought that was doing fine. Bright and early one Monday morning I started for work, still not letting the others know anything about it. But they found it out before sundown. The Captain came over to the new place and brought some kind of officer of the law. The officer pulled out a long piece of paper from his pocket and read it to my employer. When this was done I heard my new boss say:

"I beg your pardon, Captain. I didn't know this Negro was bound out to you, or I wouldn't have hired him."

"He certainly is bound out to me," said the Captain. "He belongs to me until he is twenty-one, and I'm going to make him know his place."

So I was carried back to the Captain's. That night he made me strip off my clothing down to the waist, ordered his foreman to give me thirty lashes with a buggy whip across my bare back, and stood by until it was done. After that experience the Captain made me stay on his place night and day—but my uncle still continued to "draw" my money.

I was a man nearly grown before I knew how to count from one to one hundred. I was a man nearly grown before I ever saw a colored teacher. I never went to school a day in my life. Today I can't write my own name, though I can read a little. I was a man nearly grown before I ever rode on a railroad train, and then I went on an excursion from Elberton to Athens. What was true of me was true of hundreds of other Negroes around me —'way off there in the country, fifteen or twenty miles from the nearest town.

When I reached twenty-one the Captain told me I was a free man, but he urged me to stay with him. He said he would treat me right, and pay me as much as anybody else would. The Captain's son and I were about the same age, and the Captain said that, as he owned my mother and uncle during slavery, and as his son didn't want me to leave them (since I had been with them so long), he wanted me to stay with the old family. And I stayed. I signed a contract—that is, I made my mark—for one year. The Captain was to give me $3.50 a week, and furnish me a little house on the plantation—a one-room log cabin similar to those used by his other laborers.

During that year I married Mandy. For several years Mandy had been the house-servant for the Captain, his wife, his son and his three daughters, and they all seemed to think a good deal of her. As an evidence of their regard they gave us a suit of furniture, which cost about $25, and we set up housekeeping in one of the Captain's two-room shanties. I thought I was the biggest man in Georgia. Mandy still kept her place in the "Big House" after our marriage. We did so well for the first year that I renewed my contract for the second year, and for the third, fourth and fifth year I did the same thing. Before the end of the fifth year the Captain had died, and his son, who had married some two or three years before, took charge of the plantation. Also, for two or three years, this son had been serving at Atlanta in some big office to which he had been elected. I think it was in the Legislature or something of that sort—anyhow, all the people called him Senator. At the end of the fifth year the Senator suggested that I sign up a contract for ten years; then, he said, we wouldn't have to fix up papers every year. I asked my wife about it; she consented; and so I made a ten-year contract.

Not long afterward the Senator had a long, low shanty built on his place. A great big chimney, with a wide, open fireplace, was built at one end of it and on each side of the house, running lengthwise, there was a row of frames or stalls just large enough to hold a single mattress. The places for these mattresses were fixed one above the other; so that there was a double row of these stalls or pens on each side. They looked for all the world like stalls for horses. Since then I have seen cabooses similarly arranged as sleeping quarters for railroad laborers.

Nobody seemed to know what the Senator was fixing for. All doubts were put aside one bright day in April when about forty able-bodied Negroes, bound in iron chains, and some of them handcuffed, were brought out to the Senator's farm in three big wagons. They were quartered in the long, low shanty, and it was afterward called the stockade. This was the beginning of the Senator's convict camp. These men were prisoners who had been leased by the Senator from the State of Georgia at about $200 each per year, the State agreeing to pay for guards and physicians, for necessary inspection, for inquests, all rewards for escaped convicts, the cost of litigation and all other incidental expenses.

When I saw these men in shackles, and the guards with their guns, I was scared nearly to death. I felt like running away, but I didn't know where to go. And if there had been any place to go to, I would have had to leave my wife and child behind. We free laborers held a meeting. We all wanted to quit. We sent a man to tell the Senator about it. Word came back that we were all under contract for ten years and that the Senator would hold us to the letter of the contract, or put us in chains and lock us up—the same as the other prisoners. It was made plain to us by some white people we talked to that in the contracts we had signed we had all agreed to be locked up in a stockade at night or at any other time that our employer saw fit; further, we learned that we could not lawfully break our contract for any reason and go and hire ourselves to somebody else without the consent of our employer; and, more than that, if we got mad and ran away, we could be run down by bloodhounds, arrested without process of law, and be returned to our employer, who, according to the contract, might beat us brutally or administer any kind of punishment that he thought proper. In other words, we had sold ourselves into slavery—and what could we do about it? The white folks had all the courts, all the guns, all the hounds, all the railroads, all the telegraph wires, all the newspapers, all the money, and nearly all the land—and we had only our ignorance, our poverty and our empty hands. We decided that the best thing to do was to shut our mouths, say nothing, and go back to work. And most of us worked side by side with those convicts during the remainder of the ten years.

But this first batch of convicts was only the beginning. Within six months another stockade was built, and twenty or thirty other convicts were brought to the plantation, among them six or eight women! The Senator had bought an additional thousand acres of land, and to his already large cotton plantation he added two great big sawmills and went into the lumber business. Within two years the Senator had in all 200 Negroes working on his plantation— about half of them free laborers, so called, and about half of them convicts. The only difference between the free laborers and the others was that the free laborers could come and go as they pleased, at night—that is, they were not locked up at night, and were not, as a general thing, whipped for slight offenses.

The troubles of the free laborers began at the close of the ten-year period. To a man they all refused to sign new contracts—even for one year, not to say anything of ten years. And just when we thought that our bondage was at an end we found that it had really just begun. Two or three years before, or about a year and a half after the Senator had started his camp, he had established a large store, which was called the commissary. All of us free laborers were compelled to buy our supplies—food, clothing, etc. —from that store. We never used any money in our dealings with the commissary, only tickets or orders, and we had a general settlement once each year, in October. In this store we were charged all sorts of high prices for goods, because every year we would come out in debt to our employer. If not that, we seldom had more than $5 or $10 coming to us—and that for a whole year's work. Well, at the close of the tenth year, when we kicked and meant to leave the Senator, he said to some of us with a smile (and I never will forget that smile—I can see it now):

"Boys, I'm sorry you're going to leave me. I hope you will do well in your new places—so well that you will be able to pay me the little balances which most of you owe me."

Word was sent out for all of us to meet him at the commissary at 2 o'clock. There he told us that, after we had signed what he called a written acknowledgement of our debts, we might go and look for new places. The storekeeper took us one by one and read to us statements of our accounts. According to the books there was no man of us who owed the Senator less than $100; some of us were put down for as much as $200. 1 owed $165, according to the bookkeeper. These debts were not accumulated during one year, but ran back for three and four years, so we were told—in spite of the fact that we understood that we had had a full settlement at the end of each year. But no one of us would have dared to dispute a white man's word—oh, no; not in those days. Besides, we fellows didn't care anything about the amounts—we were after getting away; and we had been told that we might too, if we signed the acknowledgement. We would have signed anything, just to get away. So we stepped up, we did, and made our marks. That same night we were rounded up by a constable and ten or twelve white men, who aided him, and we were locked up, every one of us, in one of the Senator's stockades. The next morning it was explained to us by the two guards appointed to watch us that, in the papers we had signed the day before, we had not only made acknowledgement of our indebtedness, but that we had also agreed to work for the Senator until the debts were paid by hard labor. And from that day forward we were treated just like convicts. Really we had made ourselves lifetime slaves, or peons, as the laws called us. But call it slavery, peonage, or what not, the truth is we lived in a hell on earth what time we spent in the Senator's peon camp.

I lived in that camp, as a peon, for nearly three years. My wife fared better than I did, as did the wives of some of the other Negroes, because the white men about the camp used these unfortunate creatures as their mistresses. When I was first put in the stockade my wife was still kept for a while in the "Big House," but my little boy, who was only nine years old, was given away to a Negro family across the river in South Carolina, and I never saw or heard of him after that. When I left the camp my wife had had two children by some one of the white bosses, and she was living in a fairly good shape in a little house off to herself. But the poor Negro women who were not in the class with my wife fared about as bad as the helpless Negro men. Most of the time the women who were peons or convicts were compelled to wear men's clothes. Sometimes, when I have seen them dressed like men, and plowing or hoeing or hauling logs or working at the blacksmith's trade, just the same as men, my heart would bleed and my blood would boil, but I was powerless to raise a hand. It would have meant death on the spot to have said a word. Of the first six women brought to the camp, two of them gave birth to children after they had been there more than twelve months—and the babies had white men for their fathers!

The stockades in which we slept, were, I believe, the filthiest places in the world. They were cesspools of nastiness. During the thirteen years that I was there I am willing to swear that a mattress was never moved after it had been brought there, except to turn it over once or twice a month. No sheets were used, only dark-colored blankets. Most of the men slept every night in the clothing that they had worked in all day. Some of the worst characters were made to sleep in chairs. The doors were locked and barred, each night, and tallow-candles were the only lights allowed. Really the stockades were but little more than cow sheds, horse stables, or hog pens. Strange to say, not a great number of these people died while I was there, though a great many came away maimed and bruised and, in some cases, disabled for life. As far as I can remember only about ten died during the last ten years that I was there, two of these being killed outright by the guards for trivial offenses.

It was a hard school that peon camp was, but I learned more there in a few short months by contact with those poor fellows from the outside world than ever I had known before. Most of what I learned was evil, and I now know that I should have been better off without the knowledge, but much of what I learned was helpful to me. Barring two or three severe and brutal whippings which I received, I got along very well, all things considered; but the system is damnable. A favorite way of whipping a man was to strap him down to a log, flat on his back, and spank him fifty or sixty times on his bare feet with a shingle or a huge piece of plank. When the man would get up with sore and blistered feet and an aching body, if he could not then keep up with the other men at work he would be strapped to the log again, this time face downward, and would be lashed with a buggy trace on his bare back. When a woman had to be whipped it was usually done in private, though they would be compelled to fall down across a barrel or something of the kind and receive the licks on their backsides.

The working day on a peon farm begins with sunrise and ends when the sun goes down; or, in other words, the average peon works from ten to twelve hours each day, with one hour (from 12 o'clock to 1 o'clock) for dinner. Hot or cold, sun or rain, this is the rule. As to their meals, the laborers are divided up into squads or companies, just the same as soldiers in a great military camp would be. Two or three men in each stockade are appointed as cooks. From thirty to forty men report to each cook. In the warm months (or eight or nine months out of the year) the cooking is done on the outside, just behind the stockades; in the cold months the cooking is done inside the stockades. Each peon is provided with a great big tin cup, a flat tin pan and two big tin spoons. No knives or forks are ever seen, except those used by the cooks. At meal time the peons pass in single file before the cooks, and hold out their pans and cups to receive their allowances. Cow peas (red or white, which when boiled turn black), fat bacon and old-fashioned Georgia cornbread, baked in pones from one to two and three inches thick, made up the chief articles of food. Black coffee, black molasses and brown sugar are also used abundantly. Once in a great while, on Sundays, biscuits would be made, but they would always be made from the kind of flour called "shorts." As a rule, breakfast consisted of coffee, fried bacon, cornbread, and sometimes molasses—and one "helping" of each was all that was allowed. Peas, boiled with huge hunks of fat bacon, and a hoe-cake, as big as a man's hand, usually answered for dinner. Sometimes this dinner bill of fare gave place to bacon and greens (collard or turnip) and pot liquor. Though we raised corn, potatoes and other vegetables, we never got a chance at such things unless we could steal them and cook them secretly. Supper consisted of coffee, fried bacon and molasses. But, although the food was limited to certain things, I am sure we all got a plenty of the things allowed. As coarse as these things were, we kept, as a rule, fat and sleek and as strong as mules. And that, too, in spite of the fact that we had no special arrangements for taking regular baths, and no very great effort was made to keep us regularly in clean clothes. No tables were used or allowed. In summer we would sit down on the ground and eat our meals, and in winter we would sit around inside the filthy stockades. Each man was his own dishwasher—that is to say, each man was responsible for the care of his pan and cup and spoons. My dishes got washed about once a week!

Today, I am told, there are six or seven of these private camps in Georgia —that is to say, camps where most of the convicts are leased from the State of Georgia. But there are hundreds and hundreds of farms all over the State where Negroes, and in some cases poor white folks, are held in bondage on the ground that they are working out debts, or where the contracts which they have made hold them in a kind of perpetual bondage, because, under those contracts they may not quit one employer and hire out to another except by and with the knowledge and consent of the former employer.

One of the usual ways to secure laborers for a large peonage camp is for the proprietor to send out an agent to the little courts in the towns and villages, and where a man charged with some petty offense has no friends or money the agent will urge him to plead guilty, with the understanding that the agent will pay his fine, and in that way save him from the disgrace of being sent to jail or the chain-gang! For this high favor the man must sign beforehand a paper signifying his willingness to go to the farm and work out the amount of the fine imposed. When he reaches the farm he has to be fed and clothed, to be sure, and these things are charged up to his account. By the time he has worked out his first debt another is hanging over his head, and so on and so on, by a sort of endless chain, for an indefinite period, as in every case the indebtedness is arbitrarily arranged by the employer. In many cases it is very evident that the court officials are in collusion with the proprietors or agents, and that they divide the "graft" among themselves. As an example of this dickering among the whites, every year many convicts were brought to the Senator's camp from a certain county in South Georgia, 'way down in the turpentine district. The majority of these men were charged with adultery, which is an offense against the laws of the great and sovereign State of Georgia! Upon inquiry I learned that down in that county a number of Negro lewd women were employed by certain white men to entice Negro men into their houses; and then, on a certain night, at a given signal, when all was in readiness, raids would be made by the officers upon these houses, and the men would be arrested and charged with living in adultery. Nine out of ten of these men, so arrested and so charged, would find their way ultimately to some convict camp, and, as I said, many of them found their way every year to the Senator's camp while I was there. The low-down women were never punished in any way. On the contrary, I was told that they always seemed to stand in high favor with the sheriffs, constables and other officers. There can be no room to doubt that they assisted very materially in furnishing laborers for the prison pens of Georgia, and the belief was general among the men that they were regularly paid for their work. I could tell more, but I've said enough to make anybody's heart sick. This great and terrible iniquity is, I know, widespread throughout Georgia and many other Southern States.

But I didn't tell you how I got out. I didn't get out—they put me out. When I had served as a peon for nearly three years—and you remember that they claimed I owed them only $165—when I served for nearly three years one of the bosses came to me and said that my time was up. He happened to be the one who was said to be living with my wife. He gave me a new suit of overalls, which cost about seventy-five cents, took me in a buggy and carried me across the Broad River into South Carolina, set me down and told me to "git." I didn't have a cent of money, and I wasn't feeling well, but somehow I managed to get a move on me. I begged my way to Columbia. In two or three days I ran across a man looking for laborers to carry to Birmingham, and I joined his gang. I have been here in the Birmingham district since they released me, and I reckon I'll die either in a coal mine or an iron furnace. It don't make much difference which. Either is better than a Georgia peon camp. And a Georgia peon camp is hell itself!

SUGGESTIONS FOR FURTHER READING

Rayford W. Logan called the last quarter of the 19th century the low point in African-American history in his book, *The Negro in American Life and Thought: The Nadir, 1877–1901* (1954). Leon Litwack looks at the development of racial segregation in *Trouble in Mind: Black Southerners in the Age of Jim Crow* (1998). The continued development of a black intellectual tradition is described in Howard Brotz (ed.), *Negro Social and Political Thought, 1850–1920* (1966), August Meier, *Negro Thought in America, 1880–1915*★ (1963), and William Toll, *The Resurgence of Race: Black Social Theory from Reconstruction to the Pan African Conference* (1979). The racial attitudes of whites are discussed in George Frederickson, *The Black Image in the White Mind: The Debate on Afro American Character and Destiny, 1817–1914* (1971) and Joel Williamson, *A Rage for Order: Black-White Relations in the American South since Emancipation*★ (1984).

The disenfranchisement of southern blacks is described in Paul Lewinson, *Race, Class and Party: A History of Negro Suffrage and White Politics in the South* (1932), J. Morgan Kousser, *The Shaping of Southern Politics: Suffrage Restriction and the Establishment of the One Party South, 1880–1910*★ (1974) and Darlene Clark Hine, *Black Victory: The Rise and Fall of the White Primary in Texas* (1978). See also Helen G. Edmonds, *The Negro and Fusion Politics in North Carolina, 1894–1901* (1951) and Eric Anderson, *Race and Politics in North Carolina, 1872–1901*★ (1981). An important study is Charles A. Lofgren, *The Plessy Case: A Legal-Historical Interpretation*★ (1987).

Developments outside the South are covered in David Gerber, *Black Ohio and the Color Line, 1860–1915*★ (1976), Nell Irwin Painter, *Black Migration to Kansas after Reconstruction*★ (1977), and a series of studies of black urbanization, including Elizabeth Pleck, *Black Migration and Poverty: Boston, 1865–1900* (1979), David Katzman, *Before the Ghetto*★ [Detroit] (1973), Kenneth Kusmer, *A Ghetto Takes Shape: Black Cleveland, 1870–1930*★ (1976), and Roger Lane, *Roots of Violence in Black Philadelphia, 1860–1900*★ (1986).

Studies of African-Americans in the South during this period include Loren Schweninger, *Black Property Owners in the South, 1790–1915*★ (1990), Howard N. Rabinowitz, *Race Relations in the Urban South, 1865–1890*★ (1978), Charles E. Wynes, *Race Relations in Virginia, 1870–1902* (1961), George B. Tindall, *South Carolina Negroes, 1877–1900* (1961), and Frenise A. Logan, *The Negro in North Carolina, 1879–1894* (1964).

Important works dealing with the period are Jacqueline Jones Royster (ed.), *Southern Horrors and Other Writings: The Anti-Lynching Campaign of Ida B. Wells, 1892–1900*★ (1996), Willard B. Gatewood, Jr., *Black Americans and the White Man's Burden, 1898–1903* (1975), and William H. Harris, *The Harder We Run: Black Workers since the Civil War* (1982).

★ Books marked by an asterisk are available in paperback.

7

The Organization
of Protest

INTRODUCTION

Out of the despair of the 1890s emerged the most powerful black man ever to operate on the American scene, Booker T. Washington. Born into slavery about 1856, he was a man of driving ambition and obvious ability. By 1895, when he made his famous Atlanta Exposition address, he had achieved national prominence. Washington decided to concentrate on the traits that "decent" whites were prepared to allow black men to develop. He emphasized thrift, hard work, self-help, and industrial education and played down political and social rights. From his base as principal of Tuskegee Normal and Industrial Institute in Alabama, Washington tried to direct the affairs of black people in America.

Because of his policy of apparent accommodation to the racial policies of the dominant society, Washington became the conduit through which white financial support and federal political appointments flowed to the black community. Washington seemed to hold the average ignorant rural black to blame for his condition and encouraged him to better himself through thrift and accumulation—the gospel of wealth philosophy. What he failed to realize was that the rural black would gladly have been thrifty had there been anything for him to save. Washington never really came to grips with the rural South. He was more interested in organizing the growing black middle class, and to that end he founded, with the financial backing of Andrew Carnegie, the National Negro Business League to preach the virtues of black business development in black communities. Washington seemed convinced that if black people could accumulate enough wealth, they could win the acceptance of white society.

It must be pointed out that, though Washington's public posture was accommodative, privately he was actively engaged in trying to reduce the discrimination suffered by blacks. He spent a great deal of money and effort behind the scenes trying to halt disfranchisement and segregation. In retrospect, it appears that his greatest failing was his desire for personal power and prestige. He made every effort possible to stifle criticism of himself and his policies by other blacks who often felt that other voices should be heard even while they supported his policies.

By 1903, it was clear that Washington's greatest competition for the leadership of the black community would come from the brilliant and aggressive William Edward Burghardt Du Bois. Du Bois, the first black to receive a Ph.D. from Harvard, had as his original ambition to make a complete study of the history and the present condition of black people in America. Although he had worked with Washington on several projects in the first years of the century, Du Bois found Washington's inflexibility and lack of receptivity to criticism a barrier to their further cooperation.

In 1905, with the support of other black intellectuals, Du Bois founded the Niagara Movement to protest against the increasing discrimination met by blacks in the United States and to work for the reestablishment of black people's right to vote and the elimination of race or color distinctions wherever they occurred. Although the concrete gains of the Movement were few, its manner of operation was the prototype for that of many future organizations.

Washington strongly opposed the Niagara group and used every method at his disposal to hinder its development. He bribed newspaper editors to ignore or attack the Movement and its leaders, placed undercover agents in its midst to warn him of impending programs, prevented members of the group from receiving political office, and had funds cut off from schools where the leaders of the Movement taught. Not surprisingly, this opposition was seriously detrimental to the growth of the Movement.

As the Niagara Movement was beginning to lose strength, a new organization was coming into being as a result of the desire of certain Northern white philanthropists and social workers to offer an alternative to Washington's program for racial uplift. Some of these whites had previously supported Washington, but had come to feel that his monopoly in the field of race relations was not best for black people. In 1909, a call went out for a National Negro Conference, to be held in New York City. Many members of the Niagara Movement attended, along with a number of liberal whites who were political Progressives. The next year, the National Association for the Advancement of Colored People (NAACP) was founded to carry out the program formulated at the National Negro Conference. Du Bois was the only officer of the original NAACP who was black.

Although Du Bois would have preferred to work primarily with an all-black organization, it became clear to him that the financial support necessary for such a group would not be forthcoming as long as Washington dominated the philanthropic scene. Thus, he agreed to serve as director of research for the fledgling NAACP. When he left Atlanta, where he had been doing scholarly work at Atlanta University, it is said that the city administration gave a sigh of relief, for he had earned a reputation for being troublesome.

Once in New York, against the advice of some of the NAACP board members, Du Bois began to publish a monthly journal, *The Crisis*. This publication was his major interest until he broke with the Association in 1934. Fortunately for Du Bois, *The Crisis* quickly became self-supporting. This freed him from the need for financial support from the Association, which had initially sought to limit his control over the journal and the views presented in it. During the Depression, when the circulation of *The Crisis* dropped rapidly, the NAACP had to subsidize its production once again, and the leadership of the Association seized the opportunity to reassert its control over the journal and attacked Du Bois for his growing separatism.

Du Bois responded with a vigorous attack on the leadership, which he considered to be more interested in keeping the support of whites than in advancing the cause of blacks. Finally, convinced that the black people had to take charge of their own liberation, Du Bois left the Association and returned to his work at Atlanta University, from which issued some of his most important writings, notably *Black Reconstruction in America* and the autobiographical *Dusk of Dawn*.

By 1915, the year of the death of Booker T. Washington and the year of the Association's first major court victory, in which the Oklahoma "grandfather" clause was declared unconstitutional by the Supreme Court, the NAACP was dearly embarked on its course as the most important contemporary defense organization for blacks.

In recent decades, the NAACP has come under increasing criticism from militant blacks because of its middle-class values and its public posture of moderation. But it must be remembered that as recently as the 1950s several Southern states attempted to ban the Association because of its radicalism.

Education before Equality

The Atlanta Exposition Address, 1895

BOOKER T. WASHINGTON

When called upon to make one of the opening addresses at the Cotton States and International Exposition in Atlanta in the fall of 1895, Booker T. Washington took the opportunity to express his solution to the "Negro problem." Correctly sensing the mood of the white world, both North and South, as well as that of many blacks, he made the proposal known as the Atlanta Compromise. Appealing to the nativist tendencies of his audience, he reminded them of what he called the familiarity and fidelity of the Southern black man, and, rejecting social equality as an immediate goal, he spoke of building a new South on agricultural and industrial cooperation between the races. A firm believer in inevitable progress, Washington rejected forced equality in favor of an equality that he thought the black man could earn through education and hard work.

The following selection, taken from Washington's autobiography, includes the address as originally delivered, as well as comments about the response it drew.

The Atlanta Exposition, at which I had been asked to make an address as a representative of the Negro race ... was opened with a short address from Governor Bullock. After other interesting exercises, including an invocation from Bishop Nelson, of Georgia, a dedicatory ode by Albert Howell, Jr., and addresses by the President of the Exposition and Mrs. Joseph Thompson, the President of the Woman's Board, Governor Bullock introduced me with the words, "We have with us to-day a representative of Negro enterprise and Negro civilization."

When I arose to speak, there was considerable cheering, especially from the coloured people. As I remember it now, the thing that was uppermost in my mind was the desire to say something that would cement the friendship of the races and bring about hearty cooperation between them. So far as my outward surroundings were concerned, the only thing that I recall distinctly now is that when I got up, I saw thousands of eyes looking intently into my face. The following is the address which I delivered: —

Mr. President and Gentlemen of the
Board of Directors and Citizens:

One-third of the population of the South is of the Negro race. No enterprise seeking the material, civil, or moral welfare of this section can

FROM Booker T. Washington, *Up From Slavery* (Boston, 1901), pp. 217–27.

disregard this element of our population and reach the highest success. I but convey to you, Mr. President and Directors, the sentiment of the masses of my race when I say that in no way have the value and manhood of the American Negro been more fittingly and generously recognized than by the managers of this magnificent Exposition at every stage of its progress. It is a recognition that will do more to cement the friendship of the two races than any occurrence since the dawn of our freedom.

Not only this, but the opportunity here afforded will awaken among us a new era of industrial progress. Ignorant and inexperienced, it is not strange that in the first years of our new life we began at the top instead of at the bottom; that a seat in Congress or the state legislature was more sought than real estate or industrial skill; that the political convention of stump speaking had more attractions than starting a dairy farm or truck garden.

A ship lost at sea for many days suddenly sighted a friendly vessel. From the mast of the unfortunate vessel was seen a signal, "Water, water; we die of thirst!" The answer from the friendly vessel at once came back, "Cast down your bucket where you are." A second time the signal, "Water, water; send us water!" ran up from the distressed vessel, and was answered, "Cast down your bucket where you are." And a third and fourth signal for water was answered, "Cast down your bucket where you are." The captain of the distressed vessel, at last heeding the injunction, cast down his bucket, and it came up full of fresh, sparkling water from the mouth of the Amazon River. To those of my race who depend on bettering their condition in a foreign land or who underestimate the importance of cultivating friendly relations with the Southern white man, who is their next-door neighbour, I would say: "Cast down your bucket where you are"—cast it down in making friends in every manly way of the people of all races by whom we are surrounded.

Cast it down in agriculture, mechanics, in commerce, in domestic service, and in the professions. And in this connection it is well to bear in mind that whatever other sins the South may be called to bear, when it comes to business, pure and simple, it is in the South that the Negro is given a man's chance in the commercial world, and in nothing is this Exposition more eloquent than in emphasizing this chance. Our greatest danger is that in the great leap from slavery to freedom we may overlook the fact that the masses of us are to live by the productions of our hands, and fail to keep in mind that we shall prosper in proportion as we learn to dignify and glorify common labour and put brains and skill into the common occupations of life; shall prosper in proportion as we learn to draw the line between the superficial and the substantial, the ornamental gewgaws of life and the useful. No race can prosper till it learns that there is as much dignity in tilling a field as in writing a poem. It is at the bottom of life we must begin, and not at the top. Nor should we permit our grievances to overshadow our opportunities.

To those of the white race who look to the incoming of those of
foreign birth and strange tongue and habits for the prosperity of the
South, were I permitted I would repeat what I say to my own race, "Cast
down your bucket where you are." Cast it down among the eight millions of Negroes whose habits you know, whose fidelity and love you
have tested in days when to have proved treacherous meant the ruin of
your firesides. Cast down your bucket among these people who have,
without strikes and labour wars, tilled your fields, cleared your forests,
builded your railroads and cities, and brought forth treasures from the
bowels of the earth, and helped make possible this magnificent representation of the progress of the South. Casting down your bucket among
my people, helping and encouraging them as you are doing on these
grounds, and to education of head, hand, and heart, you will find that
they will buy your surplus land, make blossom the waste places in your
fields, and run your factories. While doing this, you can be sure in the
future, as in the past, that you and your families will be surrounded by
the most patient, faithful, law-abiding, and unresentful people that the
world has seen. As we have proved our loyalty to you in the past, in nursing your children, watching by the sickbed of your mothers and fathers,
and often following them with tear-dimmed eyes to their graves, so in
the future, in our humble way, we shall stand by you with a devotion that
no foreigner can approach, ready to lay down our lives, if need be, in
defence of yours, interlacing our industrial, commercial, civil, and religious life with yours in a way that shall make the interests of both races
one. In all things that are purely social we can be as separate as the fingers, yet one as the hand in all things essential to mutual progress.

There is no defense or security for any of us except in the highest
intelligence and development of all. If anywhere there are efforts tending
to curtail the fullest growth of the Negro, let these efforts be turned into
stimulating, encouraging, and making him the most useful and intelligent
citizen. Effort or means so invested will pay a thousand per cent interest.
These efforts will be twice blessed—"blessing him that gives and him
that takes."

There is no escape through law of man or God from the inevitable:—

> The laws of changeless justice bind
>   Oppressor with oppressed;
> And close as sin and suffering joined
>   We march to fate abreast.

Nearly sixteen millions of hands will aid you in pulling the load
upward, or they will pull against you the load downward. We shall constitute one-third and more of the ignorance and crime of the South, or
one-third its intelligence and progress; we shall contribute one-third to
the business and industrial prosperity of the South, or we shall prove a

veritable body of death, stagnating, depressing, retarding every effort to advance the body politic.

Gentlemen of the Exposition, as we present to you our humble effort at an exhibition of our progress, you must not expect overmuch. Starting thirty years ago with ownership here and there in a few quilts and pumpkins and chickens (gathered from miscellaneous sources), remember the path that has led from these to the inventions and production of agricultural implements, buggies, steam-engines, newspapers, books, statuary, carving, paintings, the management of drugstores and banks, has not been trodden without contact with thorns and thistles. While we take pride in what we exhibit as a result of our independent efforts, we do not for a moment forget that our part in this exhibition would fall far short of your expectations but for the constant help that has come to our educational life, not only from the Southern states, but especially from Northern philanthropists, who have made their gifts a constant stream of blessing and encouragement.

The wisest among my race understand that the agitation of questions of social equality is the extremest folly, and that progress in the enjoyment of all the privileges that will come to us must be the result of severe and constant struggle rather than an artificial forcing. No race that has anything to contribute to the markets of the world is long in any degree ostracized. It is important and right that all privileges of the law be ours, but it is vastly more important that we be prepared for the exercises of these privileges. The opportunity to earn a dollar in a factory just now is worth infinitely more than the opportunity to spend a dollar in an opera-house.

In conclusion, may I repeat that nothing in thirty years has given us more hope and encouragement, and drawn us so near to you of the white race, as this opportunity offered by the Exposition; and here bending, as it were, over the altar that represents the results of the struggles of your race and mine, both starting practically emptyhanded three decades ago, I pledge that in your effort to work out the great and intricate problem which God has laid at the doors of the South, you shall have at all times the patient, sympathetic help of my race; only let this be constantly in mind, that, while from representations in these buildings of the product of field, of forest, of mine, of factory, letters, and art, much good will come, yet far above and beyond material benefits will be that higher good, that, let us pray God, will come, in a blotting out of sectional differences and racial animosities and suspicions, in a determination to administer absolute justice, in a willing obedience among all classes to the mandates of law. This, then, coupled with our material prosperity, will bring into our beloved South a new heaven and a new earth.

The first thing that I remember, after I had finished speaking, was that Governor Bullock rushed across the platform and took me by the hand, and that others did the same. I received so many and such hearty congratulations that I found it difficult to get out of the building. I did not appreciate to any degree, however, the impression which my address seemed to have made, until the next morning, when I went into the business part of the city. As soon as I was recognized, I was surprised to find myself pointed out and surrounded by a crowd of men who wished to shake hands with me. This was kept up on every street on to which I went, to an extent which embarrassed me so much that I went back to my boarding-place. The next morning I returned to Tuskegee. At the station in Atlanta, and at almost all of the stations at which the train stopped between that city and Tuskegee, I found a crowd of people anxious to shake hands with me.

The papers in all parts of the United States published the address in full, and for months afterward there were complimentary editorial references to it. Mr. Clark Howell, the editor of the Atlanta *Constitution*, telegraphed to a New York paper, among other words, the following, "I do not exaggerate when I say that Professor Booker T. Washington's address yesterday was one of the most notable speeches, both as to character and as to the warmth of its reception, ever delivered to a Southern audience. The address was a revelation. The whole speech is a platform upon which blacks and whites can stand with full justice to each other."

The Boston *Transcript* said editorially: "The speech of Booker T. Washington at the Atlanta Exposition, this week, seems to have dwarfed all the other proceedings and the Exposition itself. The sensation that it has caused in the press has never been equalled."

I very soon began receiving all kinds of propositions from lecture bureaus, and editors of magazines and papers, to take the lecture platform, and to write articles. One lecture bureau offered me fifty thousand dollars, or two hundred dollars a night and expenses, if I would place my services at its disposal for a given period. To all these communications I replied that my life-work was at Tuskegee; and that whenever I spoke it must be in the interests of the Tuskegee school and my race, and that I would enter into no arrangements that seemed to place a mere commercial value upon my services.

Some days after its delivery I sent a copy of my address to the President of the United States, the Hon. Grover Cleveland. I received from him the following autographed reply:—

Gray Gables, Buzzard's Bay, Mass.,
October 6, 1895

Booker T. Washington, Esq.:

My Dear Sir:

I thank you for sending me a copy of your address delivered at the Atlanta Exposition.

I thank you with much enthusiasm for making the address. I have read it with intense interest, and I think the Exposition would be fully justified if it did not do more than furnish the opportunity for its delivery. Your words cannot fail to delight and encourage all who wish well for your race; and if our coloured fellow-citizens do not from your utterances gather new hope and form new determinations to gain every valuable advantage offered them by their citizenship, it will be strange indeed.

Yours very truly,
GROVER CLEVELAND

Equality and Education

Of Mr. Booker T. Washington and Others

W. E. B. DU BOIS

In 1903, W. E. B. Du Bois, the new contender for the position of spokesman for the black community, published the essay presented next under the title "Of Mr. Booker T. Washington and Others." It was the first public sign of Du Bois' growing disenchantment with Washington, with whom he had worked earlier on various projects.

Du Bois had become increasingly suspicious of the power enjoyed by Washington as a result of the financial support of the white community. He noted that, although Washington had spoken in 1895 of increased cooperation between the races, the end of the century had brought the disfranchisement of blacks and increased color discrimination. Du Bois called for criticism by blacks of Washington's program of accommodation. According to him, it was stifling the development of the "talented tenth" of black youth capable of competing on equal terms with whites and discouraging blacks from insisting on the natural and civil rights necessary to their advancement.

From birth till death enslaved; in word, in deed, unmanned!
Hereditary bondsmen! Know ye not
Who would be free themselves must strike the blow?

BYRON

Easily the most striking thing in the history of the American Negro since 1876 is the ascendancy of Mr. Booker T. Washington. It began at the time when war memories and ideals were rapidly passing; a day of astonishing commercial development was dawning; a sense of doubt and hesitation overtook the freedmen's sons,—then it was that his leading began. Mr. Washington came, with a single definite programme, at the psychological moment when the nation was a little ashamed of having bestowed so much sentiment on Negroes, and was concentrating its energies on Dollars. His programme of industrial education, conciliation of the South, and submission and silence as to civil and political rights, was not wholly original; the Free Negroes from 1830 up to wartime had striven to build industrial schools, and the American Missionary Association had from the first taught various trades; and Price and others had sought a way of honorable alliance with the best of the Southerners. But Mr. Washington first indissolubly linked these things; he put enthusiasm, unlimited

FROM W. E. B. Du Bois, "Of Mr. Booker T. Washington and Others," *Souls of Black Folk* (Chicago, 1903).

energy, and perfect faith into this programme, and changed it from a by-path into a veritable Way of Life. And the tale of the methods by which he did this is a fascinating study of human life.

It startled the nation to hear a Negro advocating such a programme after many decades of bitter complaint; it startled and won the applause of the South, it interested and won the admiration of the North; and after a confused murmur of protest, it silenced if it did not convert the Negroes themselves.

To gain the sympathy and cooperation of the various elements comprising the white South was Mr. Washington's first task; and this, at the time Tuskegee was founded, seemed, for a black man, well-nigh impossible. And yet ten years later it was done in the word spoken at Atlanta: "In all things purely social we can be as separate as the five fingers, and yet one as the hand in all things essential to mutual progress." This "Atlanta Compromise" is by all odds the most notable thing in Mr. Washington's career. The South interpreted it in different ways: the radicals received it as a complete surrender of the demand for civil and political equality; the conservatives, as a generously conceived working basis for mutual understanding. So both approved it, and to-day its author is certainly the most distinguished Southerner since Jefferson Davis, and the one with the largest personal following.

Next to this achievement comes Mr. Washington's work in gaining place and consideration in the North. Others less shrewd and tactful had formerly essayed to sit on these two stools and had fallen between them; but as Mr. Washington knew the heart of the South from birth and training, so by singular insight he intuitively grasped the spirit of the age which was dominating the North. And so thoroughly did he learn the speech and thought of triumphant commercialism, and the ideals of material prosperity, that the picture of a lone black boy poring over a French grammar amid the weeds and dirt of a neglected home soon seemed to him the acme of absurdities. One wonders what Socrates and St. Francis of Assisi would say to this.

And yet this very singleness of vision and thorough oneness with his age is a mark of the successful man. It is as though Nature must needs make men narrow in order to give them force. So Mr. Washington's cult has gained unquestioning followers, his work has wonderfully prospered, his friends are legion, and his enemies are confounded. To-day he stands as the one recognized spokesman of his ten million fellows, and one of the most notable figures in a nation of seventy millions. One hesitates, therefore, to criticise a life which, beginning with so little, has done so much. And yet the time is come when one may speak in all sincerity and utter courtesy of the mistakes and shortcomings of Mr. Washington's career, as well as of his triumphs, without being thought captious or envious, and without forgetting that it is easier to do ill than well in the world.

The criticism that has hitherto met Mr. Washington has not always been of this broad character. In the South especially has he had to walk warily to avoid the harsh judgments,—and naturally so, for he is dealing with the one subject of deepest sensitiveness to that section. Twice—once when at the Chicago celebration of the Spanish-American War he alluded to the color-prejudice that is "eating away the vitals of the South," and once when he dined with President Roosevelt—has the resulting Southern criticism been violent enough to threaten seriously his popularity. In the North the feeling has several times forced itself into words, that Mr. Washington's counsels of submission overlooked certain elements of true manhood, and that his educational programme was unnecessarily narrow. Usually, however, such criticism has not found open expression, although, too, the spiritual sons of the Abolitionists have not been prepared to acknowledge that the schools founded before Tuskegee, by men of broad ideals and self-sacrificing spirit, were wholly failures or worthy of ridicule. While, then, criticism has not failed to follow Mr. Washington, yet the prevailing public opinion of the land has been but too willing to deliver the solution of a wearisome problem into his hands, and say, "If that is all you and your race ask, take it."

Among his own people, however, Mr. Washington has encountered the strongest and most lasting opposition, amounting at times to bitterness, and even to-day continuing strong and insistent even though largely silenced in outward expression by the public opinion of the nation. Some of this opposition is, of course, mere envy; the disappointment of displaced demagogues and the spite of narrow minds. But aside from this, there is among educated and thoughtful colored men in all parts of the land a feeling of deep regret, sorrow, and apprehension at the wide currency and ascendancy which some of Mr. Washington's theories have gained. These same men admire his sincerity of purpose, and are willing to forgive much to honest endeavor which is doing something worth the doing. They cooperate with Mr. Washington as far as they conscientiously can; and, indeed, it is no ordinary tribute to this man's tact and power that, steering as he must between so many diverse interests and opinions, he so largely retains the respect of all.

But the hushing of the criticism of honest opponents is a dangerous thing. It leads some of the best of the critics to unfortunate silence and paralysis of effort, and others to burst into speech so passionately and intemperately as to lose listeners. Honest and earnest criticism from those whose interests are most nearly touched,—criticism of writers by readers, of government by those governed, of leaders by those led,—this is the soul of democracy and the safeguard of modern society. If the best of the American Negroes receive by outer pressure a leader whom they had not recognized before, manifestly there is here a certain palpable gain. Yet there is also irreparable loss,—a loss of that peculiarly valuable education which a group receives when by search and criticism it finds and commissions its own leaders. The way in which this is done is at once the most elementary and the nicest problem of social growth. History is but the record of such group-leadership; and yet how infinitely changeful is its type and character! And of all types and kinds, what can be more instructive than the leadership of a group within a group? —that curious double movement where real progress may be negative and actual advance be relative retrogression. All this is the social student's inspiration and despair.

Now in the past the American Negro has had instructive experience in the choosing of group leaders, founding thus a peculiar dynasty which in the light of present conditions is worth while studying. When sticks and stones and beasts form the sole environment of a people, their attitude is largely one of determined opposition to and conquest of natural forces. But when to earth and brute is added an environment of men and ideas, then the attitude of the imprisoned group may take three main forms,—a feeling of revolt and revenge; an attempt to adjust all thought and action to the will of the greater group; or, finally, a determined effort at self-realization and self-development despite environing opinion. The influence of all of these attitudes at various times can be traced in the history of the American Negro, and in the evolution of his successive leaders.

Before 1750, while the fire of African freedom still burned in the veins of the slaves, there was in all leadership or attempted leadership but the one motive of revolt and revenge,—typified in the terrible Maroons, the Danish blacks, and Cato of Stono, and veiling all the Americas in fear of insurrection. The liberalizing tendencies of the latter half of the eighteenth century brought, along with kindlier relations between black and white, thoughts of ultimate adjustment and assimilation. Such aspiration was especially voiced in the earnest songs of Phyllis, in the martyrdom of Attucks, the fighting of Salem and Poor, the intellectual accomplishments of Banneker and Derham, and the political demands of the Cuffes.

Stern financial and social stress after the war cooled much of the previous humanitarian ardor. The disappointment and impatience of the Negroes at the persistence of slavery and serfdom voiced itself in two movements. The slaves in the South, aroused undoubtedly by vague rumors of the Haitian revolt, made three fierce attempts at insurrection,—in 1800 under Gabriel in Virginia, in 1822 under Vesey in Carolina, and in 1831 again in Virginia under the terrible Nat Turner. In the Free States, on the other hand, a new and curious attempt at self-development was made. In Philadelphia and New York color-prescription led to a withdrawal of Negro communicants from white churches and the formation of a peculiar socio-religious institution among the Negroes known as the African Church,—an organization still living and controlling in its various branches over a million of men.

Walker's wild appeal against the trend of the times showed how the world was changing after the coming of the cotton-gin. By 1830 slavery seemed hopelessly fastened on the South, and the slaves thoroughly cowed into submission. The free Negroes of the North, inspired by the mulatto immigrants from the West Indies, began to change the basis of their demands; they recognized the slavery of slaves, but insisted that they themselves were freemen, and sought assimilation and amalgamation with the nation on the same terms with other men. Thus, Forten and Purvis of Philadelphia, Shad of Wilmington, Du Bois of New Haven, Barbadoes of Boston, and others, strove strongly and together as men, they said, not as slaves; as "people of color," not as "Negroes." The trend of the times, however, refused them recognition save in individual and exceptional cases, considered them as one with all the despised blacks, and they soon found themselves striving to keep even the rights they formerly had of voting and working and moving as freemen. Schemers of migration and colonization arose among them; but these they refused to entertain, and they eventually turned to the Abolition movement as a final refuge.

Here, led by Remond, Nell, Wells-Brown, and Douglass, a new period of self-assertion and self-development dawned. To be sure, ultimate freedom and assimilation was the ideal before the leaders, but the assertion of the manhood rights of the Negro by himself was the main reliance, and John Brown's raid was the extreme of its logic. After the war and emancipation, the great form of Frederick Douglass, the greatest of American Negro leaders, still led the host. Self-assertion, especially in political lines, was the main programme, and behind Douglass came Elliot, Bruce, and Langston, and the Reconstruction politicians, and, less conspicuous but of greater social significance, Alexander Crummell and Bishop Daniel Payne.

Then came the Revolution of 1876, the suppression of the Negro votes, the changing and shifting of ideals, and the seeking of new lights in the great night. Douglass, in his old age, still bravely stood for the ideals of his early manhood, — ultimate assimilation *through* self-assertion, and on no other terms. For a time Price arose as a new leader, destined, it seemed, not to give up, but to re-state the old ideals in a form less repugnant to the white South. But he passed away in his prime. Then came the new leader. Nearly all the former ones had become leaders by the silent suffrage of their fellows, had sought to lead their own people alone, and were usually, save Douglass, little known outside their race. But Booker T. Washington arose as essentially the leader not of one race but of two,—a compromiser between the South, the North, and the Negro. Naturally the Negroes resented, at first bitterly, signs of compromise which surrendered their civil and political rights, even though this was to be exchanged for larger chances of economic development. The rich and dominating North, however, was not only weary of the race problem, but was investing largely in Southern enterprises, and welcomed any method of peaceful coöperation. Thus, by national opinion, the Negroes began to recognize Mr. Washington's leadership; and the voice of criticism was hushed.

Mr. Washington represents in Negro thought the old attitude of adjustment and submission; but adjustment at such a peculiar time as to make his programme unique. This is an age of unusual economic development, and Mr. Washington's programme naturally takes an economic cast, becoming a gospel of Work and Money to such an extent as apparently almost completely to overshadow the higher aims of life. Moreover, this is an age when the more advanced races are coming in closer contact with the less developed races, and the race-feeling is therefore intensified; and Mr. Washington's programme practically accepts the alleged inferiority of the Negro races. Again, in our own land, the reaction from the sentiment of war time has given impetus to race-prejudice against Negroes, and Mr. Washington withdraws many of the high demands of Negroes as men and American citizens. In other periods of intensified prejudice all the Negro's tendency to self-assertion has been called forth; at this period a policy of submission is advocated. In the history of nearly all other races and peoples the doctrine preached at such crises has been that manly self-respect is worth more than lands and houses, and that a people who voluntarily surrender such respect, or cease striving for it, are not worth civilizing.

In answer to this, it has been claimed that the Negro can survive only through submission. Mr. Washington distinctly asks that black people give up, at least for the present, three things, —

First, political power,
Second, insistence on civil rights,
Third, higher education of Negro youth, —

and concentrate all their energies on industrial education, the accumulation of wealth, and the conciliation of the South. This policy has been courageously and insistently advocated for over fifteen years, and has been triumphant for perhaps ten years. As a result of this tender of the palmbranch, what has been the return? In these years there have occurred:

1. The disfranchisement of the Negro.
2. The legal creation of a distant status of civil inferiority for the Negro.
3. The steady withdrawal of aid from institutions for the higher training of the Negro.

These movements are not, to be sure, direct results of Mr. Washington's teachings; but his propaganda has, without a shadow of doubt, helped their speedier accomplishment. The question then comes: Is it possible, and probable, that nine millions of men can make effective progress in economic lines if they are deprived of political rights, made a servile caste, and allowed only the most meagre chance for developing their exceptional men? If history and reason give any distinct answer to these questions, it is an emphatic No. And Mr. Washington thus faces the triple paradox of his career:

1. He is striving nobly to make Negro artisans business men and property-owners; but it is utterly impossible, under modern competitive methods, for workingmen and property-owners to defend their rights and exist without the right of suffrage.
2. He insists on thrift and self-respect, but at the same time counsels a silent submission to civic inferiority such as is bound to sap the manhood of any race in the long run.
3. He advocates common-school and industrial training, and depreciates institutions of higher learning; but neither the Negro common-schools, nor Tuskegee itself, could remain open a day were it not for teachers trained in Negro colleges, or trained by their graduates.

This triple paradox in Mr. Washington's position is the object of criticism by two classes of colored Americans. One class is spiritually descended from Toussaint the Savior, through Gabriel, Vesey, and Turner, and they represent the attitude of revolt and revenge; they hate the white South blindly and distrust the white race generally, and so far as they agree on definite action, think that the Negro's only hope lies in emigration beyond the borders of the United States. And yet, by the irony of fate, nothing has more effectually made this programme seem hopeless than the recent course of the United States toward weaker and darker peoples in the West Indies, Hawaii, and the Philippines,— for where in the world may we go and be safe from lying and brute force?

The other class of Negroes who cannot agree with Mr. Washington has hitherto said little aloud. They deprecate the sight of scattered counsels, of internal disagreement; and especially they dislike making their just criticism of a useful and earnest man an excuse for a general discharge of venom from small-minded opponents. Nevertheless, the questions involved are so funda- mental and serious that it is difficult to see how men like the Grimkes, Kelly Miller, J. W. E. Bowen, and other representatives of this group, can much longer be silent. Such men feel in conscience bound to ask of this nation three things:

1.   The right to vote.
2.   Civic equality.
3.   The education of youth according to ability.

They acknowledge Mr. Washington's invaluable service in counselling patience and courtesy in such demands; they do not ask that ignorant black men vote when ignorant whites are debarred, or that any reasonable restrictions in the suffrage should not be applied; they know that the low social level of the mass of the race is responsible for much discrimination against it, but they also know, and the nation knows, that relentless colorprejudice is more often a cause than a result of the Negro's degradation; they seek the abatement of this relic of barbarism, and not its systematic encouragement and pampering by all agencies of social power from the Associated Press to the Church of Christ. They advocate, with Mr. Washington, a broad system of Negro common schools supplemented by thorough industrial training; but they are surprised that a man of Mr. Washington's insight cannot see that no such educational sys- tem ever has rested or can rest on any other basis than that of the well- equipped college and university, and they insist that there is a demand for a few such institutions throughout the South to train the best of the Negro youth as teachers, professional men, and leaders.

This group of men honor Mr. Washington for his attitude of conciliation toward the white South; they accept the "Atlanta Compromise" in its broad- est interpretation; they recognize, with him, many signs of promise, many men of high purpose and fair judgment, in this section; they know that no easy task has been laid upon a region already tottering under heavy burdens. But, nev- ertheless, they insist that the way to truth and right lies in straightforward hon- esty, not in indiscriminate flattery; in praising those of the South who do well and criticising uncompromisingly those who do ill; in taking advantage of the opportunities at hand and urging their fellows to do the same, but at the same time in remembering that only a firm adherence to their higher ideals and aspirations will ever keep those ideals within the realm of possibility. They do not expect that the free right to vote, to enjoy civic rights, and to be educated, will come in a moment; they do not expect to see the bias and prejudices of years disappear at the blast of a trumpet; but they are absolutely certain that the way for a people to gain their reasonable rights is not by voluntarily throwing them away and insisting that they do not want them; that the way for a people to gain respect is not by continually belittling and ridiculing themselves; that, on the contrary, Negroes must insist continually, in season and out of season, that voting is necessary to modern manhood, that color discrimination is barbarism, and that black boys need education as well as white boys.

In failing thus to state plainly and unequivocally the legitimate demands of their people, even at the cost of opposing an honored leader, the thinking classes of American Negroes would shirk a heavy responsibility, —a responsibility to themselves, a responsibility to the struggling masses, a responsibility to the darker races of men whose future depends so largely on this American experiment, but especially a responsibility to this nation,—this common Fatherland. It is wrong to encourage a man or a people in evil-doing; it is wrong to aid and abet a national crime simply because it is unpopular not to do so. The growing spirit of kindliness and reconciliation between the North and South after the frightful difference of a generation ago ought to be a source of deep congratulation to all, and especially to those whose mistreatment caused the war; but if that reconciliation is to be marked by the industrial slavery and civic death of those same black men, with permanent legislation into a position of inferiority, then those black men, if they are really men, are called upon by every consideration of patriotism and loyalty to oppose such a course by all civilized methods, even though such opposition involves disagreement with Mr. Booker T. Washington. We have no right to sit silently by while the inevitable seeds are sown for a harvest of disaster to our children, black and white.

First, it is the duty of black men to judge the South discriminatingly. The present generation of Southerners are not responsible for the past, and they should not be blindly hated or blamed for it. Furthermore, to no class is the indiscriminate endorsement of the recent course of the South toward Negroes more nauseating than to the best thought of the South. The South is not "solid"; it is a land in the ferment of social change, wherein forces of all kinds are fighting for supremacy; and to praise the ill the South is today perpetrating is just as wrong as to condemn the good. Discriminating and broad-minded criticism is what the South needs, —needs it for the sake of her own white sons and daughters, and for the insurance of robust, healthy mental and moral development.

To-day even the attitude of the Southern whites toward the blacks is not, as so many assume, in all cases the same; the ignorant Southerner hates the Negro, the workingmen fear his competition, the money-makers wish to use him as a laborer, some of the educated see a menace in his upward development, while others—usually the sons of the masters—wish to help him to rise.

National opinion has enabled this last class to maintain the Negro common schools, and to protect the Negro partially in property, life, and limb. Through the pressure of the money-makers, the Negro is in danger of being reduced to semi-slavery, especially in the country districts; the workingmen, and those of the educated who fear the Negro, have united to disfranchise him, and some have urged his deportation; while the passions of the ignorant are easily aroused to lynch and abuse any black man. To praise this intricate whirl of thought and prejudice is nonsense; to inveigh indiscriminately against "the South" is unjust; but to use the same breath in praising Governor Aycock, exposing Senator Morgan, arguing with Mr. Thomas Nelson Page, and denouncing Senator Ben Tillman, is not only sane, but the imperative duty of thinking black men.

It would be unjust to Mr. Washington not to acknowledge that in several instances he has opposed movements in the South which were unjust to the Negro; he sent memorials to the Louisiana and Alabama constitutional conventions, he has spoken against lynching, and in other ways has openly or silently set his influence against sinister schemes and unfortunate happenings. Notwithstanding this, it is equally true to assert that on the whole the distinct impression left by Mr. Washington's propaganda is, first, that the South is justified in its present attitude toward the Negro because of the Negro's degradation; secondly, that the prime cause of the Negro's failure to rise more quickly is his wrong education in the past; and, thirdly, that his future rise depends primarily on his own efforts. Each of these propositions is a dangerous half-truth. The supplementary truths must never be lost sight of: first, slavery and race-prejudice are potent if not sufficient causes of the Negro's position; second, industrial and common-school training were necessarily slow in planting because they had to await the black teachers trained by higher institutions,—it being extremely doubtful if any essentially different development was possible, and certainly a Tuskegee was unthinkable before 1880; and, third, while it is a great truth to say that the Negro must strive and strive mightily to help himself, it is equally true that unless his striving be not simply seconded, but rather aroused and encouraged, by the initiative of the richer and wiser environing group, he cannot hope for great success.

In his failure to realize and impress this last point, Mr. Washington is especially to be criticised. His doctrine has tended to make the whites, North and South, shift the burden of the Negro problem to the Negro's shoulders and stand aside as critical and rather pessimistic spectators; when in fact the burden belongs to the nation, and the hands of none of us are clean if we bend not our energies to righting these great wrongs.

The South ought to be led, by candid and honest criticism, to assert her better self and do her full duty to the race she has cruelly wronged and is still wronging. The North—her co-partner in guilt—cannot salve her conscience by plastering it with gold. We cannot settle this problem by diplomacy and suaveness, by "policy" alone. If worse comes to worst, can the moral fibre of this country survive the slow throttling and murder of nine millions of men?

The black men of America have a duty to perform, a duty stern and delicate, —a forward movement to oppose a part of the work of their greatest
leader. So far as Mr. Washington preaches Thrift, Patience, and Industrial
Training for the masses, we must hold up his hands and strive with him, rejoicing in his honors and glorying in the strength of this Joshua called of God and
of man to lead the headless host. But so far as Mr. Washington apologizes for
injustice, North or South, does not rightly value the privilege and duty of voting, belittles the emasculating effects of caste distinctions, and opposes the
higher training and ambition of our brighter minds,—so far as he, the South,
or the Nation, does this, —we must unceasingly and firmly oppose them. By
every civilized and peaceful method we must strive for the right which the
world accords to men, clinging unwaveringly to those great words which the
sons of the Fathers would fain forget: "We hold these truths to be self-evident:
That all men are created equal; that they are endowed by their Creator with
certain unalienable rights; that among these are life, liberty, and the pursuit of
happiness."

Black Men Organize

The Niagara Movement
Declaration of Principles, 1905

*In 1905 Du Bois, following his own advice, brought together a group of black intel-
lectuals and professionals with the clear, though unstated, purpose of opposing the
Tuskegee Machine. The Niagara Movement, which held its first meeting in Canada
because of discrimination met by its members in Buffalo, New York, where the meeting first assembled, put forth a demand for racial equality in all areas of American life.*

*Although the black movement had little influence and all but the most radical of
its members joined with whites to form the National Association for the Advancement
of Colored People in 1910, its program was important because it provided a comprehensive alternative to the politics of conciliation advocated by Washington.*

*With minor changes, the "Declaration of Principles" of the Niagara Movement,
reprinted in the pages that follow, could be released again today as a summary of the
demands of blacks. Although the name of its author is not given, the document was
almost certainly written by Du Bois.*

PROGRESS. The members of the conference, known as the Niagara
Movement, assembled in annual meeting at Buffalo, July 11th, 12th and 13th,
1905, congratulate the Negro-Americans on certain undoubted evidences of
progress in the last decade, particularly the increase of intelligence, the buying
of property, the checking of crime, the uplift in home life, the advance in
literature and art, and the demonstration of constructive and executive ability
in the conduct of great religious, economic and educational institutions.

SUFFRAGE. At the same time, we believe that this class of American citizens
should protest emphatically and continually against the curtailment of their
political rights. We believe in manhood suffrage; we believe that no man is so
good, intelligent or wealthy as to be entrusted wholly with the welfare of his
neighbor.

CIVIL LIBERTY. We believe also in protest against the curtailment of our civil
rights. All American citizens have the right to equal treatment in places of public entertainment according to their behavior and deserts.

ECONOMIC OPPORTUNITY. We especially complain against the denial of
equal opportunities to us in economic life; in the rural districts of the South
this amounts to peonage and virtual slavery; all over the South it tends to crush
labor and small business enterprises; and everywhere American prejudice,
helped often by iniquitous laws, is making it more difficult for Negro-
Americans to earn a decent living.

FROM *The Niagara Movement Declaration of Principles (1905).*

EDUCATION. Common school education should be free to all American children and compulsory. High school training should be adequately provided for all, and college training should be the monopoly of no class or race in any section of our common country. We believe that, in defense of our own institutions, the United States should aid common school education, particularly in the South, and we especially recommend concerted agitation to this end. We urge an increase in public high school facilities in the South, where the Negro-Americans are almost wholly without such provisions. We favor well-equipped trade and technical schools for the training of artisans, and the need of adequate and liberal endowment for a few institutions of higher education must be patent to sincere well-wishers of the race.

COURTS. We demand upright judges in courts, juries selected without discrimination on account of color and the same measure of punishment and the same efforts at reformation for black as for white offenders. We need orphanages and farm schools for dependent children, juvenile reformatories for delinquents, and the abolition of the dehumanizing convict-lease system.

PUBLIC OPINION. We note with alarm the evident retrogression in this land of sound public opinion on the subject of manhood rights, republican government and human brotherhood, and we pray God that this nation will not degenerate into a mob of boasters and oppressors, but rather will return to the faith of the fathers, that all men were created free and equal, with certain unalienable rights.

HEALTH. We plead for health—for an opportunity to live in decent houses and localities, for a chance to rear our children in physical and moral cleanliness.

EMPLOYERS AND LABOR UNIONS. We hold up for public execration the conduct of two opposite classes of men: The practice among employers of importing ignorant Negro-American laborers in emergencies, and then affording them neither protection nor permanent employment; and the practice of labor unions in proscribing and boycotting and oppressing thousands of their fellow-toilers, simply because they are black. These methods have accentuated and will accentuate the war of labor and capital, and they are disgraceful to both sides.

PROTEST. We refuse to allow the impression to remain that the Negro-American assents to inferiority, is submissive under oppression and apologetic before insults. Through helplessness we may submit, but the voice of protest of ten million Americans must never cease to assail the ears of their fellows, so long as America is unjust.

COLOR-LINE. Any discrimination based simply on race or color is barbarous, we care not how hallowed it be by custom, expediency or prejudice. Differences made on account of ignorance, immorality, or disease are legitimate methods of fighting evil, and against them we have no word of protest; but discriminations based simply and solely on physical peculiarities, place of birth, color of skin, are relics of that unreasoning human savagery of which the world is and ought to be thoroughly ashamed.

"JIM CROW" CARS. We protest against the "Jim Crow" car, since its effect is and must be to make us pay first-class fare for third-class accommodations, render us open to insults and discomfort and to crucify wantonly our manhood, womanhood and self-respect.

SOLDIERS. We regret that this nation has never seen fit adequately to reward the black soldiers who, in its five wars, have defended their country with their blood, and yet have been systematically denied the promotions which their abilities deserve. And we regard as unjust, the exclusion of black boys from the military and naval training schools.

WAR AMENDMENTS. We urge upon Congress the enactment of appropriate legislation for securing the proper enforcement of those articles of freedom, the thirteenth, fourteenth and fifteenth amendments of the Constitution of the United States.

OPPRESSION. We repudiate the monstrous doctrine that the oppressor should be the sole authority as to the rights of the oppressed. The negro race in America stolen, ravished and degraded, struggling up through difficulties and oppression, needs sympathy and receives criticism, needs help and is given hindrance, needs protection and is given mob-violence, needs justice and is given charity, needs leadership and is given cowardice and apology, needs bread and is given a stone. This nation will never stand justified before God until these things are changed.

THE CHURCH. Especially are we surprised and astonished at the recent attitude of the church of Christ—of an increase of a desire to bow to racial prejudice, to narrow the bounds of human brotherhood, and to segregate black men to some outer sanctuary. This is wrong, unchristian and disgraceful to the twentieth century civilization.

AGITATION. Of the above grievances we do not hesitate to complain, and to complain loudly and insistently. To ignore, overlook, or apologize for these wrongs is to prove ourselves unworthy of freedom. Persistent manly agitation is the way to liberty, and toward this goal the Niagara Movement has started and asks the cooperation of all men of all races.

HELP. At the same time we want to acknowledge with deep thankfulness the help of our fellowmen from the Abolitionist down to those who today still stand for equal opportunity and who have given and still give of their wealth and of their poverty for our advancement.

DUTIES. And while we are demanding, and ought to demand, and will continue to demand the rights enumerated above, God forbid that we should ever forget to urge corresponding duties upon our people:

—The duty to vote.
—The duty to respect the rights of others.
—The duty to work.
—The duty to obey the laws.
—The duty to be clean and orderly.
—The duty to send our children to school.
—The duty to respect ourselves, even as we respect others.

This statement, complaint and prayer we submit to the American people, and Almighty God.

The NAACP
Program for Change

The Task for the
Future—A Program for 1919

NAACP

After its conception in 1910, the NAACP very quickly clarified its task. It would concern itself with the problem of achieving first-class citizenship for black people. Rather than bogging down in questions of "social equality," it would work for what it called "public equality." Though it was concerned with the problem of racial prejudice, the Association thought itself best equipped to try to provide equal protection for blacks under the Constitution.

Some critics have suggested that this policy was the result of the domination of the organization in the early years by Northern whites. Because it worked primarily in the area of legal rights, the NAACP never became an organization of the black masses, most of whom were never in a position to demand legal redress. There is no question, however, of the importance of this legal-rights struggle, which has indicated in our own times that the U. S. Constitution is only as good as its enforcement.

The document that follows states the program of the NAACP on the eve of its first decade of existence.

First and foremost among the objectives for 1919 must be the strengthening of the Association's organization and resources. Its general program must be adapted to specific ends. Its chief aims have many times been stated:

1. A vote for every Negro man and woman on the same terms as for white men and women.

2. An equal chance to acquire the kind of an education that will enable the Negro everywhere wisely to use this vote.

3. A fair trial in the courts for all crimes of which he is accused, by judges in whose election he has participated without discrimination because of race.

4. A right to sit upon the jury which passes judgment upon him.

5. Defense against lynching and burning at the hands of mobs.

FROM "The Task for the Future—A Program for 1919," *Report of the National Association for the Advancement of Colored People for the Years 1917 and 1918* (New York, 1919), pp. 76–80.

6. Equal service on railroad and other public carriers. This to mean sleeping car service, dining car service, Pullman service, at the same cost and upon the same terms as other passengers.

7. Equal right to the use of public parks, libraries and other community services for which he is taxed.

8. An equal chance for a livelihood in public and private employment.

9. The abolition of color-hyphenation and the substitution of "straight Americanism."

If it were not a painful fact that more than four-fifths of the colored people of the country are denied the above named elementary rights, it would seem an absurdity that an organization is necessary to demand for American citizens the exercise of such rights. One would think, if he were from Mars, or if he knew America only by reading the speeches of her leading statesmen, that all that would be needful would be to apply to the courts of the land and to the legislatures. Has not slavery been abolished? Are not all men equal before the law? Were not the Fourteenth and Fifteenth Amendments passed by the Congress of the United States and adopted by the states? Is not the Negro a man and a citizen?

When the fundamental rights of citizens are so wantonly denied and that denial justified and defended as it is by the lawmakers and dominant forces of so large a number of our states, it can be realized that the fight for the Negro's citizenship rights means a fundamental battle for real things, for life and liberty.

This fight is the Negro's fight. "Who would be free, himself must strike the blow." But, it is no less the white man's fight. The common citizenship rights of no group of people, to say nothing of nearly 12,000,000 of them, can be denied with impunity to the State and the social order which denies them. This fact should be plain to the dullest mind among us, with the upheavals of Europe before our very eyes. Whoso loves America and cherishes her institutions, owes it to himself and his country to join hands with the members of the National Association for the Advancement of Colored People to "Americanize" America and make the kind of democracy we Americans believe in to be the kind of democracy we shall have in fact, as well as in theory.

The Association seeks to overthrow race prejudice but its objective may better be described as a fight against caste. Those who seek to separate the Negro from the rest of Americans are intent upon establishing a caste system in America and making of all black men an inferior caste. As America could not exist "half slave and half free" so it cannot exist with an upper caste of whites and a lower caste of Negroes. Let no one be deceived by those who would contend that they strive only to maintain "the purity of the white race" and that they wish to separate the races but to do no injustice to the black man. The appeal is to history which affords no example of any group or element of the population of any nation which was separated from the rest and at the same time treated with justice and consideration. Ask the Jew who was compelled to live in the proscribed Ghetto whether being held separate he was afforded the common rights of citizenship and the "equal protection of the laws?" To raise the question is to find the answer "leaping to the eyes," as the French say.

Nor should any one be led astray by the tiresome talk about "social equality." Social equality is a private question which may well be left to individual decision. But, the prejudices of individuals cannot be accepted as the controlling policy of a state. The National Association for the Advancement of Colored People is concerned primarily with *public equality*. America is a nation—not a private club. The privileges no less than the duties of citizenship belong of right to no *separate class* of the people but to *all* the people, and to them as *individuals*. The constitution and the laws are for the protection of the minority and of the unpopular, no less than for the favorites of fortune, or they are of no meaning as American instruments of government.

Such a fight as has been outlined is worthy of the support of all Americans. The forces which seek to deny, and do deny, to the Negro his citizenship birthright, are powerful and intrenched. They hold the public offices. They administer the law. They say who may, and who may not vote, in large measure. They control and edit, in many sections, the influential organs of public opinion. They dominate. To dislodge them by legal and and constitutional means as the N.A.A.C.P. proposes to endeavor to dislodge them, requires a strong organization and ample funds. These two things attained, victory is but a question of time, since justice will not forever be denied.

The lines along which the Association can best work are fairly clear. Its fight is of the brain and the soul and to the brain and the soul of America. *It seeks to reach the conscience of America.* America is a large and busy nation. It has many things to think of besides the Negro's welfare. In Congress and state legislatures and before the bar of public opinion, the Association must energetically and adequately defend the Negro's right to fair and equal treatment. To command the interest and hold the attention of the American people for *justice to the Negro* requires money to print and circulate literature which states the facts of the situation. And the appeal must be on the basis of the facts. It is easy to talk in general terms and abstractly. The presentation of concrete data necessitates ample funds.

Lynching must be stopped. Many Americans do not believe that such horrible things happen as do happen when Negroes are lynched and burned at the stake. Lynching can be stopped when we can reach the hearts and consciences of the American people. Again, money is needed.

Legal work must be done. Defenseless Negroes are every day denied the "equal protection of the laws" because there is not money enough in the Association's treasury to defend them, either as individuals or as a race.

Legislation must be watched. Good laws must be promoted wherever that be possible and bad laws opposed and defeated, wherever possible. Once more, money is essential.

The public must be kept informed. This means a regular press service under the supervision of a trained newspaper man who knows the difference between news and gossip, on the one hand, and mere opinion on the other. That colored people are contributing their fair share to the wellbeing of America must be made known. The war has made familiar the heroic deeds of the colored soldier. The colored civilian has been, and is now, contributing equally to America's welfare. If men have proven to be heroes in warfare, they must have had virtues in peace time. That law-abiding colored people are denied the commonest citizenship rights, must be brought home to all Americans who love fair play. Once again, money is needed.

The facts must be gathered and assembled. This requires effort. Facts are not gotten out of one's imagination. Their gathering and interpretation is skilled work. Research workers of a practical experience are needed. Field investigations, in which domain the Association has already made some notable contributions, are essential to good work. More money.

The country must be thoroughly organized. The Association's nearly 200 branches are a good beginning. A field staff is essential to the upbuilding of this important branch development. A very large percentage of the branch members are colored people. As a race they have less means, and less experience in public organization, than white people. But, they are developing rapidly habits of efficiency in organization. Money, again is needed.

But, not money alone is needed.–Men and women are vital to success. Public opinion is the main force upon which the Association relies for a *victory of justice.*

Why Blacks Must Organize for Legal Rights

The Waco Horror: A Report on a Lynching

Du Bois, in his capacity as research director of the NAACP, edited The Crisis, *a monthly magazine that he launched in 1910 as a vehicle for Association propaganda, news, and his own personal views. Within ten years of its founding, it had a circulation of over 100,000, and it had been denounced by the joint Committee Investigating Seditious Activity for the New York state legislature for contributing to "revolutionary radicalism."*

The magazine gave wide coverage to incidents involving color discrimination, particularly those of a violent nature. Vivid descriptions of lynchings, riots, chain gangs, and the like filled its pages. Early issues of the journal stand today as documentation of the helpless condition of black people when confronted by whites whose concern for "law and order" did not extend to the black community.

The following report on a lynching, in all its gory detail, is characteristic of the kind of article Du Bois printed in hopes of awakening the conscience of the larger community.

1. THE CITY

The city of Waco, Tex., is the county seat of McLennan county. It is situated on the Brazos river, about half way between Dallas and Austin. It is the junction point of seven railways. The city is in a fertile agricultural region with grain and cotton as the chief products, and with nearly two hundred manufacturing establishments, representing some seventy different industries.

It had a population of 14,445 in 1890 which increased to 20,686 in 1900, and to 26,425 in 1910. The white population in these twenty years has almost exactly doubled. The colored population has increased from 4,069 to 6,067, forming thus 23 per cent of the population. The bulk of the population is native white of native parentage, there being only about 1,000 foreigners in the city.

The whole of McLennan county contained in 1910 a population of 73,250 of whom 17,234 were Negroes. This total population has nearly doubled in the last twenty years.

Waco is well laid out. The streets are broad, over sixty miles of them being paved. The sewer system of one hundred miles is excellent. There is a fine city-owned water system, and parks on the surrounding prairies.

FROM "The Waco Horror," *The Crisis*, Vol. 12 (July 1916), supplement, pp. 1–8.

There are thirty-nine white and twenty-four colored churches in Waco. By denominations the white churches are: Baptist, 14; Methodist, 9; Christian, 4; Presbyterian, 3; Jewish, 2; Episcopal, 2; Evangelistic, 1; Lutheran, 1; Catholic, 1; Christian Science, 1; Salvation Army, 1.

The colleges are: Baylor University, Baylor Academy, the Catholic College, the Independent Biblical and Industrial School, all white; and the Central Texas College and Paul Quinn, colored colleges. There are also the A. & M. College, the Gurley School, the Waco Business College, Toby's Practical Business College, the Provident Sanitarium, and the Training School.

Baylor University was founded in 1854 and has between 1,200 and 1,300 students. It is co-educational. The president is running for the United States Senate.

Two high schools serve white and colored population, and there are seven banks, including four national banks.

In other words, Waco is a typical southern town, alert, pushing and rich.

2. THE CRIME

Near the country town of Robinson, some six miles from Waco, lived a white family of four, named Fryar, who owned a small farm. This they cultivated themselves with the help of one hired man, a colored boy of seventeen, named Jesse Washington.

Jesse was a big, well-developed fellow, but ignorant, being unable either to read or write. He seemed to have been sullen, and perhaps mentally deficient, with a strong, and even daring temper. It is said that on Saturday night before the crime he had had a fight with a neighboring white man, and the man had threatened to kill him.

On Monday, May 8, while Mr. Fryar, his son of fourteen, and his daughter of twenty-three, were hoeing cotton in one part of their farm, the boy, Jesse, was plowing with his mules and sowing cotton seed near the house where Mrs. Fryar was alone. He went to the house for more cotton seed. As Mrs. Fryar was scooping it up for him into the bag which he held, she scolded him for beating the mules. He knocked her down with a blacksmith's hammer, and, as he confessed, criminally assaulted her; finally he killed her with the hammer. The boy then returned to the field, finished his work, and went home to the cabin, where he lived with his father and mother and several brothers and sisters.

When the murdered woman was discovered suspicion pointed to Jesse Washington, and he was found sitting in his yard whittling a stick. He was arrested and immediately taken to jail in Waco. Tuesday a mob visited the jail. They came in with about thirty automobiles, each holding as many as could be crowded in. There was no noise, no tooting of horns, the lights were dim, and some had no lights at all. These were all Robinson people. They looked for the boy, but could not find him, for he had been taken to a neighboring county where the sheriff obtained a confession from him. Another mob went to this county seat to get the boy, but he was again removed to Dallas. Finally, the Robinson people pledged themselves not to lynch the boy if the authorities acted promptly, and if the boy would waive his legal rights.

A second confession in which the boy waived all his legal rights was obtained in the Dallas jail. The Grand Jury indicted him on Thursday, and the case was set for trial Monday, May 15.

Sunday night, at midnight, Jesse Washington was brought from Dallas to Waco, and secreted in the office of the judge. There was not the slightest doubt but that he would be tried and hanged the next day, if the law took its course.

There was some, but not much doubt of his guilt. The confessions were obtained, of course, under duress, and were, perhaps, suspiciously clear, and not entirely in the boy's own words. It seems, however, probable that the boy was guilty of murder, and possibly of premeditated rape.

3. WACO POLITICS

Meantime, the exigencies of Waco politics are said to have demanded a lynching. Our investigator says:

"They brought the boy back to Waco because a lynching was of political value to the county officials who are running for office. Every man I talked with said that politics was at the bottom of the whole business. All that element who took part in the lynching will vote for the Sheriff. The Judge is of value to his party because he appoints the three commissioners of the jury, and these commissioners pick the Grand Jury."

The District Judge of the Criminal Court is R. I. Munroe, appointed by Governor Campbell. He is a low order of politician, and a product of a local machine. His reputation for morality is bad, and his practice at the Bar has been largely on behalf of the vicious interests.

The Sheriff of the county, S. S. Fleming, is a candidate for re-election, and has made much political capital out of the lynching. He says, in an advertisement in the *Waco Semi-Weekly Tribune:*

"Mr. Fleming is diseased with a broad philanthropy. He believes in the equality of man. He carries with him in the daily walk of his officialdom none of the 'boast of heraldry or the pomp of power.' He is just as courteous, just as obliging, just as accommodating as Sheriff as he was when selling buggies and cultivators for the hardware company. He presents to the voters for their endorsement the record made by him and his corps of splendid deputies."

Our investigator says:

"When I saw the Sheriff (Fleming) he had a beautiful story to tell. He had his story fixed up so that the entire responsibility was shifted on the Judge. The Judge admitted he could have had a change of venue, but said the mob anywhere would have done the same thing."

Meantime, the tip went out:

"The crowd began pouring into the town the day before and continued early Monday morning. The court room was packed full and a crowd of 2,000 was on the outside. The jurors could scarcely get in and out from their seats. I asked the Judge if he could not have cleared the court room, and he answered that I did not know the South. I said, 'If a person is big enough, he can get up and stop the biggest mob.' He asked, 'Do you want to spill innocent blood for a nigger?'"

"Some one had arranged it so that it would be easy to get the boy out of the courtroom. A door which opened by a peculiar device had been fixed so that it would open. One of the jurors was a convicted murderer with a suspended sentence over him."

"Lee Jenkins is the best deputy sheriff, but he is under Fleming. Barney Goldberg, the other deputy sheriff, said, 'If Lee Jenkins had had it, it would never have been, but we are working for the man higher up and must take our orders from him.' Barney Goldberg knows perfectly well that if Fleming is not re-elected, and the other candidate gets in, he will be out of a job. The other nominee for sheriff, Buchanan, is reported to be unable to read and write, but is said to have three dead 'niggers' to his 'credit.'"

"The boy, Jesse Washington, was asked what he thought about the mob coming after him. He said, 'They promised they would not if I would tell them about it.' He seemed not to care, but was thoroughly indifferent."

The trial was hurried through. The Waco *Semi-Weekly Tribune*, May 17, says: "The jury returned into court at 11:22 A.M., and presented a verdict: 'We, the jury, find the defendant guilty of murder as charged in the indictment and assess his punishment at death.' This was signed by W. B. Brazelton, foreman.

"'Is that your verdict, gentlemen?' asked Judge Munroe.

"They answered 'yes.'

"Judge Munroe began writing in his docket. He had written: 'May 15, 1916: Jury verdict of guilty,' and as he wrote there was a hush over the entire court room. It was a moment of hesitation, but just a moment. Then the tall man stared over the heads of the crowd. Fred H. Kingsbury, who was standing alongside of Judge Munroe, said, 'They are coming after him,' and as the Judge looked up, the wave of people surged forward." The court room accommodates 500 persons, but the Judge had allowed 1,500 persons to crowd in.

Our investigator continues:

"The stenographer told me that there was a pause of a full minute. He said the people crowded around him and he knew what was coming, so he slipped out of the door back of the Sheriff, with his records; and Sheriff Fleming slipped out also.

"Fleming claims that all he was called upon to do in the way of protecting the boy was to get him to court.

"A big fellow in the back of the court room yelled, 'Get the Nigger!' Barney Goldberg, one of the deputy sheriffs, told me that he did not know that Fleming had dropped orders to let them get the Negro, and pulled his revolver. Afterwards he got his friends to swear to an affidavit that he was not present. Fleming said he had sworn in fifty deputies. I asked him where they were. He asked, 'Would you want to protect the nigger?' The judge made no effort to stop the mob, although he had firearms in his desk."

4. THE BURNING

"They dragged the boy down the stairs, put a chain around his body and hitched it to an automobile. The chain broke. The big fellow took the chain off the Negro under the cover of the crowd and wound it around his own wrist, so that the crowd jerking at the chain was jerking at the man's wrist and he was holding the boy. The boy shrieked and struggled.

"The mob ripped the boy's clothes off, cut them in bits and even cut the boy. Someone cut his ear off; someone else unsexed him. A little girl working for the firm of Goldstein and Mingle told me that she saw this done."

"I went over the route the boy had been taken and saw that they dragged him between a quarter and a half a mile from the Court House to the bridge and then dragged him up two blocks and another block over to the City Hall". After they had gotten him up to the bridge, someone said that a fire was already going up at City Hall, and they turned around and went back. Several people denied that this fire was going, but the photograph shows that it was. They got a little boy to light the fire.

"While a fire was being prepared of boxes, the naked boy was stabbed and the chain put over the tree. He tried to get away, but could not. He reached up to grab the chain and they cut off his fingers. The big man struck the boy on the back of the neck with a knife just as they were pulling him up on the tree. Mr. Lester thought that was practically the death blow. He was lowered into the fire several times by means of the chain around his neck. Someone said they would estimate the boy had about twenty-five stab wounds, none of them death-dealing."

"About a quarter past one a fiend got the torso, lassoed it, hung a rope over the pummel of a saddle, and dragged it around through the streets of Waco."

"Very little drinking was done."

"The tree where the lynching occurred was right under the Mayor's window. Mayor Dollins was standing in the window, not concerned about what they were doing to the boy, but that the tree would be destroyed. The Chief of Police also witnessed the lynching. The names of five of the leaders of the mob are known to this Association, and can be had on application by responsible parties."

"Women and children saw the lynching. One man held up his little boy above the heads of the crowd so that he could see, and a little boy was in the top of the very tree to which the colored boy was hung, where he stayed until the fire became too hot."

Another account, in the Waco *Times Herald*, Monday night, says:

"Great masses of humanity flew as swiftly as possible through the streets of the city in order to be present at the bridge when the hanging took place, but when it was learned that the Negro was being taken to the City Hall lawn, crowds of men, women and children turned and hastened to the lawn."

"On the way to the scene of the burning people on every hand took a hand in showing their feelings in the matter by striking the Negro with anything obtainable, some struck him with shovels, bricks, clubs, and others stabbed him and cut him until when he was strung up his body was a solid color of red, the blood of the many wounds inflicted covered him from head to foot."

"Dry goods boxes and all kinds of inflammable material were gathered, and it required but an instant to convert this into seething flames. When the Negro was first hoisted into the air his tongue protruded from his mouth and his face was besmeared with blood."

"Life was not extinct within the Negro's body, although nearly so, when another chain was placed around his neck and thrown over the limb of a tree on the lawn, everybody trying to get to the Negro and have some part in his death. The infuriated mob then leaned the Negro, who was half alive and half dead, against the tree, he having just strength enough within his limbs to support him. As rapidly as possible the Negro was then jerked into the air at which a shout from thousands of throats went up on the morning air and dry goods boxes, excelsior, wood and every other article that would burn was then in evidence, appearing as if by magic. A huge dry goods box was then produced and filled to the top with all of the material that had been secured. The Negro's body was swaying in the air, and all of the time a noise as of thousands was heard and the Negro's body was lowered into the box."

"No sooner had his body touched the box than people pressed forward, each eager to be the first to light the fire, matches were touched to the inflammable material and as smoke rapidly rose in the air, such a demonstration as of people gone mad was never heard before. Everybody pressed closer to get souvenirs of the affair. When they had finished with the Negro his body was mutilated."

"Fingers, ears, pieces of clothing, toes and other parts of the Negro's body were cut off by members of the mob that had crowded to the scene as if by magic when the word that the Negro had been taken in charge by the mob was heralded over the city. As the smoke rose to the heavens, the mass of people, numbering in the neighborhood of 10,000 crowding the City Hall lawn and overflowing the square, hanging from the windows of buildings, viewing the scene from the tops of buildings and trees, set up a shout that was heard blocks away."

"Onlookers were hanging from the windows of the City Hall and every other building that commanded a sight of the burning, and as the Negro's body commenced to burn, shouts of delight went up from the thousands of throats and apparently everybody demonstrated in some way their satisfaction at the retribution that was being visited upon the perpetrator of such a horrible crime, the worst in the annals of McLennan county's history."

"The body of the Negro was burned to a crisp, and was left for some time in the smoldering remains of the fire. Women and children who desired to view the scene were allowed to do so, the crowds parting to let them look on the scene: After some time the body of the Negro was jerked into the air where everybody could view the remains, and a mighty shout rose on the air. Photographer Gildersleeve made several pictures of the body as well as the large crowd which surrounded the scene as spectators."

The photographer knew where the lynching was to take place, and had his camera and paraphernalia in the City Hall. He was called by telephone at the proper moment. He writes us:

"We have quit selling the mob photos, this step was taken because our 'City dads' objected on the grounds of 'bad publicity,' as we wanted to be boosters and not knockers, we agreed to stop all sale."

"F. A. GILDERSLEEVE."

Our agent continues:

"While the torso of the boy was being dragged through the streets behind the horse, the limbs dropped off and the head was put on the stoop of a disreputable woman in the reservation district. Some little boys pulled out the teeth and sold them to some men for five dollars apiece. The chain was sold for twenty-five cents a link."

"From the pictures, the boy was apparently a wonderfully built boy. The torso was taken to Robinson, hung to a tree, and shown off for a while, then they took it down again and dragged it back to town and put it on the fire again at five o'clock."

5. THE AFTERMATH

"I tried to talk to the Judge. I met him on the street and said, 'I want to talk with you about something very important.' He asked, 'What is the nature of it?' I said, 'I want to get your opinion of that lynching.' He said, 'No, I refuse to talk with you about that. What do you want it for?' I said, 'If you refuse to talk with me, there is no use of telling you what I want it for.'"

"When I met him the second time, with different clothes on, he did not recognize me. I put on a strong English accent and said I was interested in clippings from New York papers which showed that Waco had made for itself an awful name, and I wanted to go back and make the northerners feel that Waco was not so bad as the papers had represented. Then he gave me the Court records."

Our investigator continues: "I went to the newspaper offices. They were all of the opinion that the best thing to do was to hush it up. They used it as a news item, and that finished it. The Dallas *News* did not cite anything editorially because not long ago they had done something quite as bad and the boy was not guilty."

"With the exception of the *Tribune*, all the papers had simply used it as a news item and let it drop. The *Tribune* is owned by Judge McCullum, who says anything he pleases. He is nearly blind. When I read the article to him I said, 'I would like to ask you, if that had been a colored woman and a white boy, would you have protected that woman?' He answered, 'No. If it had been a colored boy and a colored woman? No.' We would not have the niggers doing anything they wanted to.' 'Do you think they would?' 'No.' "Then, they prove their superior civilization.' Then he began to tell me how he knew all about the niggers and we northerners do not. He said that as an old southerner he knew perfectly well how to handle the colored population. He told me how he was raised with them, had a colored mammy, nursed at her breast, etc.

"There is a bunch of people in Waco who are dying to see someone go forward and make a protest, but no one in Waco would do it. Ex-Mayor Mackaye and Colonel Hamilton both said, 'We do not know what to do. We are not organized to do it. It is a case of race and politics.'"

"I put out a lot of wires for a lawyer to take up the case, but no human being in Waco would take it up. I wrote to a friend in Austin and one in Houston, and the Austin friend telegraphed me that he would send me word as soon as he had found someone. I had a letter from the Houston friend who gave me the names of three lawyers, but am not sure whether they would take up a case of this kind. All have their doubts of ever getting the case into court."

"I did not dare ask much about lawyers."

"As a result of the lynching a Sunday School Convention which was to have met there, with 15,000 delegates, has been stopped."

"W. A. Brazelton, the foreman of the Jury, was very outspoken against the whole affair and blames the officials for it. He felt that as foreman of the Jury he could not lead in a protest but thought some protest ought to be made."

"Mr. Ainsworth, one of the newspaper men, seemed the only one who wanted to start a protest."

"Colonel Hamilton, a man of high standing, a northerner, and at one time a big railroad man, was outspoken against the whole affair, but said that if he led in a protest they would do the same thing to him. He said he would never register in any hotel that he came from Waco. Two Waco men did not register from Waco."

"Allan Stanford, ex-Mayor of Waco, saw the Sheriff and the Judge before the trial and received assurances that the lynching would not take place. They shut the mouths of the better element of Waco by telling them that the Robinson people had promised not to do it. They had gotten the promise of the Robinson people that they would not touch the boy during the trial, but they did not get the pledge of the disreputable bunch of Waco that they would not start the affair."

"Judge Spell said the affair was deplorable, but the best thing was to forget it."

"When representing myself as a news reporter, I asked, 'What shall I tell the people up North?' Ex-Mayor Mackaye said, 'Fix it up as well as you can for Waco, and make them understand that the better thinking men and women of Waco were not in it.' I said. 'But some of your better men were down there. The whole thing savors so rotten because the better men have not tried to protest against it. Your churches have not said a word. Dr. Caldwell was the only man who made any protest at all.'"

6. THE LYNCHING INDUSTRY

This is an account of one lynching. It is horrible, but it is matched in horror by scores of others in the last thirty years, and in its illegal, law-defying, race-hating aspect, it is matched by 2842 other lynchings which have taken place between January 1, 1885, and June 1, 1916. These lynchings are as follows:

COLORED MEN LYNCHED BY YEARS, 1885–1916

1885	78	1901	107
1886	71	1902	86
1887	80	1903	86
1888	95	1904	83
1889	95	1905	61
1890	90	1906	64
1891	121	1907	60
1892	155	1908	93
1893	154	1909	73
1894	134	1910	65
1895	112	1911	63
1896	80	1912	63
1897	122	1913	79
1898	102	1914	69
1899	84	1915	80
1900	107	1916 (5 mos.)	31
		TOTAL	2843

What are we going to do about this record? The civilization of America is at stake. The sincerity of Christianity is challenged. The National Association for the Advancement of Colored People proposes immediately to raise a fund of at least $10,000 to start a crusade against this modem barbarism. Already $2,000 is promised, conditional on our raising the whole amount.

Interested persons may write to Roy Nash, secretary, 70 Fifth Avenue, New York City.

SUGGESTIONS FOR FURTHER READINGS

Booker T. Washington's importance is brilliantly analyzed in Louis R. Harlan's two volumes of biography, *Booker T. Washington: The Making of a Black Leader, 1865–1901*★ (1972) and Booker T. Washington: *The Wizard of Tuskegee, 1901–1915*★ (1983). See also Louis R. Harlan and Raymond W. Smock (eds.), *The Booker T. Washington Papers*, 13 vols. (1972—1984). Of the many works of W. E. B. Du Bois, the ones to read first are *The Souls of Black Folk*★ (1903) and the autobiographical *Dusk of Dawn*★ (1940). Biographical studies include David

Levering Lewis, *W. E. B. Du Bois: Biography of a Race, 1868–1919* (1993), Francis L. Broderick, *W. E. B. Du Bois: Negro Leader in a Time of Crisis* (1959) and Elliott Rudwick, *W. E. B. Du Bois: A Study in Minority Group Leadership*★ (1960). See also Adolph L. Reed, Jr., *W. E. B. Du Bois and American Political Thought*★ (1997). A leader with Du Bois in the Niagara Movement is portrayed in Stephen R. Fox, *The Guardian of Boston: William Monroe Trotter*★ (1970)

For the early history of the NAACP, see Charles F. Kellogg, *NAACP: A History of the National Association for the Advancement of Colored People*★ (1973). The formation of the Urban League is described in Nancy J. Weiss, *The National Urban League, 1910–1940* (1974). The excellent collection of documents edited by Francis L. Broderick and August Meier, *Negro Protest Thought in the Twentieth Century*★ (1966) gives a many-sided view of the development of African-American intellectual and political life from the late nineteenth century up to 1964.

Studies of lynching during this period include W. Fitzhugh Brundage, *Lynching in the New South: Georgia and Virginia, 1880–1930*★ (1993), Stewart Tolnay and E. M. Beck, *A Festival of Violence: An Analysis of Southern Lynchings, 1882–1930*★ (1995), and Dominic J. Capeci, Jr., *The Lynching of Cleo Wright (1998)*.

Aspects of black life in the early twentieth century are covered in Pete Daniel, *The Shadow of Slavery: Peonage in the South, 1901–1969* (1972), John Dittmer, *Black Georgia in the Progressive Era, 1900–1920*★ (1977), and James Borchert, *Alley Life in Washington: Family, Community, Religion, and Folklife in the City, 1850–1970*★ (1980). A Revival of black emigrationism is explored in Edwin S. Redkey, *Black Exodus: Black Nationalist and Back-to-Africa Movements, 1890—1910*★ (1969).

★ Books marked by an asterisk are available in paperback.

8

✦

The Great Migration
Brings a New Mood

INTRODUCTION

The mass movement of Southern blacks to the North in the second decade of the twentieth century is one of the most important migrations in American history. Most of it was the result of economic changes brought about by the First World War. Many of the burgeoning industries of the North made a practice of staffing their factories with immigrants from Europe, but the war halted this tide. And many of those already at work marched off to war, leaving empty factory jobs in Northern cities. Between the years 1910 and 1920, the black population increased in Detroit by 611.3 percent, in Cleveland by 307.8 percent, in Gary (Indiana) by 1,283.6 percent, and in Chicago by 148.2 percent.

It was not only the pull of industry that drew blacks from the South during this period. Southern agriculture was undergoing severe difficulties, as the boll weevil moved up from Mexico and ravaged cotton crop after cotton crop. The tenant-farmer and sharecropper systems were driving rural blacks deeper and deeper into despair. When a black newspaper, the Chicago *Defender*, began to encourage blacks to migrate northward and Northern industry began to send labor recruiters to the South, the response was overwhelming.

At first, the white South sighed with relief; it was finally to be rid of the troublesome blacks. But as the migration grew, the whites realized the threat it posed to the Southern system and began to strike out at the migrants and those who encouraged them. In many places the Chicago *Defender* was banned, and to be caught with it in one's possession became an offense punishable by imprisonment. Jacksonville, Florida, required labor recruiters from the North to buy a license for $1,000 or go to jail for sixty days. Macon, Georgia, upped the license fee to $25,000 and insisted that the recruiter have recommendations from ten local ministers, ten local manufacturers, and twenty-five local businessmen. In Alabama, fines and jail sentences awaited anyone who was found guilty of encouraging labor to leave. In Mississippi, recruiters were arrested, trains were stopped, and ticket agents were threatened by whites. Yet the movement north gathered momentum.

When the war ended and the soldiers returned to find their jobs taken over by blacks, the inevitable racial clashes occurred. Whites, anxious to reaffirm the old caste lines, acted in ways intended to negate the economic and psychological gains made by blacks during the war, but the newly settled black laborers and the many black men returning from military service in Europe were in no mood to be pushed around. Sporadic violence broke out throughout the nation. Several black men were lynched in the uniform of the United States Army—one, simply because he wore the uniform. In 1918, in Chicago, the homes of many blacks who had bought property on the edges of white communities were bombed. All this served as a prelude to the summer of 1919, when there were twenty-two race riots in U. S. cities, in both the North and the South.

The first of the riots to attract national attention was in Washington, D.C., in the middle of July. The conflict began when two hundred white servicemen invaded a black neighborhood to avenge an alleged "jostling" incident involving two black men and the wife of a white sailor. Little was done by law-enforcement authorities to control the whites until blacks began to arm themselves and fight back. The four days of rioting left several dead and many wounded.

The most violent outbreak of the summer occurred in Chicago in late July, when whites caused the drowning of a black swimmer who had crossed the invisible line dividing the black from the white area at a local bathing beach. When a white policeman refused to arrest those who had caused the drowning, but instead arrested a black on a minor charge, incensed blacks attacked the policeman. The outbreak that followed lasted for a week, during which white and black mobs fought all over Chicago. At the end of the week, fifteen whites and twenty-three blacks lay dead, and countless blacks and whites were wounded.

The year 1919 marked a turning point in American history as far as racial violence is concerned. Blacks fought back openly against white attacks in greater numbers and to greater effect than ever before. In this sense, the "new Negro" spoken about so widely in the 1920s emerged from the bloody street fights of the summer of 1919.

The Great Migration created more than white reaction in Northern cities. It also created the first mass nationalist movement among American blacks— that of Marcus Garvey, a West Indian who had come to the United States during the First World War. The Garvey movement based its program on the conviction that blacks must create their own independent nation, because they would never receive justice in a white man's country. Though his organization attracted mainly West Indian immigrants at first, Garvey was ready to appeal to the black migrant from the South who found that the Northern Promised Land offered neither promise nor land. Garvey proposed to set up his "Zion" in Africa, the ancestral homeland of black people. Opposed by both white authorities and black intellectuals, Garvey was convicted on a questionable charge of mail fraud, sent to prison, and then released and deported, but the black nationalist political consciousness he aroused is a force still much in evidence in certain black movements.

A different, ironically antithetical response of blacks to the Great Migration emerged in the 1920s in the cultural nationalist movement called the Harlem Renaissance. Whereas political nationalism of the Garvey type anticipates the formation of an all-black society, cultural nationalism asserts the values of the past in an attempt to develop a cultural identity that can support a self-conscious racial elite and, so far as it reaches the black masses, develop in them racial pride and self-assurance. The black writers and artists of the Harlem Renaissance used the folk materials of the rural black past and the ghetto black present to assert the values of the black experience. Needless to say, there was considerable disagreement as to what these values were. From the ambivalence of works such as Jean Toomer's *Cane* to the certainties of those like James Weldon Johnson's *God's Trombones*, the creations of black artists and intellectuals strove with one another to express the complex meaning of blackness.

Why Blacks Chose
to Leave the South

Letters of African-American
Migrants of 1916–1918

Perhaps the most valuable sources of information about why black people left the South for Northern cities are the letters they wrote to the Chicago Defender *asking for help. Many of the letters written between 1916 and 1918 were collected by Emmett J. Scott, for a time Booker T. Washington's secretary, and were published in 1919 in the fledgling* Journal of Negro History.*

The letters, reprinted here as they were written, speak for themselves. Futility, frustration, rage, and despair can be seen in every line. Not only were individuals anxious to leave their old lives in the South, but whole groups were prepared to drop everything and migrate in the hope of finding something better. The Defender *certainly exaggerated the promise of the North, but thousands responded to its enticements and, following the route of the old Underground Railroad, caught the Illinois Central to the Promised Land.*

JACKSONVILLE, FLA., 4-25-17.

Dear Sir: in reading a copy of the Chicago defender note that if i get in touch with you you would assist me in getting imployment. i am now imployed in Florida East coast R R service road way department any thing in working line myself and friends would be very glad to get in touch with as labors. We would be more than glad to do so and would highly appreciate it the very best we can advise where we can get work to do, fairly good wages also is it possible that we could get transportation to the destination. We are working men with familys. Please answer at once. i am your of esteem. We are not particular about the electric lights and all i want is fairly good wages and steady work.

MARCEL, MISS., 10/4/17.

Dear Sir: Although I am a stranger to you but I am a man of the so called colored race and can give you the very best of reference as to my character and ability by prominent citizens of my community by both white and

FROM Emmett J. Scott (ed.), "Letters of Negro Migrants of 1916–1918," *Journal of Negro History*, vol. 4 (July and October 1919), pp. 292, 293, 302, 304, 317, 320, 325, 329, 333, 413, 419, 420, 424, 434, 435, 437, 438, 442, 443, 450, 451, 452. Reprinted by permission of the Association for the Study of African-American Life and History, Inc.

colored people that knows me although am native of Ohio whiles I am a northern desent were reared in this state of Mississippi. Now I am a reader of your paper the Chicago Defender. After reading your writing ever wek I am compell & persuade to say that I know you are a real man of my color you have I know heard of the south land & I need not tell you any thing about it. I am going to ask you a favor and at the same time beg you for your kind and best advice. I wants to come to Chicago to live. I am a man of a family wife and 1 child I can do just any kind of work in the line of common labor & I have for the present sufficient means to support us till I can obtain a position. Now should I come to your town, would you please to assist me in getting a position I am willing to pay whatever you charge I dont want you to loan me not 1 cent but help me to find an occupation there in your town now I has a present position that will keep me employed till the first of Dec. 1917. now please give me your best advice on this subject. I enclose stamp for reply.

FAYETTE, GA., JANUARY 17, 1917.

Dear Sir: I have learned of the splendid work which you are doing in placing colored men in touch with industrial opportunities. I therefore write you to ask if you have an opening anywhere for me. I am a college graduate and understand Bookkeeping. But I am not above doing hard labor in a foundry or other industrial establishment. Please let me know if you can place me.

LEXINGTON, MISS., MAY 12–17.

My dear Mr. H ——:–I am writing to you for some information and assistance if you can give it.

I am a young man and am disable, in a very great degree, to do hard manual labor. I was educated at Alcorn College and have been teaching a few years: but ah: me the Superintendent under whom we poor colored teachers have to teach cares less for a colored man than he does for the vilest beast. I am compelled to teach 150 children without any assistance and receives only $27.00 a month, the white with 30 gets $100.

I am so sick I am so tired of such conditions that I sometime think that life for me is not worth while and most eminently believe with Patrick Henry "Give me liberty or give me death." If I was a strong able bodied man I would have gone from here long ago, but this handicaps me and, I must make inquiries before I leap.

Mr. H——, do you think you can assist me to a position I am good at stenography typewriting and bookkeeping or any kind of work not to rough or heavy. I am 4 feet 6 in high and weigh 105 pounds.

I will gladly give any other information you may desire and will greatly appreciate any assistance you may render me.

SELMA, ALA., MAY 19, 1917.

Dear Sir: I am a reader of the Chicago Defender I think it is one of the Most Wonderful Papers of our race printed. Sirs I am writeing to see if You all will please get me a job. And Sir I can wash dishes, wash iron nursing work in groceries and dry good stores. Just any of these I can do. Sir, who so ever you get the job from please tell them to send me a ticket and I will pay them. When I get their as I have not got enough money to pay my way. I am a girl of 17 years old and in the 8 grade at Knox Academy School. But on account of not having money enough I had to stop school. Sir I will thank you all with all my heart. May God Bless you all. Please answer in return mail.

MOBILE, ALA., APRIL 21, 1917.

Dear Sirs: We have a club of 108 good men wants work we are willing to go north or west but we are not abel to pay rail road fare now if you can help us get work and get to it please answer at once. Hope to hear from you.

MOBILE, ALA., MAY 11, 1917.

Dear sir and brother: on last Sunday I addressed you a letter asking you for information and I have received no answer. but we would like to know could 300 or 500 men and women get employment? and will the company or thoes that needs help send them a ticket or a pass and let them pay it back in weekly payments? We have men and women here in all lines of work we have organized a association to help them through you.

We are anxiously awaiting your reply.

GRAHAM, LA., MAY 18, 1917.

Dear sir: a word of infermation and a ancer from you please there are about 12 or 15 of us with our famlys leaving the south and we can hear of collored peples leaving the south but we are not luckey enough to leave hear. Dr. —— clame to be an agent to sind peples off and we has bin to him so minnie times and has fail to get off untill we dont no what to do so if you will place us about 15 tickets or get some one else to do so we are honest enough to come at once and labor for you or the one that sind them until we pay you if so requir. If we war able we wood Sur leave this torminting place but the job we as got and what we get it we do well to feed our family so please let me here from you at once giveing full detale of my requess.

MOBILE, ALA., 4-26-17.

Dear Sir Bro.: I take great pane in droping you a few lines hopeing that this will find you enjoying the best of health as it leave me at this time present.

Dear sir I seen in the Defender where you was helping us a long in securing a posission as brickmason plaster cementers stone mason. I am writing to you for advice about comeing north. I am a brickmason an I can do cement work an stone work. I written to a firm in Birmingham an they sent me a blank stateing $2.00 would get me a ticket an pay 10 per ct of my salary for the lst month and $24.92c would be paid after I reach Detroit and went to work where they sent me to work. I had to stay there until I pay them the sum of $24.92c so I want to leave Mobile for there. if there nothing there for me to make a support for my self and family. My wife is seamstress. We want to get away the 15 or 20 of May so please give this matter your earnest considera-tion an let me hear from you by return mail as my bro. in law want to get away to. He is a carpenter by trade, so please help us as we are in need of your help as we wanted to go to Detroit but if you says no we go where ever you sends us until we can get to Detroit. We expect to do whatever you says. There is nothing here for the colored man but a hard time wich these southern crackers gives us. We has not had any work to do in 4 wks. and every thing is high to the colored man so please let me hear from you by return mail. Please do this for your brother.

NEW ORLEANS, LA., 4–23–17.

Dear Editor: I am a reader of the Defender and I am askeso much about the great Northern drive on the 15th of May. We want more understanding about it for there is a great many wants to get ready for that day & the depot agents never gives us any satisfaction when we ask for they dont want us to leave here, I want to ask you to please publish in your next Saturdays paper just what the fair will be on that day so we all will know & can be ready. So many women here are wanting to go that day. They are all working women and we cant get work here so much now, the white women tell us we just want to make money to go North and we do so please kindly ans. this in your next paper if you do I will read it every word in the Defender, had rather read it then to eat when Saturday comes, it is my hearts delight & hope your paper will continue on in the south until every one reads it for it is a God sent bless-ing to the Race. Will close with best wishes.

ALEXANDRIA, LA., JUNE 6, 1917.

Dear Sirs: I am writeing to you all asking a favor of you all. I am a girl of seventeen. School has just closed I have been going to school for nine months and I now feel like I aught to go to work. And I would like very very well for you all to please forward me to a good job: but there isnt a thing here for me to do, the wages here is from a dollar and a half a week. What could I earn Nothing. I have a mother and father my father do all he can for me but it is so hard. A child with any respect about her self or his self wouldnt like to see there mother and father work so hard and earn nothing I feel it my duty to help. I would like for you all to get me a good job and as I havent any money to come on please send me a pass and I would work and pay every cent of it back and get me a good quite place to stay. My father have been getting the defender for three or four months but for the last two weeks we have failed to get it. I dont know why. I am tired of down hear in this——/I am afraid to say. Father seem to care and then again dont seem to but Mother and I am tired tired of all this I wrote to you all because I believe you will help I need your help hopeing to here from you all very soon.

NEWBERN, ALA., 4/7/1917.

Dear Sir. I am in receipt of a letter from——of ——, ——, in regards to placing two young women of our community in positions in the North or West, as he was unable to give the above assistance he enclosed your address. We desire to know if you are in a position to put us in touch with any reliable firm or private family that desire to employ two young women; one is a teacher in the public school of this county, and has been for the past six years having duties of a mother and sister to care for she is forced to seek employment else where as labor is very cheap here. The other is a high school pupil, is capable of during the work of a private family with much credit.

Doubtless you have learned of the great exodus of our people to the north and west from this and other southern states. I wish to say that we are forced to go when one things of a grown man wages is only fifty to seventy five cents per day for all grades of work. He is compelled to go where there is better wages and sociable conditions, believe me. When I say that many places here in this state the only thing that the black man gets is a peck of meal and from three to four lbs. of bacon per week, and he is treated as a slave. As leaders we are powerless for we dare not resent such or to show even the slightest disapproval. Only a few days ago more than 1000 people left here for the north and west. They cannot stay here. The white man is saying that you must not go but they are not doing anything by way of assisting the black man to stay. As a minister of the Methodist Episcopal Church (north) I am on the verge of starvation simply because of the above conditions. I shall be glad to know if there is any possible way by which I could be of real service to you as director of your society. Thanking you in advance for an early reply, and for any suggestions that you may be able to offer.

With best wishes for your success, I remain,
very sincerely yours.

TROY, ALA., 3-24-17.

Dear Sir. I received you of Feb. 17 and was very delighted to hear from you in regards of the matter in which I written you about. I am very anxious to get to Chicago and realy believe that if I was there I would very soom be working on the position in which I writen you about. Now you can just imagine how it is with the colored man in the south. I am more than anxious to go to Chicago but have not got the necessary fund in which to pay my way and these southern white peoples are not paying a man enough for his work down here to save up enough money to leave here with. Now I am asking you for a helping hand in which to assist me in getting to Chicago. I know you can do so if you only will.

Hoping to hear from you at an early date and looking for a helping hand and also any information you choose to inform me of,

I remain as ever yours truly.

HAWKINSVILLE, GA., APR. 16, 1917.

My dear friends: I writen you some time ago and never received any answer at all. I just was thinking why that I have not. I writen you for employ on a farm or any kind of work that you can give me to do I am willing to do most any thing that you want me to so dear friends if you just pleas send ticket for me I will come up thear just as soon as I receives it I want to come to the north so bad tell I really dont no what to do. I am a good worker a young boy age of .23. The reason why I want to come north is why that the people dont pay enough for the labor that a man can do down here so please let me no what can you do for me just as soon as you can I will pay you for the ticket and all so enything on your money that you put in the ticket for me, and send any kind of contrak that you send me.

ALEXANDRIA, LA., 4/23/17.

Gentlemens: Just a word of information I am planning to leave this place on about May 11th for Chicago and wants ask you assistence in getting a job. My job for the past 8 years has been in the Armour Packing Co. of this place and I cand do anything to be done in a branch house and are now doing the smoking here I am 36 years old have a wife and 2 children. I has been here all my life but would be glad to go wher I can educate my children where they can be of service to themselves, and this will never be here.

Now if you can get a job with eny of the packers I will just as soon as I arrive in your city come to your pace and pay you for your troubel. And if I cant get on with packers I will try enything that you have to effer.

CRESCENT, OKLA., APRIL 30, 1917.

Sir: I am looking for a place to locate this fall as a farmer. Do you think you could place me on a farm to work on shares. I am a poor farmer and have not the money to buy but would be glad to work a mans farm for him. I am desirous of leaving here because of the school accommodations for children as I have five and want to educate them the best I can. Prehaps you can find me a position of some kind if so kindly let me know I will be ready to leave here this fall after the harvest is layed by. I am planting cotton.

AUGUSTA, GA., APRIL 27, 1917.

Sir: Being a constant reader of your paper, I thought of no one better than you to write for information.

I'm desirous of leaving the south but before so doing I want to be sure of a job before pulling out. I'm a member of the race, a normal and colloege school graduate, a man of a family and can give reference. Confidentially this communication between you and me is to be kept a secret.

My children I wished to be educated in a different community than here. Where the school facilities are better and less prejudice shown and in fact where advantages are better for our people in all respect. At present I have a good position but I desire to leave the south. A good position even tho' its a laborer's job paying $4.50 or $5.00 a day will suit me till I can do better. Let it be a job there or any where else in the country, just is it is east or west. I'm quite sure you can put me in touch with some one. I'm a letter carrier now and am also a druggist by profession. Perhaps I may through your influence get a transfer to some eastern or western city.

Nevada or California as western states, I prefer, and I must say that I have nothing against Detroit, Mich.

I shall expect an early reply. Remember keep this a secret please until I can perfect some arrangements.

MACON, GA., APRIL 1, 1917.

Dear Sir: I am writing you for information I want to come north east but I have not sufficient funds and I am writing you to see if there is any way that you can help me by giving me the names of some of the firms that will send me a transportation as we are down here where we have to be shot down here like rabbits for every little orfence as I seen an orcurince hapen down here this after noon when three depties from the shrief office an one Negro spotter come out and found some of our raice mens in a crap game and it makes me want to leave the south worse than I ever did when such things hapen right at my door. hopeing to have a reply soon and will in close a stamp from the same.

PALESTINE, TEX., 1/2/17.

Dear Sir: I hereby enclose you a few lines to find out some few things if you will be so kind to word them to me. I am a southerner lad and has never ben in the north no further than Texas and I has heard so much talk about the north and how much better the colard people are treated up there than they are down here and I has ben striveing so hard in my coming up and now I see that I cannot get up there without the ade of some one and I wants to ask you Dear Sir to please direct me in your best manner the stept that I shall take to get there and if there are any way that you can help me to get there I am kindly asking you for your ade. And if you will ade me please notify me by return mail because I am sure ancious to make it in the north because these southern white people ar so mean and they seems to be getting worse and I wants to get away and they wont pay enough for work for a man to save up enough to get away and live to. If you will not ade me in getting up there please give me some information how I can get there I would like to get there in the early spring, if I can get there if possible. Our Southern white people are so cruel we collord people are almost afraid to walke the streets after night. So please let me hear from you by return mail. I will not say very much in this letter I will tell you more about it when I hear from you please ans. soon to Yours truly.

NEW ORLEANS, LA., MAY 21, 1917.

Dear Sir. As it is my desire to leave the south for some portion of the north to make my future home I desided to write to you as one who is able to furnish proper information for such a move. I am a cook of plain meals and I have knowledge of industrial training. I received such training at Tuskegee Inst. some years ago and I have a letter from Mrs. Booker T. Washington bearing out such statement and letters from other responsible corporations and individuals and since I know that I can come up to such recommendations, I want to come north where it is said such individuals are wanted. Therefore will you please furnish me with names and addresses of railroad officials to whom I might write for such employment as it is my desire to work only for railroads, if possible. I have reference to officials who are over extra gangs, bridge gangs, paint gangs and pile drivers over any boarding department which takes in plain meals. I have 25 years experience in this line of work and understand the method of saving the company money.

You will please dig into this in every way that is necessary and whatever charges you want for your trouble make your bill to me, and I will mail same to you.

Wishing you much success in your papers throughout the country, especially in the south as it is the greatest help to the southern negro that has ever been read.

DAPNE, ALA., 4/20/17.

Sir. I am writing you to let you know that there is 15 or 20 familys wants to come up there at once but cant come on account of money to come with and we cant phone you here we will be killed they dont want us to leave here & say if we dont go to war and fight for our country they are going to kill us and wants to get away if we can if you send 20 passes there is no doubt that every one of us will com at once. we are not doing any thing here we cant get a living out of what we do now some of these people are farmers and som are cooks barbers and black smiths but the greater part are farmers & good worker & honest people & up to date the trash pile dont want to go no where. These are nice people and respectable find a place like that & send passes & we all will come at once we all wants to leave here out of this hard luck place if you cant use us find some place that does need this kind of people we are called Negroes here. I am a reader of the Defender and am delighted to know how times are there & was to glad to, know if we could get some one to pass us away from here to a better land. We work but cant get scarcely any thing for it & they dont want us to go away & there is not much of anything here to do & nothing for it Please find some one that need this kind of people & send at once for us. We dont want anything but our wareing and bed clothes & have not got no money to get away from here with & beging to get away before we are killed and hope to here from you at once. We cant talk to you over the phone here we are afraid to they dont want to hear one say that he or she wants to leave here if we do we are apt to be killed. They say if we dont go to war they are not going to let us stay here with their folks and it is not any thing that we have done to them. We are law abiding people want to treat every bordy right. these people wants to leave here but we cant we are here and have nothing to go with if you will send us some way to get away from here we will work till we pay it all if it takes that for us to go or get away. Now get busy for the south race. The conditions are horrible here with us. they wont give us anything to do & say that we wont need anything but something to eat & wont give us anything for what we do & wants us to stay here. Write me at once that you will do for us we want & opertunity that all we wants is to show you what we can do and will do if we can find some place. we wants to leave here for a north drive somewhere. We see starvation ahead of us here. We want to imigrate to the farmers who need our labor. We have not had no chance to have anything here thats why we plead to you for help to leave here to the North. We are humane but we are not treated such we are treated like brute by our whites here we dont have no privilige no where in the south. We must take anything they put on us. Its hard if its fair. We have not got no cotegous diseases here. We are looking to here from you soon.

Black Poets Sing

The literary output of the Harlem Renaissance of the 1920s was prodigious. Whether this was the result of a new burst of black talent or merely the result of the downtown publishers' "discovery" of talent that had always existed is impossible to determine. The fact remains that much of the writing of this movement has stood the test of time and entered the canon of American literature.

Selections from four poets have been chosen to illustrate some of the issues dealt with by the Renaissance.

COUNTEE CULLEN

Countee Cullen (1903–1946) was publishing poetry before his graduation from De Witt Clinton High School in New York City. He was perhaps the most distinguished black poet of the period of the Harlem Renaissance. The first poem given here is a moving statement about the anomaly of being a black poet. The second reflects the ambivalence of the black intellectual who is caught between his African past and his American present.

YET DO I MARVEL

I doubt not God is good, well-meaning, kind,
And did He stoop to quibble could tell why
The little buried mole continues blind,
Why flesh that mirrors Him must someday die,
Make plain the reason tortured Tantalus
Is baited by the fickle fruit, declare
If merely brute caprice dooms Sisyphus
To struggle up a never-ending stair.
Inscrutable His ways are, and immune
To catechism by a mind too strewn
With petty cares to slightly understand
What awful brain compels His awful hand.
Yet do I marvel at this curious thing:
To make a poet black, and bid him sing!

HERITAGE (FOR HAROLD JACKMAN)

What is Africa to me:
Copper sun or scarlet sea,
Jungle star or jungle track,

FROM *On These I Stand* by Countee Cullen: "Yet Do I Marvel"—Copyright 1925 by Harper & Brothers; renewed 1953 by Ida M. Cullen. By permission of The Estate of Ida M. Cullen. Copyrights administered by Thompson and Thompson, New York, NY.

Strong bronzed men, or regal black
Women from whose loins I sprang
When the birds of Eden sang?
One three centuries removed
From the scenes his fathers loved,
Spicy grove, cinnamon tree,
What is Africa to me?

So I lie, who all day long
Want no sound except the song
Sung by wild barbaric birds
Goading massive jungle herds,
Juggernauts of flesh that pass
Trampling tall defiant grass
Where young forest lovers lie,
Plighting troth beneath the sky.
So I lie, who always hear,
Though I cram against my ear
Both my thumbs, and keep them there,
Great drums throbbing through the air.
So I lie, whose fount of pride,
Dear distress, and joy allied,
Is my somber flesh and skin,
With the dark blood dammed within
Like great pulsing tides of wine
That, I fear, must burst the fine
Channels of the chafing net
Where they surge and foam and fret.

Africa? A book one thumbs
Listlessly, till slumber comes.
Unremembered are her bats
Circling through the night, her cats
Crouching in the river reeds,
Stalking gentle flesh that feeds
By the river brink; no more

Does the bugle-throated roar
Cry that monarch claws have leapt
From the scabbards where they slept.

Silver snakes that once a year
Doff the lovely coats you wear,
Seek no covert in your fear
Lest a mortal eye should see;
What's your nakedness to me?
Here no leprous flowers rear
Fierce corollas in the air;
Here no bodies sleek and wet,
Dripping mingled rain and sweat,
Tread the savage measures of
Jungle boys and girls in love.
What is last year's snow to me,
Last year's anything? The tree
Budding yearly must forget
How its past arose or set—
Bough and blossom, flower, fruit,
Even what shy bird with mute
Wonder at her travail there,
Meekly labored in its hair.
One three centuries removed
From the scenes his fathers loved,
Spicy grove, cinnamon tree,
What is Africa to me?

So I lie, who find no peace
Night or day, no slight release
From the unremittant beat
Made by cruel padded feet
Walking through my body's street.
Up and down they go, and back,
Treading out a jungle track.
So I lie, who never quite
Safely sleep from rain at night—
I can never rest at all
When the rain begins to fall;
Like a soul gone mad with pain
I must match its weird refrain;
Ever must I twist and squirm,
Writhing like a baited worm,
While its primal measures drip
Through my body, crying, "Strip!
Doff this new exuberance.
Come and dance the Lover's Dance!"
In an old remembered way
Rain works on me night and day.

Quaint, outlandish heathen gods
Black men fashion out of rods,
Clay, and brittle bits of stone,
In a likeness like their own,
My conversion came high-priced;
I belong to Jesus Christ,
Preacher of humility,
Heathen gods are naught to me.

Father, Son, and Holy Ghost,
So I make an idle boast;
Jesus of the twice-turned cheek,
Lamb of God, although I speak
With my mouth thus, in my heart
Do I play a double part.
Ever at Thy glowing altar
Must my heart grow sick and falter,
Wishing He I served were black,
Thinking then it would not lack
Precedent of pain to guide it,
Let who would or might deride it;
Surely then this flesh would know
Yours had borne a kindred woe.
Lord, I fashion dark gods, too,
Daring even to give You
Dark despairing features where,
Crowned with dark rebellious hair,
Patience wavers just so much as
Mortal grief compels, while touches
Quick and hot, of anger, rise
To smitten cheek and weary eyes.
Lord, forgive me if my need
Sometimes shapes a human creed.
All day long and all night through,
One thing only must I do:
Quench my pride and cool my blood,
Lest I perish in the flood,
Lest a hidden ember set
Timber that I thought was wet
Burning like the dryest flax,
Melting like the merest wax,
Lest the grave restore its dead.
Not yet has my heart or head
In the least way realized
They and I are civilized.

LANGSTON HUGHES

Langston Hughes (1902–1967) is represented here by two short lyrics that express the longing of blacks for their rightful place in the world. The first deals with what Hughes considered the inevitable acceptance of the black and the shame white America would feel when that acceptance finally came. The second reflects on the charms of blackness. Hughes' remarkable literary output included poetry, essays, novels, newspaper articles, and works of history.

I, TOO

I, too, sing America.

I am the darker brother.
They send me to eat in the kitchen
When company comes,
But I laugh,
And eat well,
And grow strong.

Tomorrow,
I'll be at the table
When company comes.
Nobody'll dare
Say to me,
"Eat in the kitchen,"
Then.

Besides,
They'll see how beautiful I am
And be ashamed—

I, too, am America.

DREAM VARIATION

To fling my arms wide
In some place of the sun,
To whirl and to dance
Till the white day is done.
Then rest at cool evening
Beneath a tall tree

While night comes on gently,
 Dark like me—
That is my dream!

To fling my arms wide
In the face of the sun,
Dance! Whirl! Whirl!
Till the quick day is done.
Rest at pale evening ...
A tall, slim tree ...
Night coming tenderly
 Black like me.

JAMES WELDON JOHNSON

James Weldon Johnson (1871–1938) had a varied career as a teacher, poet, diplomat, and the executive secretary of the NAACP. In his poetic work God's Trombones, Johnson tried to capture the imagery and the cadences of the old-time black preachers. What follows is a section from this work dealing with the promise of ultimate deliverance that played such a large part in black Christianity.

GO DOWN DEATH—A FUNERAL SERMON

Weep not, weep not,
She is not dead;
She's resting in the bosom of Jesus.
Heart-broken husband — weep no more;
Grief-stricken son — weep no more;
She's only just gone home.
Day before yesterday morning,
God was looking down from his great, high heaven,
Looking down on all his children,
And his eye fell on Sister Caroline,
Tossing on her bed of pain.
And God's big heart was touched with pity,
With the everlasting pity.

And God sat back on his throne,
And he commanded that tall, bright angel standing on
 his right hand:
Call me Death!

And that tall, bright angel cried in a voice
That broke like a clap of thunder:
Call Death! —Call Death!
And the echo sounded down the streets of heaven
Till it reached away back to that shadowy place,
Where Death waits with his pale, white horses.

And Death heard the summons,
And he leaped on his fastest horse,
Pale as a sheet in the moonlight.
Up the golden street Death galloped,
And the hoof of his horse struck fire from the gold,
But they didn't make no sound.
Up Death rode to the Great White Throne,
And waited for God's command.

And God said: Go down, Death, go down,
Go down to Savannah, Georgia,
Down in Yamacraw,
And find Sister Caroline.
She's borne the burden and heat of the day,
She's labored long in my vineyard,
And she's tired—
She's weary—
Go down, Death, and bring her to me.

And Death didn't say a word,
But he loosed the reins on his pale, white horse,
And he damped the spurs to his bloodless sides,
And out and down he rode,

Through heaven's pearly gates,
Past suns and moons and stars;
On Death rode,
And the foam from his horse was like a comet in the sky;
On Death rode,
Leaving the lightning's flash behind;
Straight on down he came.

While we were watching round her bed,
She turned her eyes and looked away,

She saw what we couldn't see;
She saw Old Death. She saw Old Death.
Coming like a falling star.
But Death didn't frighten Sister Caroline;
He looked to her like a welcome friend.
And she whispered to us: I'm going home,
And she smiled and closed her eyes.

And Death took her up like a baby,
And she lay in his icy arms,
But she didn't feel no chill.
And Death began to ride again—
Up beyond the evening star,
Out beyond the morning star,
Into the glittering light of glory,
On to the Great White Throne.
And there he laid Sister Caroline
On the loving breast of Jesus.

And Jesus took his own hand and wiped away her tears,
And he smoothed the furrows from her face,
And the angels sang a little song,
And Jesus rocked her in his arms,
And kept a-saying: Take your rest,
Take your rest, take your rest.
Weep not—weep not,
She is not dead;
She's resting in the bosom of Jesus.

CLAUDE MCKAY

Claude McKay (1890–1948) first published in his native Jamaica. He came to the United States in his early twenties to attend Tuskegee Institute and Kansas State University. Soon he moved to New York City, where he became an important novelist and journalist. He also wrote poetry, however, and the angry poem that follows was composed during the Red Summer of 1919 as blacks fought the white mobs.

IF WE MUST DIE

If we must die—let it not be like hogs
Hunted and penned in an inglorious spot,
While round us bark the mad and hungry dogs,
Making their mock at our accursed lot.
If we must die—oh, let us nobly die,

So that our precious blood may not be shed
In vain; then even the monsters we defy
Shall be constrained to honor us though dead!
Oh, Kinsmen! We must meet the common foe;
Though far outnumbered, let us show us brave,
And for their thousand blows deal one deathblow!
What though before us lies the open grave?
Like men we'll face the murderous, cowardly pack,
Pressed to the wall, dying, but fighting back!

FROM *Selected Poems of Claude McKay*: "If We Must Die." Copyright 1981 and reprinted with the permission of Twayne Publishers, a division of G. K. Hall and Co., Boston.

Free Africa for Africans

The Negro's Greatest Enemy

MARCUS GARVEY

Marcus Garvey organized the Universal Negro Improvement Association (UNIA) in Jamaica in 1914 to prepare for the time when al! the world's black people would live together in freedom from white domination. In 1916, Garvey went to New York City, where his ideas drew an enthusiastic response from rural blacks lately come to the city. After the First World War, increasingly frustrated returning servicemen and masses of unemployed urban blacks swelled the ranks of Garvey supporters. By 1919, the UNIA had thirty branches in the United States and several abroad. In 1920, an African government-in-exile was established by the UNIA with Garvey as provisional president. Through his appeal to black pride and a future black state, Garvey attracted millions of black sympathizers to his cause.

In the autobiographical article reprinted here, Garvey tells about the growing race consciousness that led him to found the UNIA. He also recounts the opposition he received from other black men in the United States—opposition that ultimately led to his imprisonment.

Garvey died in London in 1940 without ever having visited Africa, the land that held his dream.

I was born in the Island of Jamaica, British West Indies, on Aug. 17, 1887. My parents were black negroes. My father was a man of brilliant intellect and dashing courage. He was unafraid of consequences. He took human chances in the course of life, as most bold men do, and he failed at the close of his career. He once had a fortune; he died poor. My mother was a sober and conscientious Christian, too soft and good for the time in which she lived. She was the direct opposite of my father. He was severe, firm, determined, bold and strong, refusing to yield even to superior forces if he believed he was right. My mother, on the other hand, was always willing to return a smile for a blow, and ever ready to bestow charity upon her enemy. Of this strange combination I was born thirty-six years ago, and ushered into a world of sin, the flesh and the devil.

I grew up with other black and white boys. I was never whipped by any, but made them all respect the strength of my arms. I got my education from many sources—through private tutors, two public schools, two grammar or

FROM Marcus Garvey, "The Negro's Greatest Enemy," *Current History* (Old Series), vol. 18 (September 1923), pp. 951–57.

high schools and two colleges. My teachers were men and women of varied experiences and abilities; four of them were eminent preachers. They studied me and I studied them. With some I became friendly in after years, others and I drifted apart, because as a boy they wanted to whip me, and I simply refused to be whipped. I was not made to be whipped. It annoys me to be defeated; hence to me, to be once defeated is to find cause for an everlasting struggle to reach the top.

I became a printer's apprentice at an early age, while still attending school. My apprentice master was a highly educated and alert man. In the affairs of business and the world he had no peer. He taught me many things before I reached twelve, and at fourteen I had enough intelligence and experience to manage men. I was strong and manly, and I made them respect me. I developed a strong and forceful character, and have maintained it still.

To me, at home in my early days, there was no difference between white and black. One of my father's properties, the place where I lived most of the time, was adjoining that of a white man. He had three girls and two boys; the Wesleyan minister, another white man whose church my parents attended, also had property adjoining ours. He had three girls and one boy. All of us were playmates. We romped and were happy children playmates together. The little white girl whom I liked most knew no better than I did myself. We were two innocent fools who never dreamed of a race feeling and problem. As a child, I went to school with white boys and girls, like all other negroes. We were not called negroes then. I never heard the term negro used once until I was about fourteen.

At fourteen my little white playmate and I parted. Her parents thought the time had come to separate us and draw the color line. They sent her and another sister to Edinburgh, Scotland, and told her that she was never to write or try to get in touch with me, for I was a "nigger." It was then that I found for the first time that there was some difference in humanity, and that there were different races, each having its own separate and distinct social life. I did not care about the separation after I was told about it, because I never thought all during our childhood association that the girl and the rest of the children of her race were better than I was; in fact, they used to look up to me. So I simply had no regrets. I only thought them "fresh."

After my first lesson in race distinction, I never thought of playing with white girls any more, even if they might be next door neighbors. At home my sister's company was good enough for me, and at school I made friends with the colored girls next to me. White boys and I used to frolic together. We played cricket and baseball, ran races and rode bicycles together, took each other to the river and to the sea beach to learn to swim, and made boyish efforts while out in deep water to drown each other, making a sprint for shore crying out "shark, shark, shark." In all our experiences, however, only one black boy was drowned. He went under on a Friday afternoon after school hours, and his parents found him afloat half eaten by sharks on the following Sunday afternoon. Since then we boys never went back to sea.

"YOU ARE BLACK"

At maturity the black and white boys separated, and took different courses in life. I grew up then to see the difference between the races more and more. My schoolmates as young men did not know or remember me any more. Then I realized that I had to make a fight for a place in the world, that it was not so easy to pass on to office and position. Personally, however, I had not much difficulty in finding and holding a place for myself, for I was aggressive. At eighteen I had an excellent position as manager of a large printing estab-lishment, having under my control several men old enough to be my grand-fathers. But I got mixed up with public life. I started to take an interest in the politics of my country, and then I saw the injustice done to my race because it was black, and I became dissatisfied on that account. I went traveling to South and Central America and parts of the West Indies to find out if it was so elsewhere, and I found the same situation. I set sail for Europe to find out if it was different there, and again I found the same stumbling-block—"You are black." I read of the conditions in America. I read "Up From Slavery," by Booker T. Washington, and then my doom—if I may so call it—of being a race leader dawned upon me in London after I had traveled through almost half of Europe.

I asked, "Where is the black man's Government?" "Where is his King and his kingdom?" "Where is his President, his country, and his ambassador, his army, his navy, his men of big affairs?" I could not find them, and then I declared, "I will help to make them."

Becoming naturally restless for the opportunity of doing something for the advancement of my race, I was determined that the black man would not con-tinue to be kicked about by all the other races and nations of the world, as I saw it in the West Indies, South and Central America and Europe, and as I read of it in America. My young and ambitious mind led me into flights of great imagination. I saw before me then, even as I do now, a new world of black men, not peons, serfs, dogs and slaves, but a nation of sturdy men making their impress upon civilization and causing a new light to dawn upon the human race. I could not remain in London any more. My brain was afire. There was a world of thought to conquer. I had to start ere it became too late and the work be not done. Immediately I boarded a ship at Southampton for Jamaica, where I arrived on July 15, 1914. The Universal Negro Improvement Association and African Communities (Imperial) League was founded and organized five days after my arrival, with the program of uniting all the negro peoples of the world into one great body to establish a country and Government absolutely their own.

Where did the name of the organization come from? It was while speak-ing to a West Indian negro who was a passenger on the ship with me from Southampton, who was returning home to the West Indies from Basutoland with his Basuto wife, that I further learned of the horrors of native life in Africa. He related to me in conversation such horrible and pitiable tales that my heart bled within me. Retiring from the conversation to my cabin, all day and the following night I pondered over the subject matter of that conversation, and at midnight, lying flat on my back, the vision and thought came to me that I should name the organization the Universal Negro Improvement Association and African Communities (Imperial) League. Such a name I thought would embrace the purpose of all black humanity. Thus to the world a name was born, a movement created, and a man became known.

I really never knew there was so much color prejudice in Jamaica, my own native home, until I started the work of the Universal Negro Improvement Association. We started immediately before the war. I had just returned from a successful trip to Europe, which was an exceptional achievement for a black man. The daily papers wrote me up with big headlines and told of my movement. But nobody wanted to be a negro. "Garvey is crazy; he has lost his head," "Is that the use he is going to make of his experience and intelligence?" — such were the criticisms passed upon me. Men and women as black as I, and even more so, had believed themselves white under the West Indian order of society. I was simply an impossible man to use openly the term "negro"; yet every one beneath his breath was calling the black man a negro.

I had to decide whether to please my friends and be one of the "black-whites" of Jamaica, and be reasonably prosperous, or come out openly and defend and help improve and protect the integrity of the black millions and suffer. I decided to do the latter, hence my offence against "colored-black-white" society in the colonies and America. I was openly hated and persecuted by some of these colored men of the island who did not want to be classified as negroes, but as white. They hated me worse than poison. They opposed me at every step, but I had a large number of white friends, who encouraged and helped me. Notable among them were the then Governor of the Colony, the Colonial Secretary and several other prominent men. But they were afraid of offending the "colored gentry" that were passing for white. Hence my fight had to be made alone. I spent hundreds of pounds (sterling) helping the organization to gain a footing. I also gave up all my time to the promulgation of its ideals. I became a marked man, but I was determined that the work should be done.

The war helped a great deal in arousing the consciousness of the colored people to the reasonableness of our program, especially after the British at home had rejected a large number of West Indian colored men who wanted to be officers in the British army. When they were told that negroes could not be officers in the British army they started their own propaganda, which supplemented the program of the Universal Negro Improvement Association. With this and the other contributing agencies a few of the stiffnecked colored people began to see the reasonableness of my program, but they were firm in refusing to be known as negroes. Furthermore, I was a black man and therefore had absolutely no right to lead; in the opinion of the "colored" element, leadership should have been in the hands of a yellow or a very light man. On such flimsy prejudices our race has been retarded. There is more bitterness among us negroes because of the caste of color than there is between any other peoples, not excluding the people of India.

I succeeded to a great extent in establishing the association in Jamaica with the assistance of a Catholic Bishop, the Governor, Sir John Pringle, the Rev. William Graham, a Scottish clergyman, and several other white friends. I got in touch with Booker Washington and told him what I wanted to do. He invited me to America and promised to speak with me in the Southern and other States to help my work. Although he died in the Fall of 1915, 1 made my arrangements and arrived in the United States on March 23, 1916.

Here I found a new and different problem. I immediately visited some of the then so-called negro leaders, only to discover, after a close study of them, that they had no program, but were mere opportunists who were living off their so-called leadership while the poor people were groping in the dark. I traveled through thirty-eight States and everywhere found the same condition. I visited Tuskegee and paid my respects to the dead hero, Booker Washington, and then returned to New York, where I organized the New York division of the Universal Negro Improvement Association. After instructing the people in the aims and objects of the association, I intended returning to Jamaica to perfect the Jamaica organization, but when we had enrolled about 800 or 1,000 members in the Harlem district and had elected the officers, a few negro politicians began trying to turn the movement into a political club.

POLITICAL FACTION FIGHT

Seeing that these politicians were about to destroy my ideals, I had to fight to get them out of the organization. There it was that I made my first political enemies in Harlem. They fought me until they smashed the first organization and reduced its membership to about fifty. I started again, and in two months built up a new organization of about 1,500 members. Again the politicians came and divided us into two factions. They took away all the books of the organization, its treasury and all its belongings. At that time I was only an organizer, for it was not then my intention to remain in America, but to return to Jamaica. The organization had its proper officers elected, and I was not an officer of the New York division, but President of the Jamaica branch.

On the second split in Harlem thirteen of the members conferred with me and requested me to become President for a time of the New York organization so as to save them from the politicians. I consented and was elected President. There then sprung up two factions, one led by the politicians with the books and the money, and the other led by me. My faction had no money. I placed at their disposal what money I had, opened an office for them, rented a meeting place, employed two women secretaries, went on the streets of Harlem at night to speak for the movement. In three weeks more than 2,000 new members joined. By this time I had the association incorporated so as to prevent the other faction using the name, but in two weeks the politicians had stolen all the people's money and had smashed up their faction.

The organization under my Presidency grew by leaps and bounds. I started The Negro World. Being a journalist, I edited this paper free of cost for the association, and worked for them without pay until November, 1920. I traveled all over the country for the association at my own expense, and established branches until in 1919 we had about thirty branches in different cities. By my writings and speeches we were able to build up a large organization of over 2,000,000 by June, 1919, at which time we launched the program of the Black Star Line.

To have built up a new organization, which was not purely political, among negroes in America was a wonderful feat, for the negro politician does not allow any other kind of organization within his race to thrive. We succeeded, however, in making the Universal Negro Improvement Association so formidable in 1919 that we encountered more trouble from our political brethren. They sought the influence of the District Attorney's office of the County of New York to put us out of business. Edwin P. Kilroe, at that time an Assistant District Attorney, on the complaint of the negro politicians, started to investigate us and the association. Mr. Kilroe would constantly and continuously call me to his office for investigation on extraneous matters without coming to the point. The result was that after the eighth or ninth time I wrote an article in our newspaper, The Negro World, against him. This was interpreted as criminal libel, for which I was indicted and arrested, but subsequently dismissed on retracting what I had written.

During my many tilts with Mr. Kilroe, the question of the Black Star Line was discussed. He did not want us to have a line of ships. I told him that even as there was a White Star Line, we would have, irrespective of his wishes, a Black Star Line. On June 27, 1919, we incorporated the Black Star Line of Delaware, and in September we obtained a ship.

The following month (October) a man by the name of Tyler came to my office at 56 West 135th Street, New York City, and told me that Mr. Kilroe had sent him to "get me," and at once fired four shots at me from a .38-calibre revolver. He wounded me in the right leg and the right side of my scalp. I was taken to the Harlem Hospital, and he was arrested. The next day it was reported that he committed suicide in jail just before he was to be taken before a City Magistrate.

RECORD-BREAKING CONVENTION

The first year of our activities for the Black Star Line added prestige to the Universal Negro Improvement Association. Several hundred thousand dollars worth of shares were sold. Our first ship, the steamship Yarmouth, had made two voyages to the West Indies and Central America. The white press had flashed the news all over the world. I, a young negro, as President of the corporation, had become famous. My name was discussed on five continents. The Universal Negro Improvement Association gained millions of followers all over the world. By August, 1920, over 4,000,000 persons had joined the movement. A convention of all the negro peoples of the world was called to meet in New York that month. Delegates came from all parts of the known world.

Over 25,000 persons packed the Madison Square Garden on Aug. 1 to hear me speak to the first International Convention of Negroes. It was a record-breaking meeting, the first and the biggest of its kind. The name of Garvey had become known as a leader of his race.

Such fame among negroes was too much for other race leaders and politicians to tolerate. My downfall was planned by my enemies. They laid all kinds of traps for me. They scattered their spies among the employes of the Black Star Line and the Universal Negro Improvement Association. Our office records were stolen. Employes started to be openly dishonest; we could get no convictions against them; even if on complaint they were held by a Magistrate, they were dismissed by the Grand Jury. The ships' officers started to pile up thousands of dollars of debts against the company without the knowledge of the officers of the corporation. Our ships were damaged at sea, and there was a general riot of wreck and ruin. Officials of the Universal Negro Improvement Association also began to steal and be openly dishonest. I had to dismiss them. They joined my enemies, and thus I had an endless fight on my hands to save the ideals of the association and carry out our program for the race. My negro enemies, finding that they alone could not destroy me, resorted to misrepresenting me to the leaders of the white race, several of whom, without proper investigation, also opposed me.

With robberies from within and from without, the Black Star Line was forced to suspend active business in December, 1921. While I was on a business trip to the West Indies in the Spring of 1921, the Black Star Line received the blow from which it was unable to recover. A sum of $25,000 was paid by one of the officers of the corporation to a man to purchase a ship, but the ship was never obtained and the money was never returned. The company was defrauded of a further sum of $11,000. Through such actions on the part of dishonest men in the shipping business, the Black Star Line received its first setback. This resulted in my being indicted for using the United States mails to defraud investors in the company. I was subsequently convicted and sentenced to five years in a Federal penitentiary. My trial is a matter of history. I know I was not given a square deal, because my indictment was the result of a "frame-up" among my political and business enemies. I had to conduct my own case in court because of the peculiar position in which I found myself. I had millions of friends and a large number of enemies. I wanted a colored attorney to handle my case, but there was none I could trust. I feel that I have been denied justice because of prejudice. Yet I have an abundance of faith in the courts of America, and I hope yet to obtain justice on my appeal.

ASSOCIATION'S 6,000,000 MEMBERSHIP

The temporary ruin of the Black Star Line has in no way affected the larger work of the Universal Negro Improvement Association, which now has 900 branches with an approximate membership of 6,000,000. This organization has succeeded in organizing the negroes all over the world and we now look forward to a renaissance that will create a new people and bring about the restoration of Ethiopia's ancient glory.

Being black, I have committed an unpardonable offense against the very light colored negroes in America and the West Indies by making myself famous as a negro leader of millions. In their view, no black man must rise above them, but I still forge ahead determined to give to the world the truth about the new negro who is determined to make and hold for himself a place in the affairs of men. The Universal Negro Improvement Association has been misrepresented by my enemies. They have tried to make it appear that we are hostile to other races. This is absolutely false. We love all humanity. We are working for the peace of the world which we believe can only come about when all races are given their due.

We feel that there is absolutely no reason why there should be any differences between the black and white races, if each stop to adjust and steady itself. We believe in the purity of both races. We do not believe the black man should be encouraged in the idea that his highest purpose in life is to marry a white woman, but we do believe that the white man should be taught to respect the black woman in the same way as he wants the black man to respect the white woman. It is a vicious and dangerous doctrine of social equality to urge, as certain colored leaders do, that black and white should get together, for that would destroy the racial purity of both.

We believe that the black people should have a country of their own where they should be given the fullest opportunity to develop politically, socially and industrially. The black people should not be encouraged to remain in white people's countries and expect to be Presidents, Governors, Mayors, Senators, Congressmen, Judges and social and industrial leaders. We believe that with the rising ambition of the negro, if a country is not provided for him in another 50 or 100 years, there will be a terrible clash that will end disastrously to him and disgrace our civilization. We desire to prevent such a clash by pointing the negro to a home of his own. We feel that all well disposed and broad minded white men will aid in this direction. It is because of this belief no doubt that my negro enemies, so as to prejudice me further in the opinion of the public, wickedly state that I am a member of the Ku Klux Klan, even though I am a black man.

I have been deprived of the opportunity of properly explaining my work to the white people of America through the prejudice worked up against me by jealous and wicked members of my own race. My success as an organizer was much more than rival negro leaders could tolerate. They, regardless of consequences, either to me or to the race, had to destroy me by fair means or foul. The thousands of anonymous and other hostile letters written to the editors and publishers of the white press by negro rivals to prejudice me in the eyes of public opinion are sufficient evidence of the wicked and vicious opposition I have had to meet from among my own people, especially among the very lightly colored. But they went further than the press in their attempts to discredit me. They organized clubs all over the United States and the West Indies, and wrote both open and anonymous letters to city, State and Federal officials of this and other Governments to induce them to use their influence to hamper and destroy me. No wonder, therefore, that several Judges, District Attorneys and other high officials have been against me without knowing me. No wonder, therefore, that the great white population of this country and of the world has a wrong impression of the aims and objects of the Universal Negro Improvement Association and of the work of Marcus Garvey.

THE STRUGGLE OF THE FUTURE

Having had the wrong education as a start in his racial career, the negro has become his own greatest enemy. Most of the trouble I have had in advancing the cause of the race has come from negroes. Booker Washington aptly described the race in one of his lectures by stating that we were like crabs in a barrel, that none would allow the other to climb over, but on any such attempt all would continue to pull back into the barrel the one crab that would make the effort to climb out. Yet, those of us with vision cannot desert the race, leaving it to suffer and die.

Looking forward a century or two, we can see an economic and political death struggle for the survival of the different race groups. Many of our present-day national centres will have become over-crowded with vast surplus populations. The fight for bread and position will be keen and severe. The weaker and unprepared group is bound to go under. That is why, visionaries as we are in the Universal Negro Improvement Association, we are fighting for the founding of a negro nation in Africa, so that there will be no clash between black and white and that each race will have a separate existence and civilization all its own without courting suspicion and hatred or eyeing each other with jealousy and rivalry within the borders of the same country.

White men who have struggled for and built up their countries and their own civilizations are not disposed to hand them over to the negro or any other race without let or hindrance. It would be unreasonable to expect this. Hence any vain assumption on the part of the negro to imagine that he will one day become President of the Nation, Governor of the State, or Mayor of the city in the countries of white men, is like waiting on the devil and his angels to take up their residence in the Realm on High and direct there the affairs of Paradise.

SUGGESTIONS FOR FURTHER READING

General treatments of the Great Migration include Joe William Trotter (ed.), *The Great Migration in Historical Perspective*★ (1991), Florette Henri, *Black Migration: The Movement North, 1900–1920* (1976), and Arna Bontemps and Jack Conroy, *They Seek a City* (1945). See also Milton Sernett, *Bound for the Promised Land: African American Religion and the Great Migration*★ (1997).

The Chicago area has received a great deal of attention from scholars of black migration. Some valuable studies of this area are James R. Grossman, *Land of Hope: Chicago, Black Southerners, and the Great Migration*★ (1990), St. Clair Drake and Horace Cayton, *Black Metropolis* (1945), Allan H. Spear, *Black Chicago: The Making of a Negro Ghetto, 1890–1920*★ (1967), and Harold Gosnell, *Negro Politicians: The Rise of Negro Politics in Chicago*★ (1935). Black urbanization is also treated in Gilbert Osofsky, *Harlem: The Making of a Ghetto*★ (1966) and Joe William Trotter, *Black Milwaukee: The Making of an Industrial Proletariat, 1915–45* (1984).

Special studies of racial violence during this period include Elliott Rudwick, *Race Riot at East St. Louis, July 2, 1917*★ (1964), Arthur Waskow, *From Race Riot to Sit-In: 1919 and the 1960s*★ (1966), William Tuttle, *Race Riot: Chicago in the Red Summer of 1919*★ (1917), and Scott Ellsworth, *Death in a Promised Land: The Tulsa Race Riot of 1921*★ (1992).

The Harlem Renaissance is described in David Levering Lewis, *When Harlem Was in Vogue* (1981) and Nathan 1. Huggins, *Harlem Renaissance*★ (1971). Writings from black artists of the period can be found in Nathan I. Huggins (ed.), *Voices from the Harlem Renaissance* (1976) and Alain Locke (ed.), *The New Negro*★ (1925). Black college life is described in Raymond Wolters, *The New Negro on Campus: Black College Rebellions of the 1920s* (1975).

Information about the Garvey movement can be found in Amy Jacques-Garvey (ed.), *Philosophy and Opinions of Marcus Garvey*★, 2 vols., (1923–1925) and Robert A. Hill, et al., (eds.), *The Marcus Garvey and Universal Negro Improvement Association Papers*, 4 vols., (1983–). An historical evaluation of the movement is available in Judith Stein, *The World of Marcus Garvey: Race and Class in Modern Society* (1985).

★ Books marked by an asterisk are available in paperback.

9

✧

Depression and War: Struggle and Advance

INTRODUCTION

The Harlem Renaissance left the masses of American blacks virtually untouched. The same could not be said, of course, of the impact of the Great Depression of the 1930s. As a matter of fact, many of the leaders of the Renaissance found themselves on the relief rolls a decade after their heyday. The black masses, already at the bottom of the American economic pyramid, found their situation further depressed by the unemployment that swept the country. The maxim "last hired, first fired" was applied to blacks with a vengeance. In Detroit, for example, 60 percent of the black workers were jobless in 1931, compared to 12 percent of the whites. In 1937, the figures for unemployed workers throughout the North were 38.9 percent for blacks and 18.1 percent for whites.

Although the economic programs of the Roosevelt administration's New Deal provided enough support for blacks to shift the African-American political allegiance from the Republican to the Democratic party, widespread discrimination in the administration of relief continued to favor whites over blacks, particularly in the South. When the New Deal recovery programs got underway, blacks were allowed to participate in most of them. Often, however, they participated in a lower proportion than whites and sometimes at lower wages, although this came to be against government policy.

In housing and agriculture, black people faced the most discriminatory aspects of New Deal policy. The Federal Housing Administration refused to guarantee mortgages on homes that blacks sought to buy if the houses were in white communities. And the acreage reduction programs of the Agricultural

Adjustment Administration contributed to the decline in agricultural work for blacks across the South and spurred black migration from rural to urban areas.

During the 1930s, the American Communist Party (CP) actively recruited among the jobless in the industrial North and the rural South. Among their major targets was the black community. The interracial policies of the CP appealed to some blacks, and black communists participated in the attempts to organize industrial unions for the Congress of Industrial Organizations (CIO) and among tenant farmers and sharecroppers.

Although unemployment had slackened somewhat by the end of the 1930s, it took full-fledged defense and war mobilization to pull the United States out of the Great Depression. Blacks were only marginally employed in the burgeoning defense industries at the beginning of mobilization, and the Roosevelt administration took slight interest in this development until black labor took up the issue in dramatic fashion. With the support of a broad base of black leadership, A. Philip Randolph announced to the president that if he did not take action against racially discriminatory hiring in the defense industry, 50,000 to 100,000 black people would march on the national capitol to demand fair treatment. A few days before the march was set to begin, Roosevelt, either afraid of the violence that such a march might provoke or reluctant to embarrass the United States before the Allied nations, signed an executive order calling for a nondiscriminatory policy in defense production. By the end of the war, hundreds of thousands of black people had been through job training programs and had received positions in industry.

As the migration of blacks to industrial jobs in northern and western cities increased, certain patterns that had developed during the Great Migration of the 1910s and 1920s reappeared. Racial hostility reached a peak, and several major race riots exploded—one in Harlem, one in Los Angeles, and two in Detroit. The second Detroit riot, in 1943, one of the worst outbreaks of racial violence in American history, brought about a change in the attitude of public officials throughout the North. It became apparent that something had to be done to ease the conditions that led to such outbreaks, and several commissions were set up to prepare proposals for the elimination of the threat of violent race riots. Partly as a result of the work of these commissions, the conclusion of World War II was not marked by the eruptions of racial violence that had followed World War I.

After Pearl Harbor, the policy of the War Department toward blacks was as follows: The proportion of blacks to be enlisted in the armed services would be the same as the proportion of blacks in the population as a whole (approximately 10 percent), and black and white military units would remain segregated. In the Army, there was at first a reluctance to allow black soldiers into combat areas. Experimental desegregated units were sent into action, however, and proved to be so successful that the practice of recruiting black platoons within white companies was instituted. In 1945, a War Department report called for the grouping together of black and white units, the assignment of blacks to training camps outside the South, and the expansion of the corps of black officers. In 1948, President Harry Truman issued an executive order that officially put an end to segregated military service. Although patterns of racial discrimination continued to appear in the military, they were clearly contrary to government policy.

After World War II, there was no going back to the old caste patterns for black and white America. Black troops had fought valiantly for what they called the "double V"— victory abroad and victory at home. White society discovered that what it had always suspected was indeed the case—if black people are given some freedom, they will begin to feel that they have the right to more.

Domestic Slavery

The Bronx Slave Market

ELLA BAKER AND MARVEL COOKE

The situation of the black domestic worker grew desperate during the Depression. Yet as unemployment in other unskilled areas rose, more and more black people were forced to seek domestic service. The inhuman conditions under which some were hired received publicity through The Crisis, *which, after Du Bois' departure, was edited by Roy Wilkins, later to become the executive director of the NAACP.*

The next article was written by two black women who were investigating the so-called slave markets that operated at certain subway stops in New York City. They describe the degrading spectacle of women selling themselves into domestic slavery. Reflected in the article is the ethnic prejudice of the black women who found themselves working in families with unfamiliar customs and usages. This hostility to "different" customs is, regrettably, deeply ingrained in American life.

The Bronx Slave Market! What is it? Who are its dealers? Who are its victims? What are its causes? How far does its stench spread? What forces are at work to counteract it?

Any corner in the congested sections of New York City's Bronx is fertile soil for mushroom "slave marts." The two where the traffic is heaviest and the bidding is highest are located at 167th street and Jerome avenue and at Simpson and Westchester avenues.

Symbolic of the more humane slave block is the Jerome avenue "market." There, on benches surrounding a green square, the victims wait, grateful, at least, for some place to sit. In direct contrast is the Simpson avenue "mart," where they pose wearily against buildings and lamp posts, or scuttle about in an attempt to retrieve discarded boxes upon which to rest.

Again, the Simpson avenue block exudes the stench of the slave market at its worst. Not only is human labor bartered and sold for slave wage, but human love also is a marketable commodity. But whether it is labor or love that is sold, economic necessity compels the sale. As early as 8 A.M. they come; as late as 1 P.M. they remain.

Rain or shine, cold or hot, you will find them there—Negro women, old and young—sometimes bedraggled, sometimes neatly dressed—but with the invariable paper bundle, waiting expectantly for Bronx housewives to buy their strength and energy for an hour, two hours, or even for a day at the

FROM Ella Baker and Marvel Cooke, "The Bronx Slave Market," *The Crisis*, vol. 42 (November 1935), pp. 330–31, 340.

munificent rate of fifteen, twenty, twenty-five, or, if luck be with them, thirty cents an hour. If not the wives themselves, maybe their husbands, their sons, or their brothers, under the subterfuge of work, offer worldly-wise girls higher bids for their time.

Who are these women? What brings them here? Why do they stay? In the boom days before the onslaught of the depression in 1929, many of these women who are now forced to bargain for day's work on street corners, were employed in grand homes in the rich Eighties, or in wealthier homes in Long Island and Westchester, at more than adequate wages. Some are former marginal industrial workers, forced by the slack in industry to seek other means of sustenance. In many instances there had been no necessity for work at all. But whatever their standing prior to the depression, none sought employment where they now seek it. They come to the Bronx, not because of what it promises, but largely in desperation.

Paradoxically, the crash of 1929 brought to the domestic labor market a new employer class. The lower middle-class housewife, who, having dreamed of the luxury of a maid, found opportunity staring her in the face in the form of Negro women pressed to the wall by poverty, starvation and discrimination.

Where once color was the "gilt edged" security for obtaining domestic and personal service jobs, here, even, Negro women found themselves being displaced by whites. Hours of futile waiting in employment agencies, the fee that must be paid despite the lack of income, fraudulent agencies that sprung up during the depression, all forced the day worker to fend for herself or try the dubious and circuitous road to public relief.

As inadequate as emergency relief has been, it has proved somewhat of a boon to many of these women, for with its advent, actual starvation is no longer their ever-present slave driver and they have been able to demand twenty-five and even thirty cents an hour as against the old fifteen and twenty cent rate. In an effort to supplement the inadequate relief received, many seek this open market.

And what a market! She who is fortunate (?) enough to please Mrs. Simon Legree's scrutinizing eye is led away to perform hours of multifarious household drudgeries. Under a rigid watch, she is permitted to scrub floors on her bended knees, to hang precariously from window sills, cleaning window after window, or to strain and sweat over steaming tubs of heavy blankets, spreads and furniture covers.

Fortunate, indeed, is she who gets the full hourly rate promised. Often, her day's slavery is rewarded with a single dollar bill or whatever her unscrupulous employer pleases to pay. More often, the clock is set back for an hour or more. Too often she is sent away without any pay at all.

HOW IT WORKS

We invaded the "market" early on the morning of September 14. Disreputable bags under arm and conscientiously forlorn, we trailed the work entourage on the West side "slave train," disembarking with it at Simpson and Westchester avenues. Taking up our stand outside the corner flower shop whose show window offered gardenias, roses and the season's first chrysanthemums at moderate prices, we waited patiently to be "bought."

We got results in almost nothing flat. A squatty Jewish housewife, patently lower middle class, approached us, carefully taking stock of our "wares."

"You girls want work?"

"Yes." We were expectantly noncommittal.

"How much you work for?"

We begged the question, noting that she was already convinced that we were not the "right sort." "How much do you pay?"

She was walking away from us. "I can't pay your price," she said and immediately started bargaining with a strong, seasoned girl leaning against the corner lamp post. After a few moments of animated conversation, she led the girl off with her. Curious, we followed them two short blocks to a dingy apartment house on a side street.

We returned to our post. We didn't seem to be very popular with the other "slaves." They eyed us suspiciously. But, one by one, as they became convinced that we were one with them, they warmed up to friendly sallies and answered our discreet questions about the possibilities of employment in the neighborhood.

Suddenly it began to rain, and we, with a dozen or so others, scurried to shelter under the five-and-ten doorway midway the block. Enforced close communion brought about further sympathy and conversation from the others. We asked the brawny, neatly dressed girl pressed close to us about the extent of trade in the "oldest profession" among women.

"Well," she said, "there is quite a bit of it up here. Most of 'those' girls congregate at the other corner." She indicated the location with a jerk of her head.

"Do they get much work?" we queried.

"Oh, quite a bit," she answered with a finality which was probably designed to close the conversation. But we were curious and asked her how the other girls felt about it. She looked at us a moment doubtfully, probably wondering if we weren't seeking advice to go into the "trade" ourselves.

"Well, that's their own business. If they can do it and get away with it, it's all right with the others." Or probably she would welcome some "work" of that kind herself.

"Sh-h-h." The wizened West Indian woman whom we had noticed, prior to the rain, patroling the street quite belligerently as if she were daring someone not to hire her, was cautioning us. She explained that if we kept up such a racket the store's manager would kick all of us out in the rain. And so we continued our conversation in whispered undertone.

"Gosh. I don't like this sort of thing at all." The slender brown girl whom we had seen turn down two jobs earlier in the morning, seemed anxious to talk. "This is my first time up here—and believe me, it is going to be my last. I don't like New York nohow. If I don't get a good job soon, I'm going back home to Kansas City." So she had enough money to travel, did she?

CUT-RATE COMPETITION

The rain stopped quite as suddenly as it started. We had decided to make a careful survey of the district to see whether or not there were any employment agencies in the section. Up one block and down another we tramped, but not one such institution did we encounter. Somehow the man who gave us a sly "Hello, babies" as he passed was strangely familiar. We realized two things about him—that he had been trailing us for some time and that he was manifestly, plain clothes notwithstanding, one of "New York's finest."

Trying to catch us to run us in for soliciting, was he? From that moment on, it was a three-cornered game. When we separated he was at sea. When we were together, he grinned and winked at us quite boldly. ...

We sidled up to a friendly soul seated comfortably on an upturned soap-box. Soon an old couple approached her and offered a day's work with their daughter way up on Jerome avenue. They were not in agreement as to how much the daughter would pay—the old man said twenty-five cents an hour—the old lady scowled and said twenty. The car fare, they agreed, would be paid after she reached her destination. The friendly soul refused the job. She could afford independence, for she had already successfully bargained for a job for the following day. She said to us, after the couple started negotiations with another woman, that she wouldn't go way up on Jerome avenue on a wild goose chase for Mrs. Roosevelt, herself. We noted, with satisfaction, that the old couple had no luck with any of the five or six they contacted.

It struck us as singularly strange, since it was already 10:30, that the women still lingered, seemingly unabashed that they had not yet found employment for a day. We were debating whether or not we should leave the "mart" and try again another day, probably during the approaching Jewish holidays at which time business is particularly flourishing, when, suddenly, things looked up again. A new batch of "slaves" flowed down the elevated steps and took up their stands at advantageous points.

The friendly soul turned to us, a sneer marring the smooth roundness of her features. "Them's the girls who makes it bad for us. They get more jobs than us because they will work for anything. We runned them off the corner last week." One of the newcomers was quite near us and we couldn't help but overhear the following conversation with a neighborhood housewife.

"You looking for work?"

"Yes ma'am."

"How much you charge?"

"I'll take what you will give me." ... What was this? Could the girl have needed work that badly? Probably. She did look run down at the heels. ...

"All right. Come on. I'll give you a dollar." Cupidity drove beauty from the arrogant features. The woman literally dragged her "spoil" to her den. ... But what of the girl? Could she possibly have known what she was letting herself in for? Did she know how long she would have to work for that dollar or what she would have to do? Did she know whether or not she would get lunch or car fare? Not any more than we did. Yet, there she was, trailing down the street behind her "mistress."

"You see," philosophized the friendly soul. "That's what makes it bad for the rest of us. We got to do something about those girls. Organize them or something." The friendly soul remained complacent on her up-turned box. Our guess was that if the girls were organized, the incentive would come from some place else.

Business in the "market" took on new life. Eight or ten girls made satisfactory contacts. Several women—and men approached us, but our price was too high or we refused to wash windows or scrub floors. We were beginning to have a rollicking good time when rain again dampened our heads and ardor. We again sought the friendly five-and-ten doorway.

"FOR FIVE BUCKS A WEEK"

We became particularly friendly with a girl whose intelligent replies to our queries intrigued us. When we were finally convinced that there would be no more "slave" barter that day, we invited her to lunch with us at a nearby restaurant. After a little persuasion, there we were, Millie Jones between us, refreshing our spirits and appetites with hamburgers, fragrant with onions, and coffee. We found Millie an articulate person. It seems that, until recently, she had had a regular job in the neighborhood. But let her tell you about it.

"Did I have to work? And how! For five bucks and car fare a week. Mrs. Eisenstein had a six-room apartment lighted by fifteen windows. Each and every week, believe it or not, I had to wash every one of those windows. If that old hag found as much as the teeniest speck on any one of 'em, she'd make me do it over. I guess I would do anything rather than wash windows. On Mondays I washed and did as much of the ironing as I could. The rest waited over for Tuesday. There were two grown sons in the family and her husband. That meant that I would have at least twenty-one shirts to do every week. Yeah, and ten sheets and at least two blankets, besides. They all had to be done just so, too. Gosh, she was a particular woman.

"There wasn't a week, either, that I didn't have to wash up every floor in the place and wax it on my hands and knees. And two or three times a week I'd have to beat the mattresses and take all the furniture covers off and shake 'em out. Why, when I finally went home nights, I could hardly move. One of the sons had "hand trouble" too, and I was just as tired fighting him off, I guess, as I was with the work.

"Say, did you ever wash dishes for an Orthodox Jewish family?" Millie took a long, sibilant breath. "Well, you've never really washed dishes, then. You know, they use a different dishcloth for everything they cook. For instance, they have one for 'milk' pots in which dairy dishes are cooked, another for glasses, another for vegetable pots, another for meat pots, and so on. My memory wasn't very good and I was always getting the darn things mixed up. I used to make Mrs. Eisenstein just as mad. But I was the one who suffered. She would get other cloths and make me do the dishes all over again.

"How did I happen to leave her? Well, after I had been working about five weeks, I asked for a Sunday off. My boy friend from Washington was coming up on an excursion to spend the day with me. She told me if I didn't come in on Sunday, I needn't come back at all. Well, I didn't go back. Ever since then I have been trying to find a job. The employment agencies are no good. All the white girls get the good jobs.

"My cousin told me about up here. The other day I didn't have a cent in my pocket and I just had to find work in order to get back home and so I took the first thing that turned up. I went to work about 11 o'clock and I stayed until 5:00—washing windows, scrubbing floors and washing out stinking baby things. I was surprised when she gave me lunch. You know, some of 'em don't even do that. When I got through, she gave me thirty-five cents. Said she took a quarter out for lunch. Figure it out for yourself. Ten cents an hour!

MINIATURE ECONOMIC BATTLEFRONT

The real significance of the Bronx Slave Market lies not in a factual presentation of its activities; but in focusing attention upon its involved implications. The "mart" is but a miniature mirror of our economic battlefront.

To many, the women who sell their labor thus cheaply have but themselves to blame. A head of a leading employment agency bemoans the fact that these women have not "chosen the decent course" and declares: "The well-meaning employment agencies endeavoring to obtain respectable salaries and suitable working conditions for deserving domestics are finding it increasingly difficult due to the menace and obstacles presented by the slavish performances of the lower types of domestics themselves, who, unlike the original slaves who recoiled from meeting their masters, rush to meet their mistresses."

The exploiters, judged from the districts where this abominable traffic flourishes, are the wives and mothers of artisans and tradesmen who militantly battle against being exploited themselves, but who apparently have no scruples against exploiting others.

The general public, though aroused by stories of these domestics, too often think of the problems of these women as something separate and apart and readily dismisses them with a sigh and a shrug of the shoulders.

The women, themselves present a study in contradictions. Largely unaware of their organized power, yet ready to band together for some immediate and personal gain either consciously or unconsciously, they still cling to the American illusion that any one who is determined and persistent can get ahead.

The roots, then of the Bronx Slave Market spring from: (1) the general ignorance of and apathy towards organized labor action; (2) the artificial barriers that separate the interest of the relief administrators and investigators from that of their "case loads," the white collar and professional worker from the laborer and the domestic; and (3) organized labor's limited concept of exploitation, which permits it to fight vigorously to secure itself against evil, yet passively or actively aids and abets the ruthless destruction of Negroes.

To abolish the market once and for all, these roots must be torn away from their sustaining soil. Certain palliative and corrective measures are not without benefit. Already the seeds of discontent are being sown.

The Women's Day Workers and Industrial League, organized sixteen years ago by Fannie Austin, has been, and still is, a force to abolish the existing evils in day labor. Legitimate employment agencies have banded together to curb the activities of the racketeer agencies and are demanding fixed minimum and maximum wages for all workers sent out. Articles and editorials recently carried by the New York Negro press have focused attention on the existing evils in the "slave market."

An embryonic labor union now exists in the Simpson avenue "mart." Girls who persist in working for less than thirty cents an hour have been literally run off the corner. For the recent Jewish holiday, habitues of the "mart" actually demanded and refused to work for less than thirty-five cents an hour.

March for a Fair Share

The March on Washington
Movement, 1941

A. PHILIP RANDOLPH

Asa Philip Randolph has been an active agitator for the rights of black people since at least 1917, when he and a friend started publishing The Messenger, *a socialist magazine that was radically critical of American capitalism. In 1918, Randolph was arrested for opposing the entry of the United States into the First World War. Subsequently, he was described by a congressional committee as "the most dangerous Negro in America."*

In the 1920s, Randolph began organizing Pullman car porters, and in 1928, he changed the name of his magazine to The Black Worker. *In 1937, the organization called the Brotherhood of Sleeping Car Porters was certified, and Randolph triumphantly took his place at its head.*

From this position, he directed over a number of years many civil rights struggles, including the March on Washington for Jobs and Freedom of August 1963, when several hundred thousand people affirmed their belief in racial equality by gathering in Washington, DC, for a symbolic march.

The 1963 march was not without antecedents, though the most important of them never took place. In 1941, Randolph announced that he intended to lead a large number of blacks in a march on Washington to protest their exclusion from jobs in defense industry and their segregation in the armed forces. Six days before the march was to take place, Roosevelt issued an executive order barring discrimination in defense work. Randolph then canceled the march. Desegregation of the armed forces had to wait until after the war.

Presented next are Randolph's call for a march on Washington in 1941 and his subsequent message canceling the march. The latter originated as a radio address, broadcast on June 28, 1941. The discrepancy between the number of marchers originally called for and the number cited in the cancellation speech suggests the dimensions of the response to Randolph's appeal.

Greetings:

We call upon you to fight for jobs in National Defense.

We call upon you to struggle for the integration of Negroes in the armed forces, such as the Air Corps, Navy, Army and Marine Corps of the Nation.

FROM A. Philip Randolph, "Call to Negro America 'To March on Washington for Jobs and Equal Participation in National Defense,' July 1, 1941," *The Black Worker* (May 1941); and "The Negro March on Washington," *The Black Worker* (July 1941).

We call upon you to demonstrate for the abolition of Jim-Crowism in all Government departments and defense employment.

This is an hour of crisis. It is a crisis of democracy. It is a crisis of minority groups. It is a crisis of Negro Americans.

What is this crisis?

To American Negroes, it is the denial of jobs in Government defense projects. It is racial discrimination in Government departments. It is widespread Jim-Crowism in the armed forces of the Nation.

While billions of the taxpayers' money are being spent for war weapons, Negro workers are being turned away from the gates of factories, mines and mills—being flatly told, "NOTHING DOING." Some employers refuse to give Negroes jobs when they are without "union cards," and some unions refuse Negro workers union cards when they are "without jobs."

What shall we do?

What a dilemma!

What a runaround!

What a disgrace!

What a blow below the belt!

'Though dark, doubtful and discouraging, all is not lost, all is not hopeless. 'Though battered and bruised, we are not beaten, broken or bewildered.

Verily, the Negroes' deepest disappointments and direst defeats, their tragic trials and outrageous oppressions in these dreadful days of destruction and disaster to democracy and freedom, and the rights of minority peoples, and the dignity and independence of the human spirit, is the Negroes' greatest opportunity to rise to the highest heights of struggle for freedom and justice in Government, in industry, in labor unions, education, social service, religion and culture.

With faith and confidence of the Negro people in their own power for self-liberation, Negroes can break down the barriers of discrimination against employment in National Defense. Negroes can kill the deadly serpent of race hatred in the Army, Navy, Air and Marine Corps, and smash through and blast the Government, business and labor-union red tape to win the right to equal opportunity in vocational training and re-training in defense employment.

Most important and vital to all, Negroes, by the mobilization and coordination of their mass power, can cause PRESIDENT ROOSEVELT TO ISSUE AN EXECUTIVE ORDER ABOLISHING DISCRIMINATIONS IN ALL GOVERNMENT DEPARTMENTS, ARMY, NAVY, AIR CORPS AND NATIONAL DEFENSE JOBS.

Of course, the task is not easy. In very truth, it is big, tremendous and difficult.

It will cost money.

It will require sacrifice.

It will tax the Negroes' courage, determination and will to struggle. But we can, must and will triumph.

The Negroes' stake in national defense is big. It consists of jobs, thousands of jobs. It may represent millions, yes, hundreds of millions of dollars in wages. It consists of new industrial opportunities and hope. This is worth fighting for.

But to win our stakes, it will require an "all-out," bold and total effort and demonstration of colossal proportions.

Negroes can build a mammoth machine of mass action with a terrific and tremendous driving and striking power that can shatter and crush the evil fortress of race prejudice and hate, if they will only resolve to do so and never stop, until victory comes.

Dear fellow Negro Americans, be not dismayed in these terrible times. You possess power, great power. Our problem is to harness and hitch it up for action on the broadest, daring and most gigantic scale.

In this period of power politics, nothing counts but pressure, more pressure, and still more pressure, through the tactic and strategy of broad, organized, aggressive mass action behind the vital and important issues of the Negro. To this end, we propose that ten thousand Negroes MARCH ON WASHINGTON FOR JOBS IN NATIONAL DEFENSE AND EQUAL INTEGRATION IN THE FIGHTING FORCES OF THE UNITED STATES.

An "all-out" thundering march on Washington, ending in a monster and huge demonstration at Lincoln's Monument will shake up white America.

It will shake up official Washington.

It will give encouragement to our white friends to fight all the harder by our side, with us, for our righteous cause.

It will gain respect for the Negro people.

It will create a new sense of self-respect among Negroes.

But what of national unity?

We believe in national unity which recognizes equal opportunity of black and white citizens to jobs in national defense and the armed forces, and in all other institutions and endeavors in America. We condemn all dictatorships, Fascist, Nazi and Communist. We are loyal, patriotic Americans, all.

But, if American democracy will not defend its defenders; if American democracy will not protect its protectors; if American democracy will not give jobs to its toilers because of race or color; if American democracy will not insure equality of opportunity, freedom and justice to its citizens, black and white, it is a hollow mockery and belies the principles for which it is supposed to stand.

To the hard, difficult and trying problem of securing equal participation in national defense, we summon all Negro Americans to march on Washington. We summon Negro Americans to form committees in various cities to recruit and register marchers and raise funds through the sale of buttons and other legitimate means for the expenses of marchers to Washington by buses, train, private automobiles, trucks, and on foot.

We summon Negro Americans to stage marches on their City Halls and Councils in their respective cities and urge them to memorialize the President to issue an executive order to abolish discrimination in the Government and national defense.

However, we sternly counsel against violence and ill-considered and intemperate action and the abuse of power. Mass power, like physical power, when misdirected is more harmful than helpful.

We summon you to mass action that is orderly and lawful, but aggressive and militant, for justice, equality and freedom.

Crispus Attucks marched and died as a martyr for American independence. Nat Turner, Denmark Vesey, Gabriel Prosser, Harriet Tubman and Frederick Douglass fought, bled and died for the emancipation of Negro slaves and the preservation of American democracy.

Abraham Lincoln, in times of the grave emergency of the Civil War, issued the Proclamation of Emancipation for the freedom of Negro slaves and the preservation of American democracy.

Today, we call upon President Roosevelt, a great humanitarian and idealist, to follow in the footsteps of his noble and illustrious predecessor and take the second decisive step in this world and national emergency and free American Negro citizens of the stigma, humiliation and insult of discrimination and Jim-Crowism in Government departments and national defense.

The Federal Government cannot with clear conscience call upon private industry and labor unions to abolish discrimination based upon race and color as long as it practices discrimination itself against Negro Americans.

NEGROES' COMMITTEE TO MARCH ON WASHINGTON FOR EQUAL PARTICIPATION IN NATIONAL DEFENSE.

2289 7th Avenue, New York City
EDgecombe 4-4340

—WALTER WHITE
REV. WILLIAM LLOYD IMES
LESTER B. GRANGER
FRANK R. CROSSWAITH
LAYLE LANE
RICHARD PARRISH
DR. RAYFORD LOGAN
HENRY K. CRAFT
A. PHILIP RANDOLPH

The march of 100,000 Negroes on Washington for jobs in national defense which was scheduled for July 1st is off. The march is unnecessary at this time. This decision was reached by the National Committee for the mobilization of Negroes to march on Washington. The members of this Committee are Walter White, Rev. William Lloyd Imes, Lester B. Granger, Frank R. Crosswaith, Layle Lane, Richard Parrish, Dr. Rayford Logan, J. Finley Wilson, Rev. Adam C.

Powell, Jr., Noah A. Walters and E. E. Wilhams. These persons are not wild-eyed crackpots. They are not Communists. They have no sympathy with Communists, Communism, its program or policies. They are upright, plain, responsible Negro citizens, who love their country and the Negro race.

The reason for this decision is the issuance of an executive order by President Roosevelt banning discriminations in defense industries on account of race, creed, color or national origin, the attainment of which was the main and vital aim of the march-on-Washington movement. This is the first executive order which has been issued by a President of the United States in behalf of Negroes since the immortal Abraham Lincoln issued the Emancipation Proclamation in 1863.

Some of my listeners may be asking the question: "Why the proposed march of 100,000 Negroes on Washington?" The answer to this question is that Negroes were being turned down whenever they applied for jobs, regardless of qualifications, in defense industries all over the country. Conferences have been held with various representatives of the Government, but to no avail. Meanwhile, a wave of bitter resentment, disillusionment and desperation was sweeping over the Negro masses throughout the country. It was apparent that in order to avoid blind, reckless and undisciplined outbursts of emotional indignation against discriminations upon defense jobs, that some unusual, bold and gigantic effort must be made to awaken the American people and the President of the Nation to the realization that the Negroes were the victims of sharp and unbearable oppression, and that the fires of resentment were flaming higher and higher. In order that this threatening condition might be met with resolute, sober, sane and constructive action, a few Negro leaders came together at the call of the speaker and set up a national committee to mobilize 100,000 Negroes to march on Washington. The proposal met with prompt and instant response throughout the Nation. The favorable reaction of the Negro masses to this plan to march on Washington for jobs was due to a sense of frustration, futility and defeatism which had come over them as they watched their own communities assume the character of dead economic areas because of the lack of jobs and purchasing power, while in the white communities, the economic life of the people was throbbing, expanding and moving with promise and hope.

It was natural and inevitable that such a violent and disturbing contrast between the Negro and white communities was due to one thing, namely, that the white section of the population was enjoying participation and integration in national defense employment opportunities, whereas the Negro section of the population was being denied employment opportunities, and yet, both black and white peoples of America are equally taxed for the development and maintenance of our great defense program.

But when this grave situation was brought to the attention of the President, he definitely expressed his deep concern about it and his desire to see discriminations on account of race, color, creed and national origin abolished. He therefore issued a statement to the country and to the Office of Production Management, calling for the recognition of the right of workers to employment in national defense industries without regard to race, creed, color, or national origin. The Negro March-on-Washington Committee viewed this statement with admiration. We considered it commendable, but not enough. We therefore called upon the President to issue an executive order that had teeth in it which would give the Negro people some concrete assurance that they would no longer be given the runaround when they sought jobs in the great defense industries of the Nation.

In a statesmanlike and forthright manner, the President issued the following executive order:

REAFFIRMING POLICY OF FULL PARTICIPATION IN THE DEFENSE PROGRAM BY ALL PERSONS, REGARDLESS OF RACE, CREED, COLOR, OR NATIONAL ORIGIN, AND DIRECTING CERTAIN ACTION IN FURTHERANCE OF SAID POLICY.

Whereas it is the policy of the United States to encourage full participation in the national defense program by all citizens of the United States, regardless of race, creed, color, or national origin, in the firm belief that the democratic way of life within the Nation can be defended successfully only with the help and support of all groups within its borders: and

Whereas there is evidence that available and needed workers have been barred from employment in industries engaged in defense production solely because of considerations of race, creed, color, or national origin, to the detriment of workers' morale and of national unity:

Now, Therefore, by virtue of the authority vested in me by the Constitution and the statutes, and as a prerequisite to the successful conduct of our national defense production effort, I do hereby reaffirm the policy of the United States that there shall be no discrimination in the employment of workers in defense industries or government because of race, creed, color, or national origin, and I do hereby declare that it is the duty of employers and of labor organizations, in furtherance of said policy and of this order, to provide for the full and equitable participation of all workers in defense industries, without discrimination because of race, creed, color, or national origin:

And it is hereby ordered as follows:

1. All departments and agencies of the Government of the United States concerned with vocational and training programs for defense production shall take special measures appropriate to assure that such programs are administered without discrimination because of race, creed, color, or national origin;

2. All contracting agencies of the Government of the United States shall include in all defense contracts hereafter negotiated by them a provision obligating the contractor not to discriminate against any worker because of race, creed, color, or national origin;

3. There is established in the Office of Production Management a Committee on Fair Employment Practice, which shall consist of a chairman and four other members to be appointed by the President. The chairman and members of the Committee shall serve as such without compensation but shall be entitled to actual and necessary transportation, subsistence and other expenses incidental to performance of their duties. The Committee shall receive and investigate complaints of discrimination in violation of the provisions of this order and shall take appropriate steps to redress grievances which it finds to be valid. The Committee shall also recommend to the several departments and agencies of the Government of the United States and to the President all measures which may be deemed by it necessary or proper to effectuate the provisions of this order.

FRANKLIN D. ROOSEVELT

THE WHITE HOUSE,
June 25, 1941

I know that this order is certain to stir the hopes and aspirations of Negroes throughout the Nation, who only seek opportunities to work according to their qualifications. Tersely put, Negroes seek opportunity and not alms. It is the hope of the Negro March-on-Washington Committee that this executive order will represent thousands of jobs and hundreds of millions of dollars in increased wages in Negro communities, which will reflect themselves in higher standards of living, more education and recreation for the children, a greater security and assurance of more abundant life.

While the Negro March-on-Washington Committee wishes in this connection publicly to express its appreciation and gratitude to the President for his statesmanlike action in realistically facing this grave question of discrimination in defense jobs arising out of race, color, creed and national origin, and for his promulgation of this executive order, it cannot too strongly emphasize and stress the fact that this act of the President does not meet the vital and serious issue of discrimination against persons on a basis of race, color, creed and national origin in various departments of the federal government itself. It is the firm and reasoned judgment of the Negro March-on-Washington Committee that the inexcusable practice of discrimination against persons because of race, color, creed and national origin, by the government itself serves as a cue to and pattern for private employers to commit un-American and un-democratic offenses of discrimination also.

The President has declared in this executive order that it is the policy of the government not to countenance discrimination on account of race, color, creed or national origin in government service. Therefore the Negro March-on-Washington Committee wishes to express the hope that the President may find it possible, in the interest of National Unity and National Defense, at an early date, to issue a second executive order, complementing and supplementing this one, that will strike down for all times discrimination due to race, color, creed or national origin in all departments of the federal government, and which will give reality and force to our profession concerning democracy and to the great and all-out struggle our country is making to crush and destroy all subversive forces seeking to wreck our democratic way of life.

The Negro March-on-Washington Committee feels that it has done the Nation a great service in waging this fight for the abolition of discriminations in national defense industries based upon race, color, creed and national origin and the elimination of discriminations in departments of the federal government, since it will help to cleanse the soul of America of the poisons of hatreds, antagonisms and hostilities of race, religion, color and nationality and strengthen our country's foundation for national unity and national defense and give it the moral and spiritual force to achieve the preservation of our democratic faiths, traditions, ideals, values and heritages, the battle for which is being so nobly led by the President of the United States.

I, therefore, wish to announce and advise the Negro March-on-Washington Committees throughout the country that the march on Washington July 1st is unnecessary and will not take place.

I wish also to advise and urge that the Committees remain intact and watch and check the industries in their communities to determine the extent to which they are observing the executive order of the President.

Battle on the Home Front

What Caused the Detroit Riots?

WALTER WHITE

Walter White succeeded James Weldon Johnson as executive director of the NAACP in 1928, on the eve of the Great Depression. He served with distinction until his death in 1955. So light-skinned that he could easily pass for white, White was able to go places and do things connected with his work that would have been impossible for a darker man. Once, in fact, he was taken for a white man and was almost killed in a Harlem riot.

When the Detroit riot of June 1943 broke out, White had the governor of Michigan call out state troops to patrol the city and protect the black people from marauding whites. White and other members of the national office of the NAACP rushed to Detroit to set up relief programs for the blacks left homeless by the riot. Later, White wrote an analysis of the causes of the riot, which was printed with an attack on the Detroit police prepared by Thurgood Marshall.

White's report, reprinted in the following pages, reiterates the findings of almost every other investigation of a race riot undertaken in this century. The riot was triggered by a random act of violence and then fed by long pent-up hostility; the last traces of control disappeared as blacks and whites battled in the streets. Law-enforcement authorities, instead of trying to restore order, fought on the side of the whites. In the case of the Detroit riots, White defined the primary factors contributing to the buildup of hostility as job competition under the conditions of a war-boom economy and the systematic oppression of blacks in every area of social interaction. The fires of racial prejudice were fed by professional racists active in Detroit at the time.

In 1916 there were 8,000 Negroes in Detroit's population of 536,650. In 1925 the number of Negroes in Detroit had been multiplied by ten to a total of 85,000. In 1940, the total had jumped to 149,119. In June, 1943, between 190,000 and 200,000 lived in the Motor City.

According to the War Manpower Commission, approximately 500,000 in-migrants moved to Detroit between June, 1940, and June, 1943. Because of discrimination against employment of Negroes in industry, the overwhelming majority—between 40,000 and 50,000—of the approximately 50,000 Negroes who went to Detroit in this three-year period moved there during the fifteen months prior to the race riot of June, 1943. According to Governor

FROM Walter White, "What Caused the Detroit Riots?" Part I in *What Caused the Detroit Riots?* by Walter White and Thurgood Marshall (New York, 1943), pp. 5–16. Reprinted by permission of the National Association for the Advancement of Colored People or NAACP.

279

Harry S. Kelly, of Michigan, a total of 345,000 persons moved into Detroit during the same fifteen-month period. There was comparatively little out-migration as industry called for more and more workers in one of the tightest labor markets in the United States. The War Manpower Commission failed almost completely to enforce its edict that no in-migration be permitted into any industrial area until all available local labor was utilized. Thus a huge reservoir of Negro labor existed in Detroit, crowded into highly-congested slum areas. But they did have housing of a sort and this labor was already in Detroit. The coming of white workers recruited chiefly in the South not only gravely complicated the housing, transportation, educational and recreation facilities of Detroit, but they brought with them traditional prejudices of Mississippi, Arkansas, Louisiana, and other Deep South states against the Negro.

The sudden increase in Negro in-migration was due to labor scarcity which forced employers to hire Negroes, or be unable to fill government orders. The same circumstance—plus governmental and community pressures—created the necessity for modest upgrading of competent Negroes. One of the most important factors in bringing about such promotions was the unequivocal position taken by the top leadership of the United Automobile Workers–CIO.

According to the Research and Analysis Department of the UAW–CIO, the United States Employment Service, the Detroit Bureau of Governmental Research, and the Detroit branch of the National Association for the Advancement of Colored People, the overwhelming majority of the 250,000 to 300,000 white in-migrants to Detroit during the year immediately preceding the race riot came from the South. There was no surplus labor in nearby industrial centers like Chicago, Pittsburgh, Cleveland, Toledo, Akron, and Kansas City. Recruiting, therefore, was concentrated in the Deep South with the result that the already high percentage of Detroiters with South background was enormously increased. Here and there among these Southern whites were members of the UAW-CIO and other labor unions, churchmen and others who sloughed off whatever racial prejudices they had brought with them from the South. But the overwhelming majority retained and even increased their hostility to Negroes. This was particularly noticeable when Negroes were forced by sheer necessity to purchase or rent houses outside the so-called Negro area. For years preceding the riot, there had been mob attacks dating back as far as the famous Sweet case in 1925 upon the homes of Negroes. In some instances there had been police connivance in these attacks. In practically no cases had there been arrests of whites who had stoned or bombed the houses of Negroes. During July, 1941, there had been an epidemic of riots allegedly by Polish youths which had terrorized colored residents in Detroit, Hamtramck and other sections in and about Detroit. Homes of Negroes on Horton, Chippewa, West Grand Boulevard and other streets close to but outside of the so-called Negro areas were attacked by mobs with no police interference.

Detroit's 200,000 Negroes are today largely packed into two segregated areas. The larger of these is on the East Side bounded by Jefferson on the South, John R. on the West, East Grand Boulevard on the North, and Russell on the East. This area covers approximately 60 square blocks. A somewhat smaller Negro area is on the West Side bounded by Epworth Boulevard on the West, West Warren on the South, Grand River on the East along a line running Northwest to West Grand Boulevard and Tireman—an area of approximately 30 square blocks. In addition to these two wholly Negro areas, there are scattered locations throughout Detroit of mixed occupancy in which, significantly, there was during the riot less friction than in any other area.

The desperate scarcity of housing for whites, however, limited Negroes in finding places to live outside of the Negro areas. The Detroit newspapers have contained for months many advertisements offering rewards for housing of any nature or quality for whites. Meantime, but little public housing was created to meet the tragic need for housing of both whites and Negroes in Detroit. Even this was characterized by shameful vacillation and weakness in Washington which only added fuel to the flames of racial tension in Detroit. The notorious riots revolving about the question of who should occupy the Sojourner Truth Housing project in February, 1942, are an example of this. These riots resulted when fascist elements, emboldened by the vacillation of the National Housing Administration which reversed itself several times on Negro occupancy, joined with pressure of real estate interests to bring to a head the mob violence which led to the smashing of the furniture and beating of Negro tenants attempting to move into the project.

Previously, the Public Workers Administration had built the Brewster Project of 701 units in 1938 to which the United States Housing Authority had added the Brewster addition of 240 units completed in 1940 and 1941. All these provided housing for only about 3,000 Negroes, however.

From all other public housing projects erected in Detroit, Negroes were totally excluded, although Negroes and whites had lived together in complete amity in some of the areas on which these public housing projects, erected through the taxation of Negro as well as white Americans, were built.

Equally contributory to the explosion which was to come has been the attitude of the Detroit Real Estate Association. Mention has already been made of the opposition of the real estate interests to public housing in Detroit. Their contention was that such housing as Detroit needed should be created by private interests. But by the time private interests were ready to begin erections of homes and apartments for the greatly augmented population of wartime Detroit, priorities on building materials were put into effect. Meantime, every train, bus, or other public conveyance entering Detroit disgorged an ever increasing torrent of men, women, and children demanding places to live while they earned the war wages Detroit factories were paying. Overcrowding, lack of sanitation, a mounting disease rate resulting in absenteeism and a severe tax on the hospital and clinical facilities of Detroit were bad enough among whites. Among Negroes it resulted in a scandalous condition.

JOBS

Early in July, 1943, 25,000 employees of the Packard Plant, which was making Rolls-Royce engines for American bombers and marine engines for the famous PT boats, ceased work in protest against the upgrading of three Negroes. Subsequent investigation indicated that only a relatively small percentage of the Packard workers actually wanted to go on strike. The UAW-CIO bitterly fought the strike. But a handful of agitators charged by R. J. Thomas, president of the UAW-CIO, with being members of the Ku Klux Klan, had whipped up sentiment particularly among the Southern whites employed by Packard against the promotion of Negro workers. During the short-lived strike, a thick Southern voice outside the plant harangued a crowd shouting, "I'd rather see Hitler and Hirohito win than work beside a nigger on the assembly line." The strike was broken by the resolute attitude of the union and of Col. George E. Strong of the United States Aircraft Procurement Division, who refused to yield to the demand that the three Negroes be down-graded. Certain officials of the Packard Company were clearly responsible in part for the strike. C. E. Weiss, Personnel Manager, George Schwartz, General Foreman, and Robert Watts of the Personnel Division, urged the strikers to hold out in their demand that Negroes not be hired or upgraded. Weiss is alleged to have told the men that they did not have to work beside Negroes. At the time this report is written, Weiss, Schwartz, and Watts are still employed by the Packard Motor Car Company. The racial hatred created, released, and crystallized by the Packard strike played a considerable role in the race riot which was soon to follow. It also was the culmination of a long and bitter fight to prevent the employment of Negroes in wartime industry. There had been innumerable instances, unpublicized, in the Detroit area of work stoppages and slow downs by white workers, chiefly from the South, and of Polish and Italian extraction. Trivial reasons for these stoppages had been given by the workers when in reality they were in protest against employment or promotion of Negroes. A vast number of man hours and of production had been irretrievably lost through these stoppages. John S. Bugas in charge of the Detroit office of the FBI, states that his investigations prove that the Ku Klux Klan at no time has had more than 3,000 members in Detroit. Other investigations by officials and private agencies corroborate this fact. But the Klan did not need to be a large organization to cause serious disruption of war production in Detroit, because of the circumstance already mentioned—the increasing percentage of Southern whites who went to Detroit to work during 1942 and 1943.

The Willow Run Bomber plant is typical in this connection. This plant employed in July 45,000 workers. An analysis of its employes revealed that 30 percent came from outside the Detroit area, and 20.3 percent were last employed outside of Michigan. Between 40 percent and 50 percent of those employed in July, 1943, at Willow Run came originally from the Deep South. In July, practically all of the new hires were Southern. The labor turnover at Willow Run has been exceedingly high. So, too, has been the number of work stoppages whose real cause is opposition to employment of Negroes. Because of wartime censorship, it was impossible to ascertain the number of such episodes or the loss of production caused by it. But it is reasonable to assume that the experience at Willow Run has been characteristic of a large number of other Detroit plants. The activities of the Ku. Klux Klan under the name of the Forrest Club of which "Uncle Charlie" Spare seems to be the spokesman, has had its numbers and agents industriously organizing anti-Negro sentiment among those with racial prejudice against the Negro in several of the Detroit plants. "Strikes" against the employment or promotion of Negroes can be traced to these agitators in the Dodge Truck plant, the Hudson Arsenal, the Packard Plant, and other plants. The Klan has been active in Detroit as far back as the early 20's. Early in the 20's it almost succeeded in electing a Mayor of Detroit. It was shortly after this disaster was averted that a series of attacks upon the homes of Negroes took place, culminating in the Sweet case in 1925. Following this case tried before Judge Frank Murphy and in which the defendants were represented by the late Clarence Darrow, the Klan in Detroit dropped out of existence, along with its demise in other parts of the country. But agencies with similar methods and ideologies succeeded it. Though short-lived, a vicious successor was the notorious Black Legion which was characterized by Professor Elmer Akers, of the University of Michigan, in 1937 in his "A Social-Psychological Interpretation of the Black Legion" as a movement of "Vigilante nativism," which began as an offshot of the Ku Klux Klan.

Originally conceived to secure and insure jobs for white Southerners, the organization soon expanded its fields of activity to include putting down by violence, if necessary, all movements the Black Legion decided were "alien" or "un-American." After the conviction of its leader, Virgil F. Effinger, former Klansman, for the murder in 1936 of Charles A. Poole, a Detroit Catholic, the 4-year-old, crime-besmirched Black Legion virtually expired, but was followed quickly by others of similar purpose and method, among them The National Workers League (held chiefly responsible for the Sojourner Truth riot which saw the League's Parker Sage, Garland Alderman and Virgil Chandler indicted but never tried on charges of seditious conspiracy) which is reputedly financed in part by Nazi Bund and Silver Shirt money.

Gerald L. K. Smith, former assistant and protege of the late Huey Long, has been long active in stirring up discord and dissension in the Detroit area. His activities in America First, anti-union, and other similar groups have been greatly increased in effectiveness by his also being a Southerner trained in the art of demagogy by Huey Long, and provided with a fertile field due to the predominantly Southern white psychology of Detroit. Active also have been the followers of Father Coughlin, some Polish and Italian Catholic priests and laymen, and others who, wittingly or otherwise, have utilized anti-Negro sentiment for selfish and sometimes sinister objectives in much the same manner that the Nazis utilized anti-Semitism in Germany during the late 20's. Ingrained or stimulated prejudice against the Negro has been used as much against organized labor as it has been against the Negro. Employers and employers associations have been apathetic to the storm which was brewing.

Apparently they were interested only in the size and continuation of profits. It has been frequently charged and not displayed that some of the employers have financed or contributed heavily to some of the organizations which have organized and capitalized upon race prejudice as a means of checking the organization of workers in Detroit plants.

The Bureau of Labor Statistics of the U.S. Department of Labor lists the strikes in Detroit to prevent employment and upgrading of colored workers for the three month period March 1, 1943, through May 31, 1943. This record shows that 101,955 man-days or 2,226,920 man-hours of war production were lost by these stoppages. The record is as follows:

March 1, 1943 through May 31, 1943

Company	Beginning Date	Numbers of Workers Involved	Man-Days Idle	Issue
1. U.S. Rubber Company	March 19	1,064	3,955	Hiring colored workers and demand for separate sanitary facilities
2. Vickers, Inc.	March 25	40	60	Colored help placed in Production Department
3. Hudson Motor Car Co.	April 20	15	45	Hiring of colored plant guards
4. Hudson Naval Arsenal	May 17	750	750	Refusal to work with colored tool-maker
5. Packard Motor Car Co.	May 26	26,883	97,145	Upgrading of colored workers

DETROIT LABOR UNIONS AND THE NEGRO

One of the most extraordinary phenomena of the riot was the fact that while mobs attacked Negro victims outside some of the industrial plants of Detroit, there was not only no physical clash inside any plant in Detroit but not as far as could be learned even any verbal clash between white and Negro workers. This can be attributed to two factors: first, a firm stand against discrimination and segregation of Negro workers by the UAW-CIO, particularly since the Ford strike of 1941. The second factor is that when the military took over, the armed guards in the plants were ordered by the Army to maintain order at all costs and to prevent any outbreak within the plants. There is possibly a third factor, namely, that on Monday, June 21st, and to a lesser extent on succeeding days, Negroes were unable to get to the plants because of attacks upon them when they sought to return to work by roving mobs chiefly composed of boys between the ages of 17 and 25.

The Detroit riot brought into sharp focus one of the most extraordinary labor situations in the United States. Prior to the Ford strike of 1941 many Negroes in Detroit considered Ford their "great white father" because the Ford plant almost alone of Detroit industries employed Negroes. When the UAW-CIO and the UAW-AFL sought to organize Ford workers, their approach at the beginning was a surreptitious one. The unions felt that the very high percentage of Southern whites in Detroit would refuse to join the Union if Negroes were too obviously participating. But when the strike broke, far-sighted Negro leaders in Detroit took an unequivocal position in behalf of the organization of workers. A serious racial clash was averted by the intercession of thoughtful whites and Negroes. Following the winning of the NLRB election by the union, it began to take a broader and more unequivocal position that all workers and union members should share in the benefits of union agreements irrespective of race, creed, or color.

During the recent riot, R. J. Thomas, president of the UAW-CIO proposed an eight-point program which was widely published, and which helped to emphasize the basic causes of the riot. These points included: (1) creation of a special grand jury to investigate the cause of the riots and to return justifiable indictments, with a competent Negro attorney appointed as an assistant Prosecutor to work with the grand jury; (2) immediate construction and opening of adequate park and recreation facilities. Thomas called it "disgraceful that the City's normal, inadequate park space was permitted to be overtaxed further by the influx of hundreds of thousands of new war workers"; (3) immediate and practical plans for rehousing Negro slum dwellers in decent, Government-financed housing developments; (4) insistence that plant managements as well as workers recognize the right of Negroes to jobs in line with their skill and seniority; (5) a full investigation by the special grand jury of the conduct of the Police Department during the riots; (6) special care by the courts in dealing with many persons arrested. Those found guilty should be severely punished, and there must be no discrimination between white and Negro rioters; (7) the loss of homes and small businesses, as well as personal injuries, is the responsibility of the community, and the city should create a fund to make good these losses; (8) creation by the Mayor of a special bi-racial committee of ten persons to make further recommendations looking toward elimination of racial differences and frictions, this committee to have a special job in connection with high schools "where racial hatred has been permitted to grow and thrive in recent years."

VACILLATION ON FAIR EMPLOYMENT
PRACTICE COMMITTEE

A contributory factor to the breakdown of discrimination in employment in Detroit was the issuance on June 25, 1941, by President Roosevelt of Executive Order 8802 under which was established the President's Committee on Fair Employment Practice. Although limited in personnel, budget and authority, the FEPC as the affirmative expression of a moral principle had strengthened the efforts to eliminate discrimination in Detroit war plants. Members of the FEPC staff had carefully investigated charges of discrimination in Detroit areas. In a considerable number of cases negotiations with employers by FEPC representatives had resulted in the abolishing or lessening of discrimination. Employers, employes and labor unions knew that the Federal Government was opposed to denial of the right to work or to be upgraded on account of race, creed, color or national origin.

But in the summer of 1942, the FEPC was robbed of its independent status and placed under the control of the War Manpower Commission. The conviction in Detroit and other places began to grow that the FEPC was being quietly shelved and that the government no longer was insistent that discrimination in employment be abolished. This conviction grew as the FEPC became more and more inactive due to the failure to provide it with a budget for many months during the summer and fall of 1942 and during the period when it was stopped from functioning effectively.

Conviction crystallized into certainty when early in 1943, the Detroit railroad and Mexican hearings were indefinitely postponed. This certainty was fixed more definitely in the public mind by the long delay in selecting a new Chairman of the FEPC and defining its status and the nature of the sanctions with which it would be armed. As the FEPC lapsed into total inactivity fear of Federal action died among those who were guilty of discrimination. Anti-Negro organizations and individuals renewed and increased their agitation against the employment and upgrading of Negroes. Despair deepened in the Negro communities as they saw hordes of Southern whites imported into Detroit, provided with such housing as was available including tax-supported houses, apartments and dormitories, speedily upgraded to the better paid jobs while Negroes who had lived in Detroit for many years were still shut out.

Morale and morals of Negroes were affected adversely as they saw the one agency which had been created to do away with discrimination emasculated. Those Negroes who were employed found themselves with money they could not spend for decent houses or other improvements in their living standards. Some invested in War Bonds and insurance; others threw away their money in riotous living because they had been robbed of hope.

LAW ENFORCEMENT AGENCIES

Politically minded public officials have winked at the activities of agencies like the Klan, the Black Legion, the National Workers' League, the followers of Father Coughlin and other similar groups. During the 30's especially when there was keen competition for jobs because of the depression, Southern whites sought and secured jobs on the police force of Detroit and in the courts. There was a period of years when cold-blooded killings of Negroes by policemen were a constant source of bitterness among Negroes. Eventually, protest by such organizations as the Detroit branch of the NAACP and other

Negro and inter-racial groups led to a diminution and eventually a practical cessation of such killings. But a residue of distrust of the police remained. When the riot of June, 1943, broke forth, this suspicion of the police by Negroes was more than justified when 29 of the 35 killed were Negroes, 17 of them shot by police and a number of these shot in the back. The justification usually given by the police was "looting." There is no question that shameful and inexcusable looting of stores operated by whites in the East Side Negro area, particularly on Hastings and John R. Streets was perpetrated by Negroes. Part of this looting was for the sake of the loot. But part was due to bitter frenzy which had been too long bottled up in Negroes, and which was a form of vengeance both against the prejudice in Detroit from which Negroes had suffered, and against the looting of Negro homes and businesses ten days before in the Beaumont, Tex., riot of June 15–16, 1943.

Samuel Leiberman of the East Side Merchants Association reports that white policemen joined Negroes in the looting of stores on the East Side. In one instance a policeman carried two twenty-five-pound cans of lard from a store and locked it in the back of the police patrol car to be transported, apparently, to his home. There also is evidence that at least one of the 17 Negroes shot for "looting" was not looting, nor was there any evidence to substantiate such a charge.

The wilful inefficiency of the Detroit police in its handling of the riot is one of the most disgraceful episodes in American history. When the riot broke out on Sunday night, June 20, following a dispute between a white and Negro motorist on the Belle Isle Bridge, an efficient police force armed with night sticks and fire hoses could have broken up the rioting on Woodward Avenue and broken the back of the insurrection, had the police been determined to do so. Instead, the police did little or nothing, though there were a few individual instances of courage by policemen which are commendable.

More typical, however, was the following episode: An official of the Detroit educational system was riding Monday afternoon, June 21st, on a Woodward Avenue car. According to his statement, an inspector of police boarded the car with eight patrolmen. He announced that a mob was headed in that direction and that he and the patrolmen would take charge of and protect any Negroes on the car who wished such protection. Four of the eight Negroes accepted the offer. The other four chose to remain on the car. They crouched on the floor of the car and were concealed by the skirts of sympathetic white women. These four got to their destinations safely. But the four who had entrusted themselves to the police were either taken from the police by the mob and beaten unmercifully, or were turned over to the mob by the police.

After Federal troops had restored a semblance of order to Detroit, Police Commissioner John W. Witherspoon sought to shift the blame for the total failure of the Detroit Police Department to the Federal government for not sending troops sooner to police Detroit. Commissioner Witherspoon alleged that he had not been given information by the Federal authorities that a Presidential proclamation was necessary before Federal troops could be brought in. He sought also to prove that the police had been blameless. But this assertion was negated by photographs taken by the Detroit Free Press and other newspapers. Most revelatory of these is one taken on Woodward Avenue during the day of June 21st. An elderly Negro's arms are pinioned by two policemen while two mounted police sit astride their horses immediately behind. In the meantime, a white rioter strikes the helpless Negro full in the face with no indication on the part of any of the four policemen of any effort to protect the Negro.

The *Detroit Free Press* also took photographs of the same man in four separate acts of mob violence. As this report is written, this easily identified rioter is unarrested. Two other photographs show another white man engaged in two separate acts of violence against Negroes. In one of them he is about to strike a fleeing Negro with an iron bar. It is stated that this man was arrested but released almost immediately "for lack of evidence."

The faces of between 800 and 1,000 white rioters engaged in assaulting, killing, kicking or otherwise violating the law against the persons of Negroes, or engaged in wilful destruction of property such as the overturning and burning of the automobiles of Negroes are clearly identifiable. But as of the date of the writing of this report, few if any, of them have even been arrested.

The anti-Negro motivation of the Detroit police department is further illustrated by these facts and figures. It has already been pointed out that the Negro population of Detroit at the time of the riot was 200,000 or less, out of a total population of more than 2,000,000. The inevitable riot was the product of anti-Negro forces which had been allowed to operate without check or hindrance by the police over a period of many years. But 29 of the 35 persons who died during the riot were Negroes. An overwhelming majority of the more than 600 injured were Negroes. Of the 1832 persons arrested for rioting, more than 85 percent were Negroes. And this in the face of the indisputable fact that the aggressors over a period of years were not Negroes but whites.

Commissioner Witherspoon along with Attorney General Herbert J. Rushton, State Police Commissioner Oscar C. Olander, and Wayne County Prosecutor William E. Dowling were appointed by Governor Harry S. Kelly to investigate the riot. But a few days later, the investigating committee reported that there was no necessity of a Grand Jury investigation.

YOUTH OF WHITE RIOTERS

One of the most disturbing phenomena of the riot was the extreme youth of many of the rioters. The *Detroit Free Press* quoted Bugas, head of the Detroit Office of the FBI, as stating that 70 percent of the rioters were boys between the ages of sixteen and twenty-five. Other observers estimate a somewhat lower percentage; but most are agreed, and their opinions are borne out by newspaper photographs of the rioters, that not less than 50 percent of the rioters were boys and young men of this age and white women. What is perhaps a new and exceedingly dangerous factor in periods of emotional strain caused by war is indicated by the youth of the rioters. A few of them are not in the army because of deferments gained by industrial skills. But most of them fall into two categories. The first is made up of those who for physical, mental or moral reasons have been rejected by the armed services. A compensatory bravado seems to have been created in some of these young men who by the physical violence of mobbing sought to convince themselves and others that they were as physically able as those who had gone into the army. The most stable young men of their age having been syphoned off into the Army, Navy and other armed services, the restraining influence of the more normal had been removed from those left behind.

The second category seems to have been made up of those between fifteen and eighteen who are emotionally unstable because they know that should the war last longer they will go into the armed services. All soldiers know that when one goes into the war he may not return. Even if he does, whatever plans he may have made for the charting of his life will be interrupted and perhaps materially changed. The stabilizing influence of plans having been removed, it appears that there is an even greater willingness to indulge in physical violence when fear of punishment is removed, such as in a race riot. It is conceivable that other riots during the war and the immediate years thereafter may be distinctly affected by this wartime phenomenon.

THE PRESS

The Hearst-owned *Detroit Times* has for years featured crime, real or alleged, by Negroes and has been distinctly unfriendly in its attitude towards the Negro and his aspirations. But it was quick to characterize the riot of June 20–21 as "the worst disaster which has befallen Detroit since Pearl Harbor." The conservative *Detroit News* has been apathetic though not unfriendly. The *Detroit Free Press*, prior to its purchase by John B. Knight, followed the same pattern. But since its acquisition by Mr. Knight and under the editorship of Douglass Martin and Malcolm Bingay, it has followed an objective and enlightened attitude on the issue of race. It has featured news about Negro achievement such as the visit of the distinguished Negro agronomist, Dr. George Washington Carver, to Detroit at the invitation of Henry Ford, and the death of Dr. Carver. Its coverage of the riot was full, fair, and complete, both in its news, editorial and pictorial treatment. The attitude of the *Free Press* did much to restore sanity to the city.

Three widely-circulated Negro newspapers, the Michigan *Chronicle*, the Detroit *Tribune*, and the Detroit edition of the Pittsburgh *Courier*, have given full coverage during recent years to the favorable and unfavorable changes in the Negro's status in Detroit. This in large measure has contributed to a very well-informed opinion by Negroes.

THE MAYOR

During his term as president of the Detroit Council of Churches, Dr. Benjamin Bush and other Protestant ministers and laymen of both races had sought action by the City of Detroit to avert the inevitable race clash which threatened the city. The Council had repeatedly urged Mayor Edward J. Jeffries to appoint an interracial committee and to give that committee sufficient authority to tackle some of the problems of housing, police efficiency, employment, recreation and education which affected both Negroes and whites in Detroit, and the relations between the races. But Mayor Jeffries refused to act giving as his reason that such recognition of the existence of the problem might conceivably accentuate it. Six days after the riot, however, Mayor Jeffries appointed an interracial commission with William J. Norton of the Children's Fund as chairman. But Mr. Norton had served as chairman of a committee of the Detroit Urban League to investigate an interracial clash in the Northwestern High School in 1941. The report of that committee, most modest in its analysis of the problems involved and its recommendations, was neither acted upon nor even made public by the Mayor.

It would be a mistake to classify Mayor Jeffries as being anti-Negro.

His failure to meet the crisis or to take action on conditions which inevitably were leading to a crisis was due to weakness, lack of vision, and to political ambition. It was known that he aspired to be Governor of Michigan or United States Senator. With such ambition, he hesitated to offend any politically important group in the city of Detroit or the State of Michigan. In the meantime, the dry grass of race hatred mounted, waiting only until a spark set off a conflagration.

NATIONAL ASPECTS

The War Production Board on June 26 announced that more than one million man hours of production were lost forever during the riot. No figures are available of the man hours previously lost by work stoppages and slow down strikes to keep Negroes from being employed or upgraded. As the chief war production center of the country, the pattern of behaviour there has affected and will continue to affect other war production centers. Failure to correct conditions similar to those in Detroit, or failure by federal, state, and municipal governments to act against those who, deliberately or unwittingly, foment similar racial and industrial clashes cannot but jeopardize the winning of the war. General Dwight Eisenhower reported in the spring of 1943 that photographs of the Sojourner Truth Riot were used by Axis propagandists in North Africa to create prejudice against the United States. The same riot and the one of June, 1943, as well as stories of lynchings, attacks upon Negro soldiers, continued discrimination and segregation in the armed forces of the United States, the anti-Negro fulminations of men like Governor Talmadge of Georgia and Congressman Rankin of Mississippi are grist to the mill of the

Tokyo and Berlin radios which cite these outrages to the one billion brown, yellow, and black peoples of the Pacific and Africa, and to the millions of colored peoples of the Caribbean and South America as evidence of what will happen to these colored peoples if the United Nations win. Timorousness in attacking the problem and cowardice in surrender to the divisive forces of Detroit and other cities may conceivably cause the United States to lose the war or, most certainly, to prolong it unnecessarily at the sacrifice of the lives of American soldiers who would not otherwise die. One of the few bright spots of the Detroit riot has been the almost universal condemnation of the riot by Detroit members of the armed services. Typical of many of these is the following letter written by Corporal James E. Ferriero from the Station Hospital at Camp Crowder, Mo., to the Detroit Times, appearing in its issue of July 6, 1943:

> Why are these race riots going on there in Detroit and in other cities in this land—supposedly the land of freedom, equality and brotherhood?
>
> We who are doing the fighting, and will do the fighting to preserve this country from such acts of discrimination; we who recognize no discrimination in the trenches and fox-holes; we shed the same blood—one kind of blood—red. Things like race riots and strikes make us fighters think—WHAT ARE WE FIGHTING FOR?
>
> Americanism means everything to us, but it is swiftly turning to be an unfounded word. Regardless, we will continue to fight, to die for our loved ones. But we want to feel and know that we are fighting for the principles that gave birth to the United States of America.
>
> In this hospital ward, we eat, laugh, and sleep uncomplainingly together. Jim Stanley, Negro; Joe Wakamatau, Japanese; Eng Yu, Chinese; John Brennan, Irish; Paul Colosi, Italian; Don Holzheimer, German; Joe Wojiechowski, Polish; and Mike Cohen, Jewish.
>
> We were all injured in the line of duty. Yes—Hitler, Mussolini, Hirohito, all rub their fists in glee that their fifth column work of undermining our country is bearing fruit. Things like this prolong the war, and give the Axis time to strengthen their forces. They might possibly mean DEFEAT for us. Now more than ever we should pull together, and work side by side, unhampered by riots and strikes. We want to know that you are behind us 100 percent. We want to know you want us back regardless of creed, race or color.
>
> We want to know so that we can fight harder and, if need be, die willingly.

SUGGESTIONS FOR FURTHER READING

Surveys of African-American life during the Depression include Raymond Wolters, *Negroes and the Great Depression* (1970) and Harvard Sitkoff, *A New Deal for Blacks*★ (1978). Southern life during the Depression is described in a series of ethnographic studies, including Charles S. Johnson, *Shadow of the Plantation*★ (1934), Arthur F. Raper, *Preface to Peasantry* (1936), Hortense Powdermaker, *After Freedom: A Cultural Study in the Deep South* (1939), and Allison Davis and John Dollard, *Children of Bondage* (1940). See also Theodore Rosengarten, *All God's Dangers: A Life of Nate Shaw*★ (1974), and Dan T. Carter, *Scottsboro: A Tragedy of the American South*★ (1969).

Black radicalism is treated in Robin D. G. Kelley, *Hammer and Hoe: Alabama Communists during the Great Depression*★ (1990), Nell Irvin Painter, *The Narrative of Hosea Hudson: His Life as a Negro Communist in the South*★ (1979), Charles Martin, *The Angelo Herndon Case and Southern Justice*★ (1976), and Mark Naison, *Communists in Harlem during the Depression*★ (1983). On racial violence, see two works by Dominic J. Capeci, Jr.: *The Harlem Riot of 1943* (1977) and *Race Relations in Wartime Detroit: The Sojourner Truth Housing Controversy of 1942* (1984).

Urban life is dealt with in Cheryl Greenberg, *Or Does It Explode? Black Harlem in the Great Depression*★ (1991), A. H. Fauset, *Black Gods of the Metropolis*★ (1944), Arnold R. Hirsch, *Making the Second Ghetto: Race and Housing in Chicago, 1940–1960*★ (1983), and August Meier and Elliott M. Rudwick, *Black Detroit and the Rise of the UAW*★ (1979).

The March on Washington movement is treated in Herbert Garfinkel, *When Negroes March: The March on Washington Movement in the Organizational Politics of the FEPC*★ (1959). The black serviceman is dealt with in Jack D. Foner, *Blacks and the Military in American History: A New Perspective* (1974) and Richard M. Dalfiume, *Desegregation of the U. S. Armed Forces: Fighting on Two Fronts, 1939–1953* (1969).

Biographical material on Jackie Robinson can be found in Jules Tygiel, *Baseball's Great Experiment: Jackie Robinson and His Legacy*★ (1983), Tygiel (ed.), *The Jackie Robinson Reader: Perspective on an American Hero*★ (1997), and Arnold Rampersad, *Jackie Robinson*★ (1997). See also Bruce Adelson, *Brushing Back Jim Crow: The Integration of Minor-League Baseball in the American South* (1999).

★ Books marked by an asterisk are available in paperback.

10

✸

School Desegregation and the Cold War

INTRODUCTION

For a hundred years before the end of the Second World War, black people struggled with the courts of America over the question of the education of their children. In 1849, the courts of Massachusetts ruled that black children could be excluded from white schools if a black school was available. In reaction to this decision, the Massachusetts legislature passed an act desegregating the schools in 1855. Charles Sumner, a senator from Massachusetts who had been involved on the side of the blacks in the Massachusetts court case, tried unsuccessfully to get a provision for desegregated schooling included in the federal Civil Rights Act of 1875—the act declared unconstitutional by the Supreme Court in 1883. When the principle of "separate but equal" was set up in the case *Plessy v. Ferguson* in 1896, it was of course applied to education, as well as to transportation and public accommodations.

Unfortunately, there was no real attempt to make the separate schools equal. For example, in 1915, the South Carolina public school system spent an average of $23.76 per white child and only $2.91 per black child. By 1954, the entire South was spending only $115 per black pupil per year, compared with $165 per white child.

By 1945, the federal courts had eased the legal restrictions on black people in the area of voting rights and had ruled against the use of restrictive real-estate covenants to bar blacks from owning property. Yet education in the South remained as segregated as it had been in 1900. The NAACP finally decided to make a frontal attack on legally segregated school systems. Under the leadership of Thurgood Marshall, who later became the first black justice on the U. S. Supreme Court, a campaign against segregated schools was carefully planned.

Desegregation cases were initiated in South Carolina, Kansas, Virginia, and Delaware. The cases eventually reached the Supreme Court, grouped together under the designation *Brown v. Board of Education of Topeka, Kansas.* The Court, in a unanimous decision issued in May 1954, ruled that segregated schools were unconstitutional under the Fourteenth Amendment—that they were inherently unequal and deprived black children of equal protection of the laws. In its ruling, the Court gave the following explanation: "Segregation of white and colored children in public schools has a detrimental effect upon the colored children. The impact is greater when it has the sanction of the law; for the policy of separating the races is usually interpreted as denoting the inferiority of the Negro group."

Compliance with the decision began in the fall of 1954, when a few large cities—including Wilmington, Delaware; Washington, D.C.; and Baltimore, Maryland—and scattered towns in Missouri, Arkansas, and West Virginia—initiated school desegregation. By 1955, when the Supreme Court somewhat ambiguously ordered the states to proceed with desegregation with "all deliberate speed," many powerful forces opposing desegregation were being marshaled. Representative of the strength of this opposition was the Southern Manifesto of 1956, a document signed by nineteen U. S. senators and eighty-one members of the House of Representatives praising "those States which have declared the intention to resist forced integration by any lawful means."

As the threat of forced integration loomed large, many doctrines from the past were resurrected; notably the idea of nullification (now called interposition)—the idea that a state could interpose itself between its citizens and rulings of the federal government if it found the federal law inimical to the interests of its citizens. Needless to say, the only citizens with whom the states concerned themselves were the white citizens. A hundred years after the Civil War, the federal government found itself faced with another Great Rebellion—another deep division of opinion that would, before it was all over, again require the use of federal troops to protect the rights of black men.

In the fall of 1958, desegregation came to a virtual standstill as the South threatened to close its public schools rather than give in to the Court ruling. Public schools were actually shut down in Little Rock, Arkansas, and in certain counties in Virginia during the 1958–59 school year. By 1959, however, the South had relaxed its posture to some extent, and the number of black children in formerly white schools began to creep upward. In 1963, after nine years of school desegregation, 9.2 percent of the black children in public schools in the South attended classes with whites on a desegregated basis. Only Alabama, Mississippi, and South Carolina had completely segregated systems at the end of the 1962–63 school year. After 1963–64, only Mississippi held out, and it was soon to give way.

Apart from the legal barriers erected to prevent black children from entering white schools, several extralegal blocking procedures were developed.

Because most school desegregation plans required that black parents sue for their children's admission to white schools, the parents were vulnerable to various kinds of intimidation. They were fired from their jobs, their mortgages were foreclosed by banks, they were regularly evicted from rented quarters, and they were in many other ways physically and emotionally abused. What was remarkable was the persistence of parents and children in the face of such harassment.

In many places, the organizations that aided black parents and children came under attack as well. The Urban League, for example, was cut off from Community Chest fund drives. And the NAACP was viciously attacked on many levels: It was accused of being Communist dominated and was prosecuted under the various sedition laws of the Southern states; its members were barred from state jobs (a tactic particularly effective with school teachers); it was required to submit membership lists to state investigatory authorities.

A turning point in the school desegregation controversy came when it became apparent that the *Brown* ruling applied to segregated schools in the North as well as in the South. Although segregation in the North was not *de jure* (legally sanctioned), it was nevertheless *de facto* (actually in existence), and therefore it was subject to the Supreme Court ruling. Much of the Northern school segregation was the result of gerrymandered school districts based on segregated housing patterns. Although many plans for overcoming this situation have been proposed, school segregation in the North has in fact increased since 1954. For some, the struggle shifted away from school integration to the issue of community control of decentralized school systems.

Separate Schools Are Deliberately Unequal

Summary of Argument Presented to the Supreme Court of the United States, 1953 and the Supreme Court Decision

NAACP LEGAL DEFENSE AND EDUCATION FUND

In 1939, the cost of legal defense activities grew too large for the regular treasury of the NAACP to bear, and a special tax-exempt corporation was set up to raise money and carry on much of the legal work of the Association. This corporation, the NAACP Legal Defense and Education Fund, Inc., was responsible for the cases leading to the landmark Supreme Court decision of May 17, 1954, declaring racially segregated schools unconstitutional.

The argument in the Court was based on the Fourteenth Amendment to the Constitution, which provides that "no State shall make or enforce any law which shall abridge the privileges or immunities of citizens of the United States; nor shall any State deprive any person of life, liberty, or property, without due process of law; nor deny to any person within its jurisdiction the equal protection of the laws." The Fund maintained that in 1868, when the amendment was ratified, it was clearly understood by both its supporters and its opponents to preclude discrimination based on color or race.

What follows is a portion of the brief filed by the Fund with the Supreme Court late in 1953. A summary of the full brief, this section outlines the structure of the argument and indicates its basis in both legal precedent and the Fourteenth Amendment.

The brief is followed by the decision of the Supreme Court.

These cases consolidated for argument before this Court present in different factual contexts essentially the same ultimate legal questions.

The substantive question common to all is whether a state can, consistently with the Constitution, exclude children, solely on the ground that they are Negroes, from public schools which otherwise they would be qualified to attend. It is the thesis of this brief, submitted on behalf of the excluded children, that the answer to the question is in the negative: the Fourteenth Amendment prevents states from according differential treatment to American

FROM NAACP Legal Defense and Education Fund, Inc., *In the Supreme Court of the United States,* "Summary of Argument" (October term, 1953), pp. 15–20.

children on the basis of their color or race. Both the legal precedents and the judicial theories, discussed in Part I hereof, and the evidence concerning the intent of the framers of the Fourteenth Amendment and the understanding of the Congress and the ratifying states, developed in Part II hereof, support this proposition.

Denying this thesis, the school authorities, relying in part on language originating in this Court's opinion in *Plessy v. Ferguson,* 163 U.S. 537, urge that exclusion of Negroes, *qua* Negroes, from designated public schools is permissible when the excluded children are afforded admittance to other schools especially reserved for Negroes, *qua* Negroes, if such schools are equal.

The procedural question common to all the cases is the role to be played, and the time-table to be followed, by this Court and the lower courts in directing an end to the challenged exclusion, in the event that this Court determines, with respect to the substantive question, that exclusion of Negroes, *qua* Negroes, from public schools contravenes the Constitution.

The importance to our American democracy of the substantive question can hardly be overstated. The question is whether a nation founded on the proposition that "all men are created equal" is honoring its commitments to grant "due process of law" and "the equal protection of the laws" to all within its borders when it, or one of its constituent states, confers or denies benefits on the basis of color or race.

1. Distinctions drawn by state authorities on the basis of color or race violate the Fourteenth Amendment. *Shelley v. Kraemer,* 334 U.S. 1; *Buchanan v. Warley,* 245 U. S. 60. This has been held to be true even as to the conduct of public educational institutions. *Sweatt v. Painter,* 339 U. S. 629; *McLaurin v. Oklahoma State Regents,* 339 U. S. 637. Whatever other purposes the Fourteenth Amendment may have had, it is indisputable that its primary purpose was to complete the emancipation provided by the Thirteenth Amendment by ensuring to the Negro equality before the law. The *Slaughter House Cases,* 16 Wall. 36; *Strauder v. West Virginia,* 100 U. S. 303.

2. Even if the Fourteenth Amendment did not *per se* invalidate racial distinctions as a matter of law, the racial segregation challenged in the instant cases would run afoul of the conventional test established for application of the equal protection clause because the racial classifications here have no reasonable relation to any valid legislative purpose. See *Quaker City Cab Co. v. Pennsylvania,* 277 U. S. 389; *Truax v. Raich,* 239 U. S. 33; *Smith v. Cahoon,* 283 U. S. 553; *Mayflower Farms v. Ten Eyck,* 297 U. S. 266; *Skinner v. Oklahoma,* 316 U. S. 535. See also *Tunstall v. Brotherhood of Locomotive Firemen,* 323 U. S. 210; *Steele v. Louisville & Nashville R. R. Co.,* 323 U. S. 192.

3. Appraisal of the facts requires rejection of the contention of the school authorities. The educational detriment involved in racially constricting a student's associations has already been recognized by this Court. *Sweatt v. Painter,* 339 U. S. 629; *McIaurin v. Oklahoma State Regents,* 339 U. S. 637.

4. The argument that the requirements of the Fourteenth Amendment are met by providing alternative schools rests, finally, on reiteration of the separate but equal doctrine enunciated in *Plessy v. Ferguson.*

Were these ordinary cases, it might be enough to say that the *Plessy* case can be distinguished—that it involved only segregation in transportation. But these are not ordinary cases, and in deference to their importance it seems more fitting to meet the *Plessy* doctrine head-on and to declare that doctrine erroneous.

Candor requires recognition that the plain purpose and effect of segregated education is to perpetuate an inferior status for Negroes which is America's sorry heritage from slavery. But the primary purpose of the Fourteenth Amendment was to deprive the states of *all* power to perpetuate such a caste system.

5. The first and second of the five questions propounded by this Court requested enlightenment as to whether the Congress which submitted, and the state legislatures and conventions which ratified, the Fourteenth Amendment contemplated or understood that it would prohibit segregation in public schools, either of its own force or through subsequent legislative or judicial action. The evidence, both in Congress and in the legislatures of the ratifying states, reflects the substantial intent of the Amendment's proponents and the substantial understanding of its opponents that the Fourteenth Amendment would, of its own force, proscribe all forms of state-imposed racial distinctions, thus necessarily including all racial segregation in public education.

The Fourteenth Amendment was actually the culmination of the determined efforts of the Radical Republican majority in Congress to incorporate into our fundamental law the well-defined equalitarian principle of complete equality for all without regard to race or color. The debates in the 39th Congress and succeeding Congresses clearly reveal the intention that the Fourteenth Amendment would work a revolutionary change in our state-federal relationship by denying to the states the power to distinguish on the basis of race.

The Civil Rights Bill of 1866, as originally proposed, possessed scope sufficiently broad in the opinion of many Congressmen to entirely destroy all state legislation based on race. A great majority of the Republican Radicals—who later formulated the Fourteenth Amendment—understood and intended that the Bill would prohibit segregated schools. Opponents of the measure shared this understanding. The scope of this legislation was narrowed because it was known that the Fourteenth Amendment was in process of preparation and would itself have scope exceeding that of the original draft of the Civil Rights Bill.

6. The evidence makes clear that it was the intent of the proponents of the Fourteenth Amendment, and the substantial understanding of its opponents, that it would, of its own force, prohibit all state action predicated upon race or color. The intention of the framers with respect to any specific example of caste state action—in the instant cases, segregated education—cannot be determined solely on the basis of a tabulation of contemporaneous statements mentioning the specific practice. The framers were formulating a constitutional provision setting broad standards for determination of the relationship

of the state to the individual. In the nature of things they could not list all the specific categories of existing and prospective state activity which were to come within the constitutional prohibitions. The broad general purpose of the Amendment—obliteration of race and color distinctions—is clearly established by the evidence: So far as there was consideration of the Amendment's impact upon the undeveloped educational systems then existing, both proponents and opponents of the Amendment understood that it would proscribe all racial segregation in public education.

7. While the Amendment conferred upon Congress the power to enforce its prohibitions, members of the 39th Congress and those of subsequent Congresses made it clear that the framers understood and intended that the Fourteenth Amendment was self-executing and particularly pointed out that the federal judiciary had authority to enforce its prohibitions without Congressional implementation.

8. The evidence as to the understanding of the states is equally convincing. Each of the eleven states that had seceded from the Union ratified the Amendment, and concurrently eliminated racial distinctions from its laws, and adopted a constitution free of requirement or specific authorization of segregated schools. Many rejected proposals for segregated schools, and none enacted a school segregation law until after readmission. The significance of these facts is manifest from the consideration that ten of these states, which were required, as a condition of readmission, to ratify the Amendment and to modify their constitutions and laws in conformity therewith, considered that the Amendment required them to remove all racial distinctions from their existing and prospective laws, including those pertaining to public education.

Twenty-two of the twenty-six Union states also ratified the Amendment. Although unfettered by Congressional surveillance, the overwhelming majority of the Union states acted with an understanding that it prohibited racially segregated schools and necessitated conformity of their school laws to secure consistency with that understanding.

9. In short, the historical evidence fully sustains this Court's conclusion in the *Slaughter House Cases*, 16 Wall. 36, 81, that the Fourteenth Amendment was designed to take from the states all power to enforce caste or class distinctions.

10. The Court in its fourth and fifth questions assumes that segregation is declared unconstitutional and inquires as to whether relief should be granted immediately or gradually. Appellants, recognizing the possibility of delay of a purely administrative character, do not ask for the impossible. No cogent reasons justifying further exercise of equitable discretion, however, have as yet been produced.

It has been indirectly suggested in the briefs and oral argument of appellees that some such reasons exist. Two plans were suggested by the United States in its Brief as *Amicus Curiae*. We have analyzed each of these plans as well as appellees' briefs and oral argument and find nothing there of sufficient merit on which this Court, in the exercise of its equity power, could predicate a decree permitting an effective gradual adjustment from segregated to non-segregated school systems. Nor have we been able to find any other reasons or plans sufficient to warrant the exercise of such equitable discretion in these cases. Therefore, in the present posture of these cases, appellants are unable to suggest any compelling reasons for this Court to postpone relief.

Mr. Chief Justice Warren delivered the opinion of the Court.

These cases come to us from the States of Kansas, South Carolina, Virginia, and Delaware. They are premised on different facts and different local conditions, but a common legal question justifies their consideration together in this consolidated opinion.

In each of the cases, minors of the Negro race, through their legal representatives, seek the aid of the courts in obtaining admission to the public schools of their community on a nonsegregated basis. In each instance. they have been denied admission to schools attended by white children under laws requiring or permitting segregation according to race. This segregation was alleged to deprive the plaintiffs of the equal protection of the laws under the Fourteenth Amendment. In each of the cases other than the Delaware case, a three judge federal district court denied relief to the plaintiffs on the so-called "separate but equal" doctrine announced by this Court in *Plessy v.. Ferguson,* 163 U.S. 537. Under the doctrine, equality of treatment is accorded when the races are provided substantially equal facilities, even though these facilities be separate. In the Delaware case, the Supreme Court of Delaware adhered to that doctrine, but ordered that the plaintiffs be admitted to the white schools because of their superiority to the Negro schools.

The plaintiffs contend that segregated public schools are not "equal" and cannot be made "equal," and that hence they are deprived of the equal protection of the laws. Because of the obvious importance of the question presented, the Court took jurisdiction. Argument was heard in the 1952 Term, and reargument was heard this Term on certain questions propounded by the Court.

Reargument was largely devoted to the circumstances surrounding the adoption of the Fourteenth Amendment in 1868. It covered exhaustively consideration of the Amendment in Congress, ratification by the states, then existing practices in racial segregation, and the views of proponents and opponents of the Amendment. This discussion and our own investigation convince us that, although these sources cast some light, it is not enough to resolve the problem with which we are faced. At best, they are inconclusive. The most avid proponents of the post-War amendments undoubtedly intended them to remove all legal distinctions among "all persons born or naturalized in the United States." Their opponents, just as certainly, were antagonistic to both the letter and the spirit of the Amendments and wished them to have the most limited effect. What others in Congress and the state legislatures had in mind cannot be determined with any degree of certainty.

An additional reason for the inconclusive nature of the Amendment's history, with respect to segregated schools, is the status of public education at that time. In the South, the movement toward free common schools, supported by general taxation, had not yet taken hold. Education of white children was largely in the hands of private groups. Education of Negroes was almost non-existent, and practically all of the race were illiterate. In fact, any education of Negroes was forbidden by law in some states. Today, in contrast, many Negroes have achieved outstanding success in the arts and sciences as well as in the business and professional world. It is true that public school education at the time of the Amendment had advanced further in the North, but the effect of the Amendment on Northern States was generally ignored in the congressional debates. Even in the North, the conditions of public education did not approximate those existing today. The curriculum was usually rudimentary; ungraded schools were common in rural areas; the school term was but three months a year in many states; and compulsory school attendance was virtually unknown. As a consequence, it is not surprising that there should be so little in the history of the Fourteenth Amendment relating to its intended effect on public education.

In the first cases in this Court construing the Fourteenth Amendment, decided shortly after its adoption, the Court interpreted it as prescribing all state-imposed discriminations against the Negro race. The doctrine of "separate but equal" did not make its appearance in this Court until 1896 in the case of *Plessy v. Ferguson, supra,* involving not education but transportation. American courts have since labored with the doctrine for over half a century. In this Court. there have been six cases involving the "separate but equal" doctrine in the field of public education. In *Cumming v. County Board of Education,* 175 U.S. 528, and *Gong Lum v. Rice,* 275 U.S. 78, the validity of the doctrine itself was not challenged. In more recent cases, all on the graduate school level, inequality was found in that specific benefits enjoyed by white students were denied to Negro students of the same educational qualifications. *Missouri ex rel. Gaines v. Canada,* 305 U.S. 337; *Sipuel v. Oklahoma,* 332 U.S. 631; *Sweatt v. Painter,* 339 U.S. 629; *McLaurin v. Oklahoma State Regents,* 339 U.S. 63 7. In none of these cases was it necessary to re-examine the doctrine to grant relief to the Negro plaintiff. And in *Sweatt v. Painter, supra,* the Court expressly reserved decision on the question whether *Plessy v. Ferguson* should be held inapplicable to public education.

In the instant cases, that question is directly presented. Here, unlike *Sweatt v. Painter,* there are findings below that the Negro and white schools involved have been equalized, or are being equalized, with respect to buildings, curricula, qualifications and salaries of teachers, and other "tangible" factors. Our decision. therefore, cannot turn on merely a comparison of these tangible factors in the Negro and white schools involved in each of the cases. We must look instead to the effect of segregation itself on public education.

In approaching this problem, we cannot turn the clock back to 1868 when the Amendment was adopted, or even to 1896 when *Plessy v. Ferguson* was written. We must consider public education in the light of its full development and its present place in American life throughout the nation. Only in this way can it be determined if segregation in public schools deprives these plaintiffs of the equal protection of the laws.

Today, education is perhaps the most important function of state and local governments. Compulsory school attendance laws and the great expenditures for education both demonstrate our recognition of the importance of education to our democratic society. It is required in the performance of our most basic public responsibilities, even service in the armed forces. It is the very foundation of good citizenship. Today it is a principal instrument in awakening the child to cultural values, in preparing him for later professional training, and in helping him to adjust normally to his environment. In these days, it is doubtful that any child may reasonably, be expected to succeed in life if he is denied the opportunity of an education. Such an opportunity, where the state has undertaken to provide it, is a right which must be made available to all on equal terms.

We come then to the question presented: Does segregation of children in public schools solely on the basis of race, even though the physical facilities and other "tangible" factors may be equal, deprive the children of the minority group of equal educational opportunities? We believe that it does.

In *Sweatt v. Painter, supra*, in finding that a segregated law school for Negroes could not provide them equal educational opportunities, this Court relied in large part on "those qualities which are incapable of objective measurement but which make for greatness in a law school." In *McLaurin v. Oklahoma State Regents, supra*, the Court, in requiring that a Negro admitted to a white graduate school be treated like all other students, again resorted to intangible considerations: "… his ability to study, to engage in discussions and exchange views with other students, and, in general, to learn his profession." Such considerations apply with added force to children in grade and high schools. To separate them from others of similar age and qualifications solely because of their race generates a feeling of inferiority as to their status in the community that may affect their hearts and minds in a way unlikely ever to be undone. The effect of this separation on their educational opportunities was well stated by a finding in the Kansas case by a court which nevertheless felt compelled to rule against the Negro plaintiffs:

> Segregation of white and colored children in public schools has a detrimental effect upon the colored children. The impact is greater when it has the sanction of the law; for the policy of separating the races is usually interpreted as denoting the inferiority of the negro group. A sense of inferiority affects the motivation of the child to learn. Segregation with the sanction of law, therefore, has a tendency to [retard] the educational and mental development of negro children and to deprive them of some of the benefits they would receive in a racially integrated school system.

Whatever may have been the extent of psychological knowledge at the time of *Plessy v. Ferguson*, this finding is amply supported by modern authority.[1] Any language in *Plessy v. Ferguson* contrary to this finding is rejected.

We conclude that in the field of public education the doctrine of "separate but equal" has no place. Separate educational facilities are inherently' unequal. Therefore, we hold that the plaintiffs and others similarly situated for whom the actions have been brought are, by reason of the segregation complained of, deprived of the equal protection of the laws guaranteed by the Fourteenth Amendment. This disposition makes unnecessary any discussion whether such segregation also violates the Due Process Clause of the Fourteenth Amendment.

Because these are class actions, because of the wide applicability of this decision, and because of the great variety of local conditions, the formulation of decrees in these cases presents problems of considerable complexity. On reargument, the consideration of appropriate relief was necessarily subordinated to the primary question—the constitutionality of segregation in public education. We have now announced that such segregation is a denial of the equal protection of the laws. In order that we may have the full assistance of the parties in formulating decrees, the cases will be restored to the docket, and the parties are requested to present further argument on Questions 4 and 5 previously propounded by the Court for the reargument this Term. The Attorney General of the United States is again invited to participate. The Attorney General of the states requiring or permitting segregation in public education will also be permitted to appear as amici curiae upon request to do so by September 15, 1954, and submission of briefs by October 1, 1954.

It is so ordered.

---

[1] K.B. Clark, *Effect of Prejudice and Discrimination on Personality Development* (Midcentury White House Conference on Children and South, 1950); Witmer and Kotinsky, *Personality in the Making* (1952). Ch. VI; Deutseher and Chein, *The Psychological Effects of Enforced Segregation: A Surrey of Social Science Opinion, Journal of Psychology*, Vol. 26, p. 259 (1945): Chein, *What Are the Psychological Effects of Segregation Under Conditions of Equal Facilities?, 3 Int. J. Opinion and Attitude Res* 229 (1949); Brameld, *Educational Costs, in Discrimination and National Welfare* (Maclver, ed, 1949), 44–48; Frazier, *The Negro in the United States* (1949), 674–681. And see generally Myrdal, *An American Dilemma* (1944).

Little Rock Prepares for Desegregation

Governor Faubus Rouses the Mob

DAISY BATES

It first appeared that Little Rock, Arkansas, would deal with the Supreme Court decision on school desegregation as did many moderate cities outside the Deep South. Nine black students had been selected to attend the formerly all-white Central High School in the fall of 1957. Then Governor Faubus of Arkansas, previously considered a racial moderate, called out the state-controlled National Guard to prevent the black students from entering Central High, thus precipitating a clash between the federal and state powers that reached dimensions unknown since 1877. Faubus' use of armed force to prevent the carrying out of a federal court order obliged President Eisenhower to employ federal troops to force the desegregation of the Little Rock school. The black students attended the school under guard for the 1957–58 school year, but the Governor closed all the Little Rock high schools the next year rather than permit them to open on a desegregated basis.

The story of the desegregation of the Little Rock school is compellingly told in the book from which the following selection is taken. The author, Daisy Bates, was a former newspaper editor and the president of the Arkansas State NAACP. Here, she tells of the reaction of the blacks to the calling out of the National Guard and the effect of this action on the people of Little Rock the day the schools opened.

It was Labor Day, September 2, 1957. The nine pupils who had been selected by the school authorities to enter Central High School—Carlotta Walls, Jefferson Thomas, Elizabeth Eckford, Thelma Mothershed, Melba Pattillo, Ernest Green, Terrance Roberts, Gloria Ray, and Minnijean Brown—were enjoying the last day of their summer vacation. Some of them were picnicking, others swimming, playing tennis, or just visiting with friends and relatives. About midafternoon young Jefferson Thomas was on his way home from the pool and stopped at my house for a brief visit. While Jeff was raiding the refrigerator, a news flash came over the radio that the Governor would address the citizens of Arkansas that night.

FROM Daisy Bates, *The Long Shadow of Little Rock*, pp. 59–68. Reprinted with permission from *The Long Shadow of Little Rock*, by Daisy Bates, ©1962. Published by David McKay Company, Inc.

"I wonder what he's going to talk about," said Jeff. The youngster then turned to me and asked, "Is there anything they can do—now that they lost in court? Is there any way they can stop us from entering Central tomorrow morning?"

"I don't think so," I said.

About seven o'clock that night a local newspaper reporter rang my doorbell. "Mrs. Bates, do you know that national guardsmen are surrounding Central High?"

L. C. and I stared at him incredulously for a moment. A friend who was visiting us volunteered to guard the house while we drove out to Central. L. C. gave him the shotgun. We jumped into our car and drove to Central High. We parked a half block from the school. Under the street lights stretched a long line of brown Army trucks with canvas tops. Men in full battle dress—helmets, boots, and bayonets—were piling out of the trucks and lining up in front of the school.

As we watched, L. C. switched on the car radio. A newscaster was saying, "National guardsmen are surrounding Central High School. No one is certain what this means. Governor Faubus will speak later this evening."

Ahead of us we could see reporters rushing up trying to talk to the soldiers. However, it soon became clear that the guardsmen were under orders to say nothing. They remained silent.

The whole scene was incredible. "Let's go back home and hear Faubus!" I suggested.

The phone was ringing as we pulled into our driveway. An excited friend wanted to know what it all meant, what was going to happen. All I could offer was, "Listen to Faubus." As soon as I put down the receiver, the phone rang again. This time it was the father of one of the children. "What's going on, Daisy? What's going to happen?" All I could do was to give him the same answer.

On television, Governor Faubus creates almost the same impression he does in person. He customarily wears a dark suit, white shirt, and dark tie. He is a big man physically, and affects a big man's easy congeniality. He specializes in the folksy manner, fixing his unseen audience with an "I'm-right-here-with-you-good-folks" glance.

I don't recall all the details of what Governor Faubus said that night. But his words electrified Little Rock. By morning they shocked the United States. By noon the next day his message horrified the world.

Faubus' alleged reason for calling out the troops was that he had received information that caravans of automobiles filled with white supremacists were heading toward Little Rock from all over the state. He therefore declared Central High School off limits to Negroes. For some inexplicable reason he added that Horace Mann, a Negro high school, would be off limits to whites.

Then, from the chair of the highest office of the State of Arkansas, Governor Orval Eugene Faubus delivered the infamous words, "blood will run in the streets" if Negro pupils should attempt to enter Central High School.

In a half dozen ill-chosen words, Faubus made his contribution to the mass hysteria that was to grip the city of Little Rock for several months.

The citizens of Little Rock gathered on September 3 to gaze upon the incredible spectacle of an empty school building surrounded by 250 National Guard troops. At about eight fifteen in the morning, Central students started passing through the line of national guardsmen—all but the nine Negro students.

I had been in touch with their parents throughout the day. They were confused, and they were frightened. As parents voiced their fears, they kept repeating Governor Faubus' words that "blood would run in the streets of Little Rock" should their teen-age children try to attend Central—the school to which they had been assigned by the school board.

Typical of the parents was Mrs. Birdie Eckford. "Mrs. Bates," she asked, "what do you think we should do? I am frightened. Not for myself but for the children. When I was a little girl, my mother and I saw a lynch mob dragging the body of a Negro man through the streets of Little Rock. We were told to get off the streets. We ran. And by cutting through side streets and alleys, we managed to make it to the home of a friend. But we were close enough to hear the screams of the mob, close enough to smell the sickening odor of burning flesh. And, Mrs. Bates, they took the pews from Bethel Church to make the fire. They burned the body of this Negro man right at the edge of the Negro business section.

"Mrs. Bates, do you think this will happen again?"

I reminded Mrs. Eckford that Little Rock was a different city now. Different from 1927, when the lynching and the burning had taken place. True, Governor Faubus spoke of blood. But in the next breath he had said that he called out the guardsmen to protect life and property against violence. Surely he meant the lives of the Negro students as well as white! No, it was inconceivable that troops, and responsible citizens, would stand by and let a mob attack children.

The NAACP attorneys, Wiley Branton and Thurgood .Marshall, appealed to Federal Judge Ronald N. Davies for instruction. Their question was, in effect: What do we do now? The judge stated that "he was accepting the Governor's statement at face value—that his purpose in calling out the Guard was to protect 'life and property' against possible mob violence." Therefore, Judge Davies directed the school board again to put its plan for integration into operation immediately.

On the afternoon of the same day, September 3, when the school was scheduled to open, Superintendent Blossom called a meeting of leading Negro citizens and the parents of the nine children. I was not notified of the meeting, but the parents called me and asked me to be present. At the meeting Superintendent Blossom instructed the parents *not* to accompany their children the next morning when they were scheduled to enter Central. "If violence breaks out," the Superintendent told them, "it will be easier to protect the children if the adults aren't there."

During the conference Superintendent Blossom had given us little assurance that the children would be adequately protected. As we left the building, I was aware of how deeply worried the parents were, although they did not voice their fears.

About ten o'clock that night I was alone in the downstairs recreation room, my mind still occupied by the problems raised during the conference. L. C. appeared in the doorway. With him was a local reporter whom I had known for some time.

Words began pouring from the young reporter. "Look, Daisy," he said anxiously. "I know about the Superintendent's instructions. I know he said the children must go alone to Central in the morning. But let me tell you, this is murder! I heard those people today. I've never seen anything like it. People I've known all my life—they've gone mad. They're totally without reason. You must know you can't expect much protection—if any—from the city police. Besides, the city police are barred from the school grounds!"

My friend's voice took on a pleading quality, as if there were something I could do. "I swear there must have been about five hundred people at the school today," he continued. "And new recruits are pouring into the city from outlying areas. Even from other states. By morning there could be several thousand."

"What do you think we should do?" I asked him.

"I really don't know," he answered. "I really don't know."

The young reporter left. I sat huddled in my chair, dazed, trying to think, yet not knowing what to do. I don't recall how much time went by—a few minutes, an hour, or more—before some neighbors entered. One of them was the Reverend J. C. Crenchaw, President of the Little Rock branch of the NAACP.

His presence in my house immediately gave me an idea.

"Maybe," I said, "maybe we could round up a few ministers to go with the children tomorrow. Maybe then the mob wouldn't attack them. Maybe with the ministers by their side —"

Mr. Crenchaw caught on to the idea right away. "We can try, Daisy. At least we can try. Maybe this is the answer."

I called a white minister, Rev. Dunbar Ogden, Jr., President of the Interracial Ministerial Alliance. I did not know Mr. Ogden. I explained the situation, then asked if he thought he could get some ministers to go with the children to school the next morning.

"Well, Mrs. Bates, I don't know," he said. "I'll call some of the ministers and see what they think about it. You know, this is a new idea to me."

I said the idea was new to me, too; and that it had just occurred to me moments before. Tensely I waited for his return call. When it came, he sounded apologetic. The white ministers he had talked to had questioned whether it was the thing to do. Some of the Negro ministers had pointed out that the Superintendent of Schools had asked that no Negro adults go with the children, and that in view of this they felt they shouldn't go. Then he added gently, "I'll keep trying—and, God willing, I'll be there."

Next I called the city police. I explained to the officer in charge that we were concerned about the safety of the children and that we were trying to get ministers to accompany them to school the next morning. I said that the children would assemble at eight thirty at Twelfth Street and Park Avenue. I asked whether a police car could be stationed there to protect the children until the ministers arrived.

The police officer promised to have a squad car there at eight o'clock. "But you realize," he warned, "that our men cannot go any closer than that to the school. The school is off limits to the city police while it's 'occupied' by the Arkansas National Guardsmen."

By now it was two thirty in the morning. Still, the parents had to be called about the change in plan. At three o'clock I completed my last call, explaining to the parents where the children were to assemble and the plan about the ministers. Suddenly I remembered Elizabeth Eckford. Her family had no telephone. Should I go to the Union Station and search for her father? Someone had once told me that he had a night job there. Tired in mind and body, I decided to handle the matter early in the morning. I stumbled into bed.

A few hours later, at about eight fifteen in the morning, L. C. and I started driving to Twelfth Street and Park Avenue. On the way I checked out in my mind the possibilities that awaited us. The ministers might be there—or again they might not. Mr. Ogden, failing to find anyone to accompany him, understandably might not arrive. Would the police be there? How many? And what if—

The bulletin over the car radio interrupted. The voice announced: "A Negro girl is being mobbed at Central High. ..."

"Oh, my God!" I cried. "It must be Elizabeth! I forgot to notify her where to meet us!"

L. C. jumped out of the car and rushed to find her. I drove on to Twelfth Street. There were the minister—two white—Mr. Ogden and Rev. Will Campbell, of the National Council of Churches, Nashville, Tennessee—and two colored—the Reverend Z. Z. Driver, of the African Methodist Episcopal Church, and the Reverend Harry Bass, of the Methodist Church. With them also was Mr. Ogden's twenty-one-year-old son, David. The children were already there. And, yes, the police had come as promised. All of the children were there—all except Elizabeth.

Soon L. C. rushed up with the news that Elizabeth finally was free of the mob. He had seen her on a bus as it pulled away.

The children set out, two ministers in front of them, two behind. They proceeded in that formation until they approached the beginning of the long line of guardsmen. At this point they had their first brush with the mob. They were jostled and shoved. As they made their way toward the school grounds, the ministers and their charges attempted to pass the guardsmen surrounding Central High. A National Guard captain stopped them. He told Mr. Ogden he could not allow them to pass through the guard line. When Mr. Ogden asked why, the captain said it was by order of Governor Faubus.

The ministers returned to the car with the students and Mr. Ogden reported what the captain of the guardsmen had said. I told him that in view of the school board's statement the previous evening that Central High School would be open to Negro students in the morning, it was my feeling that the students should go immediately to the office of the Superintendent for further instructions.

When we arrived at the office, the Superintendent was out. When he failed to return within an hour, I suggested that we appeal to the United States Attorney, Osro Cobb, since Federal Judge Davies had ordered the Federal Bureau of Investigation, under the direction of the United States Attorney, to conduct a thorough investigation into who was responsible for the interference with the Court's integration order.

Mr. Cobb looked surprised when we entered his office. I told him that we were there because the students had been denied admittance to Central High School by the national guardsmen and we wanted to know what action, if any, his office planned to take.

After questioning the pupils, he directed them to the office of the FBI, where they gave a detailed report of what had happened to them that morning.

I might add here that during the school year the FBI interviewed hundreds of persons. Many of those who had participated in the mob could easily have been identified from photographs taken in front of the school. Yet no action was taken against anyone by the office of the United States Attorney, Osro Cobb, or the Department of Justice.

The Cold War and
Black Americans

The Career of Paul Robeson

Although the Communist Party in the United States sought to attract African-Americans into membership, it had little success. However, the party's espousal of racial causes led many blacks to view communism with less hostility than did the mainstream of American society. Of the prominent African-Americans who were sympathetic to left-wing and communist ideas, none was more well known than Paul Robeson.

Robeson was one of the most talented Americans of any color in the first half of the twentieth century. After his childhood as a minister's son in Princeton, New Jersey, he attended Rutgers University, where he was a two-time all-American football player. After he later graduated from Columbia Law School, he embarked on a multifaceted professional life that included the Broadway stage, Hollywood, musical concert and recording career, and being a political activist.

While the Cold War raged in the post-World War II years, Robeson refused to give up his friendship with the Soviet Union and fall into the rigid pattern of United States–Soviet relations. As far as Robeson was concerned, he would continue to believe that African-Americans belonged to a worldwide movement of oppressed humanity that owed allegiance to neither side in the Cold War.

Much of the time during his mature years, Robeson was involved in supporting anticolonial movements in what came to be called the "third world." Since many of those countries were seen by American authorities as sympathetic to the Soviet Union, Robeson found himself accused of un-Americanism and characterized as a threat to America's future.

In the chapter of Robeson's autobiography printed here, he offers a defense of his activities and explains that what many Americans see as pro-Soviet attitudes are actually designed to call attention to the ways in which the oppressed peoples of the world have been used as pawns in the struggle for world dominance.

In recent years my political views—or what are alleged to be my political views—have been the subject of wide discussion and controversy in public life generally and in Negro life as well. So many others have had their say on this matter that it seems only fair that I should have a chance to speak for myself, and so at this point I shall deal directly with that subject. My purpose in doing so is not to advance any partisan argument, but to set the record straight. I shall try to make clear exactly what my ideas are and how I came to hold them.

At the outset, let me point out that the controversy concerning my views and actions had its origin not among the Negro people but among the white folks on top who have directed at me the thunderbolts of their displeasure and rage. Although at various times certain Negro voices were heard joining in the condemnation that came from on high, it has been quite evident that the Negro community has its own way of looking at the matter.

One reaction, expressed by a wide range of Negro opinion extending from the most conservative to the most radical, is a keen resentment against certain ideas of my white critics. When it was said (and it was said many times) that Paul Robeson had shown himself to be ungrateful to the good white folks of America who had given him wealth and fame, and that he had had nothing to complain about, the statement was bound to rub Negroes the wrong way. They know that nothing is ever "given" to us, and they know that human dignity cannot be measured in dollars and cents. The late Walter White expressed this sentiment in an article in *Ebony*:

> "No honest American, white or Negro, can sit in judgment on a man like Robeson unless and until he has sacrificed time, talent, money and popularity in doing the utmost to root out the racial and economic evils which infuriate men like Robeson."

However, another common reaction in Negro life has been considerable confusion as to why I said or did certain things when the only result seemed to be increased difficulties for me; and then, too, it has been felt that the fire directed at me was putting many other Negroes "on the spot." I have often been asked: "Paul, are you doing right by being so outspoken in these times of hysteria?" And: "Wouldn't you be of greater service to the race if you just devoted yourself to being an artist and didn't make those speeches which get the white folks so upset?" And: "Man, what did you really say over there in Paris that caused such a fuss?"

I shall be glad to answer all such questions in these pages, and from what is happening nowadays I think that people will understand me better than would have been the case a few years ago. Recently, when Louis Armstrong denounced mistreatment of Negroes, and in stronger words than I have ever chosen, and when the response from other Negroes (including Jackie Robinson, as I was pleased to see) was a fervent Amen! —well, it looked like the "Old Ark's a-movering" for real!

It has been largely forgotten, and perhaps not known at all to many younger people, that my basic views on world affairs are nothing new. More than twenty years have passed since I first visited the Soviet Union and voiced my friendly sentiments about the peoples of that land, and before that I had expressed a keen interest in the life and culture of the African peoples and a deep concern for their liberation. Indeed, before the "cold war" brought about a different atmosphere, those broader interests of mine were considered by many Negroes to be quite admirable; and when in 1944 I was honored by the National Association for the Advancement of Colored People with the Spingarn Medal, my activities in behalf of "freedom for all men" were said to be a special contribution that I had made. The same point was made in 1943 when I was awarded an honorary degree by Morehouse College of Atlanta, and no one on that occasion was at all disturbed when in my speech of acceptance I observed that "the tremendous strides of the various peoples in the Soviet Union have given greatest proof of the latent abilities, not only of so-called agricultural peoples presumably unfitted for intricate industrial techniques, but also of so-called backward peoples who have clearly demonstrated that they function like all others."

We know, of course, how drastically the political climate of our country changed in the postwar years, but even in the worst period of McCarthyism—which, happily, now seems to be passing—I saw no reason why my convictions should change with the weather. I was not raised that way, and neither the promise of gain nor the threat of loss has ever moved me from my firm convictions. I recall that in 1936, when I was in London, John Hamilton, then national chairman of the Republican Party, visited me with a proposition that I return to America and campaign among Negroes for Alf Landon against President Roosevelt. My reward would be that as an actor I could write my own ticket in regard to future Hollywood contracts and starring productions, since the big film magnates were staunchly Republican and hated the man in the White House. I declined the offer and today I can smile at the thought that anyone could imagine me stumping the country, urging Negroes to turn against the New Deal and return the party of Herbert Hoover to power! Much earlier in my career, in New York, I had declined the offer of an important impresario to sign me to a lucrative ten-year contract while he would take full charge of my public life. I did not have many fixed ideas in those days, but one of them happened to be a strong conviction that my own conscience should be my guide and that no one was going to lead me around by a golden chain or any other kind.

In the early days of my career as an actor, I shared what was then the prevailing attitude of Negro performers—that the content and form of a play or film scenario was of little or no importance to us. What mattered was the opportunity, which came so seldom to our folks, of having a part—any part—to play on the stage or in the movies; and for a Negro actor to be offered a starring role—well, that was a rare stroke of fortune indeed! Later I came to understand that the Negro artist could not view the matter simply in terms of his individual interests, and that he had a responsibility to his people who rightfully resented the traditional stereotyped portrayals of Negroes on stage and screen. So I made a decision: If the Hollywood and Broadway producers did not choose to offer me worthy roles to play, then I would choose not to accept any other kind of offer. When, during the war years, I had the chance to appear before American audiences in a major Shakespearean production (fifteen years after I had first done so in London), I was deeply gratified to know that my people felt, as Dr. Benjamin Mays put it, that I had "rendered the Negro race and the world a great service in Othello by demonstrating that Negroes are capable of great and enduring interpretations in the realm of the theatre as over against the typical cheap performances that Hollywood and Broadway too often insist on Negroes doing".

Progress has been made and today there are greater opportunities for Negro performers. But it is still a hard struggle to win an equal place for them in the theatre, films, radio and television; and I am very happy and proud to see that so many of our brilliant young actors, singers and dancers are fighting for decent scripts, for roles that are worthy of their artistic talents. Years ago when I refused to sing before a segregated audience the story was headline news, and today I am happy to note that many others also have taken that stand, and that nowadays it is considered news—and bad news, by our people—whenever a prominent Negro artist agrees to perform under Jim Crow arrangements. We have every right to take great pride in the new and rising generation of our artists and we ought to support them in their struggle for equal opportunity. Their notable effort to represent faithfully our people in the arts makes such support a duty for us all.

It was in London, in the years that I lived among the people of the British Isles and traveled back and forth to many other lands, that my outlook on world affairs was formed. This fact is a key to an understanding of why I may differ in certain attitudes from many others of my generation in Negro life.

Having begun my career as a concert singer and actor in the United States, I first went abroad, like many other Negro performers, to work at my profession. If today the opportunities for Negro artists are still very limited in our country, it was many times worse thirty years ago. After several trips back and forth, I decided to stay in Europe and to make my home in London. My reasons were quite the same as those which over the years have brought millions of Negroes out of the Deep South to settle in other parts of the country. It must be said, however, that for me London was infinitely better than Chicago has been for Negroes from Mississippi.

Others have written about the success I achieved in the greater opportunities I found in England, but that is not my story here. I was, of course, deeply gratified to gain a prominent place in the theatre, in films, as concert singer and popular recording artist. Even more gratifying was the friendly welcome I received in English society. At first it was mostly "high society" —the upper-class people who patronized the arts and largely comprised the concert audiences; and I found myself moving a great deal in the most aristocratic circles. Here I was treated (in the old-fashioned phrase that still has meaning in England) as a gentleman and a scholar. My background at Rutgers and my interest in academic studies were given much more weight than such matters are given in America where bankrolls count more than brains and where bookish people are often derided as "eggheads" when they are not suspected of being "subversive." And so I found in London a congenial and stimulating intellectual atmosphere in which I felt at home. And, to an American Negro, the marked respect for law and order which is common among all classes throughout the British Isles was especially pleasing. They simply would not put up with a Faubus over there.

In those happy days, had someone suggested that my home should be "back home" in Jim Crow America I would have thought he was out of his mind. Go *back*—well, what in Heaven's name *for*? Later, when I changed my base in

English life and found myself more at home among the common people, I liked that country even better and, beyond an occasional trip to the States, I thought that I was settled for life.

But London was the center of the British Empire and it was there that I "discovered" Africa. That discovery, which has influenced my life ever since, made it clear that I would not live out my life as an adopted Englishman, and I came to consider that I was an African.

Like most of Africa's children in America, I had known little about the land of our fathers, but in England I came to know many Africans. Some of their names are now known to the world—Nkrumah and Azildwe, and Kenyatta who is imprisoned in Kenya. Many of the Africans were students, and I spent long hours talking with them and taking part in their activities at the West African Students Union building. Somehow they came to look upon me as one of them; they took pride in my successes; and they made Mrs. Robeson and me honorary members of the Union. Besides these students, who were mostly of princely origin, I also came to know another class of Africans—the seamen in the ports of London, Liverpool and Cardiff. They too had their organizations, and had much to teach me about their lives and their various peoples.

As an artist it was natural that my first interest in Africa was cultural. Culture? The foreign rulers of that continent insisted that there was no culture worthy of the name in Africa. But already musicians and sculptors in Europe were astir with their discovery of African art. And as I plunged, with excited interest, into my studies of Africa at the London School of Oriental Languages, I came to see that African culture was indeed a treasure-store for the world. Those who scorned the African languages as so many "barbarous dialects" could never know, of course, the richness of those languages and of the great philosophy and epics of poetry that have come down through the ages in these ancient tongues.

I studied many of these African languages, as I do to this day: Yoruba, Efik, Twi, Ga and others. Here was something important, I felt, not only for me as a student but for my people at home, and I expressed that thought in an article, "The Culture of the Negro," published in *The Spectator* (June 15, 1934), from which I quote these lines:

> It is astonishing and, to me, fascinating to find a flexibility and subtlety in a language like Swahili, sufficient to convey the teachings of Confucius, for example, and it is my ambition to guide the Negro race by means of its own peculiar qualities to a higher degree of perfection along the lines of its natural development. Though it is a commonplace to anthropologists, these qualities and attainments of Negro languages are entirely unknown to the general public of the Western world and, astonishingly enough, even to Negroes themselves. I have met Negroes in the United States who believed that the African Negro communicated his thoughts by means of gestures, that, in fact, he was practically incapable of speech and merely used sign language!

It is my first concern to dispel this regrettable and abysmal ignorance of the value of its own heritage in the Negro race itself. ...

I felt as one with my African friends and became filled with a glowing pride in these riches, new found to me. I learned that along with the towering achievements of the cultures of ancient Greece and China there stood the culture of Africa, unseen and denied by the imperialist looters of Africa's material wealth. I came to see the roots of my own people's culture, especially in our music which is still the richest and most healthy in America. Scholars had traced the influence of African music to Europe—to Spain with the Moors, to Persia and India and China, and westward to the Americas. And I came to learn of the remarkable kinship between African and Chinese culture (of which I hope to write at length some day).

My pride in Africa, and it grew with the learning, impelled me to speak out against the scorners. I wrote articles for the *New Statesman and Nation*, *The Spectator* and elsewhere championing the real but unknown glories of African culture. I argued and discussed the subject with men like H. G. Wells, and Laski, and Nehru; with students and savants.

Now, there was a logic to this cultural struggle I was making, and the powers-that-be realized it before I did. The British Intelligence came one day to caution me about the political meaning of my activities. For the question loomed of itself: *If African culture was what I insisted it was, what happens then to the claim that it would take 1,000 years for Africans to be capable of self-rule?*

It was an African who directed my interest in Africa to something he had observed in the Soviet Union. On a visit to that country he had traveled east and had seen the Yakuts, a people who had been classed as a "backward race" by the Czars. He had been struck by the resemblance between the tribal life of the Yakuts and his own people of East Africa. What would happen to a people like the Yakuts now that they had been freed from colonial oppression and were part of the construction of a socialist society?

Well, I went to see for myself and on my first visit to the Soviet Union in 1934 I saw how the Yakuts and the Uzbeks and all the other formerly oppressed nations were leaping ahead from tribalism to modern industrial economy, from illiteracy to the heights of knowledge. Their ancient cultures blooming in new and greater richness. Their young men and women mastering the sciences and arts. A thousand years? No. Less than twenty!

So, through my interest in Africa I came to visit and to study what was going on in the Soviet Union. I have told many times how pleased I was to find a place where colored people walked secure and free as equals. Others had observed that fact before I did and others have seen it since. Not long ago I read in the *Afro-American* a report by Dr. William E. Reed, dean of the school of agriculture at the Agricultural and Technical College in North Carolina, on his recent visit to the Soviet Union, in which he said:

I saw no signs of racial discrimination. I think it is fair to say that racial discrimination is non-existent in the U.S.S.R. ... I saw no difference between the way colored and white people live in the U.S.S.R. They are not segregated anywhere; those who attend church worship in the same churches; they attend the same schools.

That's how it is. I can't imagine that any Negro would not be pleased to see it, and I certainly was. So I thought that it would be a good thing to send my boy to school in the Soviet Union, and he did attend public school there for two years. Much has been made of that simple fact, but Paul, Jr., who later went to high school in Springfield, Massachusetts, and graduated from Cornell in New York, says that the Moscow school was a wonderful experience, that he had good teachers and good playmates, that he learned the language well— and why should that disturb anybody? (Evidently it did disturb the State Department because that fact was cited as one of the reasons why I should be denied a passport!)

I came to believe that the experiences of the many peoples and races in the Soviet Union—a vast country which embraces one-sixth of the earth's surface—would be of great value for other peoples of the East in catching up with the modern world. Today, with so many of these peoples in Asia and Africa gaining their freedom, there are many among them, including outstanding leaders, who say that they find in the Soviet achievements and those of the new China much that is of value. In a country like India, for example, there is a widespread opinion that socialism, in one form or another, must be considered as a possible solution of their problems.

I felt, too, that the rapidly growing power of the Soviet Union in world affairs would become an important factor in aiding the colonial liberation movement; and when, not long ago, the world saw how vigorously and effectively the Soviet Union moved to block Western imperialism from retaking the Suez Canal from emancipated Egypt, the truth of this view seemed amply confirmed. Here in New York, at the United Nations, we have all been able to see with our own eyes that on every issue that has come up the Soviet Union and the other socialist countries have voted in support of the colored peoples of the world. Some people say this is merely a matter of playing politics, but wouldn't it be wonderful for colored people everywhere if the U.S. delegation to the U.N. also played politics by voting that way?

Asia and Africa are looking at world developments with their eyes wide open and they don't miss a thing. As the influential newspaper *West African Pilot* put it in an editorial (June 30, 1953)

> We know no more about Communism than what its American and British detractors have pushed across to us as propaganda. ... But judging from what we see and experience from day to day, we feel that all this talk of the so-called 'free world' and 'iron curtain' is a camouflage to fool and bamboozle colonial peoples. It is part and parcel of power politics into which we refuse to be drawn until we are free to choose which ideology suits us best.

For the time being, we shall judge every nation strictly on the merits of the attitude of that nation towards our national aspirations. We have every cause to be grateful to the Communists for their active interest in the fate of colonial peoples and for their constant denunciation of the evils of imperialism. It is then left to the so-called 'free' nations to convince us that they are more concerned about our welfare than the Communists, and in this regard we believe more in action than in mere words.

The Bible says "by their deeds shall ye know them," and the colored nations cannot go wrong by taking that ancient truth as their guide.

My views concerning the Soviet Union and my warm feelings of friendship for the peoples of that land, and the friendly sentiments which they have often expressed toward me, have been pictured as something quite sinister by Washington officials and other spokesmen for the dominant white group in our country. It has been alleged that I am part of some kind of "international conspiracy."

The truth is: *I am not and never have been involved in any international conspiracy or any other kind, and do not know anyone who is.* It should be plain to everybody—and especially to Negroes—that if the government officials had a shred of evidence to back up that charge, you can bet your last dollar that they would have tried their best to put me *under* their jail! But they have no such evidence, because that charge is a lie. By an arbitrary and, as I am insisting in the courts, *illegal* ruling they have refused me a passport. In a later chapter I shall discuss the issues involved in that case, but here let me say that the denial of my passport is proof of nothing except the State Department's high-handed disregard of civil liberties.

In 1946, at a legislative hearing in California, I testified under oath that I was not a member of the Communist Party, but since then I have refused to give testimony or to sign affidavits as to that fact. There is no mystery involved in this refusal. As the witchhunt developed, it became clear that an important issue of Constitutional rights was involved in the making of such inquiries, and the film writers and directors who became known as the Hollywood Ten challenged the right of any inquisitors to violate the First Amendment's provisions of free speech and conscience. They lost their fight in the courts and were imprisoned. but since then the Supreme Court has made more liberal rulings in similar cases. The fundamental issue, however, is still not resolved, and I have made it a matter of principle, as many others have done, to refuse to comply with any demand of legislative committees or departmental officials that infringes upon the Constitutional rights of all Americans.

On many occasions I have publicly expressed my belief in the principles of scientific socialism, my deep conviction that for all mankind a socialist society represents an advance to a higher stage of life—that it is a form of society which is economically, socially, culturally, and ethically superior to a system based upon production for private profit. History shows that the processes of social change have nothing in common with silly notions about "plots" and "conspiracies." The development of human society—from tribalism to feudalism, to capitalism, to socialism—is brought about by the needs and aspirations of mankind for a better life. Today we see that hundreds of millions of people—a majority of the world's population—are living in socialist countries or are moving in a socialist direction, and that newly emancipated nations of Asia and Africa are seriously considering the question as to which economic system is the better for them to adopt. Some of their most outstanding leaders argue that the best road to their peoples' goals is through a socialist development and they point to the advances made by the Soviet Union, the People's Republic of China and other socialist countries as proof of their contention.

I do not intend to argue here for my political viewpoint, and, indeed, the large question as to which society is better for humanity is never settled by argument. The proof of the pudding is in the eating. Let the various social systems compete with each other under conditions of peaceful coexistence, and the people can decide for themselves. I do not insist that anyone else must agree with my judgment, and so I feel that no one is justified in insisting that I must conform to his beliefs. Isn't that fair?

In the wide acquaintanceships that I have had over the years, I have never hesitated to associate with people who hold non-conformist or radical views, and this has been true since my earliest days in the American theatre where I first met people who challenged the traditional order of things. And so today, Benjamin J. Davis is a dear friend of mine and I have always been pleased to say so; and he has been for many years a leader of the Communist Party of this country. I have known Ben Davis for a long time: I admired him when, as a young lawyer in Atlanta, he bravely defended a framed-up Negro youth and eventually won the case; I admired him later when, as a City Councilman in New York, he championed the rights of our people; and I admired him when, during his imprisonment, he began a legal fight to break down the Jim Crow system in the Federal penitentiaries. How could I *not* feel friendly to a man like that?

I firmly believe that Ben Davis and his colleagues were unjustly convicted, as Justice Black and Justice Douglas insisted in their dissenting opinion; and I think that their dissent in that case will be upheld in the course of history, as was the lone dissent in 1896 of Justice Harlan in the *Plessy versus Ferguson* case which was reversed in 1954 by a unanimous Court decision that the infamous "separate but equal" doctrine was unconstitutional and that Jim Crow schools were therefore unlawful. Indeed, already in several other Smith Act cases convicted persons have been vindicated by higher court action. In one case that was appealed to a Federal court, Judge William H. Hastie's forthright stand for civil liberties and against the convictions was a minority opinion; but since then, as a result of other decisions by that court and the U.S. Supreme Court, the Smith Act victims have been completely vindicated.

The main charge against me has centered upon my remarks at the World Peace Conference held in Paris in 1949, and what I said on that occasion has been distorted and misquoted in such a way as to impugn my character as a loyal American citizen. I went to Paris from England where, the night before I left, I met with the Coordinating Committee of Colonial Peoples in London, together with Dr. Y. M. Dadoo, president of the South African Indian Congress. The facts about that meeting and what I said in Paris are contained in the testimony I gave before the House Committee on Un-American Activities (a more accurate term is "Un-American Committee"!) at a hearing to which I was summoned on June 12, 1956. (This was *seven years* after another person, who was not in Paris and who did not know what I said there, was called before that Committee to give his views on what I was supposed to have said!)

Referring to the London meeting and my remarks next day in Paris, I testified as follows:

It was 2,000 students from various parts of the colonial world, from populations that would range from six to 700 million people, not just fifteen million. They asked me to address this [Paris] Conference and say in their name that they did not want war. That is what I said. There is no part of my speech in Paris which says that fifteen million Negroes would do anything. ... But what is perfectly clear today is that 900 million other colored people have told you they will not [go to war with the Soviet Union]. Is that not so? Four hundred million in India and millions everywhere have told you precisely that the colored people are not going to die for anybody and they are going to die for their independence. We are dealing not with fifteen million colored people, we are dealing with hundreds of millions. ... However, I did say, in passing, that it was unthinkable to me that any people would take ap arms in the name of an Eastland to go against anybody, and, gentlemen, I still say that. I thought it was healthy for Americans to consider whether or not Negroes should fight for people who kick them around.

What should happen, would be that this U.S. Government should go down to Mississippi and protect my people. That is what should happen.

Chairman Walter, co-author of the racist Walter-McCarran Immigration Act which I shall describe in a later chapter, did not like what I was saying and he started banging his gavel for me to stop. But I wasn't quite finished and I went on to say:

I stand here struggling for the rights of my people to be full citizens in this country. They are not—in Mississippi. They are not—in Montgomery. That is why I am here today. ... You want to shut up every colored person who wants to fight for the rights of his people!

Following that hearing, I was deeply moved and gratified by many comments in the Negro press which showed a sympathetic understanding of the position I took in Washington. Since not a line about Negro editorial opinion on this subject appeared in the white newspapers of this country, which never miss a chance to scandalize my name and to quote any Negro who can be induced to do so, let me here give excerpts from some of the Negro newspaper comments on my testimony:

Afro-American (Baltimore), June 23, 1956:

MR. ROBESON IS RIGHT

If he stands up before a Congressional committee and tells its members what colored people are saying all over the nation with reference to segregation, disfranchisement and discrimination on account of color, he's only doing in Washington what's being done in the rest of the U.S. by red-blooded Americans, white and colored. ...

We agree with Mr. Robeson that its [the Committee's] members could more profitably spend their time ... bringing in for questioning such un-American elements as those white supremacists and manifesto signers who have pledged themselves to defy and evade the very Constitution they had previously sworn to uphold and maintain.

Sun-Reporter (San Francisco), June 23, 1956:

Robeson as far as most Negroes are concerned occupies a unique position in the U.S., or the world, for that matter. Whites hate and fear him simply because he is the conscience of the U.S. in the field of color relations. Those Negroes who earn their living by the sweat of their brows and a few intellectuals idolize the man. He says the things which all of them wish to say about color relations, and the manner in which he says these things attracts the eye of the press of the world.

Charlottesville-Albemarle Tribune (Virginia), June 22, 1956:

THE HOUSE UN-AMERICAN ACTIVITIES COMMITTEE FIASCO

"Paul Robeson is a great artist and a deeply sympathetic human being. His own success did not blind him to the wrongs suffered by his race. ... To deny him the right to travel, to sing and to speak as he pleases; to put him in the pillory of a Congressional Committee and let lesser men bait him, is more hurtful to American prestige abroad than any intemperate statement he ever made."

Pittsburgh Courier (Pennsylvania), July 7, 1956:

There is a great fear that he would embarrass the U.S. abroad in regard to the Negro question. This is sheer foolishness. The world is well aware of the treatment which America accords its Negro population. The foreign press on occasion gives more space to these events than the American press. ... The Till case, the Autherine Lucy case and other such events are world property. What on earth could Robeson say that has not already been said about these sad affairs? . . . This denial is robbing him of some of the most important years of his life.

California Voice (Oakland), June 22, 1956:

Robeson embodies the unrestrained and righteous rage that has broken bonds. His is the furious spirit wearied with tedious checker playing that stretches through nearly a hundred years in order to gain the rights guaranteed a hundred years ago.

Robeson's cry is for justice, happiness and freedom here and now, while we live, not in some far away time in the future. His is the voice ... that shouts down the promises of by-and-by and bellows 'No! Now!'

A sensitive, tormented soul, he is that Other Self, the Alter Ego that a million Negroes try in self defense to disown. His protest is the authenic Protest of the Negro . ... And when Paul Robeson says, 'I don't think a Negro will fight for an Eastland,' Robeson is right.

None of these newspapers is left-wing in character, and, in making their comments from which I have quoted, several of them made that fact perfectly clear. "We are not Communists," said the *Afro-American*, "nor do we follow the Communist line. Moreover, we do not approve of some of the activities and statements attributed to Mr. Robeson."

That's fair enough, I say, and while expressing my heartfelt gratitude for the understanding shown by the Negro press for my basic position, let me also say this: How much more *democratic* are my people's newspapers than are the general newspapers of our country! Here is an example of a quality of spirit that the Negro people have in abundance and which is so lacking in much of American life. The crusade for freedom that they are interested in is right here at home. Americans who wish for peace among nations—and I believe the vast majority of them do—can join with my people in singing our old-time song—

> I'm going to lay dawn my sword and shield
> Down by the riverside ...
> I'm going to study war no more!

At Paris in 1949, I was convinced—and time has only served to deepen that conviction—that a war with the Soviet Union, a Third World War, was unthinkable for *anybody* who is not out of his mind. Certainly the majority of the colored peoples of the world have since made it clear that they want peace, and at their great conference held in Bandung, Indonesia, in 1955 they united on a program to promote peace. The reason why war is unthinkable to the peoples of Asia and Africa is spelled out in these words from the resolution adopted at Bandung:

The Conference considered that disarmament and the prohibition of the production, experimentation and use of nuclear and thermonuclear weapons of war are imperative to save mankind and civilization from the fear and prospect of wholesale destruction. It considered that the nations of Asia and Africa assembled here have a duty towards humanity and civilization to proclaim their support for disarmament and for prohibition of these weapons and to appeal to nations principally concerned and to world opinion, to bring about such disarmament and prohibition.

I would have liked to have gone to that historic gathering as an observer, but since my passport was denied I sent a message of greetings. (That message was itself later cited by the State Department as still another reason why I should not be permitted to travel!) In my message to Bandung, as in my speech at Paris, I stressed the urgent necessity of preventing another war and pointed out the direct interest that the colored peoples have in the maintenance of peace. I wrote:

Discussion and mutual respect are the first ingredients for the development of peace among nations. If other nations of the world follow the example set by the Asian-African nations, there can be developed an alternative to the policy of force and an end to the threat of H-Bomb war. The people of Asia and Africa have a direct interest in such a development since it is a well known fact that atomic weapons have been used only against the peoples of Asia. There is at present a threat to use them once more against an Asian people.

I fully endorse the objectives of the Conference to prevent any such catastrophe, which would inevitably bring about suffering and annihilation to all the peoples of the world. Throughout the world all decent people must applaud the aims of the Conference to make the maximum contribution of the Asian and African countries to the cause of world peace.

I also pointed out that the meeting of colored peoples of the East was highly significant to colored peoples of the West as well:

To the Negro people of the United States and the Caribbean Islands it was good news—great good news—to hear that the Bandung Conference had been called "to consider problems of special interest ... racialism and colonialism": Typical of the Negro people's sentiments are these words from one of our leading weekly newspapers [New York Amsterdam News]: "Negro Americans should be interested in the proceedings at Bandung. We have fought this kind of fight for more than 300 years and have a vested interest in the outcome."

No one can doubt that we do indeed have that "vested interest," and we ought to reach out in every way possible to strengthen our ties with the rising world's majority. As for me, when anyone asks me today what is the viewpoint I support in world affairs, I point to the Ten Principles of Bandung which are as follows:

1. Respect for fundamental human rights and for the purposes and principles of the Charter of the United Nations.

2. Respect for the sovereignty and territorial integrity of all nations.

3. Recognition of the equality of all races and of the equality of all nations large and small.

4. Abstention from intervention or interference in the internal affairs of another country.

5. Respect for the right of each nation to defend itself singly or collectively, in conformity with the Charter of the United Nations.

6. (a) Abstention from the use of arrangements of collective defense to serve the particular interests of any of the big powers.

    (b) Abstention by any country from exerting pressures on other countries.

7. Refraining from acts or threats of aggression or the use of force against the territorial integrity or political independence of any country.

8. Settlement of all international disputes by peaceful means, such as negotiations, conciliation, arbitration or judicial settlement as well as other peaceful means of the parties' own choice, in conformity with the Charter of the United Nations.

9. Promotion of mutual interests and cooperation.

10. Respect for justice and international obligations.

These principles I wholeheartedly support. On this platform I take my stand.

SUGGESTIONS FOR FURTHER READING

For a survey of the recent period, see Harvard Sitkoff, *The Struggle for Black Equality, 1954–1992*★ (1993). The story of the beginnings of school desegregation is brilliantly told in Richard Kluger, *Simple Justice: The History of Brown v. Board of Education and Black America's Struggle for Equality*★ (1970). The continuing process is described in Benjamin Muse, *Ten Years of Prelude: The Story of Integration Since the Supreme Court's 1954 Decision* (1964), J. Harvie Wilkinson III, *From Brown to Bakke: The Supreme Court and School Integration, 1954–1978*★ (1979), and Raymond Wolters, *The Burden of Brown: Thirty Years of School Desegregation* (1984). The legal aspects of change in racial policy are surveyed in Jack Greenberg, *Race Relations and American Law* (1959), Albert Blaustein and C. C. Ferguson (eds.), *Desegregation and the Law* (1957), and Mary Francis Berry, *Black Resistance/White Law: A History of Constitutional Racism in America* (1971). See also Mark V. Tushnet, *Making Civil Rights Law: Thurgood Marshall and the Supreme Court, 1936–1961*★ (1994).

Special issues in desegregation are analyzed in Richard A. Pride and J. David Woodward, *The Burden of Busing: The Politics of Desegregation in Nashville, Tennessee* (1985), Bernard Schwartz, *Swann's Way: The School Busing Case and the Supreme Court* (1986), Davison M. Douglas, *Reading, Writing, and Race: The Desegregation of the Charlotte Schools*★ (1995), and J. Anthony Lukas, *Common Ground* [Boston] (1985). See also E. Culpepper Clark, *The Schoolhouse Door: Segregation's Last Stand at the University of Alabama*★ (1993).

For race relations during the 1950s, see Numan V. Bartley, *The Rise of Massive Resistance: Race and Politics in the South during the 1950s* (1969) and Robert Frederick Burk, *The Eisenhower Administration and Black Civil Rights*★ (1984).

On the role of race in the Cold War, see Brenda Gayle Plummer, *Rising Wind: Black Americans and U. S. Foreign Affairs, 1935–1960*★ (1997). Martin Duberman has written the standard biography in *Paul Robeson*★ (1988). A collection of essays appear in Jeffrey C. Stewart (ed.), *Paul Robeson: Artist and Citizen*★ (1998).

★ Books marked by an asterisk are available in paperback.

11

❂

The Nonviolent
Civil Rights Movement

INTRODUCTION

The prototypes of the nonviolent direct-action campaigns of the late 1950s
and the early 1960s are found in A. Philip Randolph's March on
Washington movement and the Congress of Racial Equality (CORE). The latter was organized by religious pacifists in 1942 in an attempt to apply
Gandhian techniques to the racial struggle in America. Its founder, James
Farmer, was black, but CORE was made up primarily of whites until the
1960s. Although CORE was not directly involved in the events that led to the
nonviolent movement among Southern students in the 1960s, its skill in the
analysis of, and training for, nonviolent protests was put at the service of the
students once the movement began.

The tactic of massive nonviolent direct action appeared on the scene of
American race relations with the Montgomery, Alabama, bus boycott of 1955.
Rosa Parks, a black woman, decided not to stand up when ordered to give her
seat to a white person on a Montgomery bus, thus breaking city law. She was
arrested, and the nonviolent civil rights movement was on. For more than a
year, blacks refused to ride the buses in an attempt to bring about a slight
modification in the seating arrangements on public transportation. As a result
of the boycott, they were subjected to intimidation, arrest, and economic
reprisals of various sorts. On November 13, 1956, the Supreme Court ruled
that bus segregation violated the Constitution, and the Montgomery boycott
was declared ended. In the aftermath of the decision that finally forced a
change in Southern customs, several black churches were bombed.

The churches were an appropriate target for hostile whites, for it was from them that the boycott leadership had emerged. A Montgomery church furnished the movement with the man who served as its symbolic head until his assassination in 1968, Martin Luther King, Jr. Fresh from graduate school and just beginning to act as pastor of a Baptist church in Montgomery, King was elected to serve as head of the boycott committee. From there he joined with others to found the Southern Christian Leadership Conference (SCLC), which was to be a civil rights organization of major importance in the decades to come.

As the use of the boycott technique spread, an event occurred that changed all the rules and tactics of the protest movements. On February 1, 1960, four black college students "sat in" at a lunch counter in a Woolworth store in Greensboro, North Carolina. For some reason, this act provided the spark that set off the latent dynamite of Southern race relations. Within a matter of weeks, tens of thousands of students all over the South were engaged in sit-in campaigns. The number of arrests and violent acts of retaliation by whites soared. It has been estimated that at least 20,000 persons were arrested as a result of participation in nonviolent demonstrations in the South between 1960 and 1963.

In April 1960, the SCLC decided to call a conference of college students involved in the demonstrations. From this conference emerged the Student Nonviolent Coordinating Committee (SNCC), which was henceforth to guide the fortunes of the student movement. At the beginning, SNCC's philosophy was one of religious nonviolence, patterned after the ideas of Martin Luther King. But even then, most of the students accepted nonviolence as a practical measure, not as a total philosophy of life. Later, when SNCC shifted away from the demonstration as a technique, not so much a change in philosophy as a change in tactics was required. Under the leadership of brilliant young blacks, SNCC transformed the college campus scene in America from one of passive alienation to one of militant commitment.

The most direct contribution of CORE to the nonviolent action movement came with the Freedom Rides of 1961, undertaken to test the South's submission to the Supreme Court ruling outlawing segregation in bus and train terminals. Although their buses were bombed and burned, many continued their journeys, and over three hundred persons ended up in the Jackson, Mississippi, jail. The Freedom Rides marked the beginning of a shift of civil rights activity from the upper to the lower South, where most nonviolent direct-action campaigns were to meet with little or no success.

As SNCC began to be active in the rural Deep South, primarily trying to get the poor blacks to register for the vote, the students began to move away from their previous "middle-class" goals. This led to a rift between SNCC and King and the SCLC—a rift that became a complete split at the conclusion of the summer of 1964. Until this time, many whites had participated in the organizational activities of SNCC, and in the summer of 1964, often called Freedom Summer, Mississippi was invaded by hundreds of college students, black and white, from North and South, in an attempt to focus national attention on the state's denial of basic rights to its black citizens. In terms of this immediate goal, the summer was a great success, for it brought the horrors of Mississippi dramatically before the public eye.

Perhaps even more important in the long run, Freedom Summer marked a turning point in the black student movement. When it became apparent that it was the "whiteness" of the summer that attracted the news media, the black students decided that they had to cast out their white allies and become an all-black movement. Only in that way, they felt, could they build a movement that would ensure the coming of true liberation for black people. As long as the nation cared for blacks only when they were accompanied by whites, there would be no certainty of freedom for blacks taken alone.

The disenchantment of many blacks with what they considered the "political" approach of white liberals was strengthened when, in August 1964 at the Democratic Party Convention, the Mississippi Freedom Democratic Party (MFDP), a predominantly black organization loyal to the national Democratic party, was let down by Hubert Humphrey. The MFDP had agreed to accept a compromise proposal seating all members of the regular Democratic party and of the MFDP who would sign a pledge of loyalty and dividing the vote of the Mississippi delegation between the two groups on the basis of the number of delegates seated by each. But Humphrey, working for the vice-presidential nomination, had the Credentials Committee reject the agreed-upon compromise in favor of allowing the MFDP two at-large votes. The new compromise was rejected by the MFDP over the objections of civil rights leaders like Martin Luther King, Jr.—a clear sign that the integrationist phase of the movement for black liberation was coming to a close.

The Student Sit-Ins Begin

Greensboro, NC, February 1, 1960

FRANKLIN McCAIN

It was obviously an idea whose time had come. With little forethought and less plan-
ning, four freshmen at all-black North Carolina A&T College decided they needed to
"do something" to express their unwillingness any longer to accept the racial status quo
in the South. Their project was a simple one. They went into a Woolworth variety store,
purchased some items, and then sat down at the lunch counter and asked to be served.
This seemingly ordinary act reverberated over the next several weeks as thousands of
black and some white students took part in the lunch counter sit-ins. Activist students
met in Raleigh, NC, over Easter and organized the Student Nonviolent Coordinating
Committee (SNCC), which became the backbone of the nonviolent civil rights move-
ment.

Ironically, the sit-in tactic was one of long standing in the struggle for racial justice.
The Congress of Racial Equality (CORE) was founded in the 1940s in an effort to
desegregate eating facilities around the nation's capital. Labor unions, most famously
the United Auto Workers, also employed the technique. Although SNCC adopted
nonviolence as a tactic, at the beginning, the students acted on their own, not under the
influence of any organization or existing movement. Many assumed that the students
drew their inspiration from Martin Luther King, Jr., and the Montgomery bus boy-
cott, but the students were hardly aware of that event of several years earlier.

Once the movement expanded, activists were sometimes willing to accept the assis-
tance and guidance of more experienced organizers, and often SNCC and CORE
worked side by side on desegregation campaigns. Generational tensions developed,
however, as the students grew increasingly reluctant to grant leadership roles to the older
generation of clergy represented by King's Southern Christian Leadership Conference
(SCLC) or the NAACP.

For many months, this was truly a youth movement, one like the United States
had never seen before, and its legacy brought us significant change in racial customs and
hard-fought advances in racial equality.

FEBRUARY 1, 1960: THE SOUTH'S FIRST SIT-IN

It was one of those group friendships that spring up among college freshmen. In
their first semester at all-black North Carolina A&T College in Greensboro, he and
Ezell Blair, Jr., David Richmond, and Joseph McNeil became inseparable. They would
study together, eat together, and, "as young freshmen often do in college dormitories late
at night, when they finish studying or when they want to cop out from studying ...
resort to the old fashion type bull session."

Through the fall, their talks continued. He remembers them as "elementaty
philosophers," young idealists talking about justice and injustice, hypocrisy, how imper-
fectly their society embodied its own ideals. Slowly their talks swung to a debate as old

as philosophy itself: at what point does the moral man act against injustice? "... I think the thing that precipitated the sit-in, the idea of the sit-in, more than anything else, was that little bit of incentive and that little bit of courage that each of us instilled within each other."

The planning process was on a Sunday night, I remember it quite well. I think it was Joseph who said, "It's time that we take some action now. We've been getting together, and we've been, up to this point, still like most people we've talked about for the past few weeks or so—that is, people who talk a lot but, in fact, make very little action." After selecting the technique, then we said, "Let's go down and just ask for service." It certainly wasn't titled a "sit-in" or "sit-down" at that time. "Let's just go down to Woolworth's tomorrow and ask for service, and the tactic is going to be simply this: we'll just stay there." We never anticipated being served, certainly, the first day anyway. "We'll stay until we get served." And I think Ezell said, "Well, you know that might be weeks, that might be months, that might be never." And I think it was the consensus of the group, we said, "Well, that's just the chance we'll have to take."

What's likely to happen? Now, I think that that was a question that all of us asked ourselves. ... What's going to happen once we sit down? Of course, nobody had the answers. Even your wildest imagination couldn't lead you to believe what would, in fact, happen.

Why Woolworth's?

They advertise in public media, newspapers, radios, television, that sort of thing. They tell you to come in: "Yes, buy the toothpaste; yes, come in and buy the notebook paper. .... No, we don't separate your money in this cash register, but, no, please don't step down to the hot dog stand. ..." The whole system, of course, was unjust, but that just seemed like insult added to injury. That was just like pouring salt into an open wound. That's inviting you to do something. ...

Once getting there ... we did make purchases of school supplies and took the patience and time to get receipts for our purchases, and Joseph and myself went over to the counter and asked to be served coffee and doughnuts. As anticipated, the reply was, "I'm sorry, we don't serve you here." And of course we said, "We just beg to disagree with you. We've in fact already been served; you've served us already and that's just not quite true." The attendant or waitress was a little bit dumbfounded, just didn't know what to say under circumstances like that. And we said, "We wonder why you'd invite us in to serve us at one counter and deny service at another. If this is a private club or private concern, then we believe you ought to sell membership cards and sell only to persons who have a membership card. If we don't have a card, then we'd know pretty well that we shouldn't come in or even attempt to come in." That didn't go over too well, simply because I don't really think she understood what we were talking about, and for the second reason, she had no logical response to a statement like that. And the only thing that an individual in her case or position could do is, of course, call the manager. [Laughs] Well, at this time, I think we were joined by Dave Richmond and Ezell Blair at the counter with us, after that dialogue.

Were you afraid at this point?

Oh, hell yes, no question about that. [Laughs] At that point there was a policeman who had walked in off the street, who was pacing the aisle … behind us, where we were seated, with his club in his hand, just sort of knocking it in his hand, and just looking mean and red and a little bit upset and a little bit disgusted. And you had the feeling that he didn't know what the hell to do. You had the feeling that this is the first time that this big bad man with the gun and the club has been pushed in a corner, and he's got absolutely no defense, and the thing that's killing him more than anything else—he doesn't know what he can or what he cannot do. He's defenseless. Usually his defense is offense, and we've provoked him, yes, but we haven't provoked him outwardly enough for him to resort to violence. And I think this is just killing him; you can see it all over him.

People in the store were—we got mixed reactions from people in the store. A couple of old ladies … came up to pat us on the back sort of and say, "Ah, you should have done it ten years ago. It's a good thing I think you're doing."

These were black ladies.

No, these are white ladies.

Really?

Yes, and by the same token, we had some white ladies and white men to come up and say to us, "Nasty, dirty niggers, you know you don't belong here at the lunch counter. There's a counter—" There was, in fact, a counter downstairs in the Woolworth store, a stand-up type counter where they sold hot dogs. …

But at any rate, there were expressions of support from white people that first day?

Absolutely right. Absolutely. And I think probably that was certainly some incentive for additional courage on the part of us. And the other thing that helped us psychologically quite a lot was seeing the policeman pace the aisle and not be able to do anything. I think that this probably gave us more strength, more encouragement, than anything else on that particular day, on day one.

Unexpected as it was, the well-wishing from the elderly white women was hardly more surprising than the scorn of a middle-aged black dishwasher behind the counter. She said, "That's why we can't get anyplace today, because of people like you, rabble-rousers, troublemakers. …. This counter is reserved for white people, it always has been, and you are well aware of that. So why don't you go on out and stop making trouble?"

He has since seen the woman at, of all places, a reunion commemorating the event in which she played so unsupportive a role.

[She said] "Yes, I did say it and I said it because, first of all, I was afraid for what would happen to you as young black boys. Secondly, I was afraid of what would happen to me as an individual who had a job at the Woolworth store. I might have been fired and that's my livelihood. ..."

It took me a long time to really understand that statement ... but I know why she said it. She said it out of fear more than anything else. I've come to understand that, and my elders say to me that it's maturity that makes me understand why she said that some fifteen years ago.

But, moved by neither praise nor scorn, he and the others waited for the waitress to return with the manager, a career Woolworth's employee named C.L. Harris.

That was real amusin' as well [laughing] because by then we had the confidence, my goodness, of a black truck. And there was virtually nothing that could move us, there was virtually nothing probably at that point that could really frighten us off. ... If it's possible to know what it means to have your soul cleansed—I felt pretty clean at that time. I probably felt better on that day than I've ever felt in my life. Seems like a lot of feelings of guilt or what-have-you suddenly left me, and I felt as though I had gained my manhood, so to speak, and not only gained it, but had developed quite a lot of respect for it. Not Franklin McCain only as an individual, but I felt as though the manhood of a number of other black persons had been restored and had gotten some respect from just that one day.

But back to Mr. Harris, who was the store manager, he was a fairly nice guy to talk to on that day. I think what he wanted to do more than anything else was to—initially—was to kill us with kindness, to say, "Fellas, you know this is just not the way we do business. Why don't you go on back to your campus? If you're just hungry, go downstairs," and that sort of thing.

We listened to him, paid him the courtesy of listening to what he had to say. We repeated our demands to him, and he ended up by saying, "Well, you know, I don't really set policy for this store. The policy for serving you is set by corporate headquarters." and of course, we found out that that was just a cop out. Corporate headquarters said, "No, it's up to local communities to set standards and set practices and that sort of thing, and whatever they do is all right with us." You know, the usual sort of game of rubber checkers.

The only reason we did leave is the store was closing. We knew, of course, we had to leave when the store was closing. We said to him, "Well, we'll have plenty of time tomorrow, because we'll be back to see you." [Laughs] I don't think that went over too well. But by the time we were leaving, the store was just crowded with people from off the streets and on the streets .... As a matter of fact, there were so many people standin' in front of the store, we had to leave from the side entrance.

But back at the campus, there was just a beehive of activity. Word had spread. As a matter of fact, word was back on campus before we ever got back. There were all sorts of phone calls to the administration and to people on the faculty and staff. The mayor's office was aware of it and the governor's office was aware of it. I think it was all over North Carolina within a matter of just an hour or so.

That night they met with about fifty campus leaders to form the Student Executive Committee for Justice.

The movement started out as a movement of nonviolence and as a Christian movement, and we wanted to make that very clear to everybody, that it was a movement that was seeking justice more than anything else and not a movement to start a war. ... We knew that probably the most powerful and potent weapon that people have literally no defense for is love, kindness. That is, whip the enemy with something that he doesn't understand.

How much was the example of Dr. King and the Montgomery Bus Boycott in your mind in that regard?

Not very much. The individual who had probably most influence on us was Gandhi, more than any single individual. During the time that the Montgomery Bus Boycott was in effect, we were tots for the most part, and we barely heard of Martin Luther King. Yes, Martin Luther King's name was well-known when the sit-in movement was in effect, but to pick out Martin Luther King as a hero. ... I don't want you to misunderstand what I'm about to say: Yes, Martin Luther King was a hero. ... No. he was not the individual that we had upmost in mind when we started the sit-in movement. ...

Most journalists and historians have been quite wrong about the impetus for the first sit-in, he insists. Although all of the students had read extensively on the Montgomery movement, they were not, as has been widely reported, directly inspired by a Fellowship of Reconciliation "comic book" entitled "Martin Luther King and the Montgomery Story." They had not heard of CORE's Chicago sit-in twenty years earlier. Nor were he and the others persuaded, as one history of the sit-ins has it, to make their protest by Ralph Johns, an eccentric white NAACP member who ran a haberdashery near the campus. The subject irritates him. Dignified even in his light-hearted moments, he now becomes even more formal.

Credit for the initiation of the sit-in movement has been granted to one or two ministers, the NAACP, Ralph Johns, CORE, at least a dozen people, and it's rather amusing when you do read some of these articles. I think it's a game. The same type tactic that has been used over and over and over by the white news media and the white press to discredit blacks with particular types of achievement. You don't have to look at the sit-in movement to see that. You can think of things like, well, for instance, the surveying of the laying out of the city of Washington, D.C., or the invention of the traffic signal, or the concept of Labor Day, or even Perry's expedition to the North Pole. These are the kinds of things that come into my mind when I think about the attempt to discredit the people who actually started the sit-in movement.

So what you're saying is ... the most simple explanation applies?

Four guys met, planned, and went into action. It's just that simple.

On the second day, they were joined by over twenty other A&T students, and they kept most of the stools occupied all day. On the fourth day the first white students joined them from the University of North Carolina Women's College in Greensboro. By the second week sit-ins had spread to a half-dozen North Carolina towns.

From the Greensboro area there must have been people from six or seven university campuses who wanted to participate, who wanted to help sit-in, who wanted to help picket. We actually got to the point where we had people going down in shifts. It got to the point wherein we took all the seats in the restaurants. We had people there in the mornings as soon as the doors were open to just take every seat in the restaurant or at the lunch counter. ...

As a manager, you've got to do something. You just can't continue to have people come in and sit around. The cash registers have to ring. What happened is that after we started to take all of the seats in the restaurants, they started to pull the stools up in the restaurants. So we just started to stand around then and take all the standing room. ... I think at the height of the sit-in movement in Greensboro, we must have had at least, oh, ten or fifteen thousand people downtown who wanted to sit-in, but obviously there weren't that many chairs in downtown Greensboro for people to sit in. ...

It spread to places like the shopping centers, the drugstores in the shopping centers, the drive-ins .... No place was going to be left untouched. The only criteria was that if it did not serve blacks, it was certainly going to be hit ...

With such success came attention.

The Congress of Racial Equality offered a funny sort of help, and that kind of help was, in effect, "If you let us control the show, we'll show you how the thing is supposed to be done." And four seventeen-year-old guys were just not in the mood to let someone take their show. That was our position. Our position was, we were probably as much experts about this as anybody else. We were experts because we had had one experience already, and that's more than most people had had.

We got a lot of attention from the Communist party. [Laughs] The Communist party sent representatives down to Greensboro to assist us in any way that we deemed appropriate. If it meant actual participation, they offered to sit in with us. If it meant you needed X number of dollars to do this, or if you needed air fare to go here or there, if you needed anything, they made it known that money was available, assistance was available. Just don't sit down here in Greensboro and want for things that you need. But you know, again, it was a Christian movement, and Christians and Communists just don't mix.

Did you avail yourself of any of that?

No, we didn't need it. Even if we had needed it, there was no reason to affiliate with the Communist party. We were in the driver's seat. ... Remember, too, you had four guys who were pretty strong-willed, pretty bull-headed, and who were keenly aware that people would rush in and try to take over the Movement, so to speak. And we were quite aware of that, and we felt—not felt—were very independent. ... As a matter of fact, we were criticized on several occasions for being too damned independent. But I still don't regret it.

Did the success that you experienced cause strains among the four of you?

Never. There was enough to go around. [Laughs]

Within a year the students had forced the desegregation of Greensboro's theaters and lunch counters. "The four," however, passed quickly from the Movement scene, Blair to become a teacher in Massachusetts, McNeil a banker in New York. Richmond still lives in Greensboro, and McCain, a chemist, settled in Charlotte, one hundred miles to the south, where he is a development engineer for Celanese Corporation.

His final observation on Greensboro:

I'm told that the chamber of commerce wastes no time in letting prospective industry or businesses know that this is where the sit-in movement originated some fourteen, fifteen years ago, way back in 1960. This is another reason that we can call ourself the Gate City ... the gateway to the New South. ...

So, it's rather amusing the way they have ... used it to their advantage, something that as a matter of fact they were staunchly against at that particular time. But I think that's only smart. It's only good business to do that. I'm sure if I were the chamber of commerce, I'd do the same thing.

The Philosophy of
Nonviolent Coercion

Letter from Birmingham Jail

MARTIN LUTHER KING, JR.

It was a happy coincidence that twenty-seven-year-old Martin Luther King, Jr., had recently accepted a pastorate in Montgomery, Alabama, when the bus boycott broke out. Since his days as a seminary student, King had been developing a nonviolent philosophy of life based on the writings of Gandhi and the New Testament. As a result, King became the philosopher of the movement for nonviolent coercion.

After King brought the movement into Birmingham, Alabama, in 1963, he was arrested and jailed, along with Ralph Abernathy and Fred Shuttlesworth, on Good Friday for leading a protest march. A group of Alabama clergymen wrote King a letter while he was in jail, accusing him of coming in from the outside to stir up trouble and even to foment violence.

From the jail, King wrote a letter of reply to their charges. The letter, reprinted in the following pages, stands as an explanation and a vindication of nonviolent direct action as well as a repudiation of the charge that organized civil rights workers coming into the South fell into the category of "outside agitators." This document, perhaps more than any other from the period, catches the flavor of the nonviolent movement that brought such significant changes in the patterns of social interaction in many towns and cities of the South.

My Dear Fellow Clergymen:

While confined here in the Birmingham city jail, I came across your recent statement calling my present activities "unwise and untimely." Seldom do I pause to answer criticism of my work and ideas. If I sought to answer all the criticisms that cross my desk, my secretaries would have little time for anything other than such correspondence in the course of the day, and I would have no time for constructive work. But since I feel that you are men of genuine good will and that your criticisms are sincerely set forth, I want to try to answer your statement in what I hope will be patient and reasonable terms.

I think I should indicate why I am here in Birmingham, since you have been influenced by the view which argues against "outsiders coming in." I have the honor of serving as president of the Southern Christian Leadership Conference, an organization operating in every southern state, with head-quarters in Atlanta, Georgia. We have some eighty-five affiliated organizations across the South, and one of them is the Alabama Christian Movement for Human Rights. Frequently we share staff, educational and financial resources with our affiliates. Several months ago the affiliate here in Birmingham asked us to be on call to engage in a nonviolent direct-action program if such were deemed necessary. We readily consented, and when the hour came we lived up to our promise. So I, along with several members of my staff, am here because I was invited here. I am here because I have organizational ties here.

But more basically, I am in Birmingham because injustice is here. Just as the prophets of the eighth century B.C. left their villages and carried their "thus saith the Lord" far beyond the boundaries of their home towns, and just as the Apostle Paul left his village of Tarsus and carried the gospel of Jesus Christ to the far corners of the Greco-Roman world, so am I compelled to carry the gospel of freedom beyond my own home town. Like Paul, I must constantly respond to the Macedonian call for aid.

Moreover, I am cognizant of the interrelatedness of all communities and states. I cannot sit idly by in Atlanta and not be concerned about what happens in Birmingham. Injustice anywhere is a threat to justice everywhere. We are caught in an inescapable network of mutuality, tied in a single garment of destiny. Whatever affects one directly, affects all indirectly. Never again can we afford to live with the narrow, provincial "outside agitator" idea. Anyone who lives inside the United States can never be considered an outsider anywhere within its bounds.

You deplore the demonstrations taking place in Birmingham. But your statement, I am sorry to say, fails to express a similar concern for the conditions that brought about the demonstrations. I am sure that none of you would want to rest content with the superficial kind of social analysis that deals merely with effects and does not grapple with underlying causes. It is unfortunate that demonstrations are taking place in Birmingham, but it is even more unfortunate that the city's white power structure left the Negro community with no alternative.

In any nonviolent campaign there are four basic steps: collection of the facts to determine whether injustices exist; negotiation; self-purification; and direct action. We have gone through all these steps in Birmingham. There can be no gainsaying the fact that racial injustice engulfs this community. Birmingham is probably the most thoroughly segregated city in the United States. Its ugly record of brutality is widely known. Negroes have experienced grossly unjust treatment in the courts. There have been more unsolved bombings of Negro homes and churches in Birmingham than in any other city in the nation. These are the hard, brutal facts of the case. On the basis of these conditions, Negro leaders sought to negotiate with the city fathers. But the latter consistently refused to engage in good-faith negotiation.

Then, last September, came the opportunity to talk with leaders of Birmingham's economic community. In the course of the negotiations, certain promises were made by the merchants—for example, to remove the stores' humiliating racial signs. On the basis of these promises, the Reverend Fred Shuttlesworth and the leaders of the Alabama Christian Movement for Human Rights agreed to a moratorium on all demonstrations. As the weeks and months went by, we realized that we were the victims of a broken promise. A few signs, briefly removed, returned; the others remained.

As in so many past experiences, our hopes had been blasted, and the shadow of deep disappointment settled upon us. We had no alternative except to prepare for direct action, whereby we would present our very bodies as a means of laying our case before the conscience of the local and the national community. Mindful of the difficulties involved, we decided to undertake a process of self-purification. We began a series of workshops on nonviolence, and we repeatedly asked ourselves: "Are you able to accept blows without retaliating?" "Are you able to endure the ordeal of jail?" We decided to schedule our direct-action program for the Easter season, realizing that except for Christmas, this is the main shopping period of the year. Knowing that a strong economic-withdrawal program would be the by-product of direct action, we felt that this would be the best time to bring pressure to bear on the merchants for the needed change.

Then it occurred to us that Birmingham's mayoralty election was coming up in March, and we speedily decided to postpone action until after election day. When we discovered that the Commissioner of Public Safety, Eugene "Bull" Connor, had piled up enough votes to be in the run-off, we decided again to postpone action until the day after the run-off so that the demonstrations could not be used to cloud the issues. Like many others, we waited to see Mr. Connor defeated, and to this end we endured postponement after postponement. Having aided in this community need, we felt that our direct-action program could be delayed no longer.

You may well ask: "Why direct action? Why sit-ins, marches and so forth? Isn't negotiation a better path?" You are quite right in calling for negotiation. Indeed, this is the very purpose of direct action. Nonviolent direct action seeks to create such a crisis and foster such a tension that a community which has constantly refused to negotiate is forced to confront the issue. It seeks so to dramatize the issue that it can no longer be ignored. My citing the creation of tension as part of the work of the nonviolent-resister may sound rather shocking. But I must confess that I am not afraid of the word "tension." I have earnestly opposed violent tension, but there is a type of constructive, non-violent tension which is necessary for growth. Just as Socrates felt that it was necessary to create a tension in the mind so that individuals could rise from the bondage of myths and half-truths to the unfettered realm of creative analysis and objective appraisal, so must we see the need for nonviolent gad-flies to create the kind of tension in society that will help men rise from the dark depths of prejudice and racism to the majestic heights of understanding and brotherhood.

The purpose of our direct-action program is to create a situation so crisis-packed that it will inevitably open the door to negotiation. I therefore concur with you in your call for negotiation. Too long has our beloved Southland been bogged down in a tragic effort to live in monologue rather than dialogue.

One of the basic points in your statement is that the action that I and my associates have taken in Birmingham is untimely. Some have asked: "Why didn't you give the new city administration time to act?" The only answer that I can give to this query is that the new Birmingham administration must be prodded about as much as the outgoing one, before it will act. We are sadly mistaken if we feel that the election of Albert Boutwell as mayor will bring the millennium to Birmingham. While Mr. Boutwell is a much more gentle person than Mr. Connor, they are both segregationists, dedicated to maintenance of the status quo. I have hope that Mr. Boutwell will be reasonable enough to see the futility of massive resistance to desegregation. But he will not see this without pressure from devotees of civil rights. My friends, I must say to you that we have not made a single gain in civil rights without determined legal and nonviolent pressure. Lamentably, it is an historical fact that privileged groups seldom give up their privileges voluntarily. Individuals may see the moral light and voluntarily give up their unjust posture; but, as Reinhold Niebuhr has reminded us, groups tend to be more immoral than individuals.

We know through painful experience that freedom is never voluntarily given by the oppressor; it must be demanded by the oppressed. Frankly, I have yet to engage in a direct-action campaign that was "well timed" in the view of those who have not suffered unduly from the disease of segregation. For years now I have heard the word "Wait!" It rings in the ear of every Negro with piercing familiarity. This "Wait" has almost always meant "Never." We must come to see, with one of our distinguished jurists, that "justice too long delayed is justice denied."

We have waited for more than 340 years for our constitutional and God-given rights. The nations of Asia and Africa are moving with jetlike speed toward gaining political independence, but we still creep at horse-and-buggy pace toward gaining a cup of coffee at a lunch counter. Perhaps it is easy for those who have never felt the stinging darts of segregation to say, "Wait." But when you have seen vicious mobs lynch your mothers and fathers at will and drown your sisters and brothers at whim; when you have seen hate-filled policemen curse, kick and even kill your black brothers and sisters; when you see the vast majority of your twenty million Negro brothers smothering in an airtight cage of poverty in the midst of an affluent society; when you suddenly find your tongue twisted and your speech stammering as you seek to explain to your six-year-old daughter why she can't go to the public amusement park that has just been advertised on television, and see tears welling up in her eyes when she is told that Funtown is closed to colored children, and see ominous clouds of inferiority beginning to form in her little mental sky, and see her beginning to distort her personality by developing an unconscious bitterness toward white people; when you have to concoct an answer for a five-year-old son who is asking: "Daddy, why do white people treat colored people so mean?"; when you take a cross-country drive and find it necessary to sleep night after night in the uncomfortable corners of your automobile because no motel will accept you; when you are humiliated day in and day out by nagging signs reading "white" and "colored"; when your first name becomes "nigger," your middle name becomes "boy" (however old you are) and your last name becomes "John," and your wife and mother are never given the respected title "Mrs."; when you are harried by day and haunted by night by the fact that you are a Negro, living constantly at tiptoe stance, never quite knowing what to expect next, and are plagued with inner fears and outer resentments; when you are forever fighting a degenerating sense of "nobodiness"—then you will understand why we find it difficult to wait. There comes a time when the cup of endurance runs over, and men are no longer willing to be plunged into the abyss of despair. I hope, sirs, you can understand our legitimate and unavoidable impatience.

You express a great deal of anxiety over our willingness to break laws. This is certainly a legitimate concern. Since we so diligently urge people to obey the Supreme Court's decision of 1954 outlawing segregation in the public schools, at first glance it may seem rather paradoxical for us consciously to break laws. One may well ask: "How can you advocate breaking some laws and obeying others?" The answer lies in the fact that there are two types of laws: just and unjust. I would be the first to advocate obeying just laws. One has not only a legal but a moral responsibility to obey just laws. Conversely, one has a moral responsibility to disobey unjust laws. I would agree with St. Augustine that "an unjust law is no law at all."

Now, what is the difference between the two? How does one determine whether a law is just or unjust? A just law is a man-made code that squares with the moral law or the law of God. An unjust law is a code that is out of harmony with the moral law. To put it in the terms of St. Thomas Aquinas: An unjust law is a human law that is not rooted in eternal law and natural law. Any law that uplifts human personality is just. Any law that degrades human personality is unjust. All segregation statutes are unjust because segregation distorts the soul and damages the personality. It gives the segregator a false sense of superiority and the segregated a false sense of inferiority. Segregation, to use the terminology of the Jewish philosopher Martin Buber, substitutes an "I-it" relationship for an "I-thou" relationship and ends up relegating persons to the status of things. Hence segregation is not only politically, economically and sociologically unsound, it is morally wrong and sinful. Paul Tillich has said that sin is separation. Is not segregation an existential expression of man's tragic separation, his awful estrangement, his terrible sinfulness? Thus it is that I can urge men to obey the 1954 decision of the Supreme Court, for it is morally right; and I can urge, them to disobey segregation ordinances, for they are morally wrong.

Let us consider a more concrete example of just and unjust laws. An unjust law is a code that a numerical or power majority group compels a minority group to obey but does not make binding on itself. This is difference made legal. By the same token, a just law is a code that a majority compels a minority to follow and that it is willing to follow itself. This is sameness made legal.

Let me give another explanation. A law is unjust if it is inflicted on a minority that, as a result of being denied the right to vote, had no part in enacting or devising the law. Who can say that the legislature of Alabama which set up that state's segregation laws was democratically elected? Throughout Alabama all sorts of devious methods are used to prevent Negroes from becoming registered voters, and there are some counties in which, even though Negroes constitute a majority of the population, not a single Negro is registered. Can any law enacted under such circumstances be considered democratically structured?

Sometimes a law is just on its face and unjust in its application. For instance, I have been arrested on a charge of parading without a permit. Now, there is nothing wrong in having an ordinance which requires a permit for a parade. But such an ordinance becomes unjust when it is used to maintain segregation and to deny citizens the First-Amendment privilege of peaceful assembly and protest.

I hope you are able to see the distinction I am trying to point out. In no sense do I advocate evading or defying the law, as would the rabid segregationist. That would lead to anarchy. One who breaks an unjust law must do so openly, lovingly, and with a willingness to accept the penalty. I submit that an individual who breaks a law that conscience tells him is unjust, and who willingly accepts the penalty of imprisonment in order to arouse the conscience of the community over its injustice, is in reality expressing the highest respect for law.

Of course, there is nothing new about this kind of civil disobedience. It was evidenced sublimely in the refusal of Shadrach, Meshach and Abednego to obey the laws of Nebuchadnezzar, on the ground that a higher moral law was at stake. It was practiced superbly by the early Christians, who were willing to face hungry lions and the excruciating pain of chopping blocks rather than submit to certain unjust laws of the Roman Empire. To a degree, academic freedom is a reality today because Socrates practiced civil disobedience. In our own nation, the Boston Tea Party represented a massive act of civil disobedience.

We should never forget that everything Adolf Hitler did in Germany was "legal" and everything the Hungarian freedom fighters did in Hungary was "illegal." It was "illegal" to aid and comfort a Jew in Hitler's Germany. Even so, I am sure that, had I lived in Germany at the time, I would have aided and comforted my Jewish brothers. If today I lived in a Communist country where certain principles dear to the Christian faith are suppressed, I would openly advocate disobeying that country's antireligious laws.

I must make two honest confessions to you, my Christian and Jewish brothers. First, I must confess that over the past few years I have been gravely disappointed with the white moderate. I have almost reached the regrettable conclusion that the Negro's great stumbling block in his stride toward freedom is not the White Citizen's Counciler or the Ku Klux Klanner, but the white moderate, who is more devoted to "order" than to justice; who prefers a negative peace which is the absence of tension to a positive peace which is the presence of justice; who constantly says: "I agree with you in the goal you seek, but I cannot agree with your methods of direct action"; who paternalistically believes he can set the timetable for another man's freedom; who lives by a mythical concept of time and who constantly advises the Negro to wait for a "more convenient season." Shallow understanding from people of good will is more frustrating than absolute misunderstanding from people of ill will. Lukewarm acceptance is much more bewildering than outright rejection.

I had hoped that the white moderate would understand that law and order exist for the purpose of establishing justice and that when they fail in this purpose they become the dangerously structured dams that block the flow of social progress. I had hoped that the white moderate would understand that the present tension in the South is a necessary phase of the transition from an obnoxious negative peace, in which the Negro passively accepted his unjust plight, to a substantive and positive peace, in which all men will respect the dignity and worth of human personality. Actually, we who engage in nonviolent direct action are not the creators of tension. We merely bring to the surface the hidden tension that is already alive. We bring it out in the open, where it can be seen and dealt with. Like a boil that can never be cured so long as it is covered up but must be opened with all its ugliness to the natural medicines of air and light, injustice must be exposed, with all the tension its exposure creates, to the light of human conscience and the air of national opinion before it can be cured.

In your statement you assert that our actions, even though peaceful, must be condemned because they precipitate violence. But is this a logical assertion? Isn't this like condemning a robbed man because his possession of money precipitated the evil act of robbery? Isn't this like condemning Socrates because his unswerving commitment to truth and his philosophical inquiries precipitated the act by the misguided populace in which they made him drink hemlock? Isn't this like condemning Jesus because his unique God-consciousness and never-ceasing devotion to God's will precipitated the evil act of crucifixion? We must come to see that, as the federal courts have consistently affirmed, it is wrong to urge an individual to cease his efforts to gain his basic constitutional rights because the quest may precipitate violence. Society must protect the robbed and punish the robber.

I had also hoped that the white moderate would reject the myth concerning time in relation to the struggle for freedom. I have just received a letter from a white brother in Texas. He writes: "All Christians know that the colored people will receive equal rights eventually, but it is possible that you are in too great a religious hurry. It has taken Christianity almost two thousand years to accomplish what it has. The teachings of Christ take time to come to earth." Such an attitude stems from a tragic misconception of time, from the strangely irrational notion that there is something in the very flow of time that will inevitably cure all ills. Actually, time itself is neutral; it can be used either destructively or constructively. More and more I feel that the people of ill will have used time much more effectively than have the people of good will. We will have to repent in this generation not merely for the hateful words and actions of the bad people but for the appalling silence of the good people. Human progress never rolls in on wheels of inevitability; it comes through the tireless efforts of men willing to be co-workers with God, and without this hard work, time itself becomes an ally of the forces of social stagnation. We must use time creatively, in the knowledge that the time is always ripe to do right. Now is the time to make real the promise of democracy and transform our pending national elegy into a creative psalm of brotherhood. Now is the time to lift our national policy from the quicksand of racial injustice to the solid rock of human dignity.

You speak of our activity in Birmingham as extreme. At first I was rather disappointed that fellow clergymen would see my nonviolent efforts as those of an extremist. I began thinking about the fact that I stand in the middle of two opposing forces in the Negro community. One is a force of complacency, made up in part of Negroes who, as a result of long years of oppression, are so drained of self-respect and a sense of "somebodiness" that they have adjusted to segregation; and in part of a few middle-class Negroes who, because of a degree of academic and economic security and because in some ways they profit by segregation, have become insensitive to the problems of the masses. The other force is one of bitterness and hatred, and it comes perilously close to advocating violence. It is expressed in the various black nationalist groups that are springing up across the nation, the largest and best-known being Elijah Muhammad's Muslim movement. Nourished by the Negro's frustration over the continued existence of racial discrimination, this movement is made up of people who have lost faith in America, who have absolutely repudiated Christianity, and who have concluded that the white man is an incorrigible "devil."

I have tried to stand between these two forces, saying that we need emulate neither the "do-nothingism" of the complacent nor the hatred and despair of the black nationalist. For there is the more excellent way of love and non-violent protest. I am grateful to God that, through the influence of the Negro church, the way of nonviolence became an integral part of our struggle.

If this philosophy had not emerged, by now many streets of the South would, I am convinced, be flowing with blood. And I am further convinced that if our white brothers dismiss as "rabble-rousers" and "outside agitators" those of us who employ nonviolent direct action, and if they refuse to support our nonviolent efforts, millions of Negroes will, out of frustration and despair, seek solace and security in black-nationalist ideologies—a development that would inevitably lead to a frightening racial nightmare.

Oppressed people cannot remain oppressed forever. The yearning for free-dom eventually manifests itself, and that is what has happened to the American Negro. Something within has reminded him of his birthright of freedom, and something without has reminded him that it can be gained. Consciously or unconsciously, he has been caught up by the Zeitgeist, and with his black brothers of Africa and his brown and yellow brothers of Asia, South America and the Caribbean, the United States Negro is moving with a sense of great urgency toward the promised land of racial justice. If one recognizes this vital urge that has engulfed the Negro community, one should readily understand why public demonstrations are taking place. The Negro has many pent-up resentments and latent frustrations, and he must release them. So let him march; let him make prayer pilgrimages to the city hall; let him go on freedom rides—and try to understand why he must do so. If his repressed emotions are not released in nonviolent ways, they will seek expression through violence; this is not a threat but a fact of history. So I have not said to my people: "Get rid of your discontent." Rather, I have tried to say that this normal and healthy discontent can be channeled into the creative outlet of nonviolent direct action. And now this approach is being termed extremist.

But though I was initially disappointed at being categorized as an extremist, as I continued to think about the matter I gradually gained a measure of satisfaction from the label. Was not Jesus an extremist for love: "Love your enemies, bless them that curse you, do good to them that hate you, and pray for them which despitefully use you, and persecute you." Was not Amos an extremist for justice: "Let justice roll down like waters and righteousness like an ever-flowing stream." Was not Paul an extremist for the Christian gospel: "I bear in my body the marks of the Lord Jesus." Was not Martin Luther an extremist: "Here I stand; I cannot do otherwise, so help me God." And John Bunyan: "I will stay in jail to the end of my days before I make a butchery of my conscience." And Abraham Lincoln: "This nation cannot survive half slave and half free." And Thomas Jefferson: "We hold these truths to be self-evident, that all men are created equal ..." So the question is not whether we will be extremists, but what kind of extremists we will be. Will we be extremists for hate or for love? Will we be extremists for the preservation of injustice or for the extension of justice? In that dramatic scene on Calvary's hill three men were crucified. We must never forget that all three were crucified for the same crime —the crime of extremism. Two were extremists for immorality, and thus fell below their environment. The other, Jesus Christ, was an extremist for love, truth, and goodness, and thereby rose above his environment. Perhaps the South, the nation and the world are in dire need of creative extremists.

I had hoped that the white moderate would see this need. Perhaps I was too optimistic; perhaps I expected too much. I suppose I should have realized that few members of the oppressor race can understand the deep groans and passionate yearnings of the oppressed race, and still fewer have the vision to see that injustice must be rooted out by strong, persistent and determined action. I am thankful, however, that some of our white brothers in the South have grasped the meaning of this social revolution and committed themselves to it. They are still all too few in quantity, but they are big in quality. Some— such as Ralph McGill, Lillian Smith, Harry Golden, James McBride Dabbs, Ann Braden and Sarah Patton Boyle —have written about our struggle in eloquent and prophetic terms. Others have marched with us down nameless streets of the South. They have languished in filthy, roach-infested jails, suffering the abuse and brutality of policemen who view them as "dirty nigger-lovers." Unlike so many of their moderate brothers and sisters, they have recognized the urgency of the moment and sensed the need for powerful "action" antidotes to combat the disease of segregation.

Let me take note of my other major disappointment. I have been so greatly disappointed with the white church and its leadership. Of course, there are some notable exceptions. I am not unmindful of the fact that each of you has taken some significant stands on this issue. I commend you, Reverend Stallings, for your Christian stand on this past Sunday, in welcoming Negroes to your worship service on a nonsegregated basis. I commend the Catholic leaders of this state for integrating Spring Hill College several years ago.

But despite these notable exceptions, I must honestly reiterate that I have been disappointed with the church. I do not say this as one of those negative critics who can always find something wrong with the church. I say this as a minister of the gospel, who loves the church; who was nurtured in its bosom; who has been sustained by its spiritual blessings and who will remain true to it as long as the cord of life shall lengthen.

When I was suddenly catapulted into the leadership of the bus protest in Montgomery, Alabama, a few years ago, I felt we would be supported by the white church. I felt that the white ministers, priests and rabbis of the South would be among our strongest allies. Instead, some have been outright opponents, refusing to understand the freedom movement and misrepresenting its leaders; all too many others have been more cautious than courageous and have remained silent behind the anesthetizing security of stained-glass windows.

In spite of my shattered dreams, I came to Birmingham with the hope that the white religious leadership of this community would see the justice of our cause and, with deep moral concern, would serve as the channel through which our just grievances could reach the power structure. I had hoped that each of you would understand. But again I have been disappointed.

I have heard numerous southern religious leaders admonish their worshipers to comply with a desegregation decision because it is the law, but I have longed to hear white ministers declare: "Follow this decree because integration is morally right and because the Negro is your brother." In the midst of blatant injustices inflicted upon the Negro, I have watched white churchmen stand on the sideline and mouth pious irrelevancies and sanctimonious trivialities. In the midst of a mighty struggle to rid our nation of racial and economic injustice, I have heard many ministers say: "Those are social issues, with which the gospel has no real concern." And I have watched many churches commit themselves to a completely otherworldly religion which makes a strange, un-Biblical distinction between body and soul, between the sacred and the secular.

I have traveled the length and breadth of Alabama, Mississippi and all the other southern states. On sweltering summer days and crisp autumn mornings I have looked at the South's beautiful churches with their lofty spires pointing heavenward. I have beheld the impressive outlines of her massive religious-education buildings. Over and over I have found myself asking: "What kind of people worship here? Who is their God? Where were their voices when the lips of Governor Barnett dripped with words of interposition and nullification? Where were they when Governor Wallace gave a clarion call for defiance and hatred? Where were their voices of support when bruised and weary Negro men and women decided to rise from the dark dungeons of complacency to the bright hills of creative protest?"

Yes, these questions are still in my mind. In deep disappointment I have wept over the laxity of the church. But be assured that my tears have been tears of love. There can be no deep disappointment where there is not deep love. Yes, I love the church. How could I do otherwise? I am in the rather unique position of being the son, the grandson and the great-grandson of preachers. Yes, I see the church as the body of Christ. But, oh! How we have blemished and scarred that body through social neglect and through fear of being non-conformists.

There was a time when the church was very powerful—in the time when the early Christians rejoiced at being deemed worthy to suffer for what they believed. In those days the church was not merely a thermometer that recorded the ideas and principles of popular opinion; it was a thermostat that transformed the mores of society. Whenever the early Christians entered a town, the people in power became disturbed and immediately sought to convict the Christians for being "disturbers of the peace" and "outside agitators." But the Christians pressed on, in the conviction that they were "a colony of heaven," called to obey God rather than man. Small in number, they were big in commitment. They were too God-intoxicated to be "astronomically intimidated." By their effort and example they brought an end to such ancient evils as infanticide and gladiatorial contests.

Things are different now. So often the contemporary church is a weak, ineffectual voice with an uncertain sound. So often it is an archdefender of the status quo. Far from being disturbed by the presence of the church, the power structure of the average community is consoled by the church's silent—and often even vocal—sanction of things as they are.

But the judgment of God is upon the church as never before. If today's church does not recapture the sacrificial spirit of the early church, it will lose its authenticity, forfeit the loyalty of millions, and be dismissed as an irrelevant social club with no meaning for the twentieth century. Every day I meet young people whose disappointment with the church has turned into outright disgust.

Perhaps I have once again been too optimistic. Is organized religion too inextricably bound to the status quo to save our nation and the world? Perhaps I must turn my faith to the inner spiritual church, the church within the church, as the true *ekklesia* and the hope of the world. But again I am thankful to God that some noble souls from the ranks of organized religion have broken loose from the paralyzing chains of conformity and joined us as active partners in the struggle for freedom. They have left their secure congregations and walked the streets of Albany, Georgia, with us. They have gone down the highways of the South on tortuous rides for freedom. Yes, they have gone to jail with us. Some have been dismissed from their churches, have lost the support of their bishops and fellow ministers. But they have acted in the faith that right defeated is stronger than evil triumphant. Their witness has been the spiritual salt that has preserved the true meaning of the gospel in these troubled times. They have carved a tunnel of hope through the dark mountain of disappointment.

I hope the church as a whole will meet the challenge of this decisive hour. But even if the church does not come to the aid of justice, I have no despair about the future. I have no fear about the outcome of our struggle in Birmingham, even if our motives are at present misunderstood. We will reach the goal of freedom in Birmingham and all over the nation, because the goal of America is freedom. Abused and scorned though we may be, our destiny is tied up with America's destiny. Before the pilgrims landed at Plymouth, we were here. Before the pen of Jefferson etched the majestic words of the Declaration of Independence across the pages of history, we were here. For more than two centuries our forebears labored in this country without wages; they made cotton king; they built the homes of their masters while suffering gross injustice and shameful humiliation—and yet out of a bottomless vitality they continued to thrive and develop. If the inexpressible cruelties of slavery could not stop us, the opposition we now face will surely fail. We will win our freedom because the sacred heritage of our nation and the eternal will of God are embodied in our echoing demands.

Before closing I feel impelled to mention one other point in your statement that has troubled me profoundly. You warmly commended the Birmingham police force for keeping "order" and "preventing violence." I doubt that you would have so warmly commended the police force if you had seen its dogs sinking their teeth into unarmed, nonviolent Negroes. I doubt that you would so quickly commend the policemen if you were to observe their ugly and inhumane treatment of Negroes here in the city jail; if you were to watch them push and curse old Negro women and young Negro girls; if you were to see them slap and kick old Negro men and young boys; if you were to observe them, as they did on two occasions, refuse to give us food because we wanted to sing our grace together. I cannot join you in your praise of the Birmingham police department.

It is true that the police have exercised a degree of discipline in handling the demonstrators. In this sense they have conducted themselves rather "nonviolently" in public. But for what purpose? To preserve the evil system of segregation. Over the past few years I have consistently preached that nonviolence demands that the means we use must be as pure as the ends we seek. I have tried to make clear that it is wrong to use immoral means to attain moral ends. But now I must affirm that it is just as wrong, or perhaps even more so, to use moral means to preserve immoral ends. Perhaps Mr. Connor and his policemen have been rather nonviolent in public, as was Chief Pritchett in Albany, Georgia, but they have used the moral means of nonviolence to maintain the immoral end of racial injustice. As T. S. Eliot has said: "The last temptation is the greatest treason: To do the right deed for the wrong reason."

I wish you had commended the Negro sit-inners and demonstrators of Birmingham for their sublime courage, their willingness to suffer and their amazing discipline in the midst of great provocation. One day the South will recognize its real heroes. They will be the James Merediths, with the noble sense of purpose that enables them to face jeering and hostile mobs, and with the agonizing loneliness that characterizes the life of the pioneer. They will be old, oppressed, battered Negro women, symbolized in a seventy-two-year-old woman in Montgomery, Alabama, who rose up with a sense of dignity and with her people decided not to ride segregated buses, and who responded with ungrammatical profundity to one who inquired about her weariness: "My feets is tired, but my soul is at rest." They will be the young high school and college students, the young ministers of the gospel and a host of their elders, courageously and nonviolently sitting in at lunch counters and willingly going to jail for conscience' sake. One day the South will know that when these disinherited children of God sat down at lunch counters, they were in reality standing up for what is best in the American dream and for the most sacred values in our Judaeo-Christian heritage, thereby bringing our nation back to those great wells of democracy which were dug deep by the founding fathers in their formulation of the Constitution and the Declaration of Independence.

Never before have I written so long a letter. I'm afraid it is much too long to take your precious time. I can assure you that it would have been much shorter if I had been writing from a comfortable desk, but what else can one do when he is alone in a narrow jail cell, other than write long letters, think long thoughts and pray long prayers?

If I have said anything in this letter that overstates the truth and indicates an unreasonable impatience, I beg you to forgive me. If I have said anything that understates the truth and indicates my having a patience that allows me to settle for anything less than brotherhood, I beg God to forgive me.

I hope this letter finds you strong in the faith. I also hope that circumstances will soon make it possible for me to meet each of you, not as an integrationist or a civil-rights leader but as a fellow clergyman and a Christian brother. Let us all hope that the dark clouds of racial prejudice will soon pass away and the deep fog of misunderstanding will be lifted from our fear-drenched communities, and in some not too distant tomorrow the radiant stars of love and brotherhood will shine over our great nation with all their scintillating beauty.

Yours for the cause of Peace and Brotherhood,

MARTIN LUTHER KING, JR.

Black Political Action in the South

Life in Mississippi:
An Interview with Fannie Lou Hamer

The Mississippi Freedom Democratic Party (MFDP) was organized in the spring of 1964 in order to provide a political voice for blacks in the state who were deprived of a voice in the regular party. The MFDP elected delegates to the Democratic National Convention in August and demanded that they be seated. Although it was disappointed in its attempt to gain seats for its delegates and real representation at the convention for the black Democrats of Mississippi, the incident brought useful publicity to the struggle for civil rights in the Deep South.

Fannie Lou Hamer was one of the delegates of the MFDP to the National Convention, and her speech before the Credentials Committee in August was carried over national television. When she described how Mississippi policemen had beaten her as she tried to register to vote, the entire nation heard.

Following is an interview with Mrs. Hamer conducted by J. H. O'Dell, an editor of Freedomways. *In it, she describes the dangers involved in threatening the status quo in her home state and indicates her intention to plunge ahead with the work for change.*

O'DELL*:* Mrs. Hamer, it's good to see you again. I understand you have been to Africa since we last talked? I would like for you to talk about your African trip today.

HAMER*:* It was one of the proudest moments in my life.

O'DELL*:* That is a marvelous experience for any black American particularly for anyone who has lived here all of his life. Then, too, we want to talk about some of your early childhood experiences which helped to make you the kind of person you are and provided the basis for your becoming so active in the Freedom Movement.

HAMER*:* I would like to talk about some of the things that happened that made me know that there was something wrong in the South from a child. My parents moved to Sunflower County when I was two years old. I remember, and I will never forget, one day—I was six years old and I was playing beside the road and this plantation owner drove up to me and stopped and asked me "could I pick cotton." I told him I

FROM "Life in Mississippi: An Interview with Fannie Lou Hamer." Reprinted from *Freedomways*, vol. 5, no. 2, 1965.

didn't know and he said, "Yes, you can. I will give you things that you want from the commissary store," and he named things like cracker-jacks and sardines—and it was a huge list that he called off. So I picked the 30 pounds of cotton that week, but I found out what actually happened was he was trapping me into beginning the work I was to keep doing and I never did get out of his debt again. My parents tried so hard to do what they could to keep us in school, but school didn't last but four months out of the year and most of the time we didn't have clothes to wear. My parents would make huge crops of sometimes 55 to 60 bales of cotton. Being from a big family where there were 20 children, it wasn't too hard to pick that much cotton. But my father, year after year, didn't get too much money and I remember he just kept going. Later on he did get enough money to buy mules. We didn't have tractors, but he bought mules, wagons, cultivators and some farming equipment. As soon as he bought that and decided to rent some land, because it was always better if you rent the land, but as soon as he got the mules and wagons and everything, somebody went to our trough— a white man who didn't live very far from us—and he fed the mules Paris Green, put it in their food and it killed the mules and our cows. That knocked us right back down. And things got so tough then I began to wish I was white. We worked all the time, just worked and then we would be hungry and my mother was clearing up a new ground trying to help to feed us for $1.25 a day. She was using an axe, just like a man, and something flew up and hit her in the eye. It eventually caused her to lose both her eyes and I began to get sicker and sicker of the system there. I used to see my mother wear clothes that would have so many patches on them, they had been done over and over and over again. She would do that but she would try to keep us decent. She still would be ragged and I always said if I lived to get grown and had a chance, I was going to try to get something for my mother and I was going to do something for the black man of the South if it would cost my life; I was determined to see that things were changed. My mother got down sick in '53 and she lived with me, an invalid, until she passed away in 1961. And during the time she was staying with me sometime I would be worked so hard I couldn't sleep at night. ...

O'DELL: What kind of work were you doing?

HAMER: I was a timekeeper and sharecropper on the same plantation I was fired from. During the time she was with me, if there was something I had to do without, I was determined to see that she did have something in her last few years. I went almost naked to see that my mother was kept decent and treated as a human being for the first time in all of her life. My mother was a great woman. To look at her from the suffering she had gone through to bring us up—20 children: 6 girls and 14 boys, but still she taught us to be decent and to respect ourselves, and that is one of the things that has kept me going, even after she passed. She tried so hard to make life easy for us. Those are the things that forced me to try to do something different and when this Movement came to Mississippi I still feel it is one of the greatest things that ever happened because only a person living in the State of Mississippi knows what it is like to suffer; knows what it is like to be hungry; knows what it is like to have no clothing to wear. And these people in Mississippi State, they are not "down"; all they need is a chance. And I am determined to give my part not for what the Movement can do for me, but what I can do for the Movement to bring about a change in the State of Mississippi. Actually, some of the things I experienced as a child still linger on; what the white man has done to the black people in the South!

One of the things I remember as a child: There was a man named Joe Pulliam. He was a great Christian man; but one time, he was living with a white family and this white family robbed him of what he earned. They didn't pay him anything. This white man gave him $150 to go to the hill, (you see, I lived in the Black Belt of Mississippi) ... to get another Negro family. Joe Pulliam knew what this white man had been doing to him so he kept the $150 and didn't go. This white man talked with him then shot him in the shoulder and Joe Pulliam went back into the house and got a Winchester and killed this white man. The other white fellow that was with him he "outrun the word of God" back to town. That gave this Negro a chance to go down on the bayou that was called Powers Bayou and he got in a hollowed-out stump where there was enough room for a person. He got in there and he stayed and was tracked there, but they couldn't see him and every time a white man would peep out, he busted him. He killed 13 white men and wounded 26 and Mississippi was a quiet place for a long time. I remember that until this day and I won't forget it. After they couldn't get him, they took gas—one man from Clarksdale used a machine gun—(Bud Doggins)—they used a machine gun and they tried to get him like that and then they took gas and poured it on Powers Bayou. Thousands of gallons of gas and they lit it and when it burned up to the hollowed-out stump, he crawled out. When they found him, he was unconscious and he was lying with his head on his gun but the last bullet in the gun had been snapped twice. They dragged him by his heels on the back of a car and they paraded about with that man and they cut his ears off and put them in a showcase and it stayed there a long, long time—in Drew, Mississippi. All of those things, when they would happen, would make me sick in the pit of my stomach and year after year, everytime something would happen it would make me more and more aware of what would have to be done in the State of Mississippi.

O'DELL: What do you think will have to be done? .

HAMER: The only thing I really feel is necessary is that the black people, not only in Mississippi, will have to actually upset this applecart. What

I mean by that is, so many things are under the cover that will have to be swept out and shown to this whole world, not just to America. There is so much hypocrisy in America. This thing they say of "the land of the free and the home of the brave" is all on paper. It doesn't mean anything to us. The only way we can make this thing a reality in America is to do all we can to destroy this system and bring this thing out to the light that has been under the cover all these years. That's why I believe in Christianity because the Scriptures said: "The things that have been done in the dark will be known on the house tops."

Now many things are beginning to come out and it was truly a reality to me when I went to Africa, to Guinea. The little things that had been taught to me about the African people, that they were "heathens," "savages," and they were just downright stupid people. But when I got to Guinea, we were greeted by the Government of Guinea, which is *Black People*—and we stayed at a place that was the government building, because we were the guests of the Government. You don't know what that meant to me when I got to Guinea on the 12th of September. The President of Guinea, Sekou Touré came to see us on the 13th. Now you know, I don't know how you can compare this by me being able to see a President of a country, when I have just been there two days; and here I have been in America, born in America, and I am 46 years pleading with the President for the last two to three years to just give us a chance —and this President in Guinea recognized us enough to talk to us.

O'DELL: How many were in your delegation?

HAMER: It was eleven of us during that time, and I could get a clear picture of actually what had happened to the black people of America. Our foreparents were mostly brought from West Africa, the same place that we visited in Africa. We were brought to America and our foreparents were sold; white people bought them; white people changed their names … and actually … here, my maiden name is supposed to be Townsend; but really, what is my maiden name …? What is my name? This white man who is saying "it takes time." For three hundred and more years they have had "time," and now it is time for them to listen. We have been listening year after year to them and what have we got? We are not even allowed to think for ourselves. "I know what is best for you," but they don't know what is best for us! It is time now to let them know what they owe us, and they owe us a great deal. Not only have we paid the price with our names in ink, but we have also paid in blood. And they can't say that black people can't be intelligent, because going back to Africa, in Guinea, there are almost 4 million people there and what he, President Touré, is doing to educate the people: as long as the French people had it they weren't doing a thing that is being done now. I met one child there eleven years old, speaking three languages. He could speak English, French and Malinke. Speaking my language actually better than I could. And this hypocrisy—they tell us here in America. People should go there and see. It would bring tears in your eyes to make you think of all those years, the type of brain-washing that this man will use in America to keep us separated from our own people. When I got on that plane, it was loaded with white people going to Africa for the Peace Corps. I got there and met a lot of them, and actually they had more peace there in Guinea than I have here. I talked to some of them. I told them before they would be able to clean up somebody else's house you would have to clean up yours; before they can tell somebody else how to run their country, why don't they do something here. This problem is not only in Mississippi. During the time I was in the Convention in Atlantic City, I didn't get any threats from Mississippi. The threatening letters were from Philadelphia, Chicago and other big cities.

O'DELL: You received threatening letters while you were at the Convention?

HAMER: Yes. I got pictures of us and they would draw big red rings around us and tell what they thought of us. I got a letter said, "I have been shot three times through the heart. I hope I see your second act." But this white man who wants to stay *white*, and to think for the Negro, he is not only destroying the Negro, he is destroying himself, because a house divided against itself cannot stand and that same thing applies to America. America that is divided against itself cannot stand, and we cannot say we have all this unity they say we have when black people are being discriminated against in every city in America I have visited.

I was in jail when Medgar Evers was murdered and *nothing*, I mean *nothing* has been done about that. You know what really made me sick? I was in Washington, D.C. at another time reading in a paper where the U.S. gives Byron de la Beckwith—the man who is charged with murdering Medgar Evers—they were giving him so much money for some land and I ask "Is this America?" We can no longer ignore the fact that America is NOT the "land of the free and the home of the brave." I used to question this for years—what did our kids actually fight for? They would go in the service and go through all of that and come right out to be drowned in a river in Mississippi. I found this hypocrisy is all over America.

The 20th of March in 1964, I went before the Secretary of State to qualify to run as an official candidate for Congress from the 2nd Congressional District, and it was easier for me to qualify to run than it was for me to pass the literacy test to be a registered voter. And we had four people to qualify and run in the June primary election but we didn't have enough Negroes registered in Mississippi. The 2nd Congressional District where I ran, against Jamie Whitten, is made up of 24 counties. Sixty-eight percent of the people are Negroes, only 6–8 percent are registered. And it is not because Negroes don't want to register. They try and they try and they try. That's why it was important for us to set up the "Freedom Registration" to help us in the Freedom Democratic Party.

O'DELL: This was a registration drive organized by the Movement?

HAMER: Yes. The only thing we took out was the Constitution of the State of Mississippi and the interpretation of the Constitution. We had 63,000 people registered on the Freedom Registration form. And we tried from every level to go into the regular Democratic Party medium. We tried from the precinct level. The 16th of June when they were holding precinct meetings all across the state, I was there and there was eight of us there to attend the meeting, and they had the door locked at 10 o'clock in the morning. So we had our own meeting and elected our permanent chairman and secretary and regulars and alternates and we passed a resolution as the law requires and then mailed it to Oscar Townsend, our permanent chairman. This is what's happening in the State of Mississippi. We had hoped for a change, but these people (Congressmen) go to Washington and stay there 25 and 30 years and more without representing the people of Mississippi. We have never been represented in Washington. You can tell this by the program the federal government had to train 2,400 tractor drivers. They would have trained Negro and white together, but this man, Congressman Jamie Whitten, voted against it and everything that was decent. So, we've got to have somebody in Washington who is concerned about the people of Mississippi.

After we testified before the Credentials Committee in Atlantic City, their Mississippi representative testified also. He said I got 600 votes but when they made the count in Mississippi, I was told I had 388 votes. So actually it is no telling how many votes I actually got.

O'DELL: In other words, a Mr. Collins came before the Credentials Committee of the Democratic National Convention and actually gave away the secret in a sense, because the figure he gave was not the same figure he gave to you as an official candidate?

HAMER: That's right. He also said I had been allowed to attend the precinct meeting which was true. But he didn't say we were locked out of the polling place there and had to hold our meeting on the lawn.

O'DELL: So now you have a situation where you had the basis for a Freedom Democratic Party. You have had four candidates to run for Congress. You had a community election where 63,000 of our folk showed their interest in the election. How do you size up the situation coming out of Atlantic City? What impressions did you get from your effort in Atlantic City to be seated, and how do you feel the people back home are going to react to this next period you are going into?

HAMER: The people at home will work hard and actually all of them think it was important that we made the decision that we did make *not to compromise*; because we didn't have anything to *compromise* for. Some things I found out in the National Convention I wasn't too glad I did find out. But we will work hard, and it was important to actually really bring this out to the open, the things I will say some people knew about and some people didn't; this stuff that has been kept under the cover for so many years. Actually, the world and America is upset and the only way to bring about a change is to upset it more.

O'DELL: What was done about the beating you and Miss Annelle Ponder, your colleague in the citizenship school program, experienced while in jail? Was any action taken at all?

HAMER: The Justice Department filed a suit against the brutality of the five law officials and they had this trial. The trial began the 2nd of December 1963 and they had white jurors from the State of Mississippi, and the Federal Judge Clayton made it plain to the jurors that they were dealing with "nigras" and that "who would actually accuse such upstanding people like those law officials"—be careful what they was doing because they are law-abiding citizens and were dealing with agitators and niggers. It was as simple as that. And those police were cleared. They were on the loose for about a week before I left for Atlantic City. One of those men was driving a truck from the State Penitentiary. One night he passed my house and pointed me out to one of the other men in the State Penitentiary truck and that same night I got a threat: "We got you located Fannie Lou and we going to put you in the Mississippi River." A lot of people say why do they let the *hoodlums* do that? But it is those people supposed to have class that are doing the damage in Mississippi. You know there was a time, in different places, when people felt safe going to a law official. But I called them that day and got the answer back, "You know you don't look to us for help."

O'DELL: This threat: the man called you up and said "we've got you spotted"; I gather from that that the river has some special meaning to us living there in Mississippi?

HAMER: Yes. So many people have been killed and put in the Mississippi River. Like when they began to drag the river for Mickey and Chaney and Andy.[1] Before he was to go to Oxford, Ohio, Mickey was telling me his life had been threatened and a taxi driver had told him to be careful because they was out to get him.

When they (the sailors) began to drag the river they found other people and I actually feel like they stopped because they would have been shook up to find so many if they had just been fishing for bodies. The Mississippi is not the only river. There's the Tallahatchie and the Big Black. People have been put in the river year after year, these things *been* happening.

---

[1] Michael Schwerner, James Chaney and Andrew Goodman.

O'DELL: The general policy of striking fear in people's hearts. In other words, it is like lynching used to be. They used to night ride. ...

HAMER: They still night ride. The exact count was 32 churches they had burned in the State of Mississippi and they still ride at night. and throw bombs at night. You would think they would cut down with Mrs. Chaney. But since they murdered James Chaney, they have shot buckshot at his mother's house. And hate won't only destroy us. It will destroy these people that's hating as well. And one of the things is, they are afraid of getting back what they have been putting out all of these years. You know the Scripture says "be not deceived for God is not mocked; whatsoever a man sow that shall he also reap." And *one day*, I don't know how they're going to get it, but they're going to get some of it back. They are scared to death and are more afraid now than we are.

O'DELL: How active is the White Citizen's Council? Has it the kind of outlet through TV and radio and so forth that Negroes are aware of its presence?

HAMER: They announce their programs. In fact, one day I was going to Jackson and I saw a huge sign that U.S. Senator John Stennis was speaking that night for the White Citizens Council in Yazoo City and they also have a State Charter that they may set up for "private schools." It is no secret.

O'DELL: Does it seem to be growing? Is the white community undergoing any change as a result of all the pressure that has been put now with the Mississippi Summer Project and the killing of the three civil rights workers? What effect is it having on the white community?

HAMER: You can't ever tell. I have talked to two or three whites that's decent in the State of Mississippi, but you know, just two or three speaking out. I do remember, one time, a man came to me after the students began to work in Mississippi and he said the white people were getting tired and they were getting tense and anything might happen. Well, I asked him "how long he thinks *we* had been getting tired"? I have been *tired* for 46 years and my parents was *tired* before me and their parents were *tired*; and I have always wanted to do something that would help some of the things I would see going on among Negroes that I didn't like and I don't like now.

O'DELL: Getting back just for a minute to Atlantic City. You all were in the national spotlight because there was nothing else happening in the Democratic National Convention other than your challenge to the Mississippi delegation and I would like to go back to that and pull together some of the conclusions you might have drawn from that experience.

HAMER: In coming to Atlantic City, we believed strongly that we were right. In fact, it was just right for us to come to challenge the seating of the regular Democratic Party from Mississippi. But we didn't think when we got there that we would meet people, that actually the other leaders of the Movement would differ with what we felt was right. We would have accepted the Green proposal. But, when we couldn't get that, it didn't make any sense for us to take "two votes at large." What would that mean to Mississippi? What would it have meant to us to go back and tell the Mississippi people? And actually, I think there will be great leaders emerging from the State of Mississippi. The people that have the experience to know and the people not interested in letting somebody pat you on the back and tell us "I think it is right." And it was very important for us not to accept a compromise and after I got back to Mississippi, people there said it was the most important step that had been taken. We figured it was right and it was right, and if we had accepted that compromise, then we would have been letting the people down in Mississippi. Regardless of leadership, *we have to think for ourselves!*

O'DELL: In other words, you had two battles on your hands when you went to Atlantic City?

HAMER: Yes. I was in one of the meetings when they spoke about accepting two votes and I said I wouldn't dare think about anything like this. So, I wasn't allowed to attend the other meetings. It was quite an experience.

O'DELL: There will be other elections and other conventions and the people in Mississippi should be a little stronger.

HAMER: I think so.

O'DELL: Well, it's good to know that the people you have to work with every day are with *you.*

HAMER: Yes, they are with us one hundred percent.

O'DELL: That's encouraging because it makes the work that much easier. Is there any final thing you want to say that is part of this historic statement of life in Mississippi for yourself as a person who lives there?

HAMER: Nothing other than we will be working. When I go back to Mississippi we will be working as hard or harder to bring about a change, but things are not always pleasant there.

O'DELL: You will probably have the support of more people than you have ever had, all around the country.

HAMER: Yes, actually since the Convention I have gotten so many letters that I have tried to answer but every letter said they thought this decision, not to accept the compromise, was so important. There wasn't one letter I have gotten so far that said we should have accepted the compromise—not one.

O'DELL: So, those are the people who are interested in your work, and as you get back into the main swing of things you will be keeping in touch with those people so that they should be asked to help in any way they can regardless of where they live. It is national and international public pressure that is needed.

Are you aware that there has been any coverage of the African trip by the Mississippi press? Have they made any comments on it?

HAMER: I don't know about the press, but I know in the town where I live everybody was aware that I was in Africa, because I remember after I got back some of the people told me that Mayor Durr of our town said he just wished they would boil me in tar. But, that just shows how ignorant he is, I didn't see any tar over there. But I was treated much better in Africa than I was treated in America. And you see, often I get letters like this: "Go back to Africa."

Now I have just as much right to stay in America—in fact, the black people have contributed more to America than any other race, because our kids have fought here for what was called "democracy"; our mothers and fathers were sold and brought here for a price. So all I can say when they say "go back to Africa," I say "when you send the Chinese back to China, the Italians back to Italy, etc., and you get on that Mayflower from whence you came, and give the Indians their land back, who really would be here at home?" It is our right to stay here and we will stay and stand up for what belongs to us as American citizens, because they can't say that we haven't had patience.

O'DELL: Was there a lot of interest in your trip among the African people that you met?

HAMER: Yes. I saw how the Government was run there and I saw where black people were running the banks. I saw, for the first time in my life, a black stewardess walking through a plane and that was quite an inspiration for me. It shows what black people can do if we only get the chance in America. It is there within us. We can do things if we only get the chance. I see so many ways America uses to rob Negroes and it is sinful and America can't keep holding on, and doing these things. I saw in Chicago, on the street where I was visiting my sister-in-law, this "Urban Renewal" and it means one thing: "Negro removal." But they want to tear the homes down and put a parking lot there. Where are those people going? Where will they go? And as soon as Negroes take to the street demonstrating, one hears people say, "they shouldn't have done it." The world is looking at America and it is really beginning to show up for what it is really like. "Go Tell It on the Mountain." We can no longer ignore this, that America is not "the land of the free and the home of the brave."

O'DELL: Thank you, Mrs. Fannie Lou Hamer, Vice-Chairman of the Freedom Democratic Party of Mississippi; courageous fighter for human rights.

We Shall Overcome:
Freedom Songs

The nonviolent civil rights movement was a singing movement. Every aspect of its development was marked by song. Some of the songs were traditional songs of protest; others were adaptations of Spirituals or labor union songs; still others were composed on the spot by participants in the movement. The songs that follow are typical of the hundreds that strengthened the will of the marchers and protesters.

WE SHALL OVERCOME

"We Shall Overcome" was the unofficial theme song of the freedom movement. Adapted from a union version of an old Spiritual by the staff of the Highlander Folk School in Tennessee, it was sung wherever the movement went.

We shall overcome, we shall overcome,
We shall overcome someday.
Oh, deep in my heart, I do believe,
We shall overcome someday.

We are not afraid, we are not afraid,
We are not afraid today.
Oh, deep in my heart, I do believe,
We shall overcome someday.

We are not alone, we are not alone,
We are not alone today.
Oh, deep in my heart, I do believe,
We are not alone today.

The truth will make us free, the truth will make us free,
The truth will make us free someday.
Oh, deep in my heart, I do believe,
We shall overcome someday.

We'll walk hand in hand, we'll walk hand in hand,
We'll walk hand in hand someday.
Oh, deep in my heart, I do believe,
We shall overcome someday.

The Lord will see us through, the Lord will see us through,
The Lord will see us through someday.
Oh, deep in my heart, I do believe,
We shall overcome someday.

Black and white together, black and white together,
Black and white together now.
Oh, deep in my heart, I do believe,
We shall overcome someday.

We shall all be free, we shall all be free,
We shall all be free someday.
Oh, deep in my heart, I do believe,
We shall overcome someday.

IF YOU MISS ME FROM THE BACK OF THE BUS

"If You Miss Me from the Back of the Bus" is an example of the kind of song that won great popularity in the movement—a song with a simple melody and lyrics that could be adapted to a variety of situations. This version, sung by the members of SNCC, centers around the areas of protest in which the students were most involved.

If you miss me from the back of the bus,
    and you can't find me nowhere,
Come on up to the front of the bus,
    I'll be ridin' up there.
I'll be ridin' up there, I'll be ridin' up there,
Come on up to the front of the bus,
    I'll be ridin' up there.

If you miss me from the front of the bus,
    and you can't find me nowhere,
Come on up to the driver's seat,
    I'll be drivin' up there.
I'll be drivin' up there, I'll be drivin' up there,
Come on up to the front of the bus,
    I'll be drivin' up there.

If you miss me from Jackson State,
    and you can't find me nowhere,
Come on over to Ole Miss,
    I'll be studyin' over there.
I'll be studyin' over there, I'll be studyin' over there,

Come on over to Ole Miss,
  I'll be studyin' over there.

If you miss me from knockin' on doors,
  and you can't find me nowhere,
Come on down to the registrar's room,
  I'll be the registrar there.
I'll be the registrar there, I'll be the registrar there,
Come on down to the registrar's room,
  I'll be the registrar there.

If you miss me from the cotton field,
  and you can't find me nowhere,
Come on down to the court house,
  I'll be votin' right there.
I'll be votin' right there, I'll be votin' right there,
Come on down to the court house,
  I'll be votin' right there.

If you miss me from the picket line,
  and you can't find me nowhere,
Come on down to the jail house,
  I'll be roomin' down there.
I'll be roomin' down there, I'll be roomin' down there,
Come on down to the jail house,
  I'll be roomin' down there.

If you miss me from the Mississippi River,
  and you can't find me nowhere,.
Come on down to the city pool,
  I'll be swimmin' in there.
I'll be swimmin' in there, I'll be swimmin' in there,
Come on down to the city pool,
  I'll be swimmin' in there.

AIN'T GONNA LET NOBODY TURN ME 'ROUND

"Ain't Gonna Let Nobody Turn Me 'Round" was introduced to the movement in Albany, Georgia, by Ralph Abernathy during the summer of 1962. Because of its adaptability, it was subsequently used widely in the movement. The proper names that appear in this version are those of public officials in Albany and Terrell counties, Georgia.

Ain't gonna let nobody turn me 'round,
  turn me 'round, turn me 'round,
Ain't gonna let nobody turn me 'round,

I'm gonna keep on a walkin', keep on a talkin',
Marching up to freedom land.

Ain't gonna let Nervous Nelly turn me 'round,
    turn me 'round, turn me 'round,
Ain't gonna let Nervous Nelly turn me 'round,
I'm gonna keep on a walkin', keep on a talkin',
Marching up to freedom land.

Ain't gonna let Chief Pritchett turn me 'round,
    turn me 'round, turn me 'round,
Ain't gonna let Chief Pritchett turn me 'round,
I'm gonna keep on a walkin', keep on a talkin',
Marching up to freedom land.

Ain't gonna let Mayor Kelly turn me 'round,
    turn me 'round, turn me 'round,
Ain't gonna let Mayor Kelly turn me 'round,
I'm gonna keep on a walkin', keep on a talkin',
Marching up to freedom land.

Ain't gonna let segregation turn me 'round,
    turn me 'round, turn me 'round,
Ain't gonna let segregation turn me 'round,
I'm gonna keep on a walkin', keep on a talkin',
Marching up to freedom land.

Ain't gonna let Z. T. turn me 'round,
    turn me 'round, turn me 'round,
Ain't gonna let Z. T. turn me 'round,
I'm gonna keep on a walkin' , keep on a talkin',
Marching up to freedom land.

Ain't gonna let no jailhouse turn me 'round,
    turn me 'round, turn me 'round,
Ain't gonna let no jailhouse turn me 'round,
I'm gonna keep on a walkin' , keep on a talkin',
Marching up to freedom land.

Ain't gonna let no injunction turn me 'round,
    turn me 'round, turn me 'round,
Ain't gonna let no injunction turn me 'round,
I'm gonna keep on a walkin', keep on a talkin',
Marching up to freedom land.

FREEDOM IS A CONSTANT STRUGGLE

"Freedom Is a Constant Struggle" was composed by the Freedom Singers, members of SNCC who traveled around the country singing freedom songs and trying to build up support for the students. When the deaths of the civil rights workers James Chaney,

Michael Schwerner, and Andrew Goodman in Mississippi were announced to a mass meeting of students during Freedom Summer, the group responded with this passionate and compassionate song.

> They say that freedom is a constant struggle,
> They say that freedom is a constant struggle,
> They say that freedom is a constant struggle,
> Oh Lord, we've struggled so long,
> We must be free, we must be free.
>
> They say that freedom is a constant crying,
> They say that freedom is a constant crying,
> They say that freedom is a constant crying,
> Oh Lord, we've cried so long,
> We must be free, we must be free.
>
> They say that freedom is a constant sorrow,
> They say that freedom is a constant sorrow,
> They say that freedom is a constant sorrow,
> Oh Lord, we've sorrowed so long,
> We must be free, we must be free.
>
> They say that freedom is a constant moaning,
> They say that freedom is a constant moaning,
> They say that freedom is a constant moaning,
> Oh Lord, we've moaned so long,
> We must be free, we must be free.
>
> They say that freedom is a constant dying,
> They say that freedom is a constant dying,
> They say that freedom is a constant dying,
> Oh Lord, we've died so long,
> We must be free, we must be free.

SUGGESTIONS FOR FURTHER READING

The best single volume on the civil rights movement is Robert Weisbrot, *Freedom Bound: A History of the Civil Rights Movement*★ (1991). The first two volumes of Taylor Branch's magnificent study of the period are *Parting the Waters: America in the King Years, 1954–1962*★ (1988) and *Pillar of Fire: America in the King Years, 1963–1965*★ (1998). Other important works on King include three books by David Garrow: *Protest at Selma: Martin Luther King, Jr., and the Voting Rights Act of 1965*★ (1978), *The F.B.I. and Martin Luther King, Jr.,: From "Solo " to Memphis*★ (1981), and *Bearing the Cross: Martin Luther King, Jr., and the Southern Christian Leadership Conference*★ (1987). Recent works on King include Michael

Eric Dyson, *I May Not Get There with You: The True Martin Luther King, Jr.* (1999) and Gerald D. McKnight, *The Last Crusade: Martin Luther King, Jr., the F.B.I. and the Poor Peoples Campaign*★ (1998).

For information about the Montgomery Bus Boycott, see Stewart Burns (ed.), *Daybreak of Freedom*★ (1997). Participants in the nonviolent movement tell their story in *My Soul Is Rested. Movement Days in the Deep South Remembered*★ (1977), edited by Howell Raines. The student activists are described in *Clayborne Carson, In Struggle: SNCC and the Black Awakening in the 1960s*★ (1981), Howard Zinn, *SNCC: The New Abolitionists* (1964), and the autobiographical *Coming of Age in Mississippi*★ (1968), by Anne Moody. Biographies of important women in the movement include Douglas Brinkley, *Rosa Parks* (2000) and Chana Kai Lee, *The Life of Fannie Lou Hamer* (1999). See also Belinda Robnett, *How Long? How Long? African American Women and the Struggle for Civil Rights*★ (1997).

Important studies of individual communities include John Dittmer, *Local People: The Struggle for Civil Rights in Mississippi*★ (1994), Glenda Alice Rabby, *The Pain and the Promise: The Struggle for Civil Rights in Tallahassee, Florida* (1999), and Adam Fairclough, *Race and Democracy: The Civil Rights Struggle in Louisiana, 1915–1972*★ (1995).

The political impact of the movement for civil rights is analyzed in Doug McAdam, *Political Process and the Development of Black Insurgency, 1930–1970*★ (1985) and Steven F. Lawson, *Black Ballots: Voting Rights in the South, 1944–1969*★ (1976). See also Carl Brauer, *John F. Kennedy and the Second Reconstruction*★ (1977).

Other useful works are Glenn T. Eskew, *But for Birmingham: The Local and National Movements in the Civil Rights Struggle*★ (1997), Stephen J. Whitfield, *A Death in the Delta: The Story of Emmett Till*★ (1988), and David M. Oshinsky, *"Worse Than Slavery ": Parchman Farm and the Ordeal of Jim Crow Justice*★ (1997).

★Books marked by an asterisk are available in paperback.

12

⊛

The Militant Black Liberation Movement

INTRODUCTION

After the Freedom Summer of 1964, the focus of the movement for the liberation of black people began to shift from the South to the urban ghettoes of the North and West. As more and more legal battles were won, it became apparent that these victories had little relevance to the masses of black people, many of whom remained mired in poverty and fear generated by helplessness before the economic and political power of the white community. After the nonviolent direct action campaigns had desegregated lunch counters and public facilities, these gains, compared with the demands of real freedom, began to seem inconsequential to many blacks—especially to the militant young. The murderers of black and white civil-rights workers throughout the South went free, even those who had publicly boasted of their crimes. Racism was revealed to be not merely the sum of individual whites' hostility to blacks but an attitude insidiously built into the institutions of American society—a more elusive target than had been imagined.

As the popular press, along with racial liberals and moderates, applauded the real gains black people had made in the South through legal defense and non-violent direct action, there occurred a series of explosions—variously called riots, insurrections, and civil disorders—that turned the attention of the nation to the black ghettoes of northern and western cities. Black people living in poverty and despair were venting their often suppressed hostility through attacks on the things that they saw as most directly oppressing them—their slum dwellings and the white ghetto merchants. Most of the disturbances were triggered by incidents involving the visible symbol of white oppression—the police. Built on the frustrations of the black ghetto dweller and the student activists, black nationalism again became an openly advocated alternative.

The new nationalism drew much of its inspiration from the successful struggles for liberation carried on by formerly colonized peoples of Africa and Asia. The key concept was "self-determination." Black people must be free to decide for themselves what they will do, where they will live, how and what they will study, and how they will carry out the plans for their general liberation from the oppressors.

At first it seemed that leadership for the new nationalism might come from the Lost–Found Nation of Islam (the Black Muslims), led by Elijah Muhammad. This movement had attracted a considerable number of members and many sympathizers among urban ghetto dwellers through its clear-cut descriptions of the crimes committed against black people by "white devils." When it became apparent that the Muslims were essentially a conservative group, more interested in the salvation of black souls and the building up of its own organization than in making a frontal attack on racist institutions and seeking the liberation of all blacks, a split occurred in the Muslim movement. The dissidents, led by Malcolm X, minister of the New York City Muslims, formed the Muslim Mosque, Inc., and Malcolm founded the Organization of Afro-American Unity to carry out his plans for racial liberation. As a result of the hostility created by the split in the Muslim forces, Malcolm was killed by a black assassin in February 1965. His death was a profound tragedy for both black and white America, for it seemed that he might have been the leader who could mold a movement out of the frustrated ghetto dwellers whose anger so often led to self-destruction. Almost every segment of subsequent black liberation movements has claimed Malcolm X as one of its martyrs.

Meanwhile, in the South, after the ambiguous success of Freedom Summer, in which the attention of the nation had indeed been focused on Mississippi but little progress had been made in terms of real social change, SNCC virtually went into seclusion. For a year, its members worked quietly, organizing voters in rural communities and rethinking the organization's philosophy—finding support for the aggressive-defensive policies enunciated by Malcolm X. SNCC made its new posture public in May 1966 with the election of Stokely Carmichael as its chairman and the announcement that it intended to call upon black Americans to build and maintain control of independent institutions through which they could implement social change.

Carmichael gave the new philosophy a watchword in June 1966 when he shouted the words that sent a shock wave through the ranks of the civil-rights organizations and chills down the spine of white America—"Black Power." Why this particular phrase set off such an uproar is a subject for study by social psychologists, but it was clear that the two words conjured up a host of devils in the minds of whites and a host of possibilities in the minds of blacks. The potency of the new slogan was revealed as almost every old civil-rights organization and several new ones took positions explaining what the words meant to them.

An important development in this period was the increasing visibility and militancy of the black student movement on both predominantly black and predominantly white campuses. One reason for the change was the enrollment of large numbers of ghetto youths in the colleges. As they encountered what seemed to them to be the irrelevancies of higher education—a plaint heard from many white student groups in the same period—they began to insist on courses of study that would help them establish their identities and aid them in reconstructing the ghettoes from which they came. In the face of the increasing militancy, the established authorities of the larger society tried to put down the incipient rebellion. This led to several violent clashes between police and young black militants, many of whom were students. This process continued to reveal the patterns of structural racism in American society.

Conditions in the Urban Ghetto

Cries of Harlem

HARYOU-ACT

The gains of the nonviolent civil rights movement and the legal programs of the NAACP had little relevance to the ghetto dweller, for whom the conditions of life steadily worsened as more and more people were crushed together and confined in the "black" sections of the nation's cities. In 1964 and 1965, the black urban ghettoes exploded, and the cities of the North and the West replaced the South as the focus of protest activity. Since that time, the urban black has dominated the racial scene.

Harlem Youth Opportunities Unlimited, Inc. (HARYOU) was established in 1962 to try to bring some order to the urban chaos. Its magnificent study of 1964, Youth in the Ghetto: A Study of the Consequences of Powerlessness, *provided an analysis of the problems of ghetto youth that has not been surpassed. The statements that follow were taken from that work and give insight into the conditions of the ghetto and the state of mind of the ghetto dweller.*

—No, you have to survive. You have to survive, if you don't ... Well, I'll say if you don't have the proper education that you should have, and you go *downtown* and work, they don't pay you any money worthwhile. You can work all your life and never have anything, and you will always be in debt. So you take to the streets, you understand? You take to the streets and try to make it in the street, you know what you have; out here in the street you try to make it. All right. Being out in the street takes your mind off all these problems. You have no time to think about things because you're trying to make some money. So this is why I'm not up to par on different organizations. I don't belong to any, but perhaps I should. But I haven't taken the time to see or to try to figure it out. I've been trying to make it so hard and trying to keep a piece of money. I'm trying not to work like a dog to get it, and being treated any sort of way to get it. How to make another buck enters your mind. As far as bettering the community, this never enters your mind because it seems to me, well, I'm using my opinions—to me the white man has it locked up. The black man is progressing, but slowly. The only solution I see to it, I mean, if you are actually going to be here awhile, you have to stay healthy and not die, for one thing.

FROM "Cries of Harlem," *Youth in the Ghetto*, by HARYOU-ACT (New York, 1964), pp. 314, 315–18, 319–20, 323, 334, 336–37, 341. Reprinted with permission of HARYOU-ACT.

The other thing is while you're here you want to live the best that you can. And since Whitey has all the luxuries, I mean, he has it all locked up, you want to get a piece of it, so you have to make some kind of money so you can get it. You can't get what he's got, definitely, but you can get enough to make you feel comfortable. So you're always scheming how to, you know, how to make some money. —

— DRUG ADDICT, MALE,
AGE ABOUT 37.

—Now, they had been complaining to the Department of Health about conditions in the building, about all the violations; no lights in the hall, the rats and roaches literally moving the tenants out of the building, and about six months ago the plumbing in the basement got jammed up somehow or other and there has been standing water in the basement, and the flies and maggots and everything else have been breeding there. Now, yesterday, I understand something happened in one apartment; rats forced the woman out of her apartment. She couldn't at all control the rats; they were running all over the kitchen and all throughout the house and everything. So, last night, the picket line was decided on. —

—Where is the apartment? —

—Where is the apartment? I think it's apartment 2W in —— West 117th Street. So, during the picket line, four tenants who live in this building were out and most of the members of the Leadership Training Program here at HARYOU. There was a meeting with the Deputy Commissioner and in this meeting, all of the violations were pointed out to this man and he said that he would send inspectors to the building today. He suggested that the tenants organize their own council and pool their rents and have repairs made themselves. Now, up until this point, the tenants have been trying to keep the halls clean and you know, keep roaches down, and put down rat poisoning, but the situation got completely out of hand and the health conditions there are so bad that it is really what could break out to be a real health epidemic in that whole block because in ——, the building next to it has been vacated completely and, on occasions, workmen with their trucks have been dumping refuse into this building and other people in the neighborhood throw their garbage down to this building and there is a great accumulation of rats and roaches and everything there. At — you have maggots and mosquitoes and flies breeding in the basement and rats running all over the building. This naturally spreads on to ——, and then on down the whole block.

As far as press coverage of the whole situation, I don't know about that. The Deputy Commissioner did send out inspectors and I understand that they have just left the building and have gone back down to the Health Department to make a report. Now the thing is that this could, as actually happened before, be tied up in a whole lot of red tape, you know. The Commissioner said that he would try and find the landlord. The tenants have been complaining for months about conditions. He said that they had tried to find the landlord and they believe that the landlord has just disappeared because the city can't find him. Mr. Gray and some of the tenants say that they know where the landlord is and, in fact, they said that Mr. Gray had spoken to the landlord on the phone. And they have been in contact with the landlord's lawyers, but the city still says that they can't serve a summons on him until they find him. So this could mean being tied up in red tape for a few months more and the fact is that these people can't live under these conditions for a few months more.—

—Yeah, well, one woman said that the rats had chewed the clothes off her baby. That was one thing that was brought out this morning. I don't know about any others. —

—From what I understand, most of the tenants there have children and need from five to six rooms. Now in the past, when they were paying rent, they were only paying around $40 to $45 a month rent and I don't think I know of any place, and I don't think that anybody else does really, where they can get six rooms for $40, you know.—

—I think since this building has been jammed up down there in the basement, if there are large puddles of water down in the basement, I think that's a situation where the tenants should move out immediately; water can get under the building and the whole building can collapse. So I think they should move out immediately.—

—The Deputy Commissioner mentioned that today but the thing is finding places large enough and at rents that they can afford.

They have been filing complaints at the Health Department I know. Then, today the Commissioner came down after the complaints that the people had filed and he had sent inspectors to the building and obviously that's all that's been done.

The tenants said, "We have rats running all over the building!" and he said, "Yes, in May, you reported that. You reported that there was a lot of garbage and there were conditions that could breed rats." Then they said, like the stairs were broken down or something, and he said, "Yes, in February, you know, you reported that and we sent out an inspector," blah, blah, blah. This is all he has been doing is sending out inspectors. —

—What is the next step?—

—A live-in! It is a very nice office. That would be the step for tomorrow morning if nothing constructive is done today. No, this is for tomorrow because they are waiting for the word of what's going to be done from the Health Department because the inspectors just left the building to report back to the Health Department.—

–GIRL, AGE 15.

—There's only one teacher that can control them and that was our lady teacher. She was a lady, a big fat lady. Her name was Miss P. and she always argues, and she hits you sometimes, but she was strict. She had big "buns," she was a lady about forty, you know. And the other teachers they used to fool with you, you know, but nobody never could do nothing to her. The whole school respected her; she was the only one that could keep a class organized. And then what happened, when the men teachers—you know, the young men teachers—they come to school and want to show off, you know, so they caught it more.

You know what happened, when I came to this class, my first class; I went to class, and you couldn't do no kind of work. The teacher was so scared to turn his back on the boys, real scared, and they throw a book at him, and the teacher is so scared, they tell him come on and fight, and they all sit down and laugh. They don't care, they like that, so they fight.

Then you'd be sitting down in front and they'd say "Hey, Moe." They call him names. "Hey, Moe, come here, you crazy thing." So he walks out to get the principal and they lock the door, and he can't get back in and the principal can't get in the door. And the next thing you know they take a book, throw it out the window—breaks the class up and then they can't do nothing.

Then we have the lady teachers. They get behind the lady teachers, they feel her ass, they feel her whole body, and the teacher don't say nothing because she's scared.

One class they was able to control was typewriting, because everybody like typewriting, so they controlled it. She was a young teacher. She was kind of skinny, you know, but I tell you, she going to be fighting them, so nobody ain't going to touch her. You go to school, find typewriters broken; you're lucky if you find one typewriter that's good, so everybody's fighting all the time for that, you know.

You have four classes of gym; say four times thirty, that's a lot of people. What happens you can't play basketball 'cause they are so crowded. So you got to do exercise, line up and do exercise; nobody ever do exercise. So what happens, everybody keeps on their nice clean clothes, nobody puts on gym clothes, so they make you get on the floor—everybody with nice clean pants on—they get mad, so one guy says, "I'm not getting on the floor," so the teacher goes on over there; he fight with him a little while, then he tell everybody go in the back and stand there, go in the back and just stand up, or else you gonna get hit. So you go back and you stand up.

Everybody wants to play basketball, that's one of the main things in life, so people get a basketball and they go out in the yard and play basketball. Then the Dean runs out in the yard and catches them and write them up, and every time it's the same thing. The same ones playing basketball, 'cause that's what they like.

Sometimes the school would be crowded, you know, 'cause it's cold outside, so you go to school that day.—

–BOY, AGE 15.

—Now when a white kid gets to be 17 or 18, he's ready to go into business. Any subject that you choose to take, or any place that you choose to go, he's qualified because this is his education, he's been taught this. And when he goes to college and comes out, I mean he's ready to master anything that he chooses to take up. But here, I should get the same education, but I can't do it. Even though I'm willing to work and sweat for it, I mean I can't do it. They don't want me to do it! Why? This is what I can't understand. If I'm willing to get out—okay, so I'm willing to take the shovel and go out to dig a ditch. All right, so they're paying $6 an hour for digging this ditch. I'm willing to take a shovel and go dig it; why won't they let me? But the white boys. ... Take years ago, I mean all you could find on the shovel was black men.—

—So you're saying that they are taking the jobs away from the black man? —

—That's what they're doing because the unions have it in. They organize and run the prices so high that, I mean, it's too much money for the black man, they figure, to be making. —

–MAN, AGE ABOUT 30.

—Now we have sense enough to know, the majority of us out here, that to say, for example, the NAACP, when they find work for the members, they think the masses out here should be satisfied because they gave one NAACP member a six thousand a year job. Here are fifteen million hungry people and they should be happy over it? No, it won't last. And I see many things that are going to happen because I am one of the masses. I live with them each and every day, I sleep with them, and I am on the corners with them. When I find work, I will work. And I think that as far as radio and television, I think I am qualified to stand on my own there. They say the old thing is "The first to be fired and the last to be hired." Well, as long as you are black you will get this. You can walk down here and go into the employment office, and before you get up to the desk the head is being shaken—no work. Anything, other than black, behind you, come behind you—"Oh, yes, sit down. Stand over there. We have something for you. Maybe we can find something for you." And two to one, when they leave they have employment. We don't have it. Right here in Harlem, thirty to forty million dollars a year leaves here, and we don't get any of it. —

–MAN, AGE 35.

—The white merchants you see in Harlem, that have kids, we send them to college. But how many Negroes do you know in this community send their kids to college? We pay for all the white merchants' kids, for all their school-ing. We do this, understand what I mean, through dealing with these people. But the rate of colored kids in comparison to the white is very few. I think we should be trying to do—what we actually should be trying to do is take the money we have, instead of spending it in bars, building churches, as this fellow said, I think we should be trying to take the money and invest it in some wor-thy business for Whitey! They work for Whitey, and definitely Whitey is not going to have anyone working for him that is not qualified to make him a dollar, or to save him one. If we can do it for him, we can do it for ourselves. That's what we need, the buck! Get that, and you have everything! —

–MAN, AGE 30.

—Last night, for instance, the officer stopped some fellows on 125th Street, Car No. ———, that was the number of the car, and because this fellow spoke so nicely for his protection and his rights, the officer said, "All right, everybody get off the street or inside!" Now, it's very hot. We don't have air-conditioned apartments in most of these houses up here, so where are we going if we get off the streets? We can't go back in the house because we almost suffocate. So, we sit down on the curb, or stand on the sidewalk, or on the steps, things like that, till the wee hours of the morning, especially in the summer when it's too hot to go up. Now where were we going? But he came out with his night-stick and wants to beat people on the head, and wanted to—he arrested one fellow. The other fellow said, "Well, I'll move, but you don't have to talk to me like a dog."

—I think we should all get together—everybody—all get together and every time one draws back his stick to do something to us, or hits one of us on the head, take the stick and hit him on his head, so he'll know how it feels to be hit on the head, or kill him, if necessary. Yes, kill him, if necessary. That's how I feel. There is no other way to deal with this man. The only way you can deal with him is the way he has been dealing with us.

–MAN, AGE 35.

—Churches don't mean us no good. We've been having churches all our lives under the same conditions, and look at the condition we're still in. The church must not have meant anything. See, when you go to church you don't learn how to read and write, and count, at church. You learn that in school. See what I mean? So what good the churches doing us? They are not doing us any good! You could build some factories or something in Harlem and give our people some work near home. That would do us more good than a church. —

–MAN, AGE ABOUT 45.

The Ballot or the Bullet

MALCOLM X

Malcolm X (formerly Malcolm Little) was born in Nebraska in 1925. His father was a militant Baptist clergyman who was also an organizer for Garvey's UNIA. When Malcolm was a child, the family was threatened by the Ku Klux Klan and other racist groups. Eventually, his father was murdered "by person or persons unknown," in the words of the law-enforcement officials who investigated the case.

In his late teens, Malcolm drifted into a life of petty crime and then into a career as a successful hustler. He was caught, arrested, and jailed, and it was while in jail that he was converted to Elijah Muhammad's Nation of Islam. After his release, his remarkable talents led him straight to the number-two spot in the Muslim organization. In 1964, he withdrew from the Nation of Islam and set up an orthodox Muslim mosque, as well as a black protest organization, the Association of Afro-American Unity. The last year of his life was spent trying to develop a comprehensive program for black liberation.

Shortly after his break with Elijah Muhammad, Malcolm began participating in meetings intended to help formulate a new position on the process of black liberation. The address reprinted here was delivered April 3, 1964 at a symposium in Cleveland where he appeared with journalist Louis Lomax who supported CORE's philosophy of nonviolence. Malcolm, on the other hand, spoke about the need to develop a sense of black nationalism among African-Americans so that they could come to control political, economic, and social affairs in the black community. The U. S. Constitution gave the ballot to the people so that they might choose their representatives and, through them, govern their communities. Should this process be denied, the alternative seemed plain: "The Ballot or the Bullet."

Less than a year after he delivered this speech, Malcolm was dead, felled by an assassin's bullet.

Mr. Moderator, Brother Lomax, brothers and sisters, friends and enemies: I just can't believe everyone in here is a friend and I don't want to leave anybody out. The question tonight, as I understand it, is "The Negro Revolt, and Where Do We Go From Here?" or "What Next?" In my little humble way of understanding it, it points toward either the ballot or the bullet.

Before we try and explain what is meant by the ballot or the bullet, I would like to clarify something concerning myself. I'm still a Muslim, my religion is still Islam. That's my personal belief. Just as Adam Clayton Powell is a Christian minister who heads the Abyssinian Baptist Church in New York, but at the

FROM George Breitman (ed.), *Malcolm X Speaks: Selected Speeches and Statements.* Copyright 1965 by Merit Publishers; reprinted by permission of Pathfinder Press.

same time takes part in the political struggles to try and bring about rights to the black people in this country; and Dr. Martin Luther King is a Christian minister down in Atlanta, Georgia, who heads another organization fighting for the civil rights of black people in this country; and Rev. Galamison, I guess you've heard of him, is another Christian minister in New York who has been deeply involved in the school boycotts to eliminate segregated education; well, I myself am a minister, not a Christian minister, but a Muslim minister; and I believe in action on all fronts by whatever means necessary.

Although I'm still a Muslim, I'm not here tonight to discuss my religion. I'm not here to try and change your religion. I'm not here to argue or discuss anything that we differ about, because it's time for us to submerge our differences and realize that it is best for us to first see that we have the same problem, a common problem—a problem that will make you catch hell whether you're a Baptist, or a Methodist, or a Muslim, or a nationalist. Whether you're educated or illiterate, whether you live on the boulevard or in the alley, you're going to catch hell just like I am. We're all in the same boat and we all are going to catch the same hell from the same man. He just happens to be a white man. All of us have suffered here, in this country, political oppression at the hands of the white man, economic exploitation at the hands of the white man, and social degradation at the hands of the white man.

Now in speaking like this, it doesn't mean that we're anti-white, but it does mean we're anti-exploitation, we're anti-degradation, we're anti-oppression. And if the white man doesn't want us to be anti-him, let him stop oppressing and exploiting and degrading us. Whether we are Christians or Muslims or nationalists or agnostics or atheists, we must first learn to forget our differences. If we have differences, let us differ in the closet; when we come out in front, let us not have anything to argue about until we get finished arguing with the man. If the late President Kennedy could get together with Khrushchev and exchange some wheat, we certainly have more in common with each other than Kennedy and Khrushchev had with each other.

If we don't do something real soon, I think you'll have to agree that we're going to be forced either to use the ballot or the bullet. It's one or the other in 1964. It isn't that time is running out—time has run out! 1964 threatens to be the most explosive year America has ever witnessed. The most explosive year. Why? It's also a political year. It's the year when all of the white politicians will be back in the so-called Negro community jiving you and me for some votes. The year when all of the white political crooks will be right back in your and my community with their false promises, building up our hopes for a letdown, with their trickery and their treachery, with their false promises which they don't intend to keep. As they nourish these dissatisfactions, it can only lead to one thing, an explosion; and now we have the type of black man on the scene in America today—I'm sorry, Brother Lomax—who just doesn't intend to turn the other cheek any longer.

Don't let anybody tell you anything about the odds are against you. If they draft you, they send you to Korea and make you face 800 million Chinese. If you can be brave over there, you can be brave right here. These odds aren't as great as those odds. And if you fight here, you will at least know what you're fighting for.

I'm not a politician, not even a student of politics; in fact, I'm not a student of much of anything. I'm not a Democrat, I'm not a Republican, and I don't even consider myself an American. If you and I were Americans, there'd be no problem. Those Hunkies that just got off the boat, they're already Americans; Polacks are already Americans; the Italian refugees are already Americans. Everything that came out of Europe, every blue-eyed thing, is already an American. And as long as you and I have been over here, we aren't Americans yet.

Well, I am one who doesn't believe in deluding myself. I'm not going. to sit at your table and watch you eat, with nothing on my plate, and call myself a diner. Sitting at the table doesn't make you a diner, unless you eat some of what's on that plate. Being here in America doesn't make you an American. Being born here in America doesn't make you an American. Why, if birth made you American, you wouldn't need any legislation, you wouldn't need any amendments to the Constitution, you wouldn't be faced with civil-rights filibustering in Washington, D.C., right now. They don't have to pass civil-rights legislation to make a Polack an American.

No, I'm not an American. I'm one of the 22 million black people who are the victims of Americanism. One of the 22 million black people who are the victims of democracy, nothing but disguised hypocrisy. So, I'm not standing here speaking to you as an American, or a patriot, or a flag-saluter, or a flag-waver—no, not I. I'm speaking as a victim of this American system. And I see America through the eyes of the victim. I don't see any American dream; I see an American nightmare.

These 22 million victims are waking up. Their eyes are coming open. They're beginning to see what they used to only look at. They're becoming politically mature. They are realizing that there are new political trends from coast to coast. As they see these new political trends, it's possible for them to see that every time there's an election the races are so close that they have to have a recount. They had to recount in Massachusetts to see who was going to be governor, it was so close. It was the same way in Rhode Island, in Minnesota, and in many other parts of the country. And the same with Kennedy and Nixon when they ran for president. It was so close they had to count all over again. Well, what does this mean? It means that when white people are evenly divided, and black people have a bloc of votes of their own, it is left up to them to determine who's going to sit in the White House and who's going to be in the dog house.

It was the black man's vote that put the present administration in Washington, D.C. Your vote, your dumb vote, your ignorant vote, your wasted vote put in an administration in Washington, D.C., that has seen fit to pass every kind of legislation imaginable, saving you until last, then filibustering on top of that. And your and my leaders have the audacity to run around clapping their hands and talk about how much progress we're making. And what a good president we have. If he wasn't good in Texas, he sure can't be good in

Washington, D. C. Because Texas is a lynch state. It is in the same breath as Mississippi, no different; only they lynch you in Texas with a Texas accent and lynch you in Mississippi with a Mississippi accent. And these Negro leaders have the audacity to go and have some coffee in the White House with a Texan, a Southern cracker—that's all he is—and then come out and tell you and me that he's going to be better for us because, since he's from the South, he knows how to deal with the Southerners. What kind of logic is that? Let Eastland be president, he's from the South too. He should be better able to deal with them than Johnson.

In this present administration they have in the House of Representatives 257 Democrats to only 177 Republicans. They control two-thirds of the House vote. Why can't they pass something that will help you and me? In the Senate, there are 67 senators who are of the Democratic Party. Only 33 of them are Republicans. Why, the Democrats have got the government sewed up, and you're the one who sewed it up for them. And what have they given you for it? Four years in office, and just now getting around to some civil-rights legislation. Just now, after everything else is gone, out of the way, they're going to sit down now and play with you all summer long—the same old giant con game that they call filibuster. All those are in cahoots together. Don't you ever think they're not in cahoots together, for the man that is heading the civil-rights filibuster is a man from Georgia named Richard Russell. When Johnson became president, the first man he asked for when he got back to Washington, D.C., was "Dicky"—that's how tight they are. That's his boy, that's his pal, that's his buddy. But they're playing that old con game. One of them makes believe he's for you, and he's got it fixed where the other one is so tight against you, he never has to keep his promise.

So it's time in 1964 to wake up. And when you see them coming up with that kind of conspiracy, let them know your eyes are open. And let them know you got something else that's wide open too. It's got to be the ballot or the bullet. The ballot or the bullet. If you're afraid to use an expression like that, you should get on out of the country, you should get back in the cotton patch, you should get back in the alley. They get all the Negro vote, and after they get it, the Negro gets nothing in return. All they did when they got to Washington was give a few big Negroes big jobs. Those big Negroes didn't need big jobs, they already had jobs. That's camouflage, that's trickery, that's treachery, window-dressing. I'm not trying to knock out the Democrats for the Republicans, we'll get to them in a minute. But it is true—you put the Democrats first and the Democrats put you last.

Look at it the way it is. What alibis do they use, since they control Congress and the Senate? What alibi do they use when you and I ask, "Well, when are you going to keep your promise?" They blame the Dixiecrats. What is a Dixiecrat? A Democrat. A Dixiecrat is nothing but a Democrat in disguise. The titular head of the Democrats is also the head of the Dixiecrats, because the Dixiecrats are a part of the Democratic Party. The Democrats have never kicked the Dixiecrats out of the party. The Dixiecrats bolted themselves once, but the Democrats didn't put them out. Imagine, these lowdown Southern segregationists put the Northern Democrats down. But the Northern Democrats have never put the Dixiecrats down. No, look at that thing the way it is. They have got a con game going on, a political con game, and you and I are in the middle. It's time for you and me to wake up and start looking at it like it is, and trying to understand it like it is; and then we can deal with it like it is.

The Dixiecrats in Washington, D. C., control the key committees that run the government. The only reason the Dixiecrats control these committees is because they have seniority. The only reason they have seniority is because they come from states where Negroes can't vote. This is not even a government that's based on democracy. It is not a government that is made up of representatives of the people. Half of the people in the South can't even vote. Eastland is not even supposed to be in Washington. Half of the senators and congressmen who occupy these key positions in Washington, D.C., are there illegally, are there unconstitutionally.

I was in Washington, D.C., a week ago Thursday, when they were debating whether or not they should let the bill come onto the floor. And in the back of the room where the Senate meets, there's a huge map of the United States, and on that map it shows the location of Negroes throughout the country. And it shows that the Southern section of the country, the states that are most heavily concentrated with Negroes, are the ones that have senators and congressmen standing up filibustering and doing all other kinds of trickery to keep the Negro from being able to vote. This is pitiful. But it's not pitiful for us any longer; it's actually pitiful for the white man, because soon now, as the Negro awakens a little more and sees the vise that he's in, sees the bag that he's in, sees the real game that he's in, then the Negro's going to develop a new tactic.

These senators and congressmen actually violate the constitutional amendments that guarantee the people of that particular state or county the right to vote. And the Constitution itself has within it the machinery to expel any representative from a state where the voting rights of the people are violated. You don't even need new legislation. Any person in Congress right now, who is there from a state or a district where the voting rights of the people are violated, that particular person should be expelled from Congress. And when you expel him, you've removed one of the obstacles in the path of any real meaningful legislation in this country. In fact, when you expel them, you don't need new legislation, because they will be replaced by black representatives from counties and districts where the black man is in the majority, not in the minority.

If the black man in these Southern states had his full voting rights, the key Dixiecrats in Washington, D.C., which means the key Democrats in Washington, D.C., would lose their seats. The Democratic Party itself would lose its power. It would cease to be powerful as a party. When you see the amount of power that would be lost by the Democratic Party if it were to lose the Dixiecrat wing, or branch, or element, you can see where it's against the interests of the Democrats to give voting rights to Negroes in states where the

Democrats have been in complete power and authority ever since the Civil War. You just can't belong to that party without analyzing it.

I say again, I'm not anti-Democrat, I'm not anti-Republican, I'm not anti-anything. I'm just questioning their sincerity, and some of the strategy that they've been using on our people by promising them promises that they don't intend to keep. When you keep the Democrats in power, you're keeping the Dixiecrats in power. I doubt that my good Brother Lomax will deny that. A vote for a Democrat is a vote for a Dixiecrat. That's why, in 1964, it's time now for you and me to become more politically mature and realize what the ballot is for; what we're supposed to get when we cast a ballot; and that if we don't cast a ballot, it's going to end up in a situation where we're going to have to cast a bullet. It's either a ballot or a bullet.

In the North, they do it a different way. They have a system that's known as gerrymandering, whatever that means. It means when Negroes become too heavily concentrated in a certain area, and begin to gain too much political power, the white man comes along and changes the district lines. You may say, "Why do you keep saying white man?" Because it's the white man who does it. I haven't ever seen any Negro changing any lines. They don't let him get near the line. It's the white man who does this. And usually, it's the white man who grins at you the most, and pats you on the back, and is supposed to be your friend. He may be friendly, but he's not your friend.

So, what I'm trying to impress upon you, in essence, is this: You and I in America are faced not with a segregationist conspiracy, we're faced with a government conspiracy. Everyone who's filibustering is a senator—that's the government. Everyone who's finagling in Washington, D.C., is a congressman—that's the government. You don't have anybody putting blocks in your path but people who are a part of the government. The same government that you go abroad to fight for and die for is the government that is in a conspiracy to deprive you of your voting rights, deprive you of your economic opportunities, deprive you of decent housing, deprive you of decent education. You don't need to go to the employer alone, it is the government itself, the government of America, that is responsible for the oppression and exploitation and degradation of black people in this country. And you should drop it in their lap. This government has failed the Negro. This so-called democracy has failed the Negro. And all these white liberals have definitely failed the Negro.

So, where do we go from here? First, we need some friends. We need some new allies. The entire civil-rights struggle needs a new interpretation, a broader interpretation. We need to look at this civil-rights thing from another angle—from the inside as well as from the outside. To those of us whose philosophy is black nationalism, the only way you can get involved in the civil-rights struggle is give it a new interpretation. That old interpretation excluded us. It kept us out. So, we're giving a new interpretation to the civil-rights struggle, an interpretation that will enable us to come into it, take part in it. And these handkerchief-heads who have been dillydallying and pussyfooting and compromising—we don't intend to let them pussyfoot and dillydally and compromise any longer.

How can you thank a man for giving you what's already yours? How then can you thank him for giving you only part of what's already yours? You haven't even made progress, if what's being given to you, you should have had already. That's not progress. And I love my Brother Lomax, the way he pointed out we're right back where we were in 1954. We're not even as far up as we were in 1954. We're behind where we were in 1954. There's more segregation now than there was in 1954. There's more racial animosity, more racial hatred, more racial violence today in 1964, than there was in 1954. Where is the progress?

And now you're facing a situation where the young Negro's coming up. They don't want to hear that "turn-the-other-cheek" stuff, no. In Jacksonville, those were teenagers, they were throwing Molotov cocktails. Negroes have never done that before. But it shows you there's a new deal coming in. There's new thinking coming in. There's new strategy coming in. It'll be Molotov cocktails this month, hand grenades next month, and something else next month. It'll be ballots, or it'll be bullets. It'll be liberty, or it will be death. The only difference about this kind of death—it'll be reciprocal. You know what is meant by "reciprocal"? That's one of Brother Lomax's words, I stole it from him. I don't usually deal with those big words because I don't usually deal with big people. I deal with small people. I find you can get a whole lot of small people and whip hell out of a whole lot of big people. They haven't got anything to lose, and they've got everything to gain. And they'll let you know in a minute: "It takes two to tango; when I go, you go."

The black nationalists, those whose philosophy is black nationalism, in bringing about this new interpretation of the entire meaning of civil rights, look upon it as meaning, as Brother Lomax has pointed out, equality of opportunity. Well, we're justified in seeking civil rights, if it means equality of opportunity, because all we're doing there is trying to collect for our investment. Our mothers and fathers invested sweat and blood. Three hundred and ten years we worked in this country without a dime in return—I mean without a *dime* in return. You let the white man walk around here talking about how rich this country is, but you never stop to think how it got rich so quick. It got rich because you made it rich.

You take the people who are in this audience right now. They're poor, we're all poor as individuals. Our weekly salary individually amounts to hardly anything. But if you take the salary of everyone in here collectively it'll fill up a whole lot of baskets. It's a lot of wealth. If you can collect the wages of just these people right here for a year, you'll be rich—richer than rich. When you look at it like that, think how rich Uncle Sam had to become, not with this handful, but millions of black people. Your and my mother and father, who didn't work an eight-hour shift, but worked from "can't see" in the morning until "can't see" at night, and worked for nothing, making the white man rich, making Uncle Sam rich.

This is our investment. This is our contribution—our blood. Not only did we give of our free labor, we gave of our blood. Every time he had a call to arms, we were the first ones in uniform. We died on every battlefield the white man had. We have made a greater sacrifice than anybody who's standing up in America today. We have made a greater contribution and have collected less. Civil rights, for those of us whose philosophy is black nationalism, means: "Give it to us now. Don't wait for next year. Give it to us yesterday, and that's not fast enough."

I might stop right here to point out one thing. Whenever you're going after something that belongs to you, anyone who's depriving you of the right to have it is a criminal. Understand that. Whenever you are going after something that is yours, you are within your legal rights to lay claim to it. And anyone who puts forth any effort to deprive you of that which is yours, is breaking the law, is a criminal. And this was pointed out by the Supreme Court decision. It outlawed segregation. Which means segregation is against the law. Which means a segregationist is breaking the law. A segregationist is a criminal. You can't label him as anything other than that. And when you demonstrate against segregation, the law is on your side. The Supreme Court is on your side.

Now, who is it that opposes you in carrying out the law? The police department itself. With police dogs and clubs. Whenever you demonstrate against segregation, whether it is segregated education, segregated housing, or anything else, the law is on your side, and anyone who stands in the way is not the law any longer. They are breaking the law, they are not representatives of the law. Any time you demonstrate against segregation and a man has the audacity to put a police dog on you, kill that dog, kill him, I'm telling you, kill that dog. I say it, if they put me in jail tomorrow, kill—that—dog. Then you'll put a stop to it. Now, if these white people in here don't want to see that kind of action, get down and tell the mayor to tell the police department to pull the dogs in. That's all you have to do. If you don't do it, someone else will.

If you don't take this kind of stand, your little children will grow up and look at you and think "shame." If you don't take an uncompromising stand—I don't mean go out and get violent; but at the same time you should never be nonviolent unless you run into some nonviolence. I'm nonviolent with those who are nonviolent with me. But when you drop that violence on me, then you've made me go insane, and I'm not responsible for what I do. And that's the way every Negro should get. Any time you know you're within the law, within your legal rights, within your moral rights, in accord with justice, then die for what you believe in. But don't die alone. Let your dying be reciprocal. This is what is meant by equality. What's good for the goose is good for the gander.

When we begin to get in this area, we need new friends, we need new allies. We need to expand the civil-rights struggle to a higher level—to the level of human rights. Whenever you are in a civil-rights struggle, whether you know it or not, you are confining yourself to the jurisdiction of Uncle Sam. No one from the outside world can speak out in your behalf as long as your struggle is a civil-rights struggle. Civil rights comes within the domestic affairs of this country. All of our African brothers and our Asian brothers and our Latin-American brothers cannot open their mouths and interfere in the domestic affairs of the United States. And as long as it's civil rights, this comes under the jurisdiction of Uncle Sam.

But the United Nations has what's known as the charter of human rights, it has a committee that deals in human rights. You may wonder why all of the atrocities that have been committed in Africa and in Hungary and in Asia and in Latin America are brought before the UN, and the Negro problem is never brought before the UN. This is part of the conspiracy. This old, tricky, blue-eyed liberal who is supposed to be your and my friend, supposed to be in our corner, supposed to be subsidizing our struggle, and supposed to be acting in the capacity of an adviser, never tells you anything about human rights. They keep you wrapped up in civil rights. And you spend so much time barking up the civil-rights tree, you don't even know there's a human-rights tree on the same floor.

When you expand the civil-rights struggle to the level of human rights, you can then take the case of the black man in this country before the nations in the UN. You can take it before the General Assembly. You can take Uncle Sam before a world court. But the only level you can do it on is the level of human rights. Civil rights keeps you under his restrictions, under his jurisdiction. Civil rights keeps you in his pocket. Civil rights means you're asking Uncle Sam to treat you right. Human rights are something you were born with. Human rights are your God-given rights. Human rights are the rights that are recognized by all nations of this earth. And any time any one violates your human rights, you can take them to the world court. Uncle Sam's hands are dripping with blood, dripping with the blood of the black man in this country. He's the earth's number-one hypocrite. He has the audacity—yes, he has—imagine him posing as the leader of the free world. The free world!—and you over here singing "We Shall Overcome." Expand the civil-rights struggle to the level of human rights, take it into the United Nations, where our African brothers can throw their weight on our side, where our Asian brothers can throw their weight on our side, where our Latin-American brothers can throw their weight on our side, and where 800 million Chinamen are sitting there waiting to throw their weight on our side.

Let the world know how bloody his hands are. Let the world know the hypocrisy that's practiced over here. Let it be the ballot or the bullet. Let him know that it must be the ballot or the bullet.

When you take your case to Washington, D.C., you're taking it to the criminal who's responsible; it's like running from the wolf to the fox. They're all in cahoots together. They all work political chicanery and make you look like a chump before the eyes of the world. Here you are walking around in America, getting ready to be drafted and sent abroad, like a tin soldier, and when you get over there, people ask you what are you fighting for, and you have to stick your tongue in your cheek. No, take Uncle Sam to court, take him before the world.

By ballot I only mean freedom. Don't you know—I disagree with Lomax on this issue—that the ballot is more important than the dollar? Can I prove it? Yes. Look in the UN. There are poor nations in the UN; yet those poor nations can get together with their voting power and keep the rich nations from making a move. They have one nation—one vote, everyone has an equal vote. And when those brothers from Asia, and Africa and the darker parts of this earth get together, their voting power is sufficient to hold Sam in check. Or Russia in check. Or some other section of the earth in check. So, the ballot is most important.

Right now, in this country, if you and I, 22 million African-Americans— that's what we are—Africans who are in America. You're nothing but Africans. Nothing but Africans. In fact, you'd get farther calling yourself African instead of Negro. Africans don't catch hell. You're the only one catching hell. They don't have to pass civil-rights bills for Africans. An African can go anywhere he wants right now. All you've got to do is tie your head up. That's right, go anywhere you want. Just stop being a Negro. Change your name to Hoogagagooba. That'll show you how silly the white man is. You're dealing with a silly man. A friend of mine who's very dark put a turban on his head and went into a restaurant in Atlanta before they called themselves desegregated. He went into a white restaurant, he sat down, they served him, and he said, "What would happen if a Negro came in here?" And there he's sitting, black as night, but because he had his head wrapped up the waitress looked back at him and says, "Why, there wouldn't no nigger dare come in here."

So, you're dealing with a man whose bias and prejudice are making him lose his mind, his intelligence, every day. He's frightened. He looks around and sees what's taking place on this earth, and he sees that the pendulum of time is swinging in your direction. The dark people are waking up. They're losing their fear of the white man. No place where he's fighting right now is he winning. Everywhere he's fighting, he's fighting someone your and my complexion. And they're beating him. He can't win any more. He's won his last battle. He failed to win the Korean War. He couldn't win it. He had to sign a truce. That's a loss. Any time Uncle Sam, with all his machinery for warfare, is held to a draw by some rice-eaters, he's lost the battle. He had to sign a truce. America's not supposed to sign a truce. She's supposed to be bad. But she's not bad any more. She's bad as long as she can use her hydrogen bomb, but she can't use hers for fear Russia might use hers. Russia can't use hers, for fear that Sam might use his. So, both of them are weaponless. They can't use the weapon because each's weapon nullifies the other's. So the only place where action can take place is on the ground. And the white man can't win another war fighting on the ground. Those days are over. The black man knows it, the brown man knows it, the red man knows it, and the yellow man knows it. So they engage him in guerrilla warfare. That's not his style. You've got to have heart to be a guerrilla warrior, and he hasn't got any heart. I'm telling you now.

I just want to give you a little briefing on guerrilla warfare because, before you know it, before you know it—It takes heart to be a guerrilla warrior because you're on your own. In conventional warfare you have tanks and a whole lot of other people with you to back you up, planes over your head and all that kind of stuff. But a guerrilla is on his own. All you have is a rifle, some sneakers and a bowl of rice, and that's all you need—and a lot of heart. The

Japanese on some of those islands in the Pacific, when the American soldiers landed, one Japanese sometimes could hold the whole army off. He'd just wait until the sun went down, and when the sun went down they were all equal. He would take his little blade and slip from bush to bush, and from American to American. The white soldiers couldn't cope with that. Whenever you see a white soldier that fought in the Pacific, he has the shakes, he has a nervous condition, because they scared him to death.

The same thing happened to the French up in French Indochina. People who just a few years previously were rice farmers got together and ran the heavily-mechanized French army out of Indochina. You don't need it—modern warfare today won't work. This is the day of the guerrilla. They did the same thing in Algeria. Algerians, who were nothing but Bedouins, took a rifle and sneaked off to the hills, and de Gaulle and all of his highfalutin' war machinery couldn't defeat those guerrillas. Nowhere on this earth does the white man win in a guerrilla warfare. It's not his speed. Just as guerrilla warfare is prevailing in Asia and in parts of Africa and in parts of Latin America, you've got to be mighty naive, or you've got to play the black man cheap, if you don't think some day he's going to wake up and find that it's got to be the ballot or the bullet.

I would like to say, in closing, a few things concerning the Muslim Mosque, Inc., which we established recently in New York City. It's true we're Muslims and our religion is Islam, but we don't mix our religion with our politics and our economics and our social and civil activities—not any more. We keep our religion in our mosque. After our religious services are over, then as Muslims we become involved in political action, economic action and social and civic action. We become involved with anybody, anywhere, any time and in any manner that's designed to eliminate the evils, the political, economic and social evils that are afflicting the people of our community.

The political philosophy of black nationalism means that the black man should control the politics and the politicians in his own community; no more. The black man in the black community has to be re-educated into the science of politics so he will know what politics is supposed to bring him in return. Don't be throwing out any ballots. A ballot is like a bullet. You don't throw your ballots until you see a target, and if that target is not within your reach, keep your ballot in your pocket. The political philosophy of black nationalism is being taught in the Christian church. It's being taught in the NAACP. It's being taught in CORE meetings. It's being taught in SNCC [Student Nonviolent Coordinating Committee] meetings. It's being taught in Muslim meetings. It's being taught where nothing but atheists and agnostics come together. It's being taught everywhere. Black people are fed up with the dilly-dallying, pussyfooting, compromising approach that we've been using toward getting our freedom. We want freedom *now*, but we're not going to get it saying "We Shall Overcome." We've got to fight until we overcome.

The economic philosophy of black nationalism is pure and simple. It only means that we should control the economy of our community. Why should white people be running all the stores in our community? Why should white people be running the banks of our community? Why should the economy of our community be in the hands of the white man? Why? If a black man can't move his store into a white community, you tell me why a white man should move his store into a black community. The philosophy of black nationalism involves a re-education program in the black community in regards to economics. Our people have to be made to see that any time you take your dollar out of your community and spend it in a community where you don't live, the community where you live will get poorer and poorer, and the community where you spend your money will get richer and richer. Then you wonder why where you live is always a ghetto or a slum area. And where you and I are concerned, not only do we lose it when we spend it out of the community, but the white man has got all our stores in the community tied up; so that though we spend it in the community, at sundown the man who runs the store takes it over across town somewhere. He's got us in a vise.

So the economic philosophy of black nationalism means in every church, in every civic organization, in every fraternal order, it's time now for our people to become conscious of the importance of controlling the economy of our community. If we own the stores, if we operate the businesses, if we try and establish some industry in our own community, then we're developing to the position where we are creating employment for our own kind. Once you gain control of the economy of your own community, then you don't have to picket and boycott and beg some cracker downtown for a job in his business.

The social philosophy of black nationalism only means that we have to get together and remove the evils, the vices, alcoholism, drug addiction, and other evils that are destroying the moral fiber of our community. We ourselves have to lift the level of our community, the standard of our community to a higher level, make our own society beautiful so that we will be satisfied in our own social circles and won't be running around here trying to knock our way into a social circle where we're not wanted.

So I say, in spreading a gospel such as black nationalism, it is not designed to make the black man re-evaluate the white man—you know him already—but to make the black man re-evaluate himself. Don't change the white man's mind—you can't change his mind, and that whole thing about appealing to the moral conscience of America—America's conscience is bankrupt. She lost all conscience a long time ago. Uncle Sam has no conscience. They don't know what morals are. They don't try and eliminate an evil because it's evil, or because it's illegal, or because it's immoral; they eliminate it only when it threatens their existence. So you're wasting your time appealing to the moral conscience of a bankrupt man like Uncle Sam. If he had a conscience, he'd straighten this thing out with no more pressure being put upon him. So it is not necessary to change the white man's mind. We have to change our own mind. You can't change his mind about us. We've got to change our own minds about each other. We have to see each other with new eyes. We have to see each other as brothers and sisters. We have to come together with warmth so we can develop unity and harmony that's necessary to get this problem solved ourselves. How can we do this? How can we avoid jealousy? How can we avoid the suspicion and the divisions that exist in the community? I'll tell you how.

I have watched how Billy Graham comes into a city, spreading what he calls the gospel of Christ, which is only white nationalism. That's what he is. Billy Graham is a white nationalist; I'm a black nationalist. But since it's the natural tendency for leaders to be jealous and look upon a powerful figure like Graham with suspicion and envy, how is it possible for him to come into a city and get all the cooperation of the church leaders? Don't think because they're church leaders that they don't have weaknesses that make them envious and jealous—no, everybody's got it. It's not an accident that when they want to choose a cardinal [as Pope] over there in Rome, they get in a closet so you can't hear them cussing and fighting and carrying on.

Billy Graham comes in preaching the gospel of Christ, he evangelizes the gospel, he stirs everybody up, but he never tries to start a church. If he came in trying to start a church, all the churches would be against him. So, he just comes in talking about Christ and tells everybody who gets Christ to go to any church where Christ is; and in this way the church cooperates with him. So we're going to take a page from his book.

Our gospel is black nationalism. We're not trying to threaten the existence of any organization, but we're spreading the gospel of black nationalism. Anywhere there's a church that is also preaching and practicing the gospel of black nationalism, join that church. If the NAACP is preaching and practicing the gospel of black nationalism, join the NAACP. If CORE is spreading and practicing the gospel of black nationalism, join CORE. Join any organization that has a gospel that's for the uplift of the black man. And when you get into it and see them pussyfooting or compromising, pull out of it because that's not black nationalism. We'll find another one.

And in this manner, the organizations will increase in number and in quantity and in quality, and by August, it is then our intention to have a black nationalist convention which will consist of delegates from all over the country who are interested in the political, economic and social philosophy of black nationalism. After these delegates convene, we will hold a seminar, we will hold discussions, we will listen to everyone. We want to hear new ideas and new solutions and new answers. And at that time, if we see fit then to form a black nationalist party, we'll form a black nationalist party. If it's necessary to form a black nationalist army, we'll form a black nationalist army. It'll be the ballot or the bullet. It'll be liberty or it'll be death.

It's time for you and me to stop sitting in this country, letting some cracker senators, Northern crackers and Southern crackers, sit there in Washington, D.C., and come to a conclusion in their mind that you and I are supposed to have civil rights. There's no white man going to tell me anything about *my* rights. Brothers and sisters, always remember, if it doesn't take senators and congressmen and presidential proclamations to give freedom to the white man, it is not necessary for legislation or proclamation or Supreme Court decisions to give freedom to the black man. You let that white man know, if this is a country of freedom, let it be a country of freedom; and if it's not a country of freedom, change it.

We will work with anybody, anywhere, at any time, who is genuinely interested in tackling the problem head-on, nonviolently as long as the enemy is nonviolent, but violent when the enemy gets violent. We'll work with you on the voter-registration drive, we'll work with you on rent strikes, we'll work with you on school boycotts—I don't believe in any kind of integration; I'm not even worried about it because I know you're not going to get it anyway; you're not going to get it because you're afraid to die; you've got to be ready to die if you try and force yourself on the white man, because he'll get just as violent as those crackers in Mississippi, right here in Cleveland. But we will still work with you on the school boycotts because we're against a segregated school system. A segregated school system produces children who, when they graduate, graduate with crippled minds. But this does not mean that a school is segregated because it's all black. A segregated school means a school that is controlled by people who have no real interest in it whatsoever.

Let me explain what I mean. A segregated district or community is a community in which people live, but outsiders control the politics and the economy of that community. They never refer to the white section as a segregated community. It's the all-Negro section that's a segregated community. Why? The white man controls his own school, his own bank, his own economy, his own politics, his own everything, his own community—but he also controls yours. When you're under someone else's control, you're segregated. They'll always give you the lowest or the worst that there is to offer, but it doesn't mean you're segregated just because you have your own. You've got to *control* your own. Just like the white man has control of his, you need to control yours.

You know the best way to get rid of segregation? The white man is more afraid of separation than he is of integration. Segregation means that he puts you away from him, but not far enough for you to be out of his jurisdiction; separation means you're gone. And the white man will integrate faster than he'll let you separate. So we will work with you against the segregated school system because it's criminal, because it is absolutely destructive, in every way imaginable, to the minds of the children who have to be exposed to that type of crippling education.

Last but not least, I must say this concerning the great controversy over rifles and shotguns. The only thing that I've ever said is that in areas where the government has proven itself either unwilling or unable to defend the lives and the property of Negroes, it's time for Negroes to defend themselves. Article number two of the constitutional amendments provides you and me the right to own a rifle or a shotgun. It is constitutionally legal to own a shotgun or a rifle. This doesn't mean you're going to get a rifle and form battalions and go out looking for white folks, although you'd be within your rights—I mean, you'd be justified; but that would be illegal and we don't do anything illegal. If the white man doesn't want the black man buying rifles and shotguns, then let the government do its job. That's all. And don't let the white man come to you and ask you what you think about what Malcolm says—why, you old Uncle Tom. He would never ask you if he thought you were going to say, "Amen!" No, he is making a Tom out of you.

So, this doesn't mean forming rifle clubs and going out looking for people, but it is time, in 1964, if you are a man, to let that man know. If he's not going to do his job in running the government and providing you and me with the protection that our taxes are supposed to be for, since he spends all those billions for his defense budget, he certainly can't begrudge you and me spending $12 or $15 for a single-shot, or double-action. I hope you understand. Don't go out shooting people, but any time, brothers and sisters, and especially the men in this audience—some of you wearing Congressional Medals of Honor, with shoulders this wide, chests this big, muscles that big—any time you and I sit around and read where they bomb a church and murder in cold blood, not some grownups, but four little girls while they were praying to the same god the white man taught them to pray to, and you and I see the government go down and can't find who did it.

Why, this man—he can find Eichmann hiding down in Argentina somewhere. Let two or three American soldiers, who are minding somebody else's business way over in South Vietnam, get killed, and he'll send battleships, sticking his nose in their business. He wanted to send troops down to Cuba and make them have what he calls free elections—this old cracker who doesn't have free elections in his own country. No, if you never see me another time in your life, if I die in the morning, I'll die saying one thing: the ballot or the bullet, the ballot or the bullet.

If a Negro in 1964 has to sit around and wait for some cracker senator to filibuster when it comes to the rights of black people, why, you and I should hang our heads in shame. You talk about a march on Washington in 1963, you haven't seen anything. There's some more going down in '64. And this time they're not going like they went last year. They're not going singing "We Shall Overcome." They're not going with white friends. They're not going with placards already painted for them. They're not going with round-trip tickets. They're going with one-way tickets.

And if they don't want that non-nonviolent army going down there, tell them to bring the filibuster to a halt. The black nationalists aren't going to wait. Lyndon B. Johnson is the head of the Democratic Party. If he's for civil rights, let him go into the Senate next week and declare himself. Let him go in there right now and declare himself. Let him go in there and denounce the Southern branch of his party. Let him go in there right now and take a moral stand—right now, not later. Tell him, don't wait until election time. If he waits too long, brothers and sisters, he will be responsible for letting a condition develop in this country which will create a climate that will bring seeds up out of the ground with vegetation on the end of them looking like something these people never dreamed of. In 1964, it's the ballot or the bullet. Thank you.

Black Revolutionary Nationalism

The Philosophy and Platform of the Black Panther Party

A new organization of militant young blacks appeared on the West Coast in 1966. Borrowing the emblem of a black political movement in Lowndes County, Alabama, they called themselves the Black Panther Party for Self Defense. The panther was an apt symbol, for although it is not an aggressive animal, it fiercely defends itself when cornered.

Founded in Oakland by Huey Newton and Bobby Seale, the Panthers attracted many young blacks because of their uncompromising position on racial liberation and their affirmation of black strength and black pride. Not surprisingly, they also attracted the hostility of law-enforcement authorities from coast to coast, who systematically tried to suppress the party and put most Panther leaders in jail at one time or another.

The first selection presented next is an interview with Huey Newton, conducted by the Liberation News Service, while Newton was in jail awaiting trial on the charge of killing a policeman during a Panther–police shootout. Basing his theories partly on the analysis of colonial resistance found in Frantz Fanon's The Wretched of the Earth, *Newton speaks of the need for economic and political revolution and the possibility of cooperation between black and white radicals.*

Following the interview, the platform of the Black Panther Party is reproduced. This statement, drawn up in October 1966, is based on the theory of self-determination typical of nationalist movements and contains specific criticisms of some of the policies that have led to the oppression of black people. The document concludes with some familiar words about the justice, and even the necessity, of revolution when a government loses the consent of the governed.

QUESTION: The question of nationalism is a vital one in the black movement today. Some have made a distinction between cultural nationalism and revolutionary nationalism. Would you comment on the differences and give us your views?

HUEY P. NEWTON: Revolutionary nationalism first is dependent upon a people's revolution with the end goal being the people in power. Therefore, to be a revolutionary nationalist you would by necessity have to be a socialist. If you are a reactionary nationalist your end goal is the oppression of the people.

FROM Huey Newton, "Huey Newton Speaks from jail," *motive* vol. 29 (October 1968), pp. 8–16. Reprinted by permission.

Cultural nationalism, or pork chop nationalism, as I sometimes call it, is basically a problem of having the wrong political perspective. It seems to be a reaction instead of a response to political oppression. The cultural nationalists are concerned with returning to the old African culture and thereby regaining their identity and freedom. In other words, they feel that the African culture automatically will bring political freedom.

The Black Panther Party, which is a revolutionary group of black people, realizes that we have to have an identity. We have to realize our black heritage in order to give us strength to move on and progress. But as far as returning to the old African culture, it's unnecessary and not advantageous in many respects. We believe that culture itself will not liberate us. We're going to need some stronger stuff.

A good example of revolutionary nationalism was the revolution in Algeria when Ben Bella took over. The French were kicked out, but it was a people's revolution because the people ended up in power. The leaders that took over were not interested in the profit motive where they could exploit the people and keep them in a state of slavery. They nationalized the industry and plowed the would-be profits into the community. That's what socialism is all about in a nutshell. The people's representatives are in office strictly on the leave of the people. The wealth of the country is controlled by the people and they are considered whenever modifications in the industries are made.

The Black Panther Party is a revolutionary Nationalist group and we see a major contradiction between capitalism in this country and our interests. We realize that this country became very rich upon slavery and that slavery is capitalism in the extreme. We have two evils to fight, capitalism and racism. We must destroy both racism and capitalism.

QUESTION: Directly related to the question of nationalism is the question of unity within the black community. There has been some question about this since the Black Panther Party has run candidates against other black candidates in recent California elections. What is your position on this matter?

HUEY: A very peculiar thing has happened. Historically, you have what Malcolm X calls the field nigger and the house nigger. The house nigger had some privileges. He got the worn-out clothes of the master and he didn't have to work as hard as the field black. He came to respect the master to such an extent that he identified with the master, because he got a few of the leftovers that the field blacks did not get. And through this identity with him, he saw the slavemaster's interest as being his interest. Sometimes he would even protect the slavemaster more than the slavemaster would protect himself. Malcolm makes the point that if the master's house happened to catch on fire, the house Negro would work harder than the master to put the fire out and save the master's house, while the field black was praying that the house burned down. The house black identified with the master so much that, when the master would get sick, the house Negro would say, "Master, we's sick!"

Members of the Black Panther Party are the field blacks; we're hoping the master dies if he gets sick. The black bourgeoisie seem to be acting in the role of the house Negro. They are pro–administration. They would like a few concessions made, but as far as the overall setup, they have more material goods, a little more advantage, a few more privileges than the black have-nots, the lower class, and so they identify with the power structure and they see their interest as the power structure's interest. In fact, it's against their interest.

The Black Panther Party was forced to draw a line of demarcation. We are for all of those who are for the promotion of the interests of the black have-nots, which represents about 98 percent of blacks here in America. We're not controlled by the white mother country radicals nor are we controlled by the black bourgeoisie. We have a mind of our own and if the black bourgeoisie cannot align itself with our complete program, then the black bourgeoisie sets itself up as our enemy.

QUESTION: The Black Panther Party has had considerable contact with white radicals since its earliest days. What do you see as the role of these white radicals?

HUEY: The white mother country radical is the offspring of the children of the beast that has plundered the world exploiting all people, concentrating on the people of color. These are children of the beast that seek now to be redeemed because they realize that their former heroes, who were slavemasters and murderers, put forth ideas that were only façades to hide the treachery they inflicted upon the world. They are turning their backs on their fathers.

The white mother country radical, in resisting the system, becomes a somewhat abstract thing because he's not oppressed as much as black people are. As a matter of fact, his oppression is somewhat abstract simply because he doesn't have to live in a reality of oppression.

Black people in America, and colored people throughout the world, suffer not only from exploitation, but they suffer from racism. Black people here in America, in the black colony, are oppressed because we're black and we're exploited. The whites are rebels, many of them from the middle class and as far as any overt oppression this is not the case. Therefore, I call their rejection of the system a somewhat abstract thing. They're looking for new heroes. They're looking to wash away the hypocrisy that their fathers have presented to the world. In doing this, they see the people who are really fighting for freedom. They see the people who are really standing for justice and equality and peace throughout the world. They are the people of Vietnam, the people of Latin America, the people of Asia, the people of Africa, and the black people in the black colony here in America.

This presents something of a problem in many ways to the black revolutionary, especially to the cultural nationalist. The cultural nationalist doesn't understand the white revolutionaries because he can't see why anyone white would turn on the system. He thinks that maybe this is some more hypocrisy being planted by white people.

I personally think that there are many young white revolutionaries who are sincere in attempting to realign themselves with mankind, and to make a reality out of the high moral standards that their fathers and forefathers only expressed. In pressing for new heroes, the young white revolutionaries found these heroes in the black colony at home and in the colonies throughout the world.

The young white revolutionaries raised the cry for the troops to withdraw from Vietnam, to keep hands off Latin America, to withdraw from the Dominican Republic and also to withdraw from the black community or the black colony. So we have a situation in which the young white revolutionaries are attempting to identify with the oppressed people of the colonies against the exploiter.

The problem arises, then, in what part they can play. How can they aid the colony? How can they aid the Black Panther Party or any other black revolutionary group? They can aid the black revolutionaries first, by simply turning away from the establishment, and secondly, by choosing their friends. For instance, they have a choice between whether they will be a friend of Lyndon Baines Johnson or a friend of Fidel Castro. A friend of mine or a friend of Johnson's. These are direct opposites. After they make this choice, then the white revolutionaries have a duty and a responsibility to act.

The imperialistic or capitalistic system occupies areas. It occupies Vietnam now. It occupies areas by sending soldiers there, by sending policemen there. The policemen or soldiers are only a gun in the establishment's hand, making the racist secure in his racism, the establishment secure in its exploitation. The first problem, it seems, is to remove the gun from the establishment's hand. Until lately, the white radical has seen no reason to come into conflict with the policeman in his own community. I said "until recently," because there is friction now in the mother country between the young revolutionaries and the police; because now the white revolutionaries are attempting to put some of their ideas into action, and there's the rub. We say that it should be a permanent thing.

Black people are being oppressed in the colony by white policemen, by white racists. We are saying they must withdraw.

As far as I'm concerned, the only reasonable conclusion would be to first realize the enemy, realize the plan, and then when something happens in the black colony—when we're attacked and ambushed in the black colony—then the white revolutionary students and intellectuals and all the other whites who support the colony should respond by defending us, by attacking the enemy in their community.

The Black Panther Party is an all black party, because we feel, as Malcolm X felt, that there can be no black–white unity until there first is black unity. We have a problem in the black colony that is particular to the colony, but we're willing to accept aid from the mother country as long as the mother country radicals realize that we have, as Eldridge Cleaver says in *Soul on Ice,* a mind of our own. We've regained our mind that was taken away from us and we will decide the political, as well as the practical, stand that we'll take. We'll make the theory and we'll carry out the practice. It's the duty of the white revolutionary to aid us in this.

QUESTION: You have spoken a lot about dealing with the protectors of the system, the armed forces. Would you like to elaborate on why you place so much emphasis on this?

HUEY: The reason that I feel so strongly is simply because without this protection from the army, the police and the military, the institutions could not go on in their racism and exploitation. For instance, as the Vietnamese are driving the American imperialist troops out of Vietnam, it automatically stops the racist imperialist institutions of America from oppressing that particular country. The country cannot implement its racist program without guns. The guns are the military and the police. If the military were disarmed in Vietnam, then the Vietnamese would be victorious.

We are in the same situation here in America. Whenever we attack the system, the first thing the administrators do is to send out their strong-arm men. If it's a rent strike, because of the indecent housing we have, they will send out the police to throw the furniture out the window. They don't come themselves. They send their protectors. To deal with the corrupt exploiter, we are going to have to deal with his protector, which is the police who take orders from him. This is a must.

QUESTION: Would you like to be more specific on the conditions which must exist before an alliance or coalition can be formed with the predominantly white groups? Would you comment specifically on your alliance with the California Peace and Freedom Party?

HUEY: We have an alliance with the Peace and Freedom Party because it has supported our program in full, and this is the criterion for a coalition with the black revolutionary group. If it had not supported our program in full, then we would not have seen any reason to make an alliance with them, because we are the reality of the oppression. They are not. They are only oppressed in an abstract way; we are oppressed in the real way. We are the real slaves! So it's a problem that we suffer from more than anyone else and it's our problem of liberation. Therefore we should decide what measures and what tools and what programs to use to become liberated. Many of the young white revolutionaries realize this and I see no reason not to have a coalition with them.

QUESTION: Other black groups seem to feel that from past experience it is impossible for them to work with whites and impossible for them to form alliances. What do you see as the reasons for this and do you think that the history of the Black Panther makes this less of a problem?

HUEY: There was a somewhat unhealthy relationship in the past with the white liberals supporting the black people who were trying to gain their freedom. I think that a good example of this would be the relationship that SNCC had with its white liberals. I call them white liberals because they differ strictly from the white radicals. The relationship was that the whites controlled SNCC for a very long time. From the very start of SNCC until recently, whites were the mind of SNCC. They controlled the program of SNCC with money and they controlled the ideology, or the stands SNCC would take. The blacks in SNCC were completely controlled program-wise; they couldn't do any more than the white liberals wanted them to do, which wasn't very much. So the white liberals were not working for self-determination for the black community. They were interested in a few concessions from the power structure. They undermined SNCC's program.

Stokely Carmichael came along, and realizing this, started Malcolm X's program of Black Power. Whites were afraid when Stokely said that black people have a mind of their own and that SNCC would seek self-determination for the black community. The white liberals withdrew their support, leaving the organization financially bankrupt. The blacks who were in the organization, Stokely and H. Rap Brown, were left angry and bewildered with the white liberals who had been aiding them under the guise of being sincere.

As a result, the leadership of SNCC turned away from the white liberal, which was good. I don't think they distinguished between the white liberal and the white revolutionary; because the revolutionary is white also, and they are very much afraid to have any contact with white people—even to the point of denying that the white revolutionaries could help by supporting programs of SNCC in the mother country. Not by making programs, not by being a member of the organization, but simply by resisting.

I think that one of SNCC's great problems is that they were controlled by the traditional administrator: the omnipotent administrator, the white person. He was the mind of SNCC. SNCC regained its mind, but I believe that it lost its political perspective. I think that this was a reaction rather than a response. The Black Panther Party has NEVER been controlled by white people. We have always had an integration of mind and body. We have never been controlled by whites and therefore we don't fear the white mother country radicals. Our alliance is one of organized black groups with organized white groups. As soon as the organized white groups do not do the things that would benefit us in our struggle for liberation, that will be the point of our departure. So we don't suffer in the hang-up of a skin color. We don't hate white people; we hate the oppressor.

QUESTION: You indicate that there is a psychological process that has historically existed in white-black relations in the U.S. that must change in the course of revolutionary struggle. Would you like to comment on this?

HUEY: Yes. The historical relationship between black and white here in America has been the relationship between the slave and the master; the master being the mind and the slave the body. The slave would carry out the orders that the mind demanded him to carry out. By doing this, the master took the manhood from the slave because he stripped him of a mind. In the process, the slave-master stripped himself of a body. As Eldridge Cleaver puts it, the slave-master became the omnipotent administrator and the slave became the super-masculine menial. This puts the omnipotent administrator into the controlling position or the front office and the super-masculine menial into the field.

The whole relationship developed so that the omnipotent administrator and the super-masculine menial became opposites. The slave being a very strong body doing all the practical things, all of the work becomes very masculine. The omnipotent administrator in the process of removing himself from all body functions realizes later that he has emasculated himself. And this is very disturbing to him. So the slave lost his mind and the slave-master his body.

This caused the slave-master to become very envious of the slave because he pictured the slave as being more of a man, being superior sexually, because the penis is part of the body. The omnipotent administrator laid down a decree when he realized that in his plan to enslave the black man, he had emasculated himself. He attempted to bind the penis of the slave. He attempted to show that his penis could reach further than the super-masculine menial's penis. He said "I, the omnipotent administrator, can have access to the black woman." The super-masculine menial then had a psychological attraction to the white female (the ultra-feminine freak) for the simple reason that it was forbidden fruit. The omnipotent administrator decreed that this kind of contact would be punished by death.

At the same time, in order to reinforce his sexual desire, to confirm, to assert his manhood, he would go into the slave quarters and have sexual relations with the black women (the self-reliant Amazon), not to be satisfied but simply to confirm his manhood. If he could only satisfy the self-reliant Amazon then he would be sure that he was a man. Because he didn't have a body, he didn't have a penis, but psychologically wanted to castrate the black man. The slave was constantly seeking unity within himself: a mind and a body. He always wanted to be able to decide, to gain respect from his woman, because women want one who can control.

I give this outline to fit into a framework of what is happening now. The white power structure today in America defines itself as the mind. They want to control the world. They go off and plunder the world. They are the policemen of the world exercising control especially over people of color.

The white man cannot gain his manhood, cannot unite with the body, because the body is black. The body is symbolic of slavery and strength. It's a biological thing as he views it. The slave is in a much better situation because his not being a full man has always been viewed psychologically. And it's always easier to make a psychological transition than a biological one. If he can only recapture his mind, then he will lose all fear and will be free to determine his destiny. This is what is happening today with the rebellion of the world's oppressed people against the controller. They are regaining their mind and they're saying that we have a mind of our own. They're saying that we want freedom to determine the destiny of our people, thereby uniting the mind with their bodies. They are taking the mind back from the omnipotent administrator, the controller, the exploiter.

QUESTION: You have mentioned that the guerilla was the perfect man and this kind of formulation seems to fit directly with the guerilla as a political man. Would you comment on this?

HUEY: The guerilla is a very unique man. This is in contrast to Marxist-Leninist orthodox theories where the party controls the military. The guerilla is not only the warrior, the military fighter; he is also the military commander as well as the political theoretician. Regis Debray says "poor the pen without the guns, poor the gun without the pen." The pen being just an extension of the mind, a tool to write down concepts, ideas. The gun is only an extension of the body, the extension of our fanged teeth that we lost through evolution. It's the weapon, it's the claws that we lost, it's the body. The guerilla is the military commander and the political theoretician all in one.

What we have to do as a vanguard of the revolution is to correct this through activity The large majority of black people are either illiterate or semi–literate. They don't read. They need activity to follow. This is true of any colonized people. The same thing happened in Cuba where it was necessary for twelve men with the leadership of Che and Fidel to take to the hills and then attack the corrupt administration, to attack the army who were the protectors of the exploiters in Cuba. They would have leafleted the community and they could have written books, but the people would not respond. They had to act and the people could see and hear about it and therefore become educated on how to respond to oppression.

In this country black revolutionaries have to set an example. We can't do the same things that were done in Cuba because Cuba is Cuba and the U. S. is the U. S. Cuba had many terrains to protect the guerilla. This country is mainly urban. We have to work out new solutions to offset the power of the country's technology and communication. We do have solutions to these problems and they will be put into effect. I wouldn't want to go into the ways and means of this, but we will educate through action. We have to engage in action to make the people want to read our literature. They are not attracted to all the writing in this country; there's too much writing. Many books make one weary.

QUESTION: Kennedy before his death, and to a lesser extent Rockefeller and Lindsay and other establishment liberals, have been talking about making reforms to give black people a greater share of the pie and thus stop any developing revolutionary movement. Would you comment on this?

HUEY: I would say this: If a Kennedy or a Lindsay or anyone else can give decent housing to all of our people; if they can give full employment to our people with a high standard; if they can give full control to the black people to determine the destiny of their community; if they can give fair trials in the court system by turning the structure over to the community; if they can end their exploitation of people throughout the world; if they can do all these things, they will have solved the problems. But I don't believe under this present system, under capitalism, that they will be able to solve these problems.

I don't think black people should be fooled by their come-ons because everyone who gets in office promises the same thing. They promise full employment and decent housing; the Great Society, the New Frontier. All of these names, but no real benefits. No effects are felt in the black community, and black people are tired of being deceived and duped. The people must have full control of the means of production. Small black businesses cannot compete with General Motors. That's just out of the question. General Motors robbed us and worked us for nothing for a couple hundred years and took our money and set up factories and became fat and rich and then talks about giving us some of the crumbs. We want full control. We're not interested in anyone promising that the private owners are going to all of a sudden become human beings and give these things to our community. It hasn't ever happened and, based on empirical evidence, we don't expect them to become Buddhists overnight.

QUESTION: The Panthers' organizing efforts have been very open. Would you like to comment about the question of an underground political organization versus an open organization at this point in the struggle?

HUEY: Some of the black nationalist groups feel that they have to be underground because they'll be attacked, but we don't feel that you can romanticize being underground. They say we're romantic because we're trying to live revolutionary lives, and we are not taking precautions. But we say that the only way we would go underground is if we're driven underground. All real revolutionary movements are driven underground.

This is a pre-revolutionary period and we feel it is very necessary to educate the people while we can. So we're very open about this education. We have been attacked and we will be attacked even more in the future, but we're not going to go underground until we get ready to go underground because we have a mind of our own. We're not going to let anyone force us to do anything. We're going to go underground after we educate all of the black people and not before that time. Then it won't really be necessary for us to go underground because you can see black anywhere. We will just have the stuff to protect ourselves and the strategy to offset the great power that the strong-arm men of the establishment have and are planning to use against us.

QUESTION: Do you see the possibility of organizing a white Panther Party in opposition to the establishment, possibly among poor and working whites?

HUEY: As I said before, Black Power is people's power and as far as organizing white people we give white people the privilege of having a mind and we want them to get a body. They can organize themselves. We can tell them what they should do, but their responsibility, if they're going to claim to be white revolutionaries or white mother country radicals, is to arm themselves and support the colonies around the world in their just struggle against imperialism. Anything more than that they will have to do on their own.

QUESTION: What do you mean by Black Power?

HUEY: Black Power is really people's power. The Black Panther Program, Panther Power as we call it, will implement this people's power. We have respect for all of humanity and we realize that the people should rule and determine their destiny. Wipe out the controller. To have Black Power doesn't humble or subjugate anyone to slavery or oppression. Black Power is giving power to people who have not had power to determine their destiny. We advocate and we aid any people who are struggling to determine their destiny. This is regardless of color. The Vietnamese say Vietnam should be able to determine its own destiny. Power of the Vietnamese people. We also chant power of the Vietnamese people. The Latins are talking about Latin America for the Latin Americans. Cuba, si and Yanqui, no. It's not that they don't want the Yankees to have any power; they just don't want them to have power over them. They can have power over themselves. We in the black colony in America want to be able to have power over our destiny, and that's black power.

QUESTION: How would you characterize the mood of black people in America today? Are they disenchanted, wanting a larger slice of the pie, or alienated, not wanting to integrate into Babylon? What do you think it will take for them to become alienated and revolutionary?

HUEY: I was going to say disillusioned, but I don't think that we were ever under the illusion that we had freedom in this country. This society definitely is a decadent one and we realize it. Black people cannot gain their freedom under the present system, the system that is carrying out its plans to institutionalize racism. Your question is what will have to be done to stimulate them to revolution. I think it's already being done. It's a matter of time now for us to educate them to a program and show them the way to liberation. The Black Panther Party is the beacon light to show black people the way to liberation.

You notice the insurrections that have been going on throughout the country; in Watts, in Newark, in Detroit. They were all responses of the people demanding that they have freedom to determine their destiny, rejecting exploitation. The Black Panther Party does not think that the traditional riots, or insurrections, that have taken place are the answer. It is true that they have been against the Establishment, they have been against authority and oppression within their community; but they have been unorganized. However, black people have learned from each of these insurrections.

They learned from Watts. I'm sure that the people in Detroit were educated by what happened in Watts. Perhaps this was wrong education. It sort of missed the mark. It wasn't quite the correct activity, but the people were educated through the activity. The people of Detroit followed the example of the people in Watts, only they added a little scrutiny to it. The people in Detroit learned that the way to put a hurt on the administration is to make Molotov cocktails and to go into the streets in mass numbers. So this was a matter of learning. The slogan went up, "burn, baby, burn." People were educated through the activity and it spread throughout the country. The people were educated on how to resist, but perhaps incorrectly.

THE PLATFORM

1. We want freedom. We want power to determine the destiny of our Black Community.

We believe that black people will not be free until we are able to determine our destiny.

2. We want full employment for our people.

We believe that the federal government is responsible and obligated to give every man employment or a guaranteed income. We believe that if the white American businessmen will not give full employment, then the means of production should be taken from the businessmen and placed in the community so that the people of the community can organize and employ all of its people and give a high standard of living.

FROM The Black Panther Party, "Platform and Program of the Black Panther Party" (October 1966). Reprinted with permission.

3. We want an end to the robbery by the white man of our Black Community.

We believe that this racist government has robbed us and now we are demanding the overdue debt of forty acres and two mules. Forty acres and two mules was promised 100 years ago as restitution for slave labor and mass murder of black people. We will accept the payment in currency which will be distributed to our many communities. The Germans are now aiding the Jews in Israel for the genocide of the Jewish people. The Germans murdered six million Jews. The American racist has taken part in the slaughter of over fifty million black people; therefore, we feel that this is a modest demand that we make.

4. We want decent housing, fit for shelter of human beings.

We believe that if the white landlords will not give decent housing to our black community, then the housing and the land should be made into cooperatives so that our community, with government aid, can build and make decent housing for its people.

5. We want education for our people that exposes the true nature of this decadent American society. We want education that teaches us our true history and our role in the present-day society.

We believe in an educational system that will give to our people a knowledge of self. If a man does not have knowledge of himself and his position in society and the world, then he has little chance to relate to anything else.

6. We want all black men to be exempt from military service.

We believe that black people should not be forced to fight in the military service to defend a racist government that does not protect us. We will not fight and kill other people of color in the world who, like black people, are being victimized by the white racist government of America. We will protect ourselves from the force and violence of the racist police and the racist military, by whatever means necessary.

7. We want an immediate end to POLICE BRUTALITY and MUR-DER of black people.

We believe we can end police brutality in our black community by organizing black self-defense groups that are dedicated to defending our black community from racist police oppression and brutality. The Second Amendment to the Constitution of the United States gives a right to bear arms. We therefore believe that all black people should arm themselves for self-defense.

8. We want freedom for all black men held in federal, state, county and city prisons and jails.

We believe that all black people should be released from the many jails and prisons because they have not received a fair and impartial trial.

9 We want all black people when brought to trial to be tried in court by a jury of their peer group or people from their black communities, as defined by the Constitution of the United States.

We believe that the courts should follow the United States Constitution so that black people will receive fair trials. The 14th Amendment of the U.S. Constitution gives a man a right to be tried by his peer group. A peer is a person from a similar economic, social, religious, geographical, environmental, historical and racial background. To do this the court will be forced to select a jury from the black community from which the black defendant came. We have been, and are being tried by all-white juries that have no understanding of the "average reasoning man" of the black community.

10. We want land, bread, housing, education, clothing, justice and peace. And as our major political objective, a United Nations-supervised plebiscite to be held throughout the black colony in which only black colonial subjects will be allowed to participate, for the purpose of determining the will of black people as to their national destiny.

When, in the course of human events, it becomes necessary for one people to dissolve the political bands which have connected them with another, and to assume, among the powers of the earth, the separate and equal station to which the laws of nature and nature's God entitle them, a decent respect to the opinions of mankind requires that they should declare the causes which impel them to the separation.

We hold these truths to be self-evident, that all men are created equal; that they are endowed by their Creator with certain unalienable rights; that among these are life, liberty, and the pursuit of happiness. **That, to secure these rights, governments are instituted among men, deriving their just powers from the consent of the governed; that, whenever any form of government becomes destructive of these ends, it is the right of the people to alter or to abolish it, and to institute a new government, laying its foundation on such principles, and organizing its powers in such form, as to them shall seem most likely to effect their safety and happiness**. Prudence, indeed, will dictate that governments long established should not be changed for light and transient causes; and, accordingly, all experience hath shown, that mankind are more disposed to suffer, while evils are sufferable, than to right themselves by abolishing the forms to which they are accustomed. **But, when a long train of abuses and usurpations, pursuing invariably the same object, evinces a design to reduce them under absolute despotism, it is their right, it is their duty, to throw off such government, and to provide new guards for their future security.**

The Meaning of Black Power

Toward Black Liberation

STOKELY CARMICHAEL

Carmichael undertook to explain the meaning of black power in the fall of 1966. Speaking often and writing much about the subject, he developed a theory that closely resembled the black nationalism enunciated by Malcolm X.

In the article that follows, Carmichael attacks the unjustified sensationalism with which the press approached the notion of black power. He goes on to point out how the press tended to divide the civil rights movement into "responsible" and "irresponsible" groups, thus diminishing the possibility of cooperation among all black people.

In his analysis of powerlessness, which he considered to be the heart of the race problem, Carmichael distinguished between individual and institutional racism and suggested that the same tactics would not work to eliminate both. What was needed was for black people to gain control over their lives, economically, socially, and politically, so that they would no longer have to submit to the institutions of a racist white world. The practical working out of this plan Carmichael left to others.

One of the most pointed illustrations of the need for Black Power, as a positive and redemptive force in a society degenerating into a form of totalitarianism, is to be made by examining the history of distortion that the concept has received in national media of publicity. In this "debate," as in everything else that affects our lives, Negroes are dependent on, and at the discretion of, forces and institutions within the white society which have little interest in representing us honestly. Our experience with the national press has been that where they have managed to escape a meretricious special interest in "Git Whitey" sensationalism and race-war mongering, individual reporters and commentators have been conditioned by the enveloping racism of the society to the point where they are incapable even of objective observation and reporting of racial *incidents*, much less the analysis of *ideas*. But this limitation of vision and perceptions is an inevitable consequence of the dictatorship of definition, interpretation, and consciousness, along with the censorship of history that the society has inflicted upon the Negro—and itself.

Our concern for black power addresses itself directly to this problem, the necessity to reclaim our history and our identity from the cultural terrorism and depredation of self-justifying white guilt.

FROM Stokely Carmichael, "Toward Black Liberation," *The Massachusetts Review*, vol. 7 (Autumn 1966), pp. 639–51. Reprinted from *The Massachusetts Review*, © 1966 *The Massachusetts Review*, Inc.

To do this we shall have to struggle for the right to create our own terms through which to define ourselves and our relationship to the society, and to have these terms recognized. This is the first necessity of a free people, and the first right that any oppressor must suspend. The white fathers of American racism knew this—instinctively it seems—as is indicated by the continuous record of the distortion and omission in their dealings with the red and black men. In the same way that southern apologists for the "Jim Crow" society have so obscured, muddied and misrepresented the record of the reconstruction period, until it is almost impossible to tell what really happened, their contemporary counterparts are busy doing the same thing with the recent history of the civil rights movement.

In 1964, for example, the National Democratic Party, led by L. B. Johnson and Hubert H. Humphrey, cynically undermined the efforts of Mississippi's Black population to achieve some degree of political representation. Yet, whenever the events of that convention are recalled by the press, one sees only that version fabricated by the press agents of the Democratic Party. A year later the House of Representatives in an even more vulgar display of political racism made a mockery of the political rights of Mississippi's Negroes when it failed to unseat the Mississippi Delegation to the House which had been elected through a process which methodically and systematically excluded over 450,000 voting-age Negroes, almost one half of the total electorate of the state. Whenever this event is mentioned in print it is in terms which leaves one with the rather curious impression that somehow the oppressed Negro people of Mississippi are at fault for confronting the Congress with a situation in which they had no alternative but to endorse Mississippi's racist political practices.

I mention these two examples because, having been directly involved in them, I can see very clearly the discrepancies between what happened, and the versions that are finding their way into general acceptance as a kind of popular mythology. Thus the victimization of the Negro takes place in two phases—first it occurs in fact and deed, then, and this is equally sinister, in the official recording of those facts.

The "Black Power" program and concept which is being articulated by SNCC, CORE, and a host of community organizations in the ghettoes of the North and South has not escaped that process. The white press has been busy articulating their own analyses, their own interpretations, and criticisms of their own creations. For example, while the press had given wide and sensational dissemination to attacks made by figures in the Civil Rights movement—foremost among which are Roy Wilkins of the NAACP and Whitney Young of the Urban League—and to the hysterical ranting about black racism made by the political chameleon that now serves as Vice-President, it has generally failed to give accounts of the reasonable and productive dialogue which is taking place in the Negro community, and in certain important areas in the white religious and intellectual community. A national committee of influential Negro Churchmen affiliated with the National Council of Churches, despite their obvious respectability and responsibility, had to resort to a paid advertisement to articulate their position, while anyone shouting the hysterical yappings of "Black Racism" got ample space. Thus the American people have gotten at best a superficial and misleading account of the very terms and tenor of this debate. I wish to quote briefly from the statement by the national committee of Churchmen which I suspect that the majority of Americans will not have seen. This statement appeared in the *New York Times* of July 31, 1966.

> *We an informal group of Negro Churchmen in America are deeply disturbed about the crisis brought upon our country by historic distortions of important human realities in the controversy about "black power." What we see shining through the variety of rhetoric is not anything new but the same old problem of power and race which has faced our beloved country since 1619.*
>
> *... The conscience of black men is corrupted because, having no power to implement the demands of conscience, the concern for justice in the absence of justice becomes a chaotic self-surrender. Powerlessness breeds a race of beggars. We are faced now with a situation where powerless conscience meets conscienceless power, threatening the very foundations of our Nation.*
>
> ... We deplore the overt violence of riots, but we feel it is more important to focus on the real sources of these eruptions. These sources may be abetted inside the Ghetto, but their basic cause lies in the silent and covert violence which white middleclass America inflicts upon the victims of the inner city.
>
> ... In short the failure of American leaders to use American power to create equal opportunity *in life* as well as *law*, this is the real problem and not the anguished cry for black power .
>
> ... Without the capacity to *participate with power, i.e.*, to have some organized political and economic strength to really influence people with whom one interacts—integration is not meaningful .
>
> ... America has asked its Negro citizens to fight for opportunity as *individuals*, whereas at certain points in our history what we have needed most has been opportunity for the *whole group*, not just for selected and approved Negroes .
>
> ... We must not apologize for the existence of this form of group power, for we have been oppressed as a group and not as individuals. We will not find our way out of that oppression until both we and America accept the need for Negro Americans, as well as for Jews, Italians, Poles, and white Anglosaxon Protestants, among others, to have and to wield group power.[1]

Traditionally, for each new ethnic group, the route to social and political integration into America's pluralistic society, has been through the organization of their own institutions with which to represent their communal needs within the larger society. This is simply stating what the advocates of black

---

[1] [©1966 by The New York Times Company.]

power are saying. The strident outcry, *particularly* from the liberal community, that has been evoked by this proposal can only be understood by examining the historic relationship between Negro and White power in this country.

Negroes are defined by two forces, their blackness and their powerlessness. There have been traditionally two communities in America. The White community, which controlled and defined the forms that all institutions within the society would take, and the Negro community which has been excluded from participation in the power decisions that shaped the society, and has traditionally been dependent upon, and subservient to the White community.

This has not been accidental. The history of every institution of this society indicates that a major concern in the ordering and structuring of the society has been the maintaining of the Negro community in its condition of dependence and oppression. This has not been on the level of individual acts of discrimination between individual whites against individual Negroes, but as total acts by the White community against the Negro community. This fact cannot be too strongly emphasized—that racist assumptions of white superiority have been so deeply ingrained in the structure of the society that it infuses its entire functioning, and is so much a part of the national subconscious that it is taken for granted and is frequently not even recognized.

Let me give an example of the difference between individual racism and institutionalized racism, and the society's response to both. When unidentified white terrorists bomb a Negro Church and kill five children, that is an act of individual racism, widely deplored by most segments of the society. But when in that same city, Birmingham, Alabama, not five but 500 Negro babies die each year because of a lack of proper food, shelter and medical facilities, and thousands more are destroyed and maimed physically, emotionally and intellectually because of conditions of poverty and deprivation in the ghetto, that is a function of institutionalized racism. But the society either pretends it doesn't know of this situation, or is incapable of doing anything meaningful about it. And this resistance to doing anything meaningful about conditions in that ghetto comes from the fact that the ghetto is itself a product of a combination of forces and special interests in the white community, and the groups that have access to the resources and power to change that situation benefit, politically and economically, from the existence of that ghetto.

It is more than a figure of speech to say that the Negro community in America is the victim of white imperialism and colonial exploitation. This is in practical economic and political terms true. There are over 20 million black people comprising ten percent of this nation. They for the most part live in well-defined areas of the country—in the shanty-towns and rural black belt areas of the South, and increasingly in the slums of northern and western industrial cities. If one goes into any Negro community, whether it be in Jackson, Miss., Cambridge, Md., or Harlem, N.Y., one will find that the same combination of political, economic, and social forces are at work. The people in the Negro community do not control the resources of that community, its political decisions, its law enforcement, its housing standards; and even the physical ownership of the land, houses, and stores *lie outside that community*.

It is white power that makes the laws, and it is violent white power in the form of armed white cops that enforces those laws with guns and nightsticks. The vast majority of Negroes in this country live in these captive communities and must endure these conditions of oppression because, and only because, *they are black and powerless*. I do not suppose that at any point the men who control the power and resources of this country ever sat down and designed these black enclaves, and formally articulated the terms of their colonial and dependent status, as was done, for example, by the Apartheid government of South Africa. Yet, one can not distinguish between one ghetto and another. As one moves from city to city it is as though some malignant racist planning-unit had done precisely this—designed each one from the same master blue-print. And indeed, if the ghetto had been formally and deliberately planned, instead of growing spontaneously and inevitably from the racist functioning of the various institutions that combine to make the society, it would be some-how less frightening. The situation would be less frightening because, if these ghettoes were the result of design and conspiracy, one could understand their similarity as being artificial and consciously imposed, rather than the result of identical patterns of white racism which repeat themselves in cities as distant as Boston and Birmingham. Without bothering to list the historic factors which contribute to this pattern—economic exploitation, political impotence, discrimination in employment and education—one can see that to correct this pattern will require far-reaching changes in the basic power-relationships and the ingrained social patterns within the society. The question is, of course, what kinds of changes are necessary, and how is it possible to bring them about?

In recent years the answer to these questions which has been given by most articulate groups of Negroes and their white allies, the "liberals" of all stripes, has been in terms of something called "integration." According to the advo-cates of integration, social justice will be accomplished by "integrating the Negro into the mainstream institutions of the society from which he has been traditionally excluded." It is very significant that each time I have heard this formulation it has been in terms of "the Negro," the individual Negro, rather than in terms of the community.

This concept of integration had to be based on the assumption that there was nothing of value in the Negro community and that little of value could be created among Negroes, so the thing to do was to siphon off the "accept-able" Negroes into the surrounding middle-class white community. Thus the goal of the movement for integration was simply to loosen up the restrictions barring the entry of Negroes into the white community. Goals around which the struggle took place, such as public accommodation, open housing, job opportunity on the executive level (which is easier to deal with than the prob-lem of semi-skilled and blue collar jobs which involve more far-reaching eco-nomic adjustments), are quite simply middle-class goals, articulated by a tiny group of Negroes who had middle-class aspirations. It is true that the student demonstrations in the South during the early sixties, out of which SNCC came, had a similar orientation. But while it is hardly a concern of a black sharecropper, dishwasher, or welfare recipeint whether a certain fifteen-dollar-a-day motel offers accommodations to Negroes, the overt symbols of white superiority and the imposed limitations on the Negro community had to be destroyed. Now, black people must look beyond these goals, to the issue of collective power.

Such a limited class orientation was reflected not only in the program and goals of the civil rights movement, but in its tactics and organization. It is very significant that the two oldest and most "respectable" civil rights organizations have constitutions which *specifically* prohibit partisan political activity. CORE once did, but changed that clause when it changed its orientation toward black power. But this is perfectly understandable in terms of the strategy and goals of the older organizations. The civil rights movement saw its role as a kind of liaison between the powerful white community and the dependent Negro one. The dependent status of the black community apparently was unimportant since—if the movement were successful—it was going to blend into the white community anyway. We made no pretense of organizing and developing institutions of community power in the Negro community, but appealed to the conscience of white institutions of power. The posture of the civil rights movement was that of the dependent, the suppliant. The theory was that without attempting to create any organized base of political strength itself, the civil rights movement could, by forming coalitions with various "liberal" pressure organizations in the white community—liberal reform clubs, labor unions, church groups, progressive civic groups—and at times one or other of the major political parties—influence national legislation and national social patterns.

I think we all have seen the limitations of this approach. We have repeatedly seen that political alliances based on appeals to conscience and decency are chancy things, simply because institutions and political organizations have no consciences outside their own special interests. The political and social rights of Negroes have been and always will be negotiable and expendable the moment they conflict with the interests of our "allies." If we do not learn from history, we are doomed to repeat it, and that is precisely the lesson of the Reconstruction. Black people were allowed to register, vote and participate in politics because it was to the advantage of powerful white allies to promote this. But this was the result of white decision, and it was ended by other white men's decision before any political base powerful enough to challenge that decision could be established in the southern Negro community. (Thus at this point in the struggle Negroes have no assurance—save a kind of idiot optimism and faith in a society whose history is one of racism—that if it were to become necessary, even the painfully limited gains thrown to the civil rights movement by the Congress will not be revoked as soon as a shift in political sentiments should occur.)

The major limitation of this approach was that it tended to maintain the traditional dependence of Negroes, and of the movement. We depended upon the good-will and support of various groups within the white community whose interests were not always compatible with ours. To the extent that we depended on the financial support of other groups, we were vulnerable to their influence and domination.

Also the program that evolved out of this coalition was really limited and inadequate in the long term and one which affected only a small select group of Negroes. Its goal was to make the white community accessible to "qualified" Negroes and presumably each year a few more Negroes armed with their passport—a couple of university degrees—would escape into middle-class America and adopt the attitudes and life styles of that group; and one day the Harlems and the Watts would stand empty, a tribute to the success of integration. This is simply neither realistic nor particularly desirable. You can integrate communities, but you assimilate individuals. Even if such a program were possible its result would be, not to develop the black community as a functional and honorable segment of the total society, with its own cultural identity, life patterns, and institutions, but to abolish it—the final solution to the Negro problem. Marx said that the working class is the first class in history that ever wanted to abolish itself. If one listens to some of our "moderate" Negro leaders it appears that the American Negro is the first race that ever wished to abolish itself. The fact is that what must be abolished is not the black community, but the dependent colonial status that has been inflicted upon it. The racial and cultural personality of the black community must be preserved and the community must win its freedom while preserving its cultural integrity. This is the essential difference between integration as it is currently practiced and the concept of black power.

What has the movement for integration accomplished to date? The Negro graduating from M.I.T. with a doctorate will have better job opportunities available to him than to Lynda Bird Johnson. But the rate of unemployment in the Negro community is steadily increasing, while that in the white community decreases. More educated Negroes hold executive jobs in major corporations and federal agencies than ever before, but the gap between white income and Negro income has almost doubled in the last twenty years. More suburban housing is available to Negroes, but housing conditions in the ghetto are steadily declining. While the infant mortality rate of New York City is at its lowest rate ever in the city's history, the infant mortality rate of Harlem is steadily climbing. There has been an organized national resistance to the Supreme Court's order to integrate the schools, and the federal government has not acted to enforce that order. Less than 15 percent of black children in the South attend integrated schools; and Negro schools, which the vast majority of black children still attend, are increasingly decrepit, over-crowded, under-staffed, inadequately equipped and funded.

This explains why the rate of school dropouts is increasing among Negro teenagers, who then express their bitterness, hopelessness, and alienation by the only means they have—rebellion. As long as people in the ghettoes of our large cities feel that they are victims of the misuse of white power without any way to have their needs represented—and these are frequently simple needs: to get the welfare inspectors to stop kicking down your doors in the middle of the night, the cops from beating your children, the landlord to exterminate the vermin in your home, the city to collect your garbage—we will continue to have riots. These are not the products of "black power," but of the absence of any organization capable of giving the community the power, the black power, to deal with its problems.

SNCC proposes that it is now time for the black freedom movement to stop pandering to the fears and anxieties of the white middle class in the attempt to earn its "good-will," and to return to the ghetto to organize these communities to control themselves. This organization must be attempted in northern and southern urban areas as well as in the rural black belt counties of the South. The chief antagonist to this organization is, in the South, the overtly racist Democratic party, and in the North the equally corrupt big city machines.

The standard argument presented against independent political organization is "But you are only 10 percent." I cannot see the relevance of this observation, since no one is talking about taking over the country, but taking control over our own communities.

The fact is that the Negro population, 10 percent or not, is very strategically placed because—ironically—of segregation. What is also true is that Negroes have never been able to utilize the full voting potential of our numbers. Where we could vote, the case has always been that the white political machine stacks and gerrymanders the political subdivisions in Negro neighborhoods so the true voting strength is never reflected in political strength. Would anyone looking at the distribution of political power in Manhattan, ever think that Negroes represented 60 percent of the population there?

Just as often the effective political organization in Negro communities is absorbed by tokenism and patronage—the time honored practice of "giving" certain offices to selected Negroes. The machine thus creates a "little machine," which is subordinate and responsive to it, in the Negro community. These Negro political "leaders" are really vote deliverers, more responsible to the white machine and the white power structure, than to the community they allegedly represent. Thus the white community is able to substitute patronage control for audacious black power in the Negro community. This is precisely what Johnson tried to do even before the Voting Rights Act of 1966 was passed. The National Democrats made it very clear that the measure was intended to register Democrats, not Negroes. The President and top officials of the Democratic Party called in almost 100 selected Negro "leaders" from the Deep South. Nothing was said about changing the policies of the racist state parties, nothing was said about repudiating such leadership figures as Eastland and Ross Barnett in Mississippi or George Wallace in Alabama. What was said was simply "Go home and organize your people into the local Democratic Party—*then* we'll see about poverty money and appointments." (Incidentally, for the most part the War on Poverty in the South is controlled by local Democratic ward heelers—and outspoken racists who have used the program to change the form of the Negroes' dependence. People who were afraid to register for fear of being thrown off the farm are now afraid to register for fear of losing their Head-Start jobs.)

We must organize black community power to end these abuses, and to give the Negro community a chance to have its needs expressed. A leadership which is truly "responsible"—not to the white press and. power structure, but to the community—must be developed. Such leadership will recognize that its power lies in the unified and collective strength of that community. This will make it difficult for the white leadership group to conduct its dialogue with individuals in terms of patronage and prestige, and will force them to talk to the community's representatives in terns of real power.

The single aspect of the black power program that has encountered most criticism is this concept of independent organization. This is presented as third-partyism which has never worked, or a withdrawal into black nationalism and isolationism. If such a program is developed it will not have the effect of isolating the Negro community but the reverse. When the Negro community is able to control local office, and negotiate with other groups from a position of organized strength, the possibility of meaningful political alliances on specific issues will be increased. That is a rule of politics and there is no reason why it should not operate here. The only difference is that we will have the power to define the terms of these alliances.

The next question usually is, "So—can it work, can the ghettoes in fact be organized?" The answer is that this organization must be successful, because there are no viable alternatives—not the War on Poverty, which was at its inception limited to dealing with effects rather than causes, and has become simply another source of machine patronage. And "Integration" is meaningful only to a small chosen class within the community.

The revolution in agricultural technology in the South is displacing the rural Negro community into northern urban areas. Both Washington, D.C. and Newark, N.J. have Negro majorities. One third of Philadelphia's population of two million people is black. "Inner city" in most major urban areas is already predominantly Negro, and with the white rush to suburbia, Negroes will in the next three decades control the heart of our great cities. These areas can become either concentration camps with a bitter and volatile population whose only power is the power to destroy, or organized and powerful communities able to make constructive contributions to the total society. Without the power to control their lives and their communities, without effective political institutions through which to relate to the total society, these communities will exist in a constant state of insurrection. This is a choice that the country will have to make.

SUGGESTIONS FOR FURTHER READING

An introduction to the black liberation movement can be found in William L. Van DeBurg, *New Day in Babylon: The Black Power Movement and American Culture, 1965–1975*★ (1992).

Conditions of life in the ghetto are compellingly revealed in two autobiographies: Claude Brown's *Manchild in the Promised Land*★ (1965) and Piri Thomas' *Down These Mean Streets*★ (1967). Kenneth Clark, in *Dark Ghetto: Dilemmas of Social Power*★ (1965), analyzes the destructive elements of black ghetto existence.

The Kerner Riot Commission Report, officially entitled *Report of the Advisory Commission on Civil Disorders*★ (1968), is a good starting place for a study of urban racial unrest. Two books dealing with specific outbreaks of violence are Robert Conot's excellent *Rivers of Blood, Years of Darkness*★ (1967), the story of the Watts uprising of 1965, and John Hersey's *The Algiers Motel Incident* [Detroit] (1968). More recent books on those areas are Gerald Home, *Fire This Time: The Watts Uprising and the 1960s*★ (1995) and Thomas J. Sugrue, *The Origin of the Urban Crisis: Race and Inequality in Postwar Detroit*★ (1996). An overview of the urban racial violence of the period is found in David Boesel and Peter Rossi (eds.), *Cities under Siege: An Anatomy of the Ghetto Riots, 1964–1968* (1971).

On the revival of black nationalism, see E. U. Essien-Udom, *Black Nationalism: The Search for an Identity in America*★ (1962) and Alfonso Pinkney, *Red, Black, and Green: Black Nationalism in the United States* (1976). The beginnings of the Nation of Islam are described in C. Eric Lincoln, *The Black Muslims in America*★ (1961). See also Claude Andrew Clegg III, *An Original Man: The Life and Times of Elijah Muhammad*★ (1997). The life of Malcolm X is described in *The Autobiography of Malcolm X*★ (1964) and Peter Goldman, *The Death and Life of Malcolm X*★ (1973). See also E. Victor Wolfenstein, *The Victims of Democracy: Malcolm X and the Black Revolution* (1981).

★ Books marked by an asterisk are available in paperback.

13

✦

Consolidation
and Reaction

INTRODUCTION

The end of the 1960s saw the decline of the southern civil rights movement as the courts put an end to racially discriminatory laws and the assassination of Martin Luther King, Jr., in 1968 left a leadership vacuum that was not filled by the young militants from SNCC or the older clergy of SCLC. Outside the South, the Black Panthers found themselves besieged by law-enforcement authorities, and dozens of Panthers were killed by the police before the close of the decade.

The notion of liberation through united action was contagious, however, and several oppressed groups in America organized themselves in an attempt to overcome barriers to inequality—women, Mexican-Americans, and American Indians, for example. The strategy of nonviolence also found expression in the mainstream of the protest movement against the war in Vietnam. SNCC activists particularly sought to persuade young blacks to avoid military service, as it became apparent that African-Americans were overrepresented both in the fighting and in the dying in Indo-China.

The past few decades actually represent a period of consolidation of the gains produced by the movements of the 1960s. The racially segregated institutions of American society cracked open, and traditional barriers seemed, for a time at least, to become less of an obstacle to black achievement. As was the case with the First Reconstruction, these changes took place with the support of the federal government, particularly the courts. Toward the end of the 1970s, however, the Second Reconstruction began to slacken. Jimmy Carter ran for the presidency in 1976 promising to complete the work of establishing racial equality. Black political support enabled Carter to defeat the incumbent Gerald Ford, and the new administration held out hope for a substantial increase in black participation in the federal government. Either through a change of mind, or, more likely, a loss of nerve, Carter disappointed his black constituency, even going so far as to dismiss his ambassador to the United Nations, Andrew Young, a former aide to Martin Luther King, Jr. In the election of 1980, blacks stayed home, contributing to the defeat of the incumbent by Ronald Reagan, whose cutbacks in domestic spending programs fell particularly hard on the poor, of whom blacks make up a disproportionate number. By 1985, slightly more than a third of American blacks lived below the poverty line, and, more important, half of the black children in America can be classified as poor, by the government's own calculations.

Not surprisingly, blacks played a decreasing role in the high levels of government in the 1980s. On the other hand, the Voting Rights Act of 1965 continued to ensure a larger role for African-Americans in local and state government. In some ways, perhaps the most unambiguous result of the civil rights movement has been the increase in the number of successful black politicians in the United States. Before 1965, there were fewer than 200 black elected officials, but, by 1967, this number had increased to more than 6,500, most of whom were serving at the municipal level. Most dramatically, twenty-eight African-Americans had been elected mayors of cities of over 50,000 population. At the same time, there has been a slow, but steady, increase in black representation in Congress. This process reflects the decision of black politicians to pursue their careers within the traditional party system and to reject the movement in the mid-1970s to form an all-black political party. After staying away from the polls in the presidential election of 1980, large numbers of African-American voters were energized by Jesse Jackson's run at the Democratic nomination in 1984.

One of the most important examples of racial reaction in the Reagan years has been the changing role of the U.S. Commission on Civil Rights. Established in 1957 to investigate charges of discrimination and violations of citizens' civil rights, the Commission served the civil rights cause well through the 1970s. As reconstituted by President Reagan in 1983, however, the Civil Rights Commission has taken the position that racial discrimination has largely been eliminated from American society, and, therefore, the Commission should no longer interest itself in advancing the interests of oppressed minorities. Consequently, the majority of the commissioners regularly oppose the use of the principle of affirmative action in reducing patterns of racial, ethnic, or gender discrimination.

The process of school desegregation since the 1954 Brown decision has been erratic, but continues. In the peak years between 1968 and 1976, there was a 50-percent decrease in the segregation of white and nonwhite students. Over the whole period since 1954, black students have shown a variety of significant educational gains. They are spending more years in school, there was a dramatic decrease in the dropout rate, and college attendance increased markedly. It must be noted, however, that the late 1980s witnessed a slowing of these trends. Whether this downturn continues will depend in large measure on the future of federal aid to education.

The past two decades clearly illustrate the historical paradox of contemporary African-American life. The black middle class has been strengthened as a result of expanded educational and employment opportunities. At the same time, life in inner-city communities has deteriorated. Presidents Reagan, Bush, and Clinton had little interest in urban affairs, and political neglect of the inner-city poor has contributed to an increased level of hopelessness in the ghetto.

With the apparent end of affirmative action impending, the growth of the black middle class may begin slowing. The problems of the inner city seem beyond solution, at least in this time of urban neglect. The future of black America is uncertain at the turn of the millennium, but it is clear that the struggle for racial justice will continue until all people are truly free.

The Rainbow Coalition

Speech to the
Democratic Convention, 1984

JESSE JACKSON

Although Jesse Jackson had called for the formation of a black political party at the National Black Political Convention in 1972, slightly over a decade later, he was establishing himself as a serious candidate for the Democratic party presidential nomination. Leading what he called the "Rainbow Coalition," Jackson entered the presidential primaries in 1984 and went to the convention with over 450 delegates pledged to support his nomination.

Jackson was no stranger to uphill struggles; he had been an SCLC aide to Martin Luther King, Jr., and was with King in 1968 when he was assassinated in Memphis. In 1971, Jackson reorganized an SCLC program in Chicago to form People United to Save Humanity (PUSH) and from that base had spoken widely about the desperate need to transform society through education and empowerment.

Although Jackson went to the San Francisco convention with little hope of gaining the nomination, he thought that his delegate strength (and the need of the Democratic party to woo the black electorate) would enable him to significantly influence the party platform. He was to be disappointed in this effort, as the party rejected his appeals to (1) cut defense spending, (2) adopt a "no first use of nuclear weapons" resolution, and (3) eliminate runoffs in primary elections.

Jackson electrified the convention on July 17 with the address reprinted next, but the delegates gave Walter Mondale the nomination on the first ballot, and the Democratic candidate went down to massive defeat in the November election.

Tonight we come together bound by our faith in a mighty God, with genuine respect for our country, and inheriting the legacy of a great party—a Democratic Party—which is the best hope for redirecting our nation on a more humane, just and peaceful course.

This is not a perfect party. We are not a perfect people. Yet, we are called to a perfect mission: our mission, to feed the hungry, to clothe the naked, to house the homeless, to teach the illiterate, to provide jobs for the jobless, and to choose the human race over the nuclear race.

We are gathered here this week to nominate a candidate and write a platform which will expand, unify, direct and inspire our party and the nation to fulfill this mission.

FROM Jesse Jackson, "The Rainbow Coalition," *Vital Speeches of the Day*, vol. 51, no. 3 (November 15, 1984), pp. 77–81. Reprinted by permission.

My constituency is the damned, disinherited, disrespected and the despised.

They are restless and seek relief. They've voted in record numbers. They have invested the faith, hope and trust that they have in us. The Democratic Party must send them a signal that we care. I pledge my best not to let them down.

There is the call of conscience: redemption, expansion, healing and unity. Leadership must heed the call of conscience, redemption, expansion, healing and unity, for they are the key to achieving our mission.

Time is neutral and does not change things.

With courage and initiative leaders change things. No generation can choose the age or circumstances in which it is born, but through leadership it can choose to make the age in which it is born an age of enlightenment—an age of jobs, and peace, and justice.

Only leadership—that intangible combination of gifts, discipline, information, circumstance, courage, timing, will and divine inspiration—can lead us out of the crisis in which we find ourselves.

Leadership can mitigate the misery of our nation. Leadership can part the waters and lead our nation in the direction of the Promised Land. Leadership can lift the boats stuck at the bottom.

I have had the rare opportunity to watch seven men, and then two, pour out their souls, offer their service and heed the call of duty to direct the course of our nation.

There is a proper season for everything. There is a time to sow and a time to reap. There is a time to compete, and a time to cooperate.

I ask for your vote on the first ballot as a vote for a new direction for this party and this nation; a vote for conviction, a vote for conscience.

But I will be proud to support the nominee of this convention for the president of the United States of America.

I have watched the leadership of our party develop and grow. My respect for both Mr. Mondale and Mr. Hart is great.

I have watched them struggle with the cross-winds and cross-fires of being public servants, and I believe that they will both continue to try to serve us faithfully. I am elated by the knowledge that for the first time in our history a woman, Geraldine Ferraro, will be recommended to share our ticket.

Throughout this campaign, I have tried to offer leadership to the Democratic Party and the nation.

If in my high moments, I have done some good, offered some service, shed some light, healed some wounds, rekindled some hope or stirred someone from apathy and indifference, or in any way along the way helped somebody, then this campaign has not been in vain.

For friends who loved and cared for me, and for a God who spared me, and for a family who understood, I am eternally grateful.

If in my low moments, in word, deed or attitude, through some error of temper, taste or tone, I have caused anyone discomfort, created pain, or revived someone's fears, that was not my truest self.

If there were occasions when my grape turned into a raisin and my joy bell lost its resonance, please forgive me. Charge it to my head and not to my heart. My head is so limited in its finitude; my heart is boundless in its love for the human family. I am not a perfect servant. I am a public servant. I'm doing my best against the odds. As I develop and serve, be patient. God is not finished with me yet.

This campaign has taught me much: that leaders must be tough enough to fight, tender enough to cry, human enough to make mistakes, humble enough to admit them, strong enough to absorb the pain, and resilient enough to bounce back and keep on moving. For leaders, the pain is often intense. But you must smile through your tears and keep moving with the faith that there is a brighter side somewhere.

I went to see Hubert Humphrey three days before he died. He had just called Richard Nixon from his dying bed, and many people wondered why. And, I asked him.

He said, "Jesse, from this vantage point, with the sun setting in my life, all of the speeches, the political conventions, the crowds and the great fights are behind me now. At a time like this you are forced to deal with your irreducible essence, forced to grapple with that which is really important to you. And what I have concluded about life," Hubert Humphrey said, "when all is said and done, we must forgive each other, and redeem each other, and move on."

Our party is emerging from one of its most hard-fought battles for the Democratic Party's presidential nomination in our history. But our healthy competition should make us better, not bitter. We must use the insight, wisdom and experience of the late Hubert Humphrey as a balm for the wounds in our party, this nation and the world. We must forgive each other, redeem each other, regroup and move on.

Our flag is red, white and blue, but our nation is rainbow—red, yellow, brown, black and white—we're all precious in God's sight. America is not like a blanket—one piece of unbroken cloth, the same color, the same texture, the same size. America is more like a quilt—many patches, many pieces, many colors, many sizes, all woven and held together by a common thread.

The white, the Hispanic, the black, the Arab, the Jew, the woman, the Native American, the small farmer, the business-person, the environmentalist, the peace activist, the young, the old, the lesbian, the gay, and the disabled make up the American quilt.

Even in our fractured state, all of us count and fit somewhere. We have proven that we can survive without each other. But we have not proven that we can win or make progress without each other. We must come together.

From Fannie Lou Hamer in Atlantic City in 1964 to the Rainbow Coalition in San Francisco today; from the Atlantic to the Pacific, we have experienced pain but progress as we ended American apartheid laws; we got public accommodations; we secured voting rights; we obtained open housing; as young people got the right to vote; we lost Malcolm, Martin, Medgar, Bobby and John and Viola.

The team that got us here must be expanded, not abandoned. Twenty years ago, tears welled up in our eyes as the bodies of Schwerner, Goodman and Chaney were dredged from the depths of a river in Mississippi. Twenty years later, our communities, black and Jewish, are in anguish, anger and pain.

Feelings have been hurt on both sides. There is a crisis in communications. Confusion is in the air. We cannot afford to lose our way. We may agree to agree, or agree to disagree on issues; we must bring back civility to these tensions.

We are co-partners in a long and rich religious history—the Judeo-Christian traditions. Many blacks and Jews have a shared passion for social justice at home and peace abroad. We must seek a revival of the spirit, inspired by a new vision and new possibilities. We must return to higher ground. We are bound by Moses and Jesus, but also connected to Islam and Mohammed.

These three great religions—Judaism, Christianity and Islam—were all born in the revered and holy city of Jerusalem. We are bound by Dr. Martin Luther King, Jr., and Rabbi Abraham Heschel, crying out from their graves for us to reach common ground. We are bound by shared blood and shared sacrifices. We are much too intelligent; much too bound by our Judeo-Christian heritage; much too victimized by racism, sexism, militarism and anti-Semitism; much too threatened as historical scapegoats to go on divided one from another. We must turn from finger-pointing to clasped hands. We must share our burdens and our joys with each other once again. We must turn to each other and not on each other and choose higher ground.

Twenty years later, we cannot be satisfied by just restoring the old coalition. Old wine skins must make room for new wine. We must heal and expand. The Rainbow Coalition is making room for Arab-Americans. They too know the pain and hurt of racial and religious rejection. They must not continue to be made pariahs. The Rainbow Coalition is making room for Hispanic-Americans who this very night are living under the threat of the Simpson-Mazzoli bill, and farm workers from Ohio who are fighting the Campbell Soup Company with a boycott to achieve legitimate workers rights.

The Rainbow is making room for the Native Americans, most exploited people of all, a people with the greatest moral claim amongst us. We support them as they seek the restoration of their ancient land. We support them as they seek the restoration of land and water rights, as they seek to preserve their ancestral homelands and the beauty of a land that was once all theirs. They can never receive a fair share for all that they have given us, but they must finally have a fair chance to develop their great resources and to preserve their people and their culture.

The Rainbow Coalition includes Asian-Americans, now being killed in our streets—scapegoats for the failures of corporate, industrial and economic policies. The Rainbow is making room for the young Americans. Twenty years ago, our young people were dying in a war for which they could not even vote. But 20 years later, Young America has the power to stop a war in Central America and the responsibility to vote in great numbers. Young America must be politically active in 1984. The choice is war or peace. We must make room for Young America.

The Rainbow includes disabled veterans. The color scheme fits in the Rainbow. The disabled have their handicap revealed and their genius concealed; while the able-bodied have their genius revealed and their disability concealed. But ultimately we must judge people by their values and their contribution. Don't leave anybody out. I would rather have Roosevelt in a wheelchair than Reagan on a horse.

The Rainbow is making room for small farmers. They have suffered tremendously under the Reagan regime. They will either receive 90 percent parity or 100 percent charity. We must address their concerns and make room for them. The Rainbow includes lesbians and gays. No American citizen ought be denied equal protection under the law.

We must be unusually committed and caring as we expand our family to include new members. All of us must be tolerant and understanding as the fears and anxieties of the rejected and of the party leadership express themselves in many different ways. Too often what we call hate—as if it were deeply rooted in some philosophy or strategy—is simply ignorance, anxiety, paranoia, fear and insecurity. To be strong leaders, we must be long-suffering as we seek to right the wrongs of our party and our nation. We must expand our party, heal our party and unify our party. That is our mission in 1984.

We are often reminded that we live in a great nation—and we do. But it can be greater still. The Rainbow is mandating a new definition of greatness. We must not measure greatness from the mansion down, but the manger up.

Jesus said that we should not be judged by the bark we wear but by the fruit that we bear. Jesus said that we must measure greatness by how we treat the least of these.

President Reagan says the nation is in recovery. Those 90,000 corporations that made a profit last year but paid no federal taxes are recovering. The 37,000 military contractors who have benefited from Reagan's more than doubling the military budget in peacetime, surely they are recovering. The big corporations and rich individuals who received the bulk of the three-year, multi-billion tax cut from Mr. Reagan are recovering. But no such recovery is under way for the least of these. Rising tides don't lift all boats, particularly those stuck on the bottom.

For the boats stuck at the bottom there is a misery index. This administration has made life more miserable for the poor. Its attitude has been contemptuous. Its policies and programs have been cruel and unfair to working people. They must be held accountable in November for increasing infant mortality among the poor. In Detroit, one of the great cities of the Western world, babies are dying at the same rate as Honduras, the most underdeveloped nation in our hemisphere.

This administration must be held accountable for policies that contribute to the growing poverty in America. Under President Reagan, there are now 34 million people in poverty, 15 percent of our nation. Twenty-three million are white, 11 million black, Hispanic, Asian and others. Mostly women and children. By the end of this year, there will be 41 million people in poverty. We cannot stand idly by. We must fight for change, now.

Under this regime we look at Social Security. The 1981 budget cuts included nine permanent Social Security benefits cuts totaling $20 billion over five years.

Small businesses have suffered under Reagan tax cuts. Only 18 percent of total business tax cuts went to them—82 percent to big business.

Health care under Mr. Reagan has been sharply cut.

Education under Mr. Reagan has been cut 25 percent.

Under Mr. Reagan there are now 9.7 million female-head families. They represent 16 percent of all families, half of all of them are poor. Seventy percent of all poor children live in a house headed by a woman, where there is no man.

Under Mr. Reagan, the administration has cleaned up only 6 of 546 priority toxic waste dumps.

Farmers' real net income was only about half its level in 1979.

Many say that the race in November will be decided in the South. President Reagan is depending on the conservative South to return him to office. But the South, I tell you, is unnaturally conservative. The South is the poorest region in our nation and, therefore, has the least to conserve. In his appeal to the South, Mr. Reagan is trying to substitute flags and prayer cloths for food, and clothing, and education, health care and housing. But President Reagan who asks us to pray, and I believe in prayer—I've come this way by the power of prayer. But, we must watch false prophecy.

He cuts energy assistance to the poor, cuts breakfast programs from children, cuts lunch programs from children, cuts job training from children and then says, when at the table, "let us pray." Apparently he is not familiar with the structure of a prayer. You thank the Lord for the food that you are about to receive, not the food that just left.

I think that we should pray. But don't pray for the food that left, pray for the man that took the food to leave. We need a change. We need a change in November.

Under President Reagan, the misery index has risen for the poor, but the danger index has risen for everybody.

Under this administration we've lost the lives of our boys in Central America, in Honduras, in Grenada, in Lebanon.

A nuclear standoff in Europe. Under this administration, one-third of our children believe they will die in a nuclear war. The danger index is increasing in this world.

With all the talk about defense against Russia, the Russian submarines are closer and their missiles are more accurate. We live in a world tonight more miserable and a world more dangerous.

While Reaganomics and Reaganism is talked about often, so often we miss the real meaning. Reaganism is a spirit. Reaganonomics represents the real economic facts of life.

In 1980, Mr. George Bush, a man with reasonable access to Mr. Reagan, did an analysis of Mr. Reagan's economic plan. Mr. Bush concluded Reagan's plan was "voodoo economics." He was right. Third-party candidate John Anderson said that the combination of military spending, tax cuts and a balanced budget by '84 could be accomplished with blue smoke and mirrors. They were both right.

Mr. Reagan talks about a dynamic recovery. There is some measure of recovery, three and a half years later. Unemployment has inched just below where it was when he took office in 1981. But there are still 8.1 million people officially unemployed, 11 milion working only part-time jobs. Inflation has come down, but let's analyze for a moment who has paid the price for this superficial economic recovery.

Mr. Reagan curbed inflation by cutting consumer demand. He cut consumer demand with conscious and callous fiscal and monetary policy. He used the federal budget to deliberately induce unemployment and curb social spending. He then waged and supported tight monetary policies of the Federal Reserve Board to deliberately drive up interest rates—again to curb consumer demand created through borrowing.

Unemployment reached 10.7 percent; we experienced skyrocketing interest rates; our dollar inflated abroad; there were record bank failures; record farm foreclosures; record business bankruptcies; record budget deficits; record trade deficits. Mr. Reagan brought inflation down by destabilizing our economy and disrupting family life.

He promised in 1980 a balanced budget, but instead we now have a record $200 billion budget deficit. Under President Reagan, the cumulative budget deficit for his four years is more than the sum total of deficits from George Washington to Jimmy Carter combined. I tell you, we need a change.

How is he paying for these short-term jobs? Reagan's economic recovery is being financed by deficit spending—$200 billion a year. Military spending, a major cause of this deficit, is projected over the next five years to be nearly $2 trillion, and will cost about $40,000 for every taxpaying family.

When the government borrows $200 billion annually to finance the deficit, this encourages the private sector to make its money off of interest rates as opposed to development and economic growth. Even money abroad—we don't have enough money domestically to finance the debt, so we are now borrowing money abroad, from foreign banks, government and financial institutions—$40 billion in 1983; $70 to $80 billion in 1984 (40 percent of our total); over $100 billion (50 percent of our total) in 1985.

By 1989, it is projected that 50 percent of all individual income taxes will be going to pay just for the interest on that debt. The U.S. used to be the largest exporter of capital, but under Mr. Reagan we will quite likely become the largest debtor nation. About two weeks ago, on July 4, we celebrated our Declaration of Independence. Yet every day, supply-side economics is making our nation more economically dependent and less economically free. Five to six percent of our gross national product is now being eaten up with President Reagan's budget deficit.

To depend on foreign military powers to protect our national security would be foolish, making us dependent and less secure. Yet Reaganomics has us increasingly dependent on foreign economic sources. This consumer-led but deficit-financed recovery is unbalanced and artificial.

We have a challenge as Democrats: support a way out. Democracy guarantees opportunity, not success. Democracy guarantees the right to participate, not a license for either the majority or a minority to dominate. The victory for the rainbow coalition in the platform debates today was not whether we won or lost; but that we raised the right issues. We can afford to lose the vote; issues are negotiable. We cannot afford to avoid raising the right questions. Our self-respect and our moral integrity were at stake. Our heads are perhaps bloodied but not bowed. Our backs are straight. We can go home and face our people. Our vision is clear. When we think, on this journey from slaveship to championship, we've gone from the planks of the boardwalk in Atlantic City in 1964 to fighting to have the right planks in the platform in San Francisco in '84. There is a deep and abiding sense of joy in our soul, despite the tears in our eyes. For while there are missing planks, there is a solid foundation upon which to build. Our party can win. But we must provide hope that will inspire people to struggle and achieve; provide a plan to show the way out of our dilemma, and then lead the way.

In 1984, my heart is made to feel glad because I know there is a way out. Justice. The requirement for rebuilding America is justice: The linchpin of progressive politics in our nation will not come from the North; they in fact will come from the South. That is why I argue over and over again—from Lynchburg, Va., down to Texas, there is only one black congressperson out of 115. Nineteen years later, we're locked out of the Congress, the Senate and the governor's mansion. What does this large black vote mean? Why do I fight to end second primaries and fight gerrymandering and (*unintelligible*) and at large. Why do we fight over that? Because I tell you, you cannot hold someone in the ditch and linger there with them. If we want a change in this nation, reinforce that Voting Rights Act—we'll get 12 to 20 black, Hispanic, female and progressive congresspersons from the South. We can save the cotton, but we've got to fight the boll weevil—we've got to make a judgment.

It's not enough to hope ERA will pass; how can we pass ERA? If blacks vote in great numbers, progressive whites win. It's the only way progressive whites win. If blacks vote in great numbers, Hispanics win. If blacks, Hispanics and progressive whites vote, women win. When women win, children win. When women and children win, workers win. We must all come up together. We must come up together.

I tell you, with all of our joy and excitement, we must not save the world and lose our souls; we should never short-circuit enforcement of the Voting Rights Act at every level. If one of us rises, all of us must rise. Justice is the way out. Peace is a way out. We should not act as if nuclear weaponry is negotiable and debatable. In this world in which we live, we dropped the bomb on Japan and felt guilty. But in 1984, other folks also got bombs. This time, if we drop the bomb, six minutes later, we, too, will be destroyed. It's not about dropping the bomb on somebody; it's about dropping the bomb on everybody. We must choose developed minds over guided missiles, and think it out and not fight it out. It's time for a change.

Our foreign policy must be characterized by mutual respect, not by gunboat diplomacy, big stick diplomacy and threats. Our nation at its best feeds the hungry. Our nation at its worst will mine the harbors of Nicaragua; at its worst, will try to overthrow that government; at its worst, will cut aid to American education and increase aid to El Salvador; at its worst our nation will have partnership with South Africa. That's a moral disgrace. It's a moral disgrace. It's a moral disgrace.

When we look at Africa, we cannot just focus on apartheid in southern Africa. We must fight for trade with Africa, and not just aid to Africa. We cannot stand idly by and say we will not relate to Nicaragua unless they have elections there and then embrace military regimes in Africa, overthrowing Democratic governments in Nigeria and Liberia and Ghana. We must fight for democracy all around the world, and play the game by one set of rules.

Peace in this world. Our present formula for peace in the Middle East is inadequate; it will not work. There are 22 nations in the Middle East. Our nation must be able to talk and act and influence all of them. We must build upon Camp David and measure human rights by one yardstick and as we (*unintelligible*) too many interests and two few friends.

There is a way out. Jobs. Put Americans back to work. When I was a child growing up in Greenville, S.C., the Rev. (*unintelligible*) who used to preach every so often a sermon about Jesus. He said, if I be lifted up, I'll draw all men unto me. I didn't quite understand what he meant as a child growing up. But I understand a little better now. If you raise up truth, it's magnetic. It has a way of drawing people. With all this confusion in this convention—there is bright lights and parties and big fun—we must raise up the simple proposition: if we lift up a program to feed the hungry, they'll come running. If we lift up a program to study war no more, our youth will come running. If we lift up a program to put American (*sic*) back to work, an alternative to welfare and despair, they will come working. If we cut that military budget without cutting our defense, and use that money to rebuild bridges and put steelworkers back to work, and use that money, and provide jobs for our citizens, and use that money to build schools and train teachers and educate our children, and build hospitals and train doctors and train nurses, the whole nation will come running to us.

As I leave you now, vote in this convention and get ready to go back across this nation in a couple of days, in this campaign, I'll try to be faithful by my promise. I'll live in the old barrios, and ghettos and reservations, and housing projects. I have a message for our youth. I challenge them to put hope in their brains, and not dope in their veins. I told them like Jesus, I, too, was born in a slum, but just because you're born in a slum, does not mean the slum is born in you, and you can rise above it if your mind is made up. I told them in every slum, there are two sides. When I see a broken window, that's the slummy side. Train that youth to be a glazier, that's the sunny side. When I see a missing brick, that's the slummy side. Let that child in the union, and become a brick-mason, and build, that's the sunny side. When I see a missing door, that's the slummy side. Train some youth to become a carpenter, that's the sunny side. When I see the vulgar words and hieroglyphics of destitution on the walls, that's the slummy side. Train some youth to be a painter, an artist—that's the sunny side. We need this place looking for the sunny side because there's a brighter side somewhere. I am more convinced than ever that we can win. We'll vault up the rough side of the mountain; we can win. I just want young America to do me one favor.

Exercise the right to dream. You must face reality—that which is. But then dream of the reality that ought to be, that must be. Live beyond the pain of reality with the dream of a bright tomorrow. Use hope and imagination as weapons of survival and progress. Use love to motivate you and obligate you to serve the human family.

Young America, dream. Choose the human race over the nuclear race. Bury the weapons and don't burn the people. Dream of a new value system. Teachers, who teach for life, and not just for a living, teach because they can't help it. Dream of lawyers more concerned with justice than a judgeship. Dream of doctors more concerned with public health than personal wealth. Dream (*sic*) preachers and priests who will prophesy and not just profiteer. Preach and dream. Our time has come.

Our time has come. Suffering breeds character. Character breeds faith. And in the end, faith will not disappoint.

Our time has come. Our faith, hope and dreams will prevail. Our time has come. Weeping has endured for the night. And, now joy cometh in the morning.

Our time has come. No graves can hold our body down.

Our time has come. No lie can live forever.

Our time has come. We must leave racial battleground and come to economic common ground and moral higher ground. America, our time has come.

We've come from disgrace to Amazing Grace, our time has come.

Give me your tired, give me your poor, your huddled masses who yearn to breathe free and come November, there will be a change because our time has come.

Thank you and God bless you.

Affirmative Action

STEPHEN L. CARTER

The end of legally sanctioned racial segregation in the 1950s and 1960s was a major step in the direction of racial equality. However, as had been the case with the end of slavery, the removal of formal oppression did not eliminate customary and private discrimination. It became apparent early that some form of governmental action would be necessary to enable members of minority groups to participate fully and equitably in American life. The term "affirmative action" came to be connected with Title VII of the Civil Rights Act of 1964.

Through the presidencies of Lyndon Johnson and Richard Nixon, government rulings in affirmative action cases opened labor unions, business firms, and educational institutions to many minority group members and women. This process did not take place without opposition, of course, and the accusation of "reverse discrimination" was hurled both at government directives and those who took advantage of them. There is no doubt, however, that many African-Americans found employment and educational opportunities where they had previously been denied access. Over the years, white backlash led to many legal proceedings designed to restrict or overturn affirmative action rulings. It proved ironic, then, that the most successful attack on affirmative action was led by a black businessman and university regent in California. Ward Connerly's leadership in getting Proposition 209 adopted in 1996 by the California electorate led to his becoming the primary spokesman for the anti–affirmative action forces nationally. The main article of Proposition 209 "Prohibits the state, local governments, districts, public universities, colleges and schools, and other governmental instrumentalities from discriminating against or giving preferential treatment to any individual or group in public employment, public education, or public contracting on the basis of race, sex, color, ethnicity, or national origin." Since 1996, both Texas and Florida have dropped affirmative action legislation, Texas as a result of a lawsuit and Florida because the governor sought to preempt a legal attack.

Beneficiaries of affirmative action are not of one mind about the value of the policy. Supreme Court Justice Clarence Thomas, who took advantage of affirmative action throughout his higher education, strongly opposes the practice. On the other hand, Stephen L. Carter, a professor at Yale Law School, expresses his support for the policy in his book Reflections of an Affirmative Action Baby, *a section of which follows. The conservative turn in government policy in the 1990s suggests that affirmative action has had its day, and it remains to be seen how racial minorities will manage to find their rightful place in American life.*

I got into law school because I am black.

As many black professionals think they must, I have long suppressed this truth, insisting instead that I got where I am the same way everybody else did. Today I am a professor at the Yale Law School. I like to think that I am a good

---

one, but I am hardly the most objective judge. What I am fairly sure of, and can now say without trepidation, is that were my skin not the color that it is, I would not have had the chance to try.

For many, perhaps most, black professionals of my generation, the matter of who got where and how is left in a studied and, I think, purposeful ambiguity. Some of us, as they say, would have made it into an elite college or professional school anyway. (But, in my generation, many fewer than we like to pretend, even though one might question the much-publicized claim by Derek Bok, the president of Harvard University, that in the absence of preferences, only 1 percent of Harvard's entering class would be black.) Most of us, perhaps nearly all of us, have learned to bury the matter far back in our minds. We are who we are and where we are, we have records of accomplishment or failure, and there is no rational reason that anybody—employer, client, whoever—should care any longer whether racial preference played any role in our admission to a top professional school.

When people in positions to help or hurt our careers do seem to care, we tend to react with fury. Those of us who have graduated professional school over the past fifteen to twenty years, and are not white, travel career paths that are frequently bumpy with suspicions that we did not earn the right to be where we are. We bristle when others raise what might be called the qualification question—"Did you get into school or get hired because of a special program?"—and that prickly sensitivity is the best evidence, if any is needed, of one of the principal costs of racial preferences. Scratch a black professional with the qualification question, and you're likely to get a caustic response, such as this one from a senior executive at a major airline: "Some whites think I've made it because I'm black. Some blacks think I've made it only because I'm an Uncle Tom. The fact is, I've made it because I'm good."

Given the way that so many Americans seem to treat receipt of the benefits of affirmative action as a badge of shame, answers of this sort are both predictable and sensible. In the professional world, moreover, they are very often true: relatively few corporations are in a position to hand out charity. The peculiar aspect of the routine denial, however, is that so many of those who will bristle at the suggestion that they themselves have gained from racial preferences will try simultaneously to insist that racial preferences be preserved and to force the world to pretend that no one benefits from them. That awkward balancing of fact and fiction explains the frequent but generally groundless cry that it is racist to suggest that some individual's professional accomplishments would be fewer but for affirmative action; and therein hangs a tale.

For students at the leading law schools, autumn brings the recruiting season, the idyllic weeks when law firms from around the country compete to lavish upon them lunches and dinners and other attentions, all with the professed goal of obtaining the students' services—perhaps for the summer, perhaps for a longer term. The autumn of 1989 was different, however, because the nation's largest firm, Baker & McKenzie, was banned from interviewing students at the University of Chicago Law School, and on probation—that is, enjoined to be on its best behavior—at some others.

The immediate source of Baker & McKenzie's problems was a racially charged interview that a partner in the firm had conducted the previous fall with a black third-year student at the school. The interviewer evidently suggested that other lawyers might call her "nigger" or "black bitch" and wanted to know how she felt about that. Perhaps out of surprise that she played golf, he observed that "there aren't too many golf courses in the ghetto." He also suggested that the school was admitting "foreigners" and excluding "qualified" Americans.

The law school reacted swiftly, and the firm was banned from interviewing on campus. Other schools contemplated taking action against the firm, and some of them did. Because I am black myself, and teach in a law school, I suppose the easiest thing for me to have done would have been to clamor in solidarity for punishment. Yet I found myself strangely reluctant to applaud the school's action. Instead, I was disturbed rather than excited by this vision of law schools circling the wagons, as it were, to defend their beleaguered minority students against racially insensitive remarks. It is emphatically not my intention to defend the interviewer, most of whose reported questions and comments were inexplicable and inexcusable. I am troubled, however, by my suspicion that there would still have been outrage—not as much, but some—had the interviewer asked only what I called at the beginning of the chapter the qualification question.

I suspect this because in my own student days, something over a decade ago, an interviewer from a prominent law firm addressed this very question to a Yale student who was not white, and the student voices—including my own—howled in protest. "Racism!" we insisted. "Ban them!" But with the passing years, I have come to wonder whether our anger might have been misplaced.

To be sure, the Yale interviewer's question was boorish. And because the interviewer had a grade record and résumé right in front of him, it was probably irrelevant as well. (It is useful here to dispose of one common but rather silly anti-afrmative action bromide: the old question, "Do you really want to be treated by a doctor who got into medical school because of skin color?" The answer is, or ought to be, that the patient doesn't particularly care how the doctor got *into* school; what matters is how the doctor got *out.* The right question, the sensible question, is not "What medical school performance did your grades and test scores predict?" but "What was your` medical school performance?") But irrelevance and boorishness cannot explain our rage at the qualification question, because lots of interviewers ask questions that meet the tests of boorishness and irrelevance.

The controversy is not limited to outsiders who come onto campus to recruit. In the spring of 1991, for example, students at Georgetown Law School demanded punishment for a classmate who argued in the school newspaper that affirmative action is unfair because students of color are often admitted to law school on the basis of grades and test scores that would cause white applicants to be rejected. Several universities have considered proposals that would deem it "racial harassment" for a (white?) student to question the qualifications of nonwhite classmates. But we can't change either the truths or the myths about racial preferences by punishing those who speak them.

This clamor for protection from the qualification question is powerful evidence of the terrible psychological pressure that racial preferences often put on their beneficiaries. Indeed, it sometimes seems as though the programs are not supposed to have any beneficiaries—or, at least, that no one is permitted to suggest that they have any.

And that's ridiculous. If one supports racial preferences in professional school admissions, for example, one must be prepared to treat them like any other preference in admission and believe that they make a difference, that some students would not be admitted if the preferences did not exist. This is not a racist observation. It is not normative in any sense. It is simply a fact. A good deal of emotional underbrush might be cleared away were the fact simply conceded, and made the beginning, not the end, of any discussion of preferences. For once it is conceded that the programs have beneficiaries, it follows that some of us who are professionals and are not white must be among them. Supporters of preferences must stop pretending otherwise. Rather, some large segment of us must be willing to meet the qualification question head-on, to say, "Yes, I got into law school because of racial preferences. So what?"—and, having said it, must be ready with a list of what we have made of the opportunities the preferences provided.

Now, this is a costly concession, because it carries with it all the baggage of the bitter rhetorical battle over the relationship between preferences and merit. But bristling at the question suggests a deep-seated fear that the dichotomy might be real. Indeed, if admitting that racial preferences make a difference leaves a funny aftertaste in the mouths of proponents, they might be more comfortable fighting against preferences rather than for them.

So let us bring some honesty as well as rigor to the debate, and begin at the beginning. I have already made clear my starting point: I got into a top law school because I am black. Not only am I unashamed of this fact, but I can prove its truth.

As a senior at Stanford back in the mid-1970s, I applied to about half a dozen law schools. Yale, where I would ultimately enroll, came through fairly early with an acceptance. So did all but one of the others. The last school, Harvard, dawdled and dawdled. Finally, toward the end of the admission season, I received a letter of rejection. Then, within days, two different Harvard officials and a professor contacted me by telephone to apologize. They were quite frank in their explanation for the "error." I was told by one official that the school had initially rejected me because "we assumed from your record that you were white." (The words have always stuck in my mind, a tantalizing reminder of what is expected of me.) Suddenly coy, he went on to say that the school had obtained "additional information that should have been counted in your favor"—that is, Harvard had discovered the color of my skin. And if I had already made a deposit to confirm my decision to go elsewhere, well, that, I was told, would "not be allowed" to stand in my way should I enroll at Harvard.

Naturally, I was insulted by this miracle. Stephen Carter, the white male, was not good enough for the Harvard Law School; Stephen Carter, the black male, not only was good enough but rated agonized telephone calls urging him to attend. And Stephen Carter, color unknown, must have been white: How else could he have achieved what he did in college? Except that my college achievements were obviously not sufficiently spectacular to merit acceptance had I been white. In other words, my academic record was too good for a black Stanford University undergraduate, but not good enough for a white Harvard law student. Because I turned out to be black, however, Harvard was quite happy to scrape me from what it apparently considered somewhere nearer the bottom of the barrel.

My objective is not to single out Harvard for special criticism; on the contrary, although my ego insists otherwise, I make no claim that a white student with my academic record would have been admitted to any of the leading law schools. The insult I felt came from the pain of being reminded so forcefully that in the judgment of those with the power to dispose, I was good enough for a top law school only because I happened to be black.

Naturally, I should not have been insulted at all; that is what racial preferences are for—racial preference. But I was insulted and went off to Yale instead, even though I had then and have now absolutely no reason to imagine that Yale's judgment was based on different criteria than Harvard's. Hardly anyone granted admission at Yale is denied admission at Harvard, which admits a far larger class; but several hundreds of students who are admitted at Harvard are denied admission at Yale. Because Yale is far more selective, the chances are good that I was admitted at Yale for essentially the same reason I was admitted at Harvard—the color of my skin made up for what were evidently considered other deficiencies in my academic record. I may embrace this truth as a matter of simple justice or rail against it as one of life's great evils, but being a member of the affirmative action generation means that the one thing I cannot do is deny it. I will say it again: I got into law school because I am black. So what?

The Travail of Black Youth

Jail Time

NATHAN MCCALL

Although the African-American middle class has grown exponentially in recent years as certain barriers to education and employment have fallen, in the inner city black families continue to face debilitating environmental stresses such as deteriorating housing, poor schools, drug trafficking, single-parent households, and the lack of job opportunities. And while unemployment in the general society is at its lowest level in decades, among urban black youth the rate remains unacceptably high.

One result of the inner-city crisis is an increasing turn of black youth to antisocial activities—petty and not so petty crime. In an attempt to maintain an acceptable level of control in urban neighborhoods, law-enforcement authorities have often adopted procedures that have brought them into direct conflict with the alienated black youth of the inner city. For the police, the prevention of crime takes precedence over the protection of civil liberties, and crime prevention in the inner city means the suppression of black youth. In the most extreme cases of racial profiling in crime control, a young black person is considered suspect by his very presence on the street. Accusations of standing while black (SWB) have led to the arrest and incarceration of thousands of black youth, leading to an increasing disrespect for the law and its enforcers. On a number of occasions, dramatic and violent clashes between the police and young African-Americans have been resolved by police bullets. Too often, the police have resorted to gunfire when the "suspect" has appeared suspicious, but has not actually been accused of specific criminal behavior.

Too many young black men end up with criminal records after serving jail time for their lawbreaking. Unfortunately, jail time does not serve as a useful deterrent to later criminal activity. On the other hand, some youthful (and not so youthful) offenders use their period of incarceration to reconsider the pattern of their lives and make serious attempts to break the cycle of criminality so easily fallen into. The Black Muslims have done much of their successful recruiting in prisons, for example. The selection that follows provides another example of the productive use of jail time. As a young man, Nathan McCall was arrested for armed robbery, a crime of which he was guilty. While in prison, McCall determined to use his intelligence and education to find a way out of the labyrinth of crime into which he had been drawn. After his release, McCall became a journalist, eventually working for the Washington Post. His brilliant autobiography serves as a cautionary tale for young African-Americans.

Although it is the ghetto youth who find themselves most often subject to suspicion and arrest, the use of racial profiling by law-enforcement authorities has led to the entrapment of middle- and upper-class black males as well. Many prominent blacks have found themselves stopped by patrol cars for what is essentially the crime of driving while black (DWB). As long as racial prejudice remains operative in American society, the crime of simply having the wrong color skin will continue to plague the African-American community.

I was standing in my cell doorway, checking out the scene on the floor below, when a white convict appeared in the doorway across from mine. He stood stark still and looked straight ahead. Without saying a word, he lifted a razor blade in one hand and began slashing the wrist of the other, squirting blood everywhere. He kept slashing, rapid-fire, until finally he dropped the razor and slumped to the floor, knocking his head against the bars as he went down.

Other inmates standing in their doorways spotted him and yelled, "Guard! Guard! Guard!" Guards came running, rushed the unconscious inmate to the dispensary, and ordered a hallboy to clean up the pool of blood oozing down the walkway. Later, when. I asked the hallboy why the dude had tried to take himself out, he said, "That *time* came down on him and he couldn't take the pressure. You know them white boys can't handle time like us brothers. They weak."

It was a macho thing for a guy to be able to handle his time. Still, every once in a while, time got to everybody, no matter how tough they were. Hard time came in seasonal waves that wiped out whole groups of cats, like a monsoon. Winter was easiest on everybody. There was the sense that you really weren't missing anything on the streets because everyone was indoors. Spring and summer were hell. The Dear John letters started flowing in, sending heartbroken dudes to the fence for a clean, fast break over and into the countryside. Fall was a wash. The weather was nice enough to make you think of home, but winter was just ahead, giving you something to look forward to. Time.

I saw the lifers go through some serious changes about time. Some days, those cats carried theirs as good as anybody else, but other days, they didn't. You could look in their eyes sometimes and tell they had run across a calendar, one of those calendars that let you know what day of the week your birthday will fall on ten years from now. Or you could see in the wild way they started acting and talking that they were on the edge. Then it was time to get away from them, go to the other side of the prison yard, and watch the fireworks. They went *off*. Especially the brothers. They were determined not to go down kicking and screaming and slashing their wrists like the white boys. The brothers considered themselves too hard for that. When the time got to be too much for them, they'd go fuck with somebody and get themselves in a situation where there was no win. It was their way of saying, "Go on, kill me. Gimme a glorious way to get outta this shit."

My time started coming down on me when I realized I'd reached the one-year mark and had at least two to go. I tried to cling tighter to Liz, but that didn't work. After I was transferred from the jail to Southampton, it seemed we both backed out on the marriage plans. She didn't bring it up, and neither

FROM Nathan McCall, *Makes Me Wanna Holler: A Young Black Man in America*. New York: Random House, 1994, pp. 180–190. Reprinted by permission of Random House, Inc.

did I. Liz's visits and letters slacked off, and I felt myself slipping out of touch with the outside world. When Liz did visit, she seemed distant and nervous, like there was something she wanted to tell me but couldn't get out. That drove me crazy, along with about a hundred thousand other irritations that constantly fucked with my head.

I thought a lot about the irony of the year 1976: It was the year Alex Haley published the slave epic *Roots* and the country was celebrating the two hundredth year of its freedom from tyranny. It seemed that every time I opened a magazine or walked past a TV set, there was talk about the yearlong bicentennial celebration. I'd heard white people brag about being free, white, and twenty-one. There I was, black, twenty-one, and in the penitentiary. It seemed I'd gotten it all wrong.

It's a weird feeling being on the edge and knowing that there's not much you can do about it but hang on. You can't get help for prison depression. You can't go to a counselor and say, "Look, I need a weekend pass. This punishment thing is taking more out of me than I think it was intended to take."

I didn't want to admit to myself that the time was getting to me that much, let alone admit it to somebody else. So I determined to do the macho thing: suffer quietly. Sometimes it got so bad I had to whisper to myself, "Hold on, Nate. Hold on."

Frustrated and depressed, I went to the prison and bought a green spiral-bound tablet and started a journal, partly out of a need to capture my fears and feelings, and partly to practice using the new words I learned. I adopted a journal theme—a quote I ran across by the writer Oliver Wendell Holmes—as encouragement to keep me pushing ahead and holding on:

> I find the great thing in this world is not so much where we stand as in what direction we are moving. To reach the port of heaven, we must sail, sometimes with the wind and sometimes against it—but we must sail, and not drift, nor lie at anchor.

It made me feel better sometimes to get something down on paper, just like I felt it. It brought a kind of relief to be able to describe my pain. It was like, if I could describe it, it lost some of its power over me. I jotted down innermost thoughts I couldn't verbalize to anyone else, recorded what I saw around me, and expressed feelings inspired by things I read. Often, the thoughts I wrote down reflected my struggle with time.

> Each day I inspire myself with the hope that by some miracle of God or act of legislature I will soon regain my freedom. However, from occasional conversations, I find that many other inmates have entertained the same hope—for years.

May 21, 1976

Even the guys doing less than life had a hard time. Anything in the double digits—ten years to serve, twenty, forty, sixty—could be a backbreaker. I had a buddy, Cincinnati. Real outgoing cat. Every time you saw him, he was talking beaucoup trash. But Cincinnati was doing a hard forty, and it drove him up a wall at least twice a week. He fought it by trying to keep super-busy. With a white towel hung loosely over his shoulder and several cartons of cigarettes tucked under his arm, Cincinnati (we called him that because that's where he was from) would bop briskly across the yard, intent on his missions. He'd stop and jawbone with a group of guys hanging out near the canteen, then hand a carton of cigarettes to one of them and hurry off to the next meeting.

Cincinnati was one of several major dealers at Southampton who used the drug-peddling skills they'd learned on the streets to exploit the crude prison economy. In that economy, cigarettes replaced money as the medium of exchange. Favors and merchandise were negotiated in terms of their worth in packs of cigarettes. For twelve cartons of cigarettes, a guy could take out a contract to have somebody set up on a drug bust, or get them double-banked or shanked. Eight packs could get you a snappy pair of prison brogans from one of the brothers on the shoe-shop crew. For three packs each week, laundry workers would see to it your shirts and pants were crisply starched. Cincinnati liked to get his gray prison shirts starched so that he could turn up the collar and look real cool.

The really swift dealers found ways to convert a portion of their goods to forbidden cash, which they used to bribe guards to get them reefer and liquor, or saved for their eventual return to the streets.

Cincinnati, who was about two years older than me and had logged a lot more street time, was penitentiary-rich. He decorated his cell with plush blue towels and stockpiled so much stuff that the rear wall of his cell looked like a convenience store. It was stacked from floor to ceiling with boxes of cookies, cigarettes, and other stuff he sold, "two for one," to inmates seeking credit until payday.

Watching cats like him, I often thought about Mo Battle and his theory about pawns. Cincinnati handled time and played chess like he lived: He failed to think far ahead and he chased pawns all over the board. In his free time off from the kitchen, where he worked, he busied himself zigzagging across the prison yard, collecting outstanding debts and treating his petty "bidness" matters like they were major business deals.

Cincinnati was playful and cheery most of the time. He was as dark as night and had a shiny gold tooth that gleamed like a coin when he smiled. Short and squat, he had a massive upper body and a low center of gravity, like Mike Tyson. In fact, his voice, high-pitched and squeaky, sounded a lot like Tyson's, too. It was the kind of voice that sounded like it belonged to a child. But nobody mistook Cincinnati for a child. He was a tank, and could turn from nice guy to cold killer in a split second.

He addressed everybody as "bro'." I'd see him on the yard and say, "Yo, Cincinnati, what's happ'nin'?" And if he was in a good mood, he'd say, "Bro' Nate, life ain't nothin' but a meatball."

But time came down on Cincinnati, like it did on everybody else. He had to do at least ten of his forty years before going up for parole. I could tell when he was thinking about it. I'd run into him on the yard and say, "What's happ'nin', Cincinnati?" He'd shake his head sadly and say, "Bro' Nate, I'm busted, disgusted, and *can't* be trusted."

Cincinnati was so far away from home that he never got visits. On visiting days, he usually went out to the main sidewalk on the yard and looked through the fence as people visiting other inmates pulled into the parking lot.

Other times, I could tell how depressed he was by the way he handled defeat on the chessboard. I beat him all the time and taunted him, but sometimes he didn't take it well. Just before I put him in checkmate, he'd get frustrated and knock one of his big arms against the board, sending the pieces crashing to the floor. Then he'd look up with a straight face and say, "Oh, I'm sorry, Bro' Nate. I didn't mean to do that."

We were playing chess one day when Cincinnati stared at the board a long time without making a move. I got impatient. "Go on and move, man! You gonna lose anyway!"

Ignoring me, Cincinnati kept his eyes glued to the board and didn't speak for a long time. After a while, he said, "Bro' Nate, I'm gonna make a break for the fence. I been thinking about it a long time. I got a lotta money saved up. I can get outta state. You wanna come?"

Any inmate who says he's never thought about escaping is either lying or telling the sad truth. The sad truth is, the only dudes who don't think about making a break are those who are either so institutionalized that their thoughts seldom go beyond the prison gates, or who were so poor in the streets that they had been rescued and are glad to be someplace where they are guaranteed three hots and a cot.

There were a few desperate, fleeting moments when I thought half-seriously about making a run. Southampton is ringed by a tall barbed-wire fence with electrical current running through it, but everybody knew the heat was turned off much of the time. Sometimes, I'd stare at that fence and think about how to scale it. I pictured myself tossing my thick winter coat on top of the barbed wire to test the heat and protect my hands, climbing quickly to the top, and leaping to the other side to make my dash before tower guards could get off a good shot. I'd mapped an escape route based on what I'd seen of the area while traveling with the gun gang. I'd thought it through like a chess match, move for move. That's why I didn't try. When I thought it through, I always saw a great chance of getting busted or leading such a miserable life on the run that it would be another form of imprisonment.

Looking at Cincinnati, I jokingly turned down his offer to run. "Naw, brotherman. I'm gonna squat here. I'm expecting a visit from my lady this weekend. I'd hate for her to come and find me gone. Besides, I can handle my bid. You do the crime, you gotta do the time, Jack!"

I forgot about our conversation until a week or two later, when the big whistle at the guard tower sounded, signaling all inmates to go to their cells to be counted. The whistle blew at certain times every day, but on this day, it sounded at an odd hour, meaning there was something wrong. After we went to our cells, the word spread that Cincinnati had made a break. He'd hidden in the attic of the school building, then scrambled over the fence after a posse left the compound to hunt for him.

Following the count, guys in my building (I was in C-3 by then) grew real quiet. Every time someone escaped, I got quiet and privately rooted for him to get away. I sat on my bunk thinking about Cincinnati, trying to picture him out in the pitch dark, his black face sweating, ducking through bushes, hotly pursued by white men with guns and barking dogs. I imagined him low-running across some broad field, dodging lights and listening for suspicious sounds. I imagined the white country folks, alerted to the escape, grabbing their shotguns and joining the hunt.

Some weeks after Cincinnati made his break, he got caught somewhere in the state. It saddened me. He was shipped to a maximum-security prison more confining than Southampton, and he got more time tacked on to the forty years that was already giving him hell.

> Prison paranoia is a dangerous thing. It can affect a person to the extent that he becomes distrustful of anyone and everyone. Even though my woman has displayed no signs of infidelity, I find myself scrutinizing her behavior each week (in the visiting room), searching her eyes for the slightest faltering trait. I search in hope that I discover none, but hope even more that if there is, I will detect it before it discovers me and slithers back into some obscure hiding place.
>
> June 4, 1976

I walked into the crowded visiting room and took a seat at the table with Liz. My intuition told me that something was up. She'd come alone, without my parents or my son, and her brown eyes, usually bright and cheery, were sad and evasive. In a letter she'd sent to me earlier in the week, she had said there was something she wanted to discuss. I sensed what it was, and I'd come pre-pared.

We exchanged small talk, then there was this awkward silence. Finally, I spoke, relieving her of a burden I sensed was killing her. "You're seeing some-one else, aren't you?"

She nodded. "Yes."

There was a long pause as she waited for my reaction. I looked down at the floor and thought about what I'd just heard. My worst fear had come true. Liz couldn't hang. I'd have to do the time alone. I understood. She'd done the best she could. She'd been a helluva lot more supportive and reliable than I would have been under the circumstances. The best I could do was be grateful for what she'd done. Take it and grow, as she used to say. I tried to put on a brave face; and I said, "I understand, really. ... Well, nothing I can do about that but wish you the best. I would like you to hang in there with me, but really, I don't know when I'm gettin' outta here."

She listened quietly and nodded as I talked. When I finished, she didn't say much. We sat there, bummed out, looking at each other. Mr. and Miss Manor. Liz wished me well. Her eyes watered. Then she said good-bye, and left.

I practically ran back to my cell that Saturday morning. I wanted to get back there before the tear ducts burst. It was like trying to get to the bathroom before the bladder gives out. I made it, went inside, and flopped down on a stool. I turned on the stereo, slid in one of my favorite gospel tapes, *Amazing Grace*, by Aretha Franklin, and closed my eyes. The tape opened with a song called "Mary, Don't You Weep." The deep strains of a full gospel choir, comforting the sister of Lazarus after his death, sang in a rich harmony that sent shivers through me:

> Hush, Mary, don't you weep.
> Hush, Mary, don't you weep.

When I heard those words, the floodgate burst and the tears started, streaming down my face. Streaming. The pain ran so deep it felt physical, like somebody was pounding on my chest. I'd never been hurt by a woman before. I had never cared enough to be hurt by one. I sat there, leaning on the cell door, listening to Aretha and crying. Inmates walked past and I didn't even lift my head. I didn't care who saw me or what they thought. I was crushed. Wasted. I cried until tears blurred my vision. Then I got up, picked up my washcloth, rinsed it in the sink, held it to my face, and cried some more. Liz was gone. I remembered that she had once told me, "I'll follow you into a ditch if you lead me there." Well, I had led her there, but she'd never promised to stay.

Sometimes I'd get grinding migraines that lasted for hours on end. I figured it was caused by the pain of losing Liz, and the stress and tension hounding me. When the frequency of the headaches increased, I came up with ways to relieve the stress. I'd leave the place. I'd stretch out on my bunk, block out all light by putting a cloth over my eyes, and go into deep meditation or prayer. Starting with my toes, I'd concentrate hard and command every one of my body parts to chill. Often, by the time I reached my head the tension was gone.

Then I'd take my imagination and soar away from the prison yard. I'd travel to Portsmouth or some faraway, fictional place. Or I'd venture beyond the earth and wander through the galaxy, pondering the vastness of what God has done. I developed a hell of an imagination by doing those mental workouts, and it put me in touch with my spirit in wondrous ways. When the concentration was really good, I'd lose all feeling in my body, and my spirit would come through, making me feel at one with the universe. It was like being high: It felt so good, but I couldn't figure out a way to make it last.

I just witnessed a brutal fight in the cafeteria. The atmosphere was certainly conducive to violence: hot, odorous air filled with noise and flies. The two combatants went at each other's throats as if their lives meant nothing to them. After being confined for an extended period of time, life does tend to lose its value. I pray that I can remember my self-worth and remain cool.

July 27, 1976

A group of us from Tidewater were sitting around, sharing funny tales from the streets and telling war stories about crazy things we'd done. When my turn came, I told a story about a near stickup on Church Street in Norfolk. "Yeah, man, we ran across a dude who had nothing but chump change on him. We got mad 'cause the dude was broke, so we took his change and started to take his pants. He had on some yellow, flimsy-looking pants, so we made him walk with us under a streetlamp so we could get a better look at them. When we got under the streetlamp, we could see the pants were cheap. And they were dirty. So we let the dude slide, and keep his pants ..."

Everybody was laughing. Everybody but a guy from Norfolk named Tony. Squinting his eyes, he leaned over and interrupted, "Did you say the guy had on yellow pants?"

"Yeah."

"Goddammit, that was me y'all stuck up that night!" he said, pointing a finger at me.

Everything got quiet. The guys looked at me, then at Tony, then back at me. Somebody snickered, and everybody else joined in. I laughed, too, until I looked at Tony and realized he still wasn't laughing. He was hot. He looked embarrassed and mad as hell.

To lighten the mood, I extended my hand playfully and said, "Wow, man, I'm sorry' bout that. You know I didn't know you then."

Tony looked at my hand like he wanted to spit on it. "Naw, man. That shit ain't funny." The way he said it, I knew he wasn't going to let the thing drop. I knew that stupid macho pride had him by the throat and was choking the shit out of him.

A week or two after the exchange, he came into the library, where I was working, sat in a corner, and started tearing pages out of magazines. The library was filled with inmates. I walked over to the table and said, "Yo, Tony, you can't tear the pages outta the magazines, man. Other people have to read 'em."

He looked up, smiled an evil smile, then ripped out another page and said, "What you gonna do 'bout it? You ain't no killer." The room grew quiet. I felt like all eyes were on me, waiting to see what I would do. I started thinking fast. Tony was stout and muscular and I figured he'd probably do the moonwalk on me if he got his hands on me. He was sitting down and I was standing. I glanced at an empty chair near him. I thought, *I could sneak him right off the bat, grab that chair, and wrap it around his head.* Then I thought about the potential consequences of fighting at work. I could lose my job, get kicked out of the library. I thought, *I gotta let it slide. I have to.* I looked at Tony, shrugged my shoulders, and said, "I ain't gonna do nothin', man. The magazines don't belong to *me.*"

Tony sat there, staring at me, and tore more pages out of magazines. I walked away.

Later that night, I thought about it some more. I thought about how he'd come off. I thought, He *disrespected me.* I was too scared to let that man get away with disrespecting me. I felt I had faith that God would take care of me, but whenever I got that scared about something, I relied on what I knew best—faith in self. So I prayed, then set God aside for the time being and put together a shank like I'd learned to make while in the Norfolk jail. I melded a razor blade into a toothbrush handle, leaving the sharp edges sticking out, like a miniature tomahawk. I told one of my buddies what I intended to do. "I gotta get that niggah, man. He disrespected me and tried to chump me down."

The next day, we went looking for Tony on the yard. We spotted him leaving the dispensary with a partner. While my friend kept a lookout for guards, I approached Tony. Without saying anything, I pulled the razor blade and swung it at his throat. He jumped back. I lunged at him again and he flung his arms in front of his face, blocking the blow. The razor slashed his coat. He held up his hands and said, "Hold it, hold it, hold it, man! Be cool. Everything's cool. We all right, man. I ain't got no beef with you."

I pointed the razor at him. "Niggah, don't you never take me to be no chump!"

"All right, bro', I was just playing with you yesterday."

I turned and walked away, relieved that he'd backed down and grateful that none of the guards standing on the yard had seen what went down.

My parents came to see me that afternoon. I went into the visiting room still hyper from the scene with Tony. As we talked, I looked at them and wondered what they'd say if they knew I had just risked everything I'd worked for to prove a manhood point. I wondered if Tony was going to try to get some get-back or pay somebody to try to shank me when my back was turned. I wondered if the time was coming down on me so badly that I was losing my grip.

At chow time that evening, my homie Pearly Blue came to the table and sat next to me. There was a slight smirk on his face. I sensed he was feeling a certain delight in knowing he'd warned me to hang tight with my homies to keep hassles away. "Yo, man, I heard you had a run-in with Tony."

"Yeah, a small beef."

"I told you these old rooty-poot niggahs will try you if they think you walk alone. ...You know if you need to make another move on him, the homies can take care of it."

I kept looking straight ahead as I ate. "Naw, man. I got it under control."

I had no problems from Tony the remainder of the time I was at Southampton.

The one thing that seemed to soothe everybody in the joint was music. The loudest, most fucked-up brothers in the place chilled out when they had on a set of headphones. Some white inmates had musical instruments—guitars, saxophones, flutes—and they practiced in their cells at night. Most of the brothers didn't like hearing white music. The brothers would holler through the cell bars, "Cut that hillbilly shit out!"

But one white guy, from some rural Virginia town, was exempt from the hassles. He was a fairly good guitar player, and an even better singer. Every night, before the lights went out, he calmed the building with music. He sang

the same song, and it reverberated throughout the place. He strummed his guitar and sang the John Denver tune "Take Me Home, Country Roads." He sang
in a voice so clean it sounded like he was standing on a mountain crooning
down into one of those luscious green valleys he was singing about:

> Country rooaads
> Take me hoomme,
> To the plaaace
> Where I beloooonng …

When those lyrics floated into my cell, I'd sit quietly, lean my had against the
concrete wall, and listen. That song reminded me of how lonely I was and
made me think of home. It made me think of Liz. It made me think of my
son, my family, my neighborhood, my life. Sometimes, when he sang that song,
tears welled in my eyes and I'd wipe them away, get into bed, and think some
more.

That song seemed to calm everybody in the building, even the, baad-asses
who were prone to yell through their cells. It had the soothing effect of a
lullaby sung by a parent to a bunch of children.

Gangsta Rap and
American Culture

MICHAEL ERIC DYSON

From drumbeats in the slave quarters to gangsta rap performances on street corners in Compton or the South Bronx, African-American musical innovations have been seen as subversive by white society and have provided blacks with an outlet for frustration and an expression of creative protest. A cultural history that includes jazz, blues, rhythm and blues, and rap has provided black musicians and audiences with a deeply satisfying experience that was independent of the cultural mainstream of American society. When the popularity of black musical forms became too threatening to that mainstream it could always be coopted. The oft-told tale of the way in which Elvis Presley began the process of transmuting rhythm and blues into rock and roll is merely one example. Although white society often found the transformed performances subversive and antiauthoritarian, such attitudes were easier to accept from white artists. If the emergence of rock and roll had not coincided with the movements for racial justice and antiwar protest in the 1960s and 1970s, the belief among the young that their music challenged the authority of society's elders would likely not have been so pronounced. There is a difference between protest music that springs from alienation and music that attempts to break the stranglehold the dominant culture has on the oppressed community.

The rise of conservatism and racism in the 1980s and 1990s led to deteriorating conditions in poor communities. Among the variety of responses to the changing environment of the ghetto were the crack epidemic, gang violence, and the verbal violence of rap music. The misogyny and homophobia of much of gangsta rap lyrics exposes the bigoted attitudes in the black community and also reflects the attitudes of American society generally. Social critics who are appalled by the expressions of hostility in gangsta rap are rarely as critical of the conditions out of which that musical style emerged. Michael Eric Dyson, the author of the next passage, sees gangsta rap as an authentic response to the oppression felt by alienated black youth and calls upon opinion leaders in the society to focus more on the racial and economic oppression in American society and less on the offensive lyrics of rap performers.

The recent attacks on the entertainment industry, especially gangsta rap, by Senator Bob Dole, former Education Secretary William Bennett, and political activist C. Delores Tucker, reveal the fury that popular culture can evoke in a wide range of commentators. As a thirty-five-year-old father of a sixteen year-old son and as a professor and ordained Baptist minister who grew up in

Detroit's treacherous inner city, I too am disturbed by many elements of gangsta rap. But I'm equally anguished by the way many critics have used its artists as scapegoats. How can we avoid the pitfall of unfairly attacking black youth for problems that bewitched our culture long before they gained prominence? First, we should understand what forces drove the emergence of rap. Second, we should place the debate about gangsta rap in the context of a much older debate about "negative" and "positive" black images. Finally, we should acknowledge that gangsta rap crudely exposes harmful beliefs and practices that are often maintained with deceptive civility in much of mainstream society, including many black communities.

If the fifteen-year evolution of hip-hop teaches us anything, it's that history is made in unexpected ways by unexpected people with unexpected results. Rap is now safe from the perils of quick extinction predicted at its humble start. But its birth in the bitter belly of the '70s proved to be a Rosetta stone of black popular culture. Afros, "blunts," funk music, and carnal eruptions define a "back-in-the-day" hiphop aesthetic. In reality, the severe '70s busted the economic boom of the '60s. The fallout was felt in restructured automobile industries and collapsed steel mills. It was extended in exported employment to foreign markets. Closer to home, there was the depletion of social services to reverse the material ruin of black life. Later, public spaces for black recreation were gutted by Reaganomics or violently transformed by lethal drug economies.

Hip-hop was born in these bleak conditions. Hip-hoppers joined pleasure and rage while turning the details of their difficult lives into craft and capital. This is the world hip-hop would come to "represent": privileged persons speaking for less visible or vocal peers. At their best, rappers shape the tortuous twists of urban fate into lyrical elegies. They represent lives swallowed by too little love or opportunity. They represent themselves and their peers with aggrandizing anthems that boast of their ingenuity and luck in surviving. The art of "representin'" that is much ballyhooed in hip-hop is the witness of those left to tell the afflicted's story.

As rap expands its vision and influence, its unfavorable origins and its relentless quest to represent black youth are both a consolation and challenge to hip-hoppers. They remind rappers that history is not merely the stuff of imperial dreams from above. It isn't just the sanitizing myths of those with political power. Representing history is within reach of those who seize the opportunity to speak for themselves, to represent their own interests at all costs. Even rap's largest controversies are about representation. Hip-hop's attitudes toward women and gays continually jolt in the unvarnished malevolence they reveal. The sharp responses to rap's misogyny and homophobia signify its central role in battles over the cultural representation of other beleaguered groups. This is particularly true of gangsta rap.

While gangsta rap takes the heat for a range of social maladies from urban violence to sexual misconduct, the roots of our racial misery remain buried beneath moralizing discourse that is confused and sometimes dishonest. There's no doubt that gangsta rap is often sexist and that it reflects a vicious misogyny that has seized our nation with frightening intensity. It is doubly wounding for black women who are already beset by attacks from outside their communities to feel the thrust of musical daggers to their dignity from within. How painful it is for black women, many of whom have fought valiantly for black pride, to hear the dissonant chord of disdain carried in the angry epithet "bitch."

The link between the vulgar rhetorical traditions expressed in gangsta rap and the economic exploitation that dominates the marketplace is real. The circulation of brutal images of black men as sexual outlaws and black females as "ho's" in many gangsta rap narratives mirrors ancient stereotypes of black sexual identity. Male and female bodies are turned into commodities. Black sexual desire is stripped of redemptive uses in relationships of great affection or love.

[G]angsta rappers, however, don't merely respond to the values and visions of the marketplace; they help shape them as well. The ethic of consumption that pervades our culture certainly supports the rapacious materialism shot through the narratives of gangsta rap. Such an ethic, however, does not exhaust the literal or metaphoric purposes of material wealth in gangsta culture. The imagined and real uses of money to help one's friends, family, and neighborhood occupies a prominent spot in gangsta rap lyrics and lifestyles.

Equally troubling is the glamorization of violence and the romanticization of the culture of guns that pervades gangsta rap. The recent legal troubles of Tupac Shakur, Dr. Dre, Snoop Doggy Dogg, and other gangsta rappers chastens any defense of the genre based on simplistic claims that these artists are merely performing roles that are divorced from real life. Too often for gangsta rappers, life does indeed imitate and inform art.

But gangsta rappers aren't *simply* caving in to the pressure of racial stereotyping and its economic rewards in a music industry hungry to exploit their artistic imaginations. According to this view, gangsta rappers are easily manipulated pawns in a chess game of material dominance where their consciences are sold to the highest bidder. Or else gangsta rappers are viewed as the black face of white desire to distort the beauty of black life. Some critics even suggest that white record executives discourage the production of "positive rap" and reinforce the desire for lewd expressions packaged as cultural and racial authenticity.

But such views are flawed. The street between black artists and record companies runs both ways. Even though black artists are often ripe for the picking —and thus susceptible to exploitation by white and black record labels—many of them are quite sophisticated about the politics of cultural representation. Many gangsta rappers helped to create the genre's artistic rules. Further, they have figured out how to financially exploit sincere and sensational interest in "ghetto life." [G]angsta rap is no less legitimate because many "gangstas" turn out to be middle-class blacks faking home boy roots. This fact simply focuses attention on the genre's essential constructedness, its literal artifice. Much of gangsta rap makes voyeuristic whites and naive blacks think they're getting a slice of authentic ghetto life when in reality they're being served colorful exaggerations. That doesn't mean, however, that the best of gangsta rappers don't provide compelling portraits of real social and economic suffering.

Critics of gangsta rap often ignore how hip-hop has been developed without the assistance of a majority of black communities. Even "positive" or "nation-conscious" rap was initially spurned by those now calling for its revival in the face of gangsta rap's ascendancy. Long before white record executives sought to exploit transgressive sexual behavior among blacks, many of us failed to lend support to politically motivated rap. For instance, when political rap group Public Enemy was at its artistic and popular height, most of the critics of gangsta rap didn't insist on the group's prominence in black cultural politics. Instead, Public Enemy and other conscientious rappers were often viewed as controversial figures whose inflammatory racial rhetoric was cause for caution or alarm. In this light, the hue and cry directed against gangsta rap by the new defenders of "legitimate" hip-hop rings false.

Also, many critics of gangsta rap seek to curtail its artistic freedom to transgress boundaries defined by racial or sexual taboo. That's because the burden of representation falls heavily on what may be termed the race artist in a far different manner than the one I've described above. The race artist stands in for black communities. She represents millions of blacks by substituting or sacrificing her desires and visions for the perceived desires and visions of the masses. Even when the race artist manages to maintain relative independence of vision, his or her work is overlaid with, and interpreted within, the social and political aspirations of blacks as a whole. Why? Because of the appalling lack of redeeming or nonstereotypical representations of black life that are permitted expression in our culture.

This situation makes it difficult for blacks to affirm the value of nontraditional or transgressive artistic expressions. Instead of viewing such cultural products through critical eyes—seeing the good and the bad, the productive and destructive aspects of such art—many blacks tend to simply dismiss such work with hypercritical disdain. A suffocating standard of "legitimate" art is thus produced by the limited public availability of complex black art. Either art is seen as redemptive because it uplifts black culture and shatters stereotypical thinking about blacks, or it is seen as bad because it reinforces negative perceptions of black culture.

That is too narrow a measure for the brilliance and variety of black art and cultural imagination. Black folk should surely pay attention to how black art is perceived in our culture. We must be mindful of the social conditions that shape perceptions of our cultural expressions and that stimulate the flourishing of one kind of art versus another. (After all, die-hard hip-hop fans have long criticized how gangsta rap is eagerly embraced by white record companies while "roots" hip-hop is grossly underfinanced.)

But black culture is too broad and intricate—its artistic manifestations too unpredictable and challenging—for us to be obsessed with how white folk view our culture through the lens of our art. And black life is too differentiated by class, sexual identity, gender, region, and nationality to fixate on "negative" or "positive" representations of black culture. Black culture is good and bad, uplifting and depressing, edifying and stifling. All of these features should be represented in our art, should find resonant voicing in the diverse tongues of black cultural expressions.

[G]angsta rappers are not the first to face the grueling double standards imposed on black artists. Throughout African-American history, creative personalities have sought to escape or enliven the role of race artist with varying degrees of success. The sharp machismo with which many gangsta rappers reject this office grates on the nerves of many traditionalists. Many critics argue that since gangsta rap is often the only means by which many white Americans come into contact with black life, its pornographic representations and brutal stereotypes of black culture are especially harmful. The understandable but lamentable response of many critics is to condemn gangsta rap out of hand. They aim to suppress gangsta rap's troubling expressions rather than critically engage its artists and the provocative issues they address. Or the critics of gangsta rap use it for narrow political ends that fail to enlighten or better our common moral lives.

Tossing a moralizing *j'accuse* at the entertainment industry may have boosted Bob Dole's standing in the polls over the short term. It did little, however, to clarify or correct the problems to which he has drawn dramatic attention. I'm in favor of changing the moral climate of our nation. I just don't believe that attacking movies, music, and their makers is very helpful. Besides, right-wing talk radio hosts wreak more havoc than a slew of violent films. They're the ones terrorist Timothy McVeigh was inspired by as he planned to bomb the Federal Building in Oklahoma City.

A far more crucial task lies in getting at what's wrong with our culture and what it needs to get right. Nailing the obvious is easy. That's why Dole, along with William Bennett and C. Delores Tucker, goes after popular culture, especially gangsta rap. And the recent attempts of figures like Tucker and Dionne Warwick, as well as national and local lawmakers, to censor gangsta rap or to outlaw its sale to minors are surely misguided. When I testified before the U.S. Senate's Subcommittee on juvenile justice, as well as the Pennsylvania House of Representatives, I tried to make this point while acknowledging the need to responsibly confront gangsta rap's problems. Censorship of gangsta rap cannot begin to solve the problems of poor black youth. Nor will it effectively curtail their consumption of music that is already circulated through dubbed tapes and without the benefit of significant airplay.

A crucial distinction needs to be made between censorship of gangsta rap and edifying expressions of civic responsibility and community conscientiousness. The former seeks to prevent the sale of vulgar music that offends mainstream moral sensibilities by suppressing the First Amendment. The latter, however, is a more difficult but rewarding task. It seeks to oppose the expression of misogynistic and sexist sentiments in hip-hop culture through protest and pamphleteering, through community activism, and through boycotts and consciousness raising.

What Dole, Bennett, and Tucker shrink from helping us understand—and what all effective public moralists must address—is why this issue now? Dole's answer is that the loss of family values is caused by the moral corruption of popular culture, and therefore we should hold rap artists, Hollywood moguls, and record executives responsible for our moral chaos. It's hard to argue with Dole on the surface, but a gentle scratch reveals that both his analysis and answer are flawed.

Too often, "family values" is a code for a narrow view of how families work, who gets to count as a legitimate domestic unit, and consequently, what values are crucial to their livelihood. Research has shown that nostalgia for the family of the past, when father knew best, ignores the widespread problems of those times, including child abuse and misogyny. Romantic portrayals of the family on television and the big screen, anchored by the myth of the Benevolent Patriarch, hindered our culture from coming to grips with its ugly domestic problems.

To be sure, there have been severe assaults on American families and their values, but they have not come mainly from Hollywood, but from Washington with the dismantling of the Great Society. Cruel cuts in social programs for the neediest, an upward redistribution of wealth to the rich, and an unprincipled conservative political campaign to demonize poor black mothers and their children have left latter-day D. W Griffiths in the dust. Many of gangsta rap's most vocal black critics (such as Tucker) fail to see how the alliances they forge with conservative white politicians such as Bennett and Dole are plagued with problems. Bennett and Dole have put up roadblocks to many legislative and political measures that would enhance the fortunes of the black poor they now claim in part to speak for. Their outcry resounds as crocodile tears from the corridors of power paved by bad faith.

Moreover, many of the same conservative politicians who support the attack on gangsta rap also attack black women (from Lani Guinier to welfare mothers), affirmative action, and the redrawing of voting districts to achieve parity for black voters. The war on gangsta rap diverts attention away from the more substantive threat posed to women and blacks by many conservative politicians. [G]angsta rap's critics are keenly aware of the harmful effects that genre's misogyny can have on black teens. Irionically, such critics appear oblivious to how their rhetoric of absolute opposition to gangsta rap has been used to justify political attacks on poor black teens.

That doesn't mean that gratuitous violence and virulent misogyny should not be opposed. They must be identified and destroyed. I am wholly sympathetic, for instance, to sharp criticism of gangsta rap's ruinous sexism and homophobia, though neither Dole, Bennett, nor Tucker have made much of the latter plague. "Fags" and "dykes" are prominent in the genre's vocabulary of rage. Critics' failure to make this an issue only reinforces the inferior, invisible status of gay men and lesbians in mainstream and black cultural institutions. Homophobia is a vicious emotion and practice that links mainstream middle-class and black institutions to the vulgar expressions of gangsta rap.

There seems to be an implicit agreement between gangsta rappers and political elites that gays, lesbians, and bisexuals basically deserve what they get.

But before we discard the genre, we should understand that gangsta rap
often reaches higher than its ugliest, lowest common denominator. Misogyny,
violence, materialism, and sexual transgression are not its exclusive domain. At
its best, this music draws attention to complex dimensions of ghetto life
ignored by many Americans. Of all the genres of hip-hop—from socially conscious rap to black nationalist expressions, from pop to hardcore—gangsta rap
has most aggressively narrated the pains and possibilities, the fantasies and fears,
of poor black urban youth. gangsta rap is situated in the violent climes of
postindustrial Los Angeles and its bordering cities. It draws its metaphoric capital in part from the mix of myth and murder that gave the Western frontier a
dangerous appeal a century ago.

[G]angsta rap is largely an indictment of mainstream and bourgeois black
institutions by young people who do not find conventional methods of
addressing personal and social calamity useful. The leaders of those institutions
often castigate the excessive and romanticized violence of this music without
trying to understand what precipitated its rise in the first place. In so doing,
they drive a greater wedge between themselves and the youth they so desperately want to help.

If Americans really want to strike at the heart of sexism and misogyny in
our communities, shouldn't we take a closer look at one crucial source of these
blights: religious institutions, including the synagogue, the temple, and the
church? For instance, the central institution of black culture, the black church,
which has given hope and inspiration to millions of blacks, has also given us
an embarrassing legacy of sexism and misogyny. Despite the great good it has
achieved through a heroic tradition of emancipatory leadership, the black
church continues to practice and justify *ecclesiastical apartheid*. More than 70
percent of black church members are female, yet they are generally excluded
from the church's central station of power, the pulpit. And rarely are the few
ordained female ministers elected pastors.

Yet black leaders, many of them ministers, excoriate rappers for their verbal sexual misconduct. It is difficult to listen to civil rights veterans deplore the
hostile depiction of women in gangsta rap without mentioning the vicious
sexism of the movements for racial liberation of the 1960s. And of course the
problem persists in many civil rights organizations today.

Attacking figures like Snoop Doggy Dogg or Tupac Shakur—or the companies that record or distribute them—is an easy out. It allows scapegoating
without sophisticated moral analysis and action. While these young black
males become whipping boys for sexism and misogyny, the places in our culture where these ancient traditions are nurtured and rationalized—including
religious and educational institutions and the nuclear family—remain immune
to forceful and just criticism.

Corporate capitalism, mindless materialism, and pop culture have surely
helped unravel the moral fabric of our society. But the moral condition of our

nation is equally affected by political policies that harm the vulnerable and poor. It would behoove Senator Dole to examine the glass house of politics he abides in before he decides to throw stones again. If he really wants to do something about violence, he should change his mind about the ban on assault weapons he seeks to repeal. That may not be as sexy or self-serving as attacking pop culture, but it might help save lives.

[G]angsta rap's greatest "sin" may be that it tells the truth about practices and beliefs that rappers hold in common with the mainstream and with black elites. This music has embarrassed mainstream society and black bourgeois culture. It has forced us to confront the demands of racial representation that plague and provoke black artists. It has also exposed our polite sexism and our disregard for gay men and lesbians. We should not continue to blame gangsta rap for ills that existed long before hip-hop uttered its first syllable. Indeed, gangsta rap's in-your-face style may do more to force our nation to confront crucial social problems than countless sermons or political speeches.

SUGGESTIONS FOR FURTHER READING

Women in African-American history are surveyed in Jacqueline Jones, *Labor of Love, Labor of Sorrow: Black Women, Work, and the Family from Slavery to the Present*★ (1985) and Gerda Lerner (ed.), *Black Women in White America*★ (1973). Black feminism is explored in Paula Giddings, *When and Where I Enter: The Impact of Black Women on Race and Sex in America*★ (1984) and two books by bell hooks: *Ain't I a Woman? Black Women and Feminists*★ (1981) and *Feminist Theory: From Margin to Center*★ (1984). For the impact of the civil rights movement on emergent feminism, see Sara Evans, *Personal Politics: The Roots of Women's Liberation in the Civil Rights Movement and the New Left*★ (1979).

Black political development is described in Steven F. Lawson, *In Pursuit of Power: Southern Blacks and Electoral Politics, 1965–1982* (1985) and Paul Kleppner *Chicago Divided. The Making of a Black Mayor*★ (1985).

The origins of affirmative action can be found in Paul D. Moreno, *From Direct Action to Affirmative Action: Fair Employment Law and Policy in America, 1933–1972*★ (1997). The controversy over affirmative action is explored in Nathan Glazer, *Affirmative Discrimination*★ (1975) and Gertrude Ezorsky, *Racism and Justice: The Case for Affirmative Action*★ (1991).

On conditions in the ghetto, see Michael Katz, *The Undeserving Poor: From the War on Poverty to the War on Welfare*★ (1989) and William J. Wilson, *The Truly Disadvantaged*★ (1987). The problem of crime and racial justice is explored in David Cole, *No Equal Justice: Race and Class in the American Criminal Justice System*★ (1999).

For the development of black musical style, see W. T. Lhamon, Jr., *Raising Cain: Blackface Performance from Jim Crow to Hip Hop* (1998). Works that deal with rap and hip hop include Tricia Rose, *Black Noise: Rap Music and Black Culture in Contemporary America*★ (1994), Andrew Ross and Tricia Rose (eds.), *Microphone Fiends*★ (1994), and Nelson George, *Hip Hop America*★ (1998).

★ Books marked by an asterisk are available in paperback.

General Reading Suggestions

Several surveys of African-American history are available. The best of these are John Hope Franklin and Alfred A. Moss, *From Slavery to Freedom: A History of American Negroes*★, 8th ed., (2000), August Meier and Elliott Rudwick, *From Plantation to Ghetto: An Interpretive History of American Negroes*★ , 3e., (1976), and Lerone Bennett, *Before the Mayflower: A History of the Negro in America*★ (1962). See also the essays collected in the following anthologies: August Meier and Elliott Rudwick (eds.), *The Making of Black America: Essays in Negro Life and History*★, 2 vols. (1969), Melvin Drimmer (ed.), *Black History: A Reappraisal* (1968), and Dwight Hoover (ed.), *Understanding Negro History* (1968). Two excellent interpretations of African-American history are Vincent Harding, *There Is a River: The Black Struggle for Freedom in America*★ (1981) and Mary Francis Berry and John Blassingame, *Long Memory: The Black Experience in America*★ (1982).

The most comprehensive collection of African-American documents is Herbert Aptheker (ed.), *A Documentary History of the Negro People in the United States*★, 2 vols. (1951). An outstanding new anthology is Manning Marable and Leith Mullings (eds.), *Let Nobody Turn Us Around: Voices of Resistance, Reform, and Renewal* (2000).

For information on black athletes, see Arthur Ashe, *A Hard Road to Glory: The History of the African-American Athlete, 1619 to the Present*, 3 vols. (1993).

Darlene Clark Hine and her colleagues have prepared *Black Women in America: An Historical Encyclopedia*★, 2 vols. (1996).

For biographical information, see Leon Litwack and August Meier (eds.), *Black Leaders of the Nineteenth Century*★ (1991) and John Hope Franklin and August Meier (eds.), *Black Leaders of the Twentieth Century*★ (1993).

For an introduction to black creative writing, see the following: James A. Emanuel and Theodore L. Gross (eds.), *Dark Symphony: Negro Literature in America*★ (1968), Abraham Chapman (ed.), *Black Voices: An Anthology of Afro-American Literature*★ (1968), John Henrik Clarke (ed.), *American Negro Short Stories*★ (1966), Arna Bontemps (ed.), *American Negro Poetry*★ (1963), and Langston Hughes and Arna Bontemps (eds.), *The Poetry of the Negro, 1746–1949: An Anthology* (1949).

Two studies of particular interest to students of African-American history are August Meier and Elliott Rudwick, *Black History and the Historical Profession, 1915–1980*★ (1986) and Darlene Clark Hine (ed.), *The State of Afro-American History: Past, Present, and Future* (1986).

In 1971, James McPherson and his colleagues at Princeton edited *Blacks in America: Bibliographical Essays*. While this work is now out of date, it is comprehensive for the earlier period.

★ Books marked by an asterisk are available in paperback.